READERS AND WRITERS
IN THE
MIDDLE GRADES

Second Edition

Martha Combs

University of Nevada, Reno

Merrill
Prentice Hall

Upper Saddle River, New Jersey
Columbus, Ohio

Library of Congress Cataloging-in-Publication Data

Combs, Martha.
   Readers and writers in the middle grades / Martha Combs.—2nd ed.
     p. cm.
   Rev. ed. of: Developing competent readers and writers in the middle grades. © 1997.
   Includes bibliographical references and index.
   ISBN 0-13-048344-3
     1. Reading (Middle school) 2. English language—Composition and exercise—Study
and teaching (Middle school) 3. Young adult literature—Study and teaching (Middle
School) I. Combs, Martha. Developing competent readers and writers in the middle
grades. II. Title.

   LB1632 .C576 2003
   428.4'071'2--dc21
                                   2002069228

Vice President and Publisher: Jeffery W. Johnston
Editor: Linda Ashe Montgomery
Editorial Assistant: Evelyn Olson
Production Editor: Linda Hillis Bayma
Production Coordination and Text Design: Carlisle Publishers Services
Design Coordinator: Diane C. Lorenzo
Photo Coordinator: Sandy Schaefer
Cover Designer: Ali Mohrman
Cover Art: Riley Wolfington
Production Manager: Pamela D. Bennett
Director of Marketing: Ann Castel Davis
Marketing Manager: Darcy Betts Prybella
Marketing Coordinator: Tyra Cooper

This book was set in Goudy by Carlisle Publishers Services. It was printed and bound by Courier Kendallville, Inc. The cover was printed by Phoenix Color Corp.

Photo Credits: Ken Karp/PH College, p. 3; Anne Vega/Merrill, pp. 14, 27, 32, 55, 107, 197, 207, 215, 223; Robert Vega/Merrill, p. 43; Tom Watson/Merrill, pp. 71, 233, 363; Anthony Magnacca/Merrill, pp. 83, 121, 153, 170, 281, 307; Scott Cunningham/Merrill, pp. 92, 131, 249, 371; KS Studios/Merrill, p. 273; Linda Peterson/Merrill, p. 347.

Pearson Education Ltd.
Pearson Education Australia Pty. Limited
Pearson Education Singapore Ptd. Ltd.
Pearson Education North Asia Ltd.
Pearson Education Canada, Ltd.
Pearson Educación de Mexico, S.A. de C.V.
Pearson Education—Japan
Pearson Education Malaysia Pte. Ltd.
Pearson Education, *Upper Saddle River, New Jersey*

Merrill
Prentice Hall

10 9 8 7 6 5 4 3 2 1
ISBN 0-13-048344-3

For Jimmie Russell,
a wonderful teacher and mentor
to students at Oklahoma Baptist University.

Preface

This text is about engaging students from fourth through eighth grade in literacy experiences. Our focus is on students who are 10 to 14 years old, who are often referred to as early adolescents. *Great Transitions* (1996), the concluding report from the Carnegie Council on Adolescent Development, reaffirms for us that

> Adolescence is one of the most fascinating and complex transitions in the life span: a time of accelerated growth and change second only to infancy; a time of expanding horizons, self-discovery, and emerging independence; a time of metamorphosis from childhood to adulthood. (p. 7)

What a challenge we face as teachers of adolescents!

This book is intended to help expand your knowledge of this age group and to explore ways of engaging these students in meaningful literacy learning. To help you focus on your own learning, I present instructional approaches that others have used successfully with middle grade students. We will examine each approach in some depth, to more fully consider the possibilities it may hold for each of you and your students (or prospective students). We will eavesdrop on middle grade teachers as they engage students in whole-class, small-group, and individual reading and writing experiences.

As we follow these teachers, you will experience some of their thinking and decision making. I believe these two areas, *teacher thinking* and *decision making,* are among the most difficult areas to learn. Throughout this course, you must work to confront and understand your own thinking and decision making, the knowledge base you draw on for teaching, and how you carry through on your decisions. The teachers in this text can be your teachers, the "more knowledgeable others" (Vygotsky, 1962) who will help you advance your understanding of teaching middle grade students.

TEXT FEATURES

To support and extend your thinking, this text includes the following features:

- *In This Chapter.* At the beginning of each chapter an overview of chapter highlights helps you anticipate the contents and prepare yourself for study.
- *Before You Get Started.* This alerts you to works of literature that receive significant attention in a chapter. Knowledge of these books will enhance your

study. It is particularly important to have a copy of the literature for reference.

- *Building a Theory Base . . . and Putting Theory into Practice.* The content of most chapters is divided into two sections: one that provides appropriate background in educational theories related to the chapter topic and a second section that illustrates possible classroom applications.
- *Sample scripts, lesson frameworks, and units.* These elements are presented throughout as examples of theory applied to classroom practice.
- *Emphasis on teacher thinking and decision making.* In addition, we explore instructional approaches in depth, providing opportunities for you to develop your thinking and decision making.
- *Your Turn . . . My Turn. . . .* This feature encourages you to participate in your reading and to be a decision maker for classroom practice. Opportunities occur throughout this text to stop and reflect on the reading, to use your background of experience, and to apply knowledge from your reading.
- *Take a Moment to Reflect.* At the end of each chapter we recap chapter highlights to let you check your understanding of the most important issues in the chapter.
- *Appendices.* These provide added information about using authentic literature, suggested literature for study, background information in phonics, and sample word lists for study.

Teaching in today's classrooms challenges you to engage students in creative and critical ways, preparing young adolescents for a most uncertain world. This text provides ways for you to examine your own creative and critical thinking about the reading and writing processes of early adolescents and will challenge you to be a better decision maker, to consider issues in literacy that are critical for your students' future, and to gain the confidence that provides literate environments for middle grade students. You must not accept students' failure to become engaged with print and the thinking that it stimulates. Every student must enjoy the power and personal satisfaction that literacy provides. As a teacher of middle grade students, you are a key to that power!

ACKNOWLEDGMENTS

This book is very much a team effort. Without the expertise of my colleagues at Merrill/ Prentice Hall, this text would not be a reality. My editor, Linda Montgomery, believed in my vision and encouraged me to persevere, and I thank her for that. Her efforts in the development of this text were enthusiastically supported by Jeff Johnston. The preparation of this manuscript for production has been under the careful direction of Linda Bayma, whose expertise has made the entire process a wonderful experience for me. My thanks to everyone at Carlisle Publishers Services, who refined my thinking and brought consistency to my ideas. Thank you all so very much!

I would like to express my thanks to the reviewers of this book for their thoughtful comments and suggestions: Helen R. Abadiano, Central Connecticut State University; Larry K. Andrews, University of Nebraska—Lincoln; Carol J. Fuhler, Iowa State University; Karen Robinson, Otterbein College; and Joan Simmons, University of Wisconsin—Oshkosh.

The artwork at the beginning of each chapter was created by one of my daughters, Heather Combs. Thank you, Heather, for breathing life into my idea.

My life as a teacher and learner continues to be touched by so many other teachers and learners, in particular the undergraduate and graduate students at the University of Nevada, and by so many teachers in Washoe, Douglas, and Lyon Counties, Nevada. I am especially grateful to Lou Loftin, Kim Muncy, and Kristen Felten for sharing their stories.

Finally, to my husband, Randy Koetting, for your love, support, and encouragement during this past year. You keep me grounded in what matters!

Martha Combs

REFERENCES

Carnegie Council on Adolescent Development. (1996). *Great transitions*. Washington, DC: Author.

Vygotsky, L. S. (1962). *Thought and language* (E. Hanfmann & G. Vakar, Eds. & Trans.). Cambridge, MA: MIT Press.

Discover the Companion Website Accompanying This Book

The Prentice Hall Companion Website: A Virtual Learning Environment

Technology is a constantly growing and changing aspect of our field that is creating a need for content and resources. To address this emerging need, Prentice Hall has developed an online learning environment for students and professors alike—Companion Websites—to support our textbooks.

In creating a Companion Website, our goal is to build on and enhance what the textbook already offers. For this reason, the content for each user-friendly website is organized by topic and provides the professor and student with a variety of meaningful resources. Common features of a Companion Website include:

For the Professor

Every Companion Website integrates *Syllabus Manager*™, an online syllabus creation and management utility.

- *Syllabus Manager*™ provides you, the instructor, with an easy, step-by-step process to create and revise syllabi, with direct links into the Companion Website and other online content without having to learn HTML.
- Students may log on to your syllabus during any study session. All they need to know is the web address for the Companion Website and the password you've assigned to your syllabus.
- After you have created a syllabus using *Syllabus Manager*™, students may enter the syllabus for their course section from any point in the Companion Website.
- Clicking on a date, the student is shown the list of activities for the assignment. The activities for each assignment are linked directly to actual content, saving time for students.
- Adding assignments consists of clicking on the desired due date, then filling in the details of the assignment—name of the assignment, instructions, and whether it is a one-time or repeating assignment.
- In addition, links to other activities can be created easily. If the activity is online, a URL can be entered in the space provided, and it will be linked automatically in the final syllabus.
- Your completed syllabus is hosted on our servers, allowing convenient updates from any computer on the Internet. Changes you make to your syllabus are immediately available to your students at their next logon.

For the Student

- *Topic Overviews*—outline key concepts in topic areas
- *Strategies*—these websites provide suggestions and information on how to implement instructional strategies and activities for each topic
- *Web Links*—a wide range of websites that allow the students to access current information on everything from rationales for specific types of instruction, to research on related topics, to compilations of useful articles and more
- *Electronic Bluebook*—send homework or essays directly to your instructor's e-mail with this paperless form
- *Message Board*—serves as a virtual bulletin board to post—or respond to—questions or comments to/from a national audience
- *Chat*—real-time chat with anyone who is using the text anywhere in the country—ideal for discussion and study groups, class projects, etc.

To take advantage of these and other resources, please visit the *Readers and Writers in the Middle Grades*, Second Edition, Companion Website at

www.prenhall.com/combs

Contents

4 READ-ALOUD AND WHOLE-CLASS LITERATURE STUDY 82

7 USING INFORMATION TEXTS AND TEXTBOOKS EFFECTIVELY   196

8 UNDERSTANDING WRITING PROCESSES   222

INFORMAL WRITING: USING WRITING TO SUPPORT LEARNING

248

WRITER'S WORKSHOP: GUIDING STUDENTS' DEVELOPMENT AS WRITERS   272

WORD STUDY: EXTENDING KNOWLEDGE OF WORDS IN READING AND WRITING   306

TEACHING WITH AN INTEGRATED LANGUAGE ARTS BASAL SERIES

346

INTEGRATING LEARNING EXPERIENCES: LINKING LANGUAGE LEARNING OPPORTUNITIES   370

READERS AND WRITERS
IN THE
MIDDLE GRADES

chapter 1

Readers and Writers in the Middle Grades: An Introduction

In this chapter . . .

We begin to develop an understanding of:

- The intellectual, physical, psychological, social, and moral and ethi[...] development of middle grade students,

- Language issues of early adolescents,

- National standards for literacy development,

- Recommendations for middle grade education,

- Learning environments that encourage and support the developm[...] of competence and independence,

- A teacher's role as a mediator,

- Valuing the diversity of our students, and

- The role of assessment for teachers and students.

Something to Think About . . .

To orient ourselves to issues of literacy among early adolescents, consider these two quotes from respected educators:

> A growing body of knowledge shows that what happens to students between the ages of ten and fourteen determines not only their future success in school, but success in life as well. (Wiles & Bondi, 1993, p. 24)

> Early adolescence provides one of the last chances to help students become independent, confident producers and comprehenders of language. Students who do not develop the ability to use language in an academic setting by the time they leave middle school often drop out or experience failure in high school. If teachers could somehow capture the excitement and necessity of student communication and relate it to the content they want students to learn, perhaps educators would find the key to motivation and success for middle grade students. (Irvin, 1998, pp. 1–2)

Building a Theory Base . . .

How do we describe literacy development for early adolescents? What types of literacy experiences might these students find meaningful and challenging? To address these questions, we must have an understanding of the students we are likely to find in grades 4 through 8. In addition, we must develop a strong theoretical and pedagogical knowledge base about language and literacy from which to make appropriate decisions for instruction.

TOWARD AN UNDERSTANDING OF MIDDLE GRADE STUDENTS

With the exception of the years from birth to age 3, there is no other period in life when we experience the magnitude of change that occurs during early adolescence, approximately 10 to 14 years of age. Do you recall this period in your own life? Eichhorn (1966) refers to this period of development as *transescence*, which he describes as

> the stage of development which begins before the onset of puberty and extends through the early stages of adolescence. Since puberty does not occur for all precisely at the same chronological age in human development, the transescent designation is based on the many physical, social, emotional, and intellectual changes in body chemistry that appear before the time in which the body gains a practical degree of stabilization over these complex pubescent changes. (p. 3)

Transescence suggests a process of "becoming" that can be filled with uncertainty and anxiety. *Turning Points 2000: Educating Adolescents in the 21st Century* (Jackson & Davis, 2000), an update to the landmark 1989 Carnegie report concerning the education of middle grade students, reaffirms the need to understand and attend to their unique needs:

> There is a crucial need to help adolescents at this early age to acquire a durable basis for self esteem, flexible and inquiring minds, reliable and close human relationships, a sense of belonging in a valued group, and a way of being useful beyond one's self. They need to find constructive expression for their inherent curiosity and exploratory energy, as well as a basis for making informed, deliberate decisions—especially on matters that have large and perhaps lifelong consequences, such as education and health. (p.ix)

Considering the ideas above, it is important to consider the educational experiences we might provide for middle grade students. At this time it might be helpful to study the information presented in Figures 1.1 through 1.5, excerpted from *Caught in the Middle* (California State Department of Education, 1987), *Turning Points: Preparing American Youth for the 21st Century* (Carnegie Council on Adolescent Development, 1989), and *Turning Points 2000: Education Adolescents in the 21st Century* (Jackson & Davis, 2000), to confirm or challenge our understandings about the development of middle grade students. As we consider the literacy needs of early adolescents, our ability to make decisions concerning their literacy needs should be supported by our understanding of the developmental issues that face this group of students.

LANGUAGE OF EARLY ADOLESCENTS

We are aware that early adolescence is a time of expanded social interests and experiences. It is also a time when new thinking abilities allow consideration of many possibilities and a time when peers become more influential (National Middle School Association, 1995). The sweeping changes that are characterictic of early adolescents also impact their continued development of skill with language (Owens, 2001).

As we consider the challenges that face this age group, we must always remember that language is the foundation of literacy and, subsequently, success in school. Language is both the object of knowledge and the medium through which knowledge is acquired (Cazden, 1982). In this text, language is defined as a socially shared code or conventional system for representing concepts through the use of arbitrary symbols and rule-governed combinations of those symbols (Owens, 2001).

■ FIGURE 1.1

Intellectual development
of middle grade students

Middle grade students display the following *intellectual* development:

1. Display a wide range of individual intellectual development as their minds experience the transition from the concrete-manipulatory stage to the capacity for abstract thought. This transition ultimately makes possible:
   • Propositional thought,
   • Consideration of ideas contrary to fact,
   • Reasoning with hypotheses involving two or more variables,
   • Appreciation for the elegance of mathematical logic expressed in symbols,
   • Insight into the nuances of poetic metaphor and musical notation,
   • Analysis of the power of political ideology,
   • Ability to project thought into the future, to anticipate, and to formulate goals,
   • Insight into the sources of previously unquestioned attitudes, behaviors, and values, and
   • Interpretation of larger concepts and generalizations of traditional wisdom expressed through sayings, axioms, and aphorisms.
2. Are intensely curious.
3. Prefer active over passive learning experiences; favor interaction with peers during learning activities.
4. Exhibit a strong willingness to learn things they consider to be useful; enjoy using skills to resolve real-life problems.
5. Are egocentric; argue to convince others; exhibit independent, critical thought.
6. Consider academic goals as a secondary level of priority; personal-social concerns dominate thoughts and activities.
7. Experience the phenomenon of metacognition—the ability to know what one knows and does not know.
8. Are intellectually at risk; face decisions that have the potential to affect major academic values with lifelong consequences.

To provide appropriate guidance and support for middle grade students' literacy development, it is helpful for us to consider the language of early adolescents. In their home and community, early adolescents speak a social dialect to adults, younger children, and peers. In school they are also expected to have acquired and use an academic dialect as they converse with teachers and other students and for learning from text (Chamot & O'Malley, 1994). In addition, to separate themselves from other social groups, early adolescents develop a dialect of jargon or slang that is reserved for their peer group (Larson & McKinley, 1995).

Early adolescents use social, academic, and peer forms of language. All three forms of language have their own vocabulary, meaning, and context in which they are used. Early adolescents may shift from one dialect to another without realizing that they have adjusted their speech for the social, academic, or peer audience (Adger, 1998).

LANGUAGE FOR SOCIAL PURPOSES

The social dialect(s) that early adolescents develop is based on the cultural norms of the group with which they associate themselves. A social dialect is informal and may not be gramatically correct when compared to the form of English that is expected in school. The

Physical development of
middle grade students

Middle grade students display the following *physical* development:

1. Experience accelerated physical development marked by increases in weight, height, heart size, lung capacity, and muscular strength.
2. Mature at varying speeds. Girls tend to be taller than boys for the first 2 years of early adolescence and are ordinarily more physically developed than boys.
3. Experience bone growth faster than muscle development; uneven muscle/bone development results in lack of coordination and awkwardness; bones may lack protection of covering muscles and supporting tendons.
4. Reflect a wide range of individual differences that begin to appear in prepubertal and pubertal stages of development. Boys tend to lag behind girls. Marked individual differences are seen in physical development for boys and girls. The greatest variability in physiological development and size occurs at about age 13.
5. Experience biological development 5 years sooner than adolescents of the last century; the average age of menarche has dropped from 17 to 12 years of age.
6. Face responsibility for sexual behavior before full emotional and social maturity has occurred.
7. Show changes in body contour including temporarily large noses, protruding ears, long arms; have posture problems.
8. Are often disturbed by body changes:
   • Girls are anxious about physical changes that accompany sexual maturation, and
   • Boys are anxious about receding chins, cowlicks, dimples, and change in their voices.
9. Experience fluctuations in basal metabolism that can cause extreme restlessness at times and equally extreme listlessness at other moments.
10. Have ravenous appetites and peculiar tastes; may overtax digestive system with large quantities of improper foods.
11. Lack physical health; have poor levels of endurance, strength, and flexibility; as a group are fatter and unhealthier.
12. Are physically at risk; causes of death are homicide, suicide, accident, and leukemia.

Psychological development
of middle grade students

Middle grade students display the following *psychological* development:

1. Are often erratic and inconsistent in their behavior; anxiety and fear are contrasted with periods of bravado; feelings shift between superiority and inferiority.
2. Have chemical and hormonal imbalances that often trigger emotions that are frightening and poorly understood; may regress to more childish behavior patterns at this point.
3. Are easily offended and are sensitive to criticism of personal shortcomings.
4. Tend to exaggerate simple occurrences and believe that personal problems, experiences, and feelings are unique to themselves.
5. Are moody, restless; often feel self-conscious and alienated; lack self-esteem; are introspective.
6. Are searching for adult identity and acceptance even in the midst of intense peer group relationships.
7. Are vulnerable to naive opinions, one-sided arguments.
8. Are searching to form a conscious sense of individual uniqueness—"Who am I?"
9. Have emerging sense of humor based on increased intellectual ability to see abstract relationship; appreciate the "double entendre."
10. Are basically optimistic, hopeful.
11. Are psychologically at risk; at no other point in human development is an individual likely to encounter so much diversity in relation to oneself and others.

Social development of
middle grade students

Middle grade students display the following *social* development:

1. Experience often traumatic conflicts due to conflicting loyalties to peer groups and family.
2. Refer to peers as sources for standards and models of behavior; media heroes and heroines are also singularly important in shaping behavior and fashion.
3. May be rebellious toward parents but still strongly dependent on parental values; want to make own choices, but the authority of the family is a critical factor in ultimate decisions.
4. Are impacted by high level of mobility in society; may become anxious and disoriented when peer group ties are broken because of family relocation to other communities.
5. Are often confused and frightened by new school settings that are large and impersonal.
6. Act out unusual and drastic behavior at times; may be aggressive, daring, boisterous, argumentative.
7. Are fiercely loyal to peer group values; sometimes cruel or insensitive to those outside the peer group.
8. Want to know and feel that significant adults, including parents and teachers, love and accept them; need frequent affirmation.
9. Sense negative impact of adolescent behaviors on parents and teachers; realize thin edge between tolerance and rejection; feelings of adult rejection drive adolescent into the relatively secure social environment of the peer group.
10. Strive to define sexual characteristics; search to establish positive social relationships with members of the same and opposite sex.
11. Experience low risk-trust relationships with adults who show lack of sensitivity to adolescent characteristics and needs.
12. Challenge authority figures; test limits of acceptable behavior.
13. Are socially at risk; adult values are largely shaped conceptually during adolescence; negative interactions with peers, parents, and teachers may compromise ideals and commitments.

Moral and ethical
development of middle
grade students

Middle grade students display the following *moral and ethical* development:

1. Are essentially idealistic; have a strong sense of fairness in human relationships.
2. Experience thoughts and feelings of awe and wonder related to their expanding intellectual and emotional awareness.
3. Ask large unanswerable questions about the meaning of life; do not expect absolute answers but are turned off by trivial adult responses.
4. Are reflective, analytical, and introspective about their thoughts and feelings.
5. Confront hard moral and ethical questions with which they are unprepared to cope.
6. Are at risk in the development of moral and ethical choices and behaviors; primary dependency on the influences of home and church for moral and ethical development seriously compromises adolescents for whom these resources are absent; adolescents want to explore the moral and ethical issues which are confronted in the curriculum, in the media, and in the daily interactions they experience in their families and peer groups.

social dialect is comprised of elements found in most conversations, such as requests, explanations, greetings, salutations, questions, and the like. Social conversations are usually spontaneous, with immediate responses. The topics of conversations usually are familiar and supported by firsthand experiences in some form.

Early adolescents interact in social settings to process their own life experiences and to understand what they observe in the world. It is through such social interactions that they acquire the knowledge of the world on which we will draw to help them learn academic subjects. The familiarity of social settings provides an opportunity to acquire new vocabulary and an understanding of how that vocabulary relates to existing knowledge. If interactions within social settings have been primarily verbal, or verbal interactions tied to physical activity, and students have come to rely on that mode of communication for learning, then we must provide meaningful learning opportunities in school to help students make connections between verbal and written forms of communication.

LANGUAGE FOR ACADEMIC PURPOSES

As children enter school settings, they encounter a form and use of language that differs from their home and community. The spontaneous speech of more intimate social contexts is replaced with more restricted interactions that occur within the larger groups that are so characteristic of school. The focus of the interactions within this larger group becomes increasingly complex and removed from meaningful contexts. Unlike social interactions, middle grade students find that interactions in the school setting are filled with impersonal topics, delayed communication feedback between themselves and their teachers, and the expectation for more formal uses of standard English (Richards, Platt, & Platt, 1992).

By early adolescence, students are expected to take in a great deal of information in short periods of time, information that is increasingly removed from students' firsthand experiences in the world outside of school. The structure of sentences used by both teachers and authors of texts, from which students are expected to learn, becomes longer and more complex. However, opportunities to learn to formulate such complex sentences, structures that are very different from those used in social settings, are limited by the restricted oral interactions between students and teachers. Oral interactions, the way in which we first learn to expand our knowledge and use of language, are often limited to responding to direct questions during instruction (Chamot & O'Malley, 1994).

In addition to the use of a more formal communication style, middle grade students are expected to have acquired an understanding of the language of instruction used by their teachers and the authors of texts (e.g., main idea, paragraph, summarize, comprehend). This language is partly what distinguishes social forms from academic forms of language. The other adults in students' lives do not talk like their teachers and, consequently, provide little opportunity to help students acquire skill in effectively using academic language.

Middle grade students are also expected to understand and use the technical vocabulary of the academic disciplines they study. For example, the study of ecosystems in science includes such vocabulary as carnivore, herbivore, omnivore, producer, and consumer. If this vocabulary is new, (i.e., is not included in the social dialect that the student brings to school), then acquiring the vocabulary in order to understand concepts about ecosystems will present significant challenges unless we change the nature of interactions between teachers and students in the middle grade classrooms.

LANGUAGE FOR COMMUNICATION WITH PEERS

Early adolescents often use a special language that separates them from both adults and younger children (Larson & McKinley, 1995). This peer dialect is spontaneous, may be contextual, and usually requires only lower order thinking skills. It promotes closeness and solidarity and is filled with jargon and slang, the "words of the hour," special codes, secret meanings, and, sometimes, hand signals (Eder, Evans, & Parker, 1995). The more familiarity between the participants, the less that needs to be said.

Moving between these forms of language, and selecting language that is appropriate to the context, is a challenge for early adolescents. They may change forms of language, such as moving from academic to peer, without realizing they have done so. Such a shift may make the language they use incomprehensible for the context in which it occurs, such as during classroom instruction. With language forming the foundation of all literacy development, we must continue to make ourselves aware of the possibilities for language development among our middle grade students. Throughout this text we will raise questions about our expectations for the language our students use and its role in their literacy development.

Throughout this text you will have opportunities to step back from your reading to consider your thoughts about particular issues. Here is such an opportunity.

As you begin this text that focuses on the literacy development of students between the ages of 10 and 14, does reading information such as the contents of the previous sections call up memories of personal experiences during that part of your life? Do you flashback to particular incidents in your life as a middle grade student? When those reflections occur, how do you deal with them?

• • •

I recall vividly the intensity of feelings that I had about my friends, my apathy about doing homework, the pain and loss I felt when my favorite teacher died and we planted a tree in her memory, my excitement about what I learned in drafting class, and my fear of being up in front of my peers to lead a debate about presidential candidates. When I was learning to teach, I frequently wondered if my experiences as a student would mirror the experiences of my prospective students.

As a student, I also gained thousands of hours of experience watching teachers "do their work." When I became a teacher, I had to learn how to shift my thinking from a student's perspective and the new role that I would assume. There were times when other educators offered me ideas and information that supported my experiences, yet on many other occasions the ideas and experiences that came my way contradicted my own experiences and the beliefs about teaching that emerged from those experiences. There are few other professions in which people gain so many hours of experience as participants before they begin to practice that profession.

Our experiences as students are powerful. It is important to recognize and value our experiences as students, but it is also imperative that we consider when our experiences may contradict ideas and information that we should assimilate to change our perceptions and beliefs about teaching and learning. It is important for you to take time to consider how your past experiences influence your beliefs about education.

• • •

STANDARDS FOR LITERACY IN THE MIDDLE GRADES

Traditionally, definitions of literacy have centered around one's ability to use language to effectively participate in society. That use of language was described, in particular, as possessing the skill to read and write standard English. During the past 100 years, however, changes in technology have created "a cultural environment that has extended and reshaped the role of language and the written word" (Hobbs, 1996). Such dramatic changes compel us to recognize that multiple literacies exist today and must be connected to the culture and contexts in which they are used.

Each of us has an extensive educational history, a history of thousands of hours in school settings, that pushes us to think of literacy as reading and writing print. With today's communication technologies we must reteach ourselves to think of literacy more broadly. Consider this new definition of literacy, adopted by educators who identify themselves with the "media literacy" movement: "Literacy is the ability to access, analyze, evaluate, and communicate messages in a variety of forms" (Hobbs, 1996, p. 3). If teachers of early adolescents defined literacy in these broad terms, how might it impact school-based literacy experiences? Do you think that teachers might also begin to consider the out-of-school literacy experiences students have as an essential part of what is valued in the school curriculum?

The preceding view of literacy is also supported by the Standards for the English Language Arts developed jointly by the National Council of Teachers of English (NCTE) and the International Reading Association (IRA) and published in 1996. You can access information about these standards on the NCTE website (http://www.ncte.org/standards). The standards, presented in Figure 1.6, are intended to be viewed as interrelated parts of a whole. As you read each of these 12 standards, consider the images of literacy they describe and the role of language in literacy.

As we read documents such as the English language arts standards, we are reminded that language helps to define who we are as human beings. It is the "basis of human community. With it we inform, persuade, challenge, support, and entertain each other" (Dias, Beer, Ledwell-Brown, Pare, & Pittenger, 1992, p. 187). In a middle grade curriculum, it is through the language arts (listening, speaking, reading, writing, and viewing) that we provide early adolescents with opportunities to learn to use language, to learn about language, and to learn through language. In the chapters that follow, multiple opportunities are presented to challenge and expand your personal definitions and understandings of language and literacy.

Our role as teachers of early adolescents can have a far-reaching impact. We should guide our students to be literate individuals who are competent to deal with the problems that face us as world citizens. The curriculum and learning environment that we provide for middle grade students is an essential part of their development as literate individuals.

BEST PRACTICES IN LITERACY INSTRUCTION

As we consider the attributes of a literacy program that will support and extend the competence of all of our middle grade students, we will draw on the results of a synthesis of 10

■ **F I G U R E   1.6**

Standards for the
English language arts
From *Standards for the
English Language Arts*, by
the International Reading
Association and the
National Council of Teachers
of English, copyright 1996 by
the International Reading
Association and the National
Council of Teachers of English.
Reprinted with permission.

1. Students read a wide range of print and nonprint texts to build an understanding of themselves, and of the cultures of the United States and the world; to acquire new information; to respond to the needs and demands of society and the workplace; and for personal fulfillment. Among these texts are fiction and nonfiction, classic and contemporary works.
2. Students read a wide range of literature from many periods in many genre to build an understanding of the many dimensions (e.g., philosophical, ethical, aesthetic) of human experience.
3. Students apply a wide range of strategies to comprehend, interpret, evaluate, and appreciate texts. They draw on their prior experience, their interactions with other readers and writers, their knowledge of word meaning and of other texts, their word identification strategies, and their understanding of textual features (e.g., sound–letter correspondence, sentence structure, context, graphics).
4. Students adjust their use of spoken, written, and visual language (e.g., conventions, style, vocabulary) to communicate effectively with a variety of audiences and for different purposes.
5. Students employ a wide range of strategies as they write and use different writing process elements appropriately to communicate with different audiences for a variety of purposes.
6. Students apply knowledge of language structure, language conventions (e.g., spelling and punctuation), media techniques, figurative language, and genre to create, critique, and discuss print and nonprint texts.
7. Students conduct research on issues and interests by generating ideas and questions and by posing problems. They gather, evaluate, and synthesize data from a variety of sources (e.g., print and nonprint texts, artifacts, people) to communicate their discoveries in ways that suit their purpose and audience.
8. Students use a variety of technological and information resources (e.g., libraries, databases, computer networks, video) to gather and synthesize information and to create and communicate knowledge.
9. Students develop an understanding of and respect for the diversity of language use, patterns, and dialects across cultures, ethnic groups, geographic regions, and social roles.
10. Students whose first language is not English make use of their first language to develop competency in the English language arts and to develop understanding of content across the curriculum.
11. Students participate as knowledgeable, reflective, creative, and critical members of a variety of literacy communities.
12. Students use spoken, written, and visual language to accomplish their own purposes (e.g., for learning, enjoyment, persuasion, and the exchange of information).

research-based best practices in literacy reported by Linda Gambrell and Susan Mazzoni (1999), and supported by a study of outstanding fifth-grade teachers from across the nation (Pressley 1998). As middle grade teachers we should strive to understand and practice the following:

1. Teach reading for authentic meaning-making literacy experiences: for pleasure, to be informed, and to perform a task.
2. Use high-quality literature.

3. Integrate a comprehensive word study/phonics program into reading/writing instruction.

4. Use multiple texts that link and expand concepts.

5. Balance teacher- and student-led discussions.

6. Build a whole-class community that emphasizes important concepts and builds background knowledge.

7. Work with students in small groups while other students read and write about what they have read.

8. Give students plenty of time to read in class.

9. Give students direct instruction in decoding and comprehension strategies that promote independent reading. Balance direct instruction, guided instruction, and independent learning.

10. Use a variety of assessment techniques to inform instruction (Gambrell & Mazzoni, 1999, p. 14).

Throughout this text we will explore each of these components to learn how to provide balanced learning of literacy skills and processes for all of our students.

RECOMMENDATIONS FOR MIDDLE GRADE EDUCATION

With the uncertainty of transescence, early adolescents need to develop views of themselves as valuable, able, and responsible people. School experiences, including literacy experiences, must promote feelings of security, support, and success. The curriculum should engage students in issues that are important to them, to help them resolve conflicting viewpoints, and to reexamine their own views in light of the views of others. Meaningful reading and writing are excellent tools for such exploration.

Middle grade education received special recognition with the publication of *Turning Points: Preparing American Youth for the 21st Century* (Carnegie Council on Adolescent Development, 1989) and was reaffirmed with the recent update of the report in *Turning Points 2000: Educating Adolescents in the 21st Century* (Jackson & Davis, 2000). These studies of middle grade education recommended the following:

- Develop and implement a curriculum that is grounded in rigorous academic standards for what students should know and be able to do, recognizing that standards should be flexible to reflect changes in society.

- The curriculum must be relevant to the concerns of adolescents and based on how students learn best.

- Teachers should fully understand the needs of young adolescents and use instructional methods designed to prepare all students to achieve higher standards and become lifelong learners.

- Organize relationships in school to create a climate of intellectual development and a caring community of shared educational purpose.

- Schools for young adolescents should provide a safe and healthy environment.

- Parents and communities should be involved in supporting learning and healthy development.

The council's recommendations closely parallel the descriptions of 10- to 14-year-olds presented earlier in Figures 1.1 through 1.5. It will be helpful to refer to this information as we explore the development of language and literacy experiences for young adolescents.

LEARNING ENVIRONMENTS IN THE MIDDLE GRADES

Building on the previous recommendations, this text focuses on developmental theories that provide the base for constructing learning environments that encourage and support competent, independent behavior (Holdaway, 1979; Vygotsky, 1962, 1978). Such environments for middle grade students should include the following:

- "Knowledgeable others" who model clearly purposeful and successful use of the skills/strategies to be learned,
- Support and encouragement for approximations toward mature behavior,
- A noncompetitive learning atmosphere,
- Opportunities for practice that are motivated and paced by the learner,
- Opportunities for learners to correct and evaluate their own growth, and
- Encouragement and support that lead toward independent functioning.

In the sections that follow, examples from Hiro's fifth-grade and Kristen's seventh-grade developmental reading classrooms are used to illustrate how teachers consciously create classroom learning environments that support early adolescent development.

KNOWLEDGEABLE OTHERS

Each of us, regardless of our stage of development, sees "knowledgeable others" model behaviors with obvious purpose and success, and we may try to emulate these behaviors. These knowledgeable others help us form expectations for the behaviors we hope to attain. They also help us set benchmarks for ourselves, so that we may evaluate our development as individuals. As we observe the literacy behaviors of knowledgeable others, we learn about personal, as well as "real-world," reasons to read and write.

Manning (1995) suggests that "many adolescents particularly do not understand who they are or why they behave as they do" (p. 658). He suggests that, for adolescents, knowledgeable others live in children's and young adult literature, particularly biography and historical fiction. Early adolescents can find in the lives of others "some purpose, direction, and fulfillment in their own" (p. 658).

In his fifth-grade classroom, Hiro models reading for pleasure during independent free-choice reading periods. His face and body show his pleasure. He even laughs aloud on occasion. During writer's workshop, Hiro writes for the first 10 minutes of each class, while the students are also writing. Periodically he shares his writing to get feedback from the students. To model how competent readers think about their reading, Kristen shares some of her strategies by thinking out loud while reading books that are familiar to her seventh-grade students. Hiro and Kristen each serve as a knowledgeable other for their students.

SUPPORTING APPROXIMATIONS

Developmental processes, such as learning to read and write, mature slowly over many years. There are times in our learning when our performance is less than proficient, and even quite poor in comparison to mature performance. How the knowledgeable others in our lives respond to us as we attempt to learn greatly influences our willingness to persevere. If those around us support us and recognize our attempts, we are more likely to sustain our efforts. If, however, those around us expect more immediate success or perfection, we may question our ability to learn and may expend less effort in the process.

As teachers, we must recognize that many middle grade students are not yet mature readers and writers and that they need our continued support for their approximations toward new, more mature literacy behaviors. We also must remember that it is through students' interactions with us, their teachers, in the sociocultural environment of the classroom that they learn to read, write, and engage in academic discourse (Goatley, Brock, & Raphael, 1995, p. 355).

Hiro and Kristen support their students' attempts through conferences and compliments. During both reading and writing instruction, they have face-to-face conferences with students. Hiro makes careful notes about student progress during each conference. By referring to his notes and to samples of student work, Hiro is able to identify even the smallest progress that his students make in their reading and writing. He is then able to make specific compliments to support students' approximations toward more complex behavior, such as recognizing an author's use of foreshadowing to develop tension in a plot. In addition to her conferences, Kristen writes specific compliments in students' reading journals as she responds to letters that students write to her.

NONCOMPETITIVE ENVIRONMENTS

An environment that encourages and supports students' willingness to take risks in their attempts to learn will not emphasize competition among students. Competition that aids learning occurs within ourselves, when we push ourselves to learn something new.

Holdaway (1980) extends our understanding of competition when he states: "The real business of learning is concerned with performing better today than yesterday or last week;

■ *How will you assist your students in expanding their conversational skills to support and extend their academic learning?*

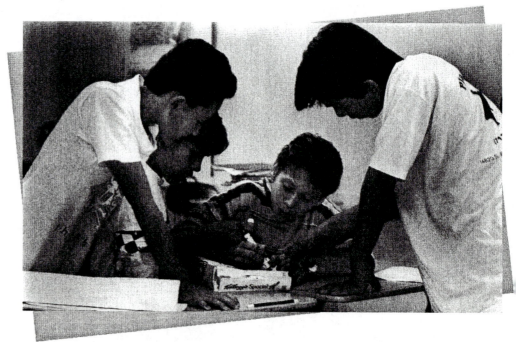

it has absolutely nothing to do with performing better than someone else. [Students] want
to learn any developmental task in order to be the same as their peers, not better than
them" (p. 18).

Early adolescence is already filled with periods of great uncertainty. Competitive environments only cause greater doubt as students question their ability to be successful.
There are more losers than winners in competitions; students in middle grade classrooms
have more to gain in inclusive, collaborative literacy environments.

The students in Hiro's and Kristen's classes keep individual records about the books
they read. There are no class charts that compare the amount of reading that students do.
Instead, Hiro has students reflect on their reading each week and make comparisons to previous weeks. Students individually graph the amount of time and number of pages read
each week, then write a self-evaluation of their reading progress. Students are easily able
to see their own improvement. Kristen asks her seventh-grade students to complete personal self-assessments in their reading logs at the midpoint and end of each grading period.

SELF-MOTIVATED, SELF-PACED PRACTICE

Learning complex processes such as reading and writing requires a great deal of practice.
When our own desire drives our learning, we are more likely to practice. Choice fuels that
desire and fosters a sense of control over our learning.

Independent learners typically set their own goals for learning and pace themselves to
suit their goals. In Hiro's classroom, students select their own reading materials and determine a reading pace that fits them and the text. They also decide when they will write responses to texts and when they wish to pursue an extension project for a text they found
meaningful. Both Kristen's and Hiro's students participate in reader's and writer's workshops, forms of individualized reading and writing that allow for student choice.

SELF-CORRECTION AND SELF-EVALUATION

Mature readers and writers are responsible for monitoring the accuracy and quality of their
own thinking. For middle grade students to achieve similar independence, they must develop the ability to monitor the quality of their own learning.

The reading and writing curriculum in middle grade classrooms must treat students as
worthwhile individuals who know something about themselves as learners. We must encourage them to trust their knowledge of themselves, combined with corrective feedback
from reliable sources, to move toward independence.

In Hiro's classroom, students keep a learning portfolio that reflects their assessment
of themselves as readers, writers, and learners. They add new work samples and self-
evaluation reports at least once each grading period. Hiro works with his students to
help them develop personal criteria for judging the value of their efforts. Kristen's students also are learning to evaluate themselves as readers and as learners. In addition,
Kristen works with members of her middle school team to help her students follow
through with self-evaluation in other subject areas.

INDEPENDENCE IS THE GOAL

Our goal for students in school, as in life, should be independence! Independent learners are
confident in their own abilities and are competent users of skills and strategies. Luis Moll

(1994) reminds us that our role as teachers is to enable and guide activities that involve students as thoughtful learners in socially meaningful tasks. Of central concern is how we facilitate the students' "taking over" or appropriation of the learning activity (p. 180).

If we are to successfully promote independence, we must set up and sustain developmental learning environments. We should let students' successes in independent learning outside of school teach us about the possibilities for learning in school.

As you read about Kristen's and Hiro's classrooms, can you envision yourself in your own classroom, creating a classroom environment for student learning? How do you envision your own classroom? What current beliefs do you hold about teaching and learning that might impact the learning environment in your classroom?

BECOMING A TEACHER-MEDIATOR

As teachers, we are a critical part of the learning environments we create for students. We serve as a "more knowledgeable other" for our students, assisting them in becoming independent and competent individuals. How will you function in this role? In this text, the role of teacher is seen as that of a mediator between learners and various types of texts (Dixon-Krauss, 1994), a mediator whose goal is to move students toward independence as readers, writers, and thinkers.

This view of teacher as mediator is influenced by the research of Russian psychologist Lev Vygotsky (1978), who describes the relationship between learners' development and instruction as a *zone of proximal development*. The zone is the range between where learners function independently (actual development) and where they function with the assistance of a more knowledgeable other (potential development). In Vygotsky's (1962) view, instruction should lead development. He states: "What the child can do in cooperation today he can do alone tomorrow. Therefore the only good kind of instruction is that which marches ahead of development and leads it; it must be aimed not so much at the ripe as at the ripening functions" (p. 104).

What does Vygotsky's theory suggest for us as middle grade teachers? We must think of instruction as paving the way for students to move from their present level of independent functioning to a higher level by providing assistance in tasks that students cannot yet do by themselves. To do this, we must know our students well enough to provide learning experiences that are *just ahead* of what they currently do independently. What a challenge, especially when we may meet several classes of students each day!

As we provide instruction within a student's zone of proximal development, we should (1) mediate or augment a student's learning through our social interactions with the student and (2) be flexible and adjust our support/assistance (amount and type) based on the feedback we receive from the student during the learning activity (Dixon-Krauss, 1996).

We cannot completely determine our role before we begin to interact with students. To help students move toward independence, we must determine our role based on what students show us they need from us as the more knowledgeable other. During any learning experience, the type of support we provide can range from vague hints to explicit responses. Student feedback during learning activities should tell us about the role they need us to take.

VALUING DIVERSITY IN THE MIDDLE GRADES

The diversity of society shows itself in middle grade classrooms. We find students that differ in their backgrounds of knowledge, their ability to make use of their experiences, their preferences for learning, and their motivation to engage in new learning experiences. As a result of the changes experienced by 10- to 14-year-olds, classroom diversity is accentuated.

DIVERSITY IN OUR SOCIETY

Diversity has always existed in our society, whether it be of gender, social class, ethnic groups, learning styles, physical or mental abilities, personal interests, religious beliefs, first language, or the like (Harris, 1994). It is the unique contributions of each of these groups, and the individuals within each group, that have made the United States the country that it is (Ramirez & Ramirez, 1994).

The United States is experiencing tremendous growth in cultural diversity. In the 1999–2000 school year, the U.S. Department of Education estimated that of the 46.8 million students enrolled in public schools, approximately 38% of the students were considered to be part of a minority group (e.g., American Indian, Asian Pacific Islander, Black, Hispanic). Such diversity brings cultural uniqueness among students that should become a part of the school curriculum. According to Moll and Gonzalez (1994), the emphasis in education should be on "students' novel use of cultural resources, including people, ideas, and technologies, to facilitate and direct their intellectual work" (p. 453).

Many middle grade students who are members of a minority group are also recent immigrants to the United States. English is not their first language. Learning a second language is a challenging, and often difficult, task that takes time. The issues of learning a second language while also being expected to participate in an academic environment present a growing challenge for middle grade teachers. The ability to function in an academic environment will take as long as 5 to 7 years (Cummins, 1981). English language learners (ELLs) will need numerous opportunities to actively participate in collaborative learning experiences with sensitive English speakers whose language can be a model (Padron, 1998).

When we know such diversity exists, as it does, it is our responsibility to use that knowledge constructively in our teaching. As Asa Hilliard (1994) reminds us,

> Diversity is the norm in human society, even when homogeneity appears on the surface. . . . When educators do not notice diversity, when they give negative notice, or when they lose the opportunity to give positive notice of the natural diversity that is always there, they create a bogus reality for teaching and learning. (p. x)

We must also remember that such variation occurs not only across learners, but also within individuals (Smart & Smart, 1973). For example, as students develop at different rates it is quite possible for a student to be able to think abstractly in one subject area but not in another.

DIVERSITY AMONG LEARNERS

As students reach the middle grades they will have many and varied literacy experiences, both in and out of school. Because we know that great diversity exists among our students we should be committed to providing learning experiences that are culturally responsive. We should understand and build on students' home culture and language. Culturally responsive instruction does not mean that we must match students' home situations exactly, but rather we must connect to their patterns of participation and values expressed in such situations (Au & Kawakami, 1994). For students who are learning English for the first time, Yolanda Padron (1998) reminds us that "Prior knowledge is a key ingredient in making sense of text. ELL students whose cultural background and language may differ from an author's may have difficulties with texts because they do not have the prior knowledge to understand them" (p. 115).

Literacy activities will be responsive if they engage students in purposeful communication with a real audience. As a part of the mainstream culture, schools reflect society's definitions of "not only *what* counts as reading when reading really counts, but also *who* counts as a reader" (Alvermann, 2001, p. 689). We must work toward helping all students feel that the literacies they are developing, including out-of-school literacies, are valued. Across all subject areas and topics of study, we must engage students in exploring the range of ideas that others share through print and nonprint sources. From CD-ROMs to information trade books to brochures and public documents, from novels about personal experiences of other early adolescents to biographies of extraordinary people living ordinary lives to popular culture magazines, from adopted textbooks to handbooks explaining strategies for navigating through video games, our students must become aware of the possibilities that literacy offers.

Our literacy programs must include opportunities for students to pursue their passions, the things that are intensely interesting to them during early adolescence. We know that middle grade students are questioning many things, particularly themselves. We must immerse them in literacy programs that support their exploration and development of personal interests in lifelong learning.

Have you considered ways in which your own cultural background might influence your views of students whose life experiences, particularly cultural and economic, are dramatically different than your own? How can you draw on your background knowledge of human development and psychology to consider the challenges that might lie ahead in today's diverse classrooms? Is it possible that you will need to find ways to increase your own life experiences with people who are very different from yourself?

• • •

ASSESSMENT AND EVALUATION IN LITERACY

In effective learning environments, assessment and instruction are inexorably linked (Spandel & Stiggins, 1990). As we develop literacy experiences, we must constantly consider each student's progress in light of what we know about that individual, as well as what we know is possible based on developmental learning theory and current knowledge of literacy learning. After all, the main purpose of assessment and evaluation is to guide and improve the decisions that we make that directly and indirectly affect what our students learn.

DEFINING ASSESSMENT AND EVALUATION

In this text, we use the term *assessment* to refer to the gathering of data through observations, conferences, and samples of student work to inform our curricular and instructional decisions. The term *evaluation* refers to the way in which we place value on the data collected according to our instructional purposes or expected outcomes.

TYPES OF ASSESSMENTS

We examine three types of assessments throughout this text: diagnostic, formative, and summative. Figure 1.7 provides an example of each type of assessment as applied to a unit of study in sixth grade that focuses on the causes and impact of severe drought, as in the Dust Bowl of the 1930s.

We collect diagnostic data when students are new to us or when we are about to begin a new unit of study. We evaluate diagnostic data to learn more about our students' strengths and areas in which they need our added support to learn what is expected in a particular subject area or grade level. Diagnostic data help us make decisions about how to approach particular concepts or topics in ways that will connect with our students' existing knowledge, skills, and strategies.

Formative assessment uses data that we collect from a variety of ongoing learning activities that, when combined, lead to a broad concept or generalization. Formative assessment data help to show how students are forming their understandings about that concept or generalization. As we engage students in learning experiences, both students and teacher should have a clear understanding of the intended outcome. We are concerned not only with completed products but also with the processes students use to learn.

Summative assessment uses data that provide a thorough understanding of students' knowledge and skills that are acquired over a period of time, such as the culmination of a unit of study or end of the school year. Summative evaluations are used to demonstrate the achievement of curriculum goals or standards.

■ **FIGURE 1.7**

Diagnostic, formative, and summative assessment

The Dust Bowl–Sixth Grade

Diagnostic Assessment: At the beginning of a unit of study that focuses on understanding the causes and impact of severe drought we ask students to write/draw things they think about/know about droughts. Students' responses will help us identify their understanding of the essential language/vocabulary that is needed to develop a deeper understanding of this topic.

Formative Assessment: Formative assessment and evaluation might include observed changes in knowledge and attitudes as reflected in each student's journal responses while reading and discussing *Out of the Dust* by Karen Hesse, combined with notes the teacher makes in response to whole-class discussions about life in western Oklahoma during the severe drought of the 1930s. Knowledge and attitudes are impacted by students' comprehension of texts such as *Out of the Dust.*

Summative Assessment: At the culmination of the unit of study, students might write and produce a play that demonstrates their understanding not only of life during that historical period, but also of the scientific principles that attempt to explain drought and their ability to use language in a variety of forms to effectively communicate what they have learned.

BEST PRACTICES IN ASSESSMENT AND EVALUATION

To build a whole picture of what students know and do as readers and writers, we should be active participants with our students in assessment and evaluation of their learning. Assessment should be intended to help students. We can do this by actively engaging students in the assessment and evaluation of their own learning to enable them to transfer knowledge and abilities to their life experiences, to enrich their learning outside of school settings.

When we work from a developmental perspective we cannot hold the same expectations for all students at any one point in the school year. Multiple sources of data show us the range of performances in our classrooms. The assessments we make should be selected for appropriateness to the intended purpose, as well as appropriateness to students' learning styles, developmental level, and opportunity to learn. As we make assessment decisions, we should strive to always be fair and equitable, free of bias in what and who we value.

The ways in which we structure learning experiences will also influence what students are able to demonstrate through assessment. Knowledge that our students acquired through the mere transmission of information, such as classroom lectures, is not likely to transfer to new learning situations (Goldman, 1997). We should focus instead on other types of learning that are deemed essential to success in the world, such as the ability to think critically and to collaborate with others in problem solving.

Our assessment of students should be continuous. We should carefully observe students as they engage in authentic literacy tasks over a substantial period of time. In addition, we should use a variety of measures that reflect appropriate instructional purposes and account for diversity among learners.

As we begin to consider the role of assessment and evaluation in our classrooms, we should look to guiding principles offered by experts in the profession. Best practices in literacy assessment, synthesized from a number of sources by Winograd and Arrington (1999), include these:

In General, Assessments—

- Are part of a systematic approach to improving education that includes strengthening the curriculum, professional development for teachers, and additional support for helping those children who need it.
- Provide educators and others with richer and fairer information about all children, including those who come from linguistically and culturally diverse backgrounds.
- Are integral parts of instruction.
- Continually undergo review, revision, and improvement.
- Are based on our most current and complete understanding of literacy and children's development.
- Support meaningful standards based on the understanding that growth and excellence can take many forms.
- Use criteria and standards that are public so that students, teachers, parents, and others know what is expected.

On Behalf of Students, Assessments—

- Focus on important goals and support meaningful student learning.
- Involve students in their own learning and enhance their understanding of their own development.
- Start with what the students currently know.

- Focus on students' strengths rather than just reveal their weaknesses.
- Provide information that is used to advocate for students rather than to penalize them.

On Behalf of Teachers, Assessments—
- Involve teachers (and often students) in the design and use of the assessment.
- Empower teachers to trust their own professional judgments about learners.
- Nourish trust and cooperation between teacher and students (pp. 217–218).

Throughout this text we will consider these best practices to help us identify artifacts that document student learning and inform our decisions as teachers.

As we close this chapter it is important to remember that as we enter today's classrooms we are challenged to move beyond our own recollections of school and be open for today's students to teach us about who they are as individuals and as learners. We each have at least 13,000+ hours as students in grades K–12 (Lortie, 1975) that influence our expectations of what life will be like as a teacher. We must be cautious as we draw on our own school experiences to inform us about classroom life in this rapidly changing world.

■ TAKE A MOMENT TO REFLECT . . .

Each chapter contains sections labeled "Take a Moment to Reflect." These sections are intended to give you an opportunity to review the main points presented in that chapter and to encourage you to question your own understanding of those ideas.

■ *Take a moment to reflect on these introductory thoughts on issues related to middle grade literacy . . .*

Although variation occurs within a group, in general we know that middle grade students are:

- In a period of transescence, a time of transition between childhood and adolescence;
- Intellectually diverse and moving toward the capacity for abstract thought;
- Physically maturing at varying speeds and are physically at risk;
- Psychologically erratic, inconsistent, and vulnerable;
- Socially in conflict between parents (society) and their peers and are socially at risk;
- Challenged by moral and ethical issues and are at risk when support from the home and church are absent.

Early adolescents use three forms of language:

- Social, academic, and peer; and
- Each form has its own vocabulary, meaning, and context for use.

Standards for the English language arts:

- Were jointly developed by NCTE and IRA in 1996.
- Provide a framework to guide educators in developing literacy programs.

National studies of middle grade education recommend:

- Rigorous, but flexible, standards;
- Relevant curriculum;
- Instructional methods designed for early adolescents;
- Intellectual and caring community;
- Safe and healthy environments; and
- Parent and community involvement.

■ *Best practices in literacy instruction, suggested by research, are as follows:*

- Teach reading for authentic meaning-making literacy experiences.
- Use high-quality literature.
- Integrate a comprehensive word study/phonics program into reading/writing instruction.
- Use multiple texts that link and expand concepts.
- Balance teacher- and student-led discussions.
- Build a whole-class community that emphasizes important concepts and builds background knowledge.
- Work with students in small groups while other students read and write about what they have read.
- Give students plenty of time to read in class.
- Give students direct instruction in decoding and comprehension strategies that promote independent reading. Balance direct instruction, guided instruction, and independent learning.
- Use a variety of assessment techniques to inform instruction.

■ *Developmental learning environments are excellent models for literacy learning and are characterized by:*

- "Knowledgeable others" who model clearly purposeful and successful use of the skills/strategies to be learned;
- Support and encouragement for approximations toward mature behavior;
- A noncompetitive environment for learning;
- Opportunities for learners to engage in self-motivated, self-paced practice;
- Opportunities for learners to correct and evaluate their own growth; and
- Encouragement and support that lead toward independent functioning.

■ *Teachers of middle grade students:*

- Are the "more knowledgeable other" for many students;
- Should be mediators between learners and texts in both reading and writing;
- Should aim instruction just beyond where students can function independently and should lead students' development; and
- Must use feedback from students to determine where to target instruction.

■ *Diversity is reflected:*

- In the dramatic physical, social, emotional, and cognitive changes that students experience during early adolescence;
- In the 38% of students enrolled in public schools who belong to minority groups; and
- In students who are learning to speak English as a second language.

■ *Assessment and evaluation are integral parts of literacy instruction:*

- *Assessment* refers to the gathering of data through observations, conferences, and samples of student work to inform our curricular and instructional decisions.
- *Evaluation* refers to the way in which we place value on the data collected according to our instructional purposes or expected outcomes.
- Diagnostic assessments help us identify students' strengths and needs.
- Formative assessments guide us in day-to-day planning toward a goal.
- Summative assessments help us evaluate the effectiveness of instruction on student learning.
- Assessment data should be appropriate to the intended audience and gathered continuously.
- Students should be involved in evaluation of their own learning.
- Quality assessment should include multiple sources of data.

■ REFERENCES

Adger, C. T. (1998). Register shifting with dialect resources in instructional discourse. In S. M. Hoyle & S. T. Agers (Eds.), *Kids talk: Strategic language use in later childhood*. New York: Oxfords Press.

Alvermann, D. E. (2001). Reading adolescents' reading identities: Looking back to see ahead. *Journal of Adolescent & Adult Literacy, 44*(8), 676–690.

Au, K. H., & Kawakami, A. J. (1994). Cultural congruence in instruction. In E. R. Hollins, J. E. King, & W. Hayman (Eds.), *Teaching diverse populations: Formulating a knowledge base* (pp. 5–23). Albany: State University of New York Press.

California State Department of Education. (1987). *Caught in the middle: Educational reform for young adolescents in California public schools*. Sacramento, CA: Author.

Carnegie Council on Adolescent Development. (1989). *Turning points: Preparing American youth for the 21st century*. Washington, DC: Author.

Cazden, C. B. (1982). Contexts for literacy: In the mind and in the classroom. *Journal of Reading Behavior, 14*, 413–427.

Chamot, A. U., & O'Malley, J. M. (1994). *The CALLA handbook: Implementing the cognitive academic language learning approach*. Reading, MA: Addison-Wesley Publishing Co.

Cummins, J. (1981). The role of primary development in promoting educational success for language minority students. In *Schooling and language minority students* (pp. 3–49). Los Angeles: Evaluation and Dissemination and Assessment Center, California State University.

Dias, P., Beer, A., Ledwell-Brown, J., Pare, A., & Pittenger, C. (1992). *Writing for ourselves/writing for others*. Scarborough, Ontario: Nelson Canada.

Dixon-Krauss, L. (1994, September). A mediation model for dynamic literacy instruction. Paper presented at the International Conference on L. S. Vygotsky and the Contemporary Human Sciences, Moscow, Russia.

Dixon-Krauss, L. (1996). Vygotsky's sociohistorical perspective on learning and its application to western literacy instruction. In L. Dixon-Krauss (Ed.), *Vygotsky in the classroom: Mediated literacy instruction and assessment*. White Plains, NY: Longman.

Eder, D., Evans, C., & Parker, S. (1995). *School talk, gender and adolescent culture*. New Brunswick, NJ: Rutgers University Press.

Eichhorn, D. (1966). *The middle school*. New York: Center for Applied Research in Education.

Gambrell, L. B., & Mazzoni, S. A. (1999). Principles of best practice: Finding the common ground. In L. B. Gambrell, L. M. Morrow, S. B. Neuman, & M. Pressley (Eds.), *Best practices in literacy instruction* (pp. 11–21). New York: Guilford Press.

Goldman, S. R. (1997). Learning from text: Reflections on the past and suggestions for the future. *Discourse Process, 23*, 357–398.

Goatley, V. J., Brock, C. H., & Raphael, T. E. (1995). Diverse learners participating in regular education "book clubs." *Reading Research Quarterly, 30*, 352–380.

Harris, V. J. (1994). Multiculturalism and children's literature. In F. Lehr & J. Osborn (Eds.), *Reading, language and literacy* (pp. 201–214). Hillsdale, NJ: Lawrence Erlbaum Associates.

Hilliard, A. (1994). In E. W. King, M. Chipman, & M. Cruz-Janzen (Eds.), *Educating young children in a diverse society* (p. x). Boston: Allyn and Bacon.

Hobbs, R. (1996). Expanding the concept of literacy. In R. Kubey (Ed.), *Media literacy in the information age*. New York: Transaction Press.

Holdaway, D. (1979). *Foundations of literacy*. Sydney, Australia: Ashton.

Holdaway, D. (1980). *Independence in reading*. Portsmouth, NH: Heinemann.

Irvin, J. L. (1998). *Reading and the middle school student: Strategies to enhance literacy*. Boston: Allyn and Bacon.

Jackson, A. W., & Davis, G. A. (2000). *Turning points 2000: Educating adolescents in the 21st century*. New York: Teachers College Press.

Larson, V. L., & McKinley, N. L. (1995). *Language disorders in older students: Preadolescents and adolescents*. Eau Claire, WI: Thinking Publications.

Lortie, D. (1975). *Schoolteacher*. Chicago: University of Chicago Press.

Manning, J. C. (1995). "Ariston metron." *The Reading Teacher, 48*, 650–659.

Moll, L. C. (1994). Literacy research in community and classrooms: A sociocultural approach. In R. B. Ruddell, M. R. Ruddell, & H. Singer (Eds.), *Theoretical models and processes of reading* (pp. 179–207). Newark, DE: International Reading Association.

Moll, L. C., & Gonzalez, N. (1994). Lessons from research with language minority children. *Journal of Reading Behavior, 26*, 439–456.

National Middle School Association. (1995). *This we believe: Developmentally responsive middle level schools*. Westerville, OH: National Middle School Association.

Owens, R. E. (2001). *Language development: An introduction* (5th ed.). Boston: D. C. Heath and Houghton Mifflin.

Padron, Y. (1998). Latino students and reading: Understanding these English language learners' needs. In K. Beers & B. G. Samuels (Eds.), *Into focus: Understanding and creating middle school readers* (pp. 105–121). Norwood, MA: Christopher-Gordon Publishers.

Pressley, M. (1998). *Literacy instruction that works: The case for balanced literacy*. New York: Guilford Press.

Ramirez, G., & Ramirez, J. L. (1994). *Multiethnic children's literature*. Albany, NY: Delmar.

Richards, J., Platt, J., & Platt, H. (1992). *Longman dictionary of language teaching and applied linguistics* (2nd ed.). Essex, England: Longman Group Limited.

Smart, M. S., & Smart, R. C. (1973). *Adolescence*. Upper Saddle River, NJ: Merrill/Prentice Hall.

Spandel, V., & Stiggins, R. (1990). *Creating writers: Linking assessment and writing instruction*. White Plains, NY: Longman.

Standards for the English Language Arts. (1996). Champaign-Urbana, IL: National Council of Teachers of English and International Reading Association.

Vygotsky, L. S. (1962). *Thought and language* (E. Hanfmann & G. Vakar, Eds. & Trans.). Cambridge, MA: The MIT Press.

Vygotsky, L. S. (1978). *Mind in society* (M. Cole, V. John-Steiner, S. Scribner, & E. Sounerman, Eds. & Trans.). Cambridge, MA: Harvard University Press.

Wiles, J., & Bondi, J. (1993). *The essential middle school*. Upper Saddle River, NJ: Merrill/Prentice Hall.

Winograd, P., & Arrington, H. J. (1999). Best practices in literacy assessment. In L. B. Gambrell, L. M. Morrow, S. B. Neuman, & M. Pressley (Eds), *Best practices in literacy instruction* (pp. 211–224). New York: Guilford Press.

chapter 2

Understanding Reading Processes

In this chapter . . .

We consider a range of issues that influence how we construct meaning with text, including:

- Our knowledge of the process of reading and making meaning,
- Stages we pass through as readers on our way to maturity,
- The role of text in constructing meaning,
- Behaviors we use to monitor our reading as we construct meaning,
- Explicit, implicit, critical, and creative/personal thinking while we re.
- Matching readers with texts of varying difficulty,
- The importance of words in constructing meaning,
- Respecting diversity in the ways that readers make meaning with texts, and
- Monitoring growth in readers through observation, conferences, a collecting samples of work.

Something to Think About . . .

> The literacy program that we plan for middle grade students should enable them to "read and write the world" to meet their needs and interests, "taking from and making of the world" what is meaningful to them. (Shannon, 1992, p. 1)

Building a Theory Base . . .

Louise Rosenblatt (1978) said that words are mere "inkspots on paper until a reader transforms them into a set of meaningful symbols" (p. 25). Thomson (1987) views this "transformation" as a process of getting better and better at making a text in our heads that has meaning for us, and as a process of becoming more intellectually and emotionally active while we read. Readers transform the symbols on a page to make and share meanings "as ways of exploring and understanding what it means to live" (Thomson, 1987, p. 13).

Constructing meaning with any one text, however, is not the same for all readers:

- Schon (1983) suggests that each reader is unique, in effect "a universe of one," and as such the meanings we make are in some way unique unto ourselves (p. 333).

- Holdaway (1980) describes the act of reading as "an individual and intensely personal thing. We cannot speak of reading as thinking without emphasizing the individual nature of the process: groups don't think" (p. 51).

- C. S. Lewis (1978), author of the classic *Chronicles of Narnia* fantasy series, suggests that any particular story can be read in different ways by different readers. The same reader also reads a text differently at different times.

- Golden and Guthrie (1986) believe that meaning does not reside in the text; rather, readers actively construct meaning, and their backgrounds and experiences influence the process.
- Bloome and Bailey (1992) suggest that, in addition to background knowledge and cultural understanding, meaning making is also influenced by our environment while we are reading and by other texts we have read.

Although our individual interpretations presumably differ, commonalities of meaning within any community of readers emerge as we share backgrounds, experiences, attitudes, and strategies as readers (Beach & Hynds, 1991, p. 455). Many adult readers have a sense of community with friends and colleagues with whom they share texts, both printed and visual (television and film). Students come to the middle grades with great variation in their experiences and ability, both in and out of school. It is our task to build a community of readers who share common experiences as they draw on their varied backgrounds.

In this text, particularly in this chapter, we consider issues that surround the reader, the text, and the literacy context to build a foundation for our theory base concerning the literacy development of early adolescents. We begin with a discussion of reading processes and the stages through which we all progress as readers.

READING PROCESS AND CONSTRUCTING MEANING

We have learned from research that reading is

"a high-speed, automatic, simultaneous operation of complex linguistic and cognitive processes. At any moment, a reader of any level of proficiency must keep in mind story meaning, sentence meaning, sentence syntax, and some metacognitive awareness of fit, while simultaneously, perceiving and identifying words, word-parts, and punctuation marks."

(Jones, 1995, p. 44)

What might Noel Jones mean by this statement? Let's read it again, this time pulling it apart and analyzing the meaningful words. In the first sentence, Jones's use of the terms in the left column can be restated as in the right column:

linguistic	Using the units and structure of our language,
cognitive	we organize what we know and think,
processes	into a series of actions leading to a particular end (meaning).
simultaneous	Several operations occur at the same time,
high-speed	as information is processed by the brain in milliseconds,
automatic	often without our conscious control.

When we read, our knowledge of language and our ability to think work together very rapidly to make meaning, often without conscious control. When meaning breaks down, we consciously use what we know and have learned from our past experience as readers to repair the breakdown. We will address such monitoring, or use of reading strategies to check meaning, in a later section.

Now, consider the remaining part of Jones's statement. At any moment in the process of making meaning, a reader must keep the following in mind:

- *Story meaning and sentence meaning.* We must not only hold in our heads the overall meaning we have constructed thus far, but also must attend to the meaning of each new sentence.
- *Sentence syntax.* To construct meaning with each new sentence, we draw on our knowledge of the grammar or structure of our language.
- *And some metacognitive awareness of fit.* We check our thinking to determine if the meanings we are making are possible and appropriate considering the structure of our language and what we know about the topic.
- *While simultaneously, perceiving and identifying words, word-parts, and punctuation marks.* At the same time, we sample just enough of the actual print on the page to confirm whether what we are thinking as we make meanings fit both the sentence and the overall meaning.

For us, as mature readers, this process of drawing on meaning, grammar, and visual cues to make meaning operates so automatically that what we do appears to be effortless. In addition, when we read we focus our attention on meaning cues, drawing on visual cues, language structure, and other sources of information only as they seem necessary to make a meaningful text in our heads. For less experienced readers, however, these processes require much more conscious control and time spent problem solving.

To emphasize the complexity of reading processes, Jones (1995, p. 45) identifies other factors affecting any act of reading:

- Personal choice (emerging from a complex mix of interests, feelings, and ideas),
- Activation of prior knowledge (calling on our organized systems for conceptualizing and understanding something),
- Level of engagement with text (the degree to which we are emotionally and intellectually involved with a text),
- Metacognitive control (awareness of our own knowledge and thought processes that support our meaning making, and our strategic use of that knowledge to monitor meaning),
- Integration of new experiences with our existing knowledge and feelings, and
- Judgment and evaluation of the meanings we make.

How might this discussion affect our sense of purpose in reading instruction? I believe our purpose should be to engage less experienced readers in acts of making meaningful texts using meaning, language, and visual cues, so that students learn to rely on meaning with only subsidiary attention to other cues, until making meaning becomes virtually automatic. We must also share our metacognitive knowledge that enables us to monitor our reading processes.

By the middle grades, students should be moving toward mature reading. To break through, students must understand what mature readers know and do. Emphasizing mature reading behaviors, then, is a main purpose of reading instruction in the middle grades.

Before moving on to a new section of text, you may find it helpful to stop for a moment to reflect on our discussion of reading processes. Without looking back in the text, describe your current understanding of reading processes.

Now, look back and see which elements of the process you included as meaningful for you. Perhaps you see those elements in yourself as a reader. The elements that you omitted may signify ideas that are not fully meaningful to you.

● ● ●

STAGES OF READING DEVELOPMENT

Reading ability develops over time in clearly identifiable stages (Holdaway, 1980; Juel, 1991). With the diversity of today's middle grade classrooms, it is likely that several stages of reading development will be represented among the students in any given class. In this text we discuss the following stages of reading development:

- Emerging,
- Developing,
- Transitional, and
- Mature.

EMERGING READERS

We are actually emergent readers from birth, as we learn to "read" the world. All during the preschool years we see print in use in our environment and, slowly, we begin to realize that the print has meaning. We know where to get hamburgers and french fries, which box holds our favorite cereal, and that the red sign on the street corner says "STOP." Our natural desire to understand leads us to explore and emulate what the significant people in our lives show us about the purposes and functions of print (Teale, 1986).

During the emerging reading stage, tremendous growth takes place. We begin to internalize purposes for print, concepts of how print works, ideas about its permanence, and concepts about words and the functions letters serve. The knowledge we develop during this time is very important, but not more important than the attitudes and motivations we, as children, have toward print and its usefulness in our lives.

We are contextual readers during this stage; we need a familiar context to be able to use the print knowledge we are acquiring. We can "read" picture books that have been read to us, but we are most comfortable with patterned repetitive text with illustrations that are highly predictable.

Emerging readers typically read texts that range from the beginning reading level to those that average midyear first-grade students can comfortably read and understand.

DEVELOPING READERS

Over time we begin to sense the patterns of our language as we gain competence with the directional nature of print. We consciously try to match the visual cues of print with what we know as we read aloud. In this stage our reading is "outside of ourselves" because we haven't yet learned to internalize our thoughts through inner speech (Vygotsky, 1978). Our reading is more like word-to-word matching (Holdaway, 1980), when we are literally glued to the print in our efforts to make sense.

In our early reading we find ourselves rerunning text or self-correcting quite a bit as we struggle to make sense of print. If we spend a lot of time in text that is relatively easy we build the confidence that helps us persevere when text is more difficult. Practicing in easy text also gives us time to organize what we know about print.

As our confidence grows, our ability to monitor and correct our own reading becomes more natural. Self-correction demonstrates our ability to make meaning through the integrated use of meaning, language, and visual cues. If the adults around us continue to correct our miscues during oral reading, it takes away our drive to self-correct.

Toward the end of this stage, typically around the early third-grade reading level, we move toward silent reading, and our reading becomes more of a private, rather than public, affair. In this transition, our oral reading becomes subvocalized. When we read to ourselves others may hear murmurs, but not words. It is silent reading that lets us focus on our reactions to a text, rather than on the words. Now, we can truly begin to read for personal satisfaction and understanding. Developing readers typically read text that ranges in difficulty from the middle first-grade to the early third-grade reading level.

TRANSITIONAL READERS

Early in the transitional stage we experience some difficulty moving back and forth between oral and silent reading. We have learned how to monitor our oral reading (assuming the surrounding adults allow us to) and are now learning to effectively monitor our silent reading.

The more we move into silent reading, the more likely we are to become truly absorbed in our reading. This also is about the time we move from picture books to chapter books or novels, which provide more extensive description and more development of plot and characters.

Spending our time in the privacy of silent reading helps us begin to sense our own "style" of reading. As a part of our style, we begin to sense the rate at which we can comfortably move through a variety of texts, the amount of attention we must give to different reading tasks, and the range of strategies we have that help us make meaning with text.

Later in this stage, we become more flexible in our reading. Reading extensively in easy texts lets us feel what fluent reading is like. Extensive, fluent reading is necessary for us to add to our understanding of how we make adjustments in our reading depending on the demands of the text. As we move toward the end of this stage, we are reading texts that are typically at about sixth-grade reading level and are preparing to break into mature reading. Transitional readers typically read texts that range in difficulty from the early third-grade to the sixth-grade reading level.

MATURE READERS

This is the current reading stage for most literate adults. There is no upper limit to this stage, but rather it "constitutes a body of learning strategies which allow the mature reader to extend and develop new skills or refinements of skill to meet changing life purposes" (Holdaway, 1980, p. 30). It is during this stage that our reading becomes "interest-and-vocation-centered" (p. 30). Our comprehension becomes quite rapid, first in areas where we spend the most time reading and have the greatest familiarity and understanding. Mature readers not only read texts at the sixth-grade reading level and above but also use reading strategies in specific ways to construct meaning (see upcoming section).

As we consider stages of development, we are thinking broadly about reading behaviors. Behaviors in the early part of a stage may look very different from those at the end of

■ *What factors will you consider when you select texts for your students?*

that same stage. As we move from one stage to another, new tasks with increased difficulty may cause us to exhibit "old" behaviors until we are able to gain greater control over new behaviors. Our ability to construct meaning at each developmental level is both text driven and knowledge driven. In the upcoming sections we will consider various issues related to both the texts we read and our knowledge of reading.

THE ROLE OF TEXT

In the classroom, we typically view texts as written documents, such as textbooks or pieces of literature. The language that authors select to put forth their ideas, the structure of the ideas presented, the form in which the ideas are presented, and the topics addressed impact how we construct meaning. Our ability to construct meaning from texts is both text driven and knowledge driven (Goldman & Rakestraw, 2000).

Text-driven processing is influenced by both the content and organization of a text, while knowledge-driven processing is influenced by prior knowledge of the content and past reading experiences. The more variation in types of texts we use in a classroom, the more we enable students to develop a broad base of knowledge for anticipating the types of information that ought to be included in particular types of texts and the ways that writers of such texts might relate such information. What we know as readers influences our potential to accurately interpret and use an author's style of conveying information to construct meaning.

While it is important to consider the construction of meaning, it is also important to consider what forms of text we select for engaging students, whose interest is served by the texts that we select, and the voices that are and are not present in our classroom. Texts may be formal or informal; oral, written, or enacted; permanent or fleeting. How broad or narrow our view is of what constitutes text can consequently expand or limit the opportunities our students have to learn (Wade & Moje, 2000). For example, if we use only adopted textbooks, texts that contain "official" or sanctioned knowledge, our students will experience only that view of the world. Is a "one-view approach" to the complexity of today's world appropriate for our students?

Consider the texts that we create throughout our lives. We *textualize*, or make texts of, our experiences and the world in which we live. This textualizing of our experiences enables us to share and reshare our experience as a set of words, signs, representations, and so on. Our experiences can also be represented as forms that are not typically thought of as texts: Architecture, rock formations, the stars in the sky, the wind, the ocean, emotion—these can all be texts (Bloome & Egan-Robertson, 1993, p. 311). The existence of a text, however, relies on what people do with that text, how it is valued, and its intended purpose. We must consider how the texts of our students' lives can be reflected in their school experiences.

The sociocultural research of Shirley Bryce Heath (1994) teaches us that the texts that each of us has access to are cultural tools that shape not only what we know, but how we know and learn. With the diversity of students in today's classrooms, we must consider carefully how we define "text" and what we consider as "appropriate" texts for the classroom. To provide for students from all types of cultural and economic backgrounds, we should make available a wide and varied range of texts, or cultural tools. We must take care not to dismiss the texts our students use in their lives outside of school. We are challenged to learn ways to incorporate students' texts into the curriculum, working with them to make connections among the various texts they explore.

In your view, what counts as "text"? How do your background experiences influence your view(s) about text? Are some texts more valuable, more worthwhile, more important than others? What or who does/should determine that value, worth, importance? If we believe that middle grade students are at an important point in their development as individuals and as citizens, how do we consider what they value, consider worthy, and see as important as we select texts for learning experiences that will be meaningful?

• • •

BECOMING STRATEGIC READERS

For middle grade students to be successful in the reading that academic success demands, they must be motivated to become proficient at self-regulating their own reading of text. Self-regulation, according to Pressley (1998), is choosing to be cognitively active as readers. As competent readers, we know that reading should make sense and, consequently, we are motivated to monitor our own construction of meaning. We recognize when meaning breaks down and deliberately use our knowledge of reading at appropriate times and under a variety of conditions to repair breakdowns when they occur. In other words, we become strategic in our reading, actively transacting with texts and deciding for ourselves which strategic processes to use when we confront challenging texts (Pressley, 1998).

Strategies are actions that we select deliberately to achieve particular goals (Paris, Wasik, & Turner, 1991). Strategies that readers use include, but are not limited to, the following actions:

- Predicting,
- Seeking clarification when uncertain,

- Looking for patterns and principles in arguments presented in text,
- Analyzing problems (including the use of backward reasoning and visualization),
- Summarizing,
- Adapting ideas in text (including rearranging parts of ideas in text), and
- Negotiating interpretations of texts in groups (Collins, 1991, cited in Pressley, 1998, p. 217).

This ability to self-monitor means that we can function independently with a variety of forms of print (Holdaway, 1980). Figure 2.1 shows a variety of ways in which strategic readers monitor their reading.

To develop effective comprehension skills and strategies in our students, they must understand that strategic readers:

■ **FIGURE 2.1**

Being strategic readers

When we monitor, we use a variety of strategies to make meaning:

We use our prior knowledge.
- We know that we can use what we already know to acquire further knowledge or information.
- We understand the reading task and its purpose(s).

We anticipate and make reasonable predictions.
- We draw on prior reading experiences to anticipate what we might need to do to make meaning.
- As we read, we use what seems reasonable to anticipate upcoming text (words or ideas). We sample just enough text to either confirm or change our predictions.

We adjust our reading strategies to meet the purposes of different types of texts.
- The presentation of ideas in narrative text is typically linear (plot sequence), but ideas in information texts can be structured in a variety of ways within the same piece (description, comparison, ordered, cause/effect, and so on). Such knowledge causes us to look for clues to how ideas are structured.
- Authors writing in a particular form (such as prose or poetry) or within a particular genre (such as fantasy or mystery) use the rules of the form or the characteristics of the genre in their writing.
- Textual information is organized in particular ways. Reference sources such as indexes, tables of contents, and glossaries can help us locate specific information. Headings, subheadings, charts and graphs, and boldface print are also clues to how information is organized within the text.
- We adjust the speed of our reading to the difficulty level of the text, our purpose(s) for reading, and our familiarity with the topic.

We monitor for meaning and self-correct miscues that disrupt meaning.
- We realize when a miscue, or a reading different from the actual text, has occurred. At that point, we activate appropriate self-correction strategies that we have learned over time.
- Repair strategies include reading on to see if key ideas are yet to come, rereading the text in question, and skipping particular sections of text because they may not be important to our purpose.

- Understand and analyze the reading task, and establish purpose and goals for the reading,
- Choose apropriate and useful strategies in light of the task,
- Monitor their own comprehension while reading, and
- Possess a positive attitude toward reading (Paris et al., 1991).

We must explicitly model and support the effective use of strategies for all students who are not yet proficient in knowing which strategies to select for particular situations and how to recognize the conditions under which those strategies should be used. Gradually we relinquish our support as students show through practice that they are able to recognize situations that require strategic reading and are able to apply strategies appropriately. Our role/responsibility as teachers changes as we move from explicitly modeling strategic reading processes to providing practice of those strategies for students.

As you examine the strategies listed in Figure 2.1, which strategies do you notice most in yourself when you read? Do you notice when you select a specific strategy, such as adjusting the rate of your reading, to fit a particular type of reading situation? Do you notice the types of texts or reading purposes that cause you to become conscious of the strategies you use as you monitor your reading?

• • •

THINKING AS WE CONSTRUCT MEANING

Our ability to construct meaning as we read is influenced by many factors, including our schema for the topic and the particular type of text, our motivation for making the text meaningful, the match between our knowledge of language and the difficulty level of the text, and our ability to effectively monitor for meaning.

A well-formed *schema* for written language helps us to organize personal experiences into abstract representations that are independent of the original stimuli (Schanklin, 1982). Our schema allows us to integrate a number of common simultaneously occurring concepts into an orderly representation (Anderson & Pearson, 1984). Abstraction allows knowledge to be used in different contexts to make sense of new experiences. Within a schema, knowledge is organized into a hierarchical framework of concepts and procedures (Adams & Collins, 1985; Schank & Abelson, 1975). If our schema does not already include an appropriate place to mentally "file" new information, we must create a new "file" within the existing framework by inferring how the new information might relate to existing concepts or procedures. When relationships are made, information in related "files" must be reconstructed. Activating our schema as readers can have a dramatic impact on our ability to comprehend text, including making inferences, how and what we attend to in text, and our ability to remember what is read.

EXPLICIT THINKING—RECALLING THE AUTHOR'S WORDS

We think in explicit ways when we are aware of the need to remember and use details. In certain reading situations, we realize that we must retain ideas from the reading for later use and that it is important to listen to the author's exact words.

Our ability to explicitly understand an author's words depends, in part, on our ability to recognize and understand the words in a text and on our knowledge of the topic. If the topic is completely unknown, we will have difficulty understanding and, most likely, will not be able to think along with the author.

IMPLICIT THINKING—THINKING BETWEEN THE AUTHOR'S WORDS

Authors do not always explicitly tell us what we may need to know. It would be impossible for an author to anticipate everything that every reader might need to know about the topic at hand. The author assumes that we know some things about the topic and that, depending on our purposes, we will "work" to make sense by filling in or linking the author's ideas. This act of filling in or linking is *implicit thinking* and is the base from which we make inferences while we read.

Anderson and Pearson (1984) identify four types of implicit thinking that we as readers use to fill in the author's ideas:

- We draw on our prior knowledge of a topic to fill in ideas that are missing in the text.
- We mentally link specific ideas that relate to an idea but that do not appear together in the text.
- We combine our prior knowledge with clues from the author (essentially a combination of the first two types of implicit thinking).
- We use logical reasoning to fill in our incomplete understanding of a text, but without enough clues from the author or our prior knowledge to check the accuracy of our thinking.

The first three types of thinking can lead us to appropriate conclusions through varying combinations of our schema and the ideas in a text. The last type, however, can be problematic if our line of reasoning leads to misconceptions about the ideas in the text.

As competent readers, we learn to think our way through a text and operate as if it should make sense. So at times we will fill in missing pieces even if it leads us to what might be an inappropriate conclusion. We will eventually be confronted by situations that contain the accurate information, and because we monitor our reading, we will question our inappropriate prior knowledge and, we hope, change our thinking.

CRITICAL THINKING—QUESTIONING AND VALUING THE AUTHOR'S IDEAS

Each of us must make critical judgments about the value or merit of an author's ideas based on a self-determined set of criteria. We develop our criteria through our experiences as readers. Making critical judgments requires us to use our background knowledge accurately and to approach reading as a thinking process.

As readers we must know that, although we consider our own ideas to make judgments, we must make those judgments in light of the author's ideas or arguments. We cannot ignore the author. We must also realize that authors have intentions. They write from a particular perspective. They have their own experiences that influence their view of the world. As we read, we question the author's view and critically consider the support that is provided. Here, as in explicit thinking, we are concerned with the ideas we will have when we leave the reading.

CREATIVE/PERSONAL THINKING—UNIQUE WAYS OF SEEING THE AUTHOR'S IDEAS

When we think in creative or personal ways, we engage with an author for personal reasons and not because we are required to achieve a specific purpose. We focus on our lived-through experience with the author, rather than on what we will take from the reading. While we may initially be influenced by the author's ideas, we soon realize that our response does not bind us to the author's way of thinking. We go beyond the author and let our own ideas take over.

THE NEEDS OF MIDDLE GRADE STUDENTS

Results of the 1998 National Assessment of Educational Progress (NAEP), the only assessment of student achievement in which the vast majority of states participate, suggest that our middle grade students continue to need opportunities to develop their abilities to construct meaning as they read. Students are asked to do the following on the NAEP assessment:

Student reading tasks:	Type of thinking:
Demonstrate basic understanding	Explicit
Develop an interpretation	Implicit
Articulate a personal reflection and response	Creative
Demonstrate a critical stance	Critical

The majority of fourth- and eighth-grade students who participate in this assessment typically do not demonstrate more than basic proficiency in their thinking about text. They are able to demonstrate explicit thinking, but need additional experiences in implicit, critical, and creative/personal thinking.

The ability to think in different ways with a variety of texts develops slowly, through many reading experiences. Students must become aware of the stance they take as readers to know the purposes for their reading and to develop their own criteria for evaluating ideas in text.

MATCHING READERS AND TEXTS

In a balanced literacy program, learning to think in literature must be balanced with learning to think in information texts if students are to be equally adept at making meaning in both types of text. As we consider texts that will engage our students in meaningful literacy experiences, we also must be concerned about the difficulty level of texts and their match with students' reading ability.

Select any text and ask several students in the same grade level to read it. What is almost effortless for some readers provides some challenge for others and is clearly too much of a challenge for still other readers. If different students read the same text in different ways, how will we know when a text is appropriate for a particular student? We can describe the match between students and texts as occurring at independent, instructional, frustration, and listening levels:

- *Independent-level text* provides very little challenge and can be understood without support.
- *Instructional-level text* is the level at which help from a more knowledgeable other is needed to make adequate meaning.

- *Frustration-level* text is challenging, and without high motivation may be too difficult for a reader to make meaning.
- *Listening-level* text is written at the highest level at which a listener can hear and make adequate meaning from the text read aloud by another.

The level of challenge that students experience in text should be related to their purposes for reading. If text is too difficult and the reader is not highly motivated to learn from the text, then the only learning that may occur is that of frustration and defeat. If text is always too easy, there is little reason to learn. There must be a balance between challenge and motivation in the selection of texts for reading.

We expect that in any classroom we will have students who represent a range of learning levels. Some students have had the benefit of instruction by more knowledgeable others, who modeled and encouraged the use of effective reading strategies. However, many students we encounter have not yet developed their potential as competent readers. They are waiting for instruction that targets their strengths and needs as readers.

INDEPENDENT-LEVEL TEXT

Text that is independent for a reader requires very little effort for success. Extensive reading at this level builds confidence in readers, habituates decoding, increases fluency, moves many competencies to an automatic level, and builds stamina to persevere when more difficult text is encountered. When students read text that is at their independent level, their comprehension and word knowledge are almost completely accurate. They know enough of the text to fill in missing understandings without the aid of more knowledgeable readers. Developmentally, students need numerous opportunities each day to develop fluency and confidence in independent-level text, especially the students who struggle with grade-level texts (Allington, 2001).

INSTRUCTIONAL-LEVEL TEXT

When students have support from a more knowledgeable other as they work with a text, they can tolerate more error than when reading at an independent level. Instructional-level text presents sufficient challenge to motivate learning, but is not too easy nor too difficult. Students working at this level know enough of the text that, with the support of a more knowledgeable reader, they are able to fill in from their own background to make sufficient meaning. The assistance of the more able reader, usually the teacher, provides support at key points to help students use their knowledge appropriately. Working at the instructional level, with appropriate guidance, allows readers to learn from their errors. A general rule of thumb at this level is 90% to 95% word recognition and 75% to 90% comprehension prior to instruction. With mediated support, the reading then resembles independent reading.

FRUSTRATION-LEVEL TEXT

In contrast to independent-level reading, which is very easy, frustration-level text is too difficult for students to learn from unless personal motivation to read is extremely high. Students may be able to partially read text at this level, but require great effort to sustain themselves. Unless they are highly motivated to learn from the text, sustained effort can be harmful to students' confidence and sense of themselves as readers, and may even lead to students forming misconceptions from the reading. If placement in frustration-level text comes from a source outside the child, such as the teacher, motivation to deal with the text may not be high enough to avoid harmful effects. Even though students' comprehension of a text is at a frustration level, they still want the text to make sense. As a result, students may fill in "slots" of missing information with logical, but inappropriate, ideas and may form misconceptions.

LISTENING-LEVEL TEXT

Students are typically able to listen to and understand text that is more difficult than text they can read by themselves. Children's *listening capacity* is the highest level at which they can hear and understand the majority of a text, the level at which they should be able to function as readers if decoding is not required. The support needed to assist students to make meaning from a text that we read aloud should be similar to the support needed at the instructional reading level.

COMPARING LEVELS OF TEXT

Different levels of text serve different purposes for readers and require differing levels of motivation for successful use. We may summarize the match between readers and texts as follows:

Text level	Purpose	Motivation level
Independent	Practice, self-teach	Low challenge
Instructional	Learn with help	Medium challenge
Frustration	Stretch, test self	High challenge
Listening	Potential as a reader	Medium challenge

Students need the opportunity each day to read texts of varying levels of difficulty. The amount of time that students spend in each level of difficulty should be determined by their development and confidence as readers. Try to provide a balance in the levels of text in which students work.

Emerging readers are making the transition from oral to written language and read with support from a more knowledgeable other. Students in this stage spend much of their time reading predictable texts, which begin as frustration-level texts but become instructional or somewhat independent texts through repeated readings. Language experience charts and books, which are students' own dictations, can also be quite independent and offer ease for practice. During independent reading times emerging readers may select frustration-level library books, which they may have heard read aloud, to challenge themselves.

Developing readers are working to gain control over print and need the confidence with text to be willing to persevere. These readers need some instructional-level challenge, but should spend the majority of their day reading independent-level materials. Students may self-select frustration-level text during quiet reading times, but it will not be very helpful for them in gaining control of reading processes.

Transitional readers know quite a lot about print and are ready to sustain more challenge with teacher guidance or in highly motivating self-selected materials. To help them solidify silent reading, be sure they continue to read in independent materials that offer "controlled challenge." Transitional children will be able to learn new skills and to refine old ones when the amount of challenge is monitored.

Mature readers are able to judge their needs as readers fairly well. They should maintain a balance between independent and instructional materials. However, their experience as readers enables them to sustain their reading in difficult texts, particularly if they are highly motivated to read. Mature readers have a repertoire of self-monitoring strategies they can call on to make meaning in difficult texts.

THE IMPORTANCE OF COMPREHENSION

Reading is constructing meaning! Without meaning, we are not reading. Throughout this chapter we have been considering a variety of factors that impact students' construction of meaning while they read. Competent readers display the types of behaviors that we must teach all students. The following description of reading behaviors (Pressley, 1999, p. 91) provides an overview of what competent readers, who are actively involved in constructing meaning, think about and do as they read:

- Based on their prior knowledge, good comprehenders anticipate the content of the text being read. As they read, they monitor whether their predictions are accurate. They are aware of the difficulty of the text, the familiarity of the ideas in it, and the quality of the writing.
- When they encounter information relevant to their current reading goal, they read more slowly than when processing less relevant parts of the text.
- They react as they read the text, based on prior knowledge, accepting some ideas and rejecting others. They reflect on the ideas in the text, constructing summaries and reasoning about whether the ideas in the text are sensible. They are interpretive, with prior knowledge driving interpretations.
- They often continue to process a text after a first reading, sometimes rereading or reskimming portions that seem especially important. Good readers sometimes explicitly attempt to restate important ideas or summarize the text to make certain that important points can be recalled later.

For good comprehenders, reading is a process of actively constructing meaning. Prior experiences play a large role, not only in information about the world that informs their reading but also in their understanding of what readers do mentally as they read.

If we are to provide equality of opportunity for all students to become competent, independent readers, we must explicitly teach students that they should actively self-regulate the mental processes they use to construct meaning. When we model comprehension strategies, mental processes that are invisible to our students, we begin with an explanation of the strategy, then we model self-verbalized regulation of comprehension strategies (Pressley, 1998):

> What if our students observed us reading and heard us say the following: "Well, I've learned three big things to keep in mind before I read a story and while I read it. One is to ask myself what the main idea of the story is. What is the story about? A second is to learn important details of the story as I go along. The order of the main events or their sequence is an especially important detail. A third is to know how the characters feel and why. So, get the main idea. Watch sequences. And learn how the characters feel and why. . . . While I'm reading I should pause now and then. I should think of what I'm doing. And I should listen to what I'm saying to myself. Am I saying the right things? Remember, don't worry about mistakes. Just try again. Keep cool, calm, and relaxed. Be proud of yourself when you succeed. Have a blast." (Meichenbaum & Asarnow, 1979, pp. 17–18)

With our scaffolded support, such self-verbalization instruction (also called Think Aloud, see Chapter 7) can gradually help students understand cognitive processes used during reading and to assume control for themselves.

From Louise Rosenblatt (1978, 1994) we have learned that meaning is not in text alone or in the reader's head alone. Rather, the reader's previous knowledge and experiences influence the meaning of the content that is read. Rosenblatt referred to this process as a transaction between reader and text, in which readers are thought of as "active meaning-makers who use their knowledge of language and the world to construct interpretations of text in light of the particular situations within which they [texts] are read" (Borasi & Siegel, 2000, p. 26).

Michael Pressley (1998) urges us to provide transactional strategy instruction in order to help all students develop the ability to effectively construct meaning. By transactional strategy instruction, he means that we should provide students with instruction that:

- Explains how to carry out the strategies,
- Models a particular strategy,
- Practices strategies with our guidance and assistance as needed,
- Teaches why the strategy is important, and
- Teaches when and where to apply the strategy (pp. 213–214).

Students who acquire and use comprehension strategies, particularly low-achieving students, also acquire more content from their daily learning experiences (Brown, Pressley, Van Meter, & Schuder, 1996). The most common strategies on which we might focus our comprehension instruction are:

- Overviewing,
- Predicting,
- Selectively reading,
- Questioning,
- Constructing mental images that represent text content,
- Seeking clarifications,
- Responding to text based on prior knowledge,
- Interpreting,
- Summarizing, and
- Rehearsing information they want to remember for later.

These are the comprehension processes that are typically found in skilled readers (Pressley, 1998, 1999).

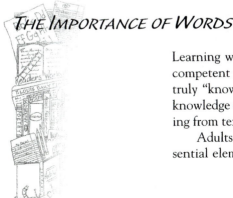

THE IMPORTANCE OF WORDS

Learning words, and then learning to use them effectively, is essential to our becoming competent readers and writers. Word knowledge is actually applied knowledge. When we truly "know" a word, we can recognize it and use it, even in unique contexts. We use knowledge of the word in combination with other types of knowledge to construct a meaning from text (Nagy & Scott, 2000, p. 273).

Adults who read competently often assume that mere knowledge of words is the essential element in reading. However, we know that reading is more than understanding words alone, yet our knowledge of words strongly influences reading comprehension (Anderson & Freebody, 1981; Davis, 1944). Reading is a complex system of knowledge and skills. Within this system, knowledge and activities involved in visually recognizing individual printed words are useless by themselves and are possible only as they are guided by complementary knowledge and activities of language comprehension. However, if individual word recognition processes do not operate properly, the system itself cannot function (Adams, 1990, p. 3).

We add to our knowledge of words incrementally, in many steps over our lifetime (Clark, 1973, 1993). This view of learning words helps to explain how a great deal of vocabulary can be gained incidentally from contexts in which we listen to and read the language of others. Yet, we do not come to fully understand all the words we encounter. In school, a student may have as many as 40 instructional encounters with a word, yet still not have full understanding of the word (Beck, Perfetti, & McKeown, 1982; McKeown, Beck, Omanson, & Perfetti, 1983; McKeown, Beck, Omanson, & Pople, 1985).

Adding to and refining our knowledge of words is challenging. "The vocabulary of written English consists of a relatively small number of words that occur frequently and an extremely large number of words that occur only infrequently" (Winsor, Nagy, Osborn, & O'Flahavan, 1993, p. 5). Consider the example presented in Figure 2.2.

Words often have more than one meaning, and the more frequently a word appears in the language, the more meanings it is likely to have. Multiple meanings of words can range from being completely unrelated to being so close that the shade of meaning separating the two may exist only in the mind of a compulsive lexicographer (Anderson & Nagy, 1991). Word meanings are flexible and are affected in some way by the context in which they occur (Green, 1989; Nagy, 1997). We cannot simply teach dictionary definitions of a word as if its meaning is isolated from the possible contexts in which the word may be found. In reality, the meaning of a word we encounter must be inferred from its context, even if the word is already familiar to us. Consider the meaning of *symphony* in the phrase "a soft distant *symphony* of rushing wind" (Polacco, 1996, p. 25). In many cases the required inferences are easy, but figurative language is certainly not without its challenges for students,

■ FIGURE 2.2

Occurrence of words in English

Anderson, Wilson, and Fielding (1988) estimate that the average fifth-grade student reads about 1 million words in a year, counting both in- and out-of-school reading. At least 10%, or 10,000, of these million words will be seen only once during that year.* Of these 10,000 words:

- 40% (4,000) are derivatives of more frequent words (*debt* to *indebtedness*),
- 13% (1,300) are inflections of more frequent words (*merge* to *merges, merit* to *merited*),
- 15% (1,500) are proper nouns,
- 22% (2,200) are in several categories (capitalizations, numbers, deliberate misspellings, mathematical expressions), and
- 10% (1,000) are truly new words.[†]

Sources: *From Growth in Reading and How Children Spend Their Time Outside of School by R. C. Anderson, P. T. Wilson, and L. G. Fielding, 1988, *Reading Research Quarterly, 23,* 285–303.
[†]From Winsor et al. (1993). *Structural analysis: Toward an evaluation of instruction.* Center for the Study of Reading, Technical Report No. 581. (ERIC Document Reproduction Service No. ED 360 625).

especially English language learners (ELLs). We must teach all students to expect English words to be used with unique shades of meaning.

As adults, we know words today that we did not know even a few months ago. The more we read and the more varied subjects and types of texts we explore, the greater our chances of encountering unfamiliar words. As competent readers and writers, we have internalized our knowledge of words we know on sight, our use of context to derive meaning, and our knowledge of letter–sound patterns (phonics) and of meaningful parts of words (morphology). We use this knowledge to help us make meaning.

Word awareness or word consciousness should be an important goal of our literacy instruction with our middle grade students. If students are to take an active role in word learning, assuming increasing responsibility for their own vocabulary growth, they need at least some information about the nature of word knowledge and the processes by which it is acquired. Therefore, we must provide instruction in metalinguistic abilities, those abilities that enable students to manipulate words parts, in order to learn new words (Nagy & Scott, 2000). We must help our students understand how to think about words, the ways in which English words are formed, and the ways in which English words are related (Beck et al., 1982).

Students' understanding of words and word learning processes also depends on the type of vocabulary instruction they experience.

> A diet of synonyms and short glossary definitions runs the danger of failing to produce a usable knowledge of those words, and creates simplistic beliefs that can interfere with future word learning. The quality of vocabulary instruction must therefore be judged not just on whether it produces immediate gains in students' understanding of specific words, but also on whether it communicates an accurate picture of the nature of word knowledge and reasonable expectations about the word learning process. (Nagy & Scott, 2000, p. 281)

■ *How do you think your students will differ as readers? How will you respect and support their differences?*

What strategies do you use to figure out words that are unfamiliar to you? How do you get those new words to become more than just "gist" to you, to understand their meaning in ways that enable you to be flexible, to adjust word meanings to various contexts? Discuss your word learning strategies with several peers. Compare and contrast the strategies that each of you use so you become aware of the variety of strategies available to competent readers.

• • •

RESPECTING DIVERSITY AMONG READERS

From our discussion in this chapter, we understand that students construct meaning in different ways and at different levels. To respect students' diversity in constructing meaning, we must consider the impact of at least three issues in our literacy program:

- Language knowledge,
- Literacy experiences, and
- Personal strategies for making meaning.

IMPACT OF LANGUAGE KNOWLEDGE

Acquiring language differs from student to student (Jaggar, 1975). The students in our classrooms will possess a range of words in their listening and speaking vocabularies. Some students will be learning English for the first time. Some students will know more than one language. We must consider this range of language acquisition and knowledge as we plan for learning experiences.

Students have expectations for how language is used and the purposes it serves based on its use in their familiar environments. Students' understanding of language is the basis for meaningful classroom communications, including reading and writing activities. As we develop instructional experiences, we must consider both the knowledge base and language structures required for successful learning. For example, if we consider using Paulsen's book *Hatchet* as a class text, what language issues could arise? We might realize that some students have had limited experiences with flying or survival in a wilderness and the language that surrounds such experiences. For other students, the structure of Paulsen's sentences and descriptive techniques will prove to be a barrier to constructing meaning.

We know that language knowledge is related to one's background experiences. As we re-examine *Hatchet*, thinking about both the content of the plot and the language, we realize that our students will relate to the book in different ways. Our plans will be focused on enabling all students to make meaning at some level. We think about ways to make the story and the language seem more concrete and accessible for both students who have life experiences that are different from those depicted in the book and those who have different language backgrounds.

We will provide many opportunities for students to work collaboratively in small groups to increase the meaningful use of English, especially for ELL students. In addition, we might select drama as a teaching strategy because it creates a physical bridge between a student's language and the language of the story. Students might act out Brian's actions and the mood of the story. Drama helps to make the language more concrete for ELL students and may be motivating to students who see little purpose for print. Drama also allows students who have a strong language background to help tell the story verbally. This is only one example of what could be done to involve all students, while respecting and enhancing their language background. I will present other examples of adapting instruction for the diverse needs of students throughout this text.

IMPACT OF LITERACY EXPERIENCES

In addition to their individual life experiences, middle grade students differ in the quality and quantity of their literary experiences (Allington, 1994; Irvin, 1998). Some students read extensively and become deeply engaged with literature, others struggle with required reading, and some choose not to read for school or for pleasure. Students who read extensively have greater opportunities than students who are not committed readers to learn about the ways authors use literary elements and information structures to engage us and to influence our thinking. They also practice more at using personal meaning-making strategies as they evolve into mature readers.

One of the most significant differences between students who are successful in reading and writing and those who are not is time—the time spent practicing literacy skills through meaningful reading and writing. As with other endeavors, students who practice more frequently are likely to get better at using their skills. To help all students be successful, we should consider ways to increase the time students spend actually reading and writing both inside and outside of school.

We must be keenly aware of our students' diverse reading experience as we plan classroom activities. For example, if we use *Hatchet* in a whole-class literature study, our plans must account for students' differing familiarity with chapter books and with a writing style such as Paulsen's, as well as for their varied life experiences with such personal issues as parental divorce, being alone, and being put in a situation that requires self-reliance. Our students will react to such events with differing amounts of courage, denial, tenacity, and problem-solving skills, and we must allow for both the presence and the expression of a range of student response.

IMPACT OF PERSONAL STRATEGIES FOR CONSTRUCTING MEANING

Language background and print experience will impact students' expectations for print and, possibly, their motivation to make sense out of print. Students have strategies for coping with print. We must discover what those strategies are and if they are useful in more complex reading tasks. Be especially conscious of ELL students. Remember that students who are acquiring a second language may feel very uncertain about their ability to transfer what they know and use in their first language as they try to learn in a second language (Padron, 1998). They may demonstrate very little of what they actually know.

When I think about respecting diversity in students, I often think of Mei Mei, the young Chinese protagonist of *I Hate English!* (Levine, 1989). English seemed very strange to her, and she feared that if she learned to speak English she might forget Chinese. Her teacher was sensitive to what Mei Mei was experiencing and searched for meaningful experiences that would let Mei Mei see that she could value both Chinese and English.

As we engage students, especially ELLs, we will keep in mind that systematic instruction directed at specific strategies or aspects of students' knowledge generally has positive effects (Fitzgerald, 1995). However, we also are aware that language is best learned through extensive and meaningful interactions. Once again we are reminded to strive for a balance in the ways that we organize learning experiences for our students.

LITERACY ASSESSMENT—DOCUMENTING GROWTH IN READING PROCESSES

To document students' reading processes, we should systematically collect data and reflect on what the data suggest about each of them as a reader, writer, and learner. As we collect data for each student, we make records that are added to our assessment portfolio so that we can document student growth over time. The items selected for this portfolio should create a broad picture both of a student's strengths and of areas that may need attention.

As students move toward maturity as readers, we must understand the quality of thinking and the processes each student uses to make meaning. This requires collecting data that demonstrates the following:

- What is understood about the types and purposes of written language;
- How a student thinks as a reader, including the strategies the student effectively uses to make meaning;
- How a student handles text of varying levels of difficulty, independently and with support; and
- The ways of constructing meaning that a student uses independently and with support.

How can we document what a student is thinking, what meaning a student makes of a reading experience? Through observing and conferring with students, we can begin to see patterns in their reading behaviors and responses to reading experiences. We can collect samples of work they write in response to their reading. These forms of assessment data begin to paint a picture of a student's process of making meaning with written language.

OBSERVATIONS

Observing the process a student uses provides us with a window or view on how a particular student arrives at a product. This allows the teacher to make good decisions about how she or he might assist during the process or restructure the process in order to best support more effective use of strategies and development as readers and writers (Rhodes & Nathenson-Mejia, 1992, p. 502).

Learning to watch our students is not an easy task with the amount of activity that goes on in a classroom. We can begin by asking, "What do I know about the ways this student constructs meaning and how did I gain that knowledge?" This question should make us think about the following:

- Our purposes for instruction,
- Learning activities that grow out of those purposes, and
- Observations we make of students during instruction.

We interpret our observations based on our knowledge of students' development and on our goals for instruction. We make notes about what we observe so that, over time, our notes serve as more detailed reminders of responses than do our recollections of the events.

Anecdotal Records. As we identify behaviors that should develop from the learning opportunities we provide, we need to develop a system for recording our observations. "Anecdotal records can be written about products or can include information about both process and product" (Rhodes & Nathenson-Mejia, 1992, p. 502).

Dated anecdotal records are essential in a process classroom, and they provide more detail than a mere checklist. Whereas a checklist is quick and may show a variety of behaviors, it usually does not provide illustrations of specific behaviors. Checklists also rely on checking for predetermined skills. Anecdotal records allow us, the student, and the context for learning to determine the focus for what we record.

Over time, we use these anecdotal records to make inferences about student behaviors, to identify patterns of behavior, and to identify strengths and weaknesses. We use anecdotal records for instructional planning, for discussing growth with students and parents, and for generating new questions about teaching, learning, and assessment (Rhodes & Nathenson-Mejia, 1992).

Records of Reading Performance. An accurate way to observe students' reading strategies is by taking a running record (Clay, 1979/1985) or administering an informal reading inventory (IRI). Running records and IRIs result in written records that reflect the strategies a reader uses to monitor meaning while reading orally. To create a written record, observe a student's oral reading, record what the student actually says while reading, and later, analyze any *miscues*, words that differ from those in the actual text (Goodman, 1972). We can take a running record on any piece of text, but they are most beneficial with those texts that students are using in the classroom.

We can use IRIs to document reading strategies, but historically IRIs have been used to determine instructional, independent, and frustration reading levels. Published IRIs typically include several passages at each level of difficulty, along with questions to ask about students' comprehension of text. Students read a variety of passages, orally and silently, increasing in difficulty, until they reach their frustration level.

Whether we use text that is familiar to students or the preselected passages of an IRI, observing and documenting students' reading is necessary for accurately monitoring progress. In Chapter 6, we discuss running records in depth.

CONFERRING ABOUT READING

In addition to observation, we also learn about how readers make meaning by talking with them. When we confer with students, our primary purpose is to listen to what students can teach us about the way they think and make meaning. We may focus the talk or probe for more information, but we cannot learn from them unless we listen.

As we move about a classroom while students are working, we might stop beside students and ask how the reading is going, giving them the opportunity to communicate their perceptions of a text and their ability to make meaning from that text. Students' comments may range from an explicit retelling to insightful, creative, or critical responses to the text. They may even read a portion of the text to us as a way of sharing their response.

During a quiet reading time, we might sit in the library area of the classroom with a student and share a reading. As naturally as possible, we inquire about the student's responses to the text. Conferring in this context should resemble an informal conversation.

We can also create opportunities during small-group reading experiences to let students inform us about their thinking if, in response to a student's comments, we ask, "What makes you think that?" Small groups also provide opportunity for students to confer with one another.

Conferring with students can place them in a position to read aloud to demonstrate the level of text they can handle comfortably or the levels of thinking they use to make meaning. The text may or may not be familiar. We discuss the reading to allow students to explain their thinking and response to reading situations. To gather data for assessment, you must ask students about their thinking.

OTHER EVIDENCE OF LEARNING

Written work also provides data about students' thinking and meaning making. Through illustrations and writing, students indicate their responses to texts read both aloud and independently. Over time, these responses can show a growing depth of understanding about types and purposes of written language and levels of making meaning that might not be represented in anecdotal or conference records. It is important to date all samples and save them regularly in a work folder. Over time, samples from the work folder are selected to become part of a literacy assessment portfolio.

To document meaning making in reading, video- or audiotape students' reading and responses three or four times per school year. Use a separate cassette or videotape for each student. These recordings, combined with written samples collected over time, will form a rich, comprehensive picture of students' growth as competent readers.

STANDARDIZED TEST RESULTS

We use standardized tests to compare students against a norm that has been established by a representative population of students at the same grade level. The norm for a particular test is established by administering test items to a representative sample of students in order to set a scoring standard. The test is given to enough students to establish the types of items that students at a particular grade level should be able to answer correctly. Theoretically, students at the same grade level, taking the test at approximately the same time in the school year, can be compared to the norm set by the original norming group.

To use standardized test scores wisely in our assessment of student learning, these two questions should be answered prior to using the test scores for evaluation:

- How well does the content of the test reflect the knowledge, skills, and dispositions that the school district values for its students?
- How well does the format of the test (typically multiple choice) match the ways in which educators believe students can best show their knowledge, skills, and dispositions?

In the next chapter, Chapter 3, we focus on features of texts, both narrative and information, that can impact students' ability to construct meaning. In Chapters 4 through 7, we apply our knowledge of theory to classroom practices that engage students in read-alouds, literature study, independent reading, and working with textbooks in content areas. The diversity of today's classrooms demands that we know a broad range of instructional frameworks for creating stimulating learning environments for middle grade students.

■ TAKE A MOMENT TO REFLECT . . .

- ■ *Reading is:*
  - A high-speed;
  - Automatic;
  - Simultaneous operation of;

- Complex linguistic; and
- Cognitive processes.

■ *To make meaning, readers must use:*

- Story and sentence meaning;
- Sentence syntax or structure;
- Words, word-parts, and punctuation; and
- Metacognitive awareness of how these pieces fit together.

■ *Readers go through identifiable stages of development:*

Emerging readers:

- Learn that print has meaning, purpose, and function;
- "Read" familiar contexts and patterns; and
- Range from preschool to the middle first-grade reading level.

Developing readers:

- Are "glued to print;"
- Consciously try to match visual cues to meaning;
- Are oral, word-by-word readers;
- Are learning to monitor their own reading;
- Are beginning to self-correct miscues;
- Move toward silent reading late in this stage; and
- Range from the middle first- through the early third-grade reading level.

Transitional readers:

- Early in this stage, experience some difficulty moving between oral and silent reading;
- Are learning how to monitor silent reading;
- Can begin to sense their style of reading as they sink into silent reading;
- Begin to be more flexible; and
- Are able to adjust their reading to the task and text range from the early third- through the sixth-grade reading level

Mature readers:

- Develop learning strategies that allow for extension and development of new skills or refinement of known skills to meet changing life purposes;
- Read rapidly, especially in familiar content areas;
- Are interest and vocation centered;
- Range from the sixth-grade to the adult reading level; and
- Continue reading throughout adult life.

■ *The texts we read influence how we construct meaning:*

- Text-driven processing is influenced by both content and organization of a text.
- Knowledge-driven processing is influenced by prior knowledge of the content and past reading experiences.

■ *Texts come in a variety of forms—formal, informal, oral, written, enacted, permanent, fleeting.*

■ *Texts are cultural tools, sometimes created out of our experience, shaping what we know, how we know it, and how we learn.*

■ *Readers monitor meaning making by:*

- Using prior knowledge;
- Anticipating or making predictions;
- Self-correcting miscues; and
- Adjusting reading to meet different purposes in a variety of texts.

■ *Readers think in different ways while they read:*

- Explicit thinking—knowing what the author actually said;
- Implicit thinking—using knowledge to fill in around the author's ideas;
- Critical thinking—judging the value of the author's ideas; and
- Creative/personal thinking—going beyond the author's ideas and valuing their own ideas.

■ *Students will process text at one of four levels, depending on their stage of reading development and the complexity of the text:*

- Independent;
- Instructional;
- Frustration; or
- Listening.

■ *Readers who are good comprehenders:*

- Anticipate the content of the text being read;
- Monitor whether their predictions are accurate;
- Are aware of the difficulty of the text, the familiarity of the ideas in it, and the quality of the writing;
- Adjust the pace of reading to their purpose(s) to process the most relevant parts of the text;
- React as they read the text, based on prior knowledge, accepting some ideas and rejecting others;
- Reflect on the ideas in the text, constructing summaries and reasoning about whether the ideas in the text are sensible;
- Are interpretive, with prior knowledge driving interpretations;
- Continue to process a text after a first reading, sometimes rereading or reskimming portions that seem especially important; and
- Sometimes explicitly attempt to restate important ideas or summarize the text to make certain that important points can be recalled later.

■ *Words are important to comprehension:*

- Knowledge and flexibility with words is essential to constructing meaning with text.
- Words may appear in more than one context, with different meanings.

- Words, and their meanings, may be related by meaningful units.
- Knowing how to learn new words is essential to continued growth in comprehension.

■ *Expecting and respecting diversity among meaning makers in the classroom can promote meaningful instruction when teachers consider students':*

- Language background;
- Experience with literature; and
- Personal meaning-making strategies.

■ *Assessment and evaluation of meaning making includes:*

- Observation and anecdotal records;
- Conferring with students;
- Collecting samples of work; and
- Understanding standardized test data.

■ REFERENCES

Adams, J., & Collins, A. (1985). A schema-theoretic view of reading. In H. Singer & R. B. Ruddell (Eds.), *Theoretical models and processes of reading* (3rd. ed., pp. 404–425). Newark, DE: International Reading Association.

Adams, M. J. (1990). *Beginning to read: Thinking and learning about print.* Cambridge, MA: The MIT Press.

Allington, R. L. (1994). The schools we have. The schools we need. *The Reading Teacher, 48,* 14–29.

Allington, R. L. (2001). *What really matters for struggling readers: Designing research-based programs.* White Plains, NY: Longman.

Anderson, R. C., & Freebody, P. (1981). Vocabulary knowledge. In J. Guthrie (Ed.), *Comprehension and teaching: Research reviews* (pp. 77–117). Newark, DE: International Reading Association.

Anderson, R. C., & Nagy, W. (1991). Word meanings. In R. Barr, M. Kamil, P. Mosenthal, & P. D. Pearson (Eds.), *Handbook of reading research* (Vol. 2, pp. 690–724). White Plains, NY: Longman.

Anderson, R. C., & Pearson, P. D. (1984). A schema-theoretic view of reading comprehension. In P. D. Pearson (Ed.), *Handbook of reading research* (Vol. 1, pp. 255–291). White Plains, NY: Longman.

Anderson, R. C., Wilson, P. T., & Fielding, L. G. (1988). Growth in reading and how children spend their time outside of school. *Reading Research Quarterly, 23,* 285–303.

Anglin, J. M. (1993). *Vocabulary development: A morphological analysis.* Monographs for the Society of Research in Child Development, Serial No. 238, Vol. 58, No. 10.

Beach, R., & Hynds, S. (1991). Research on response to literature. In R. Barr, M. Kamil, P. B. Mosenthal, & P. D. Pearson (Eds.), *Handbook of reading research* (Vol. 2, pp. 453–489). White Plains, NY: Longman.

Beck, I., Perfetti, C., & McKeown, M. (1982). Effects of long term vocabulary instruction on lexical access and reading comprehension. *Journal of Educational Psychology, 74,* 506–521.

Bloome, D., & Bailey, F. M. (1992). Studying language and literacy through events, particularity, and intertextuality. In R. Beach, J. L. Green, M. L. Kamil, & T. Shanahan (Eds.), *Multidisciplinary perspectives on literacy research* (pp. 181–210). Urbana, IL: National Conference on Research in English and National Council of Teachers of English.

Bloome, D., & Egan-Robertson, A. (1993). The social construction of intertextuality in classroom reading and writing lessons. *Reading Research Quarterly, 28,* 304–333.

Borasi, R., & Siegel, M. (2000). *Reading counts: Expanding the role of reading in mathematics classrooms.* New York: Teachers College Press.

Brown, R., Pressley, M., Van Meter, P., & Schuder, T. (1996). A quasi-experimental validation of transactional strategies instruction with low achieving second grade students. *Journal of Educational Psychology, 88*, 18–37.

Clark, E. V. (1973). What is a word? On the child's acquisition of semantics in his first language. In T. E. Moore (Ed.), *Cognitive development and the acquisition of language* (pp. 65–110). New York: Academic Press.

Clark, E. V. (1993). *The lexicon of acquisition.* Cambridge: Cambridge University Press.

Clay, M. (1979/1985). *The early detection of reading difficulties.* Portsmouth, NH: Heinemann.

Davis, F. B. (1944). Fundamental factors in reading comprehension. *Psychometrika, 9*, 185–197.

Fitzgerald, J. (1995). English-as-a-second-language reading instruction in the United States: A research review. *Journal of Reading Behavior, 27*, 115–152.

Golden, J. M., & Guthrie, J. T. (1986). Convergence and divergence in reader response to literature. *Reading Research Quarterly, 21*, 408–421.

Goldman, S. R. & Rakestraw, J. A. (2000). Structural aspects of constructing meaning from a text. In M. L. Kamil, P. B. Mosenthal, P. D. Pearson, & R. Barr (Eds.), *Handbook of reading research* (Vol. 3, pp. 311–335). Mahwah, NJ: Lawrence Erlbaum Associates.

Goodman, Y. (1972). Qualitative reading miscue analysis for teacher training. In R. Hodges & E. H. Rudorf (Eds.), *Language and learning to read: What teachers should know about language* (pp. 160–166). Boston: Houghton Mifflin.

Green, G. M. (1989). *Pragmatics and natural language understanding.* Hillsdale, NJ: Lawrence Erlbaum Associates.

Heath, S. B. (1994). The children of Trackton's children: Spoken and written language in social change. In R. B. Ruddell, M. R. Ruddell, & H. Singer (Eds.), *Theoretical models and processes of reading* (4th ed., pp. 208–230). Newark, DE: International Reading Association.

Holdaway. D. (1980). *Independence in reading.* Portsmouth, NH: Heinemann.

Irvin, J. L. (1998). *Reading and the middle school student: Strategies to enhance learning.* Boston: Allyn and Bacon.

Jaggar, A. (1975). Allowing for language difference. In G. S. Pinnell (Ed.), *Discovering language with children* (pp. 18–29). Urbana, IL: National Council of Teachers of English.

Jones, N. K. (1995). Learning to read: Insights from reading recovery. *Literacy, Teaching and Learning, 1*(2), 41–56.

Juel, C. (1991). Beginning reading. In R. Barr, M. L. Kamil, P. B. Mosenthal, & P. D. Pearson (Eds.), *Handbook of reading research* (Vol. 2, pp. 325–353). White Plains, NY: Longman.

Lewis, C. S. (1978). The reader and all kinds of stories. In M. Meek, A. Warlow, & G. Brown (Eds.), *The cool web: The pattern of children's reading* (pp. 76–90). New York: Atheneum.

Meichenbaum, D., & Asarnow, J. (1979). Cognitive-behavioral modification and metacognitive development: Implication for the classroom. In P. C. Kendall & S. D., Hollon (Eds.), *Cognitive-behavioral interventions* (pp. 11–35). New York: Academic Press.

McKeown, M., Beck, I., Omanson, R., & Perfetti, C. (1983). The effects of long-term vocabulary instruction on reading comprehension: A replication. *Journal of Reading Behavior, 15*, 3–18.

McKeown, M., Beck, I., Omanson, R., & Pople, M. (1985). Some effect of the nature and frequency of vocabulary instruction on the knowledge and use of words. *Reading Research Quarterly, 20*, 522–535.

Nagy, W. (1997). On the role of context in first- and second-language vocabulary learning. In N. Schmitt & M. McCarthy (Eds.), *Vocabulary: Description, acquisition and pedagogy* (pp. 64–83). Cambridge: Cambridge University Press.

Nagy, W. E., & Scott, J. A. (2000). Vocabulary processes. In M. E. Kamil, P. B. Mosenthal, P. D. Pearson,, & R. Barr (Eds.), *Handbook of reading research* (Vol. 3, pp. 269–284). Mahwah, NJ: Lawrence Erlbaum Associates.

Padron, Y. (1998). Latino students and reading: Understanding these English language learners' needs. In K. Beers & B. G. Samuels (Eds.), *Intro focus: Understanding and creating middle school readers* (pp. 105–121). Norwood, MA: Christopher-Gordon Publishers.

Paris, S. G., Wasik, B. A., & Turner, J. C. (1991). The development of strategic readers. In R. Barr, M. Kamil, P. B. Mosenthal, & P. D. Pearson (Eds.), *Handbook of reading research* (Vol. 2, pp. 401–432). White Plains, NY: Longman.

Polacco, P. (1996). *I can hear the sun: A modern myth.* New York: Putnam.

Pressley, M. (1998). *Reading instruction that works: The case for balanced teaching.* New York: Guilford Press.

Pressley, M. (1999). Self-Regulated comprehension processing and its development through instruction. In L. B. Gambrell, L. M. Morrow, S. B. Neuman, & M. Pressley (Eds.), *Best practices in literacy instruction* (pp. 90–97). New York: Guilford Press.

Rhodes, L. K., & Nathenson-Mejia, S. (1992). Anecdotal records: A powerful tool for ongoing literacy assessment. *The Reading Teacher, 45*, 502–509.

Rosenblatt, L. (1978). *The reader, the text, the poem: The transactional theory of the literary work.* Carbondale, IL: Southern Illinois University Press.

Rosenblatt, L. M. (1994). The transactional theory of reading and writing. In R. Ruddell, M. Ruddell, & H. Singer (Eds.), *Theoretical models and processes of reading* (4th ed., pp. 1057–1092). Newark, DE: International Reading Association.

Schank, R., & Abelson, R. (1975). *Knowledge structures.* Hillsdale, NJ: Lawrence Erlbaum Associates.

Schanklin, N. K. (1982). Relating reading and writing: Developing a transitional model of the writing process. In *Monographs in teaching and learning.* Bloomington: Indiana University School of Education.

Schon, D. (1983). *The reflective practitioner: How professionals think in action.* New York: Basic Books.

Shannon, P. (1992). *Becoming political: Reading and writing in the politics of literacy education.* Portsmouth, NH: Heinemann.

Teale, W. H. (1986). Home background and children's literacy development. In W. H. Teale & E. Sulzby (Eds.), *Emergent literacy: Writing and reading* (pp. 173–206). Norwood, NJ: Ablex.

Thomson, J. (1987). *Understanding teenager's reading.* Urbana, IL: National Council of Teachers of English.

Vygotsky, L. S. (1978). *Mind in society* (M. Cole, V. John-Steiner, S. Scribner, & E. Sounerman, Eds. & Trans.). Cambridge, MA: Harvard University Press.

Wade, S. E., & Moje, E. B. (2000). The role of text in classroom learning. In M. Kamil, P. B. Mosenthal, P. D. Pearson, & R. Barr (Eds.), *Handbook of reading research* (Vol. 3, pp. 609–627). Mahwah, NJ: Lawrence Erlbaum Associates.

Winsor, P., Nagy, W. E., Osborn, J., & O'Flahavan, J. (1993). *Structural analysis: Toward an evaluation of instruction.* Center for the Study of Reading, Technical Report No. 581. (ERIC Document Reproduction Service No. ED 360 625).

■ CHILDREN'S LITERATURE

Levine, E. (1989). *I hate English!* New York: Scholastic.
Paulsen, G. (1987). *Hatchet.* New York: Viking Penguin.

chapter 3

Teaching with Texts

In this chapter . . .

We explore:

- The power of the texts we select,
- The research support for literature-based reading,
- The importance of selecting diverse texts,
- Responding to texts,
- Features of narrative texts, and
- Features of information texts.

Focus Literature . . .

A Time for Andrew: A Ghost Story by Mary Downing Hahn, Clarion Publishers, New York, 1995.

Hatchet by Gary Paulsen, Aladdin Paperbacks, New York, 1999.

Looking into Classrooms . . .

Hector, Anita, and Amhal are meeting to make long-range plans for the school year. Hector excitedly relates some good news, "Yesterday, the librarian gave me reviews of some new literature. She has a little money left to order books and wants to know what we need." Anita asks, "Is there anything new that would be good for our units on 'Dealing with Change' or 'Immigration'?" Hector responds, "There are several on the list that I have read and I think our kids would really get in to." Amhal offers, "Are there any with minority characters?" "And we need more information books that are well written, with good photographs, to build background," Anita adds. These teachers realize the potential power of the texts they select for their students.

Building a Theory Base . . .

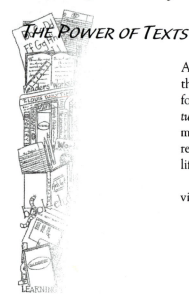

THE POWER OF TEXTS

A powerful way to engage our students with life and the world is through the use of authentic literature, works of quality literature that are complete and have not been altered for instruction. Rebecca Lukens and Ruth Cline (1995), in *A Critical Handbook of Literature for Young Adults*, define literature as "a significant truth expressed in appropriate elements and memorable language" (p. 2). Is it the "significant truth" in quality literature that reaches out, engages us, pulls us into another's world, or compels us to consider a way of life that we may never know?

McGinley and his colleagues remind us of the power of literary experiences that provide children with opportunities to:

- Envision and explore possible selves, roles, and responsibilities through the lives of story characters, both real and fictional;
- Describe or remember personal experiences or interests in their lives;
- Objectify and reflect on certain problematic emotions and circumstances as they relate to important moral and ethical dilemmas in their lives;
- Understand, affirm, or negotiate social relationships among peers, family members, and community members; and
- Raise and develop their awareness of significant social issues and social problems (McGinley & Kamberelis, 1996, p. 76; McGinley, Kamberelis, Mahoney, Madigan, Rybicki, & Oliver, 1997, pp. 55–56).

As we consider ways to engage middle grade students with high-quality texts, we can only hope to create the types of experiences described by Robert Probst (1998) when he states

> The students in these tumultuous years are beginning to shape their visions of themselves and their possibilities; the literature they read is an invitation to articulate those evolving visions, to consider all the possibilities that lie ahead, to explore the depth and range of their emotions, to question the values and beliefs that will define their character. It is an opportunity and an invitation to begin to take responsibility for becoming the people they will ultimately be. (p. 138)

Authentic literature, rich in language and ideas, should constitute a large portion of the texts we use for instruction during the middle grade years. The genres, or categories, of literature offer us a broad range of materials for engaging our students, including:

- Fiction (e.g., realistic, historical, science),
- Nonfiction,
- Biography,
- Fantasy,
- Folklore (e.g., fables, folktales, myths, legends),
- Poetry and verse, and
- Picture books.

Throughout this text, we consider ways to engage middle grade students in relevant and challenging learning experiences with a variety of literature. To add to your own learning in this text, it is important for you to become knowledgeable about the texts that are used as examples so that you can add to our conversation. You are also encouraged to identify other texts, your favorites, and relate those texts to our discussion as you make connections between theories about learning and teaching and the practices that you observe or are able to try out in classrooms.

SUPPORT FOR LITERATURE-BASED READING

Researchers have found that students in literature-based programs view reading as a meaning-making process and have higher levels of metacognitive awareness, that is, awareness of their own thinking, than students in skills-based programs (Freppon, 1991; Gambrell & Palmer, 1992). Across studies of various literature-based reading programs, students were able to construct meaning, share personal reactions, and demonstrate strategic reading behaviors such as hypothesizing, interpreting, predicting, confirming, generalizing, and evaluating (Morrow & Gambrell, 2000). In this context, literature-based reading suggests that texts for instruction are drawn from all literary genre, including nonfiction.

When literature-based reading is compared with other types of reading programs, students who participate in quality literature-based programs tend to be more strategic as readers than those in skills-based programs (Dahl & Freppon, 1995; Freppon, 1991). In addition, combining literature-based instruction with traditional basal reading instruction (see Chapter 12) was found to be more powerful than traditional instruction alone (Morrow, Pressley, Smith, & Smith, 1997). Students who participate in a program that embeds instruction in reading strategies as a part of literature-based instruction outperformed students receiving only traditional reading instruction (Baumann & Ivey, 1997; Block, 1993).

Integrating literature into content area learning also has positive effects on reading performance (Guzzetti, Kowalinski, & McGowan, 1992; Jones, Coombs, & McKinney, 1994; Smith, 1994). When a literature-based theme approach is compared to a strict textbook approach, students acquire more social studies concepts and a greater understanding of those concepts through literature-based instruction (Guzzetti et al., 1992; Jones et al., 1994). Other researchers have found that students using historical fiction novels in place of basal readers and social studies texts recalled significantly more details, main ideas, and total amount of historical information (Smith, Monson & Dobson, 1992).

In addition to fiction, a growing body of quality nonfiction is available in most content area topics. These texts provide a wide range of ideas that promote emotional responses, personal associations, imagination, prediction, and evaluation (Ross, 1994; Smith, 1994). When teaching science, math, and social studies, 95% of teachers use subject-specific texts 90% of the time (Ogens, 1990). Reliance on textbooks, however, tends to favor the accumulation of factual knowledge at the expense of the process-oriented inquiry needed to deal with science- and social studies-related issues. We must remember that the content of textbooks is often restricted to avoid controversy (Morrow & Gambrell, 2000), and space limitations may preclude attention to many topics of interest to middle grade students.

Research clearly indicates that discussing quality literature offers students opportunities to explore interpretations and respond at higher levels of abstract and critical thinking (McGee, 1992). As we are aware from discussion of learning environments in Chapter 1, learning is facilitated through the assistance of more knowledgeable members of the learning community; in particular, higher level mental processes, such as those involved in language processes and academic discourse, are enhanced through social interaction (Vygotsky, 1978). Alsami (1994) found that students who also participated in peer-led discussions of text produced significantly more elaborate and complex discussions than those who participated only in teacher-led discussions. Students' deep-level understanding of text occurred most frequently through interactions with others, especially peers (Alsami, 1995). In addition, Many and Wiseman (1992) found that the quality of literature discussions was directly related to the instructional approach. Students are more likely to clarify the text and their own experiences by making significant real-world connections to story events when discussions focus on their thoughts and personal reactions, rather than solely on analysis of a text.

Using literature for instruction also has been found to have positive effects with students who have challenges with reading. Ninety percent of a group of seventh- and eigth-grade middle school students in development reading classes using literature for reading instruction reported that they felt better about themselves as readers because with literature books they could read faster and more fluently, could remember and comprehend more of their reading, and were better able to complete reading assignments (Stewart, Paradis, Ross, & Lewis, 1996). Goatley and her colleagues (1995) have found positive benefits for special education students who were involved in a particular literature-based approach called Book Clubs, which we examine in depth in Chapter 5. Finally, students for whom English is not their first language also benefit from literature-based reading. Jimenez and Gamez (1996) found that English language learner (ELL) students began to think more strategically while using literature to learn about cognitive strategies. These positive benefits will be explored further as we examine a variety of instructional approaches to teach reading in Chapters 4 through 7.

VALUING DIVERSITY THROUGH SELECTION OF TEXTS

Texts that reflect the achievements, lifestyles, and values of the range of people in this country help students have a better understanding of who they are and what contributions they can make (Martinez & Nash, 1990; Padron, 1998). For example, we are aware that at least 38% of all public school students are members of a minority group. Hispanic students account for at least 16% of all public school enrollment and at least 31% of students in the western part of the United States. When we consider such data, we should feel compelled to engage our middle grade students in a range of quality literature that represents the rapidly changing racial and ethnic makeup of this nation.

In addition, we should select literature that is "culturally conscious" (Sims, 1983), literature that helps all of us become more familiar with the varied cultural backgrounds represented in our classrooms, the United States, and the world. Such books may focus on heritage, everyday experiences, battles against racism and discrimination, urban living, friendship, family relationships, and growing up. We may wish to look particularly for books written by members of a specific cultural group, to provide more of an insider's view.

In selecting multicultural literature, Reimer (1992) cautions us to take care that the literature selected does not present "cultural conglomerates." We must be aware of the diversity that exists, not only between groups of people, but also *within* groups. For example, we must remember that terms such as *Hispanic* refer to people from a range of countries and cultural backgrounds (e.g., Mexican-Americans, Puerto Ricans, Costa Ricans, and others). To help you consider texts for middle grades students, Appendix B contains lists of suggested books, sorted by categories, including cultural groups.

A word of caution: As individuals we identify with characters that reflect the cultural attitudes and values of the groups with which we identify (Beach, 1991). Consequently, as we encourage students to read widely in diverse texts, we must remember that their cultural identification with certain groups may cause students to resist certain texts that represent cultural memberships or various identity positions they may find unfamiliar, even somewhat uncomfortable. Our sensitivity can help students navigate this new literature toward a deeper understanding of culture and difference (Soter, 1999). Observing and understanding how students respond as members of a certain gender, social class, cultural group, and so on may help to explain their responses to texts.

READER-RESPONSE THEORY

Our understanding of literary experience is informed by theories about readers' responses to texts. In reader-response theory, meaning is believed to emerge in the *transaction* between reader and text (Rosenblatt, 1978). In this sense, a transaction is like a negotiation between two parties, a reader and a text, that brings about a change in one. A transaction between reader and text, however, cannot occur without *engagement*.

ENGAGING WITH A TEXT

Engagement with a literary text is at the heart of reader-response theory. Slatoff (1970) suggests that the very nature of a literary work is to "affect the emotions and to compel various sorts of involvement" (p. 36). Engagement is more than merely emotional response; it is a process of involving "both mind and emotion" (p. 53). Rosenblatt (1978) agrees when she states that literary study should be a "working harmony" between reason and emotion where students "develop the ability to think rationally within an emotionally colored context" (pp. 227–228).

Bruner (1986) adds that in a learning environment emotion and thought are not separate, because emotion is deeply rooted and produced within a cultural reality, where "emotion comes from the knowledge of the situation that arouses it" (p. 117). Think of yourself as a reader. How does your own emotional response to literature draw you into that literature? Do you believe that your emotional engagement calls on your mind to reason in response to the literature?

What happens when readers do not engage with a text? For these readers the words on the page are merely symbols, without meaning. But for readers with a high level of engagement the very same page of text may be pure delight, entertainment, or enlightenment.

TAKING A LITERARY STANCE

Readers both transform and are transformed by literary works. Louise Rosenblatt (1978, 1991) states that the reading experience is influenced by the stance readers take toward texts as well as the cognitive and psychological processes they bring to the reading process. As readers, we dictate—rather than the text—the stance that we take. That stance may be influenced by our reasons for selecting a particular text, something in the text may cue us to adopt a particular stance, or we may be influenced by an external force. While reading a text, we may shift our stance along a continuum, moving between the efferent and the aesthetic.

The word *efferent* comes from a Latin word meaning "to carry away." To take an *efferent stance* is to narrow our attention as we read in order to build up the meanings and ideas retained in memory. An efferent stance is a type of reading in which our primary concern is what we will carry away from the reading or what will remain with us afterward, such as the information to be acquired, the logical solution to a problem, or the actions to be carried out.

The word *aesthetic* is derived from a Greek word meaning "to sense" or "to perceive." When we take an *aesthetic stance* we turn our attention inward and center on what is being created within us during the actual reading. An aesthetic stance is a type of reading in which the reader focuses attention on the lived-through experience of the reading, the thoughts and feelings that are being stirred within the reader, the beauty of the writer's ideas and style of expression, and the past experiences that these words call up.

Robert Probst (1998) reminds us:

> If efferent reading is purposeful and directed, working toward a defined end, then aesthetic reading is exploratory and responsive, alert to unforeseen possibilities, curious about detours and digressions, playful and experimental. Above all it acknowledges the uniqueness of the reader. It respects the fact that each reader brings to the text an unduplicated history and the unique perspective that results. The experience of the text, consequently, is unique for each reader. What he makes of it, what it means, depends not simply on the words on the page, but also on who it is who reads them. (p. 128)

Rosenblatt (1985) views the possibilities for a reader's stance as an efferent–aesthetic continuum. "Since much of our linguistic activity hovers near the middle of the 'efferent–aesthetic' continuum, it becomes essential that in any particular speaking/listening/writing/reading event we adopt the predominant stance appropriate to our purpose" (p. 102). The stance that we take as readers directly affects the quality of our literary experience.

Let's apply what we know about *efferent* and *aesthetic* reading to the classroom. Imagine that you plan to engage your sixth-grade students in reading *Hatchet* (Paulsen, 1999), in which 13-year-old Brian, on his way to visit his father, who works in the Canadian oil fields, survives a plane crash and lives alone in the wilderness for 54 days. If you emphasize the survival techniques that can be learned from Brian's ordeal, what type of stance are you encouraging students to take? Why?

If, however, you respond to the way that Paulsen uses words to evoke the feelings of isolation that Brian must have felt, what type of stance would you be encouraging students to take? Why?

If you provide opportunities for students to meet in student-led literature groups and encourage them to find what is meaningful for themselves in the text, what type of stance would you be encouraging students to take? Why?

• • •

If I use *Hatchet* to form concepts about survival techniques, I am pushing students toward an *efferent stance,* to focus on what they will take away from the text that will help them understand social studies/science concepts. If I read *Hatchet* aloud to encourage students to appreciate the beauty and emotion of the text, I focus on the experience itself rather than on what students will take from it. This encourages them to take an *aesthetic stance*. If, however, students know that they will meet in student-led groups and set their own directions for discussions, the possibilities for responses can extend across the efferent–aesthetic continuum, depending on their previous literary experiences and their level of engagement with the text.

A major goal of your literacy instruction should be to help middle grade students develop a sophisticated repertoire of response options to use in a variety of literary situations. As you plan instructional experiences, you must consider how to engage students and how to help them learn to evaluate the effectiveness of the stances they take as readers.

• • •

As readers, our schema for literature and reading influences the processes we use for responding to text. In the next section, we consider various ways in which readers use intellect and emotion in response to literature.

RESPONDING TO TEXTS

Response is at the heart of reading. A student "can begin to achieve a sound approach to literature only when he reflects upon his response to it, when he attempts to understand what in the work and in himself produced that reaction and when he thoughtfully goes on to modify, reject, or accept it" (Rosenblatt, 1978, p. 76). We respond emotionally and intellectually to texts that we read. Our responses can be described through the following behaviors: engagement, conceiving, connecting, problem solving and question asking, explaining, interpreting, and judging.

ENGAGING

Engagement rests heavily on the breadth, depth, and quality of our previous literary experiences. The more positively we feel toward the act of reading in general, and toward the reading of a particular text, the more likely we are to have a high degree of engagement with that text. If our experience has taught us that reading is trying to find the "right answer" or that reading is physically hard because we are asked to read texts that are too difficult for us, then we are not likely to have positive feelings toward reading and are less likely to engage in the reading.

Our expectations for a text affect our level of engagement with it. How engaged we become in fiction, fantasy, or fact relates to our sense of reality and willingness to accept the world of a literary text as distinct from our own. How engaged we become with information text or biography relates to our interest in the topic, our desire to learn about the topic, and the relevance we see for our own lives. Without engagement, other forms of response are not probable.

CONCEIVING

Depending on the level at which we engage with a text, we develop conceptions or perceptions of that text. Readers who have difficulty defining their emotional responses to a text also have difficulty describing their conceptions of it (Miall, 1985). Personal conceptions formed in the real world influence our responses in a fictional world. Readers with a more well-organized schema for literature and reading tend to have "more elaborate and complex interpretations of the actions and behaviors of literary characters" (Hynds, 1985, p. 401). Readers who have firsthand experiences with the content of an information text are more likely to develop appropriate conceptions of the world that text describes.

CONNECTING

As readers, we connect texts with related experiences, other texts, and personal attitudes (Beach, 1987; Harste, 1986). Elaborating on our own life experiences, attitudes, and knowledge makes us better able to use that experience as we interpret texts. As we make these connections, we often draw on past literary experiences to make new interpretations. It is in our connections to text that we are able to generalize from a broad base of knowledge.

PROBLEM SOLVING AND QUESTION ASKING

When we monitor our reading and are able to articulate our difficulties in understanding text, we are better able to use problem-solving strategies to enhance understanding (Newkirk, 1984). Posing our own questions while reading helps us demonstrate better understanding than if we did not pose such questions. Mature readers interact with the author and with themselves as sense makers.

EXPLAINING

Explaining is making a clarifying statement, describing what something means to us. When we read, we may be better able to explain our personal feelings about a text rather than our interpretations. Our explanations may be based more on emotion than thought and, consequently, may lack systematic supporting evidence from the text. Our attitudes toward reading or the information provided in a text can influence our ability to explain (Black & Seifert, 1985). Text that is rich in description provides increased opportunity for engagement and the identification of supporting detail to explain our stance as readers.

INTERPRETING

Interpretation is considered to be the thinking side of constructing meaning. When we interpret as readers, we think beyond the literal meaning and "read between the lines." Our interpretations of a text are influenced by our previous literary experiences (Black & Seifert, 1985; Heath, 1985). The more experience we have as readers, at home and at school, the more likely we are to make interpretations (Martinez, 1983; Svensson, 1985). Analyzing or generalizing are more likely to occur when text is familiar.

Less experienced readers are more likely to be oriented to finding information in a text (information driven) or to following a story line (story driven), rather than to making interpretations about the author's intention (point driven) (Hunt & Vipond, 1985, 1986). They are more likely to use retelling, engaging, evaluation, or inferring in response to a text than to generalize about or analyze a text. Such behavior may be a reflection of school experiences with literature.

JUDGING

Knowledge of literature influences the processes we use as we make judgments about text. With experience, we begin to focus more on the form and complexity of text than merely on content (Britton, 1984). When less experienced readers make judgments based on content rather than on form, they are likely to negatively judge a text they do not understand. The relationship between readers' interests and their cognitive maturity also affects their making judgments about the aesthetic quality of literature (Beach & Hynds, 1991).

As readers, we use a variety of processes or strategies in our responses to texts. We seldom use one process in isolation from other response processes. "It is difficult to make generalizations about discrete response types, since responses such as explaining or describing are often embedded in superordinate strategies such as judging or interpreting" (Beach & Hynds, 1991, p. 463).

To engage students effectively in a reading and literature program, we must consider the nature of the texts we will use and how those texts influence the making of meaning. In the next sections of this chapter, we turn our attention to specific issues of narrative and informational texts. What our students know about these texts influences their level of engagement as they make meaning.

FEATURES OF NARRATIVE TEXTS

To think as mature readers, we must have a well-developed sense of how authors use literary elements. Knowing the possibilities helps us develop expectations for narrative writing. The genres of realistic fiction, fantasy, and folk literature draw heavily on narrative writing, which is characterized by the use of such literary elements as setting, characters, plot, point of view, theme, and style. We will examine here literary elements as used in children's literature and consider the importance of each element.

We draw our examples from *A Time for Andrew: A Ghost Story*, a mystery by Mary Downing Hahn (1995), in which Andrew, nicknamed Drew, is tricked into trading places in time by the ghost of Andrew, an ancestor who died of diphtheria several generations earlier. Drew must then figure out how to get back to the present. The Your Turn/My Turn sections, using *Hatchet*, by Gary Paulsen (1999), provide opportunities to apply our understanding of literary elements.

SETTING

Types of Settings. In some stories the author focuses on character development, making the setting seem somewhat unimportant. The setting is merely a *backdrop* and we do not pay much attention to it. We realize where and when the story is taking place, but we also realize that the setting does not influence our attention to the conflict the main character is experiencing. In contrast, the author may choose to use the setting in a more *integral* way, where the setting actually has a specific function in the story.

Functions of Setting. Settings serve the following functions:

1. ***Integral settings can affect the mood of a story.*** Sometimes an author uses description of the setting to create a particular mood that supports the telling of the story. For example, in *A Time for Andrew,* Hahn uses description of dreary,

windy, rainy weather and a post–Civil War house, believed to be haunted, to create an eerie mood. We expect that the setting will be important to the upcoming events, so we become engaged.

2. *Setting can illuminate a character.* Settings can be used to show us a side of a character that might not be evident in any other way. Being in Great-aunt Blythe's haunted house puts Drew in a situation he has never experienced and we see a courageous side of him that we might not see in his everyday life.

3. *Setting can act as an antagonist.* Lukens (1998) defines *antagonist* as an opposing force to the protagonist, or main character. It is the conflict between the protagonist and antagonist that creates plot in many stories. We see the setting as antagonist most prominently in stories in which characters struggle with nature or society, rather than with self or others. Nature and society push characters to show us parts of themselves we might not otherwise see.

4. *Setting can symbolize a figurative meaning.* Authors use concrete objects and color to represent abstract or implied meanings. For example, the darkness that Hahn uses to evoke feeling also symbolizes the death that overshadows Great-aunt Blythe's house. Figurative meanings are typically present in folk literature, especially myths and legends, but can also be present in other forms of narrative.

What type of setting does Gary Paulsen use in *Hatchet*? What function(s) does the setting play? What leads you to think that?

• • •

The setting in *Hatchet* is integral to the development of Paulsen's story. After the plane crash, the setting actually becomes the antagonist, the character opposing Brian. The solitude of the setting affects our anticipation of upcoming events and, consequently, affects the mood of the story.

• • •

CHARACTER

Learning about Characters. As we listen to an author describe a character, we learn about the character's physical appearance, actions, possibly the character's thoughts, and, if the author is narrating the story, we know what the author thinks about the character. Through dialogue we listen to the character's words and also what others say about the character. Then it is our job as readers to put these pieces of information together to form our own understanding of that character.

Types of Characters. Characters are described by how much is known about them and the degree to which they change during the development of the plot. Our knowledge of some characters is *round* because we know a lot about them, while our knowledge of other characters is rather *flat*. Main characters are typically round. We need to know them well if we are to engage with them in the story. Other characters are flat because we don't need to know much about them.

Characters can also be described by how much they change during the development of the plot. Some characters are affected by the events of the plot and show us how they grow and change as a result of their experiences. Characters that change are called *dynamic* characters. In contrast, some characters are *static*, showing consistent traits throughout a story. Depending on the duration of the plot, both types of characters may be needed to tell a believable story.

In *A Time for Andrew*, Drew (living) and Andrew (ghost) are round characters; we must know them well. Throughout the story we watch Drew change as a result of his experience (dynamic), while Andrew remains predominantly the same (static), in contrast to Drew. It seems logical for Andrew to remain the same, because he is a ghost. His static qualities enable us to see Drew's change more clearly.

We are likely to meet two other types of characters in various story genres: stereotyped and anthropomorphic characters. When characters are described as if they represent generalized characteristics of a group rather than as true individuals, we say they are *stereotyped*. In folk literature stereotyped characters, such as evil witches, are common because the genre is intended to teach lessons about life and the characters' traits must be easily identified. In contrast, we would not want to have stereotyped characters in realistic fiction because the author should be developing individuals who are unique and believable. If any round, flat, or stereotyped characters are living or inanimate nonhuman beings (animals, trees, vehicles, books, and so on) that act human, they are considered to be *anthropomorphic*. This type of character is often found in fantasies where the author wants the reader to suspend disbelief and respond to a fully imaginary world.

Functions of Characters.   An author uses characters to create an interesting story and also may consciously use characters to serve specific purposes. The main character, the protagonist, leads or propels the action. To keep the plot moving along, the author may create an antagonist, the opposing force(s) that pushes or challenges the main character. Sometimes the opposing force is the setting, but most often it is another character. In *A Time for Andrew*, Drew is our protagonist. His actions keep the plot moving. Andrew is the antagonist.

The author may also create a character who is a *foil*. When the author needs to push the protagonist in a particular direction or cause that character to show a particular side of him- or herself, but the antagonist cannot serve that purpose, the author creates a character with a limited, and often short-lived, role. A foil character has a specific purpose and will usually disappear after serving it. *A Time for Andrew* has several foil characters. The father serves the purpose of getting Drew to the old house so that the story can take place. We understand who Andrew is because Great-aunt Blythe serves the function of filling in background information for us.

Unity between Characters and Their Actions.   Once a character is introduced to the reader, authors should be consistent in the further development of that character in action and speech. Unity of character and action is what makes for a believable story. If an author wants the reader to invest emotionally in a character, unity is vitally important, especially in the genres of realistic and historical fiction, fantasy, and biography. There is unity of character and action in *A Time for Andrew*. Drew's actions remain true to his character.

In *Hatchet*, what type of character is Brian? How do you learn about him? Is there unity between Brian's character and his actions? What leads you to think that?

• • •

Brian is a round, dynamic character. Through the author's omniscient point of view, we are able to know all of Brian's actions and thoughts. This is necessary to the development of the story since there are no other characters in the wilderness to help disclose Brian's inner self. There is unity of character and action. What we learn about Brian through his thoughts seems consistent with his actions. Brian's thoughts give us hints about changes occurring within him before we see the changes in his actions.

• • •

PLOT

Types of Plots. As authors move characters through a series of actions and reactions, two basic types of plots emerge: progressive and episodic. In a *progressive* plot the author builds the tension between characters and events as the plot develops over a period of time. In a chapter book a progressive plot usually keeps us involved from chapter to chapter, anticipating what will happen next.

In contrast, an *episodic* plot typically focuses on one life event in a picture book, or events seem to begin anew with each new chapter in a chapter book. As readers, we do not feel the same type of tension in the development of an episode as we do with a progressive plot. While we follow a main character or two, each chapter is usually a new episode in their lives and not necessarily linked directly to the previous chapter.

The plot in *A Time for Andrew* is progressive; its series of events link together to make one story. The Little House series by Laura Ingalls Wilder is an example of episodic plots in chapter books, with each chapter beginning a new episode that may or may not be connected to the previous episode or chapter.

Order in Plots. Probably one of the most noticeable aspects of plot is order. For most stories, it makes sense for an author to tell the story in a *chronological order*. At other times it is easier for an author to "hook" us by beginning a story as a *flashback,* that is, reconstructing a story that has already occurred. Flashbacks also can be used within a progressive plot to temporarily go back and fill in missing pieces of information for us.

In *A Time for Andrew,* we begin in the present with Drew, travel back in time when Drew and Andrew trade places, follow Drew as he lives Andrew's life, occasionally visit the present to see what is happening with Andrew living Drew's life, then return permanently to the present when Drew wins back his real life. This is a progressive plot that moves between two settings.

Patterns of Action. Good stories keep us engaged, as we wait to find out what happens. The "what happens" is often tied to the solving of a problem or dilemma that faces a significant character. As we follow characters through a plot, a skillful author builds in just enough *suspense* or tension to keep us waiting to see how the situation is resolved. The author may heighten our suspense through *foreshadowing*, giving clues to coming events.

The tension may build to a *climax* or breaking point, then the author must decide what to do with the character's dilemma: end in a *cliffhanger,* or with an open or closed resolution. Some authors choose to leave us at the climax, creating a cliffhanger, and letting us decide for ourselves what else might occur. Adults often enjoy this type of participation in a plot, but children can find the lack of closure unsettling. Realistically, most of the events of our lives do not end as cliffhangers, but instead are resolved in some way. A *closed resolution* leaves little doubt in our mind about what followed the climax. Bringing closure can be reassuring for the young reader who sees life as definitive and wants to know "the answer." In contrast, some authors end with an *open resolution,* leaving some doubt in our minds about the final outcome and letting us contribute by making our own endings. Open resolutions are very effective with older students who are able to use their knowledge of life and story characters to carry on the story.

A Time for Andrew is filled with foreshadowings, which heighten the suspense of the mystery. In Chapter 2, as Drew stumbles into his great-grandfather's room, the old man says to him, "You've come back. . . . But it won't do any good. It's my house now, not yours" (p. 11). His great-grandfather had known Andrew as a boy, but we do not yet know that. The pattern of action is a climax with a closed resolution. Andrew was excellent at playing marbles. Drew beats Andrew at Ringer, a marble game, to win his way back into the present. We leave the story with Drew safely back in his own time and we know clearly what happened to Andrew and the other characters from his time. We are assured at the end that the mystery is resolved.

Conflict in Plots. Conflicts in our everyday lives influence many of our actions and reactions. We are aware of things that we do that are motivated by struggles and desires within ourselves, with other people, with our environment, or with the conventions of society. Our lives are influenced by the way we act and react with the conflicts we encounter. Because narratives tell the stories of people's lives, a narrative naturally centers around the conflicts in which people find themselves.

At least four types of conflict are found in narratives: conflict with self, conflicts with other people, conflicts with nature, and conflicts with society. Without these conflicts, how could there be tension in a plot? How could tension build to a point that a climax would be needed to resolve it? Without conflict, what would keep us interested in reading to find out what happens next?

In *A Time for Andrew*, Drew's conflict with Andrew (conflict with people) drives the plot. Once in Andrew's time, Drew is torn between returning to his own time and family and staying in Andrew's time with Hannah (conflict with self).

YOUR TURN... Describe the plot of *Hatchet*, including type, order, action, and conflict. What leads you to your conclusions?

• • •

MY TURN... The story that Gary Paulsen tells in *Hatchet* is a progressive plot, mostly chronological, with a few flashbacks to fill us in about events concerning Brian's parents. As we anticipate a rescue taking place, tensions build and subside slightly throughout, with the climax coming when the plane lands on the lake. The tensions result from Brian's conflicts with nature and with himself as he learns to live alone in the wilderness. Paulsen adds an epilogue to bring closure to the story, providing additional information about what followed the rescue.

• • •

POINT OF VIEW

Types of Point of View.   One of the choices that authors make about the way they want to engage the reader concerns point of view, or who is telling the story. Sometimes the author takes the role of an *objective narrator* who seems to be suspended over the characters and setting, with the ability to see and hear all that goes on. Then it is up to us, the readers, to judge the meaning or significance of events, actions, and speech.

If the author allows us to know the thoughts of one or more of the characters, in addition to knowing and hearing all that was done and said, the point of view becomes *omniscient*. In some plots it is important for us to know what a particular character is thinking to help us become more involved and better understand characters' motivations.

Sometimes the author allows a character to tell the story in their own, or *first-person*, point of view. We see all of the events of plot through that character's eyes. When we read a story that is written from a first-person point of view, it is important to realize that we are seeing only one view of the events and that view is influenced by the teller's feelings. First person is the point of view of *A Time for Andrew*. Drew tells us what happens to him. We have firsthand knowledge of his view of all of the events. It is hard to know about the other characters except through Drew's eyes.

From what point of view is *Hatchet* told? How does the point of view affect the story? What leads you to think that?

• • •

Hatchet is told from an omniscient point of view, which draws the reader to Brian and his dilemma. Knowing Brian's thoughts increases the possibilities for engagement between Brian and the reader.

• • •

THEME

Types of Themes.   The themes of stories help us think about important aspects of life: friendships, loyalty, death, courage, cleverness, and so on. In some genres, particularly folk literature, the theme is *explicit*, or clearly stated, but most often themes are *implicit*, and must be inferred. As readers we make inferences based on what we think is important about a story. Our inferences are influenced by our experiences as readers and in life. Because inference is involved in interpreting implicit themes, it is possible for different readers to "see" themes differently.

In *A Time for Andrew*, I feel that two main themes are (1) learning to trust ourselves and (2) meeting challenges that come our way. In the beginning, Drew's Dad is overheard telling Great-aunt Blythe that Drew is insecure and nervous, and I had the impression that Drew would shy away from things that might be hard to do. When Drew assumes Andrew's identity, he meets Hannah, Andrew's older sister, who teaches Drew how to have more faith in himself and meet challenges.

What themes do you find in Brian's story as told in *Hatchet*? What leads you to your interpretations?

• • •

One theme I see is "We can find inner strength in times of crisis." At the beginning of the book, Brian's thoughts following the pilot's death suggest that he is not very confident of himself. Over the 54 days that he must fend for himself, he shows courage and resourcefulness.

• • •

STYLE

We hear the voice of authors in their writing as they use language to engage us as readers. How well we relate to an author's style influences our engagement with that author.

Sentence Structure and Patterns. One of the first things we notice about writing is the structure of sentences. Sometimes an author will use sentence structures to accentuate certain words or ideas, getting us to notice something the author thinks is important. For example, as we are introduced to Drew in Chapter 1 of *A Time for Andrew*, his thoughts of Martin, a boy from school, tell us something about Drew's sense of himself:

> Martin—his scowling face floated between me and the rows of corn stretching away to the horizon. Whenever I dropped a ball, fumbled, or struck out, Martin was there sneering and jeering. He stole my lunch money, copied my homework, beat me up, called me names like Drew Pee-you and Death Breath. (p. 2)

Uses of Language. As we consider the maturity and experience that our students have with language, particularly with book language, we also consider the ways in which authors use words. Some authors use words to help readers make mental images or comparisons that are more concrete. Some authors play with language in new and creative ways. Some authors appeal to our senses through the use of language.

Imagery describes an author's use of words to make pictures that appeal to our senses. Imagery is also instrumental when an author tries to make pictures to help us understand something with which we may lack firsthand experience. Imagery helps the author reach out to us, encouraging us to respond to the sensations that words can evoke. Images are especially powerful when they remind us of something familiar that we connect to our own experiences, as in the following examples from *A Time for Andrew*:

- The driveway leading to Great-aunt Blythe's house is described as a "narrow green tunnel burrowing uphill through trees and shaggy bushes" (p. 2).

- We "see" Great-aunt Blythe with the words "The wind ballooned her T-shirt and swirled her gray hair. If she spread her arms, she might fly up into the sky like Mary Poppins" (p. 3).

Figurative language occurs when authors use words "in a nonliteral way, giving them meaning beyond their usual, everyday definitions" (Lukens, 1998, p. 143). Our language is full of multiple meanings and phrases we cannot interpret literally. We need experience with figurative language to fully appreciate many stories.

Personification accentuates human behavior, calling attention to qualities of inanimate objects that might otherwise go unnoticed, as when Drew says, "I walked to the bottom of the steps and peered up into the shadows. Not a sound from the floor above. . . . Like me, the house held its breath and listened" (p. 7).

To accentuate the qualities of an object or person, an author may use a *simile*, a comparative relationship between unlike things. Similes usually include the words *as, like*, or *than* to show the relationship in the comparison, as in "a spiral of dust and dead leaves danced up the driveway toward us like a miniature cyclone" (p. 5).

Devices of sound appeal to what readers find pleasing to the ear. *Onomatopoeia* uses words for sounds that suggest their meaning, like *crunch, swooosh*, and *r-r-r-ing*. *Alliteration*, the repetition of consonant or vowel sounds, accentuates particular words and phrases. Try this one from *A Time for Andrew*: "The wisteria's purple petals speckled the floor like confetti and clung to an old wooden swing" (p. 12). Read the sentence aloud and listen to the repeated *p* and *k* sounds.

What do you notice about Paulsen's writing style and use of language to tell Brian's story in *Hatchet*?

• • •

Paulsen appeals to my senses with the words he chooses. He uses imagery so that I can "see" Brian in the wilderness and be drawn into his isolation, yet see how he is maturing. It also seems as if Paulsen deliberately structures some sentences to "punch" certain words, to make me take special notice. For example, in Chapter 1, we hear Brian's thoughts:

> The burning eyes did not come back, but memories did, came flooding in. The words. Always the words.
>
> Divorce.
> The Secret.
> Fights.
> Split.
> The big split. . . . (pp. 5–6)

"Punching" words use the rhythm of short sentences and single words to demand my attention.

Paulsen uses words to help me conjure up mental images of Brian's surroundings. Fire is very important to Brian's existence. He describes one fire-making episode as follows:

The sparks grew with his gentle breath. The red glow moved from the sparks themselves into the bark, moved and grew and became worms, glowing red worms that crawled up the bark hairs and caught other threads of bark and grew until there was a pocket of red as big as a quarter, a glowing red coal of heat. (p. 92)

Paulsen uses simile for comparison. When the moose is charging Brian at the edge of the lake, Paulsen writes that "he saw a brown wall of fur detach itself from the forest to his rear and come down on him like a runaway truck" (p. 150).

• • •

FEATURES OF INFORMATION TEXTS

Each year, millions of us buy information texts (nonfiction, biographies, autobiographies) as our choice of reading materials. Middle grade readers' interest in these texts has also been well documented over the years (Carter & Abrahamson, 1995). As students progress in school, information texts and textbooks dominate the reading materials selected for academic learning experiences. Information texts also dominate the passages selected for assessment on standardized tests (Carter & Abrahamson, 1998). Ogens (1990) reported that 95% of the teachers they surveyed use subject-specific textbooks for about 90% of their instructional time in the content areas (math, science, social studies). In this section of the chapter, we focus on the issues that surround information texts, especially the issues that set them apart from narrative texts.

COMPARING NARRATIVE AND INFORMATION TEXTS

Narrative writers describe life situations and problems by skillfully using literary elements to develop believable settings, plots, and characters that will touch our emotions and draw us into the story. Informational writers also organize ideas to serve their purpose(s)

■ *What do you think your students will need to know about the various texts they will read both in and out of school?*

for writing. The possibilities for arranging information are many and varied. For example, to inform us about the dangers of pollution, an information text writer may identify its causes and inform us about the harmful effects or potential harm for man and nature. In contrast, a writer whose purpose is to teach us how to determine if water is polluted will need to organize ideas differently, to list the procedure for us to go through to test samples of water.

Rosenblatt (1978) reminds us that, as readers, we have different expectations for narrative and information texts and, consequently, approach the texts in different ways, for different purposes. In narrative texts, we have a great deal of latitude for interpreting an author's ideas in light of our experiences. Our purpose for reading narrative may be purely aesthetic, for the pleasure of the experience. In contrast, we usually approach information texts with different expectations. Because we expect to need to retain, use, or act on the information in such texts, we inspect the author's ideas and intentions much more closely.

The major differences between narrative and information texts seem to revolve around:

- The point of view of the author,
- The orientation of the content, and
- The linkages between sections of a text.

Narratives are typically written in first or third person, but someone is clearly telling the story. An information text, however, appears to have no narrator, leaving the reader without that source of information and more dependent on knowledge of text structure for predicting (Feathers, 1998). Narratives are oriented to people and their personal situations, whereas information texts are oriented to subject matter and the transmission of information. Finally, narrative texts are linked by the chronological events of the story. In contrast, information texts are "linked logically through techniques such as making comparisons, supporting main ideas with details, citing examples to illustrate concepts, describing, and listing facts" (Feathers, 1998, p. 264). In addition, in comparison to narrative texts, information texts tend to have these characteristics:

- Be less personal than narrative text.
- Contain more difficult vocabulary and technical terms.
- Require more extensive background information.
- Contain organizational patterns that can vary greatly.
- Be longer and, sometimes, overwhelming (Richek, Caldwell, Jennings, & Lerner, 2002, p. 218).

In light of these differences between narrative and information texts, it is important to keep in mind that students have significantly fewer extensive and intensive experiences reading information texts.

Through your experiences as a reader, what differences do you note in the way that you read and respond to narrative and information texts? How do you explain those differences?

• • •

Part of the difference I find between texts lies in my purposes for reading. Depending on my purposes, I determine how much effort I give to making meaning, especially if I find the text challenging. There are also fundamental differences in the way that texts are written, the way that ideas are organized on the page.

While authors of narrative use their own unique way (style) of telling a story (plot), I know (from my experience as a reader) that the story will focus on a particular person or group of people (characters) at a particular place in time (setting). I also know that either the author or a character will tell the story (point of view), and that through the telling of the story the author urges me to think about the lessons I learn about life (theme). Regardless of the genre in which a narrative is written (historical fiction, fantasy, and so on), narratives seem to have in common the telling of life stories. My own experiences with life help to connect me to the lives of others, even those who live in other places and times. The use of the literary elements feels "predictable." I know what to expect much of the time.

In contrast, information texts can address an infinite range of topics. I may possess little firsthand knowledge of the topics I read about, making the building or revising of my schema more difficult. The less I know about a topic, the harder it is to build a schema through reading. Unlike the use of literary elements in narrative text, the arrangement of ideas in an information text may not seem "predictable." I realize that I must work to find patterns in the ways that authors organize ideas, adjusting my thinking as I read. I know that some authors write in ways that make it difficult to follow their patterns of organization.

• • •

COMPREHENSIBLE TEXT

Text that is comprehensible and considerate of the reader should have the following:

- **Content.** Accurate, explicit, and appropriate to the audience. Only relevant information is included.
- **Structure.** Overall plan for how ideas are arranged and connected to each other.
- **Coherence.** Ideas are clearly related and organized; transitions are clearly indicated.
- **Language.** Clear, interesting, appropriate to the intended audience; terms are defined when used; does not assume too much knowledge on the part of the reader.
- **Textual aids.** Contain an ample amount to guide the reader (e.g., illustrations, headings, bolded vocabulary). Aids are strategically placed and support or extend the surrounding text.

Information text is challenging enough without the added burden of being inconsiderate of the reader. We should select high-quality, well-written, comprehensible texts for our students. However, the textbooks adopted by our school district will frequently contain text that is not comprehensible. When this occurs, we must be prepared to help students develop and use appropriate strategies to cope with inconsiderate text.

CONSTRUCTING MEANING IN INFORMATION TEXTS

We know that understanding text involves building coherent mental representations of information. As readers, we do this by relying on both *text-driven* and *knowledge-driven* processes (Goldman & Rakestraw, 2000). As we read, we separate the ideas in a text into concepts and their relationships. At the same time, our prior knowledge of the subject supports our attempts to make sense. If we are unable to create meaningful connections between ideas and concepts in the text, we must either:

- Build a new mental structure to accommodate the information (Gersbacher, 1997),
- Make inferences to connect the seemingly incoherent information (Graesser, Singer, & Trabasso, 1994), or
- Reread, reinterpret, and reorganize information from the text (Goldman & Saul, 1990).

These actions are influenced by the text, our knowledge, or a combination.

Our *text-driven* processing is influenced by both the content and organization of a text, while our *knowledge-driven* processing is influenced by our prior knowledge of the content and past reading experiences (Goldman & Rakestraw, 2000). Text-driven processing calls attention to the fact that the structure of a news story is different from that of a persuasive essay; that the structure of a persuasive essay is different from that of a friendly letter; and that the structure of a friendly letter is different from that of a chapter in a textbook. Our prior knowledge includes knowledge of the types of information that ought to be included in particular types of texts and the ways that writers of such texts might relate such information. What we know as readers influences our potential to accurately interpret and use an author's style of conveying information to construct meaning.

STRUCTURE OF INFORMATION TEXTS

Jean Fritz, author of many wonderful books for middle grade students, writes that "The art of fiction is making up facts; the art of nonfiction is using facts to make up a form" (1988, p.759). Carter and Abrahamson (1998) help us understand the importance of form when they state

> This art of using facts to make up a form represents an author's vision and achievement. Like great architects designing fine buildings, fine writers lay out a book by blending organization and content as painstakingly as Frank Lloyd Wright melded his designs with the natural world. Specific content determines what a reader will know about a specific subject: structure directs how that reader will view that content. (p. 322)

What are the possible structures and organizations of information texts? Can we identify and describe them as we are able to do with narrative? In narrative text, the rhetorical structure, or the use of language for communication, rests on the author's use of literary elements. That is not the case for information texts, also referred to as expository texts. In an attempt to describe the structure and organization of expository texts, Meyer (1985) identified five top-level rhetorical structures. Likewise, Carter and Abrahamson (1998) identified five dominant structures. Combining the work of these researchers provides the following types of structures for information texts:

- Description or enumeration,
- Ordered collections or lists,
- Cause/effect,
- Compare/contrast, and
- Problem/solution.

Few books contain only one of the possible information text structures previously identified; most contain a combination. This is especially true for the textbooks adopted for instruction in the content areas. Science texts, for example, may combine the following:

- *Enumeration*, to explain the theory or background knowledge for a concept;
- *Chronological order*, for the historical aspects of science; and
- *Cause/effect or problem/solution*, to help us understand how scientists question the natural world.

As you work with a variety of texts, can you identify the various structures that authors use? Metacognitively, are you aware of your thinking about text structures as you read? Does your awareness help you adjust the way in which you construct meaning from those texts? It is a good idea to begin to sharpen your awareness of the structures of texts in order to help children notice and work with those structures as they construct meaning.

• • •

As competent readers, we work with an author's structure and organization as we construct meaning. We may not be consciously aware that we do, but our *text-driven processing* of text relies on our ability to sense the structure and organization, anticipating the direction(s) the author might intend for us. When we read an editorial essay in the newspaper about a local pollution problem, for example, we key into the points the author makes concerning the perceived cause(s) of the pollution and the possible solutions. We read the emotion-laden language of the author who may be trying to persuade us to action and weigh our response. Our experiences with cause/effect writing (one might argue that this also could be problem/solution writing) push us to look beyond the emotion for the facts that help us make a judgment about the case presented. The rhetorical structures we previously identified are often signaled by language the author uses to describe, explain, justify, persuade, and the like.

USING OUR KNOWLEDGE OF TEXT STRUCTURES

Moore, Moore, Cunningham, and Cunningham (1998) suggest that as we work to construct meaning with an information text, our knowledge of such texts causes us to think in particular ways:

- Call up what we already know.
- Connect new ideas to what we already know.
- Predict or anticipate what is to come.
- Organize information into a useful framework.
- Generalize information into similar groupings after noting patterns or commonalities.
- Form an image using sensory information.
- Monitor internally to determine how well learning or thinking is progressing and repair breakdowns in understanding.

- Evaluate or judge the contents of passages and author's writing style.
- Apply knowledge or select the most appropriate response from all those acquired.

To construct meaning we must be actively involved with the ideas presented in a text. But that is not all that contributes to comprehension. The content and structure of the text also contribute to the meanings we are able to construct.

Consider the ways of thinking identified by Moore and his colleagues (1998). How do these ways of thinking apply to you as a reader? Do you sense yourself thinking in these ways as you work to construct meaning with the various texts that you read and study?

● ● ●

Let's take a moment to reconsider the ways of thinking identified by Moore and his colleagues (1998), this time asking what constructions of meaning might be driven by the text. Notice that seven of the ten can be directly influenced by the text:

- *Call up what we already know.* Is the topic clearly evident to us? Did the author use devices such as titles, headings, subheadings, and captions to make the scope of the topic evident?

- *Connect new ideas to what we already know.* Does the author seem sensitive to the possibility that we, the readers, might lack knowledge of some aspects of this topic? Does the author provide any support to the reader to identify new ideas and connect those ideas to the topic?

- *Predict or anticipate what is to come.* Does the author provide any information about upcoming ideas, content that will be further developed in another section of the text?

- *Organize information into a useful framework.* Does the author present the main ideas of the text in a coherent manner? Does the author provide clues, such as subheadings, as to the organization of ideas?

- *Generalize information into similar groupings after noting patterns or commonalities.* Does the form in which the author presents ideas provide clues to the patterns the author sees among the important ideas in the text?

- *Form an image using sensory information.* Does the author use language and visuals to stimulate our senses, supporting the connections we are able to make among ideas?

- *Monitor internally to determine how well learning or thinking is progressing and repairing breakdowns in understanding.* While monitoring is clearly our responsibility, our ability to repair breakdowns in understanding can be influenced by the ways the author organizes and communicates ideas through the text. Texts that are poorly written may present insurmountable challenges to us as readers.

The remaining ways of thinking are fully our responsibility as readers, but will be influenced by the meanings we construct with text:

- *Evaluate or judge the contents of passages and author's writing style.*
- *Apply knowledge or select the most appropriate response from all those acquired.*

As we discuss how we make meaning with what we read, consider how ideas in information texts are organized and what we must know to make sense of an author's ideas. We must begin to look more carefully at how well the author helps the reader make sense of the ideas. Our students deserve informational writing that is considerate of their background as readers and that supports them as they try to learn.

■ *TAKE A MOMENT TO REFLECT . . .*

- ■ *The texts we select for study can have a powerful impact on student's views of themselves, others, and the world.*

  Authentic literature includes:

  - Fiction (e.g., realistic, historical, science);
  - Nonfiction;
  - Biography;
  - Fantasy;
  - Folklore (e.g., fables, folktales, myths, legends);
  - Poetry and verse; and
  - Picture books.

  Research supports the use of quality literature:

  - To enhance strategic reading;
  - To enrich basal reading programs;
  - To be used exclusively for reading instruction; and
  - To strengthen learning, especially in the content areas.

- ■ *The texts we select should be diverse, representing the range of learners in the classroom.*

  Literary experience is influenced by:

  - The reader's level of engagement with a text; and
  - The stance, efferent (information) to aesthetic (beauty), that the reader takes.

  Readers respond to literature through their:

  - Level of engagement with a text;
  - Conceptions or perceptions of text;
  - Connections with related experiences or texts;
  - Question asking or problem solving to make meaning;
  - Explanations of personal responses;
  - Interpretations of texts and responses; and
  - Critical judgments about text.

- ■ *Narrative writing is woven around literary elements:*

  - Settings give us a real sense of place and character.
  - Character actions help us see the development of the plot.

- Themes help us bring real meaning to characters' actions.
- Plot develops out of characters' actions and reactions.
- Point of view provides one interpretation, readers can provide another.
- The author's style pulls all the elements together.

Settings can:

- Be merely a backdrop or integral to the plot;
- Set the mood;
- Show us more about a character;
- Actually be an antagonist or opposing character;
- Symbolize other meanings.

Characters:

- Serve different functions/purposes;
- Can be round or flat, dynamic or static;
- Can be a protagonist or antagonist;
- Can be a foil, serving a limited purpose;
- Can be anthropomorphic (nonhuman characters with human qualities); and
- Should have traits consistent with their actions.

Plots:

- Can be progressive or episodic;
- Can be chronological;
- May include flashbacks;
- Have patterns of action that include suspense, climax, and resolution;
- Can be cliffhangers, ending with a climax and no resolution, or can be resolved in either open or closed ways; and
- Are driven by character conflicts with self, others, nature, and/or society.

Point of view:

- Can be objective (narrator);
- Can be influenced by the thinking of one character (omniscient); or
- Can be controlled by one character (first person).

Theme:

- Can be explicitly stated and clear to the reader; or
- Can be implied by the author and interpreted by the reader.

Style:

- Authors affect readers through the style of their writing;
- How they structure sentences;
- How they use language, including imagery, figurative language; personification, simile, onomatopoeia, and alliteration.

■ *Information texts:*

- Are structured differently than narrative texts; and
- Require readers to use text-driven and knowledge-driven processing to construct meaning.

Information text structures include:

- Description or enumeration;
- Ordered collections or lists;
- Cause/effect;
- Compare/contrast; and
- Problem/solution.

While reading an information text, readers must accomplish these tasks:

- Call up what is already known.
- Connect new ideas to what is known.
- Predict or anticipate what is yet to come.
- Organize information into a useful framework.
- Generalize information into similar groupings after noting patterns or commonalities.
- Form an image using sensory information.
- Monitor internally to determine how well learning or thinking is progressing and to repair breakdowns in understanding.
- Evaluate or judge contents of passage and author's writing style.
- Apply knowledge or select the most appropriate response from all those acquired.

■ *REFERENCES*

Alsami, J. (1994). The effects of peer-led and teacher-led discussions of literature on fourth graders' sociocognitive conflicts. In C. K. Kinzer & D. J. Leu (Eds.), *Multidimensional aspects of literacy research, theory and practice: Forty-third yearbook of the National Reading Conference* (pp. 40-59). Chicago: National Reading Conference.

Alsami, J. F. (1995). The nature of fourth graders' sociocognitive conflicts in peer-led and teacher-led discussions of literature. *Reading Research Quarterly, 30*(3), 314–351.

Baumann, J. F., & Ivey, G. (1997). Delicate balances: Striving for curricular and instructional equilibrium in a second-grade, literature/strategy-based classroom. *Reading Research Quarterly, 32*(3), 244–275.

Beach, R., (1987). *Reader-response theories.* Urbana, IL: National Council of Teachers of English.

Beach, R. (1991). *A teacher's introduction to reader-response theories.* Urbana, IL: National Council of Teachers of English.

Beach, R., & Hynds, S. (1991). Research on response to literature. In R. Barr, P. B. Mosenthall, & P. D. Pearson (Eds.), *Handbook of reading research* (Vol. 2, pp. 453–489). New York: Longman.

Black, J., & Seifert, C. (1985). The psychological study of story understanding. In C. Cooper (Ed.), *Research response to literature and the teaching of literature* (pp. 190–211). Norwood, NJ: Ablex.

Block, C. C. (1993). Strategy instruction in a literature-based reading program. *Elementary School Journal, 94*(2), 139–151.

Britton, J. (1984). Viewpoints: The distinction between participant and spectator role language in research and practice. *Research in the Teaching of English, 18,* 320–331.

Bruner, J. (1986). *Actual minds, possible worlds.* Cambridge, MA: Harvard University Press.

Carter, B., & Abrahamson, R. (1995). Nonfiction—The teenagers reading of choice, or, ten research studies every reading teacher should know. *SIGNAL, 19*(2), 51–56.

Carter, B., & Abrahamson, R. F. (1998). Castles to Colin Powell: The truth about nonfiction. In K. Beers & B. G. Samuels (Eds.), *Into focus: Understanding and creating middle school readers* (pp. 313–322). Norwood, MA: Christopher-Gordon Publishers.

Dahl, K. L., & Freppon, P. A. (1995). A comparison of inner city childrens' interpretations of reading and writing instruction in the early grades in skills-based and whole language classrooms. *Reading Research Quarterly, 30*(1), 50–74.

Feathers, K. M. (1998). Fostering independent, critical content reading in the middle grades. In K. Beers & B. G. Samuels (Eds.), *Into focus: Understanding and creating middle school readers* (pp. 261–279). Norwood, MA: Christopher-Gordon Publishers.

Freppon, P. A. (1991). Children's concepts of the nature and purpose of reading in different instructional settings. *Journal of Reading Behavior, 23*(2), 139–163.

Fritz, J. (1988). Biography: Readability plus responsibility. *The Horn Book, 64*(6), 759–760.

Gambrell, L. B., & Palmer, B. (1992). Children's metacognitive knowledge about reading and writing in literature-based and conventional classrooms. In C. K. Kinzer & D. J. Leu (Eds.), *Literacy research, theory and practice: Views from many perspectives* (pp. 215–224). Chicago: National Reading Conference.

Gersbacher, M. A. (1997). Two decades of structure building. *Discourse Processes, 23,* 265–304.

Goatley, V., Brock, C. H., & Raphael, T. E. (1995). Diverse learners participating in regular education "book clubs." *Reading Research Quarterly, 30,* 352–380.

Goldman, S. R., & Rakestraw, J. A., Jr. (2000). Structural aspects of constructing meaning from text. In M. L. Kamil, P. B. Mosenthal, P. D. Pearson, & R. Barr (Eds.), *Handbook of reading research* (Vol. 3, pp. 311–335). Mahwah, NJ: Lawrence Erlbaum Associates.

Goldman, S. R., & Saul, E. U. (1990). Flexibility in text processing: A strategy competition model. *Learning and Individual Differences, 2,* 181–219.

Graesser, A. C., Singer, M., & Trabasso, T. (1994). Constructing inferences during narrative text comprehension. *Psychological Review, 101,* 371–395.

Guzzetti, B. J., Kowalinski, B. J., & McGowan, M. (1992). Using a literature-based approach to teaching social studies. *Journal of Reading, 36*(2), 114–122.

Harste, J. C. (1986). *What it means to be strategic: Good readers as informants.* Paper presented at the National Reading Conference, Austin, TX.

Heath, S. B. (1985). Being literate in America: A sociological perspective. In J. Niles & R. Lalik (Eds.), *Issues in literacy: A research perspective* (pp. 1–18). Rochester, NY: National Reading Conference.

Hunt, R., & Vipond, D. (1985). Crash-testing a transactional model of literary learning. *Reader, 14,* 23–39.

Hunt, R., & Vipond, D. (1986). Evaluations in literary reading. *Text, 6,* 53–71.

Hynds, S. (1985). Interpersonal cognitive complexity and the literary response processes of adolescent readers. *Research in the Teaching of English, 19,* 386–404.

Jimenez, R. T., & Gamez, A. (1996). Literature-based cognitive strategy instruction for middle school Latina/o students. *Journal of Adolescent & Adult Literacy, 40*(2), 84–91.

Jones, R. T., Coombs, W. T., & McKinney, C. W. (1994). A themed literature unit versus a textbook: A comparison of effects on content acquisition and attitudes in elementary social studies. *Reading Research and Instruction, 32*(2), 85–96.

Lukens, R. J. (1998). *A critical handbook of children's literature* (2nd ed.). New York: HarperCollins.

Lukens, R. J., & Cline, R. K. J. (1995). *A critical handbook of literature for young adults.* New York: HarperCollins.

Many, J. E., & Wiseman, D. L. (1992). The effect of teaching approach on third-grade students' response to literature. *Journal of Reading Behavior, 24*(3), 265–287.

Martinez, M. F. (1983). Young children's verbal responses to literature in parent-child storytime interactions (Doctoral dissertation, University of Texas at Austin, 1983). *Dissertation Abstracts International, 44,* 1044A.

Martinez, M., & Nash, M. F. (1990). Bookalogues: Talking about children's literature. *Language Arts, 67,* 599–606.

McGee, L. M. (1992). Exploring the literature-based reading revolution (Focus on research). *Language Arts, 69*(7), 529–537.

McGinley, W., & Kamberelis, G. (1996). Maniac Magee and Ragtime Tumpie: Children negotiating self and world through reading and writing. *Research in Teaching English, 30*, 75–113.

McGinley, W., Kamberelis, G., Mahoney, T., Madigan, D., Rybicki, V., & Oliver, J. (1997). Visioning reading and teaching literature through the lens of narrative theory. In T. Rogers & A. Soter (Eds.), *Reading across cultures* (pp. 42–68). New York: Teachers College Press.

Meyer, B. F. (1985). Prose analysis: Purposes, procedures, and problems. In B. K. Britton & J. B. Back (Eds.), *Understanding expository text* (pp. 11–64). Hillsdale, NJ: Lawrence Erlbaum Associates.

Miall, D. (1985). The structure of response: A repertory grid study of a poem. *Research in the Teaching of Literature, 19*, 254–268.

Moore, D. W., Moore, S. A., Cunningham, P. M., & Cunningham, J. W. (1998). *Developing readers & writers in the content areas K–12* (3rd ed.). New York: Longman.

Morrow, L. M., & Gambrell, L. B. (2000). Literature-based reading instruction. In M. Kamil, P. B. Mosenthal, P. David Pearson, & R. Barr (Eds.), *Handbook of reading research* (Vol. 3, pp. 563–586). Mahwah, NJ: Lawrence Erlbaum Associates.

Morrow, L. M., Pressley, M., Smith, J. K., & Smith, M. (1997). The effect of a literature-based program integrated into literacy and science instruction with children from diverse backgrounds. *Reading Research Quarterly, 32*(1), 54–76.

Newkirk, T. (1984). Looking for trouble: A way to unmask our readings. *College English, 46*, 756–766.

Ogens, E. (1990). A review of science education: Past failures, future hopes. *American Biology Teacher, 53*, 199–203.

Padron, Y. (1998). Latino students and reading: Understanding these English language learners' needs. In K. Beers & B. G. Samuels (Eds.), *Into focus: Understanding and creating middle school readers* (pp. 105–123). Norwood, MA: Christopher-Gordon Publishers.

Probst, R. (1998). Reader-response theory in the middle school. In K. Beers & B. G. Samuels (Eds.), *Into focus: Understanding and creating middle school readers* (pp. 125–138). Norwood, MA: Christopher-Gordon Publishers.

Reimer, K. M. (1992). Multiethnic literature: Holding fast to dreams. *Language Arts, 69*, 14–21.

Richek, M. A., Caldwell, J. S., Jennings, J. H., & Lerner, J. W. (2002). *Reading problems: Assessment and teaching strategies*. Boston: Allyn and Bacon.

Rosenblatt, L. M. (1978). *The reader, the text, and the poem: The transactional theory of the literacy work*. Carbondale, IL: Southern Illinois University Press.

Rosenblatt, L. M. (1985). Viewpoints: Transaction versus interaction—A terminological rescue operation. *Research in the Teaching of English, 19*, 96–107.

Rosenblatt, L. M. (1991). Literature—S.O.S. *Language Arts, 68*(6), 444–448.

Ross, E. (1994). *Using children's literature across the curriculum*. Bloomington, IN: Phi Delta Kappa Educational Foundation.

Sims, R. (1983). What has happened to the "all white" world of children's books? *Phi Delta Kappan, 64*, 650–653.

Slatoff, W. (1970). *With respect to readers*. Ithaca, NY: Cornell University Press.

Smith, J. (1994). Models for implementing literature in content studies. *Reading Teacher, 48*, 198–209.

Smith, J. A., Monson, J. A., & Dobson, D. (1992). A case study on integrating history and reading instruction through literature. *Social Science Education, 56*, 370–375.

Soter, A. O. (1999). *Young adult literature and the new literary theories: Developing critical readers in the middle school*. New York: Teachers College Press.

Stewart, R. A., Paradis, E. E., Ross, B. D., & Lewis, M. J. (1996). Student voices: What works in literature-based developmental reading. *Journal of Adolescent & Adult Literacy, 39*(6), 468–477.

Svensson, C. (1985). *The construction of poetic meaning: A cultural-developmental study of symbolic and nonsymbolic strategies in the interpretation of contemporary poetry*. Lund, Sweden: Liber Forlag.

Vygotsky, L. S. (1978). *Mind in society* (M. Cole, V. John-Steiner, S. Scribner, & E. Sounerman, Eds. & Trans.). Cambridge, MA: Harvard University Press.

chapter 4

Read-Aloud and Whole Class Literature Study

In this chapter . . .

We examine how middle grade students learn to engage in the study one text to explore their understandings of the author's craft, thinking like readers, and making personal connections. We consider:

- The value of read-aloud,

- How to organize whole-class literature study,

- Providing instruction through whole-class minilessons, mediated listening-thinking activities, and mediated reading-thinking activiti

- Engaging students in small-group discussions,

- Using writing to support and extend literature study, and

- Instruction that further develops students' skills and strategies as readers.

Focus Literature . . .

Hatchet by Gary Paulsen, Aladdin Paperbacks, New York, 1999.

Looking into Classrooms . . .

Last year, I didn't like reading very much. But this year I like it a lot. Mr. Loftin reads to us every day. He reads great books and we talk about them. He read us *Hatchet.* It was like I could see Brian in my mind, like when he had to get the survival pack from the plane and the plane was deep in the lake. It's really scary to think you can't survive on your own. But he did! I like to read Gary Paulsen books now. He's written some really great ones! (Brad, sixth grade)

Putting Theory into Practice . . .

THE VALUE OF READ-ALOUD

Reading aloud to students, especially in the middle grades, should be thought of as the "centerpiece of the curriculum from which all else flows" (Kristo, 1993, p. 54). Reading aloud to middle grade students, especially those who are reluctant readers, may be our "most direct way of communicating the special qualities of written language" (Holdaway, 1980, p. 17) and may be the single most important thing we do to add to their knowledge of reading in both narrative and information texts (Anderson, Hiebert, Scott, & Wilkinson, 1985; Routman, 1991). Through reading aloud we can promote students' language development, increase their achievement in reading, positively influence their writing, and provide opportunities for social interactions (Galda, Ash, & Cullinan, 2000).

When we read aloud to students, we bring print to life, awakening the sounds and rhythms of language. We provide a model of skillful oral reading that demonstrates that even competent readers continue to monitor for meaning. And perhaps most important of all, we demonstrate that reading is both worthwhile and pleasurable.

Middle grade students are intent on understanding themselves and their world. Reading aloud lets them experience literature as a "window" through which they can engage with the world, or as a "mirror" in which they see reflections of themselves (Cullinan, 1989, p. 390). Through listening to literature, "students come to find themselves, imagine others, value difference, and search for justice" (Langer, 1995, p. 1). Reading aloud to students promotes engagement with text that is essential for meaningful literature study.

Read-aloud is also our opportunity to engage students in literate thinking. We cannot assume that middle grade students are committed readers or that they know how to think their way through challenging text. Thinking about the meaning of print is a difficult task that requires a great deal of mental energy on the part of the reader. When we read aloud to students, we serve as the "decoder," enabling students to concentrate on thinking about a text's meaning.

Middle grade students may know how to read, but their knowledge is of little value if they choose not to read. Daily read-alouds enable students to use their knowledge of reading to think about ideas in texts within the structure of written language. Daily read-alouds engage students' minds and encourage their desire to read independently. Reading aloud to students requires much thought and practice. Figure 4.1 provides teaching suggestions drawn from Freeman (1992), Trelease (1989), myself, and many teachers I have watched bring books to life with students.

Prepare a favorite book for a read-aloud. Start small, with just a few students. Having a small group will allow you to focus both on students' responses and on your feelings about sharing the book. If possible, tape record your session. This will allow you to go back and listen to your expression, pacing of the reading, and ease of interaction with the students.

What book did you select? Why did you choose it? As you previewed the book, what decisions did you make about the following:

■ **FIGURE 4.1**

Tips for good
read-alouds

1. *Select books that you like or are old favorites.* When we "love" a book we are more likely to share that book with genuine enthusiasm.
2. *Preview the book.* Thorough knowledge of the text is essential to making decisions about what to emphasize during the read-aloud.
3. *Allow ample time.* Begin only when there is time to do justice to the book. Filling time in the school day by reading aloud is generally not a good idea.
4. *Connect with your audience.* Make frequent eye contact with students to let students know they are an integral part of the experience.
5. *Read with expression.* Bring the text to life by maintaining good pitch, volume, and expression while reading.
6. *When we read a picture book, students need to see the illustrations.* Much of the plot, character development, and setting is told through illustrations.
7. *When we read a chapter book, we should help students make connections to previous chapters.* Following the continued storyline of a chapter book requires a different type of thinking than with picture books. Students with limited experience will need help connecting the chapters as you read from day to day.
8. *Read in your own style.* When you are comfortable with your style, you are more likely to relax and enjoy the experience with the students.
9. *Adjust the pace as you read.* For complex parts of the story, slow down the pace of reading to give listeners time to process ideas. When the writing is primarily descriptive, allow listeners time to build mental pictures.
10. *Don't read above students' emotional level.* Students may not always be ready for the emotional demands of specific events or themes, especially in some chapter books.
11. *It's okay to abandon a book.* Sometimes, even when you preview and thoughtfully select books, you may still find that a particular choice is not a match for some students. In such cases the best solution may be to abandon the book.
12. *Make read-aloud books available to students.* As you finish a read-aloud, give the book a "place of honor" in the classroom library area. Some students will want to revisit the book and select it for their independent reading.
13. *Award winners are no guarantee.* Just because a book has won an award doesn't guarantee it to be a good read-aloud for your students. Be sure to preview all books with an ear for the way that the story sounds when read aloud and an eye to its appropriateness.
14. *Share information and anecdotes about authors and illustrators to help students make personal connections with books.* People write and illustrate books! Resources such as *Something About the Author* (Telgen, 1971–present) and *Children's Literature Review* (Selnick, 1976–present) provide personal and professional information about the people who write and illustrate the texts we share with students.

How to hold the book?
How to pace the book?
What might hinder expressive reading?
The appropriateness of the book?

How did the reading go? Would you change anything the next time? Continue to practice reading aloud to students until you notice that you no longer feel self-conscious and are not focusing on your ability to read aloud. Instead, you should focus on the interaction *between the students and the text*.

• • •

READ-ALOUD CLOSES GAPS BETWEEN READERS

Students come to the middle grades with varied reading experience and ability to make meaning with text. In any middle grade classroom, the range in reading levels may be as much as two-thirds the age of the students. For example, in sixth grade, when students are typically about 12 years old, the range of reading levels may span 8 years or more, from first or second grade to high school.

Students' experience with fluent reading, their ability to instantly recognize a large number of words, and their attitudes toward themselves as readers account for much of this variance in reading levels. Reading aloud to students removes barriers to making meaning, such as poor decoding skills, and provides all students with more equal access to the ideas or emotions in a text. Students are more likely to engage with a text when they are not hindered by the physical aspects of reading.

Reading aloud, then, has the potential to close the reading gap between students, fostering a sense of community in the classroom. Think of it as an instructional technique that treats reading as a responsive process, involving both emotion and thought.

If our students are to become more competent readers, they must learn to respond effectively to written language. Reading aloud can support students as they learn to respond to literature before we ask them to read and respond on their own. We can support and enhance students' responses during read-aloud by providing an environment that encourages "book talk" (Roser & Martinez, 1995) and by serving as a mediator or bridge between students and texts (Dixon-Krauss, 1995).

ENCOURAGING BOOK TALK

All students, regardless of their literary experiences, have thoughts and insights about the texts they hear and read. Unfortunately, some students may not believe that their thoughts and insights are worthy of being voiced. They may not have had many opportunities in school to really "talk" about books and their meanings. In the middle grades, when students are searching for meaning in their own lives, it is vitally important to provide a "book talk" environment that enables students to unlock and share their thoughts and insights. *Book talk* in this context refers to engaging students in literary talk or discussions. The term can also refer to summaries or teasers that we can provide about books to encourage and broaden students' choices of reading material.

Good book talk occurs when students "grapple with core issues, compare insightfully, observe closely, question profoundly, and relate life experiences to story situations" (Roser & Martinez, 1995, p. 33). How can this happen in our classrooms? Roser and Martinez (1995) state that good book talks are likely to occur when the following are true:

- The teacher has a *plan* for the talk.
- A *conversational setting* exists in the classroom.
- Experienced readers share their *genuine responses* to stories.
- Listeners/readers *return to stories* for a closer look.
- Books are drawn together into instructional units that *share a focus, topic, or theme*.
- Listeners/readers have opportunities to *explore their thinking* through writing.

MEDIATING BETWEEN READERS AND TEXTS

When we read aloud to students we serve as a more knowledgeable reader who provides support for their thinking and interactions with both narrative and information text. Helping students focus their attention on the salient aspects of a text during read-aloud has been shown to improve their understanding of it (Morrow, 1993). As a more knowledgeable other, we can support and encourage book talk among students.

Through our understanding of making meaning and responding to texts, we know that teachers should be mediators, adjusting the amount of assistance we provide during students' interaction with texts and providing feedback about their response. One valuable technique, a mediated listening–thinking activity, supports students' thinking and responses before, during, and after read-aloud. Over time, students internalize the strategies they learn for responding to text for independent use in new reading situations.

PLANNING A MEDIATED LISTENING–THINKING ACTIVITY

As we prepare a read-aloud that assists middle grade students in making meaning with text, we should think about our *purpose(s)* for engaging students with a particular text and *strategies* to assist students as they make meaning before, during, and after the reading. We should also *reflect* on how to adjust our support to students as they give feedback about their thinking during discussion. These steps, purpose–strategy–reflection, form an instructional cycle for mediated learning (Dixon-Krauss, 1995) that we repeat throughout a read-aloud. We adjust our level of assistance as student feedback tells us how much support they need to move toward being self-regulated learners.

Supporting readers in text is not a new idea. In the 1940s Emmet Betts (1946) suggested that teachers use a directed reading activity (DRA) to help readers prepare for reading and comprehend text during and after the reading. Later Russell Stauffer (1975) modified Betts's ideas by suggesting that teachers needed to emphasize their support of students' thinking while reading, calling his strategy a direct reading–thinking activity (DR–TA). Since that time we have learned from Vygotsky about the importance of the teacher serving as a mediator, rather than a director (see Chapter 1). Consequently, I suggest that we think of our instructional support as a mediated reading (or listening)–thinking activity.

Since we are reading aloud to students, and we will be supporting their listening to text, we will use a mediated listening–thinking activity (ML–TA). We plan an ML–TA in three segments: before reading, during reading, and after reading. As we begin to plan, we must consider the skills and strategies of our students in relation to the content of the new text and the author's style of writing.

Let's imagine that we are preparing to read *Hatchet* by Gary Paulsen (1999) to a class of middle grade students. *Hatchet* is the engaging story of 13-year-old Brian, who survives a plane crash and must learn to survive on his own in the Canadian wilderness. During the read-aloud, we want to provide support for students' thinking so that all students will successfully make meaning during the experience. Beyond enjoyment, our overall purposes for reading *Hatchet* might be to explore the following:

- *Readers' response to a dynamic character.* The main character, Brian, exhibits significant change as he learns to survive in the wilderness.
- *Coming to know a character through an omniscient narrator.* Brian is alone in the wilderness. The narrator shares Brian's thoughts, in addition to describing his actions and speech, to help the reader know Brian more completely.

- *The setting.* Elements of the wilderness, such as wild animals, weather, and isolation, act as antagonists (opposing characters) and help to reveal Brian's character.
- *Themes as revealed through a character.* Paulsen dramatizes the themes of survival and inner strength through his narrative description of Brian and his behavior.

We plan to begin the ML–TA in three segments: before, during, and after the reading:

1. *Before the reading* we will encourage students to use what they know as readers to anticipate the opening chapter as an introduction to the author's style of sharing plot, characters, setting, and theme.
2. *During the reading*, we will encourage students to:
   - *Predict,* anticipate, or wonder about what might happen (as needed).
   - *Listen* to the text being read aloud.
   - *Respond* to what is happening.
   - *Connect* new ideas to what they already know (as needed).
3. *After the reading*, we give students the opportunity to reflect on the chapter and consider their engagement with the text.

The sample ML–TA for Chapter 1 of *Hatchet,* shown in Figure 4.2, illustrates the process of mediating students' thinking and responses during read-aloud. As we think about Chapter 1 of that text, it is helpful to think about ways in which we might use our own responses to the text to support students' engagement with it. However, we must remember that as adult readers, our responses are often more complete and sophisticated than are those of most middle grade readers.

In addition to the information covered in the sample ML–TA, most texts contain essential words that we should discuss with students to support their understanding and enjoyment of the text. To decide how to handle any given essential word in a text, we consider the following questions:

- Is the word in students' listening vocabulary?
- Is the word used in a context that helps readers figure out the meaning?

If a word is essential to understanding, is in the students' listening vocabulary, and appears in a helping context, give students the opportunity to figure out the word(s) with clues from the text. If students' experiences or the context are insufficient, provide support for word meaning during reading and discussion.

To practice mediating between students and books, take the time to prepare an ML–TA using Chapter 2 of *Hatchet.* Try using the format shown in the sample ML–TA for Chapter 1 (Figure 4.2), structuring the predict–listen–respond–connect sequence to meet your specific needs. What will you try to help students notice and think about while they listen to you read Chapter 2 aloud?

• • •

Before Reading

Share information that is available to any reader who picks up the book—the title and front cover illustration and any information on the back cover that introduces the author or describes the plot.

Predict: "What ideas do you have so far about this story?" (pause for responses)
"What clues do we have for the meaning of the title, *Hatchet?*" (pause)
"Let's begin the chapter and see what else we find."

During Reading

Listen: Read pp. 1 and 2. Set the scene in the small plane and introduce the limited omniscient point of view from which the story is told, using the example on p. 2, "The thinking started. . . . Divorce. It was an ugly word, he thought."

Respond: (think aloud) "I guess that Gary Paulsen is going to let us know what Brian's thinking."

Predict: "Could this be a way that we will learn more about Brian? What do you think?" (pause for comments)

Listen: Read p. 3, introducing the "Secret" surrounding the divorce, mentioned on the back cover.

Respond: (pause reading to think aloud) "I wonder why Gary Paulsen capitalizes that word, *Secret*, each time he writes it?" (show text to students who are close by or have students look at own text; briefly pause for responses)

Listen: Read pp. 3–7, in which the pilot shows Brian a few things about steering the plane. Read this section aloud without interruption unless students need help with airplane terms, such as *rudder*, or to imagine the setup of a cockpit. (It will be important to recall this section during the reading of Chapter 2 when Brian must handle the plane by himself.) The first foreshadowing of the pilot's impending heart attack comes on p. 5: "He (pilot) took the controls back, then reached up and rubbed his left shoulder. 'Aches and pains—must be getting old.' " Pause if students comment; if not, defer discussion until pp. 6–7, where there is more information about the pilot's condition. On p. 7, Paulsen also mentions a "survival pack," filled with emergency supplies.

Respond: "What do we know about Brian so far?" (responses to Brian's thinking about his parents' divorce and visitation rights) "What do you think is happening with the pilot?" (responses to clues about the impending heart attack)

Connect: "How does this connect to the information on the back cover of the book?" (pause for responses)

Predict: "What do you expect in the remainder of this chapter?" (pause) "Let's find out."

Listen: Read from the bottom of p. 7 through p. 12 (end of chapter). Brian thinks back to when his mother had driven him to the airport and given him a hatchet. This section reveals information about Brian's relationship with his mother, and also describes the pilot's heart attack.

After Reading

Respond: (encourage open response) "What do you think about Brian's situation?"

Connect: (encourage students to think back over the events in the chapter [retelling] as they explore their responses) "What do we know so far?" (pause) "What would you do if you were Brian?"

Predict: "Based on what we know, what do you expect might happen in Chapter 2?"

■ **FIGURE 4.2**

Sample ML-TA for chapter 1 of *Hatchet*

Chapter 2 of *Hatchet* describes Brian's actions following the pilot's death. I would begin an ML–TA by recalling predictions at the end of Chapter 1. Then I would break the reading into three sections:

- Coming to grips with the dead pilot (pp. 13–mid 17)
- Developing a plan of action (pp. mid 17–24)
- The last two paragraphs, when the engine stops (p. 25)

After reading the first section, ending with "The plane flew on normally, smoothly," I would ask students to retell and respond to Brian's actions to get control of the plane. This discussion should lead to predictions of what might happen in the remainder of the chapter. After reading the second section, I would encourage students to respond to Brian's actions, asking, "What do you think about Brian's actions and his plans for landing the plane?"

After pausing for responses, I would read the last two paragraphs of the chapter and again ask for responses. This is a moving chapter. Students typically have strong responses to Brian's situation and have little difficulty sharing. Reflecting back on portions that showed how Brian tried to use what he knew from reading and prior experience sets students up for later chapters, when they must anticipate how Brian will be able to survive on his own. Connecting Chapters 1 and 2 helps students be aware of what they know about Brian to this point.

To end the ML–TA, I would reread the last sentence in the chapter, which provides an excellent point for students' predictions about Chapter 3. When teachers learn new instructional techniques or approaches, such as the ML–TA, they must practice with the technique so they feel comfortable with it and in control. So, be patient! With adequate preparation and practice, each of us becomes less concerned about our own success in conducting an ML–TA and more focused on our role in mediating between students and the text.

• • •

To review, a mediated listening–thinking activity helps students to make meaning during a read-aloud, supporting their thinking before, during, and after reading. Using an ML–TA as an assisted reading experience helps us understand the meanings that students are finding in texts we read aloud to them. Making meaning is the essence of reading and many students need help to develop their ability to understand more complex texts. Some students lack both extensive and intensive experiences with literature, and need repeated opportunities to explore text to make meaningful connections with the important ideas.

A read-aloud that is structured as an ML–TA is an excellent beginning for literature study with middle grade students. With careful planning, a daily read-aloud can become literature study, providing an inclusive experience for all readers. Daily read-aloud time can be extended into a whole-class literature study, including peer-led small-group discussions, literature logs, and other extension activities.

MOVING FROM READ-ALOUD TO WHOLE-CLASS LITERATURE STUDY

Students in the middle grades need many opportunities to explore their ideas about themselves, others, and their world. Using high-quality literature is an excellent way to engage students in personal and group exploration. While middle grade students have 5 or more years of school behind them, they may have little experience participating in the *study* of literature. Their expectations for books may come more from reading as skills work and as assigned tasks than from reading literature.

To encourage literate thinking among students, we may choose to begin with whole-class literature study. The advantage of whole-class experiences is that we are able to help students realize that readers make meaning in different ways with the same text. Whole-class studies also enable us to focus on our role as a mediator for student learning.

Introductory experiences in literature study should focus students' attention more on literary thinking and response than on the mechanics of reading. Through read-along and silent reading, students are supported by a more knowledgeable other (Vygotsky, 1962) as they think and respond, preparing for more independent approaches to literature study (see Chapters 5 and 6).

In this section of the chapter, we explore two ways to introduce middle grade students to whole-class literature study through mediated approaches. The first is read-along, in which the teacher reads aloud as students read along in their own copies of a text. The second approach is to assist students while they read the text. To illustrate both of these approaches, we visit Lou's sixth-grade classroom as he engages his students in the study of *Hatchet* (Paulsen, 1999). (*Note:* Using the same text as illustration enables us to compare and contrast suggested instructional approaches.)

On this particular day the students retrieve their copies of *Hatchet* and settle in their desks for the day's literature study. Lou begins by saying, "Yesterday, as we ended our reading of Chapter 2, the plane appeared to run out of fuel and the engine stopped. Brian [the protagonist] had been thinking about what he would do when that happened. What were some of the things Brian had been thinking?" Lou takes responses, then the class launches into an hour composed of reading along as Lou reads aloud, small-group discussions, and whole-class discussion of Brian and his struggle to survive.

Lou is introducing his students to literature study. By reading *Hatchet* aloud, he serves as the class "decoder" and leads a study in which all students can think about and respond to the text. The students in Lou's class vary widely in their experiences as readers. By reading aloud to students, Lou attempts to reduce the differences in reading achievement among the readers in his classroom.

Lou encourages students to silently read along in their copies with him as he reads aloud. Initially, Lou takes the lead and encourages students to notice particular passages, sometimes rereading those passages, enabling students to both hear and see the text. Having a personal copy allows students to study the text with Lou's assistance as a more knowledgeable reader. Students also are able to refer to the text during followup or extension activities.

Lou is using *Hatchet,* along with other works, in a study of author Gary Paulsen. He hopes to help his sixth-grade students understand how the characters in Paulsen's books use their life experiences to learn more about themselves and their world. Through this unit, Lou will extend students' literary understanding by focusing attention on the techniques that authors such as Paulsen use to reveal the personal growth of their characters.

Having students read along in their own texts is an excellent way to initiate a unit or theme study, focusing the attention of all students on the unit theme or concept. With Lou as a guide, students will study *Hatchet* as the core book (Zarrillo, 1989), or main text, of a "Gary Paulsen—Author" unit. The literature in such whole-class studies is typically teacher selected and whole-class activities are typically teacher led (Heibert & Colt, 1989). When the class has completed its study of *Hatchet,* Lou will use literature groups or self-selected independent reading to extend the author study. During this time he provides for student choice of reading materials and peer-led discussion groups.

■ *What factors will you consider as you plan for literature study with your students? How do you think you might decide what to emphsize with a particular text?*

ORGANIZING WHOLE-CLASS LITERATURE STUDY

Lou plans to use read-aloud/read-along to introduce his class to whole-class literature study as shown in Figure 4.3. Each day a block of time is set aside for a combination of whole-class and either independent or small-group activities. During each daily block, Lou coordinates strategy instruction through minilessons, read-aloud while students read-along, a period of work time that can be used to provide opportunities for students to either explore their own responses to the reading or time for small-group discussions, and time for the class sharing the results of their work time.

When Lou first began to teach reading through a literature-based approach he used a whole-class format, keeping the class together for discussions but providing some opportunity for independent and small-group response activities. Lou now realizes that in whole-group activities it is difficult to actively involve all students in the discussion, so he tries to provide opportunities for small-group discussions whenever possible.

PLANNING FOR LITERATURE STUDY

The instructional experiences Lou provides during whole-class literature study are drawn from (1) the reading/language arts curriculum standards that his school district expects him to teach, (2) the piece(s) of literature that he has selected for study, and (3) what he has determined through assessment and previous instruction that his students are ready to learn.

■ FIGURE 4.3

Overview of whole-class literature study

Whole Group:
(30–35 minutes)

- Opening, plans for the day
- Whole-class minilesson
  Workshop procedures
  Literary elements
  Listening/thinking strategies

- ML–TA
  Prediction
  Listen/read-along
  Response
  Connecting ideas

- Whole-class discussion following ML–TA
  Response
  Connecting ideas

Work Time:
(15–20 minutes)

- Independent work
  Literature logs
  Projects (art, drama, writing, etc.)

  OR

- Peer-led small groups
  Discussion guides
  Record personal/group responses

Whole Group:
(10–15 minutes)

- Follow-up sharing
  Literature logs
  Projects
  Discussion guides

- Connect with previous readings
- Anticipate next day's reading

SELECTING CURRICULUM STANDARDS

Each school district develops curriculum standards that identify what students should know at each grade level or developmental stage. Figure 4.4 presents a sample of the sixth-grade reading and literature standards for Lou's school district. We are familiar with *Hatchet*, the text Lou has selected for study. Which curriculum standards might Lou emphasize as his class studies *Hatchet?*

Let's consider Lou's purposes for the study of *Hatchet:*

- Reading for pleasure,
- Becoming aware of techniques authors use to reveal character growth (the main character of *Hatchet*, Brian, is a dynamic character),
- Exploring ways that students learn about their strengths and needs as readers and writers while studying the characters in Paulsen's books,
- Making inferences about a character that is revealed through an omniscient narrator,

■ **FIGURE 4.4**

Sample of language arts curriculum standards, sixth grade

1. Know and use word analysis skills and strategies to comprehend new words encountered in text.
2. Use reading process skills and strategies to build comprehension.
3. Read to comprehend, interpret, and evaluate literature from a variety of authors, cultures, and times.
4. Read to comprehend, interpret, and evaluate informational texts for specific purposes.
5. Write a variety of texts that inform, persuade, describe, evaluate, or tell a story and are appropriate to purpose and audience.
6. Write with a clear focus and logical development, evaluating, revising, and editing for organization, style, tone, and word choice.
7. Write using standard English grammar, usage, punctuation, capitalization, and spelling.
8. Listen to and evaluate oral communications for content, style, speaker's purpose, and audience appropriateness.
9. Speak using organization, style, tone, voice, and media aids appropriate to audience and purpose.
10. Participate in discussions to offer information, clarify ideas, and support a position.
11. Formulate research questions, use a variety of sources to obtain information, weigh the evidence, draw valid conclusions, and present findings.

- Using a discussion guide in peer-led small-group discussions to help students become more independent in their study of literature, and
- Using close reading as an appropriate strategy in the study of a chapter book.

According to his school district's curriculum standards, Lou emphasizes:

- Standard 2 (focus on strategies),
- Standard 3 (focus on issues of fiction), and
- Standard 10 (focus on developing discussion skills).

At the present time he is not emphasizing writing skills as a part of literature study, but will as he moves more toward peer-led literature study. Lou also knows that over the course of the school year he will address each of the standards in multiple ways.

DEVELOPING A PLAN FOR READING

When Lou selects a book for a literature study, he carefully reads the text and considers the content and length of each chapter and the amount of time he has for instruction each day. Then, he makes an initial plan for grouping chapters for the read-aloud (see Figure 4.5). *Hatchet* has 19 chapters and an epilogue. Most chapters are 8 to 12 pages long, and it takes Lou from 1 to 1.5 minutes to read aloud 1 page. He wants to read about 15 pages per day, allowing time for a few stops to help students clarify their initial understanding of the text, so typically he plans 20 to 25 minutes for the read-aloud portion of the workshop.

Based on the time required for read-aloud, Lou groups chapters that fit together. His reading plan requires at least 14 class meetings to complete the book, plus additional sessions to bring closure to the study. He also realizes that interruptions in the school sched-

■ **FIGURE 4.5**

Sample reading plan

Reading Plan for Read-Aloud Workshop
Hatchet (Paulsen, 1999)

Day	Chapter	# of Pages
1	1	12
2	2	13
3	3 & 4	16
4	5	12
5	6	10
6	7	12
7	8 & 9	14
8	10 & 11	15
9	12 & 13	17
10	14 & 15	18
11	16	14
12	17	11
13	18	10
14	19 & Epilogue	11
15	Closure	

ule and his students' needs and interests may require him to revise his plans. Lou's initial reading plan will take 15 days. As the read-along progresses, Lou adjusts his plan to accommodate the needs and interests of his students.

PLANNING FOR INSTRUCTION

As a part of his planning, Lou considers how he will help students develop the literary knowledge and thinking strategies they need to engage with author Gary Paulsen as he shares Brian's story in *Hatchet*. In a literature workshop, Lou provides instruction through the following:

- Mediated listening–thinking activities,
- Whole-class discussions, and
- Whole-class minilessons.

As he reads each chapter, Lou marks places in his copy where he anticipates needing to help his students think through the ideas in the text so they might meet his personal instructional goals of (1) exploring personal traits, such as believing in ourselves and making effective decisions, and (2) understanding the techniques Paulsen uses to reveal character growth. He also makes notes about possible instruction to help his students extend and refine their general understanding of literature and use of effective reading–thinking strategies.

From this reading, Lou plans an ML–TA for each chapter. In each ML–TA, Lou supports students in their interactions through his use of the predict–listen–respond–connect cycle. Depending on student feedback, Lou adjusts the amount of support he provides to enable them to make meaning with the text.

From his notes for each chapter, Lou also plans minilessons to make students aware of particular knowledge or strategies that could make their reading more pleasurable or effective. Samples of Lou's notes for the first two chapters of *Hatchet* are shown in Figure 4.6.

■ FIGURE 4.6

Teacher's planning notes for chapters 1 and 2 of *Hatchet*

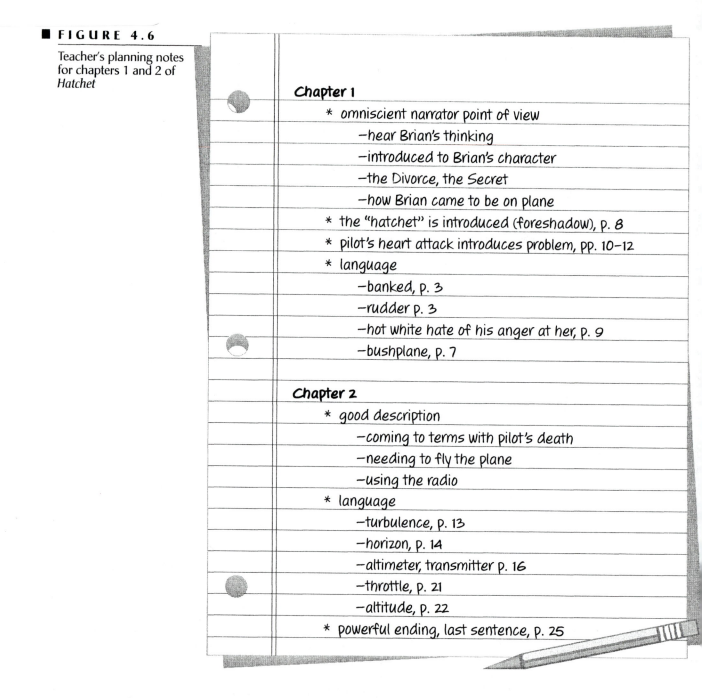

Chapter 1

   * omniscient narrator point of view

      —hear Brian's thinking

      —introduced to Brian's character

      —the Divorce, the Secret

      —how Brian came to be on plane

   * the "hatchet" is introduced (foreshadow), p. 8

   * pilot's heart attack introduces problem, pp. 10–12

   * language

      —banked, p. 3

      —rudder p. 3

      —hot white hate of his anger at her, p. 9

      —bushplane, p. 7

Chapter 2

   * good description

      —coming to terms with pilot's death

      —needing to fly the plane

      —using the radio

   * language

      —turbulence, p. 13

      —horizon, p. 14

      —altimeter, transmitter p. 16

      —throttle, p. 21

      —altitude, p. 22

   * powerful ending, last sentence, p. 25

IMPLEMENTING WHOLE-CLASS LITERATURE STUDY

When Lou is familiar with his chosen texts and is clear about instructional outcomes for his students, he begins to implement the literature study. Early in the school year Lou follows a whole-class format by keeping the class together for discussion, then allowing work time for students' personal responses to the text. After the class has studied one or two chapter books together, Lou encourages students to guide discussions by using small groups before the whole class discusses the reading in much depth.

■ FIGURE 4.7

Possible topics for
procedural minilessons

- How is listening to a book like reading a book? (emphasize thinking skills and strategies)
- Yes, I need to check my own thinking when I'm listening, just like when I'm reading.
- What do I do to help myself listen during read-aloud?
- Making predictions helps me listen and read.
- Making predictions, anticipating, thinking ahead, wondering, . . . show I am engaged with the reading.
- How does connecting back to what I already know help me make meaning?
- Why should I give the teacher feedback about my thinking during the read-aloud?
- What should I do during small-group discussions?
- How can I help our group have a good discussion?
- How can we use a discussion guide to help us in our small-group discussions?
- How do we share our group's ideas with the whole class?

In the next sections, we follow Lou as he implements each part of a literature workshop:

- Whole-class minilessons,
- Using an ML–TA to engage readers, and
- Whole-class and small-group discussions.

WHOLE-CLASS MINILESSONS

Before Lou reads to students, he begins his instruction with a minilesson. A *minilesson* is a short, 5- to 10-minute lesson that provides students with a useful "tip" for upcoming reading activities (Five, 1988; Hagerty, 1992). Lou thinks aloud about using reading or literary knowledge (skills) or a specific reading strategy. This thinking aloud helps students learn how good readers make their decisions, what information they consider, and why some possibilities get discarded (Davey, 1983).

Lou plans minilessons to teach procedures and strategies that will help students make the literature workshop successful. For *procedural minilessons,* Lou mentally walks through the daily workshop routine and tries to anticipate what may be new to his students (see Figure 4.7). For *strategic and literary minilessons,* Lou draws examples from the book being studied or books that are familiar to all of the students (see Figure 4.8).

At this particular time in the school year, the students in Lou's classroom are participating in student-led small-group discussions for the first time. To help students learn to participate in, and eventually lead, their own discussions, Lou has prepared discussion guides for each chapter of *Hatchet*. After Lou has read aloud Chapter 1, he teaches a minilesson that introduces the use of the discussion guides in the small groups (see Figure 4.9).

Typically a minilesson would precede the reading, but in this case students needed to know the content of Chapter 1 for the lesson to be effective. Through this minilesson, students in the class are able to hear and see their peers take the first steps toward peer-led discussions. Throughout the reading of *Hatchet,* Lou repeats and reinforces instruction about discussion skills to help his students become more confident and independent in their ability to lead discussions.

■ **FIGURE 4.8**

Possible topics for
strategy/literary element
minilessons

- Who's telling Brian's story? Why do we get to hear what Brian thinks?
- How do we learn about Brian by listening to his thoughts?
- What is a flashback? Why do authors use flashbacks?
- How does Gary Paulsen use flashbacks to fill us in on Brian's story?
- Is description really important?
- How does Gary Paulsen use description?
- When is a setting also a character? In *Hatchet*?
- How does Gary Paulsen use the setting to show us more about Brian?
- Is Brian changing? How can we tell?

Imagine that you are leading a literature workshop using *Hatchet* and you want to plan minilessons to help students develop their use of literary knowledge and reading strategies that will be relevant to this text. What minilesson topics might you select? Why? It may help you to think back to the sample ML–TA in Figure 4.2 and Lou's planning for Chapter 1 and 2 shown in Figure 4.6.

• • •

Chapters 1 and 2 in *Hatchet* introduce the main character, Brian, the problem the plot will develop around, the limited omniscient point of view used to tell the story, and the author's style of using language. What other topics did you identify? Any of these topics can be developed into useful minilessons:

- How does Paulsen use an omniscient narrator to help us get to know Brian as a person and draw us into the potential problems that he faces? This point of view requires the reader to make interpretations about the character. A minilesson on this topic should use text from *Hatchet* and encourage students to discuss and support their interpretations.
- Since one of Lou's objectives is to explore dynamic characters, a minilesson on this topic might engage students in brainstorming strategies they already use to learn about characters. Sharing such information not only helps students learn from each other, but also enables them to teach us about what they already know and do as readers.

• • •

ENCOURAGING STUDENTS TO READ ALONG

As stated, most minilessons precede, rather than follow, a read-along. After each minilesson, Lou introduces the chapter he will read aloud. He plans an ML–TA for each read-aloud/read-along, keeping in mind the following literary and pedagogical aspects:

- The natural breaks between events within a chapter,
- Where his students might need support to clarify actions or connect with previous events, and

(Lou has just finished reading aloud Chapter 1 of Hatchet *and has the students move into their small groups.)*

"Today is our first day to break up into small groups to talk about our reading of *Hatchet* before we talk about it as a whole-class. To help you decide *what* ideas to share in the small group, I have made a discussion guide for each of you to use in your small group meeting." (Lou places a transparency of the discussion guide on the overhead projector as copies are distributed to the students.)

"A discussion guide has ideas and questions about the book we are reading. Your small group can use these ideas and questions to help you learn to share your own ideas about the reading.

To make this discussion guide, I read Chapter 1 of *Hatchet* and tried to think about the parts of the chapter where you might say, "Why did Brian do that?" or you might wonder, "Now, what's going to happen?" or you might say to yourself, "If that was me, I would . . . ."

Let's see how a small group can use this discussion guide. I have asked one of the small groups to help me today by being part of a small-group discussion. We are going to model how your group might use the discussion guide to help you talk about Chapter 1."

(Lou joins the small group seated near the front of the classroom. Each child in the small group has a copy of the guide. The other groups can see the items on the guide, which is still on the overhead projector.)

"Pretend that I'm one of you and this is my small group. I'll begin today by reading the first question. Then each of us will share our ideas about this question. We'll go around the circle, taking turns, and listening to what each other has to say. We want to know what the other members of my group are thinking about the book. As we share, we can also makes notes on our guide sheets to help us remember important ideas."

Lou reads question 1 aloud, "What do you think about Brian's situation at the end of the chapter? What makes you think that?" Then he shares his ideas, saying "Brian is in a pretty bad situation. He doesn't know how to fly. He's probably really nervous to be all alone. But Brian seems like a thinker. He's always thinking about things that are happening. Maybe he'll keep thinking and not let himself get so scared that he can't do something. Now, will each of you take a turn and share your ideas?"

Danny: "I'll bet he's really nervous, too. No, I'll bet he's petrified. Nothing this scary has ever happened to me. I don't know what he will do." (As Danny shares, Lou models making notes on his guide sheet.)

Brad: "If I were Brian, I'd be scared and excited. I'd want to figure it out so I could live. I would want to live so much that I would figure it out. Brian watched the pilot. I'll bet he'll think of something."

Trina: "Brian doesn't seem like a chicken. I'd be scared, sure, but if I didn't do something I would die. Brian has got to do something. What good will it do to just get scared or cry? He'll die anyway. He did fly the play for a little while. Maybe he'll figure something out."

Jodie: "It said that Brian felt a white-flash of horror or terror, I can't remember which, and he couldn't breathe. That's really being scared. But he's 13. He'll do something. I'm like Trina. I think he'll try to fly the plane. He did that once already."

Lou turns to the class. "Think for a moment about what you saw us do. Who can tell us what you saw and heard?" (Takes several responses that retell the events.)

"Now, I want you to do the same thing with the members of your small group. Each of you has a copy of the discussion guide. For today, I would like you to do what you saw this group do: Read a question and give each person in the group time to share their ideas about the question. When everyone has had an opportunity to share, go on to the next question. Again, go around the group and take turns sharing your ideas. Be sure that you talk about each question.

If you finish sharing your ideas before I call the class back together, you may talk about other questions and ideas you have about this chapter. You might want to write those extra questions on the guide sheet. When we get back together as a class I'll ask you to share ideas from your small groups."

■ F I G U R E 4 . 9

Sample minilesson: First day of using discussion guide for small groups

- How he can encourage students to become more engaged with the character and use their engagement to better understand their own struggles with life.

Lou uses an ML–TA to support students' thinking and encourage response from chapter to chapter, adjusting as necessary the amount of support he provides during the read-along. If, for example, Lou notices during discussions that many students are having difficulty adjusting to the point of view of the book, he makes more frequent stops than he originally planned to help students follow the way the narrator uses Brian's thoughts to tell the story.

As Lou plans for an ML–TA, he uses the *predict–listen–respond–connect* cycle. (Refer to the sample ML–TA in Figure 4.2 and notice how the cycle is adapted to the way that Paulsen presents ideas in *Hatchet*.) Lou uses the *listen–respond* phase of the ML–TA cycle consistently while reading aloud, encouraging his listeners to share their understanding and responses. During this portion of the cycle, Lou must listen intently to student feedback so he knows how much support students need for the text to be meaningful.

He adds the *predict* phase when his listeners might anticipate upcoming events, such as by using clues about the impending heart attack to anticipate the question of who will fly the plane.

Lou uses the *connect* phase when recalling past events that might help listeners clarify meaning, such as by connecting the clues about the heart attack with information about the plane crash from the back cover of the book.

Thinking about reading aloud as phases of a *predict–listen–respond–connect* cycle provides a framework for teacher planning. The cycle calls attention to how readers think when responding to text and to where the "listeners" in a class may need support to have more meaningful interaction with the text.

ENGAGING STUDENTS IN WHOLE-CLASS DISCUSSIONS

After the read-along, students usually engage in some type of discussion, either whole class or small group. At the beginning of the school year, Lou begins with whole-class discussion rather than small groups. He intends to move into more independent reading but first wants students to feel confident when thinking about and verbalizing responses to text.

In literature study that relies on whole-class discussions to help students reflect on and clarify their understanding of text, the "After Reading" portion of the ML–TA occurs immediately following the read-along. In the "After Reading" section of the sample ML–TA for Chapter 1 of *Hatchet*, notice in Figure 4.10 how the questions focus on having students respond to the reading, retell important events, and make predictions for the next chapter. These prompts are intended to promote a well-rounded discussion of the text.

ENGAGING STUDENTS IN SMALL-GROUP DISCUSSIONS

After introducing his students to literature study through teacher-led whole-class discussions, Lou moves to student-led small-group discussions that follow the read-along. The students submit the names of three others with whom they would like to talk about the reading. Using these choices, Lou creates heterogeneous, or mixed ability, groups of four or five. Groups typically remain together for the duration of a literature study.

When small-group discussion is new for Lou's students, he provides a discussion guide to help students focus their talk. Through a whole-class minilesson (see Figure 4.9) Lou models using the guides. Students use the discussion guides until they have enough experience with small-group discussions to monitor them on their own.

■ **FIGURE 4.10**

"After reading" portion of ML–TA for chapter 1 of *Hatchet*

After the reading of Chapter 1:

Respond: Encourage open response; "Well, what do you think about Brian's situation?" (pause for responses)

Connect: Encourage students to think back over the events in the chapter (retelling) as they explore their responses; "What do we know so far?" (pause for retelling) "What would you do if you were Brian? (pause for response)

Predict: "Based on what we know, what do you expect might happen in Chapter 2?"

■ **FIGURE 4.11**

Sample small-group discussion guide for chapter 1 of *Hatchet*

Hatchet by Gary Paulsen
Discussion Guide
Chapter 1

Discuss each item with the members of your group. Record important ideas on this think-sheet for use in the whole-group discussion that will follow. Place the completed guide in your literature log.

1. What do you think about Brian's situation at the end of the chapter? What makes you think that?

2. Thinking that the pilot is dead, what would *you* do if you were Brian?

3. Look back in Chapter 1 to find parts of the story that are told through Brian's thoughts. Reread several parts to members of your group. As a reader, how do you respond to a story that is told through someone's thoughts?

Figure 4.11 presents a sample discussion guide for Chapter 1 of *Hatchet*. Notice that the items closely parallel the "After Reading" discussion suggested in the ML–TA for Chapter 1, shown in Figure 4.10. When Lou uses small-group discussions in whole-class literature study, he delays in-depth discussion of the reading until after students have had an opportunity to explore their ideas in the small groups.

Even though Lou is working with sixth-grade students, many have limited experience with reading responsively or critically or in leading their own discussions of books. To promote personal engagement, the discussion guide has open-ended questions that query students for their personal opinions and responses. Lou encourages students to provide support for their thinking from the text whenever applicable.

As Lou moves through the chapters of *Hatchet,* he makes the questions on the discussion guides more and more open. By broadening the questions, he encourages students to provide more direction for discussions. Figure 4.12 shows a sample discussion guide for Chapter 16, near the end of *Hatchet,* when Lou is encouraging students to take more control of the small-group discussions.

In the early stages of using small groups, Lou encourages the group to discuss one item at a time, with each group member sharing his or her thoughts and questions. Students' responses typically focus on simply answering the questions and not much more, and are often shallow, not the insightful thinking we hope to have as a response to good literature. But this is just what Lou expects because his students do not have much experience with peer-led discussions. From their prior experience with reading groups, students often expect Lou to take the lead, so they wait to see what he thinks they need to know. As the small-group process becomes more familiar, the "question-answering" begins to sound more like a conversation.

Lou leaves space on the discussion guides for students to record responses as appropriate. During Lou's first small-group minilesson, he suggested that students focus on discussion. They wrote responses in their guides after the discussion as a way of remembering what they wanted to share with the class. This illustrates an important point: When we begin to use discussion guides, we must carefully consider our purpose(s). If one purpose is getting students to talk, we can't let filling in the discussion guide become so important that students stop discussing in order to write answers.

■ **FIGURE 4.12**

Sample small-group discussion guide for chapter 16 of *Hatchet*

Hatchet by Gary Paulsen
Discussion Guide
Chapter 16

Discuss each item with the members of your group. Record important ideas on this think-sheet for use in the whole-group discussion that will follow. Place the completed guide in your literature log.

1. Do you think Brian has changed? When you think back on all that has happened to Brian, what *clues* do you see to Brian's change?

2. What other ideas did your group think were important to discuss today? Would you be willing to share these ideas in the whole-group discussion?

Lou circulates among the groups during the small-group discussions. He listens, but does not answer questions or tell students what responses to make. Lou believes that his students need to begin to make decisions for themselves. Their questions typically seek affirmation that they are doing the "right things." Lou responds with, "What do *you* think about . . . ?" When the students see that Lou really wants to know what they think, they stop asking and begin to trust themselves.

Also during discussions, Lou makes notes about students' responses. He studies these responses to do the following:

- Learn about students' thinking.
- Prepare for the possible directions that class discussions might take.
- Plan for the next day's read-along.
- Evaluate students' growth as literate thinkers.

Lou thinks of the small groups as a rehearsal for whole-class discussions. In the small groups, each student has the opportunity to reflect on and share personal thoughts and responses. As a result, there is greater diversity of thinking, and more students' ideas are included in the whole-class discussion.

By the time students participate in discussions of two or three chapter books in whole-class study, Lou hopes that students will direct their own discussions in the small groups. Peer-led book talks should be the goal in the middle grades.

Discussion guides focus students' attention on the aspects of each chapter that would be beneficial to discuss at the close of a literature workshop, when the whole class comes together. Try developing a discussion guide for Chapter 2 of *Hatchet*. What aspects of the chapter will you call to students' attention? Develop three open-ended discussion questions, one that encourages the reader to look back at the text, one that allows the reader to take a personal stance, and one of your own choosing.

• • •

To develop a discussion guide for Chapter 2, I looked back at the sample ML–TA for that chapter. The ML–TA for Chapter 2 is divided into three parts: Brian coming to grips with the death of the pilot, his developing a plan of action, and his reaction when the engine stops. I would use these same points to extend students' thinking as they prepare for whole-class discussion, using the following three questions:

1. *Look back.* Reread the opening paragraph for Chapter 2. Have someone in your group read the paragraph aloud. What do you think Gary Paulsen meant by this description of Brian? Why do you think he described Brian this way?
2. *Personal response.* What would you have done to figure out how to fly the airplane and communicate using the radio?
3. *Open—prediction.* What do you think Brian will do now that the engine has stopped? What do you think you would do?

• • •

WHOLE-CLASS LITERATURE STUDY WITH SILENT READING

After students gain some experience with thinking and talking about literature, they should be able to share the responsibility for reading the text as well. To accomplish this, Lou changes the read-along portion of the literature workshop to an assisted silent reading experience.

In the middle grades, a literature study using silent reading is most effective when students meet the following conditions:

- Students' reading ability is near the difficulty level of the selected text.
- They desire to read the selected text.
- They have past experience in literature study.

While Lou helps students to prepare for the silent reading, he no longer reads the text for them. He is careful, however, to be sure that students do not find themselves frustrated during the reading.

To support his students, Lou plans minilessons that will help them develop strategies for effective silent reading. He realizes that he may need to teach reading strategies that he did not emphasize in the read-along literature workshop.

In the minilessons, Lou emphasizes the use of text and models how competent readers think while they read silently. For example, as the class prepares to read Chapter 3, Lou uses a strategy minilesson to demonstrate using context and background knowledge to think about words that have multiple meanings. He places excerpts from *Hatchet* on the overhead projector, then thinks aloud so that his students will realize that good readers often must use their reasoning abilities to make meaning in their reading (Figure 4.13).

PLANNING A MEDIATED READING–THINKING ACTIVITY

The essential difference between literature study using read-along and one using silent reading is in the way the text is read. Look back at Figure 4.3, which shows ways to organize literature study. To emphasize guided silent reading we change the ML–TA to an MR–TA, mediated *reading*–thinking activity.

Like an ML–TA, an MR–TA includes predicting, responding, and connecting. However, instead of listening to text read aloud, we support students as they read the text silently to themselves. When planning an MR–TA for *Hatchet,* for example, we divide the text into manageable chunks, just as when we read aloud. Then, we help students use their ability to read silently as they learn to think more critically and responsively about literature.

In our planning, we consider the type of support students might need to interact successfully with the text. During discussion, we listen to students' feedback to learn whether they are handling the silent reading effectively. Students reading a year or more below the level of text being studied may experience some frustration during silent reading periods, unless they are highly motivated to read the selected text.

To prepare for the silent reading in an MR–TA, we think about our purpose(s) for engaging students with a text such as *Hatchet,* and the *strategies* to assist students to make meaning before, during, and after each silent reading. In addition, we *reflect* on how to adjust support to students as indicated by their feedback during discussion. We review what we know about how competent readers monitor their thinking while reading, especially in unfamiliar text. Then, we think about the content and writing style of *Hatchet,* and use what we know about our students to anticipate the needs they might have when reading.

■ FIGURE 4.13

Sample minilesson: Using context and background knowledge to determine word meaning

"When I'm reading (teacher talking), sometimes I think I know the meaning of a word, but the way it's used in the story doesn't seem to fit my word. Then I remember that in English words can have more than one meaning. So I have to look carefully at how the author used the word.

Yesterday we started reading *Hatchet* by Gary Paulsen. When we got to page 5, we came across the word *banked* and some of you questioned whether it had anything to do with money. Let's look at that part of the text again.

Remember, we were reading about Brian trying his hand at flying a plane for the first time." (Place a copy of the text on overhead with the word *banked* highlighted):

Brian turned the wheel slightly and the plane *banked* to the right, and when he pressed on the right rudder pedal the nose slid across the horizon to the right. He left off on the pressure and straightened the wheel and the plane righted itself.

"I'm thinking that the meaning of *banked* that I usually think of, as something to do with money, doesn't seem to fit in this story about flying an airplane. There must be another meaning for this word. So I look past the word, because I know that clues to word meaning can come after a word, as well as before it. As I read on, the author tells me that the nose of the plane went to the right, then, with less pressure, the plane righted itself. I think about planes I have seen flying and I get an image in my mind of what this plane might be doing. If a plane makes a turn, the wings are usually tipped. *Tipped*—maybe that fits. So I try *tipped* in place of *banked:*

Brian turned the wheel slightly and the plane *tipped* to the right,

"That makes sense to me and seems to fit with the other sentences. I think *banked* can have more than one meaning. Sometimes I can find out what meaning the author is using if I look at the other words around it for clues.

In our reading today, if we come to a word where your meaning doesn't fit with the way the author is using it, let's stop and see if we can figure it out by looking at the other words around it."

As with the ML–TA, we begin the MR–TA by introducing the text and asking open-ended questions that encourage students to use what they know as readers to anticipate both the book as a whole and the opening chapter as an introduction to the author's style of sharing plot, characters, setting, and theme. During the MR–TA, we encourage students to do the following:

1. *Predict*, anticipate, or wonder about what might happen (as needed).
2. *Read* a selected part of the text silently.
3. *Respond* to the text.
4. *Connect* new ideas to what they already know (as needed).

Following the reading, we give students the opportunity to reflect on the chapter, considering their own engagement with the text.

The sample MR–TA for Chapter 1 of *Hatchet*, shown in Figure 4.14, is one example for mediating students' thinking and responses during silent reading. We use Chapter 1 at this time so we may more effectively compare and contrast this MR–TA with the sample ML–TA in this chapter.

Before Reading

Share the information that is available to any reader who picks up the book—the title and front cover illustration, information on the back cover introducing the author and briefly describing the plot, just as in the ML-TA. Then prepare for the first segment of silent reading.

Predict: "What ideas do you have so far about this story?" (pause for responses) "What clues do we have for the meaning of the title, *Hatchet?*" (pause for responses) "Let's begin the reading to see what else we find."

During Reading

Read: "Let's each read silently to the middle of page 3, to the paragraph that ends with '. . . he hadn't noticed the burning tears.'" (students read)

Respond: "What do we know so far?" (wait for responses) "How did we find out?"

Connect: "Did you notice how the author tells us what Brian is thinking? Remember on page 2 it said, 'The thinking started.' Why do you think Gary Paulsen wants us to know what Brian is thinking?" (wait for responses) "Could this be a way that we will learn more about Brian? What do you think?" (brief pause for comments, and to think aloud) "I wonder why Gary Paulsen capitalizes that word, *Secret,* each time he writes it?" (briefly pause for responses)

Predict: "Notice how the next paragraph takes us back to the pilot and the plane. What do you think might happen now?" (listen for connections with information on the back cover of the book)

Read: Read silently to the middle of p. 5. Stop with the paragraph that ends with Brian saying, "Thank you."

Respond: "How would you feel about flying the plane?" (wait for responses)

Predict: "When you read the last two sentences on p. 5–'The words. Always the words,' what does it make you think might happen next in the story?" (pause)

Read: Read silently from the top of p. 6, beginning with "Divorce . . .," to the bottom of p. 7, ending, "Probably something he ate, Brian thought."

Respond: "What did we find out in this section?" (pause for responses) "What makes you think that?"

Connect: Sometimes authors give us clues to something that is going to happen, making us curious, wanting to read on to find out. Did you notice any clues?" (note survival pack and pilot's discomfort) "From the back cover we know there will be a crash, so we think the survival pack could be important. We also know the pilot has some type of problem."

Predict: "The last sentence we read said, 'Probably something he ate, Brian thought.' What do you think the problem might be? What makes you think that?" (pause for responses) "Let's read to find out."

Read: Read silently from the last paragraph on p. 7, beginning, "His mother had driven him from the city . . .," to the paragraph near the top of p. 10 ending with, "Brian forgot it as they took off and began flying."

Respond: "How do you think Brian feels about his mother? What leads you to believe that?" (pause)

Connect: "Brian's mother gave him a hatchet. Could this be another clue for us to think about? What do you think might be important about the hatchet?" (pause)

Predict: "The next paragraph on p. 10 begins, 'More smell now.' What do you think we might find out?" (pause for responses) "Let's read to the end of the chapter and find out."

Read: Read silently the remainder of the chapter.

After Reading

Respond: "What do you think about Brian's situation?" (brief pause for initial responses)

(When using a whole-class format, discussion continues. When using small groups, the connecting and predicting questions are placed on a discussion guide along with other items appropriate for discussion.)

Connect: "Take a few minutes to look back at the chapter. What do we know so far? What parts of the chapter are important for us to think about and remember? Be ready to share those parts with the class." (after sufficient time return to whole-class discussion of important parts)

Predict: "Chapter 1 ends with these words, 'He was alone. In the roaring plane with no pilot he was alone. Alone.' What do you think will happen in Chapter 2? What do you think Brian will do?" (pause) "If you were Brian, what would you do?" (prediction could also be a literature log entry)

■ **F I G U R E   4 . 1 4**

Sample MR–TA for chapter 1 of *Hatchet*

■ *How will you use writing to help students clarify and extend their thinking about their interactions with texts?*

The MR–TA provides a framework for mediating between students and a text that they are reading silently. We use comments and open-ended questions to encourage response and help students make connections among ideas presented in the text. How we probe student responses depends entirely on the depth of thinking in the feedback students provide.

USING LITERATURE LOGS IN WHOLE-CLASS STUDY

Some teachers choose to add a literature log to the whole-class study to give students opportunities to focus on personal responses. After whole-class or small-group discussions, students record their responses to the text in a literature or reading log. These personal responses can then be contrasted with the small-group and whole-class discussions to better understand the growth of individual students.

In whole-class literature study that uses small-group discussions, I suggest that a significant portion of the literature log entries be student's choice. Other opportunities for student response are already influenced by the questions/comments selected for the ML–TA/MR–TA and the discussion guides. Students in the middle grades should have many opportunities to explore their own thinking as well as the thinking of peers and teachers.

Many format options exist for logs or journals (see Chapter 9). We can introduce students to these various ways to structure their log or journal responses and then let them make choices about the nature of their entries. If we use logs or journals for personal response, we should provide opportunities for sharing responses during the literature study. Sharing not only provides additional purpose for making the entries, but also enriches group discussions.

In addition to personal responses, students can also record ideas and information pertinent to the literature study. For example, Lou asks students to dedicate a few pages in their logs for noting interesting and/or troublesome words. He also encourages them to illustrate, cluster, or chart their ideas as needed. The words that students record can be used for word study to extend students' vocabulary, decoding, and spelling skills.

Whole-class literature study is an excellent way to get started. Read-along involves all students initially, regardless of their reading level. Engaging students in silent reading later on provides challenge. In addition, beginning whole-class literature study by using one text can help us develop the confidence to try more challenging organizations, such as book clubs, literature circles, and individualized reader's workshops, discussed in Chapters 5 and 6.

As one example, Appendix A contains a complete whole-class literature study for *A Taste of Blackberries*. In this 1988 short chapter book, Doris Buchanan Smith shares a powerful story of two boys, Jamie and an unnamed narrator. Their friendship is cut short by Jamie's accidental death. Through the first-person voice we are able to feel children's struggles to understand the workings of the world. Smith's use of language is a rich, creative strength of this book. This literature study was developed by a group of teachers who enjoy meeting to talk about books. The study guide includes suggested lesson plans for each chapter, sample discussion guides, and suggested literature log prompts. With more experienced students, we would revise the focus of the ML–TAs/MR–TAs and discussion guides to encourage students to be more self-directed.

RESPECTING DIVERSITY THROUGH READ-ALOUD AND LITERATURE STUDY

Students bring to the classroom rich and diverse experiences that must be acknowledged, supported, and enhanced through read-aloud and literature study. The texts we select for study should take into account students' interests, world knowledge, and cultural experiences, as well as their experiences with book language.

Over the school year, we should select literature in which all students see "people like themselves" to validate their lived experience. Multicultural literature and writing reflecting a variety of lifestyles and family structures should figure prominently in our selections (see Appendix B for suggestions). In addition, the main characters with whom students interact should be both male and female, and should reflect different types of personalities and ways of solving life's problems.

Striving for balance among the types of texts, making selections across all types of narrative and information texts, provides opportunity for students with specialized knowledge to share what they know with you and with their peers. If their uniqueness is to be an asset, then we must challenge ourselves to use students' knowledge as the starting point of the curriculum.

The fewer experiences our students have with the formality of book language, the more conscious we must be in providing sustained exposure. During read-aloud we are a language bridge, mediating between students and book language. Supporting students during reading with strategies such as an ML–TA, combined with many opportunities for students to talk about their ideas with others, provides support for students who are learning to use English in academic settings.

To provide appropriate support to our students, we must become excellent "kid-watchers" (Goodman, 1985; Pappas, Kiefer, & Levstik, 1994). Whether in large- or small-group discussion we must learn to carefully observe each student, and make anecdotal records that chronicle their individual growth.

ASSESSMENT AND EVALUATION IN READ-ALOUD AND LITERATURE STUDY

To evaluate individual students' growth in a literature study, we observe their reading and writing behaviors, record observations that demonstrate effective use of strategies for making meaning in authentic literature, and sample their actual reading and writing. To monitor students, we continue to develop the teacher and student assessment portfolios.

TEACHER'S ASSESSMENT PORTFOLIO

Multiple opportunities exist for documenting student growth during whole-class literature study through observation and samples of work. Evaluation of the data will depend on our purposes for instruction and the strategies we emphasize.

Assessing and Evaluating Read-Aloud. When read-aloud is an interactive activity, as in an ML–TA, students share their general attitudes about reading as well as their attitudes about the particular text being read. By the middle grades, students who do not engage during a read-aloud are less likely to benefit from whole-class instruction. It is important to notice students' behavior during read-aloud and to consider what such behaviors suggest about students as readers.

An ML–TA enables students to share their attitudes and thinking about a text before, during, and after the reading. During each phase of an ML–TA you have the opportunity to observe student reactions and interactions. As we observe behaviors that help us better understand a student, we should make records. To help focus our observations, we can list behaviors we believe are important for middle grade students to demonstrate during read-aloud and use it as a checklist to guide our observations. Figure 4.15 shows a sample observation checklist and anecdotal record form.

To observe read-aloud behaviors, we begin by asking these questions:

- Do I know the text I am reading well enough to allow me to observe students' responses rather than think about my ability to read aloud well?
- What do I notice most about students during a read-aloud?
- Do I use my observations to adjust instruction during the read-aloud?

To improve our observation skills, we:

- Focus our attention on a few students, rather than the class as a whole, and record observations as soon after the read-aloud as possible.
- Select only one main purpose to accomplish before, during, and after the read-aloud, enabling us to focus on observing a limited number of types of student responses.

In our initial observations, it is a good idea to focus attention on a few students who most need support during the read-aloud to become engaged or to make meaning. They are our best gauge of how the read-aloud is going. To prepare to share the chosen text, set one main instructional objective for the reading, such as noticing character traits by listening to dialogue. Interactions with students should focus on our objective.

Observing Students. What does Lou watch for when his students are engaged in literature study? During read-along, Lou observes students' responses while he reads aloud, using observation forms such as the one shown in Figure 4.15. During silent reading, he observes how effectively students are able to sustain their reading, beginning with information learned through observations of independent reading. In addition, Lou carefully notes the nature of the interaction during whole-class discussions and how students attend to response activities.

Observing behaviors
during read-aloud

Name _____	Observed Behaviors during Read-Aloud		
Response to read-aloud:	**Usually**	**Sometimes**	**Rarely**
1. Shows positive response to read-aloud Comments:	_____	_____	_____
2. Participates in discussion Comments:	_____		
Shares thinking through discussion: 1. Makes meaning by using 　　Oral context 　　Background knowledge 　　Comments:	_____ _____	_____ _____	_____ _____
2. Monitors own thinking about text Comments:	_____	_____	_____
3. Uses knowledge of story elements 　　Plot development 　　Character traits 　　Setting 　　Point of view 　　Themes 　　Author's style 　　Comments:	_____ _____ _____ _____ _____	_____ _____ _____ _____ _____	_____ _____ _____ _____ _____
4. Makes connections between texts to enhance meaning Comments:	_____	_____	_____

As we found earlier in this chapter, Lou's purposes for the study of *Hatchet* are as follows:

- Reading for pleasure;
- Becoming aware of techniques authors use to reveal character growth, because the main character, Brian, is a dynamic character;
- Exploring ways in which readers learn about their strengths and weaknesses while studying the characters in Gary Paulsen's books;
- Making inferences about a character through an omniscient narrator;
- Using a discussion guide in peer-led small-group discussion to help students become more independent in their study of literature; and
- Using close reading as an appropriate strategy in the study of a chapter book.

From these purposes, Lou creates an open-ended form to record observations during the study of *Hatchet* (see Figure 4.16). The form also includes reading and writing behaviors that he emphasizes in the ML–TA and MR–TA.

While Lou does not formally conference with students during whole-class literature study, he speaks with them informally as a way of clarifying what he observes, recording the highlights on his observation forms.

Samples of Student Work. Lou places selected samples of work completed during whole-class literature study in the teacher assessment portfolio he has for each student. These pieces serve as formative assessments of student progress. Throughout the study students complete discussion guides, literature log entries, and other selected activities. Lou selects one discussion guide or log entry that represents growth for a student in a particular reading or writing behavior, often conferring with the student about the piece selected. Lou notes on the piece why he is including it in the assessment portfolio.

At the end of a grading period, usually either 6 or 9 weeks, Lou uses the items in the assessment portfolio to create a summative evaluation of student growth in the language arts. Instead of placing a numerical or letter grade on each piece as it is completed, Lou prefers to evaluate student growth over the entire grading period. He feels that a long-term, or summative, view provides a more accurate picture of what a student has accomplished.

STUDENT LEARNING PORTFOLIO

Throughout a whole-class literature study, such as *Hatchet*, students are either reading along or reading silently in the text, participating in discussions, recording their responses on discussion guides and/or literature logs, and performing other tasks.

Students should also develop a learning portfolio that will illustrate who they are as learners. Students place items in the portfolio that, when taken together, provide a picture of how they evaluate themselves as readers and writers.

Student Self-Evaluation of Read-Aloud. In addition to our evaluation of read-aloud, students should have the opportunity to evaluate their own responses. Middle grade students are able to monitor their listening–thinking processes. The more we ask students to be aware of and evaluate their own thinking and responses, the more sensitive they become to the listener's role during read-aloud. We may ask for both verbal and written self-evaluations.

Verbal self-evaluation can take place during read-aloud discussions and individual conferences. We may model self-evaluation by talking aloud about our thinking as we prepare for the reading. We encourage students to evaluate their own thinking and responses during the reading by sharing first with a partner, then with the class as a whole.

■ FIGURE 4.16

Observing behaviors
during literature study

Literature Study   Name _____ Date _____

1. Reads for pleasure:
   -shows positive response to reading
   -uses strategies effectively to enhance enjoyment

2. Character:
   -aware of ways authors reveal character growth
   -uses knowledge to learn about main character
   -learns about character through omniscient narrator

3. Literature study procedures:
   -uses discussion guide in small groups
   -takes turns, listens to others in discussions
   -makes written responses to text

4. Increases reading effectiveness:
   -learns new vocabulary in and out of context
   -uses text and personal knowledge to make predictions
   -retells and responds to important events
   -makes connections within text, between texts
   -uses a variety of strategies to make meaning
   -sustains silent reading

5. Increases writing effectiveness:
   -communicates clearly, concisely
   -uses new vocabulary in appropriate context
   -spelling appropriate for development
   -makes personal connections with text

6. Unit theme:
   -explores personal traits through reading

Written self-evaluation is easier for students if we develop a response form that queries them about their thinking and responses during the read-aloud. The form of the evaluation can be either focused or open. A focused evaluation may be a checklist for students to complete (Figure 4.17), while an open-ended response may take the form of a sentence completion or short-answer task (Figure 4.18). Still another way to encourage self-evaluation is to have students discuss their response to read-aloud in their literature

■ **FIGURE 4.17**

Focused self-evaluation
of read-aloud

Name _____ Date _____

	Usually	Sometimes	Rarely
When the teacher reads stories aloud to the class:			
1. I enjoy listening.	_____	_____	_____
2. I get involved in the story.	_____	_____	_____
3. I participate in discussions.	_____	_____	_____
4. I learn new words and phrases.	_____	_____	_____
5. I use what I already know to anticipate and follow the story.	_____	_____	_____
6. I use what I know about stories to understand:			
–the development of the plot.	_____	_____	_____
–the development and actions of the characters.	_____	_____	_____
–the role of the setting.	_____	_____	_____
–how the point of view influences the story.	_____	_____	_____
–the way the author uses language to tell the story.	_____	_____	_____
7. I use the meaning of other words in the story to figure out words I'm unsure about.	_____	_____	_____
8. If I listen carefully, I learn ways to understand more about stories.	_____	_____	_____

Comments:

logs or journals. We may choose to keep these self-evaluations in either the student's learning portfolio or teacher assessment portfolio.

Student Self-Evaluation during Literature Study. At the midpoint and at completion of a literature study, we ask students to "step back" and view their own progress as readers, writers, and thinkers. Using the purposes identified for the "Gary Paulsen—Author" unit, Lou develops an open-ended self-assessment (see Figure 4.18) to help his students consider their development of specific attitudes and behaviors. Students place completed forms in their learning portfolios.

Lou also uses the literature log throughout the literature study as a tool for finding out what individuals are thinking about the book. Periodically, Lou asks for specific feedback from students about the small groups, their ability to handle the silent reading, or any other

■ **FIGURE 4.18**

Open self-evaluation
of read-aloud

Read-Aloud Self-Evaluation

Name _____ Date _____

1. When the teacher reads stories aloud to the class, I like to

_____

_____

2. When we discuss books the teacher reads aloud, I

_____

_____

3. During a read-aloud, I learn about the development of plot by

_____

_____

4. During a read-aloud, I learn about the development of the characters by

_____

_____

5. During a read-aloud, I learn about the role of the setting by

_____

_____

6. During a read-aloud, I learn about the author's style of writing by

_____

_____

7. During a read-aloud, I learn more about thinking like a reader when the teacher

_____

_____

area in which students may need support. Students are always free to use the log for comments, questions, or concerns that they want Lou to know about. In this sense, the literature log becomes a personal dialogue between Lou and a student. It is a way for Lou to respond individually to students.

At the end of a literature study, students select one or more log entries that show something about themselves as a reader or writer that they want represented in their learning portfolio. Students indicate on blank paper or a specially prepared form (see Figure 4.19) their reasons for selecting specific items.

As students spend time being read to, they demonstrate attitudes toward reading and how they use meaning-making strategies in a listening–thinking situation. As students read independently, they demonstrate both their attitudes toward themselves as readers and their use of self-sustaining reading strategies.

■ FIGURE 4.19

Self-evaluation for
whole-class literature
study

Self-Evaluation for *Hatchet* and "Gary Paulsen–Author" Unit

Name _____

Evaluate your reading:
• Gary Paulsen lets you hear Brian's thoughts.
  How does this help you as the reader?

• What does Gary Paulsen do to help you see how Brian's character changes?

While reading Hatchet, what did you learn about . . .
• yourself as a person?

• yourself as a reader?

Evaluate your small-group discussions:
• Did the discussion guide help you participate in the discussions? Explain.

• What did *YOU* do to help your group have good discussions?

• What can you do next time to make the discussions more helpful and interesting?

During whole-class literature study, you must be aware of the choices you provide for students. Students need many opportunities to share their knowledge and strategies as well as their needs. A balance between guided activities and choice provides the flexibility you need to meet the range of interests and needs in your classroom.

■ *TAKE A MOMENT TO REFLECT . . .*

■ *Read-aloud provides:*

- Language development through exposure to rich language;
- Windows to the world, mirrors of ourselves;
- Access to literate thinking; and
- Motivation to read.

■ *Planning for read-aloud:*

- Pick books you like.
- Preview before reading, because even award winners are no guarantee.
- Allow ample time to pace the book appropriately for your students.
- Share information about authors and illustrators.
- Be conscious of how you position the book if there are relevant illustrations.
- Connect with the audience through expression and eye contact.
- Help students make connections with the reading.
- Abandon books that are above students' emotional level or are otherwise inappropriate.
- Make read-aloud books available for independent reading.

■ *Close the gap between readers through read-aloud:*

- Give all students access to a text.
- Encourage "book talk" during the read-aloud.

■ *Mediate between students and books:*

- Use ML–TA strategies before, during, and after the reading of a book to support students' interactions with a new text.

■ *Whole-class literature study provides introductory literature experiences for middle grade students:*

- ML–TA removes decoding as an obstacle to literature study.
- Reading aloud becomes reading along when students have personal copies of the text being studied.

■ *Literature study moves from:*

- Whole-group instruction;
- To small-group and independent work time; and
- Back to whole group for closure.

■ *Instruction is drawn from:*

- School district curriculum and objectives;
- The literature being studied; and
- Student needs and interests.

■ *ML–TA is built on a thinking cycle of:*

- Predict;
- Listen or read;
- Respond; and
- Connect.

■ *To implement a literature workshop:*

- Analyze the text in light of student needs and school district curriculum.
- Develop a plan for reading and study of the text.
- Plan whole-class minilessons to support both the study of the text and workshop procedures.
- Provide students with copies of the text.
- Guide student thinking using either ML–TA or MR–TA.
- Engage students in small-group or whole-class discussions about the text.

■ *Small group discussions are peer led, but are structured by teacher-made discussion guides.*

■ *Discussion guides:*

- Encourage student response and connections within and across texts.
- Become less structured as students are able to direct their own talk.

■ *Respect reading diversity among students through providing for varied:*

- Interests;
- Abilities; and
- Learning Styles.

■ *Teachers monitor growth through assessment portfolios that contain:*

- Documented observations of student performance; and
- Selected samples of student work that show strengths and areas of need.

■ *Students monitor their own growth through learning portfolios that contain:*

- Selected samples of work with justification for selection; and
- Self-evaluation of progress in literature workshop activities.

■ REFERENCES

Anderson, R. C., Hiebert, E. H., Scott, J., & Wilkinson, I. A. G. (1985). *Becoming a nation of readers*. Champaign-Urbana, IL: Center for the Study of Reading.

Betts, E. A. (1946). *Foundations of reading instruction*. New York: American Book.

Cullinan, B. E. (1989). *Literature and the child* (2nd ed.). San Diego: Harcourt Brace Jovanovich.

Davey, B. (1983). Think-aloud—Modeling the cognitive processes of reading comprehension. *Journal of Reading, 27*, 44–47.

Dixon-Krauss, L. A. (1995). Lev Semyonovich Vygotsky: The scholar/teacher. In L. A. Dixon-Krauss (Ed.), *Vygotsky in the classroom: Mediated literacy instruction and assessment* (pp. 1–5). New York: Longman.

Five, C. L. (1988, Spring). From workbook to workshop: Increasing children's involvement in the reading process. *The New Advocate*, pp. 103–113.

Freeman, J. (1992). Reading aloud: A few tricks of the trade. *School Library Journal, 38*(7), 26–29.

Galda, L., Ash, G. E., & Cullinan, B. E. (2000). Children's literature. In M. Kamil, P. B. Mosenthal, P. D. Pearson, & R. Barr (Eds.), *Handbook of reading research* (Vol. 3, pp. 361–379). Mahwah, NJ: Lawrence Erlbaum Associates.

Goodman, Y. (1985). Kidwatching: Observing children in the classroom. In A. Jaggar & M. T. Smith-Burke (Eds.), *Observing the language learner* (pp. 9–18). Newark, DE: International Reading Association.

Hagerty, P. (1992). *Reader's workshop: Real reading*. Ontario: Scholastic Canada Ltd.

Heibert, E. H., & Colt, J. (1989). Patterns of literature-based reading instruction. *The Reading Teacher, 43*, 14–20.

Holdaway, D. (1980). *Independence in reading*. Portsmouth, NH: Heinemann.

Kristo, J. (1993). Reading aloud in a primary classroom: Reaching and teaching young readers. In K. E. Holland, R. A. Hungerford, and S. B. Ernst (Eds.), *Journeying: Students responding to literature* (pp. 54–71). Portsmouth, NH: Heinemann.

Langer, J. A. (1995). *Envisioning literature: Literary understanding and literature instruction*. New York: Teachers College Press.

Morrow, L. (1993). *Literacy development in the early years* (2nd ed.). Boston: Allyn and Bacon.

Pappas, C. C., Kiefer, B. Z., & Levstik, L. S. (1994). *An integrated language perspective in the elementary school* (2nd ed.). New York: Longman.

Ramirez, G., & Ramirez, J. L. (1994). *Multiethnic children's literature*. Albany, NY: Delmar.

Roser, N. L., & Martinez, M. G. (1995). *Book talk and beyond: Children and teachers respond to literature*. Newark, DE: International Reading Association.

Routman, R. (1991). *Invitations: Changing as teachers and learners K–12*. Portsmouth, NH: Heinemann.

Selnick, G. J. (Ed.) (1976–2000). *Children's literature review* (Vols 1–40). New York: Gale Research.

Stauffer, R. (1975). *Directing the reading–thinking process*. New York: Harper and Row.

Telgen, D. (Ed). (1971–2001). *Something about the author* (Vols 1–82). Detroit, MI: Gale Research.

Trelease, J. (1989). *The new read-aloud handbook*. New York: Viking Penguin.

Tunnel, M. O., & Jacobs, J. S. (1989). Using "real" books: Research findings on literature based reading instruction. *The Reading Teacher, 42*, 470–477.

Vygotsky, L. S. (1962). *Thought and language* (E. Hanfmann & G. Vakar, Eds. & Trans.). Cambridge, MA: The MIT Press.

Zarrillo, J. (1989). Teacher's interpretations of literature-based reading. *The Reading Teacher, 43*, 22–28.

chapter 5

Book Clubs and Literature Circles: Engaging Students in Peer-Led Literature Study

In this chapter . . .

We consider how to move from whole-class to small-group literature study, providing opportunities for students to assume greater responsibility for their talk about books. This chapter introduces you book clubs and literature circles, exploring:

- Planning for book clubs and literature circles,

- Providing instruction in both approaches,

- Reading and writing to prepare for book club and literature circle meetings,
- Discussion in book clubs and literature circles, and
- Effectively using community sharing sessions.

Focus Literature

Among the Hidden by Margaret Peterson Haddix, Alladin Paperbacks, New York, 1998.

Hatchet by Gary Paulsen, Viking Penguin, New York, 1999.

Shh! We're Writing the Constitution by Jean Fritz, Scholastic, New York, 1987.

We Remember the Holocaust by David A. Adler, Trumpet Books, New York, 1989.

In Addition. . .

Appendix B contains a listing of suggested books for book club and literature circle study.

Looking into Classrooms . . .

After her seventh- and eighth-grade students' whole-class study of *Hatchet* as part of a unit theme titled "Meeting Challenges," Melodia selects five books of varying genre and difficulty for small-group literature study. She believes the selected books will provide opportunities for her students to continue their exploration of the diversity of ways that people meet challenges in their lives. Melodia knows that the lives of her middle

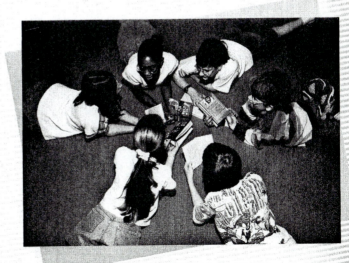

grade students are filled with daily challenges and she hopes that the selected literature will provide opportunities for rich discussions to enhance students' understandings of self and others.

Putting Theory into Practice . . .

We are aware that students in the middle grades experience dramatic changes in their bodies and lives. As they struggle to discover their independence as worthy individuals, we observe a diminishing interest in reading. This dimishing motivation to read may be linked to fewer opportunities for self-expression in their learning environments (Oldfather, 1995). Peer-led literature study may provide the impetus for becoming "part of a community of learners that enriches and extends mutual thinking and ideas, and enhances their motivation for further engagement in reading and writing" (Oldfather, 1995, p. 422).

Book clubs and literature circles offer students increased social opportunities to participate in and direct their conversations about books. Students learn to take the roles of more knowledgeable others in peer-led discussions, sharing their thinking and supporting one another as they explore new ideas. They often find that the support of the group makes a challenging book more manageable (Scott & Wells, 1998). Book clubs and literature circles can move students toward independence and mature reading.

Avid readers, especially adults, typically have opportunities to participate in book clubs, both formal and informal, that enable them to gather with others to converse about literature of personal interest (Raphael, McMahon, Goatley, Bentey, Boyd, Pardo, and Woodman, 1992). It is such "grand conversations" about books that brings many readers back to the page (Peterson & Eeds, 1990). Through their research in literacy, McMahon, Raphael, and their colleagues (Goatley, Brock, & Raphael, 1995; McMahon, 1991; Raphael, Kehus, & Damphousser, 2001; Raphael et al., 1992; Raphael & McMahon, 1994) have developed an approach to literature-based reading that uses peer-led book clubs in the classroom.

Literature circles, a term coined by Kathy Short (1986), grew out of her research in literature-based reading with Jerome Harste and Carolyn Burke in the mid–1980s. Originally, literature circles were part of the authoring cycle (Short, 1986), a curricular framework that brings together the writing process, students' life experiences, and quality literature.

Book clubs and literature circles provide curricular frameworks that encourage middle grade students "to expand and critique their understandings about their reading through dialogue with other readers" (Short, 1995, p. x) and help them develop the ability to decide *what* to share about the literature they read and *how* to share it (Goatley et al., 1995; Raphael et al., 2001). Although the majority of teachers use such small-group literature expereinces with narrative texts, multiple copies of high-quality information texts also provide excellent opportunities to engage our students in examining their views about world issues and the strategies they use to construct meaning.

What can we learn from each of these frameworks that will help us engage middle grade students in meaningful literature study? Our interest is in developing approaches that we can apply to classrooms in which students have experience with studying literature and are ready to accept more responsibility for structuring their own work.

BOOK CLUBS

A book club (McMahon, 1991; Raphael et al., 2001; Raphael & McMahon, 1994) is an approach to literature-based reading that provides balance between teacher-led and peer-led opportunities for learning. Raphael and McMahon developed the idea to answer the question, "How might literature-based instruction be created to encompass instruction in both comprehension and literature response?"(Raphael, McMahon, et al., 1992, p. 55).

In a book club, a classroom of students breaks into small peer-led groups to talk about books. Unlike whole-class literature study, described in Chapter 4, book club discussions are directed by student interests and concerns rather than teacher-made discussion guides. The teacher, however, continues to have a significant role in text selection, group instruction, and facilitating whole-class discussions.

A book club approach is most effective when students are engaged in a unit or theme that includes the study of a series of related texts. Students' study and discussion lead to making connections within and across texts, potentially deepening their engagement with the books.

A book club approach has four components: reading, writing, discussion, and instruction. The amount of time devoted to each component varies daily, depending on the text being studied, students' familiarity with book club routines, and what occurred on the previous day:

- *Reading.* Through silent reading, partner reading, choral reading, oral reading/listening, and reading at home, students receive ample reading opportunities to be ready for sharing when the clubs meet.
- *Writing.* Students reflect on their reading, then write or draw in their literature logs in preparation for sharing ideas with their peers in club meetings.
- *Discussion.* Students have opportunities to interact with and learn from others in both book clubs and community sharing sessions as they internalize their ideas about literature and life.
- *Instruction.* Teachers provide opportunities for students to learn what and how to share their literary thinking with others.

The components in the book club approach are similar to those in whole-class literature study (Chapter 4). The essential difference is that book clubs provide students with more responsibility for directing their own reading, writing, and talking about books.

GETTING STARTED WITH BOOK CLUBS

To dramatize our discussion of book clubs, we visit Lou's sixth-grade classroom once again. Lou is interested in moving his students toward more independent reading and book discussions. Instead of organizing literature study around a whole-class approach, he decides to try a book club approach using *Hatchet* (Paulsen, 1999). For this approach, Lou organizes instructional time as shown in Figure 5.1. Notice that he begins with a whole-class meeting, moves to various forms of peer-led reading and writing, then to book club meetings in which students share their reading and writing, and finally back to the whole class for sharing the outcomes of the book clubs. Lou schedules additional reading time as needed, including independent reading and time for reading at home, to help all students be prepared for book club meetings.

■ **FIGURE 5.1**

Overview of book club approach

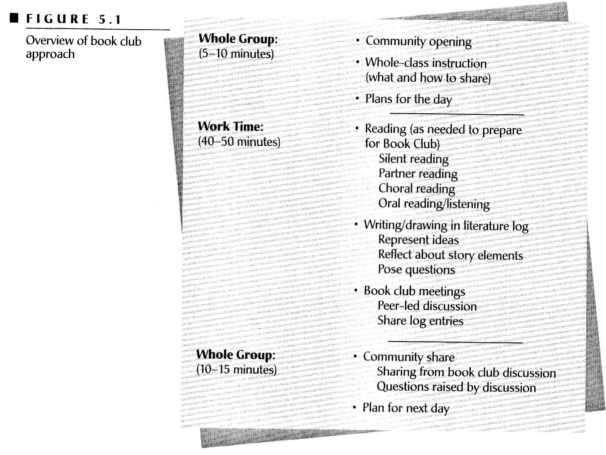

Whole Group: (5–10 minutes)	• Community opening
	• Whole-class instruction (what and how to share)
	• Plans for the day
Work Time: (40–50 minutes)	• Reading (as needed to prepare for Book Club)
	Silent reading
	Partner reading
	Choral reading
	Oral reading/listening
	• Writing/drawing in literature log
	Represent ideas
	Reflect about story elements
	Pose questions
	• Book club meetings
	Peer-led discussion
	Share log entries
Whole Group: (10–15 minutes)	• Community share
	Sharing from book club discussion
	Questions raised by discussion
	• Plan for next day

Compare the structure of whole-class literature study (Chapter 4, Figure 4.1) with that of book clubs, shown in Figure 5.1. Are any differences apparent to you?

• • •

The one difference I hope you notice is that the responsibility for the reading shifts from the teacher to the student. Teachers share the responsibility for instruction as students show us they are ready for more independence. In whole-class literature study, we moved from using only whole-class discussion to including small-group discussion with discussion guides, while continuing to guide the reading. In a book club approach, we share responsibility with students for the reading, as well as the content of the small-group discussions.

• • •

PLANNING FOR BOOK CLUBS

As Lou begins to plan for book clubs with his sixth-grade students, he considers the same factors as he did in planning whole-class literature study (see Chapter 4):

1. The language arts curriculum standards he is required to teach,
2. What *Hatchet* (or other selected texts) offers to the reader, and
3. The level of development of his students as readers and writers.

While the required curriculum standards and the selected text(s) are important, Lou knows that the actual topics he selects for instruction depend on the feedback he gets from students during community sharing sessions and his observations during book club meetings.

As Lou did for whole-class literature study, he must develop a plan for reading *Hatchet*; a plan that will enable each student to be prepared to meet with his or her book club group. During book clubs, Lou will not read the text aloud to the class; instead the students will read the text themselves. As he plans, Lou must consider the amount and type of support each student might need to successfully complete the reading. He asks himself:

- Which students will need extended reading time at school, such as during independent reading?
- Which students will need to have a copy of the book for reading at home?
- Which students will need to be matched with a more able partner to share the reading, or join a small group that will read the text orally?

For book clubs to be effective, each student must have adequate access to the ideas in the text.

To form each "club," or small group, Lou has students suggest the names of three others with whom they wish to work. Student choices typically lead to mixed-ability groups. If not, Lou makes some of the choices to be sure the groups are diverse, yet balanced by personality and reading experience. His class has seven book club groups, six with four members each and one with five.

With *Hatchet*, Lou's class begins the unit of study, considered in Chapter 4, "Gary Paulsen—Author." After completing *Hatchet*, Lou will continue the book clubs and extend the theme study by adding other Paulsen books that vary in reading level. Studying related books enables students to make connections not only within a text but also between texts. Intertextual connections strengthen students' understanding of the author's craft and their own flexibility in making meaning. Appendix B contains a listing of suggested books for literature study.

INSTRUCTION IN BOOK CLUBS

Each day Lou gathers the class together to begin their literature study and provides whole-class instruction, similar to the minilessons in the literature workshops. He focuses on the following:

- Book club procedures and how to share (taking turns, listening to others, and so on),
- Making decisions about what to share (personal responses, unresolved questions, relationships of the current text to other texts, and so on), and
- Expanding students' knowledge of literary possibilities (author's craft, development and use of particular literary elements, and so on).

Lou's decisions to provide specific instruction depend on what students already know and what support they must receive. Whenever possible, Lou demonstrates and shows concrete examples to support students' learning.

As Hill (1995) suggests, Lou keeps a running list of the instructional lessons he has developed and presented to the class, which enables him to see patterns in his instruction. The list also serves to document the skill and strategy instruction that occurs in his classroom. Lou's list includes lessons on book club procedures, effective reading and writing strategies, and decisions on what thoughts to share and how best to share them (see Figures 5.2 through 5.5).

Considering what you know about the development of middle grade students, what ideas do you have for helping them think about how to share their ideas with others in peer-led discussions? Discuss your ideas with a peer.

• • •

■ **FIGURE 5.2**

Topics for instruction in book club procedures

- What does it mean to be responsible for my own reading?
- Choosing the best way to get my reading done for a book club meeting.
- Making my learning log work for me:
  Choosing the best time to record my ideas.
  Choosing what ideas to record.
  Choosing the best way to record my ideas.
- What do we do during a book club meeting?
- How is a book club different from a reading group?
- What is a community sharing session?
- How does discussion in a book club compare to discussion in a community sharing session?

■ **FIGURE 5.3**

Topics for instruction in effective reading and writing strategies

- What do I do when I *monitor* my own reading?
- How do I *know* when reading is making sense?
- Sometimes I get confused when I read. What should I do?
- What can I do about words I don't know?
- When should I use context clues?
- When should I use phonics clues?
- How can I tell if I should try phonics or meaning units to figure out words?
- What happens if I don't agree with what the author is saying?
- Why do I get different ideas from reading than my friends do?
- When should I listen to the author? When should I listen to myself?

One thing that I especially like students to do is show respect for each other's ideas. For respect to be present in book club discussions, I must develop it in all aspects of classroom life. I cannot expect attentive listening, turn taking, or thoughtful responses in the book clubs only. Throughout the school day I, as the adult model, must show students that the behaviors I expect of them are the same behaviors that I demonstrate with them. Secondly, I must help students get to know each other in social, as well as academic, situations so they are comfortable with one another and can trust others with their thoughts. Finally, the tasks I ask students to engage in and the quality of the books I ask them to read must be worthy of their attention.

• • •

■ FIGURE 5.4

Topics for instruction in deciding what to share

- What seems important to me about this book?
- What do I notice about the way the author has put ideas together?
- Am I responding to particular ways that the author used story elements (plot, setting, character, theme, point of view, style) to tell the story? If so, what elements do I really notice?
- What questions do I ask myself as I read? Could others in my book club be asking themselves the same questions?
- When I finish reading, which of my questions are still unanswered?
- How does this story relate to me?
- How does this story relate to what I already know?
- Does this story remind me of other books I have read or know about?
- What does this book really have to say to me about life?
- I can add to the discussion by sharing things in my log (clusters or mapping, timelines, lists, charts, annotated drawings, and so on) and explaining my thinking.
- How can I learn from what I contributed to the group discussion?

■ FIGURE 5.5

Topics for instruction in deciding how to share

- How can I help others understand what is important to me about this book?
- People take turns in a discussion. How should I do that?
- What does it mean to really listen to other people's ideas?
- How can I help myself be a better listener?
- How do I show others that I really care about what they say?
- I can contribute to discussion by doing the following:
  Telling others what I think.
  Commenting on an idea shared by another student.
- When I want to know more, I can ask a question about another person's ideas.
- What can I learn from looking at my own participation in the group?

READING TO PREPARE FOR BOOK CLUBS

When Lou introduces *Hatchet* to the students, he provides a copy of a day-by-day reading plan that he has developed, shown in Figure 5.6. Students place the plan in their literature log for reference and will use it to pace their reading in preparation for book club meetings. Students typically meet with members of their book club every day.

To set the tone for the whole-class study, Lou reads aloud Chapter 1 as students follow along in their own copies. As he reads aloud, Lou uses an ML–TA format, just as he did in whole-class literature study. He talks aloud and thinks aloud to emphasize his own thinking and questioning, modeling the way proficient readers might prepare for a book club discussion. On subsequent days, students will read on their own. Lou encourages class discussion of the reading plan, including evaluation of the decisions that each student makes to accomplish the reading (silent, partners, choral, and so on). Lou encourages students to use this opportunity to discover more about their own needs as they pace their reading and to record their observations in the comments section of their plan.

Students often read ahead when they are interested in a story. When they do, Lou asks them to reread the section to be discussed that day so that it will be fresh and they will be able to make significant contributions to the discussion.

■ **F I G U R E 5 . 6**

Sample reading plan
for book clubs

Name _____   Reading Plan for _____ *Hatchet*

Date	Chapter	Pages	Comments
	1	12	
	2	13	
	3&4	16	
	5	12	
	6	10	
	7	12	
	8&9	14	
	10&11	15	
	12&13	17	
	14&15	18	
	16	14	
	17	11	
	18	10	
	19& Epilogue	11	

WRITING TO PREPARE FOR BOOK CLUBS

Students' writing in a book club approach focuses their attention on the impending discussion and helps them to take relevant stances that lead to literary understanding (Langer, 1995). Lou notices that often his students use the writing to make links between different parts of a text or across texts in the same unit of study.

At the beginning of the study, Lou models how he uses his literature log. After introducing *Hatchet* by reading Chapter 1 aloud, he places a page of his own log on the overhead projector and makes his entry in response to the chapter (Figure 5.7).

Lou then encourages students to make entries in their own logs in preparation for the book club meetings. He reminds them of the many types of entries the class has used in the past (see also Raphael & McMahon, 1994), including the following:

- *Personal comparisons or connections* the reader makes with some particular aspect of the book;
- *Questions or unresolved issues* that the reader wants to share with or get a response for from group members;
- *Important events or parts* of the book that the reader wants to remember;
- *Character charts or maps* that show physical features, actions, interactions with other characters, or any personal interest in a character that the reader explores or wants to remember;
- *Illustrations* of pictures in the reader's head (artistic and written description) in response to the author's description or reader's personal experience, along with an explanation of their importance;
- *Words and phrases* that interest the reader or that the reader wants to learn more about;
- *Something in particular that the author does* that engages the reader; and
- *Personal commentary or critique* of the story or the author's style.

The log is an excellent source of information for evaluating students' engagement with books and in book club discussions. Laura Pardo (1992), a fifth-grade teacher, has her students brainstorm an idea list for reading logs and makes it a permanent bulletin board. As her students discover new possibilities for the literature log, Laura provides the opportunity for students to teach their peers.

■ **FIGURE 5.7**

Lou's literature log entry for chapter 1 of *Hatchet*

I wouldn't like to be Brian right now. He doesn't know how to fly a plane. I'd be scared to death. Death—that's a funny word to choose!

Questions I have:
1. What is this "secret" that Brian keeps thinking about?
2. What would I do if I were Brian?
3. How would I teach myself something like flying a plane?

BOOK CLUB MEETINGS

When the members of book clubs meet, discussions are intended to be a natural outgrowth of their reading and writing about books. Unlike whole-class literature study, students are not given a teacher-made discussion guide. Instead, students share responses from their literature logs as the starting point for small-group discussions. The direction that the discussion takes then depends on the interests of the group members.

In their research with book clubs, Raphael, McMahon, and colleagues (1992) identify a number of purposes for student talk in book clubs:

- Share responses from reading logs.
- Discuss process of making responses.
- Discuss main points of a text.
- Clarify points of confusion.
- Make connections within and across texts.
- Relate ideas from text to personal feelings, experiences, and prior knowledge.
- Identify author's purposes and critique success at achieving those purposes.

These purposes demonstrate that, when provided an opportunity to direct their own discussions, students can achieve significant understanding about literature and make connections between themselves and texts.

Read the beginning of one group's discussion after reading Chapter 1 of *Hatchet*. This book club has four members, Travis, Jessie, Brad, and T. C.:

Travis:	OK, I'll start. In my log I wrote, "Right now I just want to keep reading to find out what's going to happen to Brian."
Jessie:	I wrote, "I'd be too scared to do anything. I wouldn't be able to remember what the pilot had shown me."
Brad:	Hey, Brian can't die now, this is only Chapter 1.
Travis:	I can't believe the pilot had a heart attack! I didn't know that when someone has a heart attack, they, ya' know, the smell.
Brad:	Maybe when you're in all that pain, you can't help what your body does, you can't keep gas in.
Jessie:	I have a question. What do you think the "Secret" is?
T. C.:	It must be something that made his parents break up.
Travis:	Maybe one of his parents went with someone else, ya' know, like one of them fell in love with someone else.
T. C.:	Or maybe one of them did something really embarrassing.
Brad:	Well Brian knows what it is and it sure does bother him!
T. C.:	I want to know what it is!
Jessie:	Well, I have another question then. What do you think Brian is going to do now? . . .

This discussion begins with students reading from their logs. At first the talk is somewhat stilted, then begins to sound a little more like natural conversation. In conversational groups such as this, members often take on different roles. Notice that Jessie takes the role of the "question-asker" and Brad seems to be the "clarifier."

What purposes do we see in the preceding conversation? If we consider the purposes that Raphael and her colleagues identified, we might say the following:

■ When you bring students together following small-group literature discussions, what might you learn about them as readers and as individuals?

- Travis and Jessie share responses from their logs.
- Jessie makes a personal connection with her own feelings.
- Travis and Brad discuss main points of the text (heart attack) and attempt to clarify their own confusion between the text and personal background knowledge of heart attacks.
- T. C., Travis, and Brad try to clarify their confusion about the "Secret."

How do the topics raised compare to the questions on the discussion guide used during whole-class literature study in Chapter 4 (see Figures 4.11 and 4.12.)? Is peer-led discussion a potential learning opportunity in Lou's classroom? Remember that developmental learning theory (Holdaway, 1980) suggests that learners need many opportunities to monitor, pace, and evaluate their own work as they make approximations toward more mature reading and writing. Book clubs provide such an opportunity.

COMMUNITY SHARING SESSIONS

After about 15 minutes, Lou asks the book clubs to bring their discussion to closure for that day by deciding on an idea or question to discuss with the whole class in a community sharing session. Club members know their discussion will continue tomorrow, after they have read Chapter 2 of *Hatchet*.

As the class settles into a configuration for face-to-face discussion, Lou begins by asking, "What are some of the ideas that your group thinks are most interesting or important in this chapter?" Listening to the views of others and taking turns in discussion become extremely important in this whole-class sharing session. All members do not have to participate, but all must be attentive to their classmates.

Lou has tried having one student begin the session, progressing around the circle letting students who wish to make initial comments do so, then opening up for whole-class discussion. He has found, however, that this approach leads to a rather stilted discussion and actually keeps the class from moving from reporting to conversation. Now he opens with a general question or asks if any student would like to begin.

Community sharing should be an inclusive activity. All students have participated in book clubs and have valuable ideas, comments, and questions to share with the class. Lou sees his role as facilitator and encourager, helping all students feel that their thinking will be valued. He must be sure that the ideas of all students receive respect through attentive listening and polite response by their peers.

To support students as they learn self-direction, Lou includes evaluative discussion at the end of each sharing session. The class spends a few minutes "debriefing" the day (Redman, 1995), discussing what went well and addressing possible solutions for problems. The class also looks ahead to the next day of book clubs and anticipates what will occur.

As Lou's sixth-grade class progresses through *Hatchet,* the daily book club routine will become:

- Opening,
- Peer-led reading,
- Peer-led writing,
- Peer-led book clubs, and
- Joint peer- and teacher-led sharing sessions.

Book clubs are an excellent way to move students toward independence as learners.

BOOK CLUBS WITH INFORMATION TEXTS

AMERICAN REVOLUTION BOOK CLUBS

Jean, a fifth-grade teacher, uses multiple copies of a variety of books by Jean Fritz for American Revolution book clubs. The texts present a very "reader friendly" history of that period through the lives of many of the individuals who were involved. There is even a text written from the British perspective, *Can't You Make Them Behave, King George?* The texts look like short novels, text interspersed with small illustrations and diagrams, with important documents like a copy of the Constitution in an appendix. *Shh! We're Writing the Constitution*, for example, has 48 pages of actual text.

Jean presents the text choices to her class through book talks. Students have the opportunity to examine the books and then select their first and second choice for a book club. After the groups are formed, the class decides how much must be read each day to complete the books in 1 week, typically 9 or 10 pages per day.

In keeping with book club procedures, Jean provides reading and writing time each day, prior to group meetings. She meets in small groups with students who need additional support to complete the reading. The special education and English as a second language teachers push-in to her classroom during this time to provide support to students in Jean's class. She realizes that she must increase students' engaged time with information texts to close the "experience gap" between narrative and information texts.

Jean observes students during each phase of the book club progress and provides instruction during the daily opening and focused small groups that she believes will provide the support necessary for her students to successfully comprehend their chosen texts. She teaches compare/contrast minilessons so that students are able to consider the differences between narrative texts, which they know well, and information texts, with which they have limited experiences.

Jean is very selective about the information texts that she uses in book clubs. Fritz's books are well written, and the events portrayed are historically accurate. When Jean begins these information book clubs at the beginning of the year, she starts with a whole-class text, just as Lou did with *Hatchet,* to teach the procedures of the book club. At that time she intentionally selects an information text that is below the fifth-grade reading level, so that all of the students in her class are included. Her purpose is to teach procedures, not the particular text.

WORLD WAR II BOOK CLUBS

Katarina, an eighth-grade social studies teacher, and Martin, the English teacher on her middle school team, work together to provide book club experiences in a variety of topics across the school year. At this time the class is studying World War II. Extensive high-quality literature is available on this topic.

Katarina and Martin select sets of both narrative and information texts to balance the instruction in their unit. Between English and social studies class, students will participate in both a narrative and an information book club. The teacher will use this experience to help students see the value of each type of literature and to compare/contrast their learning about history through both types of texts.

Daily reading and writing time is provided between the two classes. The teachers team together to provide support to students reading below grade level. They also share responsibility for observing discussions and providing instruction to support both the development of literacy skills/strategies and historical understanding.

One group in particular is reading *We Remember the Holocaust* by David A. Adler. This text has nine chapters, a historical chronology, and a glossary. Text is interspersed with captioned photographs. Most of the information texts for the World War II book clubs have a similar format. Martin and Katarina decide to focus their first minilessons on how to effectively use these textual aids to build background and support comprehension. Students are also asked to collect unfamiliar and interesting words for discussion in both the book clubs and in community sharing sessions.

The class develops reading plans to complete the texts over a 2-week period. Throughout the 2 weeks, Katarina and Martin provide additional background building experiences via videos, guest speakers, and independent/small-group research in areas of particular interest to the students. For Martin and Katarina, the book clubs are an excellent enhancement for their interdisciplinary units.

Now that we have discussed the book club approach, what benefits do you see in it? When might book clubs be more appropriate than whole-class studies?

• • •

The benefits I see are increased opportunity for self-direction and independence for students, while I continue to provide support through whole-class instruction, community sharing sessions, and assessment of student progress. By the time students are in the middle grades, they should have many opportunities for self-direction, but often their reading and writing experiences have not prepared them for such independence. Book clubs allow me to gradually release control of instruction by providing a predictable structure in which students learn to prepare for and monitor their own discussions.

• • •

LITERATURE CIRCLES

Kathy Short (1995) captures the essence of literature circles when she says, "Literature circles provide a curricular structure to support children in exploring their rough draft understandings of literature with other readers" (p. x). The term *rough draft* reminds us of writing processes. In literature circles, students share their "rough draft" ideas about their reading and receive response from others, causing them to reflect on their ideas and consider the ideas of others, and perhaps revise their own ideas in some way, just as they revise their writing.

Since the mid-1980s, teachers have talked about and experimented with literature circles in middle grade classrooms. While interpretations vary, many commonalities exist. The following are characteristics of most literature circles:

- Four to six students gather to talk about books they are reading.
- Groups are formed by students who choose the same book to read.
- Groups are heterogeneous, representing a range of interests and abilities.
- Groups may focus on one core book or on a number of related books.
- Books are typically related by author, genre, topic, or the study of a particular literary element.
- Students determine the pace of the reading and when the groups will meet.
- The teacher may or may not be present during the literature circles.
- In addition to discussions, students typically respond to texts through journals, logs, and projects.

Why do teachers choose literature circles? Owens (1995) cites several reasons, stating that literature circles do all of the following:

- Promote a love for literature and positive attitudes toward reading.
- Reflect a constructivist, student-centered model of literacy.
- Encourage extensive and intensive reading.
- Invite natural discussions that lead to student inquiry and critical thinking.
- Support diverse responses to text.
- Foster interaction and collaboration, provide choice, and encourage responsibility.
- Expose students to literature from multiple perspectives.
- Nurture reflection and self-evaluation.

As you can see, a number of these reasons are similar to those for using whole-class literature study and book clubs. Literature circles, however, typically offer more opportunities for student choice and decision making.

What influences the success of literature circles? Kary Brown (1995), a fifth-grade teacher, suggests that the success of literature circles (and this applies to book clubs also) is influenced by a number of factors:

- The variety and quality of books selected for study,
- The degree of choice and ownership students have,
- Students' motivation and interest in reading and talking about their chosen books,
- Students' previous experiences with literature circles,
- The amount of modeling by the teacher and other students to demonstrate aspects of literature circles such as deciding what and how to share, and
- Group dynamics.

Students' ability to work effectively in literature circles and book clubs improves over time. You will want to provide initial guidance and direction for students, reducing support in later stages.

GETTING STARTED WITH LITERATURE CIRCLES

Meet Melodia, a sixth- and seventh-grade middle school reading teacher. After introducing a unit called "Meeting the Challenge" through whole-class literature study with *Hatchet* (Paulsen, 1999), Melodia moves to literature circles so that students have the opportunity to make choices about the texts they read and become more independent in directing how their reading and writing about text will occur. She organizes rotating 75-minute blocks for literature circles, as shown in Figure 5.8. Note that the opening and closing activities resemble whole-class literature study and book clubs, while the central work time is a flexible block of activity. Herein lies the real difference between literature circles and book clubs. In literature circles, students not only choose the books they will read, but they also choose when they will read, when their groups will meet to talk about the books, and how they wish to respond to their text.

Compare the structure of a literature circle (Figure 5.8) with book clubs presented earlier in this chapter (see Figure 5.1). What similarities do you see? Are any differences apparent to you?

• • •

Both approaches open and close with what appear to be similar teacher-led whole-group activities. Even the elements in the peer-led work time seem very similar, with the exception of flexible strategy grouping and informal conferences added to the literature circle approach. The literature circle structure identifies the reading, writing, and group meetings as self-paced, which suggests more student control than in book clubs. Let's see!

• • •

■ FIGURE 5.8

Overview of literature
circle approach

Teacher-led Whole Group:
(10–15 minutes)

- Community opening
- Whole-class instruction minilessons
  (applicable to all students or texts)
- Plans for the day

Peer-led Work Time:
(40–60 minutes)

- Self-paced reading according to group plan
- Self-paced response
    Literature log
    Projects
- Literature circles meet according to group plan
- Flexible strategy groups
    By invitation
    Specific practice
- Informal conferences

Teacher-led Whole Group:
(10–20 minutes)

- Community sharing session
    Literature circle discussions
    Book talks
    Response projects
- Evaluate the day
- Plan for next day

Melodia often uses literature circles to extend whole-class literature study. After her students' whole-class study of *Hatchet*, Melodia selects five books of varying difficulty (multiple copies of each text are available) that reflect the unit theme of "Meeting the Challenge." In each text the characters learn something about themselves and others as a result of a challenging situation:

- *Among the Hidden* (Haddix, 1998). Luke, a shadow child, a third child forbidden by the Population Police, discovers another shadow child. After her untimely death, Luke decides that he, too, must not hide any longer.

- *Felita* (Mohr, 1979). Felita must leave her friends when her Puerto Rican family decides to move to a better neighborhood, only to face discrimination in the new neighborhood.

- *The Great Gilly Hopkins* (Paterson, 1978). Giladrial Hopkins, facing her third foster home in as many years, must come to terms with who she is, with a mother who does not want her, and with her need for a place to call home.

- *A Time for Andrew: A Ghost Story* (Hahn, 1995). Andrew moves through time, switching places with an ancestor, only to discover family life and values that challenge the person he is and wants to become.

- *Thunder Rolling in the Mountains* (O'Dell & Hall, 1992). Sound of Running Feet, daughter of Chief Joseph of the Nez Perce, must help her people escape to Canada or be forced to live on a reservation.

The books represent a variety of genres (mystery/suspense, realistic fiction, historical fiction, and fantasy) and a range of reading levels. They also contain strong female and male roles; illustrations of Native American, Puerto Rican, and Caucasian cultures; and family configurations that include extended, two-parent, and foster families.

Just before the class completes *Hatchet*, Melodia introduces the five books. She indicates the level of challenge of each book and makes them available for browsing. She urges students to "check the fit" of any book they think they might choose by reading a page or two (about 100 words) and noticing whether they encounter more than three to five unfamiliar words on those pages. During the class session before the literature circles begin, students submit a first and second book choice. Melodia tries to give students their first choice, while keeping the groups balanced by reading experience and personality.

PLANNING FOR LITERATURE CIRCLES

On the first day of literature circles, the students develop a reading plan for their selected book. Melodia asks each group to try to set up a plan they can complete within 3 weeks. She also reminds the groups to be sure that their plan will meet the needs of each group member and enable everyone in the group to feel successful. Melodia works with each literature circle to be sure that less experienced students are allowed ample time to complete the reading and helps them select the most effective way to do so. She also provides blank forms, similar to Lou's form (see Figure 5.6), for students to complete when their circle develops a reading plan.

Students often refer to the pacing of previous literature studies to help them decide on a reading plan. Having just completed *Hatchet*, students use that reading plan to help them decide how much to read before scheduling a literature circle. They also think about their own interactions with the text.

The group reading *Among the Hidden* (Haddix, 1998, 30 chapters, 153 pages) decides to read twice the number of pages as they did in *Hatchet* before they meet in their circles, and the group plans to meet every other day. Throughout their reading of *Hatchet*, group members found themselves wanting to read ahead, so they decide that reading more text at one time might be more satisfying. They also decide that over a weekend they can read a few extra pages. The group plans to complete the reading in 2 weeks, then plans a week to enjoy response activities and to prepare to share the book in the community session. Figure 5.9 shows the group's reading plan.

In contrast, the group that chose to read *Felita* (Mohr, 1979, 7 chapters, 112 pages, fourth-grade reading level), feels uncertain about determining its own reading schedule. They call Melodia over to their group meeting and discuss their feelings with her. She asks them how they felt about the daily reading schedule they followed for *Hatchet* and suggests they might consider such a schedule if it feels comfortable. Melodia also reminds the group that they are free to change the schedule if they gain confidence and do not need to meet each day. The group decides to follow a daily schedule, reading a chapter each day, with the exception of Chapter 2 (the group discovers that Chapter 2 is much longer than the others, so they decide to give it 2 days rather than 1). Their reading plan is shown in Figure 5.10.

Melodia asks each group to give her a copy of their reading plan. She also asks students to indicate how they will accomplish the reading. She encourages each literature circle to also talk about how they can help each other get the reading completed if necessary.

Melodia wants her students to be responsible for their decisions, but she is well aware that many lack the experience. When she knows what they are trying to accomplish, Melodia is

■ **FIGURE 5.9**

Student-developed reading plan for *Among the Hidden*

Name ___Darren___   Reading Plan for ___Among the Hidden___

Circle meets on–	Chapter #	# Pages to read	Comments
Tuesday	1–6	29	
Thursday	7–14	30	
Monday	15–19	34	
Wednesday	20–26	30	
Friday	27–30	29	
Mon–Fri			prepare to share with class

My plan is . . . to get my reading done in class and at home. I tried the book when we were choosing. It's pretty easy for me. I know most of the words. If I don't get done at school I'll take it home. My group will help me if I need it.

better able to adjust both her individual and whole-class instruction. As the literature circles begin, Melodia will combine what she knows about her students with observations of their independent and group work to anticipate when and how she might help them move toward independence.

INSTRUCTION IN LITERATURE CIRCLES

Literature circles are intended to foster independence among students. Melodia provides instruction through whole-class minilessons, flexible strategy groups, informal individual conferences, and discussion during community sharing sessions. She engages students in thinking about new literature circle procedures, continues to "nudge" their understanding of literary possibilities, and encourages them to practice strategies that competent, independent learners use to make their reading and writing satisfying.

Whole-Class Minilessons. You already know of many possibilities for minilessons. We have considered lists of possible topics in whole-class instruction and have viewed examples of actual minilessons and group instruction. We can draw on what we know:

- *General knowledge* of literature and reading background (Chapters 2 and 3)
- *Procedures* for book clubs (Chapter 5) and reader's workshop (to be discussed in Chapter 6),
- *Literary lessons* for literature study (Chapters 4 & 5), and
- *Strategy lessons* for book clubs (Chapter 5).

■ FIGURE 5.10

Student-developed
reading plan for *Felita*

Name __Zeena__   Reading Plan for __Felita__

Circle meets on–	Chapter #	# Pages to read	Comments
Tuesday	1	14	
Wednesday	2 (1/2)	12	
Thursday	2 (1/2)	12	
Friday	3	9	
Monday	4	14	
Tuesday	5	10	
Wednesday	6	11	
Thursday	7	11	
Fri–Fri			prepare for sharing

My plan is . . . to read every day at school and every night at home. I take my time when I read. Irene is going to help me by checking my reading every day and reminding me to find a quiet place. Sometimes we will read together.

Flexible Strategy Groups. During peer-led work time, Melodia invites students who have specific needs to meet with her in small groups. Typically the groups focus on strategies for effective reading and writing. Melodia emphasizes monitoring and pacing of silent reading, two areas that she observes challenge her students. These small groups also provide additional practice with selected issues raised in whole-class minilessons.

Melodia encourages students to become aware of their own needs as learners. When the class begins the unit "Meeting the Challenge," Melodia mounts a poster titled "Invitations" on the wall near the library corner and asks students to use the poster to indicate when they need particular types of strategy groups. When three or more students indicate a similar need, Melodia offers a small-group session, or she may invite students to join a strategy group. Otherwise, Melodia confers with individuals or pairs of students.

Informal Conferences. During the work time, Melodia moves about the classroom, observing students and stopping periodically to chat with them about their work. Students also initiate informal conferences with Melodia to share log entries, raise questions about a text, seek support for project plans, settle disputes in literature circles (which she mediates when appropriate), and the like. As she circulates she is careful not to disturb any student who is deeply engaged in reading, writing, or worthy conversation. Melodia makes mental notes about her interactions, and later records essential observations for ongoing student evaluation.

Whole-Class Discussions.   The class draws together for whole-class instruction at the beginning and end of each literature circle day. Minilessons are the focus of the opening class session; sharing and book talks are the focus of the closing session. Melodia plans whole-class instruction to focus on issues that the majority of students need, such as literature circle procedures and reading or writing strategies that lead to independence. She saves more specialized or individual issues for informal conferences or strategy groups.

Plans for the Day.   During each opening class meeting, Melodia checks the "status of the class" (Atwell, 1998). She asks students to tell her about their plans for the work time. They come to expect Melodia's query and focus their attention on what they intend to accomplish during the work time. Responses range from silent reading in readiness for the literature circle to putting the final touches on a project to share during the community session. From these responses, Melodia has a better idea of the role(s) she must take during work time.

READING TO PREPARE FOR LITERATURE CIRCLES

Each group develops a plan to guide their reading, which helps students learn to focus their attention during the work time, to set goals for themselves, and to pace their reading. Middle grade students benefit from this organizational tool. Melodia's role is one of support: When the reading is going well, she pulls back and lets students remain in control. When it is not going well, she moves in to help students evaluate the situation and refocus, then pulls back once again. Her goal is for students to learn to monitor their own progress.

Reading for literature circles requires greater amounts of time as books become longer and more complex. Melodia's students must increase their reading time at home or use the "free" time available during other class periods or in homeroom advisory. If Melodia was in a self-contained classroom and had the entire day with one class of students, she could also use the time typically devoted to independent reading to read literature circle books.

During the middle grades, students should sink into silent reading and become flexible readers, able to move easily between silent and oral reading. However, some students will have spent far too much time in oral reading and will not be very proficient silent readers. In addition, they may not have consolidated the skills needed to move between oral and silent reading. You will need to carefully observe students during periods of independent reading for evidence that they understand how to sustain themselves during silent reading. This may be an area for instruction during flexible strategy groups.

WRITING TO PREPARE FOR LITERATURE CIRCLES

Literature circles typically allow a great deal of choice. With book clubs, students prepare for club meetings by making entries in their literature logs. When Melodia moves to literature circles, she does not require her students to make log entries each day. Her purpose for the log does not change, but her goal changes for students. Now Melodia is working for student independence!

Melodia wants students to view writing as relevant and satisfying and to decide the appropriate times to use writing for pleasure and writing to learn. If she continues to require daily log entries, then she retains control and students will have little decision-making experience. Melodia tries to expand their knowledge of the possibilities for written response. Throughout the literature circles, Melodia (1) models a variety of ways to use the log, discussing formats and purposes for entries, (2) encourages students to share the ways they use their logs, (3) displays log entries that show how writing helps to support thinking, and (4) encourages using logs in whole-class meetings, literature circles, strategy groups, and conferences.

The request that Melodia makes of her students is to come to the literature circle meetings prepared with notes, questions, and/or specific places in their reading that warrant discussion, and be prepared to share a particularly interesting portion of text with their group.

One tool that Melodia has found useful to encourage writing is the use of "sticky" notes (such as Post-It™ notes). Students place a large sticky note on the front of their book, on which they collect interesting words and phrases and use smaller sticky notes to mark places in the text for sharing, questioning, or commenting. Students are eager to use the notes, which they sometimes refer to as their "sticky note log."

Melodia wants her students to understand writing as a purposeful act. Throughout the day, she emphasizes ways that writing captures thinking, helping readers remember details and notice changes in their ideas and feelings.

LITERATURE CIRCLE MEETINGS

Circles meet according to the reading plans that each group develops, and may range from each class session (typically three per week) to only once a week. One or two meetings per week is typical, depending on the amount of text students are able to be responsible for.

Today, the group that chose *Among the Hidden* (Haddix, 1998) is having its first meeting. Darren, Oswaldo, Rachel, Paul, and Breann have each read Chapters 1 through 6 (29 pages) according to their plan, and gather at a table in the back corner of the room with their books, literature logs, and pencils.

One member assumes responsibility at each group meeting for checking to be sure that each person is prepared and ready for discussion, then gets the discussion started. Today is Breann's turn. She asks the members if they have completed the day's reading, are prepared for discussion, and noted their work on the reading plan. Paul says he would like to share first. Breann agrees and the conversation begins.

Paul:	I didn't understand what was going on at first, but I'm starting to figure it out. I know I wouldn't want to be Luke and hide from everyone, would you?
Darren:	How can the government tell people they can't have children? Three children isn't that many. We have four in my family.
Paul:	Then two of you wouldn't be allowed to live. Would you want to have to hide like Luke? That's not living.
Rachel:	I'm the third child in my family. If I lived where Luke lives, I wouldn't get to live or I would have to hide like him.
Oswaldo:	Who are the Population Police anyway? Are they like policemen in our town? They make people follow the laws?
Breann:	But what if laws are bad for people?
Oswaldo:	Laws about how many children families can have are bad, I think, don't you?
Breann:	Their government makes a lot of laws that seem bad for people—taking land, selling hogs, children. The government is always telling people what to do.
Darren:	And no pets either! We have laws but we have freedom too. I don't think Luke lives in a democracy. A democracy wouldn't have a Population Police.
Paul:	What do you think will happen now that houses are being built behind them? It feels like something bad is going to happen.

Rachel:	Even Luke said that. Well actually the author told us that Luke felt that way.
Breann:	Luke's life is getting worse with the building of the houses. What do you think about the way his parents are acting?
Paul:	At first I thought his dad way just mean, but the more I read the more I thought that he must be very angry at the government. . . .

The conversation continues in this way for 15 to 20 minutes and ends with students checking the next reading assignment and meeting date. Similar to book club meetings, literature circle talk is influenced by notes that students have made in their literature or sticky note logs. In a book club, students make daily entries before their club meets and use the log to guide the discussion. In a literature circle, students have more freedom to use their log as it fits their purposes as readers. Consequently, topics of discussion may be both in readers' minds and written in their logs. When discussion reaches this level, it becomes more adultlike and natural.

After the circle meeting, Melodia asks students to evaluate their preparation and participation. Students use a simple form the class developed when literature circles were first introduced (see Figure 5.13). With independence as a goal, students must learn to evaluate and correct their own behavior.

COMMUNITY SHARING SESSIONS

To bring closure each day, the class gathers to share responses to books and new insights as readers and writers. This session is quite similar to the closing session for a book club approach, except that students are reading a variety of books and this session provides an opportunity for them to make intertextual connections, especially with any core books they may have in common. In Melodia's class, *Hatchet* is a core book. One of Melodia's tasks is to help students extend their understanding of the theme "Meeting the Challenge" by making connections between texts.

Orchestrating this session takes planning. Melodia asks students to indicate on a signup sheet when they wish to use class time to share response projects. She also keeps track of scheduled literature circle meetings and invites groups to share outcomes with the class, encouraging intertextual connections.

You have been introduced to two approaches to small-group literature study, book clubs and literature circles. What similarities and differences do you find in these two approaches when you compare their components, organization, teacher's role, and students' role? Compare your ideas with a colleague's.

• • •

The components of these two approaches are similar, though they may have different names. Both include some form of reading (silent reading, partner reading, and choral reading), writing (literature logs), discussion (small-group and whole-class sessions), and instruction (whole-class and flexible groups).

The overall organization is also similar. Both begin and end with whole-group meetings, the first usually including instruction that relates to either procedures, literature, or strategies. The final meeting is a sharing session, focused on what occurred in the small-group discussions. Reading, writing, and small-group discussions during work time occur in slightly different ways:

- *Literature circles.* Work time is flexible. Small groups are not doing the same things each day, and students make more decisions about the pace of their work.
- *Book clubs.* Each component occurs daily, for varying amounts of time. Although the teacher sets up the amount of reading for each day, students decide how they will accomplish it. Writing in the literature log is typically student directed, but occasionally the teacher may provide a writing prompt. Students direct book club discussions with the aid of literature log entries.

The teacher's role in both book clubs and literature circles is as a facilitator who structures the environment for learning, then steps back to let children learn how to take control of their learning. There is a slightly higher degree of teacher-initiated structure in a book club approach than with literature circles.

The students' role is more self-directed in a literature circle approach than in book clubs. Both approaches encourage independence, and structure the learning environment for students to take control of their learning.

● ● ●

RESPECTING DIVERSITY IN BOOK CLUBS AND LITERATURE CIRCLES

Book clubs and literature circles provide opportunities for students to demonstrate their independence in learning. What will independence look like in a middle grade classroom? With varying backgrounds of experience both in and out of school, students are certain to bring diversity in the ways they practice their independence.

TEACH DECISION MAKING

When given a choice, students will not always choose in ways that you might wish. We must be prepared to respect their choices and help them consider both the basis for their choices and the possibilities they did not select. Our instruction and interaction with students should help them learn that choice is a matter of identifying possibilities, considering the viability of each possibility, and making effective decisions.

When we set the pacing of group reading, we must allow for students' ability to successfully meet that pace. Sufficient reading time for each individual must be the top priority, even if it means reducing time spent on other supporting activities. Students who need extra time should have the choice of reading the literature study book during independent reading, if available. In addition, providing extra copies of books for out-of-class reading supports those students who need extended reading time. We must also plan to help group members learn to support one another.

SELECT A VARIETY OF LITERATURE

As we select books for small-group study, we should be aware of student interests and reading levels, offering if possible something of interest for everyone. While personal reading interests are provided for during independent reading, instructional materials should also have appeal for students to sustain their reading. This is particularly true for chapter books.

The manner in which we prepare students for selecting a book for small-group study is also important. Book talks and making books available beforehand for examination can help students choose books that will meet their needs and interests.

ASSESSMENT AND EVALUATION IN BOOK CLUBS AND LITERATURE CIRCLES

In Chapter 4 we considered assessment and evaluation issues that are central to any form of literature-based instruction. In this section we add to that discussion purposes for evaluation in literature study that emphasize small groups and increased independence.

TEACHER'S ASSESSMENT PORTFOLIO

We may document student growth during small-group literature study through observation, informal conferences, and samples of student work. Hill (1995), who works with teachers using a literature circle approach, suggests that monitoring student progress in small groups makes it possible for teachers to do the following:

- Provide immediate feedback to students.
- Plan for instruction.
- Assess students as readers and writers.
- Prepare progress reports for parents and students.
- Document student performance and growth.

Our purposes for instruction will ultimately determine how we choose to evaluate our students.

Observation and Informal Conferences.   A primary purpose for moving from whole-class literature study to book clubs and literature circles is to provide opportunities for students to make more decisions about their own reading and discussion of texts. These are the two areas on which we will focus as we make anecdotal notes.

In Lou's and Melodia's classrooms, students spend a great deal of time reading to prepare for book club and literature circle discussions. After whole-class lessons on selecting appropriate reading materials, developing group reading plans, and becoming aware of pacing one's own reading, Lou and Melodia must observe to see which behaviors students are able to use effectively and which require more development and support.

During reading time, Melodia and Lou observe how students choose to complete their daily reading. They encourage silent reading and provide additional support to students who have difficulty.

Lou joins one or two book club groups each day as an observer and note taker. As Lou listens in on discussions, he gathers ideas about students' engagement with the text and sees areas in which they might need support. He looks for behaviors such as sharing personal feelings and connections, discussing main points in a text, sharing the contents of literature logs, responding to others' ideas, consulting the text to support thinking, helping to clarify points of confusion, and making connections within and across texts or with the author.

He jots notes on a group record sheet (see Figure 5.11) which allows him to see trends across members of a group. The form he uses has space for five students across because most of the book clubs in his classroom have either four or five members. Melodia uses a similar procedure with literature circles.

When students select a literature circle text, Melodia observes the level of student engagement and watches for body language that suggests students' attitudes toward reading. In addition, Melodia visits with students about their choice of text and how the reading is progressing. She initially writes her observations on a grid but eventually transfers them to individual forms (see Figure 5.12) and places them in her assessment portfolio.

Samples of Student Work.   At the end of each literature study, Melodia and Lou select at least two pieces of student work to copy and place in the assessment portfolio that they keep for each student. They select work that shows an area of strength and an area that warrants attention. Literature logs, along with a list of what students have read in literature circles, serve to chronicle day-to-day work. Samples of response projects in the form of photos, creative writing, artwork, and audio- or videotapes broaden understanding of what is possible for a student. Samples of work are excellent ways to document progress that you can share with parents and administrators.

With each sample that Lou and Melodia select for placement in the assessment portfolio, they write a brief note stating their reasons for selecting the piece, emphasizing what they believe it shows about the student's progress.

STUDENT LEARNING PORTFOLIO

Just as teachers select pieces of work to represent a range of what they feel a student knows and can do during each grading period, students also select work they feel represents their learning. Students select samples of work from their literature logs, response projects, and

■ **FIGURE 5.11**

Recording observations of literature discussions

Date ___10/15___   Book Title ___Among the Hidden by Margaret Haddix___

Breann	Darren	Oswaldo	Paul	Rachel
Discussion leader today. Made sure everyone was ready. Asked questions to keep discussion going.	Made personal connections to own family. Made connections to prior knowledge about a democracy.	Asked questions to get clarification. Interested in knowing what peers think.	Showed motivation to make sense of the text. Asked questions of peers, interested in their ideas. Feeling the mood/tone of the text.	Made personal connections between text and her life. Sensed who was telling the story/point of view.

Book club/literature
circle evaluation form

Literature Study: _Among the Hidden_   Name _____

Reading:	Usually	Sometimes	Rarely
• Shows positive attitude toward reading	___	___	___
• Completes reading for group meetings	___	___	___
• Is learning to self-pace reading	___	___	___

Comments:

Writing:	Usually	Sometimes	Rarely
• Shows positive attitude toward written response	___	___	___
• Completes written response for group meetings	___	___	___
• Responds in a variety of ways	___	___	___

Comments:

Discussion:	Usually	Sometimes	Rarely
• Shares personal feelings and connections	___	___	___
• Discusses main points of text	___	___	___
• Shares literature log	___	___	___
• Consults text for support	___	___	___
• Responds to ideas of others	___	___	___
• Clarifies points of confusion	___	___	___
• Makes connections within and across texts	___	___	___
• Makes connections with author	___	___	___
• Responds to ideas of others	___	___	___
• Uses self-evaluation to improve participation	___	___	___

Comments:

■ FIGURE 5.13

Evaluation of
small-group discussion

Evaluating Our Small-Group Discussion

Name _____ Date _____

Book Title: _____

Overall our discussion today was _____
_____
_____

My participation in the group was _____
_____
_____

Something I learned in our discussion is _____
_____
_____

The best part of our discussion was _____
_____
_____

To help our discussion be more effective and interesting, I should _____
_____
_____

and our group should _____
_____
_____

I would also like to say that _____
_____
_____

a variety of self-evaluation forms. Lou and Melodia urge students to select samples of work that show different kinds of growth.

Student Self-Evaluation.   Throughout small-group literature study in Lou's sixth-grade and Melodia's sixth- and seventh-grade classrooms, students engage in a variety of activities in which they make decisions about their own behavior and performance. Even though middle grade students have several years of experience in school, these teachers do not assume that students have had much experience in self-evaluation. They realize that students need continuous guidance in this area. Students can learn how to evaluate themselves by considering criteria appropriate for their tasks and by learning to set goals for themselves.

Numerous opportunities for goal setting and self-evaluation exist in both the book club and literature circle approaches:

- After small-group meetings, Melodia asks each student to take a few moments to reflect on the dynamics of the group and whether it functions effectively. During one of the whole-class instruction sessions, Melodia and the students developed an open-ended form for recording each person's ideas (see Figure 5.13). Over the course of the school year, the class uses the form to consider the need for revisions.

- To help students learn from their own behavior, Lou periodically audiotapes or videotapes small-group discussions. Students use the tapes during a small-group meeting or community sharing session to critique the effectiveness of their own behaviors. With Lou's help, each student in the group sets a goal of one behavior to focus on for the next several weeks. The group also talks about what their discussions will look and sound like when they reach their goal(s). As a reminder to themselves, students write their goals in their literature logs. Each time the small group meets, members remind each other of their goals and support one another during group activities.
- Each group paces its reading using a reading plan. In book clubs this plan is teacher developed; in literature circles the group develops it with some teacher guidance. In either case, students must then learn to pace their reading so they are ready for small-group meetings at the appointed times. Lou works with students to help them realize how they can best pace their reading.

■ TAKE A MOMENT TO REFLECT . . .

Book clubs and literature circles move students toward independence and mature reading.

■ *Book clubs:*

- Provide balance between teacher-led and student-led reading and writing.
- Include four components that occur daily in varying amounts:
  1. Reading—teacher planned, student paced;
  2. Writing—to prepare for book club meetings;
  3. Discussion—student-led small groups and teacher-led whole group; and
  4. Instruction—whole-class lessons to support book clubs.

■ *In book clubs, a class typically studies one book at a time, but may study several related books over a period of several weeks.*

■ *Book club groups are heterogeneous, with four to five students.*

■ *Book club whole-class instruction focuses on:*

- Club procedures;
- Helping students decide what to share;
- Helping students decide how to share it; and
- Developing effective reading and writing strategies.

■ *The teacher makes a book club reading plan and provides support for students to successfully complete the reading.*

■ *Students make decisions about the most effective way to complete the daily reading, including using independent reading time and "at home" reading time.*

■ *Writing in a literature log focuses on items to share and questions to ask small-group members.*

■ *Book club meetings are student led and begin with sharing log entries.*

■ *Talk in book club meetings serves several purposes:*

- Share responses;
- Discuss process of making responses;
- Discuss main points of text;
- Clarify confusions;
- Make connections within and across texts;
- Relate to personal feelings, experiences, and knowledge; and
- Connect with or critique author.

■ *Community sharing sessions follow book club meetings and provide an opportunity for all students to share their thinking about a text.*

■ *Literature circles are small-group discussions that allow students to explore their "rough draft" thinking about a book.*

■ *In literature circles, heterogeneous groups of four to six students read different, but related, texts:*

- Student choice of text determines group membership.

■ *Whole-class minilessons provide instruction in:*

- Literature circle procedures;
- Reading and writing strategies; and
- Literary knowledge needed across related texts.

■ *In literature circles, students:*

- Determine the pace of the chosen reading;
- Develop a reading plan that all group members can accomplish, with support of the group;
- Decide what, when, and how much to write in response to their reading and for group sharing; and
- Consult logs and texts as they develop their discussion.

■ *Flexible strategy groups occur as needed to address specific needs for individuals and small groups.*

■ *Informal conferences occur as needed for teachers to monitor student progress.*

■ *Community sharing sessions occur at the end of a work time and provide opportunity for students to share responses to texts.*

■ *Teachers respect diversity by:*

- Teaching decision making; and
- Using a variety of literature that appeals to the needs and interests of all students.

■ *To monitor each student's progress, teachers document:*

- Observed behaviors; and
- Representative samples of work showing strengths and needs for an assessment portfolio.

■ *Students evaluate their own growth and performance:*

- Select samples of work.
- Provide justification for the selection.
- Place items in their learning portfolio.

■ REFERENCES

Atwell, N. (1998). *In the middle: Writing, reading and learning with adolescents* (2nd ed.). Portsmouth, NH: Heinemann.

Brown, K. (1995). Going with the flow: Getting back on course when literature circles flounder. In B. C. Hill, N. J. Johnson, & K. L. S. Noe (Eds.), *Literature circles and response* (pp. 85–93). Norwood, MA: Christopher Gordon Publishers.

Goatley, V. J., Brock, C. H., & Raphael, T. E. (1995). Diverse learners participating in regular education "book clubs." *Reading Research Quarterly, 30,* 352–380.

Hill, B. C. (1995). Literature circles: Assessment and evaluation. In B. C. Hill, N. J. Johnson, & K. L. S. Noe (Eds.), *Literature circles and response* (pp. 167–198). Norwood, MA: Christopher Gordon Publishers.

Holdaway, D. (1980). *Independence in reading.* Portsmouth, NH: Heinemann.

Langer, J. A. (1995). *Envisioning literature: Literacy understanding and literature instruction.* New York: Teachers College Press.

McMahon, S. I. (1991, April). *Book club: How written and oral discourse influence the development of ideas as children respond to literature.* Paper presented at the annual meeting of the American Educational Research Association, Chicago.

Oldfather, P. (1995). Commentary: What's needed to maintain and extend motivation for literacy in the middle grades. *Journal of Reading, 38*(6), 420–422.

Owens, S. (1995). Treasures in the attic: Building the foundation for literature circles. In B. C. Hill, N. J. Johnson, & K. L. S. Noe (Eds.), *Literature circles and response* (pp. 1–12). Norwood, MA: Christopher Gordon Publishers.

Pardo, L. S. (1992, December). *Accommodating diversity in the elementary classroom: A look at literature-based instruction in an inner city school.* Paper presented at the meeting of the National Reading Conference, San Antonio, TX.

Peterson, R., & Eeds, M. (1990). *Grand conversations: Literature groups in action.* Richmond Hill, Ontario: Scholastic-TAB.

Raphael, T. E., Goatley, V. J., McMahon, S. I., & Woodman, D. A. (1992). Teaching literacy through student book clubs: A first year teacher's experience. In B. E. Cullinan (Ed.), *Literature across the curriculum: Making it happen* (pp. 137–152). Newark, DE: International Reading Association.

Raphael, T. E., Kehus, M., & Damphousser, K. (2001). *Book club for middle school.* Lawrence, MA: Small Planet Communications.

Raphael, T. E., & McMahon, S. I. (1994). "Book clubs": An alternative framework for reading instruction. *The Reading Teacher, 48,* 102–116.

Raphael, T. E., McMahon, S. I., Goatley, V. J., Bentley, J. L., Boyd, F. B., Pardo, L. S., & Woodman, D. A. (1992). Research directions: Literature and discussion in the reading program. *Language Arts, 69,* 55–61.

Redman, P. (1995). Finding a balance: Literature circles and "teaching reading." In B. C. Hill, N. J. Johnson, & K. L. S. Noe (Eds.), *Literature circles and response* (pp. 55–70). Norwood, MA: Christopher Gordon Publishers.

Scott, J., & Wells, J. (1998). Readers take responsibility: Literature circles and the growth of critical thinking. In K. Beers & B. G. Samuels (Eds.), *Intro focus: Understanding and creating middle school readers* (pp. 177–197). Norwood, MA: Christopher Gordon Publishers.

Short, K. (1986). *Literacy as a collaborative experience.* Unpublished doctoral dissertation, Indiana University, Bloomington, IN.

Short, K. (1995). Foreword. In B. C. Hill, N. J. Johnson, & K. L. S. Noe (Eds.), *Literature circles and response* (pp. ix–xii). Norwood, MA: Christopher Gordon Publishers.

■ CHILDREN'S LITERATURE

Adler, D. A. (1989). *We remember the Holocaust*. New York: Trumpet Brooks.

Fritz, Jean (1987). *Shh! We're writing the constitution*. New York: Scholastic.

Haddix, M. P. (1998). *Among the hidden*. New York: Aladdin Paperbacks.

Hahn, M. D. (1995). *A time for Andrew: A ghost story*. New York: Clarion.

Mohr, N. (1979). *Felita*. New York: Bantam Doubleday Dell.

O'Dell, S., & Hall, E. (1992). *Thunder rolling in the mountains*. New York: Bantam Doubleday Dell.

Paterson, K. (1978). *The great Gilly Hopkins*. New York: Harper & Row.

Paulsen, G. (1999). *Hatchet*. New York: Viking Penguin.

Speare, E. G. (1983). *The sign of the beaver*. New York: Houghton Mifflin.

6

Independent Reading and Reader's Workshop Individualizing Literature Study

In this chapter . . .

We consider ways in which self-selected independent reading and writing help middle grade students mature as readers. Our study includes:

- Visiting two classrooms that practice reader's workshop: a self-contained fifth grade and a seventh- and eighth-grade middle scho[ol] reading class,

- The components of reader's workshop: time, choice, structure, response, and community,

- What teachers must do to prepare for reader's workshop, and

- How to organize the classroom, including book selection, independent reading, conferencing, response activities, and adequate instructional support.

Focus Literature . . .

A Time for Andrew: A Ghost Story by Mary Downing Hahn, Clarion Publishers, New York, 1995.

Looking into Classrooms . . .

As the seventh-grade students enter the classroom, they retrieve their literature logs from the orange bin near the door and visit with classmates as they settle into their desks. Bell tones on the intercom signal the beginning of second period. Kristen waits for the students to settle, then asks, "How does a mystery writer create a mysterious mood?" She takes responses, then says, "You have been reading a variety of mysteries for the past three weeks. As I conference with each of you and listen to your comments about your books, you seem to be noticing that one thing mystery writers do is create a mood that, as Brandon said the other day, 'has MYSTERY written all over it.' "

Putting Theory into Practice

In addition to read-alouds, independent reading is one of the most important ways that students can spend their time if they are to become fluent, competent readers (Allington, 2001; Center for the Study of Reading, 1990). Regardless of our approach to reading instruction, our students should have substantial amounts of time to read independently every day, for the following reasons:

- The more that words pass in front of a reader's eyes, the greater the opportunity that individual has to become a better reader (Allington, 1977).

- One-third or more of vocabulary growth can be accounted for by independent reading (Center for the Study of Reading, 1990).

- Reading strategies improve significantly if students read independently for at least 10 minutes per day or 1 hour per week (Anderson, Heibert, Scott, & Wilkinson, 1985).

- Students' attitudes toward reading improve through self-selected independent reading (Tunnel & Jacobs 1989).

Independent reading may occur in the classroom or at home, but it must occur!

ENCOURAGING INDEPENDENCE IN READING

Every middle grade teacher can encourage independent reading in the following ways:

- Provide blocks of time for independent reading.
- Use knowledge of what motivates students.
- Support self-monitoring behaviors.

TIME TO READ

Although students in the middle grades have participated in reading instruction for 4 to 8 years, many are not yet fluent, independent readers. To become independent, students must frequently practice reading strategies. Some middle grade students read only when it is assigned and, even then, may still not complete the reading assignment. Some students may never have experienced "reading time" in school as a connected block of time devoted just to reading. For some students, "reading" has meant a number of short periods of instruction, each filled with a different activity.

To encourage independent reading, then, our first step must be to provide ample blocks of reading time, encouraging students to sink into meaningful independent reading:

- *Provide time each day for independent reading.* Also called SSR (sustained silent reading) or DEAR (drop everything and read), everyone in the classroom reads silently for a specified period of time in books of their own choice. In content area classes in middle school, we may provide independent reading time in books related to topics the class is studying. The homeroom advisory period in the middle school also can frequently be devoted to independent reading.

- *Provide time for self-selected independent reading during periods of "work time" in the classroom.* Encourage independent reading in topics of interest or units of study, rather than assigning additional paper-and-pencil activities.

- *Establish a reading program with independent reading at the center of instruction.* We can organize literature study so that students spend large amounts of time reading independently each day.

PERSONAL MOTIVATION

To become independent readers, students must be motivated to read (Holdaway, 1980). When middle grade students look at school reading tasks, do they see tasks that are worthy of their sustained effort? Can they see themselves moving toward independence as readers?

Students who are highly motivated to learn a task have an incredible internal drive that is often able to overcome any initial setbacks encountered in new learning experiences (Holdaway, 1980). Students can sustain themselves when they see that the desired task is worth learning and can see themselves making progress toward independence.

What choices concerning independent reading would motivate middle grade students? To answer this question, we must consider the nature of middle grade students in general (see Chapter 1) and, in particular, their individual needs and interests. Our students must be able to see that their needs and interests are at the heart of classroom activities.

First, and most important, students should freely choose the texts they will read. The most motivating aspect of reading is certainly the personal meaning that individuals construct. Students are likely to find more meaning in books they choose themselves. Second, we should allow our students to choose whether and how they share with others their personal responses to books read for pleasure. As adults, we are able to choose whether we will share our response to independent reading. Students should have a similar choice. If they must always be accountable to someone other than themselves for their reading, when will their reading behavior be under their control or totally for pleasure?

SELF-MONITORING

To become independent readers, students must learn to develop their natural desire to monitor and critique their own reading performance (Holdaway, 1980). Students are able to independently monitor their own reading when their ability to make meaning is high. This is most likely to occur when reading materials are suited to a student's level of performance and desire to read. If texts are difficult, learning how to monitor one's own reading is too great a challenge and becomes self-defeating.

Your classroom reading program can support both students' sense of gaining independence, and their drive to be more independent, by providing interesting low-challenge material (material at student's independent reading level—see Chapter 2—in which their word recognition and understanding of the material is almost perfect) to build students' sense of confidence and independence.

GETTING STARTED WITH INDEPENDENT READING

Independent reading will not happen automatically in our classrooms. We must plan for it just as we plan other parts of the literacy program. Students know whether or not independent reading is really important by the way that we do the following:

- Establish a "reading" environment in the classroom.
- Provide a consistent and predictable time for independent reading.
- Make available a variety of reading materials to meet their needs and interests, including both narrative and information.

- Provide an attractive and functional place where they can have access to reading materials.
- Promote independence through self-selection.

ESTABLISH A READING ENVIRONMENT

The environment that we establish in our classroom should say "Readers live here." The classroom environment in which students live for a good part of their day should promote reading. Is there a class library that houses a variety of reading materials? Inviting displays that promote reading? Displays of student work that show the types of reading experiences they are having?

When students watch us, will they see someone who cares about reading? Will we encourage students to share their reading? Will we share our own reading with students? The reading atmosphere in our classroom shows the way that we value reading.

To promote initial interest, we may need to "sell" books to some of our students. Just because we find great books and display them in the classroom doesn't mean that students will become independent readers. We can help students be interested in books by making special introductions for new books. As a part of each read-aloud time, we can give a short talk about a new book, describing a few highlights or a summary, or pose an interesting situation that students can explore by reading the book. For chapter books, we can read part of an exciting event aloud as an enticement.

Somewhere in the classroom we should make a display of books around special topics being studied. We can then introduce the display and highlight a few books each day. Students can share what they are finding in the books in the display.

CONSISTENT AND PREDICTABLE TIME TO READ

Acquiring competence is a matter of practice over time. How much practice do middle grade students need to develop as independent readers? It will vary. Some students will read outside of school. Some students will not require as much reading practice as others. Some students may slow their own progress because they continue to select books that are almost too challenging so they can "look" like their peers.

We can respond to students' varying needs for reading time by doing the following:

- Provide a set time each day for everyone to read independently.
- Provide flexible time for choosing independent reading during work periods.
- Encourage at-home reading as a part of homework assignments.

By the middle grades, students should easily be able to sustain their reading for 30 to 45 minutes. Sustained reading, however, requires students to build stamina. Students who have not had the opportunity for sustained reading will need time and patient guidance in learning how readers keep their own reading going.

We can also build independent reading time each day by making it a choice during such instructional blocks as reading/language arts or content area activities. Devoting instructional time to independent reading, including books about a current topic of study, allows students more practice time.

Teachers who use a reader's workshop approach (discussed in the latter part of this chapter) devote a great deal of instructional time to independent reading. Reader's workshops often combine independent reading with instructional reading time to have longer blocks for student-selected independent reading.

In the hustle and bustle of the school day it is easy to let independent reading time slip away. If we want to begin to equalize differences between students' background experiences with books, we must provide time for students to read.

VARIETY OF READING MATERIALS

Students bring a variety of interests into the classroom. Will they find books to feed those interests in the classroom or school library? Students have varied reading abilities. Will they find materials to fit their levels of independence? If we believe that reading is important and we want students to read, then we must provide interesting and varied materials.

In a well-stocked classroom library, we need a minimum of 20 to 25 books per student. To begin to build a classroom library, we can check out class sets from both the school and public libraries. Class sets, typically 30 to 40 books, can be kept for 3 to 4 weeks. For students who are reading primarily picture books, we may need to circulate books more frequently. When it is time for new books, we can involve students in deciding which books to recycle.

School book clubs are another good source of inexpensive books. At the beginning of each school year we may wish to ask parents if they would be willing to buy three or four books from book clubs for the class library during the school year, or one book every 2 or 3 months. Many parents will be willing to do this. Book club prices are usually lower than those of bookstores. The class may also conduct fundraisers to buy books with the consent of the school administration.

In the class library we might want to acquire duplicate copies of some books. Some students enjoy reading the same book a friend is reading. Duplicate copies provide an opportunity for students to initiate their own literature discussions with someone who has read or is reading the same book.

EASY ACCESS TO READING MATERIALS

The classroom library should invite students to want to read. The area doesn't have to be large, but it does need to be inviting. My preference was usually to have the class library near a wall area or bulletin board where we could make a display about a featured author, a special day like Earth Day, or other topics of study for which books were available. Books were featured in other areas of the room also, but I gave particular emphasis to books in the library area.

In the early part of the school year and throughout, students can help decide how to make the library area an attractive place they like to visit. Students' involvement in planning increases their sense of ownership in the classroom.

TEACH SELF-SELECTION

We cannot assume that middle grade students are proficient at selecting appropriate reading materials just because they have been in school for a number of years. To know our students as independent readers, it is wise to discuss their interests and to observe their processes of selecting reading materials.

We can also learn about students' interests through interest inventories, interviews, and journal entries. Interest inventories are helpful in gathering initial personal information about students. Students can individually respond in writing on a form such as those shown later in Figures 6.11 and 6.12. If time is available, we may prefer to use the items from the interest inventory and interview students or have students interview each other. Face-to-face interactions typically provide opportunities for clarifying responses or probing other areas of interest indicated by a student's response.

When we know students' interests, we can suggest particular books or authors, and may order class reading materials targeted to those interests. Book displays and sharing opportunities can also highlight books of interest to particular students.

We can also make better use of the school library by providing to the media specialist/librarian a list of students' interests. The librarian may then highlight a variety of relevant books during library visits.

The difficulty level of books is another issue in selection. Ideally, students should read books that are "just right" for them. When a student selects a book she thinks she would like to read, encourage her to try it out first to see how well it suits her. Consider the "3–5 test": While the student is reading the first page or two (approximately 100 words) ask her to tuck away a finger every time she comes to an unknown word. If she bends enough fingers to drop the book, it might be too difficult for her. Then she must decide if she is willing to "work" at reading the book. Students who want to read particular books badly enough, even if they might be difficult, should be allowed to try. How will students become independent if we always try to control their choices?

Setting up and periodically restocking the classroom library presents an excellent opportunity to discuss selecting books and to practice with support. We may discuss with students about reading easy, just right, and hard books. Students should consider the amount of energy it takes to read a hard book. We can have students browse and select a book they think is "easy" for them, one that is "just right," and another that is "hard." Students can discuss how they came to that conclusion and teach each other about how they select books. The success of independent reading rests heavily on students being able to self-select appropriately.

YOUR TURN...

How will you establish an environment that encourages independent reading in your classroom? Can you explain the basis for your decisions?

• • •

USING INDEPENDENT READING AS READER'S WORKSHOP

We turn our attention now to ways in which self-selected independent reading can become the basis for reading instruction in our classroom. Our study will include:

- Visiting two classrooms that practice reader's workshop, a self-contained fifth grade, and a seventh- and eighth-grade middle school reading class;
- The components of reader's workshop: time, choice, structure, response, and community;
- What teachers must do to prepare for reader's workshop; and
- How to organize the classroom, including book selection, independent reading, conferencing, response activities, and adequate instructional support.

A GLIMPSE INTO A READER'S WORKSHOP

Kristen is a first-year developmental reading teacher. On most any day, if we visited one of her seventh- or eighth-grade reading classes at a local middle school, we would notice a hush fall over the room as students settle into the quiet reading period that is part of her reader's workshop. On this particular day in early November, the students are immersed in a study of mysteries. Kristen continues the discussion she began in the Looking into Classrooms section at the opening of the chapter . . . .

> Kristen places a text sample on the overhead projector and continues, "The mystery I am reading is *A Time for Andrew*, by Mary Downing Hahn. It's a time-warp mystery where two boys trade places in time. In the very first chapter though, on pages five and six, I already have the feeling that the mystery is starting. Look at what the author writes and listen to her words. Can you feel the mysterious mood she is creating?" Kristen reads the passage aloud in a mysterious tone. Following the reading, the class has a brief discussion about the text that Kristen shared.
>
> Kristen ends the minilesson by saying, "Each of you is reading your own mystery. How is the writer of your mystery creating a mysterious mood? When we come together for our sharing time at the end of the period, I would like for some of you to share examples of what your author is doing to create a mysterious mood.
>
> "I see that Jeff, April, Marta, and Oscar are signed up for conferences today. Which of you would like to be first? April? Okay. After I finish the four conferences, the group that is working with decoding three- and four-syllable words will meet in our group area. Is there any other business that we need to take care of as a class? Are we ready to begin the quiet reading period? Well, then let's begin. You have two minutes to get settled with your books."

Today's reader's workshop in Kristen's classroom is similar to those on most other days. Students choose books they want to read, they conference with their teacher about their reading, minilessons are provided to focus students' attention on important reading issues, silent reading is the mainstay of the program, and students are encouraged to share their responses to literature in a variety of ways (see Atwell, 1987; Five, 1988; Hagerty, 1992; Hansen, 1987).

Through self-selection of reading material, each student in Kristen's reader's workshop may be reading a different book. The students also may be beginning or ending books at different times. Self-selected reading has been used successfully with students of all ages for many years (Ducker, 1968; Holdaway, 1980; Veatch, 1959). In times past we have referred to this approach as individualized reading, but today we refer to it as reader's workshop. Regardless of its name, student choice of reading material and independent reading are at the heart.

READER'S WORKSHOP COMPONENTS

The term *reader's workshop* currently describes a range of literature-based reading programs. In this text, however, we use the term's original meaning as a reading program based on the following components: time, choice, structure, response, and community (Atwell, 1987; Five, 1988; Hagerty, 1992; Hansen, 1987; Hornsby & Sukarna, 1986).

TIME

Teachers who use reader's workshop commit consistent blocks of time to reading, particularly silent reading, because of their belief that students learn to read by reading (Holdaway, 1980).

Independent reading time is no longer considered just "recreational," it is now the center of the reading program. When time for daily independent reading is predictable, students realize that they will not be hurried and can read in more natural ways, just as adults do who enjoy pleasure reading (Hagerty, 1992). Ample time for browsing and selecting books is provided. Personal reflection is also an important part of the time devoted to reading.

In Kristen's classroom, each class period is devoted to reader's workshop. Students in this middle school meet four of their seven classes each day for 75 minutes. With the rotating block schedule, Kristen usually sees her second period students 3 days per week. Time to read remains predictable because students know that each second period will be a reader's workshop. In self-contained middle grade classrooms, teachers are usually able to have reader's workshops daily, for 1 hour or more.

CHOICE

Advocates of reader's workshops recognize the role of personal motivation in the process of making meaning with print (Hagerty, 1992; Holdaway, 1980). Learning to make appropriate personal reading choices requires practice and knowledge of the literature possibilities. Choice is a joint responsibility of both the student and teacher. Students must come to know both themselves as readers and their personal preferences for topic and style. Teachers must come to know their students' interests, make quality literature readily available, and introduce students to the possibilities in that literature.

Before Kristen began the study of mysteries, she collected 117 mysteries from her personal book collection, the school library, and each public library branch, representing a range of subgenres (mostly contemporary, historical, and fantasy), writing styles, and reading levels. Kristen managed to find multiple copies of a few books, knowing that many of her students enjoy reading the same book as a friend.

Her students' reading interests and experiences vary widely. Their reading levels range from third to eleventh grade, with most students falling somewhere between the sixth- and ninth-grade level. Since the beginning of the year, Kristen and the students have talked about making good book choices and knowing when a choice is "right" for the individual. In addition, students have completed interest inventories (see Chapter 5) and talk often with Kristen about their reading interests.

STRUCTURE

Reader's workshop requires a well-planned organization and consistency on which students can count (Hagerty, 1992). The teacher's role is that of guide and facilitator, anticipating the type and degree of support students will need to become independent readers. Reader's workshop moves from whole-group sessions to a work time, then back to the whole group for sharing. Teachers provide mediated instruction both to the class and to small groups. Unlike the previous workshop formats we have discussed, teachers also schedule individual conferences with students to monitor and evaluate their progress.

Kristen uses a predictable structure for reader's workshop. A large wall chart shows how the blocks of time are allocated. Each day Kristen posts a workshop agenda on the board. Students know who is in conference, if there are small-group meetings, if someone is presenting a project, and so on. The class uses planning sessions during each whole-group meeting to clarify agenda items. Kristen provides instructional support through minilessons and small-group strategy instruction, individual conferences and help sessions, and whole-class discussions.

RESPONSE

Reader's workshop encourages readers to explore and extend their individual responses to literature as a part of becoming independent readers. Research on reader-response theories (Beach, 1993; Rosenblatt, 1978) has shown that it is a reader's personal response to literature that encourages that reader to return to literature experiences. Response comes from the reader and cannot be controlled by an outside force. (For further discussion of reader response, refer to Chapter 3.)

Kristen's students have opportunities for response through conferences, literature logs, projects, and group sharing. Students meet regularly with Kristen to share responses to their reading. She uses this time to let students teach her about their views of the literature.

Literature logs are typically open responses that the student directs. Occasionally, Kristen will ask students to focus their response on an issue that the class is studying. During the mystery unit, students critique their mystery according to criteria that the class decides are important. In open responses, students usually choose to direct their responses toward issues in class discussions and minilessons.

Students may choose to complete an individual or group project as a response to a text. While Kristen requires two projects each 9 weeks, the students decide when they will do the projects and which books they will use. Projects may be rehearsed readings, reader's theater, a model or other art, a book talk, an innovation of the author's writing style, or the like.

A final form of response available for Kristen's students is group sharing. In this classroom, groups may be a few peers or the entire class. Students often choose to read the same book as a friend. Kristen encourages those students to get together and share their responses to the text. Another form of small-group sharing comes when students read different books but get together to discuss a common characteristic, such as plot development or writing style. During the mystery unit, students who read different books were able to share their ideas about the qualities of a good mystery. Finally, each reader's workshop ends with a community sharing session, giving students a forum for sharing both completed projects and responses to their current reading.

COMMUNITY

In a reader's workshop, students will teach each other what they know if given the opportunity and an environment that supports interaction, collaboration, and risk taking. We are well aware of the power of interaction and collaboration in learning (Johnson, 1981; Slavin, Madden, Karweit, Dolan, & Wasik, 1991; Vygotsky, 1962). Sharing sessions and cooperative work time encourage students to learn to depend on and learn from each other. The teacher is a model for how to listen to and respect the ideas of others. A sense of community in a classroom creates the feeling that everyone in the room is both teacher and learner, with knowledge to share (Hagerty, 1992). Remember, everything we know as individuals was not taught directly to us. Much of what we know we taught ourselves or learned by observing and interacting informally with more knowledgeable others. Reader's workshop encourages students to become teachers, teaching themselves and each other.

Students clearly feel the open and accepting atmosphere in Kristen's classroom. Throughout each class period, students encourage and support one another, just as Kristen provides support to each of them. Multiple opportunities for sharing their ideas encourage students to be both learners and teachers, and Kristen fosters this community atmosphere.

Time, choice, structure, response, and community—five components are needed to make reader's workshop successful. But the most important element is *you*, the teacher! A successful reader's workshop is not possible unless you have a clear understanding of your students and of the possibilities of literature.

READER'S WORKSHOP IN FIFTH GRADE

To illustrate the possibilities of reader's workshop, teacher Kim Muncy describes its operation in her fifth-grade class during the first full year of implementation. As you read Kim's story, consider the organizational issues involved in this individualized approach to literature-based reading.

Kim narrates:

During the first 10 minutes of reader's workshop we meet as a class and I provide a mini-lesson, either on a reading strategy or something I want the students to notice about the book they are reading. This is also the time I give book talks on new books I've purchased for the class library.

For the next 20 minutes everyone reads silently in the book of their choice. I let the students choose their own books because they know best what they can and want to read. (I did an interest inventory at the beginning of the year to find out what their interests were and to get to know my students. This was a big help when I added books to the class library.) During this time I don't allow any commotion or talking because I know many students are like I am and are easily distracted by the smallest noise.

For the first 10 minutes of the silent reading time, I also read. This is my opportunity to become more familiar with children's literature, and I can model what a good reader looks like, since many of my students don't have a consistent model elsewhere.

After these first 10 minutes, I begin individual conferences with the three students who had scheduled the time the day before. Each conference lasts about 7 to 10 minutes. The students bring their book, reading record, and reading log. I keep running notes on our conference.

I usually open the conference by looking at their reading log and asking them how they're doing with it. The students know how important it is to keep their log up to date. When we discussed the reading log in class, these were some of the reasons given for why the log is important:

"So we know where we left off the day before."

"So we can see how many pages we read each day."

"So we have a place to keep interesting words if we want to use them in our writing."

"So we can remember what authors wrote which books and we can look for another book by that author in the library."

Next, I review what we talked about the last time we met by looking at the notes in my folder. Sometimes the students are really impressed that I remember the details of their story and what we talked about. I ask them to tell me about what they are reading now.

If they haven't finished the book yet and need a bit more nudging, I might ask a few questions, such as:

What do you like best about your book so far?

What can you tell me about what you've read so far?

What is happening where you are reading right now?

What do you think will happen next? Why do you think that?

How do you think the story will end?

How does the author hold your attention?

Can you relate to any of the characters? Which ones? Why?

Why do you think the author chose this particular title?

If they have finished the book, I ask different questions, questions that get at overall reactions and understanding:

What else have you read by this author or about this subject?

What reaction(s) did you have to the book? Why do you think you reacted that way?

What reaction do you think the author intended for the reader?

What problems or confusion did you have while reading? How did you solve them?

What surprised you about this book? Why did it surprise you?

How does this book compare to other books you have read?

What are you planning to read next?

At some point in the conference, the students orally read a rehearsed part of the book, and then we discuss why they chose that part and what's happening in it. I take notes the entire time and continue even after they leave. My notes are on what the book is about and how I feel they are understanding what they are reading, as well as how capably they answer my nudging questions.

I just started being aware of the compliments I give the students after they read. I noticed that they leave the conference with smiles on their faces! I try to be specific, and compliment students appropriately:

I noticed how you self-corrected when you realized the reading didn't make sense. Good readers do that.

You use great voice when you read, and it's interesting to listen to you read. Good readers do that.

I noticed you emphasized important words in your story. Good readers do that.

Sometimes I make a suggestion that seems appropriate for that particular student:

As you finish this book, you might think about or try to . . . .

As you write in your reading log, you might think about or try to . . . .

When you come to words that you're not sure about, you might think about or try to . . . .

When you're ready to choose another book, you might think about or try to . . . .

After about 20 minutes of silent reading, the students have the option of working on a reading activity of their choice for the next 10 minutes. They may also continue to read silently, which is what most of my students choose. I don't force an activity after every book because I believe that students will read more if they know they have the freedom to read without having to do an activity. Isn't that really the point of reading, anyway? I believe they learn to read more by reading, not by doing extension activities. Plus, they might feel that some books are not worth the time involved in doing an extension activity.

After the activity time, I ask them to fill out their reading logs for the day. On a form that I provide [see Figure 6.5, presented later in this chapter], they record the dates they began and completed the book, number of pages read each day, its title, author, and genre, interesting words, comments, and their future plans for activities or reading. At this time I do not ask for a great deal of written response because I want students to spend more time reading, enough to really get absorbed in their books. Response comes in conferences and group discussions.

The next 10 minutes or so is share time. It brings closure to the day's workshop activities. The three students I confer with have the opportunity to share with their peers anything related to their books. This time helps them become independent readers because they are encouraged to have their own thoughts, feelings, and ideas about a particular book without anyone judging their reasons for expressing a particular idea. The audience has the chance to respond, which helps form a sense of community in this classroom.

It seems that lately students are challenging the ideas of those who are sharing by asking them why they feel a certain way about a book. Many students' answers are so direct and confident that they really make me believe they are becoming stronger readers.

If there is extra time during the share session I'll ask if anyone tried something new or learned something new that day. I also ask if anyone found an interesting word. Lately, the interesting words are quite abundant. If the students want to share an interesting word or a word that they don't understand, they must have written it in their reading log along with the page number they found it on. They share the word with the group in what I call "before, during, and after" context. They have to read the sentence that comes before the word, the sentence the word is in, and the sentence that comes after. The audience tries to figure out what the word means in context, and most of the time, they do. When someone is able to come up with the definition, we discuss how they figured it out.

There are now so many people who want to share an interesting word that I had to limit it to five a day. Some of the kids now write their interesting words on a piece of sentence strip paper and tape it on our word wall to share with others who might want to use it in writer's workshop.

For evaluation, I check their reading logs periodically, looking for effort as far as keeping it complete and up to date. What I'm finding out, though, is how many times I have to go over how to properly fill out the record form. I'm attributing this to the fact that maybe those students truly don't understand the reason for even having a reading log, and therefore they don't feel it is important.

I also ask that they complete four projects of their choice on books of their choice each 12 weeks. If they don't complete four books in 12 weeks, and I have some students who don't, I modify the evaluation to suit their needs and let them know that it's more important for them to read than to do projects. Students need to know they can pace themselves. They need to find the rhythm and speed that is best for them as readers.

ORGANIZING A READER'S WORKSHOP

As we can see from the descriptions of Kim's and Kristen's classrooms, a reader's workshop is a cohesive block of instructional time that includes both whole-group and independent/ small-group work periods. It requires a (preferably continuous, uninterrupted) block of time, usually of an hour or more, to allow students ample time for sustained silent reading. Figure 6.1 outlines the components of a reader's workshop. Compare this outline to Kristen's and Kim's programs. Although reader's workshop practice will vary from classroom to classroom, the five components—time, choice, structure, response, and community—form the foundation of all decisions teachers make as they modify the workshop to fit their students.

■ **FIGURE 6.1**

Overview of reader's workshop

Whole Group:
(10–15 minutes)
	• Community opening
	• Whole-class instruction
	    -Minilessons
	    -Workshop procedures
	    -Literary knowledge
	    -Reading strategies
	• Book talks
	• Plans for the day

Work Time:
(35–50 minutes)
	• Quiet reading period
	• Conferences
	• Response activities
	    -Literature log
	    -Small-group sharing
	        Same text
	        Related texts
	    -Independent projects
	        Art, drama, writing, readings
	• Flexible strategy groups
	• Individual help/questions
	• Making new selections

Whole Group:
(10–20 minutes)
	• Community sharing session
	    -Projects
	    -Small-group discussions
	    -Book talks
	• Evaluate the day
	• Plan for tomorrow

PREPARING FOR READER'S WORKSHOP

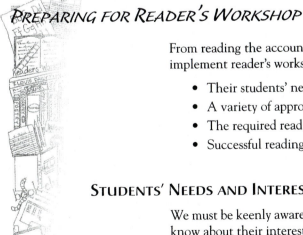

From reading the accounts of Kristen's and Kim's classrooms, we know that teachers who implement reader's workshop must be very familiar with the following:

- Their students' needs and interests,
- A variety of appropriate literature,
- The required reading/language arts curriculum standards, and
- Successful reading behaviors and attitudes.

STUDENTS' NEEDS AND INTERESTS

We must be keenly aware of our students for reader's workshop to be successful. We should know about their interests inside and outside school, and know them as readers. Using an interest inventory, as Kim did with her fifth-grade class, is a start (see Figures 6.11 and 6.12

in the assessment section at the end of this chapter). Observing students during silent reading, response, sharing, and conference activities also provides us with assessment information that will help us make appropriate group and individual instructional decisions. To truly individualize literature instruction, we must be able to document each student's progress. Careful record keeping can help us feel confident of our knowledge of students as individuals and of their growth as readers. We document students' knowledge and skill levels by using informal reading inventories or running records, conference notes, and students' reading/writing portfolios, projects, and other responses.

A VARIETY OF APPROPRIATE LITERATURE

As in any literature-based reading program, but especially with a reader's workshop, we need a broad knowledge of children's and young adult literature. That knowledge should include wide reading across genres and topics, and consideration of various authors' writing styles. Three thousand to 5,000 children's and young adult books are published each year. To stay current, we can call on the help of experts who review literature in magazines such as *Horn Book, Booklinks, The ALAN Review, School Library Journal,* and *Voices of Youth Advocates.* In addition, most professional journals, such as *The Reading Teacher, Journal of Adolescent and Adult Literacy, Language Arts, Teaching Children Mathematics, Social Studies and the Young Learner, Social Education,* and *Science and Children,* have regular columns that review and evaluate literature.

We should maintain a classroom library stocked with quality literature. In addition the school librarian should be a key person in selecting and acquiring quality literature. Books can be acquired through school district instructional material budgets, student book clubs, the school library, the public library, garage sales, and donations from parents and the community.

We should try to acquire books that provide a balance among genres and topics that appeal to both boys and girls, and whose reading levels span at least 3 to 4 years above and below each grade level you teach. The school librarian can help us with school district policies that might affect our selections. Some school districts have published lists of books approved for student use.

TEACHING THE REQUIRED READING/LANGUAGE ARTS CURRICULUM

We must quickly become familiar with the reading and language arts curriculum in our school district. Each school district develops curriculum standards that identify what students should know at each grade level. We can obtain copies of the curriculum standards for local school districts and become familiar with the knowledge and skills that are identified for the middle grades. Figure 6.2 shows an example of one school district's standards for the language arts.

If you happen to teach seventh or eighth grade in the district whose standards appear in Figure 6.2, which objectives might you select to emphasize during a reader's workshop? Why?

• • •

■ **FIGURE 6.2**

Sample of language arts
curriculum standards

1. Know and use word analysis skills and strategies to comprehend new words encountered in text.
2. Use reading process skills and strategies to build comprehension.
3. Read to comprehend, interpret, and evaluate literature from a variety of authors, cultures, and times.
4. Read to comprehend, interpret, and evaluate informational texts for specific purposes.

I could incorporate each of the district's standards into a reader's workshop. Any workshop's overall objective is to have personal purposes for reading, which include reading for pleasure and information (standards 3 and 4). As my students read silently, they would also have to use strategies to monitor their meaning making and to sustain their reading over longer periods of time (standard 2). In minilessons, strategy groups, and individual conferences I would use familiar texts to extend their knowledge of a variety of genres (standard 3) to help them make appropriate choices for reading, their knowledge of literary elements (standard 3) and author's use of literary devices to enhance their appreciation of texts (standard 3), and their knowledge of words and word meanings (standard 1). This knowledge would then help them select appropriate strategies to suit the purposes for which they are reading (standard 2).

• • •

School district curriculum standards such as those shown in Figure 6.2 may not identify the specific procedural and strategy knowledge needed for reader's workshop. We must add goals, such as the list below, to our curriculum:

- Create ideas to encourage students to share their reading processes in conferences and sharing sessions.
- Learn how to recognize students' personal strengths and needs as readers.
- Learn how to recognize when a book is not appropriate and should be abandoned.
- Learn how to help students learn to monitor their own meaning making.

SUCCESSFUL READING BEHAVIORS AND ATTITUDES

In an individualized program such as reader's workshop, we want to feel confident that students will continue to grow as readers. Therefore, we must know and understand reading processes and the types of learning environments in which literate behaviors flourish. Then, we must be able to use that knowledge to identify the appropriate reading behaviors and attitudes we expect students to exhibit. Our expectations of students will guide our decisions as we set up a reader's workshop. Careful and consistent observation of students as they select books, read independently, conference, make records of their reading, and share with their peers will help us identify students' attitudes toward reading and the reading behaviors they are using successfully.

IMPLEMENTING A READER'S WORKSHOP

Now that we are aware of the basic issues that surround reader's workshop, let's take a closer look at some of the essential elements that lead to successful implementation. As we move along, note that some elements of reader's workshop draw on what we already know about whole-class literature study, book clubs, and literature circles.

SUPPORTING INDEPENDENT READING

Middle grade students need support to mature as readers and to use independent reading time wisely. We must provide an environment that supports quiet reading and must help them learn to select appropriate reading materials.

Providing a Quiet Reading Time.   In both Kim's and Kristen's classrooms, silent reading was given priority in the reading period. Both teachers believe that students must have sustained opportunities to read if they are to become proficient silent readers. Middle grade readers must develop "the ability to persevere at a personal pace that makes efficient use of current skills" (Holdaway, 1980, p. 34). As in any activity, perseverance requires sustained practice.

In Kim's classroom, 20 of the 60 minutes devoted to reader's workshop are spent in silent reading. The commitment to this time enables Kim's students to settle into their reading. She encourages extending the independent reading beyond the quiet reading period if students choose, because Kim believes that self-selected reading is also self-paced reading. Kristen has 75-minute periods, which allow for extended blocks of quiet reading as needed. Some teachers find it difficult to have a large block of time for silent reading, so they combine the time devoted to independent reading with reader's workshop.

Selecting an Appropriate Book.   In reader's workshop students must learn to choose books that are appropriate for their interests and reading level. We support book selection daily by sharing books through read-alouds, book talks, and personal responses. Whole-group meetings in reader's workshop are excellent opportunities for everyone to share their feelings about books. When a sense of community exists in a classroom, students place importance on the views of others and allow those views to influence their selection of new books. Part of our task is to teach students how to determine book difficulty and how to decide when to abandon an inappropriate selection.

For example, Kristen begins the mystery unit by making an inviting display of selected books, and gives book talks to introduce as many books as she can. She also provides browsing time during the week prior to the unit.

Draw on what you know! Imagine that you would like to start a reader's workshop but your students have little experience selecting their own texts for reading instruction. What could you do? Your students have little experience pacing their own reading to complete a text. What could you do?

• • •

Selecting texts? Students have experience selecting library books and independent reading materials. Using what they know, I could talk about and demonstrate how I know a book is easy, just right, or challenging. I could also spend some time in literature circles, which offer text choices, before beginning reader's workshop.

Self-paced reading? Here again, literature circles may be my first step before reader's workshop. Then my students will gain experience in self-pacing while they have the support of a group of students who are reading the same text and can help with pacing decisions.

• • •

CONFERENCES WITH STUDENTS

Conferences with individual students represent one of the most difficult and time-consuming parts of reader's workshop, but they also are one of the most valuable ways for us to learn about students. Conferences are often the part of reader's workshop that makes teachers hesitant to try this approach. Kristen tries to conference with four students each day. She encourages students to indicate their readiness by signing up for a conference. Kristen prefers to see students when they are ready. She finds the talk is more productive.

From Kim's description earlier in this chapter, we know that conferences are short private meetings, lasting 7 to 10 minutes, between the teacher and a student. Conferences allow open dialogue about a book the student is reading or has just completed. This time between teacher and student is not a time for instruction. Instead, the purpose is to learn how students are handling the books they chose independently. Conferences provide us with opportunities to monitor a student's individual reading progress, to diagnose difficulties, and to encourage the use of particular strategies (Hagerty, 1992; Holdaway, 1980). Figure 6.3 summarizes student's and teacher's roles in conferences. As shown, our role is one of questioning, listening, probing responses, and making notes.

Kim and Kristen keep conference notebooks, with records of their meetings with each student. During and immediately following each conference, they note such student behaviors as the following:

- Level of response and understanding,
- Fluency,

■ **FIGURE 6.3**

Student and teacher roles in a reader's workshop conference

During a conference— a student shares ...	and the teacher ...
• personal responses to a book	• probes the responses
• a selected part of a book through oral reading	• probes the responses
• literature log entries for the book	• reviews and discusses the entries
	• encourages and guides student's efforts throughout conference
	• makes a record of conference observations

■ *When you conference with a student, what will you want to know about his or her interactions with a text? How might you find out?*

- Word recognition and self-monitoring,
- Ability to select appropriately,
- Self-pacing, and
- Self-evaluation.

Figure 6.4 shows a sample of Kim's conference notes.

Draw on what you know! You would like to start a reader's workshop, but your students have never participated in one-to-one conferences. What could you do?

• • •

I can draw on what I know about teaching small-group discussions in literature study (Chapter 5). I could develop a series of minilessons about what conferences are and what happens in a conference, perhaps modeling a conference in front of the class. Then we could discuss as a class what occurred and why.

• • •

FIGURE 6.4

Kim's conference notes from reader's workshop

Reading Conference Record	Name ___Stacy___
Book Notes	**Observations/Comments**
10/1 <u>Jeremy Thatcher, Dragon Catcher</u> (fantasy) —Jeremy runs to a place he's never seen before —gets dinosaur eggs in magic shop —has directions on how to hatch eggs —dragon sends Jeremy messages	—good reading log entries, had none before —excellent comprehension —realizes story also told through characters' thoughts —sees foreshadowing —not sure how book will end
10/13 <u>Under the Blood Red Sun</u> (historical fiction) —Japanese family moved to Hawaii in 1940s —issues of discrimination, fear	—just right, generally smooth oral reading —comprehends —struggled some with some Japanese words, but doesn't interfere with overall comprehension —chose selection for oral reading because she felt it was most interesting, helped her better understand the characters

RESPONDING TO LITERATURE

How we feel about the literature we read is what draws us back to read again and again. Students will have different responses to the same text and will express those responses in different ways. Consequently, we need to provide varied opportunities for students to show their response to the literature they read, including the occasional option of not responding.

Literature or Reading Logs. In reader's workshop, the literature log is a personal record of a student's independent reading. Ultimately, this log should reflect the direction that students are taking with their reading. In the beginning, however, it is important that students understand the purpose for the log, especially to see it as more than a required task they complete for the teacher. Recall Kim's comment about the difficulty some of her students have with the reading log. Purpose and value are very important to middle grade students; they tend not to perform well on tasks that they perceive to have little value or an unclear purpose.

Literature logs may take many possible forms (see Chapters 8 and 9 for other examples). In a reader's workshop, the log might have several sections:

- A daily reading record that includes date, book title, pages read, and space for comments;
- A page or more devoted to words of interest and words not easily recognized; and
- Responses to reading (open, focused, double-entry, story frames, dialogue letters, story map, and so on).

Student and teacher together should decide the number of entries in the log. It may not be necessary to write a response each day. The log should not become tedious, but rather should be a functional record of reading progress.

Daily Reading Record. This record becomes part of a student's history as a reader. The reading record may be used in conferences to help students consider the criteria they use to select books, and to help students evaluate the pace of their reading and their ability to persevere with a book. Note how Kim uses reading records as she discusses students' progress during conferences. Her reading log combines book selection and record of reading (see Figure 6.5). We must decide how much information we want students to put on one record form. Figure 6.6 shows a sample alternate form.

Words and Phrases from Literature. Kim encourages her students to share their interest in words with others in group meetings. By the middle grades students have a great deal of word knowledge, but may not recognize that knowledge as helpful in self-learning. Independence in word recognition means helping students become aware of their ability to work with new words and phrases.

We may choose to review word and phrase lists individually during conferences or in strategy groups to meet the needs of students who are at similar stages of development of word knowledge. We can encourage students to record page numbers to refer to the use of a word in the text, perhaps using the "before, during, and after" context technique as Kim described. Figure 6.7 shows a sample log entry for words from Kristen's class.

Responses to Reading. It is not necessary to make daily entries. In the early phase of reader's workshop, we may want to offer focused log entries to "nudge" student's interactions with literature. We may also ask students to reflect on a book and make closing comments before they move to a new selection. We should involve students in making decisions about the type and frequency of log entries.

The minilessons that we offer our students can focus on how to make different types of entries and how to select a particular type of entry. See Chapters 8 and 9 for more detail on particular types of literature log entries.

Draw on what you know! You would like to start a reader's workshop but your students have little experience selecting topics and forms for their literature log responses. What could you do?

• • •

Name ___Valentina___   Reading Log

Date	Pages Read	Genre	Title & Author	Words to Remember	Comments	Future Plans
9-18	32	fiction	Not for a Billion Gazillion Dollars, Paula Danziger	— — —	not interesting, I did not finish	— — —
9-22	1-21 22-44 45-98 99-122 123-157	fiction	Words of Stone, Kevin Henkes	simultaneous boisterous	really exciting, I liked the characters	I'll make a poster for book talks
9-30	38	fiction	Slime Lake, Tom B. Syone		boring, too easy, didn't finish	I need help in choosing books that are right for me
10-1	1-43 44-66 67-91 92-148 149-end	fantasy	The Cricket in Times Square, George Selden	deliberate miraculously menacing	good character, really believable!	I'll add a card to the "recommended book file"

■ **FIGURE 6.5**

Sample reading log

... I would begin with making daily log entries, mixing focused with open responses (choice). I would couple daily responses with minilessons and flexible strategy groups focusing on types of possible responses and how to decide what to write.   • • •

Small-Group Sharing.   Middle grade students need opportunities to share their responses to books with others, both formally and informally. After quiet reading periods,

■ **FIGURE 6.6**

Sample daily reading record

Date & Book Title	Pages Read	Comments
Nov. 12 A Time for Andrew	Ch 1 (pp. 3–11)	I chose this book because Mrs. Felten is reading it too. It sounded spooky.
Nov. 13	Ch 2 & 3 (pp. 12–21) Home pp. 22–29	This is spooky. Drew found some really old marbles in the attic.

■ **FIGURE 6.7**

Word/phrase lists in literature logs

Interesting Words/Phrases	Words/Phrases to Study
A Time for Andrew P. 2 ancestral home P. 2 his scowling face floated between me and the rows of corn P. 4 dim-witted P. 11 his face was skull-like P. 12 gurgled	A Time for Andrew P. 7 art deco P. 9 reminisced P. 11 inarticulate

students should be able to spontaneously share their ideas with others as they work. Students who have read the same books may elect to form small sharing groups during work time to compare their ideas.

In addition to spontaneous sharing, we can consider formalizing such small-group meetings. These sharing opportunities will resemble book club and literature circle meetings. As we bring students together, we can provide a "discussion guide" that suggests ways

■ FIGURE 6.8

Discussion guide for
connecting texts

Mysterious Connections. . .

We are all reading mysteries! This small group meeting is to explore how mystery writers reveal the "mystery" of their story. Gather 3–5 people together who are far enough in their books that the author has revealed the "mystery."

To get started—

1. Share the cover, title, author, and BRIEF summary of your book so far. (BRIEF means one or two sentences, not a "blow-by-blow" description of the plot.)

2. Share what the "mystery" is and how the author let you find out about it.

3. What similarities and differences do you find among the books in your group? Make notes to recall the important points. Be ready to share this information in community sharing.

How Authors Reveal the "Mystery"	
Similarities	**Differences**

to begin the conversation, particularly when students have read different, but related, books whose relationship may not be readily apparent. An open-ended discussion guide, such as Kristen uses when her class studies mysteries (see Figure 6.8), helps students make connections across texts.

Independent Projects.   The emphasis in reader's workshop is on student choice, rather than on choices the teacher directs. Students do, however, need to be aware of their options for independent projects. One idea is to make a wall chart of possible extensions, such as those in the following list. Remember, projects should *never* become more important than reading and talking about books.

Possible Response Projects

- Writing

  Letter to or from a character

  Character diary or journal

  Innovate on or change a story

  Newspaper article about a character or event

  Write a sequel

  Write a "reminder" story, "This story reminds me of. . . ."

  Write to the author of your book

- Art
    - Advertisements
    - Cartoon sequences
    - Diorama scenes
    - Wall mural
    - Family or character "photo" album
    - Collage of characters, main events, settings
    - Make a wordless book that illustrates main events
    - Make a quilt of favorite events, quotes, characters, and so on
- Reading
    - Make a display of books, poems, magazines, and newspaper articles that relate to the theme of your book
    - Find and share other books by the same author or topic
    - Research the "facts" behind your book
- Drama/Speech
    - Videotape/audiotape a scene
    - Interview a character
    - Become a character
    - Give a book talk
- Maps or Clusters
    - Physical location (settings or plots)
    - Character attributes or relationships
    - Timeline of events or character change
    - Story map (beginning–middle–end, problem–events–resolution)
- Games
    - Develop a board game about your character or story
    - Make a card game to match character attributes or story events

Draw on what you know! You want to start a reader's workshop, but your students have had no experience in selecting independent response activities and pacing their completion of the projects. What could you do?

• • •

Minilessons on selecting independent projects could certainly be helpful. The planning time that is built into the beginning of each workshop also could be a valuable time to help students think about how they will use their time, especially if they are involved in an independent project. I would not assign projects until other parts of the reader's workshop are familiar and working effectively.

• • •

INSTRUCTION IN READER'S WORKSHOP

Students' need for interaction with a more knowledgeable other does not disappear when their reading and writing become more self-directed. They will continue to need teacher guidance in reading and writing processes and strategies. Our instruction can take the form of minilessons, flexible strategy groups, and individual help.

Whole-Class Minilessons. During the opening group meeting, we may provide short focused minilessons on the following topics:

- *Procedures to help a reader's workshop run smoothly:*
    Steps and expectations of a reader's workshop.
    How to pick out a book that's right for you.
    Deciding when to abandon a book.
    How to fill out a reading record.
    Deciding how to respond to a book.
    How to decide on an extension activity (project).
    How to prepare for a conference.
    Giving a book talk.
    What to do when you finish your book.
    How to share what you read.
    What to do in discussion groups.
    How to respond as a listener when someone shares.
    How to respect books.
- *Use of a particular literary element or technique:*
    What are the different genres and their characteristics?
    What are the literary elements in a book?
    How does your author use literary elements?
    How are literary elements important in a story?
    What is the theme of your book? How can you tell?
    How is a plot organized?
    Different types of plots: going forward, going backward.
    Discussing conflict and when it might be good.
    Does there have to be a conflict?
    How does your author let you get to know a character?
    Why are some characters more important than others?
    Why would an author use a foil character?
    Discuss point of view and its importance.
    How do authors begin and end stories?
    How do authors hook your interest?
    How are fiction and information books different?
    Identifying parts of a book and how to use them.
    Fact versus opinion.
    Reality versus fantasy.

- *Appropriate use of a particular reading strategy:*
     How to deal with unknown words: pronunciation and meaning.
     How to recognize similes and metaphors.
     How to ask yourself questions while reading.
     How can you sketch for understanding?
     How to make inferences.
     Drawing conclusions.
     Recognizing and finding details.
     Summarizing.
     Finding the main idea.
     Thinking ahead (predict), thinking back (connect).
     Stopping to reflect on a story.
     How can you help yourself read information texts?

To support the continued development of reading skills and strategies in our students, we will need to share the knowledge of mature readers through all three types of minilessons. We know that we will draw the content for minilessons from observations of the students, knowledge of the books they are reading, and the existing reading/language arts curriculum. Kristen helps students focus on the characteristics of mysteries through her minilesson on how authors reveal the mystery. This minilesson was developed from curriculum standards, the mysteries her students were reading, and her knowledge of students' experiences with the characteristics of a genre.

We should use talk-aloud and think-aloud strategies in minilessons to help students learn how readers think about reading. Minilessons will be most helpful to students if we draw examples from familiar literature, such as books that are shared in whole-class read-alouds. The sample procedural minilesson shown in Figure 6.9 focuses students' thinking on preparing for a reader's workshop conference.

Flexible Strategy Groups.   One concern that teachers often express is "How can students continue to learn new skills and strategies when they are reading by themselves?" Meeting students in flexible small groups extends the ideas that we emphasize in whole-class minilessons and provides practice that some, but not all, students may need. Small groups serve a limited purpose, such as to develop a particular strategy, then are disbanded. We present ideas first to the class in minilessons. When we notice that a number of students are still not using particular literary knowledge or reading strategies, more extensive small-group work is warranted.

Topics for strategy groups can be drawn from the lists of suggested minilesson topics in this text, from our knowledge of the reading process and student literature, from our school district's curriculum, or from a basal reading series. Strategy group instruction is teacher mediated and may resemble small groups used in other literature study. To capitalize on students' motivation, Holdaway (1980) suggests letting students attend strategy groups if they feel they need help rather than mandating attendance. An invitation to join a small group encourages students to assess their own need for the skill or strategy being offered.

How do teachers make such decisions? Kim and Kristen provide examples:

- Kristen notices during conferences that some students are having difficulty with multisyllable words, especially words with unusual roots. Over a period of several weeks she offers small-group work in strategies for decoding multisyllable words in

FIGURE 6.9

Sample procedural minilesson for reader's workshop

Getting ready for a reader's workshop conference

"We've been having reading conferences for several weeks now and I've noticed that you've been remembering to bring your book and literature log to the conference. That's part of getting ready for a conference.

"Another part of getting ready takes place in your head. When I'm going to conference with you, I think back to our last conference. I think about the things you told me about your book, I look at the notes I made about our conference, and I think about the book you were reading. I also think about what I've seen you doing in reading since that last conference and the minilessons we've had that might help you enjoy reading your books more. Then I anticipate what you might say to me when we meet. That's what I do in my head.

"When you get ready for a conference with me, you should also spend some time thinking about what will happen in the conference. You'll think about what you want to tell me about your book. Since you know that our conference is also to help you be a better reader, you might think about something I can do to help you enjoy your book the most.

"Tomorrow I will be conferencing with ____ , ____ , and ____ . Each of you might spend some of your work time today getting your head ready for our conference tomorrow."

context, but only for students who demonstrated need. She draws her examples from her conference notes as well as from books students are currently reading. Following instruction, Kristen observes the students to see whether their decoding of multisyllable words shows improvement.

- Kim notices during conferences and informal talks that a number of students have little to say about the characters in their texts. Probing their responses yields little new information. Kim decides to offer several strategy group sessions on characterization. Using a familiar text, she explores examples of how characters are introduced, how they are slowly developed, and how they may change over time as a result of events and conflicts. Her focus then turns to the books students are currently reading, and to helping them apply characterization strategies. Over the next several conferences, Kim carefully observes the students' sense of character to see whether the strategy sessions are effective.

Individual Help/Questions. When Kim and Kristen are not in conferences with students, they circulate, providing support and encouragement. They answer questions and make suggestions that help students build on previous conferences or whole-class instruction. Kim thinks of this as a time to continue learning about her students as individuals and as readers.

Both teachers make notes to add to their conference records. (They find it helpful to carry a clipboard for this purpose.) Kim transfers her notes to the conference record, while Kristen, because she has many students, prefers to use sheets of computer labels, writing a student's name on each label. When a label is filled, she peels it off and places it on a page in the student's assessment portfolio. Empty labels clue her in to who she is not watching closely.

COMMUNITY SHARING SESSIONS

Formal sharing occurs during class meetings, with book talks or the sharing of projects. We might choose to organize sharing as Kim did, having those students we conference with each day also be the ones who share responses to books with their peers. Regardless, students will need coaching to decide what to share and how they want to share their responses.

Consider teaching students to use *remembers, reminders,* and *questions* (Graves, 1994) in response to someone who is sharing. After a student has shared his or her response, group members respond with:

- *Remembers,* telling the person what they remember about the shared ideas, somewhat like retelling after a story;
- *Reminders,* memories and past experiences that are cued by what was shared ("It reminds me of . . ."); and
- *Questions* about what was shared to clarify or to fill in missing information.

RESPECTING DIVERSITY IN READER'S WORKSHOP

PROVIDE FOR PERSONAL INTERESTS

Self-selected reading, in both independent reading and reader's workshop, provides an opportunity for students to pursue personal reading interests in literature of their choice. Of the different literature-based approaches we have considered, reader's workshop is the most responsive to students' needs and desires as readers. In reader's workshop, students are able to pursue passions, as well as develop interests in new areas of literature.

Knowing our students well is imperative to responding to their personal interests. Interest inventories and personal conferences are two ways to come to know students as readers. Interest inventories created by teachers for their particular students are probably the most successful for honest, open responses from students. A variety of inventories should be conducted over the course of the school year because students' interests are likely to change. We keep inventories simple and target the issues of importance in our classroom. As Kristen plans for a mystery unit in her reading class, she surveys students to know more about the types of mysteries they would be interested in reading (see Figure 6.10). In Kim's reader's workshop, students will be reading all types of texts, so Kim must have a more general sense of what is currently interesting her students. Kim might use inventories such as the samples given in Figures 6.11 and 6.12. The potential of conferences to inform us about students' interests is well documented in this chapter.

VALUE STUDENTS' JUDGMENTS

Providing for self-selection of reading material tells students that we trust their judgment. Just as adults come to know their own taste in literature, so can students. They may make some poor choices, but it is difficult to learn how to choose if we do not have the opportunity to do so.

Individual conferences provide opportunities to guide students in their personal decision making. Conferences hold students accountable for monitoring their own progress, but also provide them with support to successfully self-monitor.

Sample mystery inventory

Name _____ Date _____

Mystery's the Thing!

The most mysterious thing I have ever seen or heard about is _____

_____

_____ .

I would like to read mysteries about (check as many as you like):

_____ kids my age   _____ history (ex. Egyptians, Civil War)
_____ kids who are older than me   _____ things that can happen today
_____ grown-ups   _____ the future
_____ detectives   _____ animals
_____ sports heroes   _____ war time
_____ movie stars   _____ crimes and murder

Other types of mysteries that would interest me:

_____   _____

Sample interest inventory

Name _____ Age _____ Grade _____ Date _____

1. When you are at school, what are your favorite things to do?

2. When you are at home, what are your favorite things to do?

3. Do you have special hobbies or interests?

4. What things do you prefer to do by yourself?

5. What things do you prefer to do with your friends?

6. What things do you prefer to do with your family?

7. Do you like to read? _____ . What are your favorite books?

8. How do you know if someone is a good reader?

9. Are you a good reader? _____ . Why or why not?

■ **FIGURE 6.12**

Sample interest inventory

Name _____ Date _____

Categories	The All-Time Best . . .	The All-Time Worst . . .
movies		
television programs		
music		
magazines		
books		
computer games		
Internet sites		
hobbies		
school subjects		

In reader's workshop, students have a range of choices for log entries. The log represents another decision-making opportunity and helps students learn about their ability to make and follow through on their choices. Students' decisions should be discussed in the conferences, focusing on the rationale for their decisions.

FOSTER INDEPENDENCE

The ultimate goal for all learners should be for them to become independent readers. Extensive independent reading time and reader's workshop allow students to pace their own reading by providing large blocks of time so that, through self-pacing, they can find their own rhythms as readers.

Self-selection helps individual readers learn to effectively monitor their own reading, to recognize levels of comfort with different types of reading material. Strategic readers develop through having opportunities to monitor their own reading. It is not enough to know what a strategy is and how to do it. The real test comes when a student must decide on a particular strategy and know how to activate and use it during reading. Self-selection can support the development of self-monitoring, and will ideally lead to self-evaluation. Through self-selected reading, students can develop trust in their own judgment and in their ability to evaluate their own reading performance.

ASSESSMENT AND EVALUATION IN INDEPENDENT READING

What independent reading behaviors should we expect to see in the middle grades? How can we know that students can practice appropriate self-selection of literature? How can we assess sustained silent reading or students' engagement with texts? By the middle grades, students should have had many opportunities to read independently, including selecting appropriate books and shifting from oral to efficient silent reading behavior. We may not see such independence, however, in all students. We will need multiple strategies for gathering assessment data about our students so that we may provide the appropriate support for their continued literacy growth.

Take this opportunity to reread Kim's explanation of the organization of her reader's workshop, noting the references she makes to gathering assessment data and evaluating student progress. Note that her statements require knowledge of students gained through evaluation. Kim makes notes during conferences. She listens to students read aloud and asks them to justify their selection of text. She observes students during minilessons, community sharing, and independent reading times. Reading workshop teachers become keenly aware of how individuals think, act, make decisions, and follow through on tasks.

ADDING TO OUR TEACHER ASSESSMENT PORTFOLIO

To provide an environment that supports independent reading, we must carefully observe students to see how effectively they use their opportunities to read, and identify students who need our guidance and support. Do students seem to be engaged with the texts they have selected? For how long do individuals sustain their reading? When engagement appears to wane, what seems to be the reason? We combine our observations and students' self-evaluations to determine the adjustments needed in the classroom environment and in students' background knowledge and reading strategies to enable them to become effective independent readers. We must decide which independent reading behaviors are important and systematically observe students for occurrences. Figure 6.13 shows a sample observation form.

From a reader's workshop, what might we want to add to our teacher's assessment portfolio that reflects student growth? Where is our greatest potential for interaction with students? Conferences might be the number one choice. From other literature approaches, we are already aware of the possibilities for observation and gathering samples of students' work. Because of the unique role of conferences in reader's workshop, we will focus here on the value of these face-to-face meetings for monitoring student progress.

Both Kim and Kristen keep a conference notebook with a section for each student. During individual conferences they make notes that include the following types of observations:

- The types of texts students are selecting to read,
- Patterns of reading (completed, abandoned),
- How and what they choose to share of the text,
- The quality of rehearsed oral reading,
- Strategies they use to make meaning,
- Students' insights about the author's use of literary elements,
- Students' insights about themselves as readers, and
- Students' general level of engagement with texts.

■ **FIGURE 6.13**

Observing independent
reading behaviors

Independent Reading Behaviors

Name _____   Date _____

Independent Reading:	Usually	Sometimes	Rarely
1. Self-selects appropriate materials.	____	____	____
2. Engages in sustained reading appropriate to development and experience.	____	____	____
3. Abandons books that are inappropriate.	____	____	____
4. Is establishing personal preferences for content, style, authors, genre.	____	____	____
5. Displays positive attitudes toward personal reading.	____	____	____
6. Seeks advice about selecting reading materials when needed.	____	____	____
7. Uses library effectively.	____	____	____

Comments:

No single conference yields assessment data on each of these points, but, when taken collectively, conference notes can be a valuable source for evaluation. Conference notes become formative assessment data that guide our decisions.

Self-Selecting Texts.   As Kim looks back over her conference notes (see Figure 6.4), along with the student's reading record (see Figure 6.5 or 6.6), she is able to get a clear sense of the types of books students select to read. She can see which types of books they complete in a timely manner, those they complete reluctantly, and those they abandon. Kim feels that students' patterns of selecting texts form a base for her understanding of them as readers. She chooses to have a complete list of all books read during a grading period in each student's assessment portfolio.

Sharing Text in Conferences.   To prepare for a conference, students select and rehearse a piece of text that is meaningful in some way and that they wish to share with the teacher. In the conference the student reads the selected text aloud. Kim and Kristen think about the portions of text that students select to share and wonder what those selections suggest about each student's (1) level of engagement, (2) sense of self as a reader, and (3) insights about the author's craft. Both teachers ask students to introduce what they will read and, after the reading, probe students' responses and make notes.

Quality of Oral Reading.   When students share text in a conference, they typically read aloud text that has been rehearsed. Kim and Kristen listen carefully to the fluency level that students exhibit. After rehearsal, students should read appropriate text in a fluent and ex-

■ FIGURE 6.14

Sample scripted running record

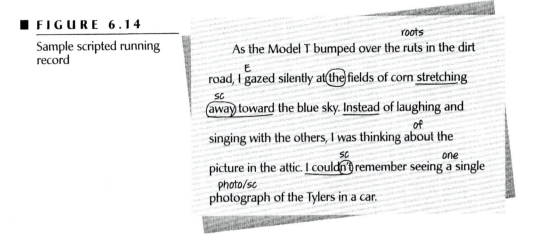

pressive manner, much like text at their independent reading level. For diagnostic purposes, it is also valuable to listen to students read text that has not been rehearsed.

Both teachers make running records reflecting a student's strategies for monitoring meaning while he or she reads orally. When making a running record, the teacher observes, records what the student actually says while reading, and later, analyzes any miscues, or words that differ from those in the actual text. Clay (1968) developed this procedure while she studied the reading behavior of young children, but it also is valuable in helping teachers listen carefully to middle grade readers. The procedure is similar to the miscue analysis developed by Goodman and Burke (1972).

You may make running records with both familiar and unfamiliar text. When text is familiar, we expect fewer errors. When text is unfamiliar, we have our best opportunity to see and hear the self-monitoring strategies that students control and use fairly automatically.

Running records can either be scripted or unscripted. For a scripted running record (see Figure 6.14), we have a typed copy of the student's text. For an unscripted running record, we make a record of the reading on a blank sheet of paper using check marks and notations of miscues.

To take a running record, we sit beside the student, but slightly behind so that our recording is less distracting. As the student reads, we make a record of the reading. It also is a good idea to tape record the reading, especially when we are new at this procedure, to be sure that we recorded accurately. These tape recordings provide concrete examples to parents/guardians and students of progress toward competent reading behavior.

Scripted Running Record. Kim typically uses scripted running records early in the school year as a way of learning what self-monitoring strategies her students use in oral reading. She assumes that the way students use strategies in oral reading will be similar to their use in silent reading. Using a variety of texts, Kim is able to determine students' independent, instructional, and frustration reading levels.

Taking a scripted running record is an excellent way to check students' ability to self-select appropriate texts for reader's workshop. Such a record ensures that students are selecting instructional- or independent-level text, not frustration-level text. On the day before Kim plans to make a scripted running record, she borrows the student's chosen book, photocopies a representative passage of about 250 words, and returns the book to the student. The next day, Kim asks the student to read the photocopied selection of text orally, tape recording the reading to be sure that she marks the running record accurately.

Kim listens carefully for accuracy in the student's reading. She asks if the selected text is familiar and whether the student has rehearsed the reading. When a student is familiar with the text, especially if he has rehearsed it, she expects the oral reading to sound like independent reading (95% to 100% accuracy), instead of instructional-level reading (90% to 95% accuracy).

Figure 6.15 shows codes that are typically used to mark a scripted running record. Note the difference between recorded miscues counted as errors and those miscues that are recorded but not considered errors. Those not counted as errors are miscues that either do not interfere with making meaning or that ultimately result in a correct reading.

For example, Kim listens to a student read a passage from *A Time for Andrew* (Hahn, 1995, p. 83). The student has just selected this text. The reading passage is taken from the middle of the text and is fairly representative of the writing in this text. A scripted running record of this reading might look like that shown in Figure 6.14, while an unscripted running record of the same text might look like that shown later in Figure 6.17.

There are 56 words in the passage in Figure 6.14. Which miscues would you count? Which miscues would not be counted? How accurately does this student read this text? Is this text appropriate for her? What leads you to that conclusion? (Remember, word recognition accuracy must be roughly 90% to 95% for instructional-level text.)

• • •

Four errors would count:

- *Roots* for *ruts*,
- Omission of *the* in the second line,
- Substituting *of* for *about* in the fourth line, and
- Substituting *one* for *a* in the fifth line.

Seven miscues would be recorded as evidence of her reading behavior, but would *not* be counted:

- Encouragement to try *gazed*, which the student then read accurately (notice the *e* for encourage),
- Repeating *stretching* _____ *toward*,
- Self-correcting the omission of *away*,
- Repetition of *instead*,
- Repetition of *I couldn't*,
- Self-correction of *couldn't*, and
- Self-correction of *photograph*.

Calculate the accuracy rate:

Total words	–	number of errors	=	words read correctly
56	–	4	=	52

Miscues that are counted:

Substitution—Student reads a word differently than the printed text.

rose
I studied his rosy face, his white hair and mustache.

Omission—Student leaves out a word printed in the text.

I studied his (rosy) face, his white hair and mustache.

Insertion—Student adds a word or words that are not in the printed text.

his
I studied his rosy face, his white hair and ʌmustache.

Teacher Tells—Student appeals to the teacher for help, teacher first responds, "Try it," student is unable to respond, then teacher tells.

T
I studied his rosy face, his white hair and mustache.

Try That Again—Student becomes completely lost in a section of text, teacher brackets passage that has caused the problem and says, "Try that again." The whole passage is coded as TTA and counted as one miscue. Any additional miscues that are made in the rereading are marked with the usual codes. Miscues from the first reading are ignored.

steadied SC round fake SC
TTA [I studied his rosy face, his white hair and mustache.]

Miscues that are recorded, but NOT counted:

Repetition—Student repeats a word or phrase. This usually indicates students have lost the meaning or they are using rereading as a strategy to figure out an unknown word. One underline is used for each repetition.

I studied his rosy face, his white hair and mustache.

Self-Correction—Student corrects own miscue *without* assistance. The original miscue does not count.

steadied SC
I studied his rosy face, his white hair and mustache.

Teacher Encourages—Student stops reading at point of unknown word, may or may not appeal for help, teacher encourages but does not tell, saying "try it," E (Encourage) is recorded, then student response is recorded.

E ✓
I studied his rosy face, his white hair and mustache.

Words Correct	÷	Total Words	=	Accuracy Rate
52	÷	56	=	0.92 = 92%

The accuracy rate tells us that our reader correctly reads 92% of the words in this text. This text is within our student's instructional level (90% to 95%).

How well does this student monitor her own reading? How might we calculate that? Self-corrections and repetitions are signs of self-monitoring. This student uses repetition to check her thinking. If she did not use repetition as an aid to self-correct her miscues (*away, couldn't,* and *photograph*), there would have been a total of seven more miscues. To calculate her rate of self-correction, compare all possible miscues to the number of corrected miscues.

$$\frac{\text{Miscues} + \text{Self-corrections}}{\text{Self-corrections}}$$

$$\frac{4 + 3}{3} = \frac{7}{3} = \frac{2.3}{1} = 2:1$$

Round off 2.3 to 2, giving a ratio of 2:1. The ratio means that for approximately every two miscues, the reader self-corrects one. That is an excellent self-correction rate. She monitors her own reading quite well.

If the student did not self-correct her miscues, her accuracy rate would have dropped to 87.5%, as shown below, putting her accuracy rate into a range that is considered to be at the frustration level:

Total words	–	Number of errors	=	Words read correctly
56	–	7	=	49

Words Correct	÷	Total Words	=	Accuracy Rate
49	÷	56	=	0.875 = 87.5%

What type of miscues occur that this reader does not self-correct? What information in the text is this student attending to? Remember from Chapter 2 that three cuing systems influence our reading: meaning (makes sense), language (sounds right), and visual (looks similar). Look at the reader's miscues. Which cuing systems seem to be influencing her miscues?

Types of Miscues

Counted Error:	Meaning	Language	Visual
roots for *ruts*	_____	_____	_____
omissions of *the*	_____	_____	_____
substitute *of* for *about*	_____	_____	_____
substitute *one* for *a*	_____	_____	_____

- *ruts* — Visual, meaning, and language miscues all could be influencing the *roots* miscue. *Roots* looks visually similar to *ruts*, it makes sense in the context of the story, and sounds right in the sentence.

- *the* — The omission of *the* could be influenced by meaning and language. The sentence still sounds right and makes sense.
- *of* and *one* — Substituting *of* for *about* (and *a* for *one*) draws on meaning and language cues. The sentences still sound right and make sense.

• • •

For three of the four miscues that were not self-corrected, we might say that this student does not attend as closely to visual cues when meaning and language cues suggest that her reading of the text is correct.

From analyzing responses on the running record, what might we conclude about this student's reading? From our analysis we can see that she makes meaning through repetition, self-correction, and miscues that preserve meaning and language structures. To help her see clearly what students are doing as readers, Kim uses a form (Figure 6.16) that shows the analysis of cues used for each miscue and self-correction. Over time, Kim's records could show patterns in a student's reading behavior that could be useful in supporting or redirecting the student's use of strategies to construct meaning.

■ FIGURE 6.16

Form for recording running record showing cuing strategies

RUNNING RECORD

Name ___Jesse___   Date ___10/7___

Text ___A Time for Andrew___

Accuracy Rate = ___87.5___ %

★ Counted Miscues = ___92___ %

Self-Correction Rate = 1: ___2___

Words in text ___56___

Reading level: ____ Ind. (96–100%)
     ✔ Inst. (90–95%)
     ____ Frus. (50–89%)

Cues Used: M = meaning
     S = language structure
     V = visual

pg.	E	SC	M	S	V
roots As the Model T bumped over the ruts in the dirt	1	–	✔	✔	✔
E road, I gazed silently at ⟨the⟩ fields of corn stretching	1	–	✔	✔	
sc ⟨away⟩ toward the blue sky. Instead of laughing and	1	1			✔
of singing with the others, I was thinking about the	1	–	✔	✔	
sc one picture in the attic. I couldn't remember seeing a single	2	1	✔	✔	
photo/sc photograph of the Tylers in a car.	1	1			✔
	7	3	4	4	3

■ **FIGURE 6.17**

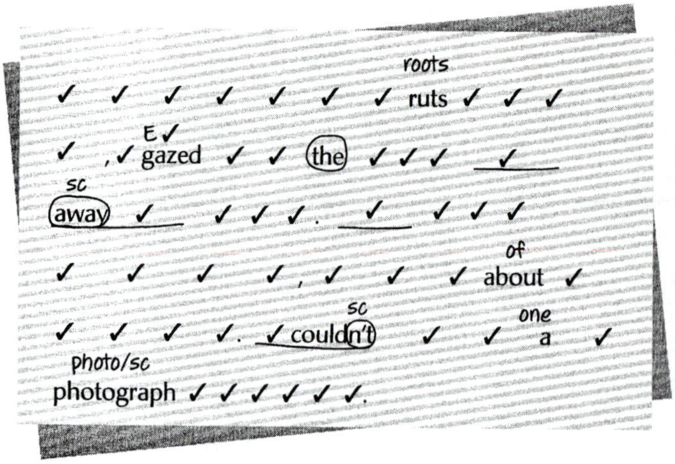

Sample unscripted
running record

Unscripted Running Record.   Sometimes Kim wants to informally assess a student's oral reading. In that case, she takes an *unscripted* running record, which she makes without making a copy of the reading text. While looking at the student's text, she uses check marks to show the student's reading accuracy. The advantage of an unscripted record is that we can make one at any time, without advance notice. Unscripted running records can be excellent records of student's oral reading.

If Kim is having a conference with the previous student, and takes an unscripted running record of the same text from *A Time for Andrew*, the record would look like the one shown in Figure 6.17. Kim would score and analyze the running record in the same manner as she would the scripted version.

ADDING TO STUDENTS' LEARNING PORTFOLIO

Students should keep records of their independent reading. The level of detail in the record should reflect how the information will be used in the classroom. Figure 6.18 shows a sample daily record-keeping form that includes the number of pages read and, when expanded appropriately, allows for recording the reading of a one chapter book over several weeks. Daily records are helpful if we are trying to encourage students to evaluate the consistency of their independent reading. In contrast, it may be sufficient to have students merely make one record of each book, as shown in Figure 6.19. The information we ask students to record should serve a purpose that students understand, such as noting reading preferences or recording how long students spend with each book or how often they abandon books. Students can help decide what to include on the record form.

We should encourage students to monitor and evaluate their own independent reading. Figure 6.20 shows a sample self-evaluation form that combines both focused and open response items. In the middle grades, independent reading takes on much greater importance because students are expected to use reading and writing for independent learning and to contribute to collaborative projects. Independent reading behaviors provide valuable insights into students' attitudes about reading and about themselves as readers.

FIGURE 6.18

Sample independent
reading record

Name _____ Daily Independent Reading Record

Date Started:		Title: Author:
Date:	Pages read:	Comment:
Date:	Pages read:	Comment:
Date:	Pages read:	Comment:
Date:	Pages read:	Comment:
Date:	Pages read:	Comment:
Date:	Pages read:	Comment:
Date:	Pages read:	Comment:
Date:	Pages read:	Comment:
Date:	Pages read:	Comment:
Date:	Pages read:	Comment:

In reader's workshop, students must learn to keep careful records of their reading. They log each book, including those they decide to abandon. They also decide which books they will write responses for and what types of responses to make.

At the end of each grading period, students in both Kristen's and Kim's classes place copies of their reading records in their learning portfolios along with self-selected responses from logs and projects that they believe show their growth as readers. Students also select responses for books that were especially challenging or meaningful. As in whole-class literature study, book clubs, and literature circles, students are expected to justify their choices. See Chapters 4 and 5 for discussions of other possibilities for helping students evaluate their performance and growth as readers.

■ **FIGURE 6.19**

Sample independent
reading record

Date Started & Date Completed or Abandoned	Title & Author	Comments

Name _____   Independent Reading Record

■ *TAKE A MOMENT TO REFLECT . . .*

■ *Independent self-selected reading:*

- Should happen every day.
- Helps students become fluent readers.
- Increases vocabulary.
- Improves reading skill.
- Improves attitude toward reading.

■ *Encourage independence with books:*

- Provide a consistent predictable time to read.
- Provide adequate time for independent practice.
- Provide a well-stocked library with easy access.
- Provide a comfortable reading environment.
- Introduce new books.
- Help students learn how to select appropriate books.

■ *Reader's workshop is an individualized reading program based on:*

- Predictable blocks of time;
- Student choice of reading material;

■ **FIGURE 6.20**

Sample self-evaluation
of independent reading

Self-Evaluation of Independent Reading

Name _____   Date _____

	Usually	**Sometimes**	**Rarely**
1. When given a choice of things to do, I choose to read.	___	___	___
2. When I read independently: I know how to select books that are right for me.	___	___	___
I can read for a period of 20 minutes or more.	___	___	___
I abandon books that are not right for me.	___	___	___
I am learning what types of books and authors I like best.	___	___	___
I monitor my own reading to be sure it's making sense to me.	___	___	___
3. When I go to a library, I know how to find what I need.	___	___	___

4. As an independent reader, I am _____

_____

5. The way I can tell a book is just right for me is _____

_____

_____

6. To be a better independent reader, I need to _____

_____

_____

- A consistent structure;
- Opportunity for students to respond to their reading; and
- A sense of community developed through collaboration and sharing.

■ *Reader's workshop is set up on a workshop framework that moves from:*

- Whole-class instruction and planning;
- To a block of independent work time; then
- Back to whole-class sharing and planning.

■ *To prepare for a reader's workshop, you must:*

- Know a great deal about students' needs and interests.
- Have access to a range of literature.

- Consider how you will meet your school district's required curriculum.
- Be able to recognize successful reading behaviors and attitudes.

■ *To implement a reader's workshop, you must:*

- Provide a quiet reading time each day.
- Help students refine their ability to select appropriate reading materials.
- Make available consistent time to confer with students about their reading.
- Encourage student response to reading by using literature or reading logs.
- Build community through small-group and whole-class sharing.
- Provide opportunities for individual expression through response projects.

■ *Instruction in a reader's workshop is provided through:*

- Whole-class minilessons that address workshop procedures, aspects of literature, and the effective use of reading strategies;
- Flexible strategy groups that are organized as the need becomes apparent through conferences, teacher observation, and student initiation;
- Individual help sessions initiated by students; and
- Interaction during community sharing sessions.

■ *We respect diversity among students in reader's workshop when we:*

- Build on their personal interests through reading.
- Value the judgments students make about their reading.
- Encourage and foster independence in reading.

■ *Student progress in independent reading is monitored through:*

- Records of texts students select to read;
- Patterns that illustrate reading behavior (completed texts, abandoned texts, level of engagement);
- Quality of rehearsed oral reading during conferences;
- Personal insights of self as reader; and
- Taking running records to document effective use of reading strategies.

■ *Running records:*

- Are scripted or unscripted records of the miscues that students make while reading.
- Can be made for any text that students read.
- Use a system of markings that show students' reading behavior.
- Can reveal patterns of effective and ineffective strategy use.
- Should be completed for each middle grade student three or four times each school year.

■ REFERENCES

Allington, R. (1977). If they don't read much, how they ever gonna get good? *Journal of Reading,* 21(2), 57–61.
Allington, R. L. (2001). *What really matters to struggling readers: Designing research-based programs.* New York: Longman.

Anderson, R. C., Heibert, E. H., Scott, J., & Wilkinson, I. A. G. (1985). *Becoming a nation of readers*. Champaign-Urbana, IL: Center for the Study of Reading.

Atwell, N. (1987). *In the middle: Writing, reading and learning with adolescents*. Portsmouth, NH: Heinemann.

Beach, R. (1993). *Reader-response theories*. Champaign-Urbana, IL: National Council of Teachers of English.

Center for the Study of Reading (1990). *Teachers and independent reading: Suggestions for the classroom*. Champaign-Urbana, IL: Author.

Clay, M. (1968). A syntactic analysis of reading errors. *Journal of Verbal Learning and Verbal Behavior, 7*, 434–438.

Clay, M. (1979). *The early detection of reading difficulties*. Portsmouth, NH: Heinemann.

Ducker, S. (1968). *Individualized reading: An annotated bibliography*. Metuchen, NJ: Scarecrow.

Five, C. L. (1988, Spring). From workbook to workshop: Increasing children's involvement in the reading process. *The New Advocate*, pp. 103–113.

Goodman, Y. M., & Burke, C. (1972). *The reading miscue inventory*. Upper Saddle River, NJ: Merrill/Prentice Hall.

Graves, D. (1994). *A fresh look at writing*. Portsmouth, NH: Heinemann.

Hagerty, P. (1992). *Reader's workshop: Real reading*. Richmond Hill, Ontario: Scholastic Canada Ltd.

Hansen, J. (1987). *When writers read*. Portsmouth, NH: Heinemann.

Holdaway, D. (1980). *Independence in reading*. Portsmouth, NH: Heinemann.

Hornsby, D., & Sukarna, D. (1986). *Read on: A conference approach to reading*. Portsmouth, NH: Heinemann.

Johnson, D. M. (1981). The effects of cooperative, competitive and individualistic goal structures on achievement: A meta-analysis. *Psychological Bulletin, 89*, 47–62.

Rosenblatt, L. M. (1978). *The reader, the text, the poem: The transactional theory of the literary work*. Carbondale, IL: Southern Illinois University Press.

Slavin, R. E., Madden, N. A., Karweit, N. L., Dolan, L. J., & Wasik, B. A. (1991). Success for all: Ending reading failure from the beginning. *Language Arts, 68*, 404–409.

Tunnel, M. O. & Jacobs, J. S. (1989). Using "real" books: Research findings on literature based reading instruction. *The Reading Teacher, 42*, 470–477.

Veatch, J. (Ed.). (1959). *Individualizing your reading program: Self-esteem in action*. New York: Putnam.

Vygotsky, L. S. (1962). *Thought and language* (E. Hanfmann & G. Vakar, Eds. & Trans.). Cambridge, MA: The MIT Press.

■ CHILDREN'S LITERATURE

Hahn, M. D. (1995). *A Time for Andrew: A ghost story*. New York: Clarion Publishers.

chapter **7**

Using Information Texts and Textbooks Effectively

In this chapter . . . .

We will expand our understanding of using information texts and textbooks in middle grade classrooms by exploring:

- Strengths and weaknesses of information texts/textbooks,
- Using information texts/textbooks for instruction,
- Evaluating information texts/textbooks, and
- Selecting appropriate instructional strategies.

Looking into Classrooms . . .

At the beginning of every school year, Jean, a fifth-grade teacher, surveys her students to determine their level of comfort and experience with information texts and textbooks. Fifth-grade students in her school district have many social studies and science standards to demonstrate. Jean knows that she will be using both adopted textbooks and a variety of information texts to teach literacy skills/strategies and content. She needs to know what background her students may have. What she typically finds is that her students believe they don't know how to independently read a chapter in a textbook. They report that their previous teachers typically read textbook information aloud in whole-class discussions and told them what the textbook was really saying. Jean wants her students to develop skills to conduct independent and small-group research and to effectively monitor their reading in information texts. Her students typically report that they are not sure how to get started with a research question and how to find what they need in particular texts. They also report that it is very hard to "keep themselves going" in a textbook chapter. Jean knows that she has much to do to close the gap between narrative and information text experiences for her students.

Putting Theory into Practice . . .

Reading and writing are functional tools not to be mastered unto themselves, but to be situated within our content area teaching (McGinley & Tierney, 1989). Students learn to use literacy skills to be participants in the content area community (Sfard, 1998), and to be confident in their ability to search and

NOTE: This chapter will address some specific issues about students' skills and strategies in information texts that were not addressed in Chapter 4, 5, or 6. Therefore, the format of this chapter is slightly different. Previewing this chapter before reading may be helpful.

locate information, explain and defend their understandings of concepts, transfer concepts by writing solutions to problems, and engage in multiple strategies for literacy learning (Guthrie, Meter, McCann, Wigfield, Bennet, Poundstone, Rice, Failbisch, Hunt & Mitchell, 1996). We want to create content area classrooms that are inquiry oriented, where "students are no longer outsiders who regard knowledge as something handed down and preserved as flat factual statements in textbooks" (Borasi & Siegel, 2000, p. 20). Consequently, in this chapter we explore the issues and strategies that are at the heart of encouraging students to be active participants in their own learning across the curriculum.

CHARACTERISTICS OF INFORMATION TEXTS/TEXTBOOKS

As a beginning point, the information texts and textbooks we select for instruction should be high-quality texts. They should be:

- Factually accurate,
- Free of stereotypes,
- Clearly illustrated to enhance and clarify the text,
- Designed to encourage analytical thinking,
- Written with clear, interesting, and appropriate language, and
- Comprehensible to the reader (Norton & Norton, 1998).

We are also aware that information texts are organized quite differently than narratives (see Chapter 3). The work of several researchers (Carter & Abrahamson, 1998; Meyer, 1985) identifies the prevailing structures found in information texts:

- Description or enumeration,
- Ordered collections or lists,
- Cause/effect,
- Compare/contrast, and
- Problem/solution.

We can see that these various structures are prevalent in our textbooks. Science textbooks, for example, may combine:

- **Enumeration,** to explain the theory or background knowledge for a concept;
- **Ordered lists,** for the historical aspects of science; and
- **Cause/effect or problem/solution,** to help us understand how scientists question and learn about the natural world.

Most information texts and textbooks use more than one of the structures identified above to address their content. Therefore, we must carefully examine the texts we intend to use for instruction to understand what our students will contend with as they construct meaning about the content.

In addition to the various structures that are possible in information texts, especially in textbooks, we must also consider other factors in the format of these texts. We need to merely examine a current textbook in science or social studies to see the many forms in which information is displayed. If we open a textbook and examine the two facing pages we find information in the form of:

- Text with headings and subheadings on both sides,
- Photo inserts with questions or captions that provide information that is often not in the text,
- Maps with legends and labels,
- Charts, diagrams, and graphs with labels,
- Focus questions intended to guide the reader,
- Factoids, small boxes with an interesting fact related to the topic,
- Problems to solve,
- Issues to think critically about,
- Bolded vocabulary words, and
- Connections to other curriculum areas.

From page to page throughout the chapter, the format changes, creating an unpredictable context each time we turn the page. We are constantly challenged to reorient ourselves to the format, to understand what we should attend to, to determine what might be most important. Visually, information text is dramatically different than narrative. It is only through extensive experiences and our guidance with such texts that our students will begin to be comfortable with the possibilities of what they might find on a page, and how to make decisions [decide] to focus their attention.

YOUR TURN...

This would be a good opportunity to select a few of your favorite information texts to examine as you consider using these texts for instruction. In addition, this is also a good time to get reacquainted with textbooks for the grade levels and subject areas that you intend to teach. As you identify current textbooks, be sure to examine the teacher's edition. It will contain copies of the pages of the student's text, as well as additional instructional support.

● ● ●

USING INFORMATION TEXTS/TEXTBOOKS FOR INSTRUCTION

A major block to students' literacy development in the content areas is inconsistent experiences with information texts (Irvin, 1998). While textbooks dominate content area instruction in the middle grades, their use varies greatly and the amount of the textbook that is actually read is in question. Armbruster and her colleagues (1991) reported that even in lessons where the textbook is the focus, students do very little actual reading. When text is read it is primarily as round-robin oral reading, one student reading at a time. Text is more likely to be read aloud, by teachers and students, when students have difficulty reading it independently. The oral reading of text, however, is frequently interrupted with teachers' questions and students' answers.

An unfortunate by-product of teachers' control of textbook reading is that students may come to depend on the teacher as the interpreter of the text, rather than developing their own skills for independently synthesizing information from the textbook. If students work with a single text in a content area, they may also come to see that textbook as the authority and limit their opportunities to critically evaluate ideas across multiple sources (Geisler, 1994).

In contrast to these narrow views of the uses of content area texts, we want to engage our students in ways that emphasize higher-order thinking skills, including inquiry, critical analysis, and synthesis of information (Bean, 2000). Students learn from their experiences and we must provide extensive and intensive reading experiences with a range of content area texts, just as we do with narrative, if students are to become competent readers across the curriculum.

GUIDELINES FOR USING INFORMATION TEXTS/TEXTBOOKS

As we consider the ways in which we will organize learning opportunities for our students in content area study, we should keep in mind the following guidelines, drawn from a synthesis of research (Irvin, 1998, pp. 173–174) and from years of my own personal experiences with middle grade students and teachers:

- Focus on the process of constructing meaning, with special consideration to the role of prior knowledge in the development of new concepts.
- Provide explicit, scaffolded strategy instruction to move students toward independent learning.
- Provide ample amounts of time for extensive and intensive reading to build and practice reading skills and the effective use of self-regulated strategies.
- Facilitate comprehension instruction before, during, and after reading.
- Provide daily opportunities for students to learn collaboratively and talk about their reading.
- Reinforce and develop reading abilities through writing.
- Make assessment compatible with the kinds of learning encouraged.

We will keep these guidelines in mind as we consider the materials and instructional strategies we will use to engage our students.

GUIDELINES FOR EVALUATING INFORMATION TEXTS/TEXTBOOKS

Knowing that students often have many fewer experiences reading and constructing meaning effectively in information texts and textbooks, we must carefully consider our selections of texts for instruction. Consider the following potential strengths and weaknesses of information texts, especially textbooks that are used in the content areas of science, social studies, and mathematics:

Strengths

- *Scope.* Text carefully lays out content from grade level to grade level, ensuring that all areas of a discipline are addressed.
- *Sequence.* Textbooks typically take a spiral approach; topics introduced at one grade level are expanded at a later level.

Weaknesses

- *Limited concept development.* Concepts may be presented in a limited amount of text. So many ideas may be presented at one time that students end up attempting to recall too many major ideas at the same time (Anderson & Armbruster, 1984; Armbruster, 1984).
- *Disconnectedness.* From chapter to chapter there may be little relationship between the topics and concepts presented. Little or no attempt may be made to show how one topic is related to another.

- *Developmentally inappropriate.* Topics may be beyond the age/stage of what the learner can conceptualize; concepts covered may assume background knowledge that readers do not have.
- *Readability.* The level of reading can become very challenging due to unfamiliar vocabulary for a large number of new/unfamiliar concepts. In an attempt to reduce the difficulty level of a text, sentences may be shortened, taking out causal connectives (*because, therefore, as a result*). Such sentences make causal relationships between key ideas more difficult to determine.

To help us make appropriate decisions about which information texts and which portions of adopted textbooks to use with our middle grade students, Wolfinger (2000) suggests that we ask ourselves 10 questions to evaluate the quality of the texts (see Figure 7.1). Being aware of the strengths and weaknesses of the texts that we use for instruction enables us to make more informed instructional decisions on behalf of our students.

With a partner or group of your peers, select a current textbook to evaluate. After careful review of the text, independently answer each of the 10 questions listed in Figure 7.1. Compare your notes with others. Clarify the differences in your evaluations.

• • •

SELECTING INSTRUCTIONAL STRATEGIES

To prepare for scaffolding students' experiences in information texts/textbooks, we should recall from Chapter 4 that to mediate between students and what is to be learned, we must carefully consider:

- Our *purpose* for engaging students in thinking about the text,
- The *strategy(ies)* to assist students as they construct meaning before, during, and after reading the text, and
- Our *reflection* on how we adjust support to students as indicated by their feedback during discussion (Dixon-Krauss, 1996).

■ FIGURE 7.1

Questions to guide textbook evaluation

1. Is the content presented accurate?
2. Is the content developmentally appropriate?
3. Is there a balance of content (e.g., in science the text covers biological, physical, and earth-space sciences)?
4. Is the content merely mentioned or is it fully developed?
5. Is an appropriate amount of content information included in each chapter?
6. Is the content accessible to the students? Can they learn it in an appropriate way?
7. Is the content meaningful to students?
8. Is the content relevant to the students?
9. Can the content be taught effectively using hands-on teaching strategies with real materials?
10. Is the content applicable to real-life situations?

■ FIGURE 7.2

Instructional strategies
and skills

Instructional Strategies	. . to teach/practice . .	Reading/Thinking Skills
Visuals of Self-Questioning		Predict
Predict and Confirm		Identify
Scavenger Hunt		Label
K-W-L Plus		Recall
Expectation Grid		Infer
List–Group–Label		Recognize patterns
Think-Aloud	→	Sequence
Say Something		Group
Think Silently		Summarize
Self-Guided Reading—Visuals		Understand cause/effect
Active Reading		Understand compare/contrast
GIST		Generalize
Reciprocal Teaching		Analyze
Topic–Detail–Main Idea		Evaluate
Recycled Stories		
QAR		
Graphic Organizers/Idea-Mapping		

In this chapter, as well as throughout this text, we examine a variety of ways to move students toward self-regulated independence as readers. We choose a *specific instructional strategy* because we believe that it is best for achieving our *purpose*. As we engage students, *reflection* on what we see them do and say tells us about the effectiveness of our decision. In addition to the multiple uses of the ML–TA/MR–TA to mediate between students and texts, a variety of instructional strategies, adapted from Wallis (1998) and shown in Figure 7.2, are available that we can use to teach and extend students' understanding of various reading/thinking skills. Students become full participants in the community of content learners when they know what strategies and skills active readers use, as well as when and how to use such skills and strategies. We must provide explicit instruction for all students to move toward full participation in our classrooms.

CONTENT MEDIATED READING–THINKING ACTIVITY (CONTENT MR–TA)

We begin our examination of instructional strategies for content area learning with a basic procedure for engaging students in text, content MR–TA, then we consider other specific strategies to enhance reading information text.

Let's visit a sixth-grade classroom, where the teacher, Jasmine, wants her students to think about how they link the author's ideas with what they already know. It is early in the school year and Jasmine is trying to provide some explicit guidance and support for her students because their experiences with independent use of strategies for constructing meaning in information texts appear to be rather limited. In tandem with modeling thinking while reading such texts, Jasmine will also provide many opportunities for her students to practice using the strategies independently and in small groups.

From Chapter 4 we are familiar with an MR–TA (mediated reading–thinking activity) as a procedure for guiding students in their interactions with narrative texts. A narra-

■ FIGURE 7.3

Comparing MR–TA in
narrative and information
texts

MR–TA	Content MR–TA
Before the reading, reader thinks— *What is this possibly going to be about? *What do I already know?	*Before the reading, reader thinks—* *What is this going to be about? *What information do I already know about this topic? *By looking at the text can I tell what I might need to think about to understand the author's ideas?
During the reading, we think— *How does this fit with what came before? *How does this fit with what I already know? *What will happen next? *Do I need to change what I am thinking?	*During the reading, we think—* *Am I finding the important details? *Which ideas are the main or most important ideas? *How do these ideas fit with what I already know? *Do I need to rethink my own ideas?
After the reading, we think— *How do I feel about this? *What do I want to remember about this?	*After the reading, we think—* *Now, what was that all about? *What do I really need to remember? *How will I use these ideas?

tive MR–TA focuses on using background knowledge, combined with the ideas in the text, to encourage students to anticipate and respond to the story. In information texts, however, the emphasis is not so much on personal response, as on recognizing important ideas and linking those ideas to our prior knowledge. We interact with the author's ideas as presented and use personal knowledge to support our understanding.

Given the differences in texts, it would stand to reason then that Jasmine revises the narrative MR–TA technique when she moves to information text. Figure 7.3 shows a comparison of the reader's thinking between an MR–TA for narrative texts and a content MR–TA.

In information texts, Jasmine wants to help her students realize how their reading (or listening, if she reads aloud to students using a content ML–TA) may be different than with narrative texts. Students need to know they must pay careful attention to the author's ideas. They are not as free to make personal interpretations in information texts as in narrative texts. Retaining, using, or acting on the information in the text is a purpose of the reading; therefore, students must be actively involved in linking new information to their existing schema. They must come to realize that they are responsible for monitoring what is or is not making sense.

Jasmine realizes that what her students are able to take from a text depends on what they bring to it. Students who come to us with more extensive background knowledge and more book experience may be more successful initially than less-experienced students. As Jasmine observes students' responses during content MR–TAs, she must watch the responses of her less-experienced students as a gauge of effectiveness, then provide the appropriate instruction to close the gaps among students.

To promote thinking and meaning making before, during, and after the reading of a text, Jasmine stops at key points and discusses the text by asking open-ended questions. Because of the structure of ideas in information texts, she guides students to explain the information in a text and make connections among ideas and between the text and their own knowledge. She carefully examines the structure of ideas in a particular text to guide how she supports students' thinking and connecting.

In Chapter 4, we used a *predict–read–respond–connect* cycle to mediate between students and narrative text. In a content MR–TA, because of differences between narrative and information text (readers' purposes for reading, the way the text is written, and the ways readers must think while reading), readers do not *respond* to text. Instead, readers first must *explain* the ideas they found in the text, then make connections to their schema for the topic. So, Jasmine revises the content MR–TA cycle to be *predict–read–explain–connect.*

For example, imagine that Jasmine's sixth-grade classroom is beginning a study of ancient Egypt. Chapter 3 in the adopted social studies textbook that she uses focuses on ancient Egypt, as one of several chapters about the beginnings of civilization. The unit she plans begins with a look at the Nile River as the base of Egyptian civilization. After brainstorming and clustering what students already know about the Nile (rather than ancient Egypt as a whole), she engages students in viewing a video about the Nile River Valley to help students build visual images of that time and place. Then Jasmine prepares for the textbook reading, encouraging and supporting students' thinking through a content MR–TA. She begins by asking students to preview the text and predict the information the text might contain. Figure 7.4 provides a scripted illustration of how a content MR–TA with Jasmine's social studies textbook might proceed.

A content MR–TA is a basic technique for chunking text and guiding students to realize how actively involved they should be with a text in order to comprehend. The content MR–TA also provides opportunities to teach students how to detect and use text structures, how to integrate information from visual aids for comprehension, and how to self-monitor one's reading. When Jasmine uses an ML–TA/MR–TA, she alternates her modeling with opportunities for students to make decisions about their own strategy use during reading.

What did you notice about the ways in which Jasmine modeled and guided students' thinking? It would be good to challenge yourself to develop an MR–TA for an information text that you might read with students. Ask yourself what you notice about your thinking as you read the text and how you might help students notice their own thinking while reading. This is a good time to look back at Chapters 2 and 3 to remind yourself about issues related to comprehending information texts and strategies used by good readers.

• • •

The remainder of this chapter focuses on a variety of strategies we can use to provide explicit instructions that show students a variety of ways in which they can actively construct meaning with text. Each strategy serves a purpose. Selecting a particular strategy should be directly related to our *purpose* for engaging students in thinking about a particular text, and whether we want to model thinking *strategies* before, during, and/or after reading text. As

Before Reading:

Predict: Let's think about how we make predictions before we begin to read. The heading of this section of the text is "The Geography of Ancient Egypt." I'm thinking about this heading as I read the other subheadings on pages 65–69. I'm asking myself, "What do I think I might learn about Egypt?" The heading tells me that the focus is on geography, so I ask myself, "What do I know about geography?" I know it has something to do with the land and how the people are able to live in that environment. What predictions are you making as you preview this section? *(takes responses from students, queries students about what influenced that prediction)* How do these predictions compare to the Nile web that we started? *(Students make comparisons and contrasts.)*

During Reading:

Read: Let's look at the first subheading, "The Nile River Valley." Here we want to listen carefully to see if our ideas are on track with what the author thinks is important about the Nile. *(Jasmine reads the first three paragraphs out loud to set the tone for the reading. She refers students to the map on page 66 as suggested in the second paragraph. She reminds students that textual aids, like maps, can help make visual links with the author's ideas. Then she continues to read aloud.)* What do we know so far? *(She takes students' responses.)* I noticed how the author of this textbook reminds us how much the geography of a place influences people's lives. What ideas are important to remember about the influence of the geography? Please read the remainder of this subsection silently.

Explain: What did we find out about the Nile? *(takes students' responses, queries for students' awareness of cues from the text, as well as from their heads, that lead to those ideas)*

Connect: Should we add to or revise our web? Why do we think these ideas are important? What clues in the text and in our heads lead us to say that? *(Adds to the web *flows from south to north, and *Egypt divided into Upper and Lower).*

Predict: Look at the map on page 66. What differences might there have been between Upper and Lower Egypt? What do we notice on the map that might give us some ideas? *(takes responses)* What does the next subheading make you think about? *(takes responses)*

Read: Let's read "The Overflow of the Nile" silently to check our ideas.

Explain: What did we find out about the overflow? *(takes responses)* Does the text explain why the overflow happened every summer? *(takes responses)* Perhaps we should reread the last few paragraphs to see if we can clarify our thinking. Did that help? Sometimes authors are inconsiderate and don't tell us everything or they think we know more about the topic than we do. Where else can we look for information to help us? *(Guides students to look at geographical areas of central Africa on the classroom map.)*

Connect: Do we need to add to or revise our cluster? *(takes responses)* The next section is titled "The Nile Delta." We should ask ourselves what we already know about that. *(Students refer back to the web and the map on page 66.)*

(continued)

Predict:	What else might we find out about the Nile Delta in this section? What makes us think that? The text? Our heads? *(takes responses)*
Read:	Please read this section on page 67 silently.
Explain:	What do we know about the delta? *(takes responses)* What did you find out about the comparison of the delta to the lotus flower? Does that seem important for us to remember? Why or why not? *(takes responses)*
Connect:	How do these ideas compare to the ideas on our web? *(takes responses)*
Predict:	We can tell from the subheadings and illustrations that the remaining sections have something to do with farming. Why do you think the textbook author put these sections next? *(takes responses)* As you read silently, it is important to make note of the details about farming and the Nile that you think are important to add to your understanding of life during this time in Egypt.
Read:	Students read pages 68 and 69 silently.
Explain:	What details did you notice as you read? *(takes responses)* Did anyone use the drawing on page 69 to better understand the way ancient Egyptians used irrigation? How did the drawing help? *(takes responses)* The drawing is another text aid that the author gives us to add to what we learn from the words in the text. The author expects us to use these aids to add to or revise our understanding.

After Reading:

Connect:	In the last paragraph on page 69, the textbook author states that the Nile helped to unite Egypt. What do we know that could support that statement? Where did we get our ideas? *(takes responses)* Do we need to make any other revisions to our web for today? *(takes responses)* When we finish reading it is important to try to connect the most important ideas together to make it easier to remember. What are the most important ideas we want to remember from this reading? *(takes responses)* Let's highlight those important ideas on our cluster.

we engage our students in the strategy, we must *reflect* on their response so that we can decide how to adjust our support to move students toward self-regulated use of the strategy. Students learn differently and will not find utility in the same strategies. Here is a major challenge in teaching—knowing our students well enough to help them figure out which strategies are most effective for each of them.

STRATEGIES TO BUILD BACKGROUND

Predict and Confirm. There are times when we engage students in reading text for which they have little prior knowledge. *Predict and Confirm* (Beyer, 1971) is an instructional strategy in which we provide relevant background information to students in two stages. It prepares students to make predictions that set purposes for reading. In the beginning, Predict and Confirm moves back and forth between small-group and whole-class discussions. Working together, students are guided to draw important information from the materials that serve to focus their personal predictions when the reading begins. This is an excellent strategy to use at the beginning of a unit of study or a new topic within a unit.

Procedure

- The teacher poses a general question about the topic of the reading.
- In small groups students:
    - Preview text,
    - Consider additional information provided by the teacher,
    - Discuss ideas generated by the information, and
    - Make predictions about the reading.
- Students and the teacher discuss and write predictions from small-group work.
- The teacher presents additional information, such as pictures, a video, or a story.
- Small groups, and then the whole class, discuss whether to revise or modify predictions.
- Students read the selection in the textbook using their personal predictions as the purpose for reading.
- The teacher helps the students revise their predictions, based on the reading.

The revised information can then be used as the beginning of research and writing experiences to extend students' thinking.

Scavenger Hunt. There are times when students need background information, particularly vocabulary, before starting a unit of study. Borrowing the format of scavenger hunts that are familiar to many students outside of school, teams of students work together, searching for information about a list of related items (Cunningham, Crawley, & Mountain, 1983). You will need to decide how you feel about having teams compete against each other in the hunt.

■ *Imagine yourself guiding your students in their reading and study of a textbook. What skills and strategies might you need to teach to help all children construct meaning?*

Procedure

- Teacher announces new unit of study that will begin in a few days and provides lists of some key vocabulary and concepts for that unit.
- The class is divided into teams of four to six students.
- The teams get identical lists of terms for the scavenger hunt.
- Teams are able to search a wide range of sources for initial information, such as the Internet, class and school libraries, community resources, and interviews.
- At the beginning of the unit, teams share what they found in their hunt.
- A record of the hunts, such as class charts that combine items from all groups' lists, is valuable for reference during the unit.

STRATEGIES TO ACTIVATE AND FOCUS PRIOR KNOWLEDGE

K-W-L Plus.   The K-W-L chart is a well-known tool for both reading and writing. While Donna Ogle (1986) first developed the idea to support students' comprehension of information text, many educators also use the chart to help students brainstorm for writing about specific topics. In the *Plus* version of the K-W-L, Carr and Ogle (1987) added semantic mapping and summarizing to strengthen the relationships that students made among ideas in the text.

Other variations of K-W-L charts can also be used:

- K-W-L-Q, adds a Q, "Questions from the reading" (Schmidt, 1999);
- K-W-H-L, adds an H, "How I can learn" (Bromley, 2000); and
- K-W-L-S, adds an S, "What I still need to learn" (Sippola, 1995).

The procedure begins as a teacher-guided activity, moving back and forth between the whole class and small groups. The next step is to encourage individual students to complete the steps, supported by whole-class discussion. Finally, students have a go at the procedure on their own and discuss their thinking following the completion of the activity. It is important that students understand the intention—learning to "think" like a K-W-L while reading text.

Procedure

- The teacher provides a three-column chart, on which students fill in the first column, "What I already *KNOW*." Small-group brainstorming is effective to get more students involved in the process.
- Information from the small groups is combined and categorized.
- Students preview the material to be read.
- Teacher helps students use the list/categories generated to anticipate categories of information they may find in the reading.
- The teacher leads a discussion to help students pull together information and formulate personal questions for the reading.
- Small groups then fill in the W column of the chart, "*WHAT* we think we might learn as we read."
- Students read the selection.
- Small groups discuss the reading and collaborate to fill in the L column of the chart, "What we *LEARNED* from the reading."

- Mapping: Small groups use the K-W-L worksheet to construct a web of the main ideas from the reading and how the ideas are related.
- Summarizing: Small groups use the map to produce a summary to improve comprehension.
- Extension: Identify the thinking that good readers do in each step of the process.

Expectation Grid.   Caldwell (1993) suggested this visual tool to help students independently prepare for reading. Even if we don't know much about a specific topic, we still have expectations about the types of things (categories) that could relate to that topic.

Imagine that we are talking to someone who has never heard about the discovery of King Tut's tomb. What are the types of things (categories) we might tell this person? We might describe who made the discovery (people), where it happened (location), how it happened (sequence and reason), or the impact of the discovery (cause/effect and importance). Creating an *Expectation Grid* requires that we anticipate the categories in which we might find information (see Figure 7.5). Anticipating the categories is a form of making predictions, general rather than specific. It is helpful to leave one or two grids open for an unexpected category. The grid can be completed during or after the reading. Information in the Expectation Grid can be summarized or can become the basis for further research.

Procedure

- As students prepare to read, they think about what they expect to learn from a particular reading.
- After previewing the text to be read, categories are created.
- During the reading, important information can be collected by category, which requires the student to make connections between details.
- Unexpected categories are added during the reading.
- After the reading, each category is reviewed to be sure that information is in the correct location.

List–Group–Label.   Hilda Taba (1967), an expert in social studies, was concerned with helping students learn new concepts by making connections between words/ideas. *List–Group–Label* is a flexible strategy that can be used to anticipate ideas that may appear in a specific text, but can also be revised during or after the reading to add new information. The labeled and grouped list typically resembles a web or cluster (see Figure 7.6).

Procedure

- **List.** Brainstorm as many words as possible related to a particular subject/topic/idea.
- **Group.** Rearrange ideas to indicate which words go together to form a group.
- **Label.** Identify a word or phrase that describes how the items in the group are related.

STRATEGIES TO MODEL ACTIVE READING

Think-Aloud.   Teachers are consistently encouraged to make the thinking processes of active, competent readers more accessible for all students. While reading, we think aloud (Davey, 1983), talking to students about our thinking. We tell them what we are noticing

■ **FIGURE 7.5**

Sample expectation grids

People	Location	Sequence
Reason	Historical Event	Cause/Effect
Importance		

Characteristics	Diet	Habitat
Life Cycle	Animal	Usefulness
Hunted by		

in the reading, what the words and visual aids make us think about. We try to describe the various ways in which we sense our own comprehension and how we select a strategy to repair comprehension when it seems to have broken down. In this text, *Think-Alouds* are modeled through minilessons and ML–TAs/MR–TAs. The list below, adapted from suggestions by Margaret Richek and her colleagues (2002), identifies some ways of thinking while reading that can and should be made more explicit for all students.

Thinking Processes of Active Readers
- Summarize/connect ideas as we read.
- Think ahead when we make a prediction or an inference.
- Question the text when we are not sure.
- State what is making sense, what we think we are figuring out.
- State when and how we connect to our prior knowledge.
- State when and how we make personal connections to something in the text.

■ **FIGURE 7.6**

List–Group–Label

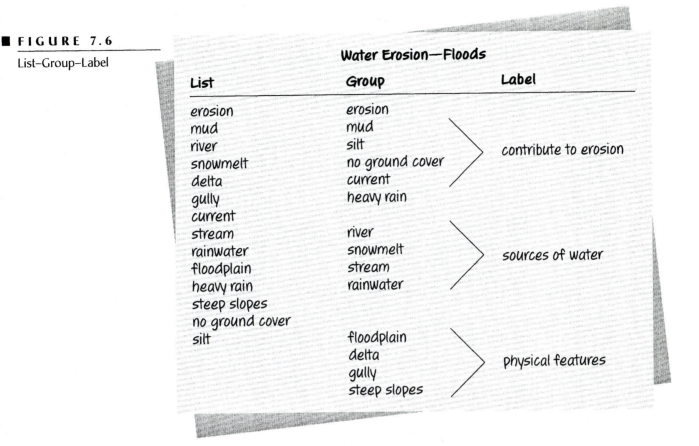

Water Erosion—Floods

List	Group	Label
erosion	erosion	
mud	mud	
river	silt	contribute to erosion
snowmelt	no ground cover	
delta	current	
gully	heavy rain	
current		
stream	river	
rainwater	snowmelt	sources of water
floodplain	stream	
heavy rain	rainwater	
steep slopes		
no ground cover		
silt	floodplain	
	delta	physical features
	gully	
	steep slopes	

Think Silently. *Think Silently* is an individual application of the Think-Aloud strategy suggested by Wallis (1998). The teacher would first model this process as a Think-Aloud. Students would then be encouraged to read silently and share how they were able to use this type of strategy to actively monitor their reading.

Procedure

- Think. . . . What predictions can I make about this text and the content?
- What visual images do I have in my mind?
- What do I already know about this?
- Do I need to read more? Think more? Read on?

Say Something/Say Something Silently. It is sometimes helpful to have insight into another's thinking about reading. *Say Something* (Harste, Short, & Burke, 1988) provides a procedure for two readers to talk to each other about their impressions of a text. After reading, when students say something to each other, they often find that each has noticed different things about a text. The two readers then have the opportunity to teach each other about their reading strategies.

Say Something Silently (Wallis, 1998) is a strategy that individual readers use to guide themselves through text. While slightly different than Say Something, Say Something Silently also promotes active reading. After learning to process reading a text with a partner, it is easier to process on one's own reading and thinking.

Procedure: Say Something
- Partners decide how to read—silently, take turns, one reader.
- Agree on first stopping point, read, stop, say something about what you just read.
- Select next stopping point and repeat steps.

Procedure: Say Something Silently
- Individual student previews; notices charts, graphs, bolded words, and so on.
- The student plans where to stop and say or write something about what was just read.
- After finishing each segment, the student makes a list of the most important ideas.

Visual Tour Guide.   It is important, while reading information text, to understand and integrate the information presented in visuals throughout the reading. Wallis (1998) suggests that readers focus on a visual in the text and ask several self-questions to guide interpretation of the visual. Self-questioning can first be modeled by the teacher as a Think-Aloud. Then, the teacher can provide practice for students to try asking self-questions about visual aids, with discussion of how students made decisions about the meaning of the visual aids. Finally, students can try the procedure on their own, with follow-up discussions.

Procedure

Individual readers look at a visual and ask self-questions:

- Where do I start?
- Have I ever seen one like this before?
- What can this visual tell me?
- Are there labels, headings, or captions that can help me?
- Is this familiar or do I need some assistance?
- How does this information fit with or add to the text?

Active Reading.   Karen Feathers (1993) suggests a procedure to encourage active reading among students. To help students "see" what they are thinking about a text, they create codes for their thinking and mark those codes on a copy of the text. This is an excellent way for students to see their own active reading processes. It would be best to teach this strategy as a whole-class or small-group shared reading of the text, making decisions about which code to place in the right-hand column. Students can also be guided to consider how to monitor for reading that is not making sense.

Procedure
- On copies of text, students create a column on the right side of the text to indicate their thinking and questions as they read.
- Depending on their purposes for reading, students develop codes for such things as
  - Main idea (MI),
  - Don't understand (DU),
  - I don't know this (!!),
  - I have questions about this (??),
  - Why is this called an _____? (Why?)

- After the first reading students are encouraged to reread to see if they can answer any of their own questions.
- Finally, they are encouraged to synthesize their thinking, separating what is known from what needs further reading or research.

GIST.   Similar to writing a telegram, the GIST strategy relies on an economy of words to convey a message. GIST focuses on reducing text to a few key ideas (Anderson, 1978). First with teacher guidance, then in small groups, partners, or individuals, students move through cycles of connecting, analyzing, and summarizing facts and details. After the reading, the key ideas are expressed as a summary of the reading.

Procedure

- Students and teacher read three to five paragraphs (or an agreed-on amount).
- Readers collaborate to reduce the key ideas of the text to 20 words that capture the gist.
- Students and teacher read more text.
- Readers collaborate to incorporate new key ideas with the previous key ideas, still limited to 20 words.
- The read and reduce cycle continues until the reading is completed.
- When complete, the readers produce a written summary that describes the key ideas of the text as a whole.

Reciprocal Teaching.   Encouraging active reading is the main purpose of *Reciprocal Teaching* (Palincsar & Brown, 1984a & b, 1986). "Students are taught to make predictions while reading, to question themselves about ideas in text, to seek clarifications when confused, and to summarize content. The adult teacher initially explains and models these strategies for students, but quickly transfers responsibility to the members of the group, with individual students taking turns leading the reading group" (Pressley, 1998, pp. 205–206). For this strategy to be effective, it is essential that the teacher model higher order questioning, to move students beyond the literal-level questions they typically ask. Herrmann (1988) suggests a few changes to the procedure to increase the explicit explanations needed for students to internalize self-monitoring strategies.

Procedure

- **Predict.** Read the title, preview visual aids, and ask the students to predict possible content.
- **Read.** Read the text aloud paragraph by paragraph.
- **Question.** After each paragraph, ask questions about the content and invite students to share possible answers. Ask students to offer additional questions.
- **Summarize.** At appropriate places, summarize what was read and share with students how you arrived at the summary. Did you use a topic sentence? Did the author offer any clues about important segments?
- **Clarify.** Discuss any words or concepts that are confusing and help the students to clarify these. As in Think-Alouds, the students must have names for what they are doing.

Topic–Detail–Main Idea.   Richek and her colleagues (2002) suggest a strategy to help students determine when texts have clear connections between details and main ideas, versus when the reader is left to make that determination. At first, the teacher guides students through the process. The teacher identifies each step—topic, details, main idea—and thinks aloud to make clear the identification of each part. Writing the topic, details, and main idea also sets up for summarization of the text.

Procedure

- Read the entire selection.
- *Topic.* Reread first paragraph, identify the topic of the paragraph. State the topic in one or two words.
- *Details.* Underline each thing the author says about the topic. These are details.
- *Main idea.* Now, you have a topic and details. Check to see if there is a main idea that connects all the details.
- If you don't find a main idea, write a sentence that tells the main idea. Ask yourself: Is the author describing something? Comparing or contrasting? Explaining a problem or solution? Explaining a cause or an effect?

Question–Answer Relationship (QAR).

To answer questions about our reading, either asked by others or ourselves, it is helpful to consider where the source of the answer might lie. QAR (Raphael, 1984) is a simple strategy that has multiple possibilities. The source of the answer is usually found in one of four places:

In the book:	In my head:
* Right there	* Author and me
* Think and search	* On my own

The intention is for students, over time, to be able to use self-questions about the source of answers and determine where to look for content in a particular text.

Procedure

- Teacher and student read a passage together.
- Teacher asks a question about the text. Teacher asks students to discuss what they think the question is asking and where in the text the answer might be found.
- Students look for the answer, then discuss how it helped them to analyze the question and speculate on where the answer might be found.
- Over time, the teacher provides fewer prompts for analyzing the question, then fewer prompts speculating on the source of the answer.

Idea-Mapping.

The value of visual representations of organized information has been recognized since David Ausubel (1968) first suggested that educators should support students' concept development through a technique he called an advanced organizer. Ausubel suggested providing a structured overview of the most important information to be read (in a visual format), then returning to the overview to confirm the important ideas and add other information gained through reading.

Since that time educators have explored a wide range of visual organizations that support students' learning before, during, and after reading, as well as for planning compositions. *Idea-Mapping* (Armbruster, 1986; Armbruster & Anderson, 1982) is a procedure for teaching students to recognize organizational patterns of information text and help them visually represent how ideas in a textbook are linked. Initially, idea maps are made beforehand by the teacher, with the intent that students will learn to construct their own maps as they are better able to detect organization structures in information texts.

■ *How will you use visual representations of ideas and their relationships to help students build their comprehension of the information they gather from various texts?*

■ **FIGURE 7.7**

Idea map for description

Main Idea	
Detail	
Detail	
Detail	
Detail	
Detail	

Procedure

- In the early stages, the teacher identifies the organizational structure and gives students a blank map that is organized appropriately for the selected text (such as Figure 7.7).
- The next step is to give students the choice of two idea maps. After reading the text, the students decide which map fits best and then complete the map.
- The third step is for students to independently choose which map to use with a particular text.
- Finally, students construct their own idea maps as they recognize the structure of the text.

ONGOING SUPPORT FOR SELF-REGULATION

Self-Questioning Flowchart.   As we teach self-regulating reading behaviors, we construct a flow chart with our students to post on the wall of the classroom (Englot-Mash, 1991; Neal & Langer, 1992). The chart, such as the one shown in Figure 7.8, serves as a constant reminder of the ways in which active readers think while they are reading. Notice that this particular chart attends to comprehending both narrative and information text.

We want our students to know that good readers are actively involved in the process of reading. We want them to be aware of the types of things that good readers think about and ask themselves as they read. The chart should be constructed jointly as a class, using students' words whenever possible. In addition, as students add new self-regulating strategies to their repertoire, the chart should be revised to reflect those strategies.

Think about yourself as an active reader. Which of these strategies seem useful to you? Which strategies do you wish a teacher might have modeled or explicitly taught you as a middle grade student to make reading in information texts feel more comfortable?

As you have the opportunity to observe in middle grade classrooms, try to be more aware of the ways in which teachers and students talk about constructing meaning with information texts and textbooks. As you reflect on those observations, also reflect on the types of strategies that might provide more opportunities for students to practice active reading, moving them toward self-regulated reading of information texts.

● ● ●

■ *TAKE A MOMENT TO REFLECT . . .*

■ *High-quality information text is:*

- Factually accurate;
- Free of stereotypes;
- Clearly illustrated to enhance and clarify the text;
- Designed to encourage analytical thinking;
- Written with clear, interesting, and appropriate language; and
- Comprehensible to the reader (Norton & Norton, 1998).

■ *Information text can have the following structures:*

- Description or enumeration;
- Ordered collections or lists;
- Cause/effect;
- Compare/contrast; or
- Problem/solution.

■ *To use information texts effectively, we should:*

- Focus on the process of constructing meaning, with special consideration given to the role of prior knowledge in the development of new concepts.

Self-questioning flowchart

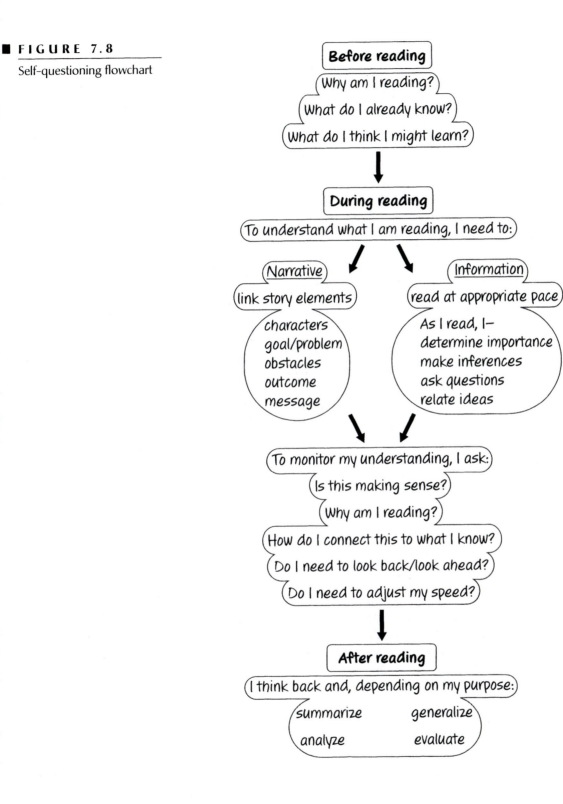

- Provide explicit, scaffolded strategy instruction to move students toward independent learning.
- Provide ample amounts of time for extensive and intensive reading to build and practice reading skills and the effective use of self-regulated strategies.
- Facilitate comprehension instruction before, during, and after reading.
- Provide daily opportunities for students to learn collaboratively and talk about their reading.
- Reinforce and develop reading abilities through writing.
- Make assessment compatible with the kinds of learning encouraged.

■ *We should evaluate texts to understand their strengths and weaknesses:*

- *Strengths:* broad scope and spiraled sequence.
- *Weaknesses:* limited concept development, disconnectedness, developmentally inappropriate, and readability level.

■ *As we preview texts for instruction we should evaluate by asking ourselves the following questions about the text:*

- Is the content presented accurate?
- Is the content developmentally appropriate?
- Is there a balance of content?
- Is the content merely mentioned or is it fully developed?
- Is an appropriate amount of content information included in each chapter?
- Is the content accessible to the students? Can they learn it in an appropriate way?
- Is the content meaningful to students?
- Is the content relevant to the students?
- Can the content be taught effectively using hands-on teaching strategies with real materials?
- Is the content applicable to real-life situations?

■ *When we plan instruction in information texts we consider:*

- Our purpose for engaging students in thinking about the text;
- The strategy(ies) to assist students as they construct meaning before, during, and after reading the text; and
- Our reflection on how we adjust support to students as indicated by their feedback during discussion.

■ *We can select from a wide variety of instructional strategies as we engage students and provide explicit instruction in effective use of strategies in information texts:*

- Mediated Reading–Thinking Activity (MR–TA);
- Predict and Confirm;
- Scavenger Hunt;
- K–W–L Plus;
- Expectation Grid;
- List–Group–Label;

- Strategies to model active reading;
- Think–Aloud;
- Think Silently;
- Say Something/Say Something Silently;
- Visual Tour Guide;
- Active Reading;
- GIST;
- Reciprocal teaching;
- Topic–Detail–Main Idea;
- Question–Answer Relationship (QAR);
- Idea-Mapping; and
- Self-Questioning Flowchart.

■ REFERENCES

Anderson, R. C. (1978). Schema-directed processes in language comprehension. In A. M. Lesgold, J. W. Pellegrino, S. D. Fakkema, & R. Glaser (Eds.), *Cognitive psychology and instruction.* New York: Plenum Press.

Anderson, T. H. & Armbruster, B. B. (1984). Content area textbooks. In R.C. Anderson, J. Osborn, & R. J. Tierney (Eds.), *Learning to read in American schools: Basal readers and content texts* (pp. 193–226). Hillsdale, NJ: Lawrence Erlbaum Associates.

Armbruster, B. B. (1984). The problems of inconsiderate text. In G. G. Duffy, L. R. Roehler, & J. Mason (Eds.), *Comprehension instruction: Perspectives and suggestions* (pp. 202–217). New York: Longman.

Armbruster, B. B. (1986). *Using frames to organize expository text.* Paper presented at National Reading Conference, Austin, TX.

Armbruster, B. B., & Anderson, T. H. (1982). *Idea-mapping: The technique and its use in the classroom* (Reading Education Report No. 36). Champaign, IL: Center for the Study of Reading, University of Illinois.

Armbruster, B. B., Anderson, T. H., Armstrong, J. O., Wise, M. A., Janisch, C., & Meyer, L. A. (1991). Reading and questioning in content-area lessons. *Journal of Reading Behavior, 23,* 35–60.

Ausubel, D. R. (1968). *Educational psychology: A cognitive view.* New York: Holt, Reinhart, & Winston.

Bean, Thomas W. (2000). Reading in the content areas: Social Constructivist dimensions. In M. L. Kamil, P. B. Mosenhall, P. D. Pearson, & R. Barr (Eds.), *Handbook of reading research* (Vol. 3, pp. 629–644). Mahwah, NJ: Lawrence Erlbaum Associates.

Beyer, B. K. (1971). *Inquiry in the social studies classroom.* Columbus, OH: Charles E. Merrill Publishing Company.

Borasi, R., & Siegel, M. (2000). *Reading counts: Expanding the role of reading in mathematics classrooms.* New York: Teachers College Press.

Bromley, K. (2000). Integrating language arts with the content areas. In K. D. Wood & T. S. Dickinson (Eds.), *Promoting literacy in grades 4–9: A handbook for teachers and administrators* (p. 220–232). Boston, MA: Allyn and Bacon.

Caldwell, J. (1993). *Developing an expectation grid for understanding expository text.* Milwaukee, WI: Cardinal Stritch College. Unpublished strategy.

Carr, E., & Ogle, D. (1987). K-W-L-Plus: A strategy for comprehension and summarization. *Journal of Reading, 30*(7), 626–631.

Carter, B., & Abrahamson, R. F. (1998). Castles to Colin Powell: The truth about nonfiction. In K. Beers & B. G. Samuels (Eds.), *Into focus: Understanding and creating middle school readers* (pp. 313–322). Norwood, MA: Christopher Gordon Publishers.

Cunningham, P., Crawley, S. G., & Mountain, L. (1983). Vocabulary scavenger hunts: A scheme for schema development. *Reading Horizons, 24,* 45–50.

Davey, B. (1983). Think aloud: Modeling the cognitive processes of reading comprehension. *Journal of Reading, 27,* 44–47.

Dixon-Krauss, L. (1996). *Vygotsky in the classroom: Mediated literacy assessment and instruction.* White Plains, NY: Longman.

Englot-Mash, C. (1991). Tying together reading strategies. *Journal of Reading, 35*(2), 150–151.

Feathers, K. M. (1993). *Infotext: Reading and learning.* Portsmouth, NH: Heinemann.

Geisler, C. (1994). *Academic literacy and the nature of expertise.* Hillsdale, NJ: Lawrence Erlbaum Associates.

Guthrie, J. T., Meter, P. V., McCann, A. D., Wigfield, A., Bennet, L., Poundstone, C. C., Rice, M. E., Failbisch, F. M., Hunt, B., & Mitchell, A. M. (1996). Growth of literacy engagement: Changes in motivation and strategies, during concept-oriented reading instruction. *Reading Research Quarterly, 31,* 306–333.

Harste, J. C., Short, K. C., & Burke, C. (1988). *Creating classrooms for authors: The reading–writing connection.* Portsmouth, NH: Heinemann.

Herrmann, B. A. (1988). Two approaches for helping poor readers become more strategic. *The Reading Teacher, 42,* 24–48.

Irvin, J. L. (1998). *Reading in the middle school.* Boston: Allyn and Bacon.

McGinley, W., & Tierney, R. J. (1989). Traversing the tropical landscape: Reading and writing as ways of knowing. *Written Communication, 6,* 243–269.

Meyer, B. F. (1985). Prose analysis: Purposes, procedures, and problems. In B. K. Britton & J. B. Back (Eds.). *Understanding expository text* (pp. 11–64). Hillsdale, NJ: Lawrence Erlbaum Associates.

Neal, J. C., & Langer, M. A. (1992, November). Open to suggestion: A framework of teaching options for content area instruction: Mediated instruction of text. *Journal of Reading, 36*(3), 227–230.

Norton, D. E., & Norton, S. E. (1998). *Through the eyes of a child: An introduction to children's literature* (5th ed.). Upper Saddle River, NJ: Merrill/Prentice Hall.

Ogle, D. M. (1986). KWL: A teaching model that develops active reading of expository text. *The Reading Teacher, 39*(6), 564–570.

Ogle, D. M. (1989). The know, want-to-know, learn strategy. In K. D. Muth (Ed.), *Children's comprehension of text* (pp. 205–223). Newark, DE: International Reading Association.

Palincsar, A. S., & Brown, A. L. (1984a). The quest for meaning from expository text: A teacher guided journey. In G. G. Duffy, L. R. Roehler, & J. Mason (Eds.), *Comprehension instruction: Perspectives and suggestions* (pp. 251–264). New York: Longman.

Palincsar, A. S., & Brown, A. L. (1984b). Reciprocal teaching of comprehension-fostering strategies and comprehension-monitoring activities. *Cognition and Instruction, 1*(2), 117–125.

Palincsar, A. S., & Brown, A. L. (1986). Interactive teaching to promote independent learning from text. *The Reading Teacher, 39*(8), 771–777.

Pressley, M. (1998). *Reading instruction that works: The case for balanced teachings.* New York: Guilford.

Raphael, T. E. (1984, January). Teaching learners about sources of information for answering comprehension questions. *Journal of Reading, 27*(4), 303–311.

Richek, M. A., Caldwell, L. S., Jennings, J. H., & Lerner, J. W. (2002). *Reading problems: Assessment and teaching strategies.* Boston: Allyn and Bacon.

Schmidt, P. R. (1999). KWLQ: Inquiry and literacy learning in science. *The Reading Teacher, 52*(7), 789–792.

Sfard, A. (1998). On two metaphors for learning and the dangers of choosing just one. *Educational Researcher, 27*(2), 4–13.

Sippola, A. E. (1995). K-W-L-S. The Reading Teacher, 49(6), 542–543.

Taba, H. (1967). *Teacher's handbook for elementary social studies.* Reading, MA: Addison-Wesley.

Wallis, J. (1998). Strategies: What connects readers to meaning. In K. Beers & B. G. Samuels (Eds.), *Into focus: Understanding and creating middle school readers* (pp. 226–243). Norwood, MA: Christopher Gordon Publishers.

Wolfinger, D. M. (2000). *Science in the elementary and middle school.* New York: Longman.

chapter 8

Understanding Writing Processes

In this chapter . . .

We explore:

- Four views of writing—as a code, a medium, a product, and a proce[ss]

- Thinking with written language, to retain, re-collect, re-create, re-construct, and re-present ideas,

- The process approach to writing, exploring writing as a recursive process including rehearsal or prewriting, composing or drafting, revising for meaning, editing for correctness, and sharing or publishing,

- Writing traits,

- Writing in the literacy program,

- Issues in maintaining legible handwriting, and

- Monitoring students' growth in writing through collecting samples [of] writing, observing, and conferring with students about their writing[.]

Something to Think About . . .

Like many adults, children often think that their lives are too dull to write about, that writers must be special people–minor gods who drop books into the library by magic. . . . Students need to know that the stories and books they see in the library are the creations of ordinary people like themselves. . . . The writing club is open to everyone. To join, all one needs are a few ideas. (Means & Linderer, 1998, p. 3)

Building a Theory Base. . .

Pat D'Arcy (1989), a British educator, writes, "We must not, at any stage, allow ourselves to forget that the act of writing is an act of making sense and of shaping meaning" (p. 1). *Writing to make sense. Writing to shape meaning.* As readers, we know what these phrases mean. From our earliest encounters with print, we have been influenced, even shaped, by the words of others.

We may think, however, that we cannot influence and shape others with our words. Our experiences with writing in school may have left us with little confidence that we can write like the authors we read. But writing is much more than the print we find in books. Look at the print that is around us today, and you will find examples of the ways writing shapes meaning, to influence, to inform, to organize, and to persuade.

VIEWS OF WRITING

Students in middle grade classrooms learn about writing by the ways they are taught to use it and by the things that teachers emphasize about it. D'Arcy (1989) states, "The writing we require from our pupils and the ways in which we respond to that writing will in their turn influence the pupils' expectations and consequently their approach to and performance in writing, possibly for life" (p. 19).

Lucy Calkins (1994) comments, "What our students do as writers will largely depend on what we expect them to do and on what they've done in the past" (p. 113). It is time to begin to consider whether students in our classrooms will see writing as a symbolic code that they must master, a medium through which they may communicate, an end product to achieve, an active process, or as a combination of these. As we consider different views of writing in the sections that follow, reflect on your own background as a writer. Which view(s) will students find at work in your classroom?

WRITING AS A CODE

If we view writing as a code, we give a great deal of attention to the correct use of language symbols. Most of us have firsthand experience with writing as a code. As students, we spent endless hours completing exercises that focused on grammar, sentence structures, spelling, and so on. We received feedback on our writing in the form of red marks on compositions. We were given specific formats into which we fit our ideas about a topic. While these practices were intended to focus our attention on the details of written language, we also learned that there was a "right" way to write.

Research in writing (Calkins, 1994; Clay, 1975; Graves, 1983, 1994) helps us realize that overemphasis on code, at the expense of meaning, can lead students not only to see writing as a tedious task, but may also lead students toward becoming inadequate writers. From our discussion about making meaning with print during reading, we know that concepts about written language are best acquired in the context of meaningful activity. Writing in the middle grades should emphasize the code of written language within the context of making and shaping meaning.

WRITING AS A MEDIUM

If we consider writing as a medium, we view it as "verbal play dough" (D'Arcy, 1989), out of which writers may make something useful. Just as an artist uses a medium as a vehicle of expression, so writers use words. Just as an artist experiments with a medium to see what it can do, a writer experiments with language without being quite sure where it will lead. An artist knows that while the medium is visible, its meaning lies within its creator and the individuals who observe it. So too the meaning of writing lies within its creator and observers.

By the way that we engage middle grade students with written language we can help them see language as a flexible and responsive medium, able to be manipulated or reshaped to meet different intentions. Students' experiences with written language affect their views about the possibilities of language. Middle grade students will come to us with a range of experiences in writing. Unfortunately, many of those experiences may have fostered negative feelings. We must be patient and provide many models and experiences that enable students to experience the flexibility and responsiveness of writing.

WRITING AS A PRODUCT

The completion of projects or tasks is important to our sense of satisfaction in our work and our lives, and is often the way that we measure our personal success. However, when completion becomes more important than the task itself, our work may become personally meaningless and unsatisfactory.

In writing, we want students to experience the self-satisfaction of finished products. We can encourage their writing to move in certain directions, but what will ultimately be most important is the direction that students think their work should take. If we expect to convince middle grade students that writing is a purposeful and satisfying tool for communication, we must remember that simply producing a written product should never become more important than the meaning that the product holds for the writer.

WRITING AS AN ACTIVE PROCESS

Research in writing during the past two decades has led us to realize that writing is an active, not a passive, process. Perhaps our own experiences with writing have taught us about this process. Writing is full of mental and physical activity that enables us to move our thinking out of our heads, down our arms, and out our fingers via pen or keyboard. The process of writing makes visible our thinking, our feelings, and the images in our heads.

Thinking of writing as an active process is tied to viewing writing as a responsive and flexible medium. For students to recognize the existence of this process, we must help them become aware of their thinking, then show them how they can capture that thinking with words. Providing varied writing experiences will help students see that writing can serve different purposes, take different forms, and be directed to different audiences.

Lucy Calkins (1994) pushes our thoughts about writing as a process even further. Her experiences with writing have taught her that "Writing does not begin with deskwork but with lifework . . . living with a sense of awareness" (p. 3). Cynthia Rylant, a children's book author, describes her own writing process as "being an artist every single day of one's life" (cited in Calkins, 1994, p. 3).

What views do you presently hold about writing? What past experiences have influenced your view?

• • •

Students must have opportunities not only to experience writing as a process, but must also come to place their own importance on writing as a medium for expression using a code that allows others to understand, and as a product that represents their thinking. Any writing program should provide a balanced view of writing. We must support students as they begin to understand that possibilities for writing exist beyond "completing tasks for the teacher."

• • •

THINKING WITH WRITTEN LANGUAGE

As we write, we think with written language (D'Arcy, 1989; Graves, 1994; Smith, 1982). Our thinking can take several forms depending on our purposes for writing (D'Arcy, 1989). Throughout our lives, we *retain* memories of our experiences with the world. At times we *re-collect*, or call up once again, these stored experiences in order to use them for some purpose. Some situations in which we find ourselves require us to *re-create* memories from our firsthand experiences, revisiting or even revising our thinking. We can also use writing to *re-construct* our ideas, arriving at new perceptions of knowledge gained through secondhand experience. Finally, writing enables us to *re-present* our thinking so that it can be seen and shared by others. (Note that D'Arcy deliberately hyphenates the terms to call attention to the fact that as we arrive at new knowledge and new understandings through writing, we draw on what we have already collected, constructed, or created.)

Our students will write by drawing on both their experiences and their knowledge of language. A writing program that encourages and supports thinking focuses on what students have retained in memory, enabling them to re-collect, re-construct, re-create, and re-present their thinking.

RETAINING EXPERIENCE

Through our senses we are constantly taking in new experiences, or "memories" as D'Arcy (1989) refers to them. Processing information through our senses is a natural way of learning (Piaget & Inhelder, 1969). Our senses influence how we interpret and retain experiences. As we *retain* experiences, we construct new schema or adapt existing schema. This process of retaining experience, especially meaningful experience, is virtually effortless and we may not realize all that we know. Talking about experience may be the first step for many students. Engaging in whole-class, small-group, and partner discussions brings ideas to the verbal level. Then, writing to explore thinking becomes a possibility.

RE-COLLECTING EXPERIENCE

"None of us are in a position to 'know what we know' until we are given opportunity to re-collect what we have retained" (D'Arcy, 1989, p. 4). *Re-collecting,* calling up past experiences or knowledge, gives us an opportunity to think about what we know. The more we re-collect what we know, the easier it is to use our experience and reshape our thinking. Experienced writers know this and write from what they know, re-collecting experiences to create believable stories.

Planning activities that enable students to re-collect what they have retained will be an essential step for successful and satisfying writing. Students can re-collect their ideas in many forms of informal writing such as notes, idea clusters, diagrams, lists, and short descriptions. The more students use writing to "see" their thinking, the more confident they will be that they have something to say.

RE-CREATING EXPERIENCE

Our firsthand experiences with the world are usually easier for us to recall than vicarious, or secondhand, experiences. When we sift through the incredible amount of detail we have retained from personal experience, certain memories stand out as significant to us. We *re-create* those experiences in our mind, perhaps highlighting some aspect differently than we had on previous occasions.

We re-create our responses to literature when we identify with the triumphs and struggles of characters. We use literature as a mirror. In its reflection, we use our own life experience combined with our literary experience to look closely at some particularly relevant event.

Writing in middle grade classrooms should enable students to re-create their lived experience and write about what they know best. Students who struggle with what to write about may be students who do not value their own lived experience. Carefully selecting for our reading program literature that connects with our students' lives can extend opportunities for re-creating experiences through writing.

RE-CONSTRUCTING EXPERIENCE

With each new experience, we gather re-collections of the past to understand the proper connections to make with the present. We adjust our ideas in light of what we know, *re-constructing*, or revising, previously held views. Much of the knowledge we gain in life is through secondhand experience, which can be more difficult to manipulate or reshape than firsthand knowledge.

Almost daily we ask students to re-construct their previous knowledge in light of new information. We introduce new concepts for which they lack firsthand experience. To enable students to use this new knowledge effectively, we should help them first re-collect what they already know. Writing, especially informal writing, can be instrumental in helping students see what they know in preparation for re-constructing their knowledge.

RE-PRESENTING EXPERIENCE

Sharing what we think connects us to the lived experience of others. The forms that such sharing takes depend in large part on our audience and our intentions for sharing. Audience and purpose shape the form and function of the writing.

To reinforce students' sense of what they know, they need many opportunities to share their thinking, considering the form that best fits their intended purpose and will make the strongest connections to their intended audience. *Re-presenting* thinking assumes that students are engaged in meaningful communication and have a vested interest in the outcome.

How will you treat writing in your classroom? How will you ask students to think with written language?

• • •

If I treat writing as an active process, my students will have numerous opportunities to represent their thinking. Informal writing, captured over time in logs or journals, provides students with opportunities to see their ideas change as they gather new information. During the process of developing a piece of writing to completion, my students may see a change in their ability to clearly re-present their thinking. By re-presenting their thinking in writing at different points in their learning, my students focus on their new knowledge. Seeing their own growth hopefully will lead to self-satisfaction as writers and learners.

• • •

PROCESS APPROACH TO WRITING—A JOURNEY IN THINKING

We turn our attention now to what we have learned about the process(es) that professional writers go through as they explore their thinking and attempt to share that thinking with others. While no journey is the same for any two people, some parts of the journey do bear close resemblance. Pat D'Arcy (1989) reminds us that:

> All journeys take time, and when the going is tough some will take longer than others. It is possible on a journey to have a rest along the way—several rests, if the journey is an extended trek over unfamiliar ground. It is possible to look back over ground already covered and to look forward at least as far as the next bend. It is useful to be able to call on help if you get stuck, and it can be reassuring to have company at least from time to time, as the journey progresses. (pp. 27–28)

In a writing program built on the process approach, pieces of writing emerge over time through a recursive, or flexible, process (Calkins, 1994; D'Arcy, 1989; Graves, 1983, 1994). To develop an idea fully, writers go through different phases with their thinking and writing, each phase serving a different purpose:

- Rehearsal or prewriting,
- Composing or drafting,
- Revising,
- Editing, and
- Publishing or sharing.

The process is considered *recursive* because writers move between phases of writing as it suits their need, not as someone directs them. Earlier we discussed different views of writing: as code, medium, product, and process. In a process approach to writing, we give attention to all four views of writing. For example, during editing, knowledge of writing as a code becomes very important. Writing as a medium comes into play as students consider their options for shaping ideas. Writing as a product is realized during the publishing phase, as students prepare their writing in a form to be shared with others. Student perceptions of writing as a *process* will undergird their efforts from start to finish.

REHEARSAL OR PREWRITING

Getting started with a piece, knowing what we want to write, and having confidence that an idea is worthwhile or that anyone else might be interested are dilemmas that all writers face. Conscious rehearsal accompanies the decision to write (Graves, 1994).

Getting Started.   If daily informal writing is an integral part of our literacy program, students will already be recognizing, examining, questioning, and exploring their thinking. Informal writing occurs in all areas of the curriculum, such as making a chart that compares and contrasts the functions of various government structures in social studies or explaining one's thinking in the solution of a problem in mathematics (see Chapter 9). If students have participated in many informal writing experiences, they will be ready to extend their thinking in more depth. If, however, students are not used to daily writing, we should provide many informal writing opportunities before expecting students to take pieces through a formal process of development, revision/editing, and publication.

To get started with a piece of writing, authors frequently do such things as the following (see Figures 8.1, 8.2, and 8.3):

- Daydream or write in their heads,
- Sketch or doodle, often labeling or making annotations,
- Brainstorm lists of words or ideas,
- Web, cluster, or outline ideas or sequences of thought,
- Read more about a topic,
- Talk with a friend,
- Free write,
- Make charts, graphs, Venn diagrams, or other graphic organizers for ideas, or
- Review notes made previously.

Experience with informal writing prepares students to think about beginning longer, more developed pieces. If our students have experience with exploring their ideas informally, they may feel comfortable and confident as they begin to plan a piece. Students' work during this phase should show great variety because they use different strategies as

■ **FIGURE 8.1**

Idea cluster for *Cinderella's Revenge*, fourth grade

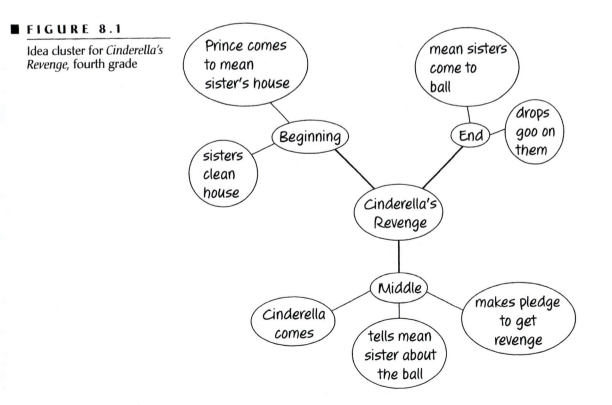

Word list for poem, "My
Family is a Rose," eighth
grade

person		part of flower
mother	keeps peace taxi *always making things	leaf
father	*protects fixes stuff works hard	thorn
sister	strong smart *stable	stem
dog	always happy *joy quiet	petals
me	friendly *gets everyone together	roots

■ FIGURE 8.3

Story map for historical
fiction, seventh grade

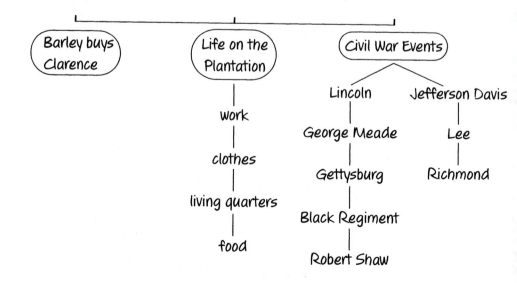

Barley's Plantation

Clarence - 48 (narrator)
Joseph - 30, strong
Phillip - 50, gray beard
Sally - 30s, tall, thin
Lily - 12, Sally's daughter

Barley buys Clarence

Life on the Plantation
|
work
|
clothes
|
living quarters
|
food

Civil War Events
Lincoln   Jefferson Davis
| |
George Meade   Lee
| |
Gettysburg   Richmond
|
Black Regiment
|
Robert Shaw

they get started. Encouraging only one strategy for all students, such as idea clustering, is limiting for those who find it easier to plan through other means, such as by making lists. Experience with informal writing helps students learn about the many different forms that their thinking can take as they prepare to develop an idea into a piece of formal writing. Observing students during informal writing also will help you know more about their preferred writing styles.

We don't want to hurry students through this planning phase. If we do, we may find they will continue to struggle with a piece that never really meets their expectations. Exploring ideas during this phase is essential if students are to find a focus.

Finding a Focus. At some point during the "getting started" phase, students will be ready to clarify their topic and direction. At this point response from another writer can be very helpful in affirming or clarifying thinking. A responsive listener must try to listen for the writer's intention, what he or she is hoping to accomplish with the writing.

Students can be trained to become responsive listeners. Notice the word *trained*. We must model what responsive listening looks and sounds like, then coach partners as they practice. We can also be one of these responsive listeners, as we hold conferences with students about the focus of their writing. D'Arcy (1989) suggests that we must look through children's writing, rather than at the writing itself. We must try to see the student's intention for the writing. Once students find their focus, sustained writing will usually follow.

COMPOSING OR DRAFTING

Sustained writing is the goal of this stage. When students have a clear sense of where they are trying to go with a piece of writing, sustaining their effort is not so difficult. Students who continue to struggle with their writing during this phase usually have not truly found their focus.

Our role during this phase is to get out of the way. As long as students are sustaining the writing, we let them go. They can use this phase to build their stamina as writers. We must remember that informal writing does not usually require sustained effort. Composing becomes the first time for many students that writing continues beyond short bursts.

During the composing phase, we begin to see something of the recursive nature of writing. Some writers move back to the strategies used during the "getting started" phase, especially when they find that they need to clarify what they know about their topic. Some writers, on occasion, move ahead into the editing phase and correct spellings or punctuation that they realize is not conventional. For others, moving back and forth between composing and revising/editing is a natural way for them to check their thinking, so we see them change, add, or delete some of their initial ideas (see Figure 8.4).

One of the reasons we should step back when students are composing is to let them become more aware of their own style as writers. Each of us benefits by knowing how we write and what processes we go through, by knowing what works for us as writers. Students can't learn about their own style if someone else is always intruding into the process.

REVISING

Revision refers to making changes for meaning and requires a writer to become a reader, rereading for meaning. While rereading ideas in the draft, the writer may recognizes gaps between her original intention and what she actually wrote. At that point she may be motivated to rework that particular part of the text. The writer may also decide to wait until a later time.

All Men Created Equal

"Going once, going twice, sold to the man in the back row for 40 dollars."

The man stood up. He was tall and lanky, with dark hair and a mustache. He was wearing a black overcoat and black socks. A big hat sat upon his head. He had a stern look on his face, but as I walked over to him he smiled a little.

"What's your name?" he asked.

"Clarence Tomkins," I replied.

"Mine's Bob Barley. Jump in the wagon."

I got in the back of the wagon quickly, and we drove off with a strong jerk. The ride lasted an hour. It was nice to get a break from work. My last owner had me working sixteen hours a day, even at night when it was dark. He finally had to sell me when my back became injured. It was apparently from the work I was doing. I was praying that this man would be different.

We got to his house and plantation. Immediately I saw three other slaves working out in the field, and as we drove up another little black girl came out of the house. She had ragged clothes on, but an apron so I guessed she worked in the house.

"Sarah," the man yelled, "I'm home with another one!"

A ~~women~~ woman came out of the house. She was petite, with blond hair. She ~~had on~~ wore a dress and apron. She looked me over for what seemed like a long time.

"Well, I guess he'll do," she said, "What's your name?"

"Clarence Tomkins."

"You had better get started. Lily here will tell you where your sleeping quarters are and everything else you need to know. Go along Lily."

The little girl took my arm and led me to a little shack over on the far side of the property.

"This is where we all sleep. There's me, Joseph, Phillip, and my ma Sally. They're out working. I work in the house cooking and cleaning. The old lady seems horrid, but she's not so bad. Just don't get in no trouble. We eat at 5:45 in the morning. Some mush and water. At 12:00 we get the same thing and at 8:00 at night we eat some bread, meat, and a small cup of milk. Sometimes I can sneak in a piece of extra bread or cheese, but not always. If you get into trouble they take away a meal, but there are no whips."

I said a silent prayer to God for both of my sisters had been killed with whips by their masters. I myself had felt the pain of a whip before.

"Any questions Clarence?" Lily asked me.

"What about clothes?" I asked. All that I had on now was a pair of old pants.

She looked me over and said "they'll probably give you a long sleeved shirt for cold weather. When it's warm though, you'll just have to work without your shirt. These are the shoes you'll get. . . ."

(story continues)

■ **FIGURE 8.4**

Sample draft, historical fiction, seventh grade

Making meaning can involve more than just changing words. Students may have to make major changes in meaning, such as restructuring sentences or rearranging the order of the whole piece. They may make minor changes such as adding punctuation to clarify meaning, and also may attend to the grammar or syntax of the language.

Donald Graves (1994) suggests that most writers follow a simple composing pattern:

select, write, read; select, write, read.

Over time, revision becomes an added step in the pattern as:

select, write, read, write, reread, and rewrite.

Revision occurs when writers are monitoring their composing phase, with the focus of their writing in mind. This sequence, however, is not automatic. Writers learn to revise through their struggle to communicate, and by understanding the possibilities inherent in the writing process.

Being able to revise requires that the writer sense other possible options in the writing. All students need guidance as they learn to look again at their writing. In fact, we may find ourself saying to a student, "Take another look at your words. What are you trying to say? Is it doing what you want? Perhaps you might consider. . . ." Students are also able to support one another in this re-seeing process. Figures 8.5 and 8.6 show a sample self-review and comments on a peer review for the historical fiction draft shown in Figure 8.4.

To some degree, a student's decisions to revise his own work is developmental. Donald Graves (1994) suggests a rough developmental sequence in revision. Students typically (1) add to a piece before they are able to sense where to (2) insert new ideas or information. After insertions, (3) finding and writing the main idea of a piece, instead of a "bed to bed" story that tells all, becomes possible. Finally, (4) lining out words, rather than erasing, is a sign that students see the words as flexible and open to revision.

If students lack sufficient knowledge of their topic or the genre in which they are writing, revision will be difficult. Similarly, if students lack a sense of audience, the focus of the writing will be unclear and revision may not target the ideas that most need

■ *Your students can learn a great deal about writing from each other. How might you teach students to share what they know about writing as they help each other revise and edit their writing?*

■ FIGURE 8.5

Self-review of historical
fiction, seventh grade

	Review Sheet	Form #1
	Name: Marie	Period: 4
	Title of Writing: All Men Created Equal	
	Draft #1	
1.	What is the strongest or most exciting part of piece?	
	The beginning—1st couple pages	
2.	Is the paper limited to 1 topic?	
	yes	
3.	What is the topic?	
	One slave's life during the Civil War	
4.	Does the lead get the writer right into the writing?	
	Yes—	
5.	Which parts don't fit in and could be taken out? . . "and as a matter	
	of fact I think I was their favorite. . ."	
6.	Where could I use more description or explanation?	
	—none—	
7.	Is there any part that could use dialogue?	
	I have it everywhere it needs to be	
8.	Is there any part that could confuse the reader?	
	Yes, when I put in about the 2 sides, I will change those few paragraphs	
9.	Have I repeated myself saying anything more than once? No—	
10.	Am I using particular words too often?	
	none—	
11.	Do I have paragraph breaks?	
	Paragraphing is fine	
12.	Is there information that could go in another place?	
	Yes, I will change it	
13.	How do I want my reader to feel?	
	Like they have a pretty good understanding of the Civil War———▶	

reworking. Finally, two issues that plague writers and block revision are lack of time to write and writing too much.

Sometimes students make a poor choice of topic and the writing does not develop. At that point, they need to know that abandoning a piece of writing is appropriate and something that writers may choose to do. The draft should be kept in the writing folder in case the writer decides to give the topic another try later.

■ FIGURE 8.6

Peer review of historical fiction draft, seventh grade

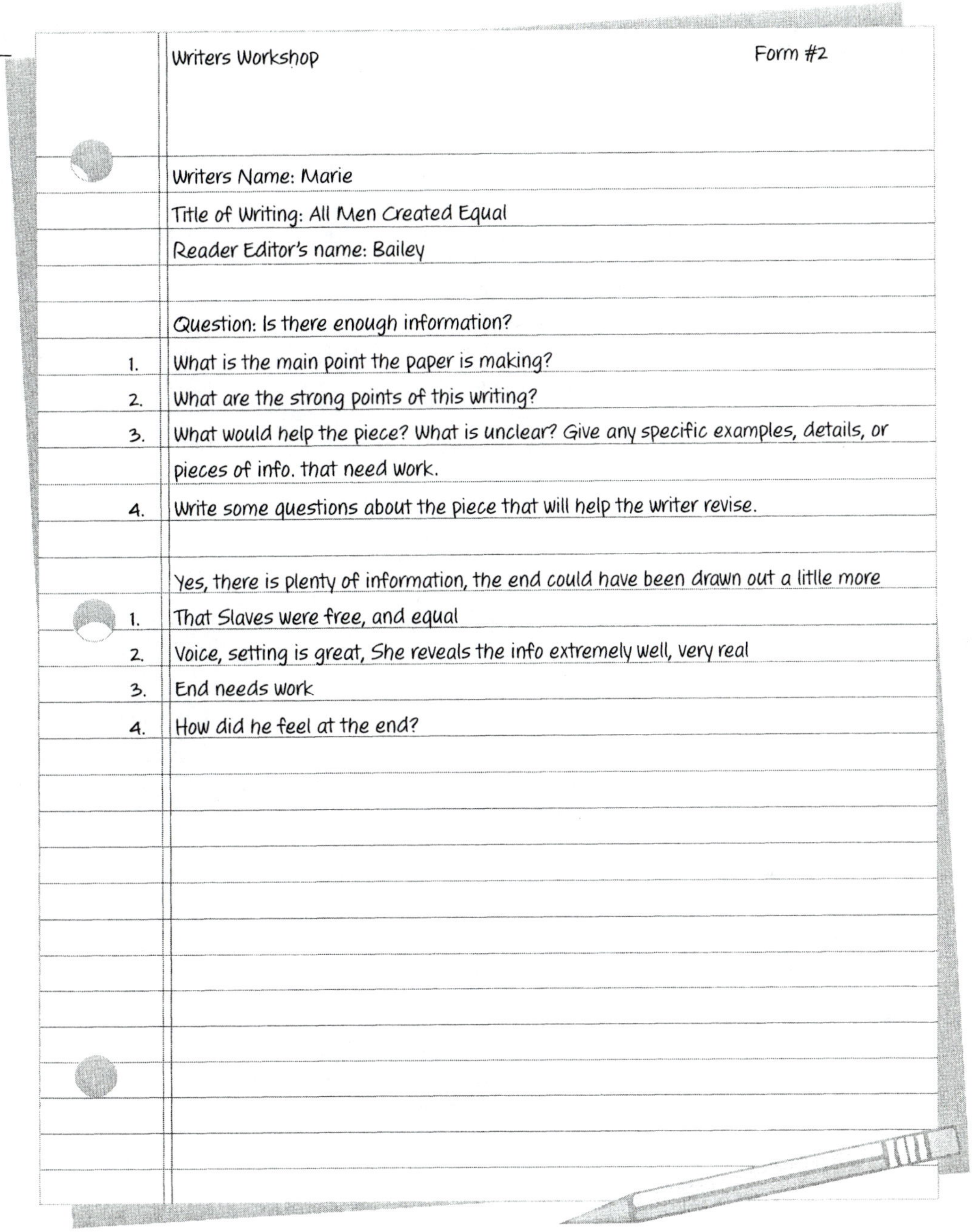

Writers Workshop	Form #2

Writers Name: Marie

Title of Writing: All Men Created Equal

Reader Editor's name: Bailey

Question: Is there enough information?

1. What is the main point the paper is making?
2. What are the strong points of this writing?
3. What would help the piece? What is unclear? Give any specific examples, details, or pieces of info. that need work.
4. Write some questions about the piece that will help the writer revise.

Yes, there is plenty of information, the end could have been drawn out a litlle more
1. That Slaves were free, and equal
2. Voice, setting is great, She reveals the info extremely well, very real
3. End needs work
4. How did he feel at the end?

EDITING

Editing requires a writer to become a reader and read for details, so that the writing is conventional and other readers are able to interpret the writing as intended. This phase will usually focus on conventions of writing such as grammar, capitalization, and spelling. Our expectations for students' level of use of conventions depends on their stage of word knowledge and spelling development (see a later section in this chapter). Here is where we must use our knowledge of students, so that we do not have unrealistic expectations of their ability, for example, to use correct spelling in their finished pieces. If we know that a student is just beginning to understand spelling patterns of derivational words, such as *composition* and *legality,* we do not expect conventional spellings without support of an editing partner or resources such as a dictionary.

We can assist students in achieving a satisfactory level of convention in their writing by helping them learn to work in editing groups. Here again, we should model for students how to read someone's writing and help them find details that might need attention. During our modeling, we must emphasize that the purpose of giving attention to correctly using the code is to be able to communicate clearly with others. For example, all writers spell words in certain ways because we have agreed, as users of American English, that we will all use the same spellings so we will know what others have written. If each of us chose our own spellings, or our own grammatical structures, we might not be able to make meaning from each other's writing.

PUBLISHING OR SHARING

As students move their writing toward completion, form may again become an issue. The best form for a piece of writing may not be evident until the draft of ideas has been completed. Between drafting and publishing, the student may realize a need to change form. For example, what began as a descriptive piece may become a poem because the student discovers that the message of the writing is better suited to poetry (see Figure 8.7). In such a case, the student moves back to the drafting and editing phases.

During the publishing, or sharing, phase, students have opportunities to publicize their writing (see Figure 8.8). In an author's chair (Graves, 1983, 1994) a student reads aloud a piece of writing to which other students respond. You also may prominently display writing in the classroom or publish it in books that are available for all to read. Students learn about writing from the writing of their classmates.

Think about the last piece of formal writing you completed. What do you know about your own writing process? What type of journey did you take with your writing?

• • •

In my own writing I have found that rehearsal consists of thinking for a long time about what I will write before I actually put anything on paper (or on disk). When I finally begin to compose, ideas come rapidly. Then I have to let it sit for a few days. I revise best when I step away for a few days and rethink what I want my audience to think or feel. Editing for conventions is relatively easy with a computer, but I find that I tend to edit as I go so there isn't much to correct with the spellcheck program.

• • •

■ FIGURE 8.7

Poem, "My Family is a Rose," eighth grade

My family is a rose.

My mother is a leaf, always making something.

My father is a thorn, protecting always.

My sister is a stem, trying hard to keep us stable.

My dog, Goldie, is the petals, always spreading joy.

And I am the roots, trying hard to hold us down from the rushing wind.

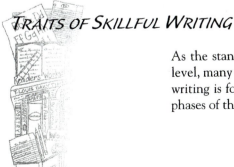

TRAITS OF SKILLFUL WRITING

As the standards movement has impacted language arts curricula at the state and local level, many states have moved to assessment of student writing. In my own state, students' writing is formally assessed at grades 4, 6, and 8. The assessment engages students in all phases of the writing process and evaluates the writing for specific traits.

Cinderella's Revenge
By Aubrey

Once upon a time like usual Cinderella was living happily ever after like in the first Cinderella, but only this time she's getting revenge. So this is how the story goes . . . .

One day the Prince came along to Pupil, Dupil, and Fupil's house. These are the mean people that Cinderella worked for.

They were in their aprons cleaning house when the Prince knocked on their door and said, "This is your royal highness." The mean girls ran to get their best clothes on but the Prince knocked down the door with them in their aprons running to their rooms.

This upset them so that they screamed, "Ahhhhhh!"

The Prince looked at them just standing in their aprons, "Oh," said the Prince, "too bad!"

"Well," said Pupil, "you have no right to walk into someone else's house without them answering. And look at us just standing here in our aprons."

There was suddenly a loud noise. Boom!!! It was the mother knocking down the door.

"Now look, Mom's mad," said Dupil.

"I am so sorry," said the Prince.

"You had better be sorry," said the sisters.

"I like you Prince," said Dupil.

"I don't like you," said the Prince.

"Well, why not?" asked Pupil with her big mean dark eyes.

"Because you are the people who are mean to Cinderella and I love her," said the Prince.

Suddenly Cinderella's guardian picked up the door that the Prince had knocked down, threw it in the air and walked into the room. The guardian said, "Here is your royal queen, Cinderella." (The girls were in shock)

Cinderella walked into the room with a nice outfit on and said, "Prince I am waiting for you. I have something to tell you. We are having a Ball this Saturday night and you are invited to attend as my guests."

"So . . ." says the Prince "what will we do to them at the ball? We could plan where they stand, put three jugs of goo above where they stand and dump it on them," said the Prince.

"Oh what sweet revenge" said Cinderella as she smiled to herself with pleasure.

AT The BALL . . .

"They're here," yelled Cinderella.

"Go place them in their spots," said the Prince.

"Okay," said Cinderella. Cinderella took them to their places and yelled at the Prince so he would drop the goo on their heads. And this is exactly what he did, the goo fell from the ceiling landed smack dab on the mean girl's heads! Maybe next time the girls will get revenge, but for now it was Cinderella's turn. And once again Cinderella lived happily ever after unlike the mean girls with the goo in their hair.

THE END!

As we are aware, 12 Standards for the English Language Arts were jointly developed by the National Council of Teachers of English and the International Reading Association (see Chapter 1). Three of these standards focus on the traits that students are expected to develop in their writing:

- *Standard 4.* Adjust use of written language (e.g., conventions, style, vocabulary) to communicate effectively with a variety of audiences and for different purposes.
- *Standard 5.* Employ a wide range of strategies in writing and use different writing process elements appropriately to communicate with different audiences for a variety of purposes.
- *Standard 6.* Apply knowledge of language structure, language conventions (e.g., spelling and punctuation), figurative language, and genre to create texts.

These national standards clearly identify expectations that students should understand and use writing processes to develop their ideas, and to effectively organize and communicate those ideas, using language as a tool.

Mark Honegger (2001) reminds us that writing is a complex task, as he identifies the traits of a skillful writer:

- The writer must match the purpose of his composition to the needs of his audience.
- The writer must have control of his content.
- The writer must organize his composition.
- The writer must write in a cohesive way so that paragraphs are both internally unified and linked to one another.
- Finally, the writer must write prose that is free of grammatical errors, that has punctuation that serves the purposes of his composition, and that is socially appropriate for the intended audience (Honegger, 2001, p. 52).

We can support students' growth as writers if we help them focus on these traits of skillful writing as they develop and share their understandings of themselves and the world.

IDEAS AND CONTENT

We cannot write well about things of which we have little knowledge! The life each of us actually lives influences, as well as limits, the background we are able to build through firsthand experiences. Therefore, we must learn to use extensive reading and other vicarious experiences (films, using primary documents, observing others, and so on) to build sufficient background to develop the language and concepts that lead to understanding. Without sufficient knowledge and understanding of a topic, our thinking is limited and will influence our ability to develop a coherent presentation or argument, especially through formal writing.

Our understanding of the purpose of the writing and the audience for whom it is intended should influence the content we select. Finding real purposes for writing can increase our students' desires to communicate with others and move their intended audience beyond us, their teacher. Published authors, myself included, typically have a clear purpose for writing and they have ideas about who their intended audience might be. This knowledge influences the ideas and content that are selected for inclusion.

We acknowledge that the students in a classroom will be diverse in any number of ways. Knowing this means that we realize they will have different background knowledge for the content we will require them to study in school. As we design writing experiences for our students, we cannot underestimate the impact of their background knowledge and experiences on their ability to be successful academically. We must accept the responsibility for adequately preparing all of our students for the ideas and content we expect them to include in their writing.

ORGANIZATION

Developing a coherent and compelling presentation of ideas relies on our ability to think clearly about topics we know and understand. If we lack sufficient background knowledge of a topic, we will be limited in our ability to organize our thoughts so that they are understandable to others. If we lack background experience with the genre or text structure (see Chapter 3) in which we are expected to write (myth/legends, persuasive essay, description, biography, and so on), what knowledge will we draw on to guide us in arranging our ideas in that particular style? How will we know the ways in which we can or should link related ideas into coherent text?

The ability to coherently organize our ideas as we write is not an isolated skill; rather it is interrelated with other writing traits, especially ideas and content. We will need to provide many background experiences in the varied genres and structures of text that we expect students to produce. Sharing the composition of a text in whole-class experiences can provide our students with a model of ways in which authors might think as they make decisions about what will and will not be included in a text and how those ideas will be organized (see Chapter 10).

Having a clear understanding of the purpose for the writing and the audience for whom it is intended helps the writer make decisions about organizing ideas and content. When the purpose for writing is personally meaningful, we are able to invest ourselves as writers, to attend more closely to the message we are crafting. Familiarity with our intended audience helps us draw on our experience with communicating ideas about this topic to skillfully select the appropriate context for our reader(s).

AUTHOR'S VOICE

The purpose of teaching writing as a process should be to help each student find his or her own voice, and to learn to express that voice clearly. Donald Graves (1994) adamantly states that voice is the driving force of the writing process. "Voice is the imprint of ourselves in our writing. . . . It's the writer's voice that gives me the best sense of his or her potential" (pp. 81–82). Kathryn Klintworth (2001) adds that "Voice is the writer's identity . . . . We must convince students that taking the risk to find their voice is a worthwhile endeavor, especially since students work hard to be just like everyone else, and being an individual often subjects a student to ridicule and ostracism. However, students at this age are also extremely passionate and energetic, and helping them to find their voices in order to infuse their writing with this passion and energy is definitely worth the time it takes" (p. 35).

Examining their own backgrounds is a way to help students begin to find their individual voices. As we help students discover their individual voices, we must be especially sensitive to those students who move between different worlds and consider the language and culture of home versus the language and culture of school. The identities that students have formed in each may be very different. Finding one's individual out-of-school identity/voice in writing requires that we recognize how dramatically different the worlds of home and school may be.

We must provide support for all students to explore, value, and share personal experiences, as well as views about themselves and the world. Donald Graves (1994) encourages us to help students select topics they know well and have a vested interest in so that their voice is clearly heard. He believes that "Voice should breathe through the entire process: rehearsal, topic choice, selection of information, composing, reading, and rewriting" (p. 82).

LANGUAGE AND CONVENTIONS

We know that students pick up much of their understanding of language through reading. For example, through active engagement with the texts they read, students can add from 600 to 5,000 words to their vocabulary each year (Nagy, Herman, & Anderson, 1985). In addition, Mark Honegger (2001), a specialist in grammar, states that "There is a general consensus that the more students read the more they are likely to pick up the feel of good style, the more their own grammatical competence increases, and the more they pick up the punctuation conventions of formal writing without the punitive nature of going through dreary drills" (p. 45). We can see how much reading instruction can potentially impact our students' writing by the ways in which we engage them with the language of quality texts, developing their interest in the particular ways that authors use language. We also can help students come to understand how punctuation and spelling are tools that aid communication.

We are aware that language develops slowly over time, through many varied experiences. Therefore, we also understand that improving students' abilities to use language skillfully in their writing will also develop slowly, through many varied reading and writing experiences. We will not make much progress with our students' development of language and conventions until they see language as a tool for communication, to be understood by others they care about.

BEST PRACTICES IN WRITING INSTRUCTION

In a review of research related to writing instruction, Karen Bromley (1999) identifies the following key components of sound writing instruction:

- Standards and assessments guide teachers and students.
- Large blocks of time are provided for reading, writing, talking, and sharing.
- Students write to construct meaning across the curriculum in a variety of forms.
- Teachers provide explicit instruction in composing and conventions.
- There is choice and authenticity in students' writing for a variety of purposes and audiences.

Jan Williamson, from the North Carolina Department of Public Instruction, echoes these goals when she states that "students learn to write with control and clarity when they:

- Write daily and have opportunities to share their writing.
- Write regularly for real, personally significant purposes and for a wide range of audiences.
- Have rich and continuous reading experiences, including published literature of merit and the work of peers and teachers.
- Have access to models of writing and writers at work.

- Are given instruction in the processes of writing.
- Can collaborate with peers for ideas and guidance in writing.
- Have one-to-one writing conferences with the teacher.
- Have explicit instruction in specific strategies and techniques of writing.
- Are taught grammatical usage and mechanics in context of their own writing and speaking.
- Are given ample opportunity to revise works to develop stronger drafts.
- Write as an extension of literature study as well as write in diverse genres such as autobiographical/biographical sketches, narratives, journal entries, personal responses, business letters, feature articles, research reports, scientific/technical writing, process essays, editorials, formal speeches, letters to the editor, fables, folklore, myths, short stories, and poems.
- Practice and use writing as a tool for learning in all disciplines, not just in English" (cited in Warner, 2001, p. 172).

Both Bromley and Williamson identify the importance of a teacher's role in helping students develop their skills as writers. As we consider the learning experiences we will provide for students, we should ask ourselves the following questions:

- For what purpose are students writing?
- Who is the audience for their writing?
- Am I giving students choices in what they write?
- Are they writing in a variety of forms in all content areas?
- How am I helping them understand and use the writing process?
- What explicit instruction am I providing?
- How am I using literature to inspire and model good writing?
- How am I helping students understand how conventions affect writing? (Marino, 1997, cited in Bromley, 1999)

To help us apply our knowledge about writing from this chapter to classroom practices in Chapters 9 and 10, we will consider illustrations of how teachers plan and implement quality instruction in writing for all students.

As you read the lists above, what ideas come to mind about your role in the development of students as writers? What ideas do you have about the role that students' background knowledge and experiences will play in their development as writers?

• • •

Maintaining Legible Handwriting

"The goal of handwriting instruction is to develop fluent and legible handwriting" (Tompkins, 1993, p. 315). By the middle grades, students have been introduced to both manuscript and cursive handwriting formation. Our focus now should be on helping students develop a personal style of handwriting that is both legible and functional for the individual.

With the focus of attention on the process of writing, as it has been for the past decade, you must not lose sight of handwriting's real purpose. Donald Graves (1994) states that "handwriting is the vehicle carrying information on its way to a destination. If it is illegible the journey may not be completed. Handwriting, like skin, shows the outside of a person. But beneath the skin beats the living organism, the life's blood, the ideas, the information" (p. 241).

To increase the legibility and function of students' handwriting, we must take care not to overemphasize its surface aspects or how the writing looks on the paper. If we do, we may inadvertently be telling students that handwriting is more important than thinking.

Our purposes in handwriting instruction should be twofold: (1) to provide instruction in patterns of formation that will allow handwriting to become fluid and eventually unconscious, and (2) to help students see the purpose of legibility as a vehicle to clear communication.

DEVELOPING FLUENT HANDWRITING

The elements of fluent handwriting are letter formation, size and proportion, spacing, slant, alignment, and line quality (Barbe, Wasylyk, Hackney, & Braun, 1994). If the formation of letters is tedious, students will soon tire in their attempts to communicate. Handwriting instruction should help students see that some methods of letter formation are less tiring for their hands. Learning to be consistent in letter formation will, in general, lead students toward fluid hand motions. To this end, some directed handwriting instruction and practice is warranted, especially when first introducing a pattern (Farris, 1991). We carefully supervise instruction and practice so that we can provide students feedback as a more knowledgeable other about the progressions they follow to make letters.

Fluency in the formation of letters becomes a factor when students are composing. As Donald Graves (1994) reminds us:

> If the familiar motor pathways are not built up through regular writing about topics the writer knows, then slowness can hamper the expression of content. The writing goes down on the page so slowly that the writer pokes along word-by-word on the page. That is, each word takes so long to write down that the next word, or even the rest of the sentence, cannot be contemplated at the same time as the one under construction. (p. 251)

The manner in which students hold a writing implement can also be a positive or negative factor in the physical exertion of writing. Some students have taught themselves to hold the pen or pencil in what appears to be an awkward position. Before we attempt to change a student's grip, we should observe the student during writing to see if the grip is functional and that the student's hand does not tire easily.

LEGIBILITY FOR COMMUNICATION

The real purpose of writing is for communication. Therefore, handwriting's true purpose is as a vehicle for communication. Handwriting instruction must emphasize the need for legibility as a vehicle for communication. A writer cannot communicate on paper using handwriting no one can read.

The most appropriate place to reinforce this idea will be in the midst of writing experiences that students will share with others. When students gather together in response pairs or editing groups, it will become apparent when someone cannot respond because the writing is not legible. The more we engage students in the sharing of their writing, the more functional opportunities we have to reinforce real reasons for legibility. When students care about communicating, they have more interest in legibility.

RESPECTING DIVERSITY IN WRITING DEVELOPMENT

If students come to school with different experiences, then we can assume that their knowledge of and interest in communicating through writing will also differ. Like reading, writing is very personal. Writers develop through a personal desire to communicate with themselves and others. In the classroom, we can support diversity by (1) honoring students' thinking and (2) supporting their independent development as writers.

HONOR STUDENTS' THINKING

When we ask students to put their ideas on paper so that they and others can see them, we are asking them to trust us with their thoughts and feelings. How we treat their ideas will tell students a great deal about how we see them as human beings, how we value them as individuals. If we view writing as an extension of the self, we will treat students' writing with respect.

It will be very easy for us, as the adult, to see things that are missing from students' writing, things that we would like to have seen them put into the writing, things that we think they know and should use. When we see missing pieces, we might be inclined to impose our own ideas on the writing. Our response to their writing should be to help them accomplish their own intentions. As we respond, we can "nudge" their writing, offering suggestions that might be helpful, but not imposing our ideas on them.

SUPPORT INDEPENDENCE

Observing developmental learning environments has taught us that students want to be independent. By supporting their independence as writers, we value students' ideas as individuals, providing many opportunities for them to show who they are. When we demonstrate various forms of writing and talk about how we make decisions as a writer, we show students how competent writers think. Modeling thinking processes supports students and reduces the "hidden curriculum" of writing, expectations that are not made explicit to all.

ASSESSMENT AND EVALUATION OF WRITING

Students develop as writers through both informal (Chapter 9) and process writing (Chapter 10) experiences. Understanding the quality of thinking and processes each student uses to produce meaningful print requires the collection of data that demonstrates the following:

- What a student understands about writing as a code, a medium, a product, and a process;
- How a student uses writing as a form of thinking to recollect, re-create, or re-construct ideas;

- How a student demonstrates skill in the various writing traits;
- How a student uses various forms of informal writing to communicate; and
- How a student uses the phases of the writing process to explore and develop personal understandings of a topic and to communicate that topic to others.

In many respects, monitoring growth in writing is easier than in reading because the results of writing are more visible. However, it is still important to go beyond the product to understand students' thinking processes and response to writing as a means of communication.

SAMPLES OF WRITING

Samples of writing serve as a starting point for assessment and evaluation. What can samples of writing show us? Over time, samples can be compared for growth in the following areas:

- Overall organization,
- Quality and appropriateness of content,
- Expression of ideas,
- Development of individual voice,
- Quality and appropriateness of word choices,
- Sentence fluency, and
- Appropriate use of conventions.

Although evaluating a student's writing for specific traits may allow us to talk about the writing in more detail, traits may not reveal aspects of the "student as writer" that we ought to know. The traits view writing as a code, a medium, and a product. What about writing as an active process?

To understand the "journey" of the ideas from the writer's mind, flowing down the arm and out of the hand, we must carefully observe the writer in different writing situations and confer with the writer about knowledge of personal writing processes.

We analyze writing traits, such as ideas/content, organization, use of conventions, and so on, in formal writing produced through the writing process. Yet much of the writing students will do in school will be informal writing, writing that will serve a specific purpose and may not be revised or edited. Observation and conferring with students will be essential to our understanding their thinking.

OBSERVING WRITERS AT WORK

When we watch someone writing, what can we observe? Do we get a glimpse of his or her "style"? In a room full of writers, will we see different styles, different levels of understanding about how one writes and why one writes, or different levels of confidence and experience as writers? What should we watch for as students write?

As we observe, we should ask, "What do I know about this student as a writer and how did I gain that knowledge?" To answer this question, we return to our instructional purposes in writing, the writing activities that have grown out of those purposes, and our observations of the student during the activities. Did we watch the student based on our knowledge of human development and our goals for instruction? Did we make anecdotal records of our observations so that, over time, our notes would serve as more detailed reminders of the student's responses than would our recollections of the events?

CONFERRING WITH WRITERS

Providing a forum for students to talk about their writing is essential to understanding their motivations and intentions as writers. Informal writings, completed as part of classroom instruction, are shared and discussed as part of developing and confirming students' understanding of selected curriculum standards. The writing process, as practiced in a writer's workshop, has response built into it through student–teacher conferences, response partners and groups, and editing partners and groups. Conferring during informal writing also provides a window into students' thinking. Talk can focus on how students organized their thinking, why they chose a particular format, whether they considered other forms, and on explaining the content of the writing. Assessment and evaluation must begin with and build on what students see in their own writing. It is important for us to consider what we will want to know about our students as writers.

■ TAKE A MOMENT TO REFLECT

■ *Writing can be viewed in at least four ways:*

- As a code using language as its symbols;
- As a medium to be manipulated and shaped;
- As a product to be completed; and
- As an active process of creating or constructing.

■ *Writing is a form of thinking that is done with written language and involves:*

- Retaining memories and experiences;
- Re-collecting those memories and experiences;
- Re-creating memories from firsthand experiences;
- Re-constructing knowledge from vicarious or secondhand experiences; and
- Re-presenting what is known that was not originally known.

■ *The writing process is like a journey that includes:*

- Getting started with an idea for a piece of writing;
- Exploring the idea to find a focus;
- Composing ideas in sustained writing;
- Revising for meaning;
- Editing for conventions; and
- Sharing the thinking that has emerged.

■ *Writing instruction should call attention to the following traits:*

- Ideas and content;
- Organization;
- Author's voice; and
- Language and conventions.

■ *Writing in literacy programs should provide:*

- Frequent and varied opportunities to write;
- Rich reading experiences to build background;
- Models of and direct instruction in writing;
- Experience with writing as a process; and
- Meaningful writing experiences across the curriculum.

■ *Attention should be given to handwriting to help students:*

- Maintain fluent formation; and
- Write legibly for communication.

■ *Writing development should:*

- Respect diversity in students' thinking; and
- Support independence in development.

■ *Assessing students' growth as writers involves:*

- Focusing on samples of writing over time;
- Anecdotal records of observations of writing behavior; and
- Conferring with students about their thinking while writing and about their writing processes.

■ *REFERENCES*

Barbe, W. B., Wasylyk, T. M., Hackney, C. S., & Braun, L. A. (1994). *Zaner-Bloser creative growth in handwriting (grades K–8)*. Columbus, OH: Zaner-Bloser.

Bromley, K. (1999). Key components of sound writing instruction. In L. B. Gambrell, L. M. Morrow, S. B. Neuman, & M. Pressley (Eds.), *Best practices in literacy instruction* (pp. 152–174). New York: Guilford Press.

Calkins, L. M. (1994). *The art of teaching writing* (rev. ed.). Portsmouth, NH: Heinemann.

Clay, M. (1975). *What did I write? Beginning writing behaviour*. Portsmouth, NH: Heinemann.

D'Arcy, P. (1989). *Making sense, shaping meaning: Writing in the context of a capacity-based approach to learning*. Portsmouth, NH: Heinemann.

Farris, P. J. (1991). Handwriting instruction should not be extinct. *Language Arts, 68*, 312–314.

Graves, D. (1983). *Teaching writing*. Portsmouth, NH: Heinemann.

Graves, D. (1994). *A fresh look at writing*. Portsmouth, NH: Heinemann.

Honegger, M. (2001). No-Grammar and grammar appreciation: Two approaches to the G-Word. In M. Warner (Ed.), *Winning ways to coach writing: A practical guide for teaching writing* (pp. 42–66). Boston: Allyn and Bacon.

Klintworth, K. (2001). Audience and voice. In M. L. Warner (Ed.), *Winning ways of coaching writing: A practical guide for teaching writing* (pp. 28–41). Boston: Allyn and Bacon.

Means, B., & Linderer, L. (1998). *Teaching writing in middle school: Tips, tricks, and techniques*. Englewood, CO: Teacher Idea Press.

Nagy, W. E., Herman, P., & Anderson, R. (1985). Learning words from context. *Reading Research Quarterly, 20*, 233–253.

Piaget, J., & Inhelder, B. (1969). *The psychology of the child*. New York: Basic Books.

Smith, F. (1982). *Writing and the writer*. London: Heinemann.

Tompkins, G. E. (1993). *Teaching writing: Balancing process and product*. Upper Saddle River, NJ: Merrill/Prentice Hall.

Warner, M. (2001). The state-mandated writing test. In M. Warner (Ed.), *Winning ways of coaching writing: A practical guide for teaching writing* (pp. 161–175). Boston: Allyn and Bacon.

chapter 9

Informal Writing: Using Writing to Support Learning

In this chapter . . .

We will consider a variety of ways that middle grade teachers

- Use informal writing across the curriculum to help students learn, and

- Use combinations of informal writing experiences in the form of learning logs to enhance instruction in literature study, a particular content area, and units or theme studies.

Looking into Classrooms . . .

The students in Marian's sixth-grade class have many opportunities to use writing to learn. In mathematics, for example, students make a K–W–L list of what they already know about a topic, what they want to learn, and (at selected points throughout the math unit) what they did learn; select a project in which they will collect and analyze data, and set up a project notebook that includes records of all work related to the project; write an explanation of which methods of collecting, reporting, and interpreting data they find easiest to use; write notes about the difficulties encountered in writing and conducting a project; and describe the task they enjoyed most during a unit of study.

Putting Theory into Practice . . .

To help students re–collect, re–create, and re–construct their experience as a tool for learning in the middle grades, we must engage them in daily writing experiences. Certainly, they will produce many formal, well-developed pieces of writing through writer's workshop, but the most valuable experiences may be those that are informal, are functional, and that occur daily. Research by Jetton and Alexander (1997), however, has documented that in most subject area classes at both the elementary and secondary levels, especially in disciplines other than English composition, students have few opportunities to engage in the construction of written text, either in class or in homework assignments. A greater focus on functional, informal writing can dramatically increase the amount of writing that students do.

Tompkins (1993) suggests that informal writing helps students capture ideas and experiences and organize their thinking. Informal writings, in contrast to the more formal pieces developed in a

writer's workshop, are shorter pieces of writing that can take many forms and that do not necessarily go through the phases of the writing process (see Chapters 8 and 10). Informal writing includes the following:

- Lists: descriptive lists, versions of K–W–L, note-taking, ordered lists, and outlines.
- Description/explanation: descriptions, explanations, and definitions, journal entries.
- Annotations: diagrams and story boards.
- Graphic organizers: web or clusters, timelines, story maps, Venn diagrams, and charts.

Informal writing gives students the opportunity to record spontaneous thinking in a familiar form. Through such opportunities, students come to see writing as a medium that is flexible and useful for thinking. Informal writing does not emphasize code or product; its primary purpose is to capture thinking in a way that the writer sees as useful. Informal writing may be revised for accuracy, edited for conventions, and may or may not be published or shared.

Informal writing should be an integral part of a middle grade literacy program in which students routinely create written records to capture their thinking and preserve it for future use. In today's world, we process so much information on a daily basis that we need mechanisms to retain, re-collect, re-create, and re-construct that information. Formal writing is not always feasible nor the most desirable type of writing to accomplish a goal (Calkins, 1994).

As we engage students in thinking about a variety of subjects, it is important to help them learn how to capture their thinking for later use. Writing their thoughts should become a "habit of mind," a way in which students capture ideas that helps them think about what they know.

Students who have not developed the habit of using writing to retain, re-collect, re-create, or re-construct their thinking will need our modeling and instruction to understand the possibilities of informal writing throughout the curriculum. Through shared writing experiences in which we lead the composing process, we may model various types of informal writing with our students. Through demonstration, on a chart or overhead projector, students share in the generation and organization of ideas. As we guide the shared writing we are able to think aloud or share our thinking about decisions we make during writing. Those shared writing experiences can become interactive when we share the pen with students.

Interactive writing, a version of shared writing in which students share the pen in the construction of texts, provides opportunities for students to demonstrate their understanding of written language as they write on the group chart and the class looks on. During interactive writing students also have opportunities to verbalize their thinking while writing.

... List the variety of ways in which you use writing throughout your day. What do these types of writing suggest to you about the skills that your students might also need to develop?

• • •

I leave notes for others, make notes for myself, take phone messages, make shopping lists or lists of things to do, make simple charts to collect related pieces of information, sketch and label drawings to explain my thinking to someone, such as when giving directions, and the like. These are all examples of informal writing.

• • •

In our daily lives, informal writing is the dominant type of writing that we do and should become an integral form of writing in our middle grade classrooms. Let's consider a variety of informal writing opportunities and how each might be used to engage middle grade students.

Lists can take a variety of forms, either random or ordered. Information on lists can also be organized into other forms such as graphic organizers and even descriptive or explanatory paragraphs. Students use lists to retain or to re-collect ideas (e.g., list of homework assignments, types of ocean animals, checklist for self-evaluating a class project, and so on) for later use.

While information in random lists does not yet have an organization imposed on it, ordered lists have an organization, sequenced by time or relationship. Sequences of events can be presented as ordered lists. Listing the steps in a process also results in an ordered list. Order can also be established by size or importance, as in understanding a place value in a number system.

DESCRIPTIVE LIST

We often make lists of information that are related to a topic. Recalling related information that is descriptive of a particular topic is helpful in our study. Some descriptive lists may have categories, with no specific order among items within each category. Descriptive writing is very prominent in middle grade texts. Making lists of attributes related to a particular topic may help students begin to prepare for descriptive writing. Phillip, an eighth-grade science teacher, wants his students to explore the systems of the human body. He realizes that students will need strategies (1) to sift through information, (2) to decide what is important, and (3) to organize and retain that information. Phillip engages students in making combinations of descriptive and ordered lists, focusing on essential vocabulary. Figure 9.1 illustrates such lists. The student made lists of the systems of the human body (descriptive), the functions of the skeletal system (descriptive), and the relationship between elements within the digestive system (ordered). These lists serve as a starting point for making connections among ideas that can later be explored through description or explanation and then finally detailed in more formal writings in a writer's workshop.

VERSIONS OF K-W-L

As a tool for writing, a K-W-L (Ogle, 1986) chart is composed of three columns in which we list what we already *Know* about a topic or concept, what we *Want* to know, and, finally, what we *Learned* after a period of study. A K-W-L chart is an excellent tool for not only helping students activate prior knowledge before, during, and after reading, but also for

Decriptive list for science, eighth grade

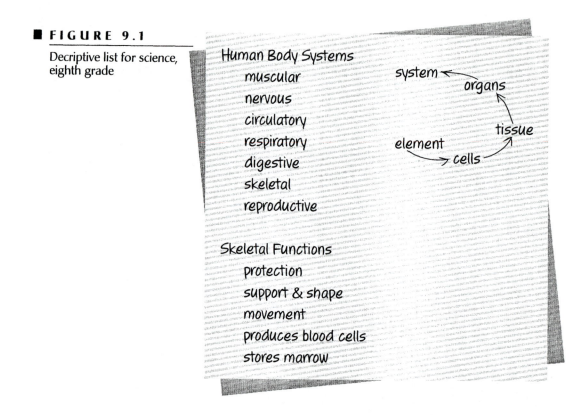

retaining and re-collecting ideas. Other versions add a column, K-W-H-L (Bromley, 2000), K-W-L-Q (Schmidt, 1999), and K-W-L-S (Sippola, 1995). In the first, "H" stands for "How I can learn?" in the second, "Q" stands for "Questions I still have," and finally, the "S" stands for "What I still want to know."

Teresa, a fourth-grade teacher, engages students in developing both personal and class K-W-H-L and K-W-L-Q charts for units of study during the year. At the beginning of the school year, Teresa asks small groups of students to brainstorm what they *Know* about what living things need to survive. Ideas from the small groups are synthesized onto a class chart. Based on that synthesis, Teresa then asks the small groups to raise questions about *What* they would like to know (see Figure 9.2). Teresa knows that if she asks students about *What* they would like to know, then she must be prepared to adjust her plans for the unit or provide opportunities for individuals to explore and share those topics. As the class plans to begin small-group research projects, Teresa encourages members of each group to complete the "H" column, thinking about *How they can learn* about their particular part of the study. The small groups will complete their research and share the results with the class. Finally, after the research is completed, both the small groups and the class as a whole will consider what was learned during the study and complete the "L" portion of the chart.

NOTE-TAKING

In the midst of an experience, students can use words, phrases, and sentences to capture and retain their thoughts. Notes made during experiences or immediately following help students retain the experience for future use. Notes are usually loosely organized around topics or categories. We should demonstrate note-taking during activities in which retain-

■ FIGURE 9.2

K-W-H-L for living
things, fourth grade

K - What I Know	W - What I Want to Learn	H - How I Can Learn	L - I Learned . . .
Living things need: food water place to live defense good temperatures know how to take care of self protection place to hide clothes or fur	What makes an animal endangered? What happens when wild animals don't have food? Can we make more water? What happens after a disaster like a forest fire? How do animals stay warm in winter?	national geographic.org Animal survival book Field trip— Desert Research Institute research Yellowstone fire	

ing ideas is important. It is also then important to help students see the value in organizing their notes into a useful form.

At the beginning of each year, Alex, a seventh-grade social studies teacher, engages students in a unit on using maps effectively. He finds that typically students are not aware of some of the types of maps that will be used during units of study in his class. As he exposes students to the variety of maps, he also demonstrates note-taking strategies. He helps students think about how to organize ideas on a page, how to show relationships, and how to select important words and phrases. Figure 9.3 shows a sample of early guided note-taking in his class.

ORDERED LIST

An ordered list is typically organized by some aspect of time, size, or relationship. Events in social studies are often ordered by time. When students place events in order by when they occurred they will have an ordered list (see Figure 9.4). To show a stronger relationship, the list of events could then be represented visually on a timeline.

Writing the steps that were followed to solve a problem in math or to complete an experiment in science results in an ordered list. The list can then be checked for accuracy of recall and questions can be raised about the reasoning attached to each step (see Figure 9.5).

■ **FIGURE 9.3**

Note-taking in social studies, seventh grade

Maps

Different maps = different information

<u>Political maps</u>
political divisions
boundaries of countries & states
capital cities

<u>Physical maps</u>
natural features of the earth

continents	mountains
oceans	plains
islands	deserts
lakes	rivers

<u>Grid map</u>
special-purpose maps, like cities
number-letter grid to locate specific place on map

<u>Distribution map</u>
use color to show how something is distributed over a particular area
darker color = more

population
rainfall
religion
languages

Such ordered lists may then have an explanatory or descriptive passage added that provides an overall understanding of student learning. For example, after listing the steps that were taken to solve a math problem, Marian asks her students to explain why the chosen method of solution seemed to be the most reasonable.

Writing the steps in directions also results in an ordered list. Jean asks her fifth-grade students to write directions for playing a game they have created about events that led to the Civil War. She stresses the importance of accuracy and clarity so that others will understand how to play the game. Directions can also be written that guide a classmate to locating particular physical features on a map. Writing directions for use by another challenges the writer to clarify thinking in order to guide the reader to a particular end.

Making My "Kid Pay" Graph

1. I brainstormed jobs that kids really do.
2. I picked 5 jobs for my graph
   clean room
   take out trash
   baby sit
   feed pets
   mow lawn

3. I made a survey of everyone in my class.
4. I had to average the answers so I could have 1 number for my graph.
5. I put the bars on my graph.
6. I discovered that most other kids get paid more for their jobs than I do.

■ FIGURE 9.5

Ordered list of events, eighth grade

Important Events in Modern Europe

1914	World War I begins
1917	United States enters the war
1919	Treaty of Versailles ends World War I
1920s	Depression in Germany
1933	Hitler becomes Nazi dictator of Germany
1935	The Holocaust begins
1939	World War II begins
1941	Japan attacks Pearl Harbor; United States enters the war
1944	D-Day
1945	United States drops atomic bombs on Japan; World War II ends
1956	Revolts against communism in Eastern Europe
1961	Berlin Wall is built
1980	Birth of Solidarity in Poland
1985	Mikhail Gorbachev becomes leader of the Soviet Union

The relationship among items may also be the basis for an ordered list. Notice the drawing of parts of the digestive system shown by the eighth-grade student in Figure 9.1. The relationship among the parts, a relationship of size and function, becomes an ordered list. Phillip encourages his students to explore meaningful ways of retaining and re-collecting information. This student has strengthened her list by using arrows to emphasize the relationship as she understands it.

OUTLINE

Note-taking can also take the form of organized lists, such as an outline. Outlines show the relationship between main ideas and supporting details. When outlining is a new tool, students should be given a formatted outline and the recording of information should be guided through a shared writing experience.

I. Main Idea
   a. supporting detail
   b. supporting detail
II. Main Idea
   a. supporting detail
   b. supporting detail

Outlines are best to use when the main ideas are easily identified.

When Armando teaches students about the branches of the American government each year, he also reinforces the usefulness of outlines for organizing information. He believes that the clear distinction between the three branches makes it easy to build an outline (see Figure 9.6). He begins with a visual of the information in the shape of a tree with three main branches, then students transfer information to an outline form. He finds that students better understand that the Roman numerals stand for each main branch of the tree and letters/numbers stand for the smaller branches.

DESCRIPTION/EXPLANATION

These forms of informal writing engage students in elaborating on their thinking. This category also includes a variety of journals, which is the most common form of informal writing we are likely to find in middle grade classrooms.

DESCRIPTION

Descriptions use words to build images of objects, people, places, and events, as do illustrations. In descriptions, students re-collect ideas they have already retained, or re-create a portion of an experience. Students in Jaime's fourth-grade class usually begin their descriptions as a list or a web/cluster. When students are comfortable with the information in their list, Jaime guides them to organize the ideas into paragraph form to provide more detail and clarity (see Figure 9.7). Such description also provides an opportunity to encourage students to see what they know about the composition of a paragraph.

■ FIGURE 9.6

Outline of three branches of government, fifth grade

Branches of Government

I. Legislative Branch
  A. Who
    1. House of Representatives
    2. Senate
  B. Responsibility
    1. power to make laws
    2. power to declare war

II. Executive Branch
  A. Who
    1. President
    2. Vice President
    3. Cabinet
  B. Responsibility
    1. make sure that laws are obeyed
    2. work with Congress to make policy

III. Judicial Branch
  A. Who
    1. Supreme Court
  B. Responsibility
    1. decides arguments about meaning of laws
    2. interprets the Constitution

EXPLANATION

An explanation is often useful when events require elaboration. In an explanation, the writer conveys more information than merely to list ideas or events that occurred. The writer provides a rationale or support for her thinking (e.g., hypothesizing about a science experiment, or reasons for selecting a particular form for a piece of process writing).

Explanation is initially developed as students are engaged in numerous teacher-led and peer-led discussions. Building on verbal discussion skills, Phillip encourages frequent opportunities for students to individually explain their thinking in preparation for discussions. Phillip is especially conscious of students' interactions with textbook reading, because he knows that the content and vocabulary are challenging for many of his students. In Figure 9.8, one student explains her thinking after reading in her science text about scientific notation.

Description: List to paragraph

Forming the Hawaiian Islands

* made by volcanoes long ago
* islands are tops of volcanoes
* melted rock, ashes, gas
* comes from deep in the earth
* cools down and hardens
* forms mountain
* built up from ocean floor of Pacific Ocean

The Hawaiian Islands were made long ago by volcanoes. A volcano is an opening in the surface of the earth. Melted rock, ashes, and gas are forced out from deep inside the earth. As the hot rocks and ashes cool, they form a mountain. The islands of Hawaii are actually the tops of volcanoes that were built up from the floor of the Pacific Ocean.

Sample explanation, eighth-grade science

Scientific Notation

Prediction —

This may be about how to write large numbers in a way you can understand.

After —

I didn't think about scientists needing a way to talk about billions and trillions of miles. Scientific numbers would have way too many 0's to be able to read. I would have to stop to count the 0's everytime. Now I have to remember that the exponent tells how many 0's there are in the number.

$$10^2 = 100$$
$$10^3 = 1,000$$
$$10^4 = 10,000$$
$$10^5 = 100,000$$

DEFINITIONS

As a part of vocabulary instruction across the curriculum, students are frequently asked to describe their understanding of a word by writing a definition. This often occurs prior to reading text that includes that word or finding how the word is defined in a dictionary. Constructing a definition requires a student to recall prior knowledge, select words to describe that understanding, and perhaps give examples to support that understanding.

In Marian's sixth-grade math class, students frequently encounter terms that can have meanings in everyday speech that are different than their use in mathematics. For example, recall the student who reported the steps she followed in developing a graph that compared what others earned for jobs they did (see Figure 9.4). After she collected her data about the amount of money her friends are paid for the jobs they do, she realized that she needed a better understanding of the word *average*, especially as it is used in math. Marian encouraged the student to first write her personal definition and give an example, then to compare that to the definition in the dictionary. Figure 9.9 shows the student's thinking.

JOURNAL ENTRIES

A journal can be a tool for helping students retain, re-collect, re-create, and re-construct thinking. Many people make written records of the everyday events in their lives in some form of journal. While the form may differ, the intention is often similar—to capture feelings and experiences for personal, not public, use. Entries in journals frequently take the form of descriptions or explanations.

We can use journals to provide both an outlet for students' personal thoughts and a daily writing opportunity. Journals may be personal or may be a dialogue between student and teacher. The purpose, however, remains as a personal outlet for each writer.

Other types of written records might be called "working journals" because writers record observations and information they will use for another purpose (Tompkins, 1993). In this text, we will refer to such working journals as *learning logs* to differentiate them from journals. Learning logs, described in an upcoming section, are intended to be a vehicle for helping students use writing as a tool for learning, particularly in content areas such as science, social studies, and mathematics.

Personal Journal Entry. Writers usually choose their own topics for their personal journals. Contents typically focus on events in the writer's life and on personal concerns. The personal journal serves as an outlet and should not be made public, except at the writer's choosing. We may choose to write responses to students' entries to stimulate their writing and to model elements of language. This type of journal entry is useful for encouraging students to express themselves and for making personal connections. Its academic functions, however, are limited.

Dialogue Journal Entry. Personal journal entries become dialogue journal entries when the writer addresses the writing to another who is expected to respond. This exchange is typically a private conversation through writing (Bode, 1989; Gambrell, 1985; Staton, 1987). Students set the direction for the conversation. Our role, if we are the responder, is that of encourager and supporter, and to nudge or stretch thinking. Our goal should be for students to become the questioners (Tompkins, 1993). Dialogue journals can be of great value in bridging the gap between talking and writing (Kreeft, 1984), helping students work out nonacademic school problems (Staton, 1980), supporting students as they think and talk about books (Barone, 1990), and providing a private forum for students to seek assistance (see Figure 9.10).

■ **FIGURE 9.9**

Definitions of average,
sixth-grade math

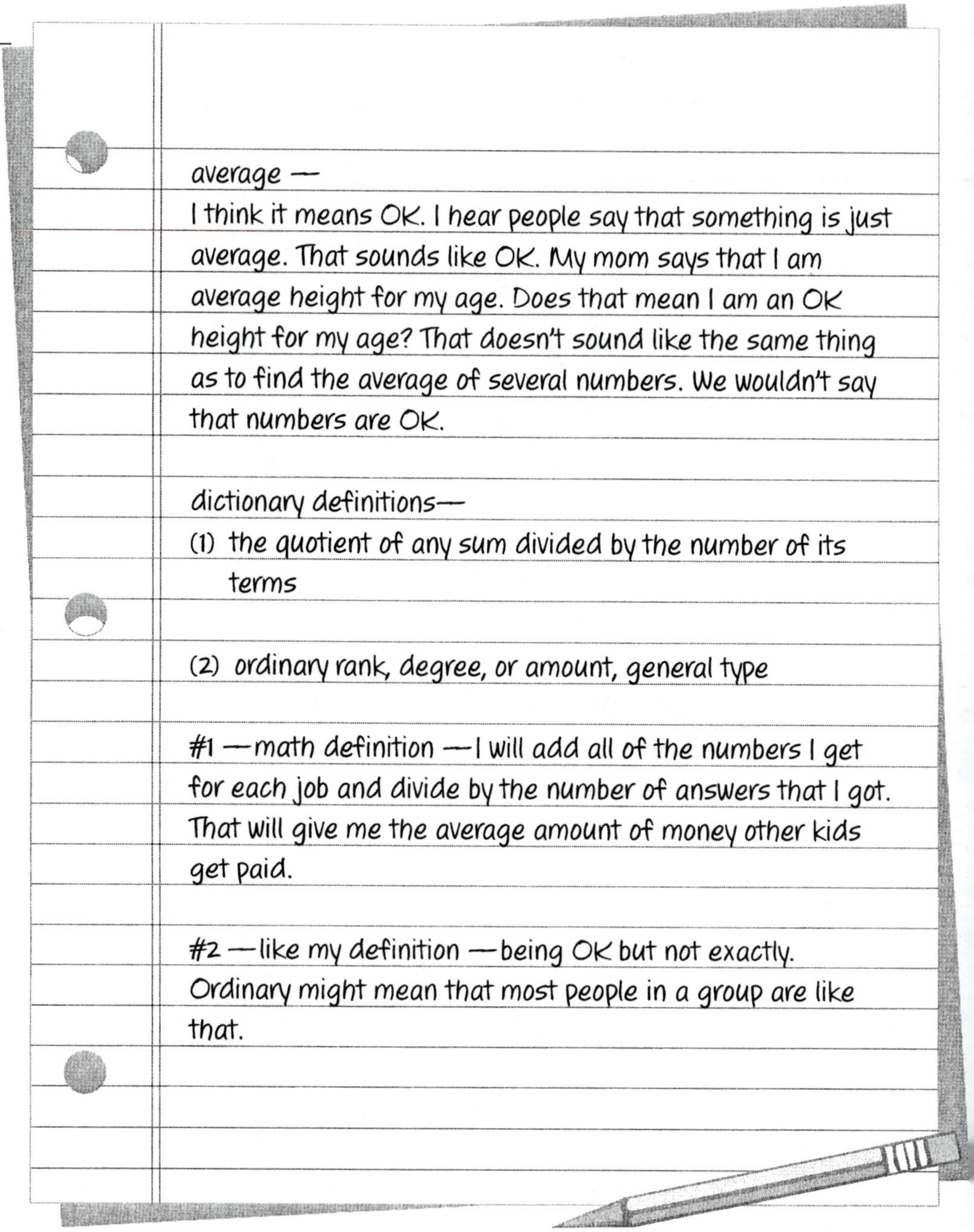

average —
I think it means OK. I hear people say that something is just
average. That sounds like OK. My mom says that I am
average height for my age. Does that mean I am an OK
height for my age? That doesn't sound like the same thing
as to find the average of several numbers. We wouldn't say
that numbers are OK.

dictionary definitions—
(1) the quotient of any sum divided by the number of its
     terms

(2) ordinary rank, degree, or amount, general type

#1 —math definition —I will add all of the numbers I get
for each job and divide by the number of answers that I got.
That will give me the average amount of money other kids
get paid.

#2 —like my definition —being OK but not exactly.
Ordinary might mean that most people in a group are like
that.

RESPONSE JOURNAL ENTRY

Students may write their responses to books they are reading, to a particular event in the classroom, or to concepts they are learning. Tompkins' (1993) review of research reveals that students' responses may include the following:

- Retellings and summaries,
- Questions related to understanding the text,
- Interaction or empathy with characters,

■ **FIGURE 9.10**

Sample dialogue journal
entry, sixth grade

Raquel's entry (student)

I am having some trouble with my project. I am afraid that when I ask other kids the questions on my survey, they will think it is dumb. Do you think my survey is dumb? How should I ask my questions so that the other kids won't laugh at me?

Marian's response (teacher)

You think that your parents don't pay you enough for the jobs you do at home and you want a way to convince them. There could be other kids in the class who feel the same way. Your project could help them too. Maybe you can start a survey by telling them why you are doing it. I think other kids will see that your project could help them too. What do you think about my suggestion?

- Predictions of what will happen and validation after reading,
- Personal experiences, feelings, and opinions related to the reading,
- Simple and elaborated evaluations, and
- Philosophical reflections.

We see that response journals can include writings that cross over different categories of informal writing, for example, retellings are similar to ordered lists. We need to frequently ask individual students to share what they think.

DOUBLE-ENTRY JOURNAL

Specific statements that authors make can evoke strong responses in readers. Originally, a double-entry journal (Berthoff, 1981) combined a quote from a text with the student's response. A double-entry journal page is divided into two columns with a quote from the text (noting chapter and page numbers for future reference) on the left and the student's response on the right (see Figure 9.11). Because the quote is provided, double-entry responses are focused and interpretable. Gail Tompkins (1993) suggests other variations for double-entry journals:

Left Side	Right Side
* Reading notes	* Discussion notes
* Prediction	* What actually happened

ANNOTATIONS

Writing can elaborate on ideas that are drawn, and vice versa. Annotations can be labels, descriptions, or explanations that comment on or clarify the illustration. Annotations may help visual learners reflect on their thinking. Some students are better able to organize their writing by first making pictorial representations.

■ **FIGURE 9.11**

Double-entry journal,
sixth grade

Name Marta	Double-Entry Journal
In the text . . . (give page number) The sun exploded the sky, just blew it up with the setting color. (page 170)	My response . . . (what I think) It reminds me of the sunset with all the pink, blue, purple, orange
Had flashes of color in his brain, explosions of color. (page 177)	It made me think of paint splattered
It was sweet and tangy—almost too sweet. (page 189)	It made me think of Island Twists Mar-O-Mango Berry Kool-Aid.®

DIAGRAMS

Drawing is a tool that many students find helpful to represent their ideas. Drawings can also provide a window into students' emerging understandings or misunderstandings. As Marian engages her sixth-grade students in concepts about geometry, she encourages them to annotate their drawings to show their thinking (see Figure 9.12).

STORY BOARDS

As students prepare to develop a storyline for a narrative, illustrating their ideas may provide stronger visual support than the traditional story map that uses key words and phrases in a sequential organization (see story map discussion in next section). Filmmakers use story boards to develop the story line when they plan a movie. Actors use the story boards to talk about the plot and possible dialogue. We encourage students to clarify their thinking about the events on the story board by annotating the board with ideas about the development of the story elements.

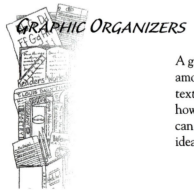

GRAPHIC ORGANIZERS

A graphic organizer is a simple way to organize our thinking. It visually shows relationships among ideas. The possibilities for graphic organizers are endless. Authors of information texts often help readers prepare for the ideas in a chapter or section by visually showing how the ideas are organized, taking the form of a web or hierarchical flowchart. Students can also use graphic representations to re-collect ideas from an existing text or re-construct ideas in a new way, drawn from a variety of resources.

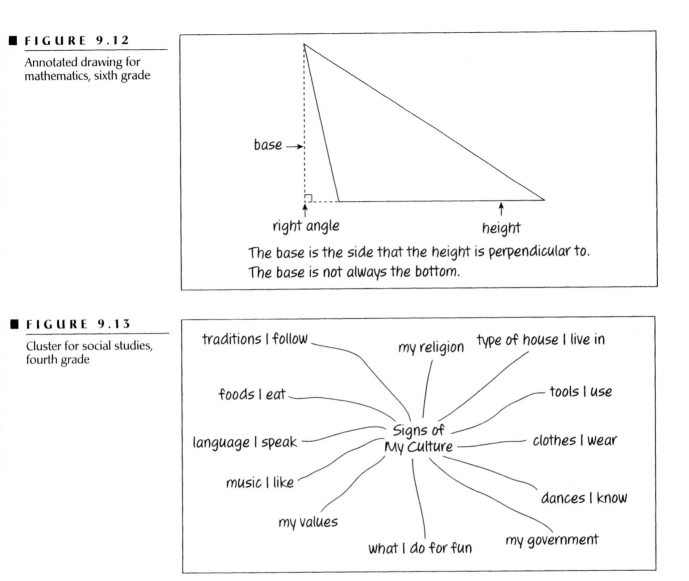

■ **FIGURE 9.12**

Annotated drawing for mathematics, sixth grade

base →

right angle   height

The base is the side that the height is perpendicular to.
The base is not always the bottom.

■ **FIGURE 9.13**

Cluster for social studies, fourth grade

traditions I follow   my religion   type of house I live in

foods I eat   tools I use

language I speak   Signs of   clothes I wear
                         My Culture

music I like   dances I know

my values   my government

what I do for fun

WEBS OR CLUSTERS

Students can arrange lists visually to show how ideas relate. Such a display can be a helpful tool for retaining and re-collecting specific ideas. A simple web/cluster may identify ideas that relate to a single topic, but it may not show how the ideas relate to one another (see Figure 9.13). Such web/clusters are useful to describe a topic or concept as long as the topic/concept is well known to students. Organized clusters of ideas help students see how important details in new topics/concepts are related. Understanding the relationships of ideas can help students add to or replace their existing schema for the topic/concept.

TIMELINES

Organizing information in chronological order on a timeline is a useful way to understand the temporal relationship among events. Timelines can recall and organize a list of life events, such as for a biography or autobiography; relive daily events, such as recalling the order of events of a class field trip; or relate world events that occurred during a similar time period but in different regions of the world. Ordered lists of chronological events, such as those shown in Figure 9.5, show visual relationships when they are recorded on a timeline. The intervals on a timeline should always be of equal size to reinforce the relationship between events.

STORY MAPS

Another type of visual representation of thinking is a story map that shows the relationship of important literary elements and the general progression of the plot. Story maps can be as simple as a beginning–middle–end progression or may identify more complicated relationships, such as problem–events–resolution. The visual representation can also be drawn to show the increasing tension in the plot leading to the climax. Story maps are a planning device to re-collect or re-tell a story or re-create a new story drawn from a variety of our literary experiences. For example, Marie, in seventh grade, uses a map (see Figure 9.14) to plan her piece of historical fiction that centers around the Civil War period and slavery. Notice how she plans to include historical facts to support her fictional characters and setting.

■ **F I G U R E 9 . 1 4**

Story map for historical fiction, seventh grade

<u>Barley's Plantation</u>

Clarence - 48 (narrator)

Joseph - 30, strong

Phillip - 50, gray beard

Sally - 30s, tall, thin

Lily - 12, Sally's daughter

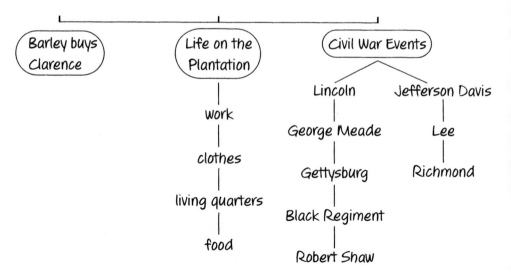

VENN DIAGRAM

The interlocking circles of a Venn diagram enable students to visually show similarities and differences between two categories of characteristics. They may re-construct their understanding of the relationship between ideas or objects as they decide how to place each item in the Venn diagram. During a fourth-grade weather unit, Jaime has his students construct a Venn diagram comparing and contrasting the concepts of weather and climate (see Figure 9.15). He uses this informal writing experience as a rehearsal for compare/contrast writing.

CHARTS

Charts can help students re-collect ideas about a topic and re-construct those ideas into related groups. Carlos, a fifth-grade teacher, selects categories that help his students identify and organize relevent information. For most topics he uses simple charts (see Figures 9.16 and 9.17), with a few categories, while Duncan, an eighth-grade social studies teacher, may use a larger number of categories and subcategories (see Figure 9.18). Determining categories and format is an important part of chartmaking. We may predetermine categories, or the categories may emerge out of unorganized ideas when examining their relationships.

For students who have little experience with setting up a chart, it is helpful for the class to participate in making decisions about what are the appropriate categories and how they are related. During a unit about ancient Egypt, Laura guided her sixth-grade students to construct a chart showing relationships among people in various social classes (see Figure 9.19). Laura provided part of the chart (shown in bold), while students worked together to complete the remaining parts (shown in italics).

What positive outcomes might you observe if students in your classroom engaged in daily informal writing experiences such as the examples discussed in this section?

• • •

■ **FIGURE 9.15**

Venn Diagram, fourth grade

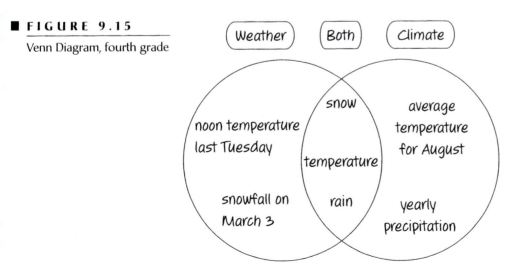

Chart for social studies,
fifth grade

Three Branches of US Government

Branch	Who	Responsibilities
Legislative	Congress -Senate -House of Representatives	make laws declare war
Executive	President Vice President Cabinet Departments	make sure laws are obeyed work with Congress
Judicial	Supreme Court -Chief Justice -8 other justices	decides about meaning of laws and Constitution

■ **FIGURE 9.17**

Social studies, fifth grade

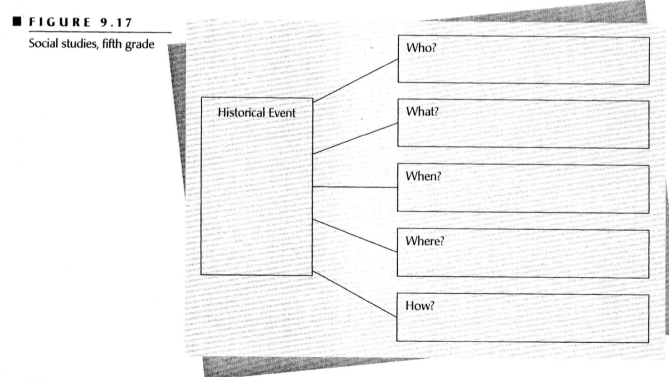

■ **FIGURE 9.18**

Chart for social studies,
eighth grade

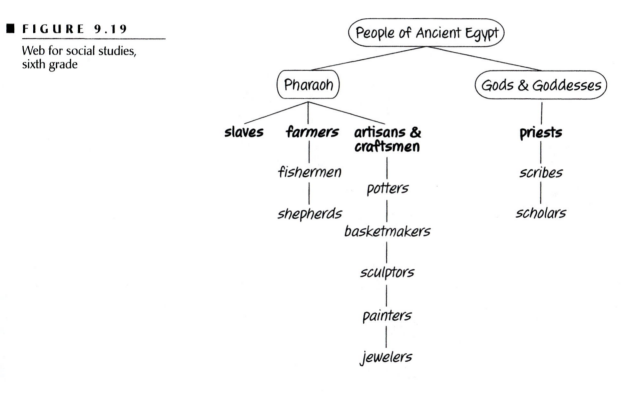

Comparing World Governments	Free and Open Elections	People Control Own Lives	Safeguard Individual Freedom	Government Controls Economy
Communism	—	—	—	+
Constitutional monarchy	+	+	+	—
Democracy	+	+	+	—
Dictatorship	—	—	—	+
Monarchy	—	—	—	+
Republic	+	+	+	—

+ attribute   — not an attribute

■ **FIGURE 9.19**

Web for social studies,
sixth grade

```
              People of Ancient Egypt
                 /            \
            Pharaoh        Gods & Goddesses
          /    |    \            |
    slaves  farmers  artisans &   priests
              |      craftsmen      |
          fishermen      |        scribes
              |        potters       |
          shepherds      |        scholars
                     basketmakers
                          |
                      sculptors
                          |
                       painters
                          |
                       jewelers
```

Students who frequently make lists of important information, arrange ideas into a coherent description, label diagrams to explain an idea, or organize their thinking into a
multilevel chart are less likely to be intimidated by formal writing experiences and more
likely to feel successful about expressing their thinking in print.

• • •

LEARNING LOGS

Learning logs that utilize a variety of informal writings are the most practical way to bring students into content area writing. Learning logs can help children record and react to their learning in all areas of the curriculum, including mathematics, science, and social studies (Fulwiler, 1985). Think of a learning log as a collection of journal-type responses and informal writings that, when taken together, can help students see growth in their thinking.

Learning logs provide great versatility. In practice, learning logs can combine the formats and intentions of the journals described earlier, as well as a variety of informal writing formats. Learning logs can stimulate writing through such variety, meeting the needs and preferences of individual students.

Our experiences with writing help us decide what thoughts we need to re-collect and what form would best represent our thinking. In our writing program, informal writing may help students see that writing is beneficial and within reach. Let's consider the possibilities for learning logs in one subject area, as well as in an integrated unit of study.

LEARNING LOGS IN LITERATURE STUDY

Using a variety of forms of writing throughout the study of a novel or a group of related novels can demonstrate to students the range of ways that we are able to retain, re-collect, re-create, and re-construct our understanding of literature and the world. For example, while participating in a whole-class literature study of *Hatchet,* by Gary Paulsen (1999), Lou's sixth-grade students might do the following:

- Write responses to the text using a particular journal style.
- Draw and label different kinds of survival equipment.
- Cluster what they know about survival or the wilderness and add to the cluster as they gain new knowledge.
- List interesting words in the text and add related words that could be used to describe the setting.
- Write personal definitions for interesting words, then add to or revise these definitions as they gain greater understanding through reading and study.
- Write a description of the setting around the lake as they interpret it from their reading.

What other types of writing might be added that could extend students' engagement with the text and topic?

CONTENT LEARNING LOGS

Learning logs are an excellent vehicle for focusing and supporting students' learning in a particular content area, such as mathematics, through informal writing. For example, while working on a chapter about interpreting data in their mathematics textbook, Marian's sixth- and seventh-grade students do the following:

- Make a K-W-L *list* of what they already know about the topic, what they want to learn, and (at selected points throughout the chapter) what they did learn.
- Make a *list* of how they spend the money they receive from jobs, doing chores, or allowances.

- Select a project in which they will collect and analyze data, and set up a project notebook that includes *records* of all work related to the project.
- Write an *explanation* of which methods of collecting, reporting, and interpreting data they find easiest to use.
- *Record* various text exercises in their learning logs.
- Construct a variety of *graphs* and explain how the structure of various graphs reflects their purpose.
- Use mean, median, and mode to write a *description* of an average school day.
- Make *Venn diagrams* that show correlations between objects or events around them.
- *Explain* various ways to misread a stem-and-leaf plot and why a key is necessary.
- Write *notes* about the difficulties encountered in writing and conducting a survey.
- *Describe* the task enjoyed most during the unit.

A number of these writing activities appear as suggestions in the mathematics textbook teacher's edition that Marian uses. She adds other writing experiences as needed to encourage and support students' thinking about interpreting data. Through such writing experiences, students are able to learn that being literate in mathematics involves an understanding of language and using language effectively to express ideas.

THEME OR UNIT LEARNING LOGS

We also can use learning logs as vehicles for collecting a variety of writings during a theme or unit of study. When Luis, teaching in a multigrade fourth- through sixth-grade classroom, teaches an integrated unit titled "Quilts," his students' learning logs contain a variety of informal writings:

- Several pages for collecting *lists* of interesting words related to quilts and quiltmaking that include correct spellings, key words for meanings, and drawings to illustrate;
- *Definitions* of unfamiliar words, with which students can compare their thinking to peer and dictionary definitions, and link to related words they know;
- *Annotated drawings* to illustrate different types of quilt designs that the class has studied or that the student has researched independently;
- *Charts* that compare and contrast quilt designs;
- *Brainstormed lists* or *clusters* that indicate what the student knows about different types of quilts, with new ideas added in a different color as they occur;
- *Descriptions* of particular patterns, with special attention to geometrical terms to explain the relationship between figures in patterns;
- *Explanations* of the origins of particular quilt patterns;
- A page set aside for a *list* of personal questions about quilts;
- Pages set aside for a *list* of quilt books that students have read with *annotations* or *responses* about the book;
- *Notes* made while watching videos about quiltmaking;
- A *record* of a field trip to a local quilter's house;
- An *interview* with someone who has made a quilt; and
- Sample patterns made from cloth and/or colored paper with *sequenced instructions*.

Students complete these informal writings during whole-class discussions, small-group work, and independent research. If a particular form of informal writing is new to students, Luis engages the class in a shared or interactive writing lesson to demonstrate what that form looks like and how it can be constructed.

What positive outcomes do you think the students in Lou's, Marian's, and Luis's classes might realize from the variety of writings in their informal learning log writing?

• • •

Many experiences in a variety of informal writing styles, as we have explored in this chapter, are essential in students' preparation for more formal processes, such as writer's workshop or research writing (see Chapter 10). As we weave writing into the literacy program, we must provide scaffolded instructional experiences and multiple, varied opportunities for students to develop confidence in themselves as writers and thinkers.

■ TAKE A MOMENT TO REFLECT . . .

- ■ *Informal writing is focused, functional writing that serves as a tool for learning, and may include:*
  - Lists: descriptive list, versions of K-W-L, note-taking, ordered list, and outlines.
  - Description/explanation: descriptions, explanations, definitions, and journal entries.
  - Annotations: diagrams and story boards.
  - Graphic organizers: web or clusters, timelines, story maps, Venn diagrams, and charts.
- ■ *Informal writing is often recorded in varying types of journals or logs:*
  - Personal journal;
  - Dialogue journal;
  - Response journal;
  - Double-entry journal; and
  - Learning logs.
- ■ *Learning logs typically include many different types of informal writing that is related by subject area or theme.*

■ REFERENCES

Barone, D. (1990). The written responses of young children: Beyond comprehension to story understanding. *The New Advocate, 3,* 49–56.

Berthoff, A. (1981). *The making of meaning: Metaphors, models, and maxims for writing teachers.* Montclair, NJ: Boynton/Cook.

Bode, B. A. (1989). Dialogue journal writing. *The Reading Teacher, 42,* 568–571.

Bromley, K. (2000). Integrating language arts with the content areas. In K. D. Wood & T. S. Dickinson (Eds.), *Promoting literacy in grades 4-9: A handbook for teachers and administrators* (pp. 220–232). Boston, MA: Allyn and Bacon.

Calkins, L. M. (1994). *The art of teaching writing* (rev. ed.). Portsmouth, NH: Heinemann.

Fulwiler, T. (1985). Writing and learning, grade 3. *Language Arts, 62,* 55–59.

Gambrell, L. B. (1985). Dialogue journals: Reading–writing interaction. *The Reading Teacher, 38,* 512–515.

Jetton, T. L., & Alexander, P. A. (1997). Instructional importance: What teachers value and what students learn. *Reading Research Quarterly, 32,* 290–308.

Kreeft, J. (1984). Dialogue writing—Bridge from talk to essay writing. *Language Arts, 61,* 141–150.

Ogle, D. (1986). K-W-L: A teaching model that develops active reading of expository text. *The Reading Teacher, 39,* 364–370.

Schmidt, P. R. (1999). KWLQ: Inquiry and literacy learning in science. *The Reading Teacher, 52*(7), 789–792.

Sippola, A. E. (1995). K-W-L-S. *The Reading Teacher, 48*(6), 542–543.

Staton, J. (1980). Writing and counseling: Using a dialogue journal. *Language Arts, 57,* 514–518.

Staton, J. (1987). The power of responding in dialogue journals. In T. Fulwiler (Ed.), *The journal book* (pp. 47–63). Portsmouth, NH: Heinemann.

Tompkins, G. E. (1993). *Teaching writing: Balancing process and product.* Upper Saddle River, NJ: Merrill/Prentice Hall.

■ *CHILDREN'S LITERATURE*

Paulsen, G. (1999). *Hatchet.* New York: Viking Penguin.

chapter 10

Writer's Workshop: Guiding Students' Development as Writers

In this chapter . . .

We explore ways to use our knowledge of writing development to support and enhance students' sense of themselves as writers, including:

- The components of writer's workshop,

- An illustration of writer's workshop in a fifth-grade classroom, as Kim narrates her first year of implementing the approach, and

- Linking writer's workshop with other areas of study.

Looking into Classrooms . . .

Writer's workshop happens every day from 9:15 to 10:15 in Kim's fifth-grade classroom. "I've never done a writer's workshop until this year. Now, I can't imagine not doing it," Kim states emphatically. She goes on to explain, "Our format for writer's workshop is very predictable. We always start out with a minilesson to provide helpful instruction about some small aspect of writing, then we have 10 minutes of quiet writing to get everyone started. For the remaining 40 minutes students write, have a conference with me, or meet with peers to get help in revising or editing a piece. Finally, a few students share what they are doing and we celebrate their successes. I have learned so much about writing from my students. Their attitudes about writing are becoming more and more positive because they have so much control over what they do, but they know I am always there to guide and support."

Putting Theory into Practice . . .

In this chapter, we discuss setting up a classroom environment to support and enhance students' writing competence. We begin with a statement by Lucy Calkins (1994) about the power of writing as a tool for learning:

> The powerful thing about writing with words is that we are really working with thoughts. Writing allows us to put our thoughts on the page and in our pockets; writing allows us to pull back and ask questions of our thoughts. It is this dynamic of creation and criticism, of pulling in to put thoughts on the page and pulling back to question, wonder, remember more, organize and rethink that makes writing such a powerful tool for learning. (p. 222)

COMPONENTS OF A WRITER'S WORKSHOP

Students learn to write through many varied experiences, both informal and formal. As they write, they simultaneously learn to capture and organize their thoughts for future use. In a writer's workshop students move through the phases of the writing process to develop formal pieces of writing. In other words, they put the writing process to work! These phases are clearly visible in the workshop (see Figure 10.1). The order of activities is optional, depending on intended outcome(s), allocated time, and what works best for students. Each part of a writer's workshop has specific purposes for supporting students' growing competence as writers.

PREDICTABLE TIME TO WRITE

If students are to become competent writers, time for writing must be predictable. The work requires time to plan, to settle in, and to get in one's stride as a writer. We should allocate a sustained block of at least 40 to 60 minutes per day (Calkins, 1994; Graves, 1994). Calkins (1994) stresses the need for consistent blocks of time to write:

> If students are going to become deeply invested in their writing, and if they are going to live toward a piece of writing and let their ideas grow and gather momentum, if they are going to draft and revise, sharing their texts with one another as they write, they need the luxury of time. If our students are going to have the chance to do their best and then to make their best better, they need long blocks of time. Sustained effort and craftsmanship are essential in writing well, yet they run contrary to the modern American way. (p. 186)

Teachers who are committed to developing competent writers look for ways to move instruction related to aspects of writing into the work of the writer's workshop. To find consistent blocks of workshop time in an already crowded school day, teachers often do the following:

- Begin the day with students writing while the teacher is occupied with administrative matters such as attendance and lunch counts.
- Complete writing tasks from other subject areas, such as theme studies.

■ **FIGURE 10.1**

Organization of writer's workshop

Whole-Group Meeting: (10–15 minutes)	• Minilesson • Plans for the day
Work Time: (20–30 minutes)	• Individual writing time • Conferring • Response partners/groups • Editing partners/groups • Publishing
Whole Group: (10–15 minutes)	• Share sessions or Author's Chair • Plans for next day

- Merge instruction in aspects of writing, such as handwriting, grammar, and spelling, that might otherwise be taught separately.
- Join reading instruction or literature studies with writing into a reader's/writer's workshop.

DEMONSTRATIONS OF WRITING

Some aspects of the writing process are not easily observed as someone writes. Students need to see writing modeled and to hear how writers think about the content and process of their writing. Minilessons and shared writing experiences provide explicit demonstrations of workshop procedures, writing processes, forms of writing, and conventional uses of language.

Minilessons. As discussed previously, minilessons are not full-length lessons. They address knowledge and strategies that are helpful for students to know at a particular time or that students are "using but confusing." Minilessons serve as a "forum for planning a day's work, a time to call writers together . . . for raising a concern, exploring an issue, modeling a technique, reinforcing a strategy" (Calkins, 1994, p. 193).

Minilessons are short and to the point, lasting 5 to 10 minutes, and are intended to "put the idea in the room" so that students can explore whether it is helpful to them and can share the idea with each other (Calkins, 1986). Minilessons plant seeds of ideas or expand on students' demonstrated awareness.

In the beginning stages of writing workshops, minilessons can help students learn workshop procedures. Later in the school year, minilessons may focus on the use of genres and literary elements or on strategies for becoming effective writers. The topics we select for minilessons should grow out of what students show through their feedback during opportunities to write.

Shared Writing Lessons. A more direct way to demonstrate writing is through shared writing lessons, in which students, with the guidance of a "more knowledgeable writer," develop a piece of writing together, and record the shared thinking on a large chart or overhead transparency. This has also been referred to as *group writing*, but "shared" is a good description of what should actually occur. The focus of what is written depends on the particular knowledge students need to see modeled.

Shared writing lessons are typically more in depth than minilessons and allow for demonstration, as well as discussion, of particular techniques in a piece of group writing. On days when we schedule shared writing, we will extend whole-group time during the workshop and shorten individual writing time and/or the sharing session.

Sometimes shared writing might actually be shared revising or shared editing, using a piece that the class has written together. Existing pieces can be considered as drafts, then used in a new way, to help students see that sometimes writers decide to change the focus of a piece. Changing the focus can change the way the author's voice sounds, the intended audience, or even the form that the writing takes (such as changing from personal narrative to poetry).

TOPIC CHOICE

Professional writers select their own topics for writing. In an effective writer's workshop students, too, choose their topics. "'Ownership' is vital if students are to make a real commitment of time and effort to the task of learning the craft of writing" (Wells, 1986,

p. 202). By the time they reach the middle grades, most students are quite capable of selecting their own topics for writing.

When students are able to select their own topics, boys and girls often make very different choices (Douglas, 1988; Graves, 1973). Boys often choose to write about the world outside of themselves with a focus on informational writing, whereas girls write with a focus toward "I" and personal narratives. The differences between students' self-selected topic choices reflect the diversity that exists in our classrooms.

RESPONSE TO WRITING

Providing opportunity for students to select their own topics requires you to take their choices seriously and respond to their writing based on what individuals are trying to accomplish. Students need the response of others "to discover what they do and do not understand" (Graves, 1994, p. 108) about their topic, the writing process, and their desire to be understood by others.

Response through Conferring.   While it can be very helpful for us to confer with students about their writing, our goal is really to help them learn to confer with themselves as writers. "Writing separates our ideas from ourselves in a way that it is easiest for us to examine, explore, and develop them" (Smith, 1982, p. 15). Early on, we must help students learn how to step back from their writing, how to *want* to step back, to see themselves in their words. Conferring with students should help them learn how to ask themselves questions about their piece as they reread and rethink their intentions.

Informal conferences happen as we circulate among students and begin conversations. We schedule *formal conferences* to have an in-depth look at a completed piece of writing or to evaluate a student's growth as a writer. Students need to confer at different points in their writing—getting focused, refocusing a draft, questioning a choice of form, thinking about getting started on a new piece, affirming that their piece is going well, receiving a nudge to take the next step, and so on. Talking with students about their writing enables us to learn who they are as writers and to become more sensitive to their individual needs for instruction.

Response Partners/Groups.   Students will probably need response to their writing that goes beyond conferences. Helping students learn how to respond to one another's writing will strengthen writing in our classrooms, allowing everyone to become a teacher. The procedure we use to enable students to get responses to their writing depends on how our classroom functions. In some classrooms, small groups can work effectively. Careful observation of students helps you decide whether partners or groups are most effective. The success of response will closely relate to the overall climate of support and respect we foster.

Editing Partners/Groups.   Encourage editing for conventions after students have gathered responses to the meaningful aspects of their writing. While some students do minor editing during writing, many students delay major editing until after completing their initial draft. They may require assistance from a more able writer to notice details in the writing that are unconventional or that need attention. Students can be very helpful to each other, teaching each other strategies for checking spelling and punctuation. Editing partners or groups will need coaching to be sensitive to the varying levels of knowledge that exist in a classroom.

Whether revising for meaning or editing for conventions, we are asking students to let the knowledge they have gained as readers also help them as writers. We should stress this point as we demonstrate revising and editing skills throughout daily writing activities.

YOUR TURN...

Have you observed a writer's workshop in a middle grade classroom? If so, what did you notice most? How did students appear to feel about the workshop?

• • •

MY TURN...

I first observed a writer's workshop in a fifth-grade class. In the beginning of the school year, the workshop seemed chaotic, but as students learned what Louise, their teacher, expected, they settled into a rhythm of writing. At first I questioned how students could learn about writing by working on their own. Then I began to notice how pairs of students helped each other when questions arose. I was also amazed that students would write for sustained periods of time without the teacher telling them. At first I was very skeptical of writer's workshop, but Louise taught me that through support and experience, teachers can help students become independent and confident writers.

• • •

PUTTING THE COMPONENTS TO WORK: WRITER'S WORKSHOP IN FIFTH GRADE

For a close look at how writer's workshop actually functions, we visit with Kim Muncy, a fifth-grade teacher in her first year of using writer's workshop as one way of teaching writing skills and strategies. Kim describes a typical day of writer's workshop in her classroom, noting the issues that she has dealt with in this first year.

GETTING STARTED

Kim Narrates:

From 9:15 to 10:15 we have writer's workshop. I've never done a writer's workshop until this year. Now, I can't imagine not doing it. Our format for writer's workshop is very predictable. We always start out with a minilesson. They are about 10 minutes long, and range from how to incorporate a writing trait, like organization or voice, in a piece of writing, to ways we can help ourselves and others edit papers. I develop minilessons around a variety of topics (examples can be found in Figures 10.2, 10.3, and 10.4).

■ **FIGURE 10.2**

Minilesson topics for workshop procedures

- How to do writer's workshop and expectations
- How to confer
- How to fill out a writing log
- Sharing writing
- Being a good listener
- Talking with friends, sharing ideas
- Evaluating your writing
- How to fill out a cover sheet before submitting it
- Understanding a grading rubric
- Publishing ideas and other extension activities

■ **FIGURE 10.3**

Minilesson topics for
writing strategies

- Matching form, purpose, and audience
- Using the phases of the writing process
- How to keep yourself going during writing time
- How to edit your, or a friend's, paper
- Taking risks
- How/when to revise (adding on, inserting, changing)
- How/when to edit
- When to abandon a piece
- How to determine which resources are best

■ **FIGURE 10.4**

Minilesson topics for
using writing traits

- *Organization:*
  Narratives—personal, fictional (story)
  Expository—research report, explanation,
    description, compare/contrast
  Persuasive—letters, speech,
    getting the reader's attention
- *Ideas and content:*
  Staying focused on your topic
  Knowing enough about your topic
- *Voice:*
  Hearing "you" in your writing
  Writing in an interesting way
- *Word choice:*
  Choosing words that fit your piece
  Describing a character, setting, or event
- *Sentence structure and fluency:*
  Using a variety of sentence forms
  Getting a "flow" to your writing
  Using the right words in the right places
- *Writing mechanics/conventions:*
  Making your writing easy to read
  Using conventions to help the reader

    I always base the topic of the minilesson on what students have demonstrated in their work and on what they've shared with me in conferences. For example, in yesterday's minilesson I shared some examples of leads that other authors use to get their writing started (see Figure 10.5). Through conferences and other discussions with students, it appeared to be a concern. This is also the time when I share my writing, because students need to know what good writing sounds and looks like as a model to draw on when they're writing.

I've noticed you enjoy reading books that capture your interest right from the start, in the first sentence or two. In writing we call that "a good lead." Did you know there is more than one kind of "good lead"? To help you think about your options for writing, let's looks at the leads for a few pieces of literature we have read to see what other authors do to get their writing off to a good start.

Sometimes authors start with a lead that fits the genre and introduces the plot. Do you remember when we studied mysteries and we especially liked *A Time for Andrew* by Mary Downing Hahn (1995)? She introduces the mystery by saying (place quote on overhead)—

"There it is." Dad slowed the car and pointed to a big brick house standing on a hill above the highway. From a distance, it looked empty, deserted, maybe even haunted. (p. 1)

Remember that Drew's dad and mom were taking him to his Aunt's house to stay for a few months. Notice how Mary Downing Hahn uses this lead to introduce that situation and create a sense of mystery right from the start. I think that is an example of a good mystery lead.

Sometimes authors choose to start by setting the scene, especially when the setting is going to play an important part. In *The Star Fisher* by Lawrence Yep (1991) we followed Joan Lee, a Chinese-American girl, as she moved to West Virginia in 1927, hoping to be accepted in the new town. (place quote on the overhead)—

I thought I knew what green was until we went to West Virginia.
As the old locomotive chugged over the pass, I could see nothing but green. Tall, thin trees covered the slopes, and leafy vines grew around the tree trunks; and surrounding the trees were squat bushes and tall grass.
And as the train rattled down into the valley, the green slopes seemed to rise upward like the waves of an ocean; and I felt as if the train were a ship sinking into a sea of green.

Lawrence Yep begins with setting to help you sense what Joan felt when she first saw her new home, West Virginia.

Sometimes an author leads off a story by introducing us to the main character, to get us interested in that character right away. In the beginning of *Maniac Magee*, Jerry Spinelli (1990) writes (place quote on overhead)—

They say Maniac Magee was born in a dump. They say his stomach was a cereal box and his heart a sofa spring.
They say he kept an eight-inch cockroach on a leash and the rats stood guard over him while he slept.
They say if you knew he was coming and you sprinkled salt on the ground and he ran over it, within two or three blocks he would be as slow as everybody else.
They say. (p. 1)

Does this description of Maniac Magee capture your interest? Does it make you want to know more about him? If so, then Jerry Spinelli wrote a good character lead.

We have looked at three options that authors use for getting the story started — focusing on plot, setting, or character. How they choose to start can have someting to do with what they want the reader to notice first. As you are working on your pieces today, look at the way you chose to lead off your piece. Do you think your lead will capture the reader's interest? Do you think your lead has something to do with what you want your reader to notice first? Perhaps some of you will be willing to share your lead at the end of today's writer's workshop.

I ask questions after the minilesson to check students' writing plans for the day:

- Who is starting a new piece today?
- Who is continuing a piece?
- Who will be rereading, revising, or reworking their writing today, and do you need any help doing this?
- Who will be editing today, and would you like to be in an editing group?

DAILY WRITING TIME

After I get an idea of who is doing what and jot down notes for myself about responses to my "check" questions, the students begin in their work folders, which hold notes, drafts, finished copies, resources, and so on.

Students choose their own topics during writer's workshop because it gives them a sense of ownership of their work. Sometimes I ask them to make choices within a particular genre, such as mystery, or a theme such as "Survival" or "Ancient Egypt." Even within these areas, students still have ownership over the specific topic and form of their writing. When I have something specific I want them to write about, we do it outside of writer's workshop.

This writing time lasts 20 to 30 minutes. While the class starts to work, I first go to those students who I know always have a hard time getting focused and started. I make sure they know what they'll be working on that day. I allow students to go to quiet areas in the room with a partner to discuss ideas and to share their work. When everyone is settled, I begin my daily conferences.

CONFERENCES

I see three or four students, who know it is their turn. (I have a rotating list of names for conferences, so the students always know when they're meeting with me.) When they come to conference, they bring their writing folders and what they are working on or what they would like to discuss. I confer with students to get to know them better, to monitor their progress, and to help them with any problems.

I usually get the conference going by saying, "Tell me about what you're working on." This is usually all it takes to get them talking. If they don't seem willing to share, I might ask "nudging" questions:

- How did you begin your piece?
- What can you tell me (if it's fiction) about your characters, setting, problem, or . . . ?
- What is happening in your piece that you're working on right now?
- What will happen next?
- How will you end your piece?
- How did you come up with your ideas?
- What are your future plans for this writing?
- What do you like best about your piece?
- What would you change if you could?
- What gave you trouble while writing?
- What did you learn as you wrote?
- How do you keep your reader interested and focused?
- What surprised you about your piece?

■ *You will need to develop ways to document the progress you observe in your students as writers. What types of notes might be helpful to you?*

• *How is this piece important to you?*
• *How does this work compare with other pieces you've written?*

By asking "nudging" questions, I'm trying to teach students how to think about what they're writing and to evaluate themselves. I believe this leads to greater independence. At the close of the conference, I always mention specific things I liked in their writing or that I noticed that were new or different.

KEEPING RECORDS

I keep running progress notes on each student, which I take during and immediately after their conference (see Figure 10.6). I keep track of titles, genres, strengths in the writing, problems I see students having, problems they say they are having, whether their log is being kept up, and any future plans they might have for publishing the piece.

In my notebook I also have a list of 5- to 10-minute small-group workshops that students can sign up for, and when each workshop will be or was given. Workshops are my way of offering group instruction based on student need. Workshops follow up minilessons, but are a bit more in depth. I call them workshops because the students think it sounds like it will be more fun than work. They sign up for a workshop they think will help them with their writing, such as one on organization, conventions, or word choice. Students can sign up at the end of a conference or any time that I am free.

FINDING TIME TO TEACH

I learned from Donald Graves (1994) that if students don't recognize they need help with a particular problem, they probably aren't ready to receive help yet. I really found this to be true

FIGURE 10.6

Kim's conference notes

Travis

9/1   -friends

        -Eric brainwashed by Dan, evil scientist

        *described characters

9/11   -wrote sequel, Laughing Waters

        -characters (Eric, Dan) show more development

10/2   -Pinball

        -man in pinball machine bouncing around

        -needs to make clearer (he feels)

        -got idea from Virtual Reality program

        *doesn't know how to keep reader interested, wants
         help here

        -used a lot of dialogue incorrectly so he signed up
         for the "_____" workshop and Zack is also helping
         him since he is a "master" at using quotations.

when I first began my workshops. I used to recommend that students come to specific workshops, and afterwards I would still find the same mistakes in their work. I realized that students may not recognize or find useful the writing ideas that I was sharing. Now I concentrate on helping students get to know themselves as writers so they are able to accept my invitations to workshops.

When I have at least two students signed up for a particular workshop, I send them a special invitation telling them where, when, and what to bring to the workshop. If for some reason a student does not come, I ask the class if anyone else is interested in that particular workshop and schedule an additional time. I always keep track of who comes, and I look to see if they implement workshop ideas in their writing.

During the workshop, we work with pieces the students are either working on or have finished. It seems that all I have to do to get them to search further in their writing is to focus their attention on a particular technique or element. Then they seem to notice it in many different places. By using their own writing for workshop lessons, they are taking charge of what needs to be added, deleted, or revised, and they are the ones who find the areas that need attention. I put our workshop minilessons on chart paper, and hang them on the walls so all students, including those who were not in a particular workshop, can refer to them if they are having difficulty with that skill.

I also keep a list of names of students who have mastered certain workshop lessons. Other students can use these "masters" as a resource if I am not available. One goal I have is to teach some of these "masters" how to teach a workshop on a skill or strategy they have mastered. How valuable it would be for them, their peers, and for me to see how they would communicate one of my workshop lessons to others!

SHARING WRITING

After 20 or so minutes of writing time, students choose to continue writing or to work on a publishing project for a finished or nearly finished piece. Publishing or celebrating students' work becomes part of their experiential base, and aids in making it their own while giving it a touch of finality. Our publishing projects have taken the following forms:

- bookmaking
- posters
- cartoon strips
- wordless books with tapes
- greeting cards
- advertisements
- videos
- plays
- pamphlets
- reader's theater
- puppet shows
- physical models

- pop-up books
- postcards
- big books
- dioramas
- newscast interviews
- pantomimes with tape
- flip book with script
- collages
- sculptures
- fact file
- TV productions

The end of writer's workshop consists of the class coming together for discussion. Some kids share excerpts of what they're writing, some share projects, and some share risks they've taken in their writing. I also ask if anyone tried what was discussed in the minilesson or workshop that day. Students schedule sharing time, and can check a posted list to prepare themselves if it's their share day. I also have emergency open slots for kids who just can't wait until their turn comes up next. The audience then has a chance to respond with what Donald Graves, in his book, A Fresh Look at Writing (1994), calls remembers, reminders, questions, and comments. Students tell the author what they remember about the piece, say if it reminds them of anything, and ask questions or make other comments about the writing.

KEEPING TRACK OF STUDENT PROGRESS

For evaluation purposes, the students are required to fill out a writing log (see Figure 10.7). They know they need to keep logs up to date and that I always check them at conferences. We also

Name _Seiko_   Writer's Workshop Log

Begin	Finish	Genre	Title	Strengths	Weaknesses	Future Plans
9/7	9/10	nonfiction	Me	used good word choice	my words were not new	maybe introduce one of my friends
9/11	I don't want to finish	fiction	Grasshoppers	I used good rhyming	my words don't sound new	none right now
9/12	9/12	commercial	Sugar Cola	neat idea	wasn't a good product	Do another commercial?
9/13	9/20	fiction adventure	Thunder Mountain	new types of rides	---------	Make more rides?
9/21	9/27	fiction baseball	Giants vs Rockies	I liked it and it's a good story	NO NEW WORDS!	make another story cause it got rained out
10/1	10/23	fiction adventure	The Home in the Woods	a good camping story	need more adventure	Write a sequel?
10/26	dumped	fiction	The Princess and the Frog (my version)	tried my ideas	kind of boring	maybe come back when I have more ideas
10/30	11/4	mystery	We're Coming Back to Get You	good quotes never used the word "said"	no new words	make it more exciting

■ **FIGURE 10.7**

Sample student writing log

284

continue to discuss as a class the importance of keeping a writing log. My students offer the following reasons for keeping their logs:

- "So we can see what kind of stories we like to write."
- "So we'll try something new."
- "So if we abandon a piece we can see it in our writing log and have another try at it if we want to."
- "We can keep track of how long it takes us to write a whole story."
- "We can work on the weaknesses that we have in our 'weaknesses' column."

Students also must turn in a completed piece every two weeks. Most do, but some turn in longer unfinished pieces. With each piece they turn in, they fill out an evaluation cover sheet that asks the following:

- What type of story did you write?
- What do you like best about your writing?
- What do you like least about your writing?
- What gave you the most difficulty?
- What do you want the reader to notice?

I have them do this so they can begin to evaluate their own work at deeper levels (see "Monitoring Students' Growth as Writers" at the end of this chapter for other examples).

I evaluate the pieces by means of a rubric that I created from a student writing guide. Everyone has copies of the guide, and if they get a low score for a certain area, they can look in their copy to get immediate feedback. If they are unhappy with a score, they know they are welcome to revise, edit, or address whatever the problem may be, to try to raise their score.

My students have come to learn that they can count on writer's workshop every day, no matter what the schedule is. On the few days that it has to be cut short, they are very disappointed.

Writer's workshop is working for me with this class of students. I truly believe this because I have seen improvement in all areas of writing traits as well as in the writing strategies of most students, including my least experienced. I have three students who were unwilling to write at the beginning of the school year. They considered a story to consist of a beginning sentence, a middle sentence, and an ending sentence. Through some incredible nudging, and by going to them first when each writing period begins, I have seen growth not only in the length of their pieces, but also in the amount of detail and voice. Now, I am trying to stretch them even further. They struggle and work hard at achieving one self-made goal at a time.

When at the end of the year we choose stories to go into each student's schoolwide portfolio, I am sure the reluctant writers will see a lot of growth. As for my stronger writers, they are learning to take risks and try new things in their writing. I'm also learning a lot as I go.

I'm not sure that my class last year could have done a writer's workshop. They were not very independent. I probably would have needed to make the workshop more structured, especially in my expectations of student roles. I may have had fewer short workshop lessons with more in-depth class lessons, and firmer guidelines for editing partners. This is something I'll have to consider in the future as I meet each new class. It won't be a barrier for me, only more of a challenge.

Writer's workshop will be a challenging approach to use in your classroom. At this point, what aspect do you feel most confident about and why? What aspect do you feel least confident about and why?

• • •

When I first tried a writer's workshop in the middle grades, I was teaching sixth grade. I was committed to the daily predictable time block needed for the students to become confident writers. I also believed that the students needed to select their own topics so that their writing would be meaningful. What I didn't feel at all confident about was how students would continue to learn about such conventions of writing as grammar and spelling if I didn't teach them directly. At the time, I didn't know many other teachers who were using a workshop approach, so I searched for articles and books by people who had, in hopes that I could learn from them.

• • •

GUIDING WRITING ACROSS THE CURRICULUM

As students move into the middle grades, expectations for writing in all areas of the curriculum take on greater significance. Students typically have many experiences with reading and writing narrative texts. For some reason, we expect that knowledge should help them read and write information texts. Data from most standardized tests, including the National Assessment of Educational Progress, administered to a large number of fourth- and eighth-grade students throughout the United States, suggest that students are not well prepared for constructing meaning with information texts.

It is scaffolded learning experiences with information texts that prepare students to read and write information text! Many students will come to us in the middle grades with few experiences with information texts, especially in the composing of such texts. We must be prepared to build their background of experience with information texts and provide support until they are able to assume personal responsibility for reading and writing such texts.

WRITING AS A TOOL IN RESEARCH

In the middle grades, we expect students to have some level of independence in searching texts for specific information and ideas, and communicating the results. Learning how to conduct effective research into meaningful questions is a skill identified by the writers of national literacy standards. In Chapter 1 we examined the Standards for the English Language Arts by the International Reading Association and the National Council of Teachers of English (1996). In addition to the three standards that focus on writing traits presented in an earlier chapter, we are aware of two additional standards that focus specifically on developing students' skills in research across the curriculum:

- *Standard 7.* Students conduct research on issues and interests by generating ideas and questions and by posing problems. They gather, evaluate, and synthesize data from a variety of sources (e.g., print and nonprint texts, artifacts, people) to communicate their discoveries in ways that suit their purpose and audience.
- *Standard 8.* Students use a variety of technological and information resources (e.g., libraries, databases, computer networks, video) to gather and synthesize information and to create and communicate knowledge.

Local school districts also identify research skills as an important expectation for student learning in language arts. For example, one school district's research standards for grades 4–8 include the following expected student outcomes:

- Formulate research questions, establish a focus/purpose for cross-curricular inquiry.
- Locate and select a variety of library resources, media, and technology to investigate a research question.
- Record information using note-taking and appropriate organizational formats.
- Document research sources; also cite sources within compositions.
- Present research findings for different purposes and audiences using charts, maps, or graphs with written text and/or multimedia.

As we examine these standards, we can see that all of the language arts are integrated into the research process. Students must read, write, and talk about their research. We can assume that while listening is not specifically identified, students develop listening skills as they interact with both their teacher and peers in this process.

The writing process, as practiced in writer's workshop, provides guidance as students search, select, synthesize, and share their learning about a topic or concept. Using a workshop framework, similar to that described by Kim Muncy earlier in this chapter, provides a dedicated block of time to provide guidance in all aspects of the writing process. As students write in all areas of the curriculum they will need experience with and instruction in a variety of text structures in order to effectively communicate their ideas to others.

WRITING ACROSS TEXT STRUCTURES

In Chapter 3 we considered the various types of structures that can be found in information texts that students will read: description/explanation, ordered/sequence, cause/effect, compare/contrast, and problem/solution. In Chapter 9 we added to this knowledge as we explored various types of informal writing which included many of the structures previously identifed.

Imagine that we are developing a sixth-grade unit about life in ancient Egypt. How might we engage students in writing across the various text structures?

- ***Description or enumeration.*** Example: Describe the life of an artisan or craftsman in ancient Egypt.
- ***Ordered or sequential.*** Example: Describe how pyramids were built.
- ***Cause/effect.*** Example: Explain the cause of the Nile overflowing its banks each year and the effect of the flooding.
- ***Compare/contrast.*** Example: Compare/contrast the life of an artisan with the life of a slave.
- ***Problem/solution.*** Example: Possible solutions for preserving the bodies of pharaohs after their death.

While students learn to construct meaning as they read these various types of texts, they may not generalize that knowledge to decisions they must make during the writing process. As we engage students with a variety of information texts, we must help them see the range of organizational patterns that authors use to achieve different purposes and understand that they can draw on these reading experiences as they compose their own texts.

How can we help students develop background experience with writing across various text structures? To demonstrate how ideas can be arranged in information writing, Ernesto, a sixth-grade teacher, helps his students see relationships among ideas and consider ways to organize those ideas. Focusing on one type of text structure at a time, he engages students in shared writings that model the structure and ways to organize ideas in that structure. Recall that shared writing occurs when a teacher and students compose together; the teacher serves as the scribe recording the group's ideas on an overhead or large chart. Ernesto finds that it is most effective to connect the demonstration of information writing to the ways ideas are organized in a unit of study. After students have some experience with a particular structure, Ernesto moves to writer's workshop so that students can try out their ideas, get responses from others, then revise and edit for sharing. Let's consider some examples from Ernesto's classroom. Figure 10.8 illustrates the variety of visual representations of text structures that Ernesto develops with his students.

Description/Enumeration.   When his students study the geography of the world's land and water ecosystems, Ernesto engages students in gathering information about the characteristics of tundra, forests, grasslands, deserts, and oceans. He helps students illustrate these descriptions in a web (see Chapter 9 for a webbing example), relating each characteristic to the central topic. Using the web and examples from information texts, Ernesto

■ **FIGURE 10.8**

Illustrating text structures in information text

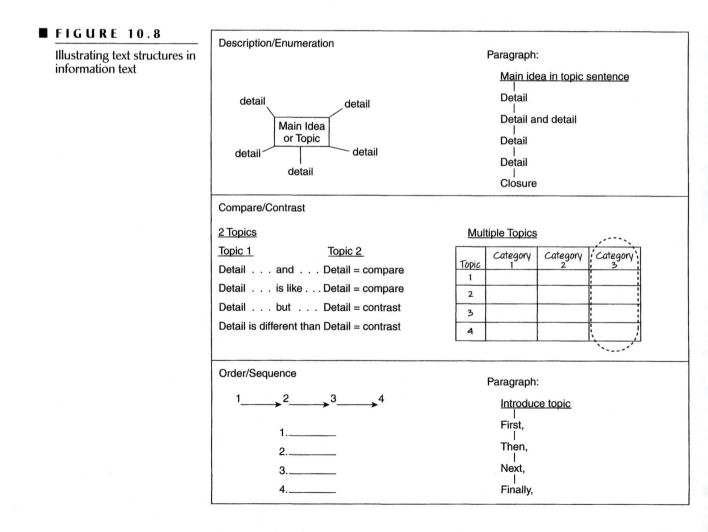

helps students see that in descriptive writing the characterictics each relate to the main topic, but may not directly relate to each other in a particular order.

To begin, he engages students in building a web of ideas/details about an individual ecosystem, then he helps students examine the web for relationships among the ideas. The web serves as prewriting for the writer's workshop, in which students will develop a paragraph that describes one ecosystem. First, through shared writing, the class uses ideas on the web to compose a paragraph that describes a forest ecosystem (see other example in Chapter 9, Figure 9.7). Then, students use the desert web to compose a descriptive paragraph about a desert ecosystem. Students in Ernesto's class are most familiar with desert ecosystems, so he has them apply what they learned about descriptive writing to that ecosystem. Over several days students make drafts of their ideas, get responses from peers, revise and edit their paragraphs, then share their writing with the class.

Compare/Contrast. As students' knowledge of the various ecosystems grows, Ernesto encourages them to begin to compare and contrast the chracterictics of several ecosystems. He has heard his students use comparison in their conversations, so Ernesto tries to relate this writing experience to the language his students use. He introduces comparison in writing by intertwining a description of one ecosystem, deserts, with another, forests. He begins with the web that the class developed for deserts and helps students identify the main ideas. Then he reintroduces the web students developed for forests according to the main points established for deserts. The class identifies details that are similar and those that are different by building a chart that has each characteristic in a category across the top, with the two ecosystems in rows on the side.

■ **FIGURE 10.8**

(Continued)

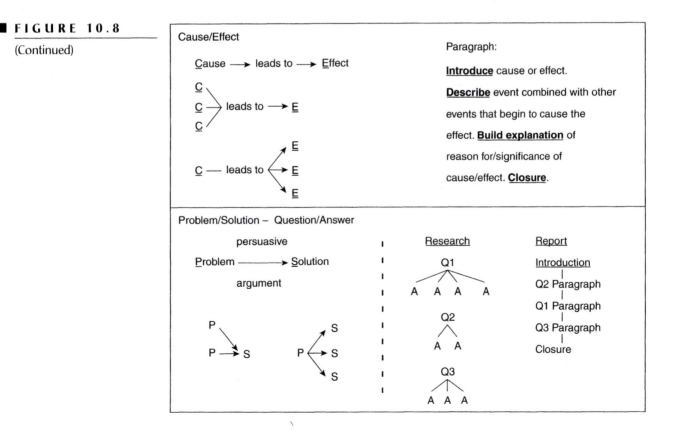

Ernesto leads the class in verbally composing statements of comparison. For similarities the class develops statements of comparison using *and*, *alike*, and *same as*, while for differences they develop statements using *but*, *different than*, and *in contrast to*. Ernesto could have used a Venn diagram (see example in Chapter 9) to compare and contrast the characteristics of two ecosystems, but he plans to add comparisons of the remaining ecosystems, so a chart format is more suited to his purposes.

Later in the unit the class-developed chart will serve as prewriting for a writer's workshop in which students will select one characteristic (top of chart), then compare/contrast each ecosystem according to that characteristic. In Ernesto's class, descriptive writing leads to comparative writing, as the scope of the unit broadens.

Order/Sequence.   Frequently we must describe a process or sequence of steps that has an order such as giving directions for making something or describing the steps we performed that lead to a particular outcome in a science experiment. At the beginning of the school year, Ernesto helps students use a timeline to identify times in their life when they learned something new (see illustration in Chapter 9). The timeline serves as prewriting for an autobiography that is intended to help students realize and appreciate the many things they have learned to do in their lives.

Cause/Effect.   Later in the year, when students are investigating and describing how elements can combine to form new substances that often have different properties (physical science), Ernesto will guide students to see the value of being able to not only correctly identify the sequence of steps they follow in making pancakes (order/sequence), but also to describe the change in physical properties of the ingredients as they move from step to step in the process (cause/effect).

Ernesto realizes that helping his students think through cause/effect relationships requires their use of background experience with physical changes to recognize how a particular cause and effect are related. He will help students rearrange their sequential list of steps, using arrows to show the direction of cause/effect relationships. Ernesto also knows that cause/effect relationships are signaled by language, giving clues about the existence and direction of the relationship. Writers use words such as *because*, *as a result*, *leads to*, or *makes* to describe/explain the relationship As his students develop their written explanation of the change in the physical properties of the ingredients in the pancakes, Ernesto will help them attend to the language that signals how causes and effects are related.

Problem/Solution.   Another type of structure that can be found in information writing is the identification of a problem and its solution(s). This structure is often associated with persuasive writing in which the author identifies a problem and presents arguments for a particular solution Ernesto knows that a strong persuasive argument can be challenging to develop, so he looks for multiple opportunities throughout the school year to engage his students in identifying problems and possible solutions that are meaningful to them. As the students studied ecosystems they became aware of the desire of the federal government to locate a nuclear waste depository in an isolated area of their desert state. Students were very motivated to study the problem and develop strong persuasive arguments, pro and con, about this possible action. This problem/solution writing took the form of letters to government officials who were involved in making the decision.

Question/answer is a similar structure to problem/solution. Ernesto uses question/answer structures to help students organize their research about a topic. During the first research project of the school year, Ernesto uses this structure in a very guided manner. After a brainstorming session to activate background knowledge and generate questions about a topic (the K and W sections of a K-W-L-Q, see Chapter 9), Ernesto places each question on a separate sheet of chart paper so that everyone can see it. As students search for information, the charts serve as a means of organizing ideas. Students write important words or phrases on the relevant charts. After enough ideas are gathered, Ernesto engages students in shared writing sessions to discuss how to organize each answer. Then, the group decides how to organize the answers to each question into a coherent order. On the overhead or another large chart, Ernesto leads a shared writing activity that shows students how to organize the questions/answers into a research report.

Subsequent question/answer research projects are more student directed, substituting a large index card or a sheet of paper for each question rather than large charts. Sometimes small groups each choose a particular question to explore. The completed research project is then a compilation of each group's efforts.

WRITER'S WORKSHOP IN CONTENT AREAS

Kim chooses to allow free choice of topics in her writer's workshop. Other teachers, particularly those in middle school, choose to focus the writer's workshop on particular types of writing that enhance content area studies or integrated units. For example, to support a social studies unit on ancient Greece, Laura, a sixth-grade teacher, may focus students' attention on how to conduct research, then report on the results of that inquiry. She may guide students to inquire about the scientific and mathematical knowledge of the Egyptians and how they used that knowledge to improve living conditions (description/explanation).

In middle school, teams of teachers often work together on interdisciplinary units. To support a team's unit of study, the English teacher often provides time in writer's workshop to develop compositions around the theme, applying content knowledge developed in science or social studies classes. For example, seventh- and eighth-grade students at a local middle school were studying about political action in their community, in particular how to influence the city parks department to put grass on their barren school grounds for a joint-use park. To make their case, students needed to learn how to write persuasive letters to local government officials (problem/solution). As Duncan, the social studies teacher, helped students research the issues, Carla, the English teacher, devoted writer's workshop time to helping students learn how to develop persuasive arguments.

Students may also continue to develop their skills in narrative, applying content knowledge. To support a unit on the Civil War, Marie's seventh-grade English teacher provided writer's workshop time for students to develop pieces that displayed their knowledge of the Civil War, developed in an interdisciplinary unit. Marie chose to write a fictional account that was made more believable by historical information. The beginning of Marie's draft, five pages at completion, is shown in Figure 10.9. Also included are samples of the story map she used to plan her piece (Figure 10.10), revision and editing prompts from her teacher which Marie used to guide her self-evaluation (Figure 10.11), a peer review (Figure 10.12), and Marie's final comments (Figure 10.13).

Choice is not taken away when teachers focus the writer's workshop. Students continue to select their own ideas about the topic while they learn how to write in particular forms for a variety of purposes. What is accomplished is an effective use of school time, increased support to students as they explore and refine their knowledge of writing, and greater opportunities for teachers to demonstrate how writers think with written language.

As we try new approaches, such as a writer's workshop, we may need models for learning, just as our students do. It will help to observe other teachers' workshops and read about

"Going once, going twice, sold to the man in the back row for 40 dollars."

The man stood up. He was tall and lanky, with dark hair and a mustache. He was wearing a black overcoat and black socks. A big hat sat upon his head. He had a stern look on his face, but as I walked over to him he smiled a little.

"What's your name?" he asked.

"Clarence Tomkins," I replied.

"Mine's Bob Barley. Jump in the wagon."

I got in the back of the wagon quickly, and we drove off with a strong jerk. The ride lasted an hour. It was nice to get a break from work. My last owner had me working sixteen hours a day, even at night when it was dark. He finally had to sell me when my back became injured. It was apparently from the work I was doing. I was praying that this man would be different.

We got to his house and plantation. Immediately I saw three other slaves working out in the field, and as we drove up another little black girl came out of the house. She had ragged clothes on, but an apron so I guessed she worked in the house.

"Sarah," the man yelled, "I'm home with another one!"

A women [woman] came out of the house. She was petite, with blond hair. She had on [wore] a dress and apron. She looked me over for what seemed like a long time.

"Well, I guess he'll do," she said, "What's your name?"

"Clarence Tomkins."

"You had better get started. Lily here will tell you where your sleeping quarters are and everything else you need to know. Go along Lily."

The little girl took my arm and led me to a little shack over on the far side of the property.

"This is where we all sleep. There's me, Joseph, Phillip, and my ma Sally. They're out working. I work in the house cooking and cleaning. The old lady seems horrid, but she's not so bad. Just don't get in no trouble. We eat at 5:45 in the morning. Some mush and water. At 12:00 we get the same thing and at 8:00 at night we eat some bread, meat, and a small cup of milk. Sometimes I can sneak in a piece of extra bread or cheese, but not always. If you get into trouble they take away a meal, but there are no whips."

I said a silent prayer to God for both of my sisters had been killed with whips by their masters. I myself had felt the pain of a whip before.

"Any questions Clarence?" Lily asked me.

"What about clothes?" I asked. All that I had on now was a pair of old pants.

She looked me over and said "they'll probably give you a long sleeved shirt for cold weather. When it's warm though, you'll just have to work without your shirt. These are the shoes you'll get. . . ."

■ FIGURE 10.9

Marie's draft about the Civil War, seventh grade

■ **FIGURE 10.10**

Marie's story map planning, seventh grade

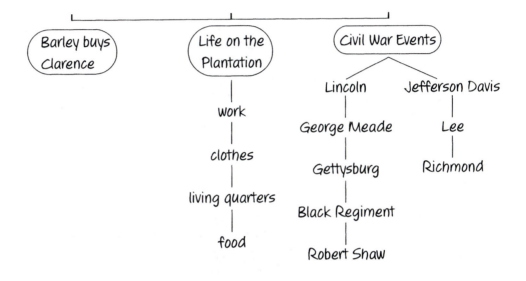

Barley's Plantation

Clarence - 48 (narrator)
Joseph - 30, strong
Phillip - 50, gray beard
Sally - 30s, tall, thin
Lily - 12, Sally's daughter

the experiences of others who share through their published writing. We, too, can learn from "more knowledgeable others." In the end, however, writer's workshop in our classroom will depend on our knowledge of writing processes and our students' needs as writers.

ATTENTION TO LANGUAGE CONVENTIONS

In a fully implemented writer's workshop, grammar, usage, mechanics, and conventions become meaningful as students revise and edit their work. As we learned in Kim's description of writer's workshop in her classroom, for example, she uses minilessons, small-group "workshops," individual conferences, and response or editing partners to teach specific aspects of using language for effective written communication. Most students need these varied forms of instruction to apply language conventions accurately and consistently.

Students' oral language and reading of literature form the base of their knowledge about the structure of English. The more widely students use language and the more they pay attention to the language of others when they listen and read, the greater opportunity they have to notice language patterns. In most cases, we should provide explicit instruction, helping students recognize what they already know about language, as well as what they still need to learn in order to communicate effectively. We should draw selected issues for explicit instruction from students' needs as writers, so they will see how the information is relevant.

Revising and editing
prompts from Marie's
teacher

		Review Sheet	Form #1
		Name: Marie	Period: 4
		Title of Writing: All Men Created Equal	
		Draft #1	
1.		What is the strongest or most exciting part of piece?	
		The beginning—1st couple pages	
2.		Is the paper limited to 1 topic?	
		yes	
3.		What is the topic?	
		One slave's life during the Civil War	
4.		Does the lead get the writer right into the writing?	
		Yes—	
5.		Which parts don't fit in and could be taken out? . . "and as a matter of fact I think I was their favorite. . ."	
6.		Where could I use more description or explanation?	
		—none—	
7.		Is there any part that could use dialogue?	
		I have it everywhere it needs to be	
8.		Is there any part that could confuse the reader?	
		Yes, when I put in about the 2 sides, I will change those few paragraphs	
9.		Have I repeated myself saying anything more than once? No—	
10.		Am I using particular words too often?	
		none—	
11.		Do I have paragraph breaks?	
		Paragraphing is fine	
12.		Is there information that could go in another place?	
		Yes, I will change it	
13.		How do I want my reader to feel?	
		Like they have a pretty good understanding of the Civil War⟶	

Peer evaluation of
Marie's piece

	Writers Workshop	Form #2

Writers Name: Marie

Title of Writing: All Men Created Equal

Reader Editor's name: Bailey

Question: Is there enough information?

1. What is the main point the paper is making?

2. What are the strong points of this writing?

3. What would help the piece? What is unclear? Give any specific examples, details, or pieces of info that need work.

4. Write some questions about the piece that will help the writer revise.

Yes, there is plenty of information, the end could have been drawn out a little more.

1. That Slaves were free, and equal

2. Voice, setting is great, She reveals the info extremely well, very real

3. End needs work

4. How did he feel at the end?

■ **FIGURE 10.13**

Marie's final comments to reflection prompts from her teacher

Writers Workshop	Form #3

Writers Name: Marie Cannon

Title of Writing: All Men Created Equal

1. What do you like about this piece of writing?

I like that it tells a story but still has a lot of information in it.

2. What was your plan for revision?

I took out words and phrases

3. What would change further if you had more time, energy, or desire?

I would make the conclusion better

Figures 10.14 and 10.15 identify basic issues in grammar, usage, mechanics, and conventions that will need attention during writer's workshop. Observation of students during writing and evaluation of their drafts and final products provide valuable direction for the instruction we should provide. As Kim found, our students will not all have the same strengths or needs. We will need to provide differentiated instruction in the uses of language and conventions, just as we provided varied levels of guided reading experiences.

Sentence Types
- declarative—statement (.)
- imperative—command (.)
- interrogative—question (?)
- exclamatory—shows strong feeling (!)
- simple sentence—contains one subject and one predicate
- compound sentence—contains two simple sentences, separated by a comma and joined by a conjunction (*and, but, or*)

Subject
- complete subject—who or what the sentence is about
- compound subject—two subjects joined by a conjunction
- subject pronouns—substitute for noun (*I, you, he, she, it, we, you, they*)

Predicate
- complete predicate—what the subject is or does
- compound predicate—two predicates joined by a conjunction
- object pronouns—(*me, you, him, her, it, us, you, them*)

Subject–Verb Agreement
- if subject is singular, verb must be singular

Negatives
- one per sentence

Nouns
- singular
- plural
- common
- proper
- possessive

Pronouns
- stand in place of noun
- can refer to a noun

Possessive Pronouns
- before noun (*my, your, his, her, its, our, their*)
- stand alone (*mine, yours, his, hers, ours, theirs*)

Verbs
- action verbs—tell what the subject of a sentence does
- helping verbs—work with the main verb, usually changes the tense
- irregular verbs—do not add the typical inflected suffixes to show past tense
- linking verbs—connect a subject with a word that names or describes the subject
- verb tense—tells the time in which action takes place (present, past, past participle, future)

Adjectives
- describe or tell more about a noun
- tell which one, how many, or what kind
- comparison (*-er, -est, more, most*)
- predicate adjectives—follow a linking verb, describe the subject
- demonstrative adjective—point out a specific person or thing (which one, which kind, how many?)

Adverbs
- describe or tell more about a verb
- tell when, where, how
- comparison (*-er, -est, more, most*)

Articles
- *a*—before a consonant
- *an*—before a vowel
- *the*

Prepositions
- connect a noun or pronoun to another word in the sentence
- common prepositions (*after, around, as, before, between, during, for, in, inside, of, over, through, to, until, with*)
- prepositional phrases—begin with a preposition and end with a noun or pronoun
- adjective prepositional phrases—function as adjectives
- adverb prepositional phrases—function as adverbs

■ **FIGURE 10.14**

Writing instruction: Topics in grammar and usage

■ FIGURE 10.15

Writing instruction:
Topics in mechanics
and conventions

Capitalization
- first word of a sentence
- titles of people, books, poems, stories, songs
- proper names
- initials
- proper nouns and pronouns
- greetings and closings of a letter
- first word of a direct quote
- abbreviations

Punctuation
- period
  declarative sentence
  imperative sentence
  abbreviation
- question mark
  interrogative sentences
- exclamation mark
  exclamatory sentence
- comma
  in a series (three or more items)
  with names (when spoken to)
  after introductory words
  between date, year
  between city, state/country
  inside quotation marks
  in greeting/closing of a letter
  before conjunction in a compound sentence
- apostrophe
  in possessives
  in contractions
- colon
  greeting of business letter
  between hour and minute (1:20 A.M.)
  listing

RESPECTING DIVERSITY IN STUDENTS' WRITING

Throughout this chapter, it should be apparent that the writing process as used in writer's workshop, by its very nature, respects what students bring to the page. Teachers who teach writing as a process honor and validate the individual's experience and language.

Writing is a process of moving one's thinking out of the mind and onto paper. While students differ in the experience and language background they bring to school, all students are thinkers and all are capable of communicating. One purpose of a writing program should be to provide whatever support and assistance students need to be able to use their language to express, explore, and appreciate their lived experiences. As students acquire new firsthand and vicarious learning experiences, they should have many opportunities to share them with us and with classmates, enriching their own and their peers' possibilities for writing.

Our writing program supports diversity of students' interests and background of experiences by letting them exercise some control over the topic or content of their writing. Having choice enables students to write from firsthand experience, to write with confidence about the content of their lives. When we allow choice, we honor the importance that students place on ideas or events that have meaning for them.

Finally, we respect diversity among students when we listen with sensitivity to the student as "writer" rather than focusing on the writing itself. Our talk with students should focus on their needs, interests, and concerns as writers. Only by listening carefully will we begin to hear each student's voice.

ASSESSMENT AND EVALUATION OF WRITING

Understanding students as writers requires that we carefully observe students as they are immersed in their writing, to confer with them about their work, and to collect a variety of samples of their writing over time.

During a grading period, students should keep all of their writing they have begun and/or completed in a work folder. From this work folder, students select writing to place in their learning portfolio and we select writing to place in our assessment portfolio. We might also choose to divide this writing into two folders for ease of handling — work in progress and past work.

The "work in progress" folder often holds three-hole paper and has pockets for loose papers. Only the most recent pieces are kept in this folder so that it is not cluttered. A running list of ideas and self-assessment checklists are also in this folder.

The "past work" folder holds all writing that is not needed on a daily basis. This folder should be accessible to the student as needed. The writing in this folder might be divided between "completed pieces" and "drafts and ideas." Even if a piece is initially abandoned, all first attempts should be kept in case the student decides to return to the piece at a later time.

TEACHER ASSESSMENT PORTFOLIO

Adding to our assessment portfolio should provide a comprehensive collection of data for evaluation.

Observing Writing.   There is a great deal of activity in a writing process classroom. We must make a conscious effort to watch students systematically. During each workshop, when students are involved in individual writing, we make careful notes about the writing behavior of one or two students, observing every student over the course of a month. We also make additional informal observation notes as needed.

What behaviors might we look for? We begin with the following:

- How students respond to minilessons and shared writing activities,
- How they settle into their writing each day,
- How they give and receive help during response and editing activities,
- The attitudes they display toward their own and others' writing,
- How they sustain themselves during independent writing, and
- What writing strategies they use.

We should routinely review our observation notes, reflecting on each student's progress. A scarcity of information for a student should tell us that we need to make more frequent and focused observations. Our observations can be collected on a checklist that focuses on the behaviors we are working to develop with an individual student (see Figure 10.16). Information from such individual records can also be collated in a class record to see patterns across students.

■ **FIGURE 10.16**

Writing behaviors checklist

Growth in Using Writing Processes

Name Dates				
Getting Started . . . • uses informal writing strategies • explores new topics • uses background experience				
Finding a Focus . . . • focuses after exploring ideas • abandons unproductive topics				
Composing . . . • shows sustained effort • meaning more important than conventions				
Revising for Meaning . . . • rereads to check meaning • receives input from others • uses input from others • changes words/sentences • changes order • adds on				
Editing for Conventions . . . • receives input from others • checks for capital letters • checks for punctuation • checks for spelling (in word knowledge stage)				

Conferring about Writing.   Teachers who use the writing process extensively in their classrooms confer with students in a number of different ways. From conferences during writer's workshop, we make notes about each student. We keep our conference notes in a separate folder or notebook or combine them with anecdotal records. These records help us to evaluate those pieces of writing that we select for our teachers' assessment portfolio.

Our conference notes should help us understand how students think as writers. We will not be able to adequately evaluate samples of writing unless we go beyond the surface of the writing and into the processes students use. The format we choose for making notes should fit the information we need about each student. Recall the notes that Kim makes during conferences (refer back to Figure 10.6).

Selecting and Evaluating Samples of Writing.   During the grading period, we select samples of each student's work for our assessment portfolio that document areas of growth as a writer, as well as areas of need. Over time, we collect samples that create a comprehensive picture of each student as a writer. It is best to photocopy selections so that originals can remain in the work folder or the student's portfolio. Our evaluation of each piece should clearly relate to our instructional goals during that marking period.

STUDENT LEARNING PORTFOLIO

During each grading period, students should have the opportunity to select pieces of writing to go into their learning portfolio. Graves (1994) suggests that along with selecting what students think is their "best" work, they should also select work that they feel represents growth in specific writing traits or strategies. For example, if developing detail or description has been a focus of that grading period, we ask students to select the piece they think is their best example of using detail or description, writing an explanation to accompany their selection. In addition, students should also have the option of selecting a piece they want in their portfolio for their own reasons, together with an explanation of why they chose it.

To help students make selections, Graves (1994) suggests frequently spending time during writer's workshop reviewing past writing and reflecting on its merits. We may wish to focus minilessons on how to reflect on one's own writing by modeling reflecting on personal writing samples. Minilessons may also encourage students to share their thinking as they reflect on their past writings.

For each piece selected, students should provide an explanation for their selection. We will need to teach students how to evaluate themselves; it is not a natural process. We should devote instructional time to self-evaluation, hold self-evaluation conferences with students to encourage particular strategies, and provide self-evaluation checklists for students.

Students should attach their self-evaluation to the finished piece of writing when they place it in their learning portfolio. We should provide a self-evaluation form on which students can record their explanation. Self-evaluations can be open ended or may ask students to rate themselves on specific criteria (see Figures 10.17 and 10.18).

The self-evaluation we encourage in students should be linked to our observations of their writing behavior and the writing strategies we have encouraged during that grading period. Students will learn more about themselves as writers if we help them focus on evaluating particular traits of their writing, instead of giving them the impression that "whatever they want to say about their writing is fine." Writing is a complex process and involves the use of many skills and strategies. We should help students evaluate by focusing their attention on particular strategies for some pieces, yet leave the evaluation of at least one piece open for them to decide the focus.

■ **FIGURE 10.17**

Open-ended self-evaluation

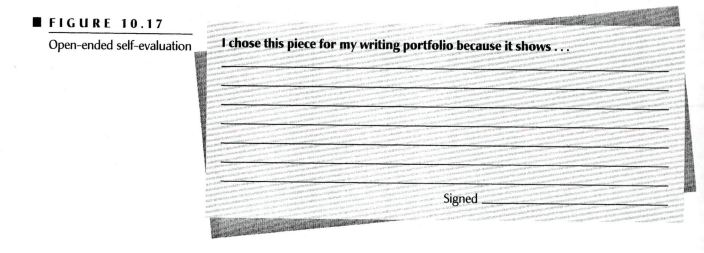

I chose this piece for my writing portfolio because it shows . . .

_____

_____

_____

_____

_____

Signed _____

■ **FIGURE 10.18**

Self-evaluation of an
instructional focus:
Description

I chose this piece for my portfolio because it shows what I learned about writing descriptions:

Do all the details relate to my topic? How do I know? _____

_____

Do the describing words (adjectives and adverbs) make good pictures? How do I help someone "see" my topic? _____

_____

_____

Does my beginning catch my reader's interest? If so, how? _____

_____

Signed _____

Evaluating Writing Traits.   Many school writing programs, even district and state assessment programs, include evaluation of writing by looking for traits considered to be characteristics of good writing:

- How ideas and content are expressed in the writing,
- How the author organized ideas to get the point across,
- How well the voice of the author is heard,
- The author's use of language, including word choice and sentence structure, and
- Use of conventions to communicate clearly with the reader.

The use of traits for evaluation provides a *rubric*, a standard of expectation, that is known to both student and teacher. The qualities of writing expressed in a rubric should reflect the classroom writing program. Rubrics help students and teachers look for similar

■ FIGURE 10.19

Rubric for evaluating
writing traits

Evaluating the Traits of My Writing

Ideas and Content:
5 = I know a lot about my topic, my ideas are interesting, the main point is clear, and my topic is not too broad.
3 = The reader usually knows what I mean. Some parts will be better when I tell just a little more about my topic.
1 = When someone else reads my writing, it will be hard for him or her to understand what I mean or what it is all about.

Organization:
5 = My beginning gets the reader's attention and makes the reader want to find out what's coming next. Every detail adds a little more to the main idea. I ended at a good place and at just the right time.
3 = The details and order make sense most of the time. I have a beginning but it may not really grab the reader. I have a conclusion but it seems to sum up my writing in a ho-hum way.
1 = The ideas and details are sort of jumbled and confused. I don't really have a beginning or an end.

Voice:
5 = My writing has lots of personality. It really sounds like me. People who know me will know it is my paper.
3 = Although readers will understand what I mean, they may not "feel" what I mean. My personality comes through sometimes. I probably need to know a little more about my topic to show, rather than tell, the reader about it.
1 = I can't really hear my voice in this writing. It was hard for me to write this paper. I really need to know much more about my topic or be more willing to take a risk about what I saw.

Use of Language:
5 = The sentences are clear and sound good when read aloud. Words fit just right.
3 = Some of my sentences are choppy or awkward, but most are clear. Some words are very general, but most times the reader will figure out what I mean.
1 = Even when I read my writing, I have to stop and reread, just to figure out some of the sentences. A lot of my sentences seem to be the same. The words I chose don't seem to be very interesting.

Use of Conventions:
5 = There are very few errors; it wouldn't take long to get this ready to publish.
3 = My spelling is correct on simple words, most of my sentences begin with capital letters and end with the right punctuation.
1 = There are a lot of spelling and grammar errors. Punctuation and capital letters seem to be missing. My paragraphs are not indented.

qualities of writing in one piece or across several pieces. Consider the rubric shown in Figure 10.19, adapted from Spandel and Culham (1993). It is intended for use by middle grade writers. Notice that the evaluation scale is 5, 3, 1, with 5 being high. Students learn that, in a given category, if their piece is better than a 3 but clearly not a 5, they select 4 as most representative of their work. Once the attributes and scale are familiar, we can attach a form similar to that shown in Figure 10.20 to each evaluated piece.

We must be careful to evaluate students' writing according to our instructional goals, those goals reflected in minilesson topics, shared writing topics, writing strategies suggested

■ FIGURE 10.20

Writing traits evaluation form

For this piece, I think my writing shows—

		1	2	3	4	5
• Ideas and Content	–	1	2	3	4	5
• Organization	–	1	2	3	4	5
• Voice	–	1	2	3	4	5
• Use of Language	–	1	2	3	4	5
• Use of Conventions	–	1	2	3	4	5

What I like the best about this piece is _____

_____

One thing I think I could have done better is _____

_____

Signed: _____

in conferences, and behaviors we have noted in anecdotal records of observations and conferences. We can convert these goals into recording forms that will let us indicate a student's overall progress in areas such as using the writing process, types of writing, organization of content, or use of conventions. The best forms are those we create, because they accurately reflect our program goals. A form such as the Writing Behaviors Checklist (Figure 10.16 shown earlier in this chapter) can serve as an excellent means for recording our evaluations of student progress over time.

Monitoring students' growth in writing is a continuous process and requires our focused attention. We cannot develop an appropriate writing program for students if we do not know them as writers. We cannot know students as writers without carefully observing and talking with them. Careful monitoring is a commitment we must make to effectively guide students as writers.

■ TAKE A MOMENT TO REFLECT . . .

■ *Writer's workshop provides:*
- A predictable time and structure for writing;
- Demonstrations of writing through minilessons and shared writing;
- A block of time for sustained writing;
- Choice of topic or content; and
- Response to writing through conferences, response groups, and sharing sessions.

■ *Minilessons:*
- Are 5- to 10-minute lessons that offer helpful suggestions;
- Can focus on the procedures of writer's workshop—
  - Writing in a particular genre;
  - Using literary elements;
  - Using conventions appropriately; and
- Are given when students demonstrate the need for specific knowledge.

■ *Writing conferences provide opportunities for:*
- Students' ideas about writing to be heard at different points in the writing process;
- Teachers to learn from students;
- Students to learn to ask themselves questions about their writing; and
- Both formal and informal one-to-one conversations about writing.

■ *Writer's workshop can be linked with study in other areas to:*
- Allow ample time for students to learn about varied forms of writing; and
- Retain control of their topic choice.

■ *We must provide many opportunities for students to use writing processes to support their learning across all areas of the curriculum, using such structures as:*
- Description/explanation;
- Order/sequence;
- Cause/effect;
- Compare/contrast; and
- Problem/solution or question/answer.

■ *We must respect the diversity of:*
- Experience and language knowledge among students; and
- Use it constructively to help students gain competence as writers.

■ *We monitor students' growth as writers through:*
- Careful observation of writing behaviors;
- One-to-one conferences;
- The collection of samples of writing in portfolios; and
- Evaluation of writing samples for traits—
  - Ideas and content;
  - Organization;
  - Voice;
  - Use of language; and
  - Use of conventions.

■ REFERENCES

Calkins, L. M. (1986). *The art of teaching writing*. Portsmouth, NH: Heinemann.

Calkins, L. M. (1994). *The art of teaching writing* (rev. ed.). Portsmouth, NH: Heinemann.

Douglas, D. J. (1988). *Factors that relate to choice of topic in a first grade process writing classroom.* Unpublished doctoral dissertation, Oklahoma State University.

Graves, D. H. (1973). *Children's writing: Research directions and hypotheses based upon an examination of the writing processes of seven year old children.* Unpublished doctoral dissertation, State University of New York at Buffalo.

Graves, D. H. (1994). *A fresh look at writing*. Portsmouth, NH: Heinemann.

Hahn, M. D. (1995). *A time for Andrew: A ghost story*. New York: Clarion Publishers.

Smith, F. (1982). *Writing and the writer*. London: Heinemann.

Spandel, V., & Culham, R. (1993). *The student-friendly guide to writing traits*. Portland, OR: Northwest Regional Educational Laboratory.

Spinelli, J. (1990). *Maniac magee*. Boston, MA: Little, Brown.

Wells, G. (1986). *The meaning makers: Children learning language and using language to learn.* Portsmouth, NH: Heinemann.

Yep, L. (1991). *The star fisher*. Victoria, Australia: Puffin.

chapter **11**

Word Study: Extending Knowledge of Words in Reading and Writing

In this chapter:

We explore possibilities for developmentally appropriate word study in the middle grades, including:

- Word study within a literacy program,

- Word knowledge in reading, including sight vocabulary, context, phonics, and morphemes,

- Word knowledge in writing, including spelling,

- Setting up word study activities,

- Content to include in instruction, and

- Assessment and evaluation of students' word knowledge development.

Looking into Classrooms . . .

The students in Jaime's multiage classroom study groups of words each week that have something in common. His fourth-, fifth-, and sixth-grade students make word cards, sort words into various groupings for study, make records of their sorts in a word study notebook, and talk about the patterns they notice with the other students in their group and with Jaime. The words they study come from their reading materials and their own writing. Since the beginning of the school year, Jaime has documented the growth of his students' knowledge about words. He knows that lack of word knowledge can be a bottleneck for comprehension and fluent writing. He stimulates his students to be curious about words in everything that they read and write.

Putting Theory into Practice . . .

To be effective communicators in our public and private lives we must be able to read, write, and think with a myriad of words. Our education, experience, and interest in communicating effectively with others determine how well we learn to use words. What interests do middle grade students have in communication? At this stage of their lives, they are striving to be understood and appreciated as individuals who are making the transition from childhood to adulthood. They often struggle with communicating both inside and outside of their peer group.

WORD STUDY IN THE LITERACY PROGRAM

Coming to "know" a word is multidimensional (Nagy, Herman, & Anderson, 1985). It involves knowledge of the word's:

- Spoken form,
- Written form,
- Grammatical behavior (its use as a particular part of speech, such as a verb),
- Collocational behavior (What other words does this word commonly occur with?), and
- Stylistic register (In what type of writing is this word likely to be found?).

To truly "know" a word requires us to have many meaningful experiences with it, with multiple opportunities to recognize the way(s) in which we are creating new connections to what we already know.

Knowing that vocabulary development goes well beyond learning dictionary definitions of words, we must provide stimulating and scaffolded learning experiences with words in a literacy program that:

- Are developmentally appropriate to students' knowledge of words,
- Provide explicit instruction and extensive practice in reading and writing new words,
- Actively engage students in developing their understanding of words and ways to learn them,
- Allow students to personalize word learning,
- Build on multiple sources of information to learn words through repeated exposures,
- Develop a strong conceptual understanding of the predictable and possible patterns in English words, and
- Cause students to recognize the relatedness of words and consciously develop strategies for active, independent word learning (Blachowicz & Fisher, 2000).

WORD KNOWLEDGE AND READING

Anderson, Wilson, and Fielding (1988) estimate that the average fifth-grade student reads about one million words in a year, counting both in- and out-of-school reading. At least 10%, or 10,000, of these million words will be seen only once during that year. Winsor, Nagy, Osborn, and O'Flahavan (1993) estimate the composition of those 10,000 words to be:

- 40% (4,000) derivatives of more frequent words (e.g., *debt* to *indebtedness*),
- 13% (1,300) inflections of more frequent words (e.g., *merge* to *merges*, *merit* to *merited*),
- 15% (1,500) proper nouns
- 22% (2,200) in several categories (capitalizations, numbers, deliberate misspellings, mathematical expressions), and
- 10% (1,000) truly new words.

With the shift from narrative to information texts that occurs in the middle grades, the vast majority of these "truly new words" are likely to be related to content area study in which students not only learn new words for familiar concepts, but they also encounter words that are both new words and new concepts. As far back as 1943, Cronbach made educators aware that learning vocabulary in a content area requires special attention to:

- The learning of specific meanings, frequently of new concepts, in the context of specific units of study;
- A receptive and expressive control of the key terms; and
- Teaching to a level of retention.

In addition to what they already know, students are learning new meanings for familiar words that are used in a special way in a particular discipline (Blachowicz & Fisher, 2000). In content area study, specific meanings for words and concepts and all they imply are central to instruction, and become the foundation for later learning (Carr, 1985).

To support vocabulary development with all learners, we must provide explicit instruction in using semantic-based techniques rather than using definitions, or definitions plus context (Marmolejo, 1990). In content area study we emphasize the relationships between words and the features that distinguish words in a particular category, such as various types of homes. We should engage students in learning experiences that develop knowledge of the essential vocabulary before we ask them to read new content. Then we expose students to words in differing contexts to facilitate their word learning (Gipe, 1979–1980; McKeown, 1985).

English language learners, especially, must have sources for encountering new words in which they can get a clear image of word meaning, either visual or auditory or both. They must be able to make strong memory connections between the forms in which they are likely to find the words and their various meanings (Hatch & Brown, 1995).

We can also teach students to use text-based clues to aid in their selection of vocabulary for individual study. We personalize their study through self-selection. Fisher, Blachowicz, and Smith (1991) found that when students in fourth- and seventh-grade literature groups are allowed to select their own words for study, students chose words at or above their grade level and they retained knowledge of their meanings. In content areas, where it may be important to focus on particular words and concepts in a chapter, there is also some supporting evidence for student self-selection.

COMPONENTS OF READING WORDS

To read the variety of words that we encounter daily, we draw on our sight vocabulary, context clues, phonics patterns, and morphological patterns. During the middle grades, students must become successful and confident users of these components to be able to make meaning with words and to continually add to their knowledge of words. Being able to unlock and understand unfamiliar words in print, or familiar words in unfamiliar contexts, opens the door for students to become powerful users of language.

Sight Vocabulary.   We recognize many words instantly, without needing to study distinguishing details. Such words are called *sight words* or our *sight vocabulary*. Meaningful words are easier for us to remember. Familiar words in our environment, words we see over and over, are usually the first ones we learn to read. To be fluent readers, we need a large storehouse of known words (Holdaway, 1980). To build this storehouse, we notice features of familiar words that help us distinguish them from other words, then store these features and words in memory for later use. As we work over time to make meaning with print, the distinguishing visual features we notice become more and more refined. With the help of more knowledgeable readers, we also begin to make associations between symbols and sounds. In our memory, we link the *phonological,* or sound, structures in words with their distinctive visual features (Ehri, 1991).

We develop our large storehouse of known words by both extensive and intensive reading. Extensive reading, across different genres and topics and for different purposes, exposes us to many different words. Intensive reading gives us the opportunity to distinguish the details in words and to link new words to words and word parts that we already know. As we come to "own" a word, we (1) learn a new concept and the labels for that concept, or (2) learn new labels for known concepts, then (3) bring new words into our productive vocabulary through our ability to use the word appropriately in a variety of contexts (Graves, 2000).

Contextual Meaning.   We must learn to use the context in which words occur to discern their meaning. *Context* involves using the *meaning cues* we derive from surrounding familiar words, phrases, and sentences, and the *language cues* of grammar and syntax to provide clues to the meaning of words that seem unfamiliar. Context should also be our main way of checking the accuracy of the visual cues we use to pronounce unfamiliar words.

We have already processed the meaning of the text up to the point of our encounter with an unfamiliar word or a known word in an unfamiliar context. Using that meaning, we look at the word for clues to letter–sound patterns and ask, "What word do I know that looks like this word (visual) and fits in this phrase/sentence/paragraph?" We then check context by asking, "Does that sound right (structure) and make sense (meaning)?"

Our ability to use contextual meaning relies on our ability to effectively integrate visual and language cues to support meaning. If reading instruction has focused our attention on visual cues more than on meaning and language cues, we may not know how to use context adequately. Successful use of context to make meaning assumes that we balance our use of all three cues as needed.

Phonics Patterns.   As we are probably aware, *phonics* is the component of word knowledge that relies on letter–sound relationships within syllables. While knowledge of phonics is highly correlated with success in reading and spelling, it is important to remember that knowledge of phonics alone does not constitute reading.

When we speak of phonics, we typically mean the *visual cues* to sounds represented by the left-to-right arrangement of consonants and vowels within syllables. To use our phonics knowledge, we must be able to match letter patterns with the possible *phonemes,* or sound units, stored in memory from oral language.

Phonics is a widely debated issue in reading instruction in the United States. English is primarily an alphabetic system, in which symbols represent the speech sounds of oral language. In an ideal alphabetic system each speech sound has its own distinctive graphic representation. Herein lies the problem with English. Sometimes the phonemic significance of a letter is modified by the following:

- The letter(s) that come immediately after (*lit/light*),
- One or more nonadjacent letters (*can/cane*),
- The identity of the word or its constituent syllables as wholes (*father/fathead*), and
- The absence of stress or accent on a syllable (*a-bout'*).

Because English is not a perfect alphabetic system, we must look for the patterns that do exist, patterns that we can emphasize with our students. We must look for letter patterns within syllables and consider the types of thinking used to identify sound patterns. To continue to develop your knowledge of phonics, in Appendix D we discuss the full range of phonics elements so that you are prepared to meet the range of readers you may find in your middle grade classroom.

In general, it is best to help students develop phonics knowledge by moving from the simple to the complex, engaging students in thinking about the following patterns:

- Single-letter patterns before double (*ran/rain*),
- Consistent patterns before variant (*street/great*), and
- Sounded patterns before silent (*not/knock*).

To be useful, instruction in phonics should focus on elements that are appearing in students' reading and writing.

Morphological Patterns. While phonics patterns enable us to understand letter–sound relationships within syllables, morphological patterns enable us to break apart multisyllable words to find morphemes—units of meaning such as roots, prefixes, suffixes—and to relate those units to determine word meaning. Morphological awareness has been found to make a significant contribution to reading ability (Carlisle, 1995; Carlisle & Nomanghoy, 1993). Figures 11.1 and 11.2 may help you distinguish between possible morphological patterns and components in words.

It is estimated that at least 60% of the new words we encounter in reading can be analyzed into parts that give substantial help in figuring out their meaning (Nagy & Anderson, 1984). Many irregularities exist, however, between English spellings and pronunciations, yet as we examine such irregularities we notice morphological relationships between words, such as *sign* and *signature*, that help us understand word meanings.

■ **F I G U R E   1 1 . 1**

Morphological units

Base
- A free morpheme that can function as a word or may have affixes attached to create words with related meanings.

Root
- A morpheme that must be bound to other morphemes to form words, such as *bine* in the word *combine*.

Affix
- General term for morphemes that must be bound to a root or base to form words.
- Prefix
  - Morpheme added before a base word or root.
  - Can be independent of the base word, as in **dis**obey.
  - Can be dependent on the root, as in **com**bine.
- Suffix
  - Morpheme added after the base or root.
  - Can be inflectional, as in *think + ing*, to change the number, verb tense, or comparison.
  - Can be derivational, as in *danger + ous*, to change usage of the word.

■ FIGURE 11.2

Morphological patterns
in words

Studying morphological patterns in words helps us see
that multisyllable words are made from combinations of
base words or roots and affixes. Some examples are:

base + base	= *over + drawn* or *shouldn't*
base + affix	= *jump + ing* or *care + ful*
affix + base/root	= *dis + obey* or *com + bine*
affix + base + affix	= *dis + loyal + ty*
base + affix + affix	= *care + ful + ly*
affix + base + affix + affix	= *un + self + ish + ly*

Understanding the shared morphological relationships between such words not only contributes to reading ability, but also to spelling ability (Nagy & Anderson, 1984).

Experts tell us that effective use of morphology in word learning depends on our metalinguistic ability, the ability to reflect on and manipulate the structural features of language (Tunmer, Herriman, & Nesdale, 1988). By fourth grade, most students achieve the
basic morphological insight that longer words can often be broken into shorter words or
pieces that give clues to their meanings (Anglin, 1993; Tyler & Nagy, 1989) To illustrate,
researchers find that between first and fifth grade, the number of root words that children
know increases by about 4,000, yet the number of derived words (words with prefixes
and/or suffixes) increases by 14,000. The bulk of the increase appears to reflect students'
morphological *problem solving*, that is, their ability to identify and understand new words
by breaking them down into their component morphemes (Anglin, 1993).

SELECTING WORDS FOR STUDY

Graves, Juel, and Graves (1998) provide some very helpful criteria for identifying vocabulary words for study in reading. Consider these questions that teachers are encouraged to
ask as they plan for student learning:

- *Is understanding the word important to understanding the selection in which it appears?*
  If the answer is no, then other words are probably more important to teach.

- *Are students able to use context or structural analysis skills to discover the word's
  meaning?* If students can use these skills, then we should provide the opportunity
  to practice them. Practice enables students to consolidate these skills and reduce
  the number of words we need to teach.

- *Can working with the word be useful in furthering students' context, morphemic
  analysis, or dictionary skills?* If the answer is yes, then working with the word can
  serve two purposes. It can aid students in learning the word, and it can help them
  acquire a strategy they can use in learning other words.

- *How useful is this word outside of the reading selection currently being taught?* The
  more frequently a word appears in materials students read, the more important it
  is for them to know the word. Additionally, the more frequently a word appears,
  the greater the chances that students will retain the word once we have taught it
  (pp. 10–11).

As we engage students in reading activities, how can we guide students in the study of words? Think back to the classrooms that we visited in previous chapters as we explored ways to organize literature-based reading. Lou, Melodia, Kim, and Kristen encourage word study during reading through teacher-mediated ML–TAs and MR–TAs, whole-class mini-lessons, individual reading conferences, and small-group discussions. Students practice using new words in all forms of literature study, as well as independent reading.

For example, as Lou plans for the reading of Chapters 1 and 2 in *Hatchet* (Paulsen, 1999), he identifies language that warrants attention within the context of each chapter, meaningful words and phrases that may need clarification depending on students' background knowledge. Focusing on language during reading activities is a valuable form of word study. Lou draws words from those books students are currently reading. Students in his sixth-grade classroom become more interested in learning new words as they realize how it adds to their understanding and, consequently, to their enjoyment of reading.

In keeping with the criteria identified previously, Lou selects words for study by considering the background of his students, the context in which the words are used, the level of word knowledge required to be able to decode each word, and the utility of the word. He believes that word study in reading focuses first on recognition and understanding, then leads to expanding vocabulary through studying related words.

Example: Possible focus words in the study of *Hatchet*, and words that might be unfamiliar. Most words are related to airplanes and flying, the subject of those chapters.

Chapter 1	Chapter 2
banked	turbulence
rudder	horizon
bushplane	altimeter
	transmitter
	throttle
	altitude

Lou also asks students to identify unfamiliar words in their reading. As they study a book, students collect words on pages of their literature log. Lou provides many opportunities in whole-class discussions for students to mention words they want to examine and discuss. Students can be quite accurate in identifying words they do and do not know (White, Slater, & Graves, 1989).

In the list above:

- The meaning of *bushplane* will be related to what students know about other compound words.
- The decoding words *rud-der, throt-tle,* and *trans-mit-ter* will be related to other syllable patterns with double letters.
- In *altitude* and *altimeter* students will be led to see the common morphemic unit, *alti*, deriving meaning by anology, and relating the meaning of *altimeter* to the meaning of *altitude*. Students will draw on their knowledge of science to find meaning in the unit, *meter*, as in *thermometer*, for additional meaning of *altimeter*.

Word study in reading is most effective as part of the study of a text, rather than in isolation. Students must have support to recognize words in their reading, then to analyze patterns and make associations with known words that are related by pattern or meaning. At any given time, the words studied in reading should be slightly more complex than those studied for writing/spelling. For example, students who can read words that typically come late in the transitional (multisyllable) stage, third- to sixth-grade reading level, should be able to write conventionally words that occur earlier in that stage (see later portions of this chapter for specific content). The new words that students study in reading activities will eventually become the words for study in their writing/spelling. Again, we see that reading development leads writing development.

SELECTING INSTRUCTIONAL STRATEGIES

Here is where we must know something about our students' background knowledge. When it comes to learning new words, it matters whether or not they already have background knowledge about the concept. Many words are simply new labels for concepts students already know. Helping our students attach new labels is supported by meeting those words in the rich context of well-written text. When students already know the concept, dictionaries can be a helpful tool, because students are able to draw on the multiple meanings provided in the definitions.

Developing vocabulary for new concepts can be quite challenging. For those words that are important and will appear frequently in students' reading, we need to build students' background for the concept. Integrating learning experiences through units of study is one of our most powerful instructional strategies for learning language. Connecting experiences that allow students to focus on concepts over a period of time provides opportunities for the language of the concept to be recycled (see Chapter 13). Linking reading to talking, viewing, writing, and doing keeps students in the mode of recycling the language about a concept. Students find themselves using the new vocabulary over and over, in a variety of contexts. We teach students how to make connections among words so they can teach themselves word-learning strategies.

Four strategies have great value for word learning:

- Use the context in which words are found to infer their meaning, including knowledge of possible multiple meanings of words (for background see Chapter 2).
- Use word parts, or morphemic units, to infer meaning, as well as make analogies with known words/word parts (for background see Chapters 2 and 11).
- Use relationships between words, such as synonyms and antonyms, to infer meaning.
- Use the dictionary to learn or verify the meaning or, possibly, the multiple meanings of a word (adapted from Graves, 2000, p. 123).

The majority of our students will need explicit instruction in the procedure and value of each strategy above. They will need for us to make clear what the strategy looks like and sounds like in use. We do this through the way we guide their thinking during ML–TA/ MR–TA exercises and strategy minilessons, by teaching from words that students record in their learning logs, through weekly word study (see later sections of this chapter), and by establishing an environment of inquiry in the classroom.

As we teach word-learning strategies, it is best to take a whole–part–whole approach.

- We embed our instruction in the act of connected reading and writing of text,
- Draw out the word(s) in question for analysis and concept building, and
- Then return to the text for practice.

As our students practice a new skill/strategy, we must remember that they are novices and cannot be expected to function as experts. We must continue to provide scaffolded support, slowly releasing our support as students demonstrate their ability to independently use strategies to construct meaning. We must also remember that learning words is only one part, albeit an important part, of constructing meaning with text. Students' knowledge of words in reading must be orchestrated with other skills/strategies to comprehend.

As your middle grade students move toward becoming mature readers, they will encounter many new words. It might be helpful for you to begin noticing and collecting words in texts that are intended for middle grade students. The more familiar you are with the types of words students might encounter, the more easily you can decide on the types of strategies that might be most effective to support their word learning.

• • •

WORD KNOWLEDGE AND WRITING

The words that students come in contact with while reading will serve as models for the patterns in the words they write. Studying words during literature-based reading enhances opportunities to notice patterns essential in writing, especially with multisyllable words. Once again, reading development leads writing development.

How can we use writing activities to encourage the study of words? During literature-based reading experiences, Lou, Melodia, Kim, and Kristen ask students to make written records in journals or logs. These records require students to think about the patterns they notice in words while reading and to use those patterns when they write. During daily writer's workshop (see Chapter 10), Kim encourages students to give careful attention to their word choices as they structure sentences and revise and edit their work.

In mathematics, social studies, and science, these teachers ask students to list, explain, chart, describe, record, label and annotate drawings, brainstorm or cluster, and make notes in learning logs. Each of these teachers asks students to use words in writing that first appear in the students' reading material. These teachers believe that attending to the words they write enables students to become competent thinkers and communicators.

Some of our students will have the ability to visualize words, and for these students spelling words conventionally may be an easier task than it is for others. These students may possess the "spelling gene" as described by Richard Gentry (1997). While spelling may appear to be a skill of rote memory, it actually relies on a conceptual understanding of three language principles. Ability in spelling is based on an understanding of alphabetic, orthographic, and morphemic principles (Henderson & Templeton, 1986):

- The *alphabetic principle* tells us that letters represent sounds, such as the letters *c-a-t* represent the sounds /c/, /a/, /t/.
- The *orthographic principle* is based on spelling patterns in a particular language, such as English words that end with a /v/ sound must be spelled with the letters *ve* as in *have* and *five*.

- The *morphemic*, or *meaning, principle* tells us that words that have related meanings should have related spelling patterns. For example, *legality* is related to *legal*, even though their pronunciations may differ. The spelling of *legal* remains the same in *legality* to show the relationship of the words by meaningful units, or morphemes.

The background knowledge required to understand and use the alphabetic, orthographic, and morphemic principles begins with attention to words in reading.

We know that students progress through stages of understanding as they move toward mature reading and writing. In the middle grades, we will find that most students are focusing on understanding multisyllable words. In the next two sections, we discuss the types of multisyllable patterns that will be the focus of word study for students in the middle grades.

As we consider stages of development, we must always remember that students may not master the reading and writing of all patterns of words in a particular stage before they begin to notice and understand word patterns in the next stage. Some phonics patterns that appear infrequently in students' reading materials may not become prevalent in students' writing until they are in a more advanced stage. Careful observation of students' use of words in reading and writing helps us be sensitive to times when we may have to help students attend to and understand particular phonics patterns.

INSTRUCTIONAL STRATEGIES TO PROMOTE WORD KNOWLEDGE

Along with the informal study of words as they appear in students' reading and writing, we can also provide a weekly program of formal word study at the appropriate level for all students. To do this, we select appropriate words for focused study of patterns, replacing the traditional spelling instruction that uses a single textbook. We dedicate approximately 15 to 20 minutes per day to word study activities, organizing the time so that either the whole class or small groups study at the same time. During this time our tasks are to observe students' word study strategies, discuss patterns, and "nudge" students to explore their thinking about words.

WHOLE-CLASS WORD BUILDING

With the diversity of knowledge about words that is likely to exist among any group of students, building words is an excellent whole-class or small-group word study activity. Building words, letter by letter or chunk by chunk, requires that students use their skills in phonemic awareness and morphemic patterns. Students use their knowledge of phonemic awareness to hear sound chunks in words, match those chunks to appropriate letters, and place letters in sequence from left to right on the desk or table in front of them. Students use their knowledge of morphemic units to hear meaningful chunks in words.

Word building provides students with the opportunity to experience firsthand that changing just one letter or the sequence of the letters within a word changes that word (Cunningham & Cunningham, 1992). This concept is essential to students' concepts about multisyllable words in the English language.

Teachers who use word building experiences for focused word study do so several days each week. It is best to study a group of words over several days, providing opportunities for students to reread patterns, rewrite patterns, discuss their observations, and speculate on other words that are related to the pattern being studied.

Options for Word Building.   At least two options for building words are available:

1. Select a longer word, such as *inspection,* that contains letters from which a number of words can be constructed (Cunningham & Hall, 1994).

   Example: provide students with letter cards,

   i-n-s-p-e-c-t-i-o-n, to build words such as

in	it	pen	nose	cent	untie
pin	pit	open	noise	cents	optic
spin	spit	opens		sent	
pine	spite		pose		tension
spine			poise	since	pension
				notice	
					inspect
				cities	inspection

2. Select particular morphemic patterns, such as the root *spec-,* from which related words can be built.

   Example: use *spec-* to build

   spec + ta + tor   re + spect + able
   spec + ta + cle   in + spec + tion
   spec + trum   spec + tac + u + lar

   Example: use *re-* and *-able* to build

   re + fill + able   re + place + able
   re + new + able   re + mov(e) + able
   re + spect + able   re + us(e) + able

Procedure for Whole-Class Word Building.   During a word building session, each student has either (1) letter cards for each letter in the word for the day, such as *i-n-s-p-e-c-t-i-o-n,* or (2) word chunks to make words that contain a morphemic pattern, such as the root *spec.* The procedure for building words, adapted from Cunningham and Hall (1994), includes the following steps:

- The teacher states the number of letters (or chunks) and the word to be made, such as "Let's build a five-letter word, *noise*" or "Let's build a three-chunk word, *inspection.*"
- The teacher then observes to see how the students proceed to build the word.
- One student, who built the word correctly, then writes the word on a large chart for all to see.
- The teacher helps the students check their spelling of the word against the model.
- The students continue building words until they have made all of the words for the day.
- After the students build the words for the day, the teacher uses large word cards to help students sort the words into groups that have similar patterns and to consider the meaning of particular words.
- To end the lesson, the teacher asks students to speculate on how a word might be spelled that contains a chunk of a word made that day (p. 8).

How do we decide which words should be the focus for a word building lesson? We must consider the range of word knowledge among our students and select words that the majority can read and spell, with a few challenging words for the more advanced students. We work together as a class, providing support to individuals as needed. Care must be taken to keenly observe the students for whom some of the longer words may be near their frustration level.

As we build words, we should also encourage children to write the words they make. Writing is an excellent reinforcement for letter–sound correspondences. A word study notebook, described in detail in an upcoming section, can be quite useful for recording word building lessons.

Selecting morphemic patterns for study should be directed by the words that are showing up in students' reading materials or words that students are trying to use in their writing. We know that utility is important. Students must be able to apply their new knowledge to print in some manner fairly soon after word building lessons.

Word building experiences can occur daily in middle grade classrooms. Word building provides opportunities for students to hear spoken words, then use letters or word chunks to construct words. Students also have opportunities to participate in sorting words by patterns and spelling by analogy, when part of a word is used to spell another. They extend their vocabulary knowledge by discussion of the relationships between words that share the same roots or affixes.

SMALL-GROUP WORD SORTING

Word study can also occur in small groups, geared to the developmental levels of our students. Students focus on sorting words with patterns that are very close to their particular developmental level. This is another way for students to see patterns in words. Students sort words by placing small cards with related words in a column for comparison.

Options for Word Sorting.   Word sorts can serve different purposes in studying patterns:

- In an *open word sort* students determine categories for the word cards, showing the patterns they notice independently (see Figure 11.3).
- In a *closed word sort* teachers direct students' attention to search for specific patterns (see Figure 11.4).

PROCEDURE FOR SMALL-GROUP WORD SORTING

A weekly schedule for small-group study of words might include the following types of activities for students:

Monday

- Begin with a new list of appropriate words.
- Students check to be sure they can read each word.
- Write the list of words in a word study notebook.
- Make a card for each word, using blank index cards.
- Take a spelling pretest with a partner (optional).

Tuesday and Wednesday

- Individually review word cards.
- Do an open sort (Tuesday) and a closed sort (Wednesday) to explore sound or meaning patterns.

■ **FIGURE 11.3**

Open word sort

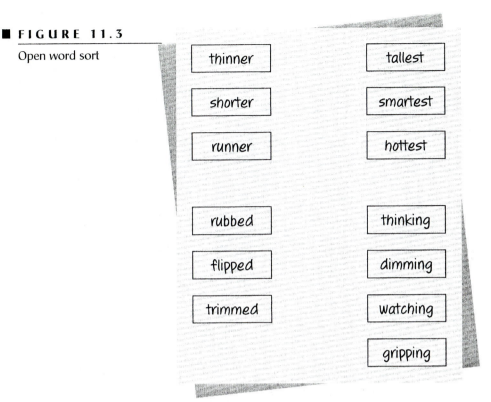

■ **FIGURE 11.4**

Closed word sort—
consonant doubled when
suffix is added

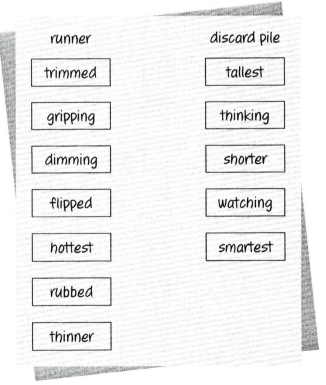

- Write the results each day in the word study notebook.
- Discuss patterns observed with partner and teacher.
- Compare the open word sort with the closed word sort.
- Discuss results with partner and teacher.

Thursday
- Individually review word cards.
- Do activity that focuses on applying patterns, such as a word hunt in familiar texts.
- Write new words that follow the focal pattern(s) in the word study notebook.
- Compare new words and word list, noting similarities and differences in the notebook.
- Discuss results with partner and teacher.

Friday
- Posttest/check patterns, including student-chosen words.
- Discuss comfort/confidence with patterns.
- Plan for next week of word study.

IMPLEMENTING AND MANAGING WEEKLY WORD STUDY

Jaime teaches in a multiage classroom, with grades four, five, and six. For his word study program, Jaime has learned that he must understand how students learn new words and relevant patterns of English words. Using this knowledge, he then develops word lists that fit patterns for the various levels of spelling that are appropriate for students in his class. He collects words from various grade levels of spelling textbooks and children's literature for these lists. (Appendix C contains sample lists of words sorted by level and pattern that may be used for word study.)

After determining each student's level of word knowledge, he creates manageable groups with similar word knowledge and instructional need. These groups allow students to study sight words that are within their reach for learning to write conventionally. He prepares weekly word charts for each group and provides blank paper grids for the students to prepare as word cards for sorting activities, cutting the grid apart into separate word cards. He circulates while students are working on sorting activities, discussing what they have noticed and mediating between what students already know and what they might need to clarify to make sense of the patterns they are studying (Vygotsky, 1962).

As Jaime implements his word study program, he helps students understand the purpose for each part of the weekly study. He teaches them to be good partners, assisting and supporting each other's efforts to learn words. To help students remember what they have learned, he has them record the results of their word sorts, as well as their thinking about the sorts, in a word study notebook.

Forming Word Study Groups. For word study to be most beneficial, students should focus on patterns that they are beginning to notice but may not yet understand. If we ask students to attend to patterns in words that are too far ahead of what they know, they will not be able to make full use of our instruction.

To learn what his students are noticing about language, Jaime looks at the developmental, or inventive, spellings in their writing. As students are learning about phonics and morphemic patterns, they often "invent" temporary spellings to stand for patterns not yet internalized (Temple, Nathan, Temple, & Burris, 1993), representing words as best they can with what they know at their independent level of performance. Jaime uses students' writing to see what they know about written language, to see levels of word knowledge:

- Some knowledge is independent, and is used conventionally.
- Some knowledge is just becoming familiar, and is used inconsistently or unconventionally.
- Some knowledge has not yet been noticed or understood, and is absent.

Jaime analyzes the way students write a focused sample of words, representing varying stages of development, asking them to write a list of words arranged in a sequence that is typical of students' development. He dictates each word, uses the word in a sentence, then repeats the word. While students write, Jaime observes students' levels of confidence. We discuss assessing and evaluating the students' stage of word knowledge in greater depth in "Assessment and Evaluation of Word Knowledge," later in this chapter.

Students will benefit most from a word study group that focuses on what they are just beginning to figure out or are using inconsistently. For example, Jaime notices that one of his fifth-grade students is aware of changes in words that end with the letter y in one-syllable words, but does not consistently apply that knowledge to multisyllable words, writing *tries* and *babies*, but *apologys*. Jaime thinks this student needs to be in a study group focusing on base words that change with the addition of inflected suffixes. In contrast, another fifth-grade student writes *nation*, *tention*, and *creation*. Jaime places this student in a group that focuses on the derivational suffixes *-ion*, *-tion*, and *-sion*, knowledge that typically develops later than inflected suffixes. Word study is most effective with a manageable number of groups. Jaime has four levels of word knowledge represented among students in his multiage classroom:

- Vowel patterns within syllables,
- The addition of inflected suffixes to base words,
- Use of various prefixes and suffixes that derive new meanings for base words, and
- Words that are related by their roots but have spelling or pronunciation changes.

For most single-grade classrooms, the range of student knowledge may not be as great, making three groups a workable number.

When it is time, Jaime asks all students to move to the section of the room where other members of their particular group will conduct their word study. Since members of a particular word study group have the same words, sitting together enables students to share their thinking with other word study partners. As Jaime circulates among the groups, he interacts with both individuals and groups of students, discussing what they have noticed about the patterns they are studying.

Developing Word Lists.   To develop lists of appropriate words for study, we must know a sufficient amount about phonics and the morphological patterns of the words that our students are encountering in their reading and writing. We can gather words from students' reading materials, their writings, and from various levels of available spelling books; then group the words into categories of related patterns. Jaime finds that building his own word study lists has made him notice word patterns and compare and contrast the difficulty level of words. (See Appendix C for sample lists.)

We must carefully select words that are appropriate to the level of development of our students. For example, when students first study base + inflected suffix words, the list should contain only words in which the base does not change (*jumping, monkeys, spoiled*). After students understand this pattern, they will be ready to consider base words that change (*baking, running, pennies*).

Instructional Activities.   As Jaime begins a week of word study, he needs to see what students already know. As preassessment, he asks students to do an open sort (see Figure 11.3). The students decide how to group the words, typically by sound, visual, or meaning patterns. In Figure 11.3, the student sorted by the visual pattern in the inflected suffix (*-er, -est, -ing, -ed*). When Jaime wants to determine students' understanding of a particular pattern or patterns, he chooses the categories and has them complete a closed sort (Figure 11.4).

A two-level sort is easiest for students, with one set of cards that fits a particular pattern and a *discard pile* for all cards that do not fit. Without a discard pile, students may feel forced to place words in a category even if they are not certain about the pattern of the word. The number of levels or groupings in a sort is determined by the number of patterns being observed or compared. For example, when Jaime's students compare syllable divisions in words, such as before or after the single middle consonant in a two-syllable word (*spi/der, riv/er*), he also includes a discard pile for words that fit in neither category. Having a discard pile creates a three-level sort because there will be three groupings of word cards. In Figure 11.3, the student made a four-level sort; Figure 11.4 shows a two-level sort.

When a pattern is new, students first complete a two-level sort, asking themselves whether a word fits into the focus category or the discard pile. As students learn more patterns, they begin to compare one with another, solidifying their understanding. For example, after sorting words as in Figure 11.4, students might think of other ways that inflected suffixes can change base words. This comparison could lead to such four-level sorts as:

1. Consonant doubling before adding the suffix (*run + n + ing*),
2. Dropping the *e* to add the suffix (*change + es*),
3. Changing *y* to *i* before adding the suffix (*candy + i + es*), and
4. A discard pile.

Try a word sort. This will be a closed sort, because the categories are determined for you. Read the words below, listening carefully for *silent consonants*. Make a three-level sort: (1) words that have one or more silent consonants at the beginning of a syllable, (2) words that have one or more silent consonants at the end of a syllable, and (3) words that do not have silent consonants.

ghostly	studio	wreck	solemn	fasten
castle	doubtful	listen	scribe	tombstone
knuckle	condemn	nestle	numb	stomach

What similarities do you find among the words in each of the first two piles?

• • •

Let's see how our thinking compares.

In the first column I placed *ghostly, knuckle, wreck, castle, nestle, listen,* and *fasten.* I see several letter combinations that typically are silent at the beginning of a syllable (*gh, wr, kn*). I also notice that four of the words (*cas-tle, nes-tle, lis-ten, fas-ten*) have a silent *t* at the beginning of the second syllable.

In the second column I have *doubtful, condemn, numb, solemn,* and *tombstone.* I notice that the syllables that include the silent consonant end with *bt, mn,* and *mb.* These consonant combinations are not easy to pronounce and, over the years, one of the consonants in each pair has been assimilated.

In my discard pile I have *studio, scribe,* and *stomach* because they do not contain silent consonants.

• • •

Word Study Notebooks.   Jaime provides each student with a word study notebook, a three-ring folder with inside pockets. Students record their words each week, keeping the words for the grading period together in the folder. Jaime often suggests that students refer to past lists and sorts to recollect what they have learned, to encourage them to continue to make connections among patterns, and to monitor the growth in their thinking.

Jaime's students make entries in their word study notebooks each day:

- *Monday:* Students record the list of words for the week.
- *Tuesday:* They record their open sort and explain the pattern(s) they observed.
- *Wednesday:* They record their closed sort and explain the pattern(s) they see. They make comparisons with Tuesday's open sort.
- *Thursday:* Students record words they find as they go on a word hunt or other related activity. Again they record what they find, thinking about the weekly pattern.
- *Friday:* Partners give each other their spelling test and help check for conventional spellings, discussing any ongoing confusion.

The writing in the notebook is informal, primarily for students' personal use. Jaime does not ask students to edit their responses, except for conventional spellings of words for study, either currently or in the past. Jaime does evaluate students' daily effort, their completion of each day's activity, the thinking shown in the open sort, level of accuracy of the closed sort, and the spelling test.

Jaime asks students to use their word study notebooks daily. His students treat the recording they do as a valued exercise, and use their notebooks during word study group meetings to support their discussions. Figures 11.5 and 11.6 show sample notebook entries.

If Jaime engaged his students in whole-class word building he would also ask students to record the results of building words in their notebooks. Recording words provides opportunities for writing to reinforce the order of letters or chunks within words and to create a permanent record for review and comparison of words.

CONTENT FOR WORD STUDY: MULTISYLLABLE PATTERNS

Students who are reading at mid-third through sixth-grade level are likely to be in the multisyllable patterns stage of word knowledge. The term *multisyllable patterns stage* describes the focus of this stage of development (Gunning, 2001). Students in this stage are ready to apply what they know about phonics patterns within single-syllable words to longer, more complex words. In this stage word study includes multisyllable words made from morphemic syllables, phonetic syllables, or a combination. See Figure 11.7 for an overview of this stage.

Monday (word list)

flipped	hottest	gripping
thinking	trimmed	watching
shorter	smartest	dimming
rubbed	tallest	
thinner	runner	

Tuesday (open sort)

flipped	thinking	thinner
trimmed	dimming	shorter
rubbed	gripping	runner
	watching	

smartest

tallest   I put words with the same

hottest   ending together.

Wednesday (closed sort)

base word changed	no change to base word
flipped	thinking
trimmed	watching
rubbed	shorter
dimming	tallest
gripping	smartest
thinner	
runner	
hottest	

Base words that changed ended with
1 consonant. Other base words ended with
2 or 3 consonants.

Thursday (word hunt—
independent reading book)

base changes

slam - slammed
strap - strapped
fill - filling
grab - grabbed

base doesn't change

stack - stacking
prompt - prompted
scratch - scratched

The consonant will probably be doubled for a word that ends with a single consonant.

Friday (test)

■ **FIGURE 11.5**

Word study notebook—multisyllable pattern stage

Word Study Notebook

Monday (word list)

century	autograph
biography	centipede
centigrade	telegraph
photograph	centimeter
percentage	telephone
television	graphics
geography	telescope

Tuesday (open sort)

century	autograph
centipede	biography
centimeter	photograph
percentage	telegraph
centigrade	graphics
	geography

television
telescope
telephone
telegraph

One part is the same in each word, but doesn't always have to be in the same place in the word.

Wednesday (closed sort)

What is the root of each word?
What does the root mean?

century	cent = 100
centipede	
percentage	
centigrade	
centimeter	

autograph	graph = to write or
biography	record
photograph	
telegraph	
graphics	
geography	

television	tele = far
telescope	
telephone	
telegraph	

Thursday (word hunt)

centennial — 100th anniversary

holograph — all handwritten by the author

Friday (test)

■ **FIGURE 11.6**

Word study notebook—morphemic pattern stage

325

Word Knowledge Stage	Focus of Learning in the Stage
Multisyllable Patterns (early third–sixth)	Phonetic syllable patterns, including schwa:
Read—Multisyllable words, phonetic and morphemic solidifying silent reading becoming flexible readers	v/cv - ci/der vc/cv - mar/ket vc/v - riv/er c+le - tri/ple
	Morphemic syllable patterns:
Write—Two- and three-syllable words, morphemic and phonetic	base + base (compound words, contractions)
	base + inflected suffix, no change to base (s, es, ed, ing)
	base + inflected suffix, base changes (consonant double, e drop, y to i)
	independent prefix + base (untie)
	base + derivational suffix (no pronunciation change)
	prefix + base + suffix (no pronunciation change)

SYLLABICATION GENERALIZATIONS

1. We encourage students to talk about the generalizations they use for familiar multisyllable words. Introduce unfamiliar words that use these generalizations.
   a. Morphemic generalizations:
      - base + base (compound, contraction)
      - prefix + base or base + suffix; this pattern could also include words with more than one affix, such as *un + break + able*
   b. Phonic generalizations:
      - V/CV—single consonant between vowels; first vowel can be open syllable (long vowel) (*fa + vor, mu + sic*),
      - VC/V—closed syllable (short vowel) (*riv + er, hab + it*),
      - VC/CV—two consonants between vowels, not a blend or digraph (*dol + lar, mar + ket*), and
      - C + le—preceding consonant stays with *le*, except for *ck* (*ta + ble, pick + le*).
2. We ask students to discriminate words according to their makeup and the syllabication generalizations that would be most helpful in decoding them.
3. Schwa—In English, most syllables in a word do not receive equal stress when the word is pronounced. When we do not stress each syllable equally in a word, we can alter the sound of the vowel in an unstressed, or unaccented, syllable,

especially if the vowel in that syllable is a single vowel. The vowel in an unstressed syllable can represent the sound of short u, as in up. When a vowel in an unstressed syllable represents the sound of short *u*, we refer to this phenomenon as a schwa. Pronounce the following words and listen for the schwa:

about = a + *bout'*   *pencil* = *pen'* + *cil*

second = *sec'* + *ond*   *signal* = *sig'* + *nal*

In *about*, a- is the unstressed syllable. It sounds like short *u*. In the other words the unstressed syllable is the second one and also sounds like short *u*.

A schwa seldom occurs in base + affixed words, because each morpheme unit is stressed. Consider the following words. Is there a schwa? Is there an unstressed syllable?

foolish = *fool* + *ish*   *repaid* = *re* + *paid*

enrage = *en* + *rage*   *raincoat* = *rain* + *coat*

Notice how each morphemic, or meaning, unit is stressed. Stressed syllables are not likely to have a schwa. A schwa is most likely to occur in words that are made of sound units rather than meaning units.

To focus students' attention on such patterns, we ask students to either build or sort words to discriminate the presence or absence of a schwa:

- Has a schwa, does not have a schwa, or
- Schwa in first syllable, schwa in second syllable, or neither.

COMPOUND WORDS

1. Students use compound words in oral language, and encounter them fairly early in written language. For study, compound words should be composed of two known sight words; only the thinking strategy for compound words is then actually new.

2. Students focus first on concrete compound words, then on those with implied meanings. They should cluster words for study around topics such as people, places, things, animal life, and time (Rinsky, 1993).

CONTRACTIONS

1. *Contractions* are base + base combinations. Typically one base word is shortened to make the contraction. Begin with more predictable contractions, in which the first base word is pronounced and does not change.

   more predictable: *we are* = *we're*

   less predictable: *will not* = *won't*

2. Students study contraction families—*not* (*can't*), *are* (*we're*), *will* (*I'll*), and *is* (*he's* and *I'm*)—to see generalizations across a family.

BASE + INFLECTED SUFFIXES (BASE DOES NOT CHANGE)

1. In the previous stage students learn to write one-syllable base words. In the multisyllable pattern stage, students learn to listen for and write both the base word and the suffix.

2. Students build words, using cards to see each word part (base, suffix). This practice can be beneficial for students who have difficulty hearing the two parts of these words.

BASE + INFLECTED SUFFIXES (BASE CHANGES)

1. In the previous stage students studied inflections in which the base word remains the same (*jump* + *s*). In this stage they are introduced to the conditions under which the base will be altered as two syllables are joined. Students should study the following generalizations:
   - When adding *-es*, *-ed*, or *-ing* to a base word that ends with *e*, the *e* in the base word is usually dropped to avoid changing the sound of the vowel in the suffix.
     horse + *es* = *horses*, not *horsees*
     rake + *ed* = *raked*, not *rakeed*
     hide + *ing* = *hiding*, not *hideing*
   - When adding *-ed* or *-ing* to a base word that ends with a single consonant, the consonant is usually doubled to preserve the short vowel sound in the base.
     grab + *ed* = *grabbed*, not *grabed*
     hop + *ing* = *hopping*, not *hoping*
   - When adding *-es* or *-ed* to a one-syllable base word that ends with *y*, the *y* is typically changed to *i* to form the vowel digraph *ie* (long *i* or long *e*). Note that *ye* is not a common vowel combination within a syllable.
     cry + *es* = *cries*   *baby* + *es* = *babies*
     cry + *ed* = *cried*   *hurry* + *ed* = *hurried*

INDEPENDENT PREFIX + BASE

1. Independent prefixes are studied before dependent prefixes because independent prefixes typically are attached to base words that students know. Dependent prefixes are attached to roots that usually do not stand alone as words.
2. Students first study words in which the prefix and base are unchanged when brought together (*un* + *tie*). The base word should be meaningful to students, so they may understand the meaning of the new prefix + base word.
3. Appropriate prefixes for study early in this stage include *un*, *pre*, and *re*. Students should focus on joining and separating prefixes and bases, with discussion of meaning changes. To build or sort words, students make separate word cards that can be joined to make new words (*re* + *pay, tie, do, view*).
4. Later in this stage students return to independent prefixes + base words and explore the following prefixes: *-dis, -en, -for, -fore, -im, -in, -inter, -mis,* and *-non*. These prefixes typically create words with more challenge than *untie* or *preview* (*im* + *patient*).

BASE + DERIVATIONAL SUFFIX

In the multisyllable pattern stage, students begin to think about words in which the suffix changes the meaning of the base word. They begin with words in which the base word remains identifiable. We focus their attention on adding to base words to examine change in meaning and part of the speech. We encourage students to think of the original base word as a spelling aid.

Can you identify the types of multisyllable words that are included in this list? To be able to respond spontaneously to students' unfamiliarity with words, you must teach yourself to see the patterns in words your students might encounter. What do you know about these words?

overdrawn   *arrangement*

• • •

overdrawn = over + drawn
    compound word with an implied meaning
arrangement = arrange + ment
    derivational suffix causes change in part of speech and meaning of word

• • •

CONTENT FOR WORD STUDY: MORPHEMIC ANALYSIS

During the morphemic analysis stage (Gunning, 2001), which typically follows the multisyllable patterns stage, students break into mature reading. We must focus here on helping them develop and use strategies for encountering a multitude of unfamiliar multisyllable words. Students will have enough background knowledge of written language to draw words for study in reading and writing from the same bank of words. Emphasis at this stage is twofold:

- Efficiently using what is already known to read and write new words and
- Adding to existing knowledge of word parts, especially Greek and Latin roots.

See Figure 11.8 for an overview of this stage.

DEPENDENT PREFIX + ROOT

Determining the meaning of words with dependent prefixes requires a different thinking strategy than that used with independent prefixes. We help students realize that the word *design* is not merely *de + sign*. Determining the meaning of each part of a dependent prefix word does not necessarily help determine the meaning of the whole. Knowing that the prefix *de* carries the meaning "in reverse, away, or down," along with the word's context, will not necessarily help determine overall meaning. Consider the meaning of the dependent prefixes below in relation to the example words.

Prefix	Example
com/con—together, with	*compress, continue*
ex—out, away	*example, expensive*
pro—forward, for	*program, profound*

■ **F I G U R E 11.8**

Overview of morphemic
analysis stage

Word Knowledge Stage	Focus of Learning in the Stage
Morphemic Analysis (sixth–adult)	dependent prefix + root (*con + cern*)
	prefix + base/root + affix (*excitement*)
Read—Multisyllable words mature flexible reading read for personal and vocational purposes	pronunciation changes occurring in stressed syllable *com pose'* *com'po si tion* *met'al* *me tal'lic*
Write—Complex, multisyllable words	change in syllable division *sign, sig'nal, sig'na ture* *grave, grav'i ty*
	Greek combining forms number prefixes (*mono, bi, tri*) scientific forms (*tele-, -meter, thermo-, astro-, -graph*)
	Latin roots and related words *spect* (to look)—*spectator, inspection, spectacles*
	Assimilated prefixes *ad + tract = attract* *in + mobile = immobile*

PRONUNCIATION CHANGES

1. Adding an affix to a base word can change the spelling of the base, sometimes causing a change in pronunciation. Adding an affix can change the syllable that is accented or stressed, also causing a change in pronunciation. We help students explore the pronunciation changes in words that present decoding and spelling challenges. We compare base words to affixed words to help students generalize the effect of adding affixes.

2. Explore patterns of pronunciation change:
   - Change in the syllable that is stressed
     stressed to unstressed (*com pose'*, *com' po si tion*)
     unstressed to stressed (*met' al*, *me tal'lic*)
   - Changes in letter sound due to where syllable divides for pronunciation
     vowel (*di/vide*, *di/vis/ion*) (long to short)
     consonant (*sign*, *sig/nal*) (silent to sounded)

GREEK COMBINING FORMS

English has borrowed prefixes and roots from Greek that frequently occur in words related to number and scientific concepts. We help students notice how they use these word parts to determine the meaning of words:

- number prefixes (*uni-, bi-, tri-, quadr-, penta-, hexa-*)
- scientific forms (*bio-, tele-, therm-, aster-, auto-, micro-, phot-, hydr-, -scop, -graph, -phon*)

Students should study words in prefix-related groupings and discuss how to deduce meaning from the combination of word parts. For example, discuss related *micro* words:

microscope	microbiology	microorganism
microscopic	microbe	microphone
microwave	microfilm	

Can students tell what *micro* means by studying these words?

LATIN ROOTS AND RELATED WORDS

English also contains many borrowed Latin word parts. While Latin roots are less obviously recognized as "words," knowing them certainly helps readers have a sense of a derived word's meaning. Provide opportunity for students in this stage to explore words that share the same root. For example, the root *dic*, meaning to "speak" or "point," can be found in the following words:

dictate	dictionary	prediction
verdict	dictator	contradict

See Appendix C for sample words for study. In addition, an excellent resource for other word parts for study is *English Vocabulary Elements* by Keith Denning and William R. Leben.

We should select words for study in this stage from students' current reading, both fiction and information texts. Students will be most interested in learning words related to what they are studying. As we plan a word study program, we must remember that early adolescents will need a meaningful learning environment to be interested in learning words.

Have another try. What patterns do you notice in these words that would be helpful for middle grade students to use to build word meanings?

    prediction   *biology*

                                           • • •

prediction = pre + dic + tion

dependent prefix must be attached to the Latin root, meaning "to speak," derivational suffix changes part of speech and use of word, such as predict to prediction

biology = bio + logy

made from two Greek combining forms, *bio* = life and *log* = study, to study life

                                           • • •

RESPECTING DIVERSITY IN WORD STUDY

Learning words is a very important part of the processes of reading and writing. Confidence in one's own ability to comprehend words greatly influences daily reading and writing performance. If middle grade students are to be successful in learning words, we must consider their experiences with print, their knowledge of how to monitor their own reading and writing, and their knowledge of the language of instruction. In addition, we must provide a variety of opportunities for students to read, write, and study words.

EXPERIENCE AFFECTS KNOWLEDGE

In learning, it is often *experience* that sets students apart from one another (Allington, 1994). As we plan a word study program, we should encourage students' differences in experience to enrich the daily "talk" about words. We should expect that students will make sense of their word study experiences in different ways and will, if given the opportunity to interact, teach each other what they understand about reading and writing words.

Teaching according to developmental levels also acknowledges this difference in experience with words. Adopting one level of a spelling or word analysis program for all students in a classroom does not acknowledge or respect the diversity of experience they bring.

ENCOURAGE SELF-MONITORING

As we encourage students to use a "context +" strategy in their work with words, we expect them also to adapt the strategy to their thinking as readers and writers. A "context +" strategy means that students are able to figure out unfamiliar words by using the context of what they are reading plus visual cues from the unfamiliar word. Students may know different chunks of words, making analogies to other known words in which those chunks appear. For example, in the word *perspective*, a student familiar with sports may recognize the root, *spect*, by making an analogy to a word like *spectator*. We must support the diverse ways in which students learn by encouraging them to think aloud about the knowledge and strategies they use as they work. We can model thinking aloud through minilessons that we teach about using the "context +" strategy.

We also encourage students to self-monitor through editing for meaning and correctness in all writing. Writing is for communication; therefore, we cultivate in our students the desire to be understood through the self-monitoring of what they write. Just as readers must monitor for the meaning they are constructing from a text, writers must also monitor for the meaning they are creating/communicating through a text. Writers read and reread their text, checking for both meaning and correctness. Designating revision/editing partners or groups during writer's workshops provides additional support for writers who are working to improve their skills with the English language.

CONSIDER THE LANGUAGE OF INSTRUCTION

For students whose first language is not English, the language of instruction can be a mystery. Who else will they hear talk about variant vowels, prefixes, or Latin roots? As teachers, we have a specialized language we use in school. How well do our students know that special language? It is our responsibility to teach the meaning of the language of instruction to all students, so all will have an equal opportunity to benefit from word study instruction. Here again, thinking aloud during instruction can provide additional information to students about how to understand and use the language of instruction.

PROVIDE A VARIETY OF OPPORTUNITIES

In this text, sorting and building words to study their patterns is a major instructional approach for word study. However, while completed words or word sorts may look similar, the thought processes students use will vary. We can encourage this variety by providing opportunity for students to share their thinking with others during word study, and by accepting students' different styles of recording in their word study notebooks. We should try to be open in our thinking about how students learn words.

Some students will learn words easily by reading many books or by writing for long periods of time. Some students will learn by saying words and spelling them aloud. Still others will find that repeatedly seeing word cards helps them to remember. Some students will have to think they are "playing" to learn words, such as with word games. Some students will be motivated to learn most when working on a computer. The instructional strategies suggested in this chapter are only a start, a foundation for a word study program. We will need to add to these ideas, especially as students teach us what works best for them.

ASSESSMENT AND EVALUATION OF WORD KNOWLEDGE

Studying growth in students' developmental knowledge of words provides a frame of reference for assessment and evaluation. What we intend to evaluate will guide the data we collect for assessment. Daily reading and writing, along with focused spelling samples, will be our most accurate way to determine:

- What students know and use independently,
- What they are beginning to notice but often confuse, and
- What they have not yet noticed about patterns in written language.

ADDING TO OUR TEACHER ASSESSMENT PORTFOLIO

Knowledge of words is an important aspect of reading and writing development. It is important to maintain records of students' level of development and growth in word knowledge across a school year, and from year to year. We will want to have information about students' knowledge of words both in context and in isolation.

OBSERVING DEVELOPMENT OF WORD KNOWLEDGE

Careful observation of reading and writing behavior, along with samples of reading and writing, enables us to ask important questions about students' growth in word knowledge. The questions that we might ask about students' growth in word knowledge will change across stages of development.

For students who are *not* yet functioning in the *multisyllable patterns stage*, we want to ask the following questions:

- Are students showing an increase in sight vocabulary that can support fluent reading?
- Do students' reading and writing reflect a growing knowledge of single- and double-vowel patterns? What behaviors suggest that students understand that some letters in English will be silent and may serve as markers for a vowel in the same syllable?
- How consistently are students able to use context plus phonics knowledge to read unfamiliar words?
- How consistently are students able to read base words within morphological patterns in which the base does not change?

In the *multisyllable patterns stage*, we want to ask the following questions:

- Does each student have a large enough sight vocabulary to read fluently in appropriate text?
- Are students able to use morphological patterns in decoding words in which the base has been changed by the joining of syllables? What behaviors have we observed?
- Are students beginning to integrate phonics and morphological patterns to decode unfamiliar multisyllable words?
- Are students becoming more consistent in conventionally representing familiar syllables in two- and three-syllable words?

In the *morphemic analysis stage*, we want to ask the following questions:

- What behaviors suggest that students are ready to break into mature reading?
- What behaviors suggest that students are developing power with words and have developed independent learning strategies?
- What behaviors suggest that students relate meaning, spelling, and pronunciation when reading and writing unfamiliar words?

We gather data to address these questions by observing students' behavior during reading and writing activities, conferring with students about their reading and writing, and collecting samples of reading and writing over time.

SAMPLES OF WORD KNOWLEDGE IN CONTEXT

To evaluate a student's knowledge of words in the context of text, we may make a running record (Clay, 1979/1985) of each student's oral reading (see assessment section of Chapter 6 for examples). As a student reads orally, we use a variety of symbols to show the various strategies the student uses in a variety of familiar and unfamiliar texts. The running record shows patterns of reading behavior, particularly the strategies on which a student relies most often to make meaning. The running record also shows which texts are independent, instructional, and frustration level for a student.

Another assessment of student's knowledge of words is through examination of daily writing samples. It is important to note the relationship between words that students are able to read accurately in the context of connected text and the words that students are able to write accurately in connected text. Taking a baseline sample of students' writing at the beginning, middle, and end of the school year is an excellent way to chart growth for an individual and for a class of students (see Chapter 8 for a discussion of writing traits). When students in a class write about the same topic under the same conditions (time, aids available, draft versus process writing), it is possible to note the range of development among them in both vocabulary and spelling.

SAMPLES OF WORD KNOWLEDGE IN ISOLATION

To complement what running records may show about students' growth in reading words, we ask individual students to write a carefully selected sample of words that represent various stages of word knowledge development. When students write the same words several times over the course of a school year, we may easily compare samples and see clearly any growth in word knowledge.

In a student's focused writing sample, we evaluate each word for the stage of word knowledge it represents. It is important also to determine what the overall sample shows about a student's knowledge of words. As we discuss the stages of development, remember that all concepts within a stage may not develop evenly or in an exact sequence. Our students will not necessarily progress through a stage at the same rate or in the same sequence.

IDENTIFYING STAGES OF WORD KNOWLEDGE

To identify and monitor students' growth in word knowledge, we collect and analyze writing samples at the beginning of the school year and two or three other times during the year. We ask students to write a sample of words that represents a variety of phonic and morphemic patterns. When we assess, we begin with word patterns that are fairly independent, progress through patterns that are likely to be at the student's instructional level, then include a few patterns at the frustration level to see what knowledge is emerging.

Sample Words for a Focused Assessment.   From the words listed below, we select an appropriate number to begin our assessment. We do not have to administer all words on the same day. We may complete our assessment over several days. After we have an initial idea of where a student is functioning, it is best to have the student write a focused list or 10 to 15 words that provide multiple examples of specific types of patterns, such as the groupings below. As we gain confidence with patterns, we are able to develop groups of words for assessment that provide relevant information in relation to the curriculum.

Syllable Patterns Stage
> Short vowels, some with blends and digraphs
>> *map, wet, wish, spot, cut*
>> *flag, went, sing, clock, just*
> Long vowels, with blends, digraphs, and silent letters
>> *wave, sleep, hide, joke, flute*
>> *stay, dream, night, hold, huge*
> Variant vowels and consonants
>> *charge, fear, third, store, nurse*
>> *chalk, brought, shook, wrong, voice*

Multisyllable Patterns Stage

<u>Phonics patterns (V/CV, VC/V)</u>

> *among, believe, spider, future*
>
> *animal, desert, visit, product, study*

<u>Phonics patterns (VC/CV, C+le)</u>

> *angry, jelly, middle, bottle, double*
>
> *farmer, surprise, wonder, hundred, mystery*

<u>Phonics patterns (VV/C, VVC/)</u>

> *author, measure, either, noisy, courage*

<u>Morphemic patterns (base + base, base + inflected suffix)</u>

> *anyone, breakfast, wouldn't*
>
> add *s, es, ed, ing* to short and long vowel words in previous stage (*charged, dreaming*), *balancing* (*e* drop)

<u>Morphemic patterns (base + derivational suffix)</u>

> *pollution, dangerous, direction, government*
>
> *happiness* (change *y* to *i*)

<u>Morphemic patterns (independent prefix + base)</u>

> *repair, unusual, impossible*

Morphemic Analysis Stage

<u>Dependent prefix + root</u>

> *exhaust, convince, compress, devour*

<u>Prefix + base/root + affix</u>

> *excitement, desirable, procedure*
>
> *ingredient, unskilled, irresistible*

<u>Pronunciation changes occurring in stressed syllable</u>

> *composition, metallic, preparation*
>
> *legality, repetition, confident*

<u>Change in syllable division</u>

> *signature, musician, mortality*
>
> *gravity, criminal, division*

<u>Greek combining forms/Latin roots</u>

> *unilateral, bicentennial, photographer*
>
> *aquarium, pedestrian, spectator*

Figure 11.9 shows a sample of spelling differences across students in fourth, sixth, and eighth grades. The sample is selected from both multisyllable patterns and morphemic analysis stages, providing a glimpse of student knowledge of both phonics and morphemic units. Such a broad sample can be given at the beginning, middle, and end of a school year to provide an overall assessment of student growth. More frequent assessments should be drawn from a narrower range of words to make appropriate decisions for short-range instructional goals.

As students gain experience with patterns of written language, we can expect to see changes in the way they represent phonic and morphemic units in words. In Figure 11.9, what do you notice about each student's word knowledge?

• • •

■ FIGURE 11.9

Focused spelling
assessment

Word	Fourth Grade	Sixth Grade	Eighth Grade
went	went	went	went
dream	dream	dream	dream
hold	hold	hold	hold
chalk	chak	chalk	chalk
voice	voys	voice	voice
future	fuchur	future	future
double	dubble	double	double
mystery	mistry	mystery	mystery
courage	curage	curage	courage
balancing	balancing	balanceing	balancing
exhaust		exaust	exaust
ingredient		ingredent	ingrediunt
composition			compusition
musician			musision
photographer			photographer

In the first section the fourth-grade student spells words conventionally in which all sounds can be heard. The *lk* in *chalk* and *ce* in *voice* present some challenge. The two-syllable words in the second section are not yet conventional, but do have most phonemes represented. This student would benefit from studying variant phonic patterns (*chalk, voice*), then focus on applying knowledge of one-syllable patterns to multisyllable words.

The sixth-grade student is somewhat successful with two-syllable words, showing the greatest confusion with variant phonetic elements (*future, courage*) and the impact of adding a suffix to a word that ends with a vowel (*balancing, e* drop). I would place this student in a multisyllable patterns group that will review syllable patterns and changes to base + inflected suffix words, especially with words that have varying phonentic patterns.

I would place the eighth-grade student in a morphemic patterns group. Spellings are conventional up to *ingredient*. In the last grouping it is apparent that this student is thinking more about a word's sound rather than using information from its morphemic (meaning) elements, as with *compusition* and **musision.** This student would benefit from study that relates meaning and sound to spelling patterns.

It is also important to examine the decoding skills of these students as an additional clue to knowledge of patterns in English spellings. Recognition of words in isolation, without the help of context, might reveal a student's level of confidence with particular phonic and morphemic patterns within multisyllable words.

• • •

We design focused word knowledge assessments by having students write several words representing knowledge from one particular stage or a portion of a stage. For example, to assess multisyllable pattern knowledge, we can select multisyllable words that review the various syllabication patterns, such as the following:

- base + base—*overdrawn, shouldn't;*
- base + affixes—*rabies, reviewing, incomplete;* and
- VCV/VCCV/C + *le—climate, level, splendid, knuckle.*

These few words focus on patterns that are typically mastered later in the multisyllable patterns stage. If students are assessed several times during a period of study (4 to 6 weeks), we would be able to compare the samples and evaluate their growth in word knowledge. Students who have moved into the morphemic analysis stage should be able to write these words conventionally.

Focused assessments are most useful when administered individually. As we watch each word being written, we are able to decide what the writing is showing and how much farther we might go with the student in gathering useful information. For example, our assessment of the fourth-grade student in Figure 11.9 could have stopped after the word *double.* At that point, we knew enough about elements that were confusing to this student.

In a focused assessment of word knowledge, we do not need to go more than one stage above where the student is working. This fourth-grade student already had two unconventional spellings in the first group of words (syllable patterns stage). The multisyllable patterns list shows the student's confusions about patterns that occur later in the multisyllable patterns stage.

In the work samples we keep to document students' growth, such samples of word knowledge will be a primary source of information about what phonics and morphemic knowledge our students know how to write independently, as well as what emerging knowledge we can make the focus of reading and writing instruction.

KEEPING RECORDS OF WORD KNOWLEDGE DEVELOPMENT

For evidence of word knowledge, we should record our observations of students' reading (see discussion of running records in Chapter 6) or a piece of focused or unfocused writing. We can create record-keeping forms, such as those shown in Figures 11.10 and 11.11, that reflect the knowledge and strategies that should develop at each stage. Such forms, combined with anecdotal notes, will provide a more complete picture of student development.

■ TAKE A MOMENT TO REFLECT . . .

■ *Word study is an integral part of a balanced literacy program. Such a program:*

- Promotes appreciation of words;
- Stimulates interest and curiosity in learning words;
- Enhances knowledge of patterns in English; and
- Provides explicit instruction and practice

The basic components of word knowledge development are sight words, context clues, phonics patterns, and morphemic patterns.

■ **FIGURE 11.10**

Sample record keeping
for multisyllable
patterns stage

Word Knowledge Development—Multisyllable Patterns Stage			
Morphemic Patterns:	**Usually**	**Sometimes**	**Rarely**
1. base + inflectional suffix			
reading			
no change to base	___	___	___
base changes	___	___	___
writing			
no change to base	___	___	___
base changes	___	___	___
2. independent prefix + base			
reading	___	___	___
writing	___	___	___
3. base + derivational suffix			
reading	___	___	___
writing	___	___	___
Syllabication Generalizations:			
1. recognizes word as primarily structural or phonetic	___	___	___
2. applies base + base, base + affix			
reading	___	___	___
writing	___	___	___
3. applies V/CV, VC/V, VC/CV, C+le			
reading	___	___	___
writing	___	___	___
4. integrates structural and phonics knowledge as needed	___	___	___
5. is aware of the possibility of a schwa, tries to apply to words	___	___	___
Self-Monitoring Strategies:			
1. uses context + beginning syllable, checked by sense and other syllables	___	___	___
2. oral reading is fluent in low-challenge materials	___	___	___
3. silent reading is rapid in low-challenge materials	___	___	___
4. decoding is becoming fairly automatic	___	___	___

■ *Sight words are:*

- Recognized automatically;
- Stored in memory by linking distinctive spelling features to the phonological (speech sound) structure of words in memory necessary for fluent reading; and
- Gained through extensive and intensive reading.

■ FIGURE 11.11

Sample record keeping
for morphemic analysis
stage

Word Knowledge Development—Morphemic Analysis Stage

Structural & Phonics Patterns:	Usually	Sometimes	Rarely
1. is refining syllabication knowledge from multisyllable patterns stage			
reading	___	___	___
writing	___	___	___
2. integrates morphemic patterns and phonics automatically to decode new words	___	___	___
3. explores relationship between pronunciation, spelling, and meaning	___	___	___
4. when unsure of pronunciation and/or spelling, refers to related words for help	___	___	___
5. recognizes/uses knowledge of dependent prefixes + root	___	___	___
Vocabulary:			
1. uses knowledge of roots to determine word meaning	___	___	___
2. continues to add to sight vocabulary	___	___	___
3. continues to add to meaning vocabulary	___	___	___
Self-Monitoring Strategies:			
1. uses "context +" strategy efficiently and effectively	___	___	___
2. moving toward mature reading	___	___	___

■ *Context is a function of constructing meaning with the meaning and structure of language:*

- Deriving meaning from surrounding text should be the main checking system for decoding.
- Thinking strategy already known in spoken language.

■ *Phonics patterns:*

- Understanding phonics patterns requires an understanding of the importance of directionality in print.
- Students' reading, writing, and questions show independent and emerging knowledge.

■ *Morphemic patterns:*

- Made from morphemes or units of meaning.
- Meaning of base words/roots can be changed by adding or changing affixes.
- Base words can function without affixes; roots usually need an affix.

- Affixes include:
  -prefixes, independent and dependent
  -suffixes, inflected and derivational.
- Structural patterns are made from combinations of base words/roots and affixes:
  -base + base
  -affix + base
  -base + affix
  -affix + base + affix.

■ *Word knowledge is developed through extensive and intensive reading:*

- Our selection of words for study is guided by the following questions:
  1. Is understanding the word important to understanding the selection in which it appears?
  2. Are students able to use context or structural analysis skills to discover the word's meaning?
  3. Can working with the word be useful in furthering students' context, morphemic analysis, or dictionary skills?
  4. How useful is this word outside of the reading selection being currently taught?
- Four strategies have great value for word learning:
  1. Use the context in which words are found to infer their meaning, including knowledge of possible multiple meanings of words.
  2. Use word parts, or morphemic units, to infer meaning, as well as make analogies with known words/word parts.
  3. Use relationships between words, such as synonyms and antonyms, to infer meaning.
  4. Use the dictionary to learn or verify the meaning or, possibly, multiple meanings of a word.

■ *Word knowledge is developed through extensive and intensive writing. Three principles guide the writing of words:*

- The alphabetic principle tells us that letters represent sounds.
- The orthographic principle is based on spelling patterns in a particular language.
- The morphemic, or meaning, principle tells us that words that have related meanings should have related spelling patterns.

■ *Word study is:*

- Daily instruction in word knowledge that serves as both word identification and spelling development;
- Focused on students' developmental stages in word knowledge;
- A planned program of weekly study of words by patterns; and
- Integrated into daily reading and writing instruction.

■ *Weekly word study programs provide:*

- Guided whole-class word building experiences; and
- Small-group developmental word sorting experiences.

■ *Word building includes:*

- Building words letter by letter to reinforce a variety of phonic and morphemic patterns; and
- Building words chunk by chunk to explore relationships among morphemic units.

■ *Word sorting includes:*

- Lists of 10 to 15 words in patterns;
- Developmentally appropriate words from stages of word knowledge;
- Sorting to focus children's attention on distinctive features; and
- Writing to retain thinking.

■ *Word sorts can be:*

- Open or closed;
- Pictures or words; or
- Multilevel.

■ *Word study in the multisyllable stage emphasizes:*

- Changes to words with the joining of syllables:
  - Inflectional suffixes, adding and dropping consonants to preserve vowel sounds; and
  - More independent prefixes.
- Syllabication
  - Noticing differences in multisyllable words;
  - Integrating the use of phonics and structural patterns;
  - Generalizations:
    base + base
    base + affix
    V/CV, VC/V, or VC/CV
    C + le
- Schwa—single vowels in unaccented syllables.
- Self-monitoring, using context + first syllable, checked by context and remaining syllables.
- Silent reading.

■ *Word study in the morphological patterns stage emphasizes:*

- Differences among words with independent and dependent prefixes;
- Addition of affixes can cause pronunciation changes in multisyllable words, but does not always cause spelling changes:
  - change in which syllable is stressed; and
  - change in where a word divides into syllables;
- Introduces the Greek and Latin influence on the English language.

■ *Students are diverse in their:*

- Experiences as readers and writers;
- Knowledge of the language of instruction; and
- Ability to monitor their writing.

■ *Word knowledge development can be monitored through:*

- Observation of students during discussions of words in daily activities;
- Samples of daily writing;
- Focused samples of selected words in isolation; and
- Miscues during running records.

■ REFERENCES

Allington, R. L. (1994). The schools we have. The schools we need. *The Reading Teacher, 48*(1), 14–29.

Anderson, R. C., Wilson, P. T., & Fielding, L. G. (1988). Growth in reading and how children spend their time outside of school. *Reading Research Quarterly, 23*, 285–303.

Anglin, J. M. (1993). *Vocabulary development: A morphological analysis.* Monographs for the Society of Research in Child Development, Serial No. 238, Vol. 58, No. 10.

Blachowicz, C. L., & Fisher, P. (2000). Vocabulary instruction. In M. L Kamil, P. B. Mosenthal, P. D. Pearson, & R. Barr (Eds.), *Handbook of reading research* (Vol. 3, pp. 503–523). Mahwah, NJ: Lawrence Erlbaum Associates.

Carlisle, J. (1995). Morphological awareness and early reading achievement. In L. Feldman (Ed.), *Morphological aspects of language processing* (pp. 189–209). Hillsdale, NJ: Lawrence Erlbaum Associates.

Carlisle, J., & Nomanghoy, D. (1993). Phonological and morphological awareness in first graders. *Applied Psycholinguistics, 14*, 177–195.

Carr, E. M. (1985). The vocabulary overview guide: A metacognitive strategy to improve vocabulary comprehension and retention. *Journal of Reading, 28*, 684–689.

Clay, M. (1979/1985). *The early detection of reading difficulties.* Portsmouth, NH: Heinemann.

Cronbach, L. J. (1943). Measuring knowledge of precise word meaning. *Journal of Educational Research, 36*, 528–534.

Cunningham, P. M., & Cunningham, J. W. (1992). Making words: Enhancing the invented spelling-decoding connection. *The Reading Teacher, 46*, 106–115.

Cunningham, P. M., & Hall, D. P. (1994). *Making words: Multilevel, hands-on, developmentally appropriate spelling and phonics activities.* Torrence, CA: Good Apple.

Denning, K., & Leben, W. R. (1995). *English vocabulary elements.* New York: Oxford University Press.

Ehri, L. C. (1987). Learning to read and spell words. *Journal of Reading Behavior, 19*, 5–31.

Ehri, L. (1991). The development of the ability to read words. In R. Barr, M. L. Kamil, P. B. Mosenthal, & P. D. Pearson (Eds.), *Handbook of reading research* (Vol. 2, pp. 354–376). New York: Longman.

Fisher, P. J. L., Blachowicz, C. L. & Smith, J. C. (1991). Vocabulary learning in literature discussion groups. In J. Zutell & S. McCormick (Eds.), Learner factors/teacher factors: Issues in literacy research and instruction: Fourtieth Yearbook of the National Reading Conference (pp. 201–209). Chicago: National Reading Conference.

Gentry, J. R. (1997). My kid can't spell: Understanding and assisting your child's literacy development. Portsmouth, NH: Heineman.

Gipe, J. P. (1979–1980). Investigating techniques for teaching word meanings. *Reading Research Quarterly, 14*, 624–645.

Graves, M. F. (2000). A vocabulary program to complement and bolster a middle-grade comprehension program. In B. M. Taylor, M. F. Graves, & P. Van Den Broek (Eds.), *Reading for meaning: Fostering comprehension in the middle grades.* New York: Teachers College Press.

Graves, M. F., Juel, C., & Graves, B. B. (1998). *Teaching reading in the 21st century*. Boston: Allyn and Bacon.

Gunning, T. G. (2001). *Building words*. Boston: Allyn and Bacon.

Hatch, E., & Brown, C. (1995). *Vocabulary, semantics, and language education*. Cambridge, England: Cambridge University Press.

Henderson, E. H., & Templeton, S. (1986). A developmental perspective of formal spelling instruction by alphabet, pattern, and meaning. *Elementary School Journal, 56*, 305–316.

Holdaway, D. (1980). *Independence in reading*. Portsmouth, NH: Heinemann.

Marmolejo, A. (1990). The effects of vocabulary instruction with poor readers: A meta-analysis. (Doctoral dissertation, Teachers College, Columbia University, New York, 1990). *Dissertation Abstracts International, 51*, 03A.

McKeown, M. G. (1985). The acquisition of word meaning from context by children of high and low ability. *Reading Research Quarterly, 20*, 482–496.

Nagy, W., & Anderson, R. C. (1984). How many words are there in printed school English? *Reading Research Quarterly, 19*, 304–330.

Nagy, W. E., Herman, P. A., & Anderson, R. C. (1985). Learning words from context. *Reading Research Quarterly, 20*, 233–253.

Rinsky, L. A. (1993). *Teaching word recognition skills* (5th ed.). Scottsdale, AZ: Gorsuch Scarisbrick.

Temple, C., Nathan, R., Temple, F., & Burris, N. (1993). *The beginnings of writing* (2nd ed.). Boston: Allyn and Bacon.

Tunmer, W. E., Herriman, M., & Nesdale, A. (1988). Metalinguistic abilities and beginning reading. *Reading Research Quarterly, 23*, 134–158.

Tyler, A., & Nagy, W. (1989). The acquisition of English derivational morphology. *Journal of Verbal Learning and Verbal Behavior, 14*, 638–647.

Vygotsky, L. S. (1962). *Thought and language* (E. Hanfmann & G. Vakar, Eds. & Trans.). Cambridge, MA: The MIT Press.

White, T. G., Slater, W. H., & Graves, M. F. (1989). Growth of reading vocabulary in diverse elementary schools: Decoding and word meaning. *Journal of Educational Psychology, 82*(2), 281–290.

Winsor, P., Nagy, W. E., Osborn, J., & O'Flahavan, J. (1993). *Structural analysis: Toward an evaluation of instruction*. Center for the Study of Reading, Technical Report No. 581. (ERIC Document Reproduction Service No. ED 360 625)

■ CHILDREN'S LITERATURE

Paulsen, G. (1999). *Hatchet*. New York: Viking Penguin.

chapter *12*

Teaching with an Integrated Language Arts Basal Series

In this chapter . . .

We explore the organization and use of a basal reading series integrating reading and language arts, including:

- A brief history of basal reading series,

- The components of a basal series,

- How a basal series is organized,

- Overview of a basal theme or unit,

- Overview of a basal lesson, and

- Planning a basal theme or unit using a combination of whole-class, small groups, and reader's workshop methods.

Before We Begin . . .

- The basal series that is described in this chapter is *Literature Works* (DeLain et al., 1996). Theme 5, Survival, is the focus of our discussion in this chapter.

- The literature selection entitled "Kinship" in the basal lesson is actually Chapter 3 of *Woodsong* by Gary Paulsen (1990).

- For comparison, locate copies of other basal reading materials being used in the school districts with which you are familiar.

Looking into Classrooms . . .

Let's imagine that we have accepted positions as sixth-grade teachers in a school district that has adopted a basal reading series for the language arts program. In our new classroom we find copies of student books, teacher's editions, and other support materials for a reading series published by Silver Burdett & Ginn (DeLain et al., 1996). As we leaf through the books, we reflect on our own reading experiences in elementary school and remember sitting at a table with other students while the teacher guided us through selections in a reading book. Those books were probably from a basal reading series!

Building a Theory Base . . .

WHAT IS A BASAL LANGUAGE ARTS SERIES?

A *basal language arts series* is a sequential set of instructional materials organized around a hierarchy of language arts skills (Goodman, Shannon, Freeman, & Murphy, 1988). The stories in current basal readers are often excerpts from quality children's literature, such as a picture book or a chapter taken from a novel. Traditionally, series editors revised these selections, substituting decodable words for some of the original language in order to teach specific vocabulary and skills (McCarthey & Hoffman, 1995). While teachers have historically used some type of published materials to teach students to read, sets of basal materials have been part of the American educational scene only since the early 1900s (Goodman et al., 1988).

A BRIEF HISTORY

Early in our nation's history, teachers taught reading with a Hornbook, a 3- by 5-inch handheld paddle holding one page of text. Students would recite the alphabet, phonetic syllables, and the Lord's Prayer from their Hornbook each day. The only book typically available for reading by adults or children was the Bible. Books for children, as we know them today, did not exist.

By the 1840s educators became concerned with carefully controlling the rate at which new words were introduced to young readers. *McGuffey Eclectic Readers* provide an example of early attempts to control vocabulary, a characteristic of most basal readers (Bohning, 1986). A page in a beginning *McGuffey Reader* might have included words, letter patterns, and controlled text:

Tab	Ann	hat	catch	see
	e	ch	s	

See Tab! See Ann!
See! Tab has the hat.
Can Ann catch Tab?

Students pronounced words and sounds, then applied them to a simple text. The text itself bore great similarity to the basal readers used in the 1950s and 1960s, with characters such as Sally, Dick, and Jane. Texts for the middle grades were didactic, intending to teach values, citizenship, and patriotism through realistic stories and biographies of important people that were written by the textbook authors.

Around the beginning of the 20th century, with dramatic increases in the school-age population, grammar schools were organized into a graded system by age for more efficient instruction. During this period industrialization had a great influence on our thinking, and schools became concerned with efficiency and standardization of the "product" of schools, the students. Teachers did not always have a high level of training and there was concern that all students would not receive similar instruction (Shannon, 1989). Such concerns led to the creation of sets of graded reading materials known as basal reading series (Betts, 1946). Each book in a series included directions to the teacher for engaging students with new vocabulary and questions to assess students' comprehension of each selection.

Basal readers have dominated reading instruction in the United States since their inception (McCallum, 1988). As early as 1935, basal readers were seen as the foundation for classroom reading programs and the source of "expert" knowledge for instruction. Arthur Gates (1935), a well-known reading educator, suggested that basal readers freed the teacher to give more attention to the proper selection of other reading materials and the proper guidance of students in their total reading program.

From the 1940s to the 1960s, classroom instruction was dominated by basal reading series, such as the *Dick and Jane New Basic Readers,* that conveyed stereotypic images of family life (Reutzel & Cooter, 1992). With rapidly expanding global competition in the 1960s and 1970s, basal readers began to reflect a growing national concern for students' ability to demonstrate their knowledge of basic skills. During this same period, the struggle for equality by various groups in the United States led to challenges of the stereotyped portrayal of characters in basal texts (Aukerman, 1981). More recently, as a result of the whole-language movement, the content of basal readers is once again changing to include high-quality literature, less isolated skills instruction, more integration of reading with other language arts and content, and greater flexibility in decision making for teachers (McCarthey & Hoffman, 1995).

Basal series, however, continue to dominate reading instruction in the United States. Textbook adoption policies and funds for purchasing instructional materials contribute greatly to the extensive use of basal readers (Goodman et al., 1988). Textbook adoption committees at state and local levels set acceptable standards for textbooks to be used in public schools. Publishers submit materials for review by the committee, and materials that are selected can be purchased with public school funds for use in schools (Farr, Tulley, & Powell, 1987).

The demands placed on publishing companies by such heavily populated states as Texas, California, and Florida, which use state adoption processes and spend large amounts of money on basal adoptions, dramatically influence the content and organization of basal materials. For example, the state of Texas proclaimed that only texts including authentic, unedited, and unabridged children's literature would be considered for reading/language arts adoptions (Texas Education Agency, 1990). Imagine how publishers respond to such a demand by a state that buys millions of dollars of their product.

School districts often adopt a basal series as the main source of instructional materials for teaching the district curriculum. Funds are provided to purchase such materials. While school districts may allow teachers to use authentic literature rather than an adopted reading series, textbook funds for purchasing the literature may be limited. In such cases, literature-based teachers do not have equal access to funds for instructional materials.

A CALL FOR CHANGE

For the past two decades basal series have been the target of criticism by groups that advocate holistic philosophies (Goodman et al., 1988; McCarthey & Hoffman, 1995; Reutzel, 1991; Shannon, 1989, 1990). The main areas of concern have been using only excerpts of literature, teaching of isolated skills, and the perceived control of teaching behaviors.

Authors of basal series select the literature that students read, provide direction to teachers, and furnish prepared practice materials for students to use. In the past the literature selected has not been authentic, but instead was often written by the editors of the series to control the level of readability and to avoid controversial issues. The readability controls led to selections in which the language was stilted, uninteresting, and difficult to understand.

Basal series have been criticized for teaching skills in isolation from meaningful contexts. In the past, workbooks that accompanied basal series provided practice that required students to "fill in" someone else's ideas. The number of different skills introduced or practiced in one lesson forced "reading" time to become "skill-and-drill" time. In addition, the placement of skills instruction within the basal series seemed arbitrary and unrelated to the selections being read.

Authors of basal readers provided preplanned lessons for teachers to use in reading instruction. Theoretically, teachers should have been free to prepare other learning experiences for children, but often the basal reading program became the only source of students' reading materials.

Teacher's editions for basal readers originally consisted of a few pages in the back of a student's book, the highlighting of new words in a selection, and a few suggestions for teaching a selection. During the 1970s, teacher's editions became scripts for the teacher to read during instruction. Scripting was seen as an attempt to provide teachers with information about new instructional strategies and to make their actions during reading instruction more standardized across the country.

The organization and language of basal teacher's editions led teachers to believe that educators who developed the series had "expert" knowledge about reading. Consequently, teachers allowed the teacher's edition to strongly influence decisions that should have been made at the classroom level. Apple (1982) refers to this as *deskilling*, when teachers do not trust their own knowledge and, instead, defer to an outside "expert." In this approach it is believed that over time, teachers become deskilled in basal approaches and techniques, becoming technicians who turn pages and follow directions.

What do these concerns suggest for literacy instruction today? Publishers of current series have been responding to past criticisms (McCarthey & Hoffman, 1995):

- Current basal series are incorporating higher quality literature selections.
- Formats and organizations of new texts are more diverse.
- Series are incorporating a greater variety of genres.
- The adaptations of authentic children's literature texts are minimal, preserving the richness of language.
- The selections contain more complex plots and more well-developed characters, and require readers to make interpretations.
- Many series now attempt to present skill and strategy instruction in meaningful contexts.
- Vocabulary evidence indicates that readability controls have been significantly reduced, if not abandoned.
- Series editors encourage teachers to be decision makers and to select activities appropriate for their children.
- Editors now include process writing, thematic units, and numerous extension activities that reflect current trends in integrated literacy instruction.

The change in basal series from 1986 to the present is dramatic, showing the influence of the movements in literature-based reading, whole language, and integrated thematic instruction.

Putting Theory into Practice . . .

The authors of a basal language arts series can offer suggestions for planning learning experiences for students, but should not make the decisions for us. We should make the decisions that we believe are best for our students. The teacher's edition for a basal series offers prepared lessons and activities, but the series' authors clearly expect that we will select what is best for our students.

If we view a basal language arts series as multiple copies of literature selections and a series of skill and strategy lesson plans with support materials, then we will use our knowledge of literacy to make effective decisions. Before we teach with basal materials, we must decide what types of experiences our students need, just as we would if we were teaching with authentic literature. Keeping our goals and standards in mind, we can select the portions of the basal materials that will help us meet those goals and standards.

Overview of an Integrated Language Arts Basal Series

Let's return to that new sixth-grade classroom. Imagine that we are looking over all of the materials that come with the reading series. We see that there are six spiral-bound teacher's editions, six units of study for one school year. Turning to the front pages of one of the volumes, we find references to the components of the program, such as those found in *Literature Works* (DeLain et al., 1996) listed below:

Literature Resources
Student Anthology
Theme Magazine
Theme Trade Books

Practice and Support Materials
Practice Book & Language Arts Handbook
Spelling Source: An Integrated Approach to Spelling
English Language Support Program

Teacher Resources
Teacher's Guide
Source Bank
Home Connections
Teaching Transparencies

Technology Resources
CD-ROM and Videodiscs
Story Tapes
Videotapes

Assessment Components
Guide to Student Portfolio and Classroom Assessment
Reading Process Assessment

Reading and Language Arts Skills Assessment
Writing Assessment Guide
Placement Inventory
Informal Reading Inventory
Phonics Inventory

From the list above, it is apparent that this basal series is quite comprehensive. What do you find in the basal series that you are able to examine? Publishers typically provide anthologies of literature selections for students, consumable materials to practice skills and strategies, supplemental materials to extend beyond the literature selections, an assessment program for monitoring students' progress, and a comprehensive teacher's manual that includes illustrations of student and supplemental materials. The impact of technology can be seen in the inclusion of CD-ROMs, laser discs, and other supporting media. While the program is comprehensive, many materials must be purchased separately.

We should be aware, however, that some school districts may not provide textbook funds for the purchase of all the materials that are considered to be a supplemental part of the program. We may only be provided with a class set of Student Anthologies (the basic literature selections), a set of Teacher's Editions, and selected workbook materials from the Practice and Support category.

While surveying basal materials, we become keenly aware that over the years instructional materials have grown into well-developed management systems for integrated classroom language arts programs. A number of basal series, including *Literature Works*, also integrate some content area materials for a more comprehensive program. For example, one of the six themed units in the sixth-grade program focuses on ancient Egypt, which is typically a topic of study in social studies during that year.

HOW PROGRAM COMPONENTS ARE ORGANIZED

Most current basal language arts series are organized around units of instruction that contain literature selections, skill and strategy instruction, extension activities, and assessment materials. In *Literature Works*, for example, the sixth-grade collection is divided into six units:

- Perspectives,
- Uncovering the Past: Ancient Egypt,
- Finding Common Ground,
- Strange Encounters,
- Survival, and
- Journeys of Change.

The publishers suggest that a teacher spend approximately 5 to 6 weeks on each theme unit.

FIRST STEPS IN PLANNING

Before we consider the contents of a basal unit and the decisions to be made, let's think about our general planning processes. If we are planning to teach a themed unit of our own, we would probably do the following:

- Determine what students need to learn by consulting district/national standards and knowledge of our students.

- Gather available resources.
- Select activities to help our students reach selected curriculum standards.
- Consider the level of instruction and support needed by students to reach the selected standards.
- Consider how to assess student learning.

All of these aspects of unit or theme planning are included in the themes developed by the authors of the basal series. Our task, then, is to decide how well their suggestions meet our goals, as well as the needs and interests of our students. As we make decisions about a basal language arts program, we find that:

- Some suggested activities are appropriate and should be kept just as they are,
- Some activities meet our goals but must be modified to meet students' needs, and
- Some are inappropriate for our goals and/or students' needs and interests and either should be discarded or revisited at a more appropriate time.

Remember: Our decision making is the key to effective use of any commercially produced teaching materials.

HOW A BASAL THEME UNIT IS ORGANIZED

We now turn our attention to one of the themes in the sixth-grade basal program of *Literature Works*, "Survival," and see how it is organized. Understanding the organization of a unit or theme in a basal series can be a key element to understanding the organization of the entire grade level.

Theme or Unit Planner.   To facilitate unit planning, the teacher's edition usually provides a chart that highlights important unit resources and activities found in the lesson plans for each selection. The Theme Planner in the *Literature Works* series contains an overview of the four selections contained in the Student Anthology. There are also suggestions for resources and activities to extend instruction and student engagement beyond the four selections. If we are to spend 5 to 6 weeks in this unit we will certainly need more reading material than the four selections provided in the student anthology. We will also need a variety of reading levels to meet the needs of the range of readers in our classroom.

Many basals now use authentic literature. For example, the following selections are included in the "Survival" unit:

- "Kinship," from *Woodsong* by Gary Paulsen (1990, Simon & Schuster)
- "Leader of the Pack," from *Champions: Stories of Ten Remarkable Athletes* by Bill Littlefield (1993, Little Brown and Company)
- "The Grandfather Tree," from *Morning Girl* by Michael Dorris (1990, Econo-Clad Publishers)
- "Four Against the Sea," from *A Boat to Nowhere* by Maurene Crane Wartski (1989, Signet)

The resources identified for extending student learning may or may not be included in the materials purchased by the school district. Copies of some of the extention materials may appear in the teacher's edition. Many of the materials shown are considered supplemental and are typically purchased separately.

Management Options.   Teacher's editions typically offer options for managing or organizing instruction. As a central focus, we may choose to use the selections in a student anthology or the suggested theme trade books. Suggestions are given for extending instruction through theme projects, the writing process, trade books, and anthology ideas. The variety of materials can be very useful in meeting the needs and interests of our students. We also may choose to combine parts of the different management options.

Ongoing Assessment.   We begin planning a theme by deciding what students should learn and what behaviors will indicate such learning. The Ongoing Assessment pages provide information about the learning goals that the basal's authors suggest and have planned for learning experiences. We can see that the focus of our chosen theme is on constructing meaning, learning about language, and appreciating language and literature. Each focus appears with appropriate learning goals and performance indicators.

We must decide which learning goals and performance indicators are appropriate for our students and at what particular time. Basal series authors carefully plan and sequence their goals throughout the series. The activities suggested typically build on previously introduced skills and strategies and generally allow sufficient learning time.

As part of our ongoing assessment, series authors encourage us to have students keep a portfolio that demonstrates their growth as readers and writers. They have developed a "Guide to Student Portfolios and Classroom Assessment." Our knowledge of portfolio assessment from other chapters in this text should help us make decisions about using materials in the basal series.

Theme Launch.   The next section in the teacher's edition is entitled "Theme Launch," and contains suggestions for capturing students' attention, suggested literature to read aloud, ideas for a theme bulletin board, and an introductory selection available on videodisc. As in all unit teaching, we need to "hook" our students right from the start. We may choose to begin with the teacher's edition suggestions and then add ideas of our own.

Literature Selections.   The "Survival" theme is presented through four literature selections, each with a fully developed lesson plan. Each plan begins with a "Selection Planner" that gives an overview of the integrated lesson plan. In this chapter, we focus on the plan for the literature selection titled "Kinship," which is actually Chapter 3 of *Woodsong*, by Gary Paulsen (1990). Our emphasis here is on considering how best to use the suggestions provided in the teacher's edition.

Other Theme Components.   The final pages of the theme plan contain other suggestions for this theme study as a whole, including the following:

- Theme Wrap-Up,
- More Books and Technology,
- Theme Magazine,
- Trade Book Support,
- Writing Process,
- Theme Project,
- Assessing Growth, and
- Home Connections.

Theme Wrap-Up.   Bringing closure to learning is an important issue in effective instruction. For the "Theme Wrap-Up," the series authors suggest ways to help students reflect on the selections and make connections to the overall theme. Rather than wait until the end of a theme, we should continually help students make connections among theme learning experiences.

More Books and Technology. The series authors have researched books related to the theme, and they suggest books on a variety of levels to better meet students' needs and interests. We may create a display of these books in the classroom, along with other related texts, for use throughout the unit. We can encourage students to make selections for independent reading at home and school. The authors also identify supplemental technology that supports the unit theme.

Theme Magazine. If we have access to the "Theme Magazine," supplemental selections in magazine format, the series authors provide suggestions for integrating these selections with other theme materials. One or more articles or activities in the Theme Magazine support or extend each major selection in the student anthology, *Collection*. The formats of the articles vary and are accessible to most students.

Trade Book Support. In the *Literature Works* series, the authors suggest two pieces of authentic literature for study in each theme. Since the selections in the student anthology are excerpts from literature, it is important that our students also engage in extended reading. Chapter books, in particular, build a stamina for reading that excerpts cannot. The trade books suggested for the "Survival" theme are *Drylongso* (Hamilton, 1992) and *The Crystal Drop* (Hughes, 1993). For each trade book, the series authors have developed plans for engaging students. We are free to include other trade books for study or substitute other texts. In earlier chapters we studied *Hatchet*, another survival story by Gary Paulsen (1999). We could choose to include a study of *Hatchet* in this survival theme. As we did in Chapter 4, I would be inclined to use this piece as a whole-class literature study to accompany other survival selections, including the sequel to *Hatchet, Brian's Winter* (Paulsen, 1996).

Writing Process. In each theme, the authors suggest at least one extended piece of writing that is taken through the writing process to publication. In this "Survival" theme, students are provided an opportunity and instruction in writing with "Exposition: Comparison and Contrast," including suggestions for helping students with each phase of the writing process. If we have a writer's workshop each day, we could use these suggestions in minilessons, shared writing, small-group instruction, and conferences.

Theme Project. Units of study typically engage students in demonstrating what they learn by letting them choose to complete open-ended projects. One project students might enjoy that appears in this unit is making a "Survival Handbook." Quality projects require time and preparation to develop, and to succeed they must be part of our initial planning.

Assessing Growth. To follow up the beginning section, "Ongoing Assessment," the series authors make suggestions for informal assessment, such as conferences and student self-assessment, as well as more formal assessment of specific skills and strategies developed in the unit. Once again, the basal series' "Portfolio Checklist" reminds us of options for assessing students' learning.

Home Connections. Finally, the series authors make suggestions for strengthening the connections among student, family, and school. Encouraging students to read at home should always be a mainstay of our literacy program. If we want students to read at home, we must make available a varied collection of appropriate texts at their instructional reading level to support and stimulate their interests. We must also work with parents/guardians to provide an environment in the home that will encourage reading.

Keeping parents/guardians informed about theme studies can also promote home connections. The series authors suggest that we consider (1) using a theme newsletter to involve families in theme-related activities and (2) encouraging family assessment of the work in a student's portfolio. These suggestions can be catalysts for other successful ways to build connections between home and school.

The basal series authors have tried to put together suggested lessons and materials that we can weave into a theme or unit. The ideas presented can be a springboard into an integrated unit of study with more emphasis in content area learning, or we may treat the material as an integrated reading/language arts unit. The direction a unit will take is our decision.

YOUR TURN...

What is your impression thus far of current basal reading/language arts programs? How do you feel about what a program of this type offers you as a teacher? Can you see yourself as a decision maker, selecting materials that meet your instructional goals and are appropriate for your students?

• • •

PLANNING TO TEACH A BASAL SELECTION

The basal lesson plan for "Kinship" will be the focus of this review and discussion. Regardless of the basal series in use, there is typically a lesson plan format that is consistent from selection to selection. We must know and understand the components and format of a lesson plan before we can make informed decisions about the use of suggested activities for a particular selection.

FORMAT OF BASAL LESSON PLANS

Each selection in *Literature Works* begins with a "Selection Planner" that provides an overview of the reading, writing, speaking, listening, and viewing lessons developed for each selection, as well as possible cross-curricular connections. The series authors intend for us to spend as much as 1 week on a single selection and related theme activities.

In this basal series, the teaching of a selection such as "Kinship" is typically broken into three parts:

- Part 1: Reading and Responding,
- Part 2: Literature-Based Instruction, and
- Part 3: Integrated Curriculum.

Part 1, "Reading and Responding" focuses on activities that typically occur before and during the reading of a selection. The teacher's edition suggests such prereading activities as building background knowledge, activating prior knowledge by making a concept web, developing vocabulary that will appear in the selection, and applying phonics and morphemic knowledge to the new vocabulary. The remaining activities in this section typically occur during the guided reading of a selection—preview and predict, setting purposes, checking predictions, and so on.

Activities in Part 1 of the lesson plan are similar to the steps in a directed reading activity (DRA) (Betts, 1946), which has dominated the format of basal reading instruction for decades. Similar to an MR–TA (see Chapters 4 and 5), a DRA emphasizes preparing students for a selection by preteaching concepts and vocabulary, guided silent reading and discussion, rereading for a closer look at key concepts, and instruction in reading skills that are often isolated from the context of the story. We also can see the influence of literature-based and holistic approaches with the inclusion of fix-up strategies, attention to literary elements and the author's craft, and written response to literature.

Part 2 of the lesson plan, "Literature-Based Instruction," focuses on activities that typically occur after the first reading. The activities in this section are enhanced by knowledge of the selection, which is often used as an illustration of the skill or strategy being developed or reinforced.

Part 3 of the lesson plan, "Integrated Curriculum," is a new addition to most basal lessons. Only recently have publishing companies attempted to integrate the language arts, and other curricular areas as appropriate. Spelling and grammar, typically taught through other commercially developed programs, are now a part of one lesson plan. We must decide whether the words identified, for spelling especially, are appropriate for our students' level of word knowledge development.

As we discuss the planning of the first selection in the "Survival" theme, "Kinship," by Gary Paulsen (1990), we will consider how each part of the lesson plan is developed. We should compare suggestions made by the series authors with our own ideas about effective reading/language arts instruction.

Part 1: Reading and Responding

Building Background. The publishers provide a summary of the selection and activities for building background for the reading of the selection. We know there is a strong relationship between students' background knowledge and their ability to make meaning with text. We can see why the series authors suggest that we help students activate their prior knowledge before reading the selection. The selection that students are about to read focuses on the ingenuity of dogs. Making a concept web about dogs, as suggested, is one option for helping students recollect their prior knowledge. The authors also suggest reading a selection in the Theme Magazine, titled "How Cold Can You Go?," which provides background on arctic environments, the setting in "Kinship."

What type of background knowledge do you think will help students prepare for the content of the selection?

• • •

While the weather certainly may be cold, Paulsen focuses on his understanding of his sled dogs. Students would benefit most by considering what they already know about the types of dogs that will appear in the story, rather than merely students' general knowledge about dogs.

• • •

Developing Vocabulary.   Basal series traditionally suggest preteaching any vocabulary in the selection that we may not yet have introduced to students. Middle grade students, especially those who read widely, are likely to have encountered a variety of the selected words in other texts. The issue we must consider is whether or not the author presents each "new word" in a context that allows students to apply their word knowledge to understand the author's intended meaning. If so, we should let students first try to use what they know. To preteach the words, a transparency is provided with sentences that contain the selected vocabulary; however, the sentences are not drawn from the context of the story. Let's examine the identified words:

- *Steeped* (steep), *mystified* (mystery), *awakening* (awake), *dwelling* (dwell), and *exaltation* (exalt) are morphological patterns that students are likely to have encountered in other forms, which combined with the context should help them figure out the gist of each word.
- *Whirlpool* is a compound word that is quite literal, and students are likely to know the component parts.
- *Alleviate* and *chagrin* may be new. Consider the context in which *alleviate* and *chagrin* appear in "Kinship":

To *alleviate* the boredom we give the dogs large bones to chew and play with. (p. 22)

There was some self-pity creeping in, and not a little *chagrin* at being stupid enough to just let them run when I did not know the country. (p. 28)

Would you preteach the suggested words, practicing the words before students read "Kinship"? Would you use the transparency with its sentences that are not drawn from the text?

• • •

Using the context of the selection, I think students can get a sense of word meaning. I want to see which word knowledge strategies they use effectively. After reading the text, I can check their understanding of word meanings in context. If I have been teaching vocabulary development using base words and affixes plus context to determine word meanings, I should give students opportunities to apply that knowledge.

• • •

Spelling Preview and Support.   In this basal series, one list of spelling words is identified for each selection. The words for this particular selection are a mixture of *-ion*, *-tion*, and *-sion* words, with spelling clues from the base word (*infect, infection; tense, tension*). These words are typically studied during the transitional stage, reading levels third through sixth grades. If our students are all reading at about sixth-grade level, this list will be appropriate. If not, we will want to create additional lists that provide words that are developmentally appropriate for students' spelling levels, as discussed in Chapter 11.

Reading Options.   The suggested reading option is "Supported Reading," providing support to students as needed during the reading. To begin the reading, we are urged to have students preview the text and predict what they will learn from the selection and complete the "W" section of their K-W-L chart (Ogle, 1986). (This suggests that the brainstorming about dogs, in the earlier section, was intended to be entered on the "K" section of the K-W-L chart, although this is not specified in the teacher's edition.)

Strategic Reading. As the reading begins, other suggestions for teacher–student interaction about the text appear in the margins of the teacher's edition pages. Comprehension, Author's Craft, Visualizing, Vocabulary, Appreciating Multilingualism and Cultural Diversity, and Fix-up Strategies are suggested for calling students' attention to particular aspects of this text. Suggestions include:

- W in the K-W-L (*What* we want to learn),
- Author's Craft—Genre,
- Comprehension—Author's Purpose,
- Reading Strategy,
- Visualize,
- Think Aloud,
- Comprehension—Compare/Contrast,
- Reading Strategy—Check Predictions,
- Author's Craft,
- Characterization,
- Theme,
- Appreciating Multiculturalism—Share Knowledge, and
- Appreciating Cultural Diversity—Appreciation and Acceptance.

What decision might you make to support students during the reading of the selection?

• • •

Since the reading of this nonfiction piece is suggested as *supported* reading, I could use an MR–TA for mediating between the students and the text. I would preview the text with students, encourage them to predict what they might learn, complete the "W" section of the K-W-L, and clarify the point of view of this autobiography (first person). I would plan stopping points in the MR–TA to incorporate most of the suggestions made in the teacher's edition. After the reading we could discuss characterization, theme, multilingualism, and diversity issues. I probably would not include the suggestions made for compound words, except for the meaning of *whirlpool*, because the suggested words seem inappropriate for this level of text.

• • •

Informal Assessment. The performance indicators provided assist us as we consider how students respond to the reading. Questions to check comprehension are also suggested. The K-W-L (Ogle, 1986) chart can be completed at this point.

Meeting Individual Differences.   Suggestions appear on each page below the story for ways to challenge students and to provide additional comprehension or language support. We know that the range of students in our classrooms will require us to adapt instruction to meet students' needs. The series authors offer ideas for such adaptations that we may incorporate after the initial reading of the text, when students' background knowledge can be used to make stronger connections.

Responding.   Students should have the opportunity after the reading to respond to the selection. The series authors suggest a variety of response opportunities:

- Personal response in a journal,
- Reader response groups, sharing journal entries,
- Creative response through writing, role playing, and designing a board game, and
- Critical response through problem solving.

Response suggestions also appear in the student text. In addition, suggestions make connections to the unit theme, survival, and to other pieces of literature.

What choices might you make for encouraging students' responses to the selection?

• • •

As we discovered with book clubs, making a personal written response helps prepare students for sharing their responses with others. I would certainly encourage journal responses to the selection. Other types of response depend on our students and their interaction with the selection. Supported reading was suggested for the reading of "Kinship," so I assume that students have already had some opportunity for discussion with their peers. In this situation, then, I might consider creative or critical responses.

• • •

PART 2: LITERATURE-BASED INSTRUCTION

This section of the basal lesson plan contains teaching ideas for skills and strategies that, for the most part, support the reading of the selection. For each selection we are provided lessons for specific aspects of literature, comprehension, word study, and study skills.

Literature: Story Structure–Theme.   This literature lesson focuses on learning to identify the theme of the selection, "Kinship." It then applies that knowledge to a selection read previously. Being able to identify the theme of a selection makes it possible for students to learn life lessons for themselves. For other selections, this section of the lesson might focus on other literary elements such as characters or point of view or setting.

Comprehension: Compare/Contrast.   In "Kinship," Paulsen describes the impact of his relationship with his dogs on his attitude and behavior. This lesson asks students to compare and contrast Paulsen's attitude and behavior before and after he observes his dog,

Columbia, trick another dog, Olaf. A Venn diagram is suggested, and a practice worksheet for comparison to another piece of literature is provided.

Word Study: Vocabulary—Compound Words. Word study can be most effective when words are related by common meaning units. This lesson suggests the study of compound words that share a common base word, *wind*. The compound word, *whirlpool*, was identified in the vocabulary list at the beginning of this selection. By this stage of word knowledge development, because students are well aware of how compound words are formed, studying related compounds can be effective for word study.

Study Skills: Forms/Applications. One reason for learning to read and write is to perform basic literate tasks such as completing forms and applications. Paulsen must complete applications when he wants to enter an Iditarod race. This lesson provides practice with forms that are either familiar to the students or that appear in the Practice Book.

Which of the four previous lessons might you include when you teach the selection "Kinship"? Explain your reasoning.

• • •

Before addressing the theme of "Kinship," I would lead students back into the selection to compare and contrast Paulsen's attitude about dogs before and after observing Columbia and Olaf. The Venn diagram is an excellent informal writing technique (see Chapter 9) to use to recollect story events for comparison. After we had a good sense of Paulsen's attitude, we would be ready to consider theme. Studying compound words can be a valuable way to expand vocabulary, but they are not an important part of this selection. While reading "Kinship," I would prefer to focus on descriptive words, which are an important part of this selection and will be needed in the expository writing for this unit. Attention to completing forms and applications would be more appropriate in a life skills unit. How did our thinking compare?

• • •

PART 3: INTEGRATED CURRICULUM

In this section, the series authors have provided lessons that make connections among the language arts and other curricular areas. While these lessons are labeled "Part 3" and appear at the end of the selection lesson plan, they are not necessarily intended to come at the end. If the suggested lesson is appropriate, we must decide where to include it in our study of the selection.

Writing Workshop: Using Sensory Words. Gary Paulsen uses many words that appeal to the senses and help to build strong images for the reader. This lesson begins with a minilesson that focuses students' attention on the use of sensory words in the selection, and that enables students to practice with familiar subjects, then apply their knowledge to writing a descriptive paragraph about a familiar subject.

Grammar Workshop: Adverbs.   This workshop begins with a minilesson about adverbs and what they are, followed by practice in identifying, describing, and using adverbs of time, place, and manner. Like the use of sensory words, knowledge of adverbs can help writers communicate more vividly, especially in comparison writing.

Viewing Workshop: Using Visual Aids to Explain.   This lesson provides an opportunity to help students explore representing their ideas in graphic form. Students are urged to consider how a visual presentation helps to make information easier to understand.

Spelling Workshop: Endings -ion, -tion, -sion.   Targeted words having these endings were introduced at the beginning of the selection. During the week students are able to practice this pattern through Daily Language Activities (editing sample sentences) and pages from the Practice Book.

Cross-Curricular Connections.   To connect with the content of the "Kinship" selection, two lessons are suggested: exploring the tundra and calculating the average speed that Iditarod dog teams travel. These suggestions would probably be interesting to students. Questions we must ask are "How much time must be committed to explore these issues adequately?" and "Do I want to devote such time at this point in the theme study?"

Which suggested lessons would you decide to use from Part 3? Would any of these suggested lessons be better accomplished through other activities already occurring in your classroom?

• • •

The Writing Process section, near the end of the theme, suggested that students should be engaged in writing an expository piece involving comparing and contrasting. In my classroom I would have a daily writer's workshop, in which I would incorporate the types of writing suggested by the series authors when they are appropriate. I would use the suggested lessons for Writing Workshop and Grammar Workshops in my minilessons for our daily writer's workshop, because these lessons help students with word choices that improve their ability to make written comparisons and contrasts. The Viewing Workshop would be saved until a point in a theme study when students are beginning to prepare visual aids for class sharing. In my classroom, I would have daily word study to support spelling development. The suggested words for the Spelling Workshop would be added to existing lists for the students in the transitional stage, the stage in which these words are appropriate for spelling instruction. I would pull together the Cross-Curricular Connections for each selection as theme choices that capture student interest and enhance our theme study, especially suggestions that require extended time.

• • •

Now that we have considered most parts of the theme plan for the unit "Survival," we must extend our planning beyond the separate selections to the theme as a whole. How will we tie lessons, materials, and activities together to achieve our goals?

TEACHING THE BASAL THEME UNIT

We might try a flexible unit plan that will cover the suggested 5 to 6 weeks and incorporate whole-class literature study, literature circles or book clubs, and the individual reading of reader's workshop. To do so, we will need a wide array of literature related to the theme.

DEVELOPING A FLEXIBLE UNIT PLAN

A flexible unit can include the following:

- Whole-class literature study to introduce the unit and provide teacher-led instruction that focuses students' attention on accomplishing the unit goals and objectives, along with our district's curriculum standards;
- Literature circles or book clubs to enable students to further explore the concepts introduced in the whole-class study and deepen their understanding, with moderate teacher guidance; and
- Reader's workshop to culminate the unit, allowing students to focus on aspects of the unit theme of particular interest to them and to apply what has been developed in the previous whole and small groups.

We might also choose to begin with a whole-class study, then spend the remaining time in reader's workshop, especially if we do not have sets of multiple copies of appropriate literature.

Figure 12.1 presents examples of how we can divide the flexible time period among the three types of study groupings. Time frames should be adjusted according to the length of the text chosen for whole-class study and the number of different texts to be read by the small groups. The figure shows 4-, 6-, and 9-week periods to illustrate flexibility.

■ *A basal reading series will provide a range of literature and suggested sequences of language arts skills. Using these materials, how might you provide for the diverse interests and reading levels of the students in your classroom?*

■ **FIGURE 12.1**

Flexible literature units

Types of Grouping	4-Week Unit	6-Week Unit	9-Week Unit
Whole-class study	1 week	1–2 weeks	2–3 weeks
Literature circle or book club	2 weeks	2–4 weeks	3–4 weeks
Reader's workshop or independent reading	1 week	1–2 weeks	2–3 weeks

SAMPLE SIX-WEEK BASAL UNIT PLAN—"SURVIVAL"

Imagine, again, that we are teaching sixth grade and are planning to teach the "Survival" unit provided in the reading/language arts basal series. Our class is already familiar with whole-class literature study. Students also have participated in literature circles and book clubs earlier in the school year. While we have not used reader's workshop as a consistent part of the reading program, students do have a predictable time for independent reading each day. The pieces are all in place for us to teach the basal theme through a flexible unit format.

To begin planning this flexible unit, let's think about the basal unit we have been discussing in this chapter. What literature is available in the unit for a whole-class study, for literature circles or book clubs, and for reader's workshop? Would we need to collect other literature for this unit? What other types of literature will we need?

We could begin our search for materials by going back to the beginning of the unit and reviewing each page, searching for suggested literature. Here are the possibilities:

- *Whole class: The Crystal Drop* (Hughes, 1993), a chapter book, and *Drylongso* (Hamilton, 1992), a picture book. The series authors share ideas for teaching with these books.
- *Literature circles/book clubs:* The four selections included in *Collection* are available in multiple copies with developed lesson plans and support activities—"Kinship," "Leader of the Pack," "The Grandfather Tree," and "Four Against the Sea."
- *Reader's workshop:* Seventeen books are listed for More Books and Technology and articles in the Theme Magazine.
- *Additional:* Suggested read-alouds are *Abel's Island* and *The Big Wave*.

Using many of the materials provided by the basal program, we might organize the 6-week unit as shown in Figure 12.2. Note how the materials provided by the basal program fulfill our needs for whole-class and small-group literature study. We will need additional books for reader's workshop beyond those suggested in the More Books and Technology section of the unit plan.

WHOLE-CLASS LITERATURE STUDY

To get the unit started with a clear focus on survival, we engage students in a whole-class literature study (see Chapter 4) using a class set of *The Crystal Drop* (Hughes,

■ **FIGURE 12.2**

Survival unit—six weeks

Whole-Class Literature Study (2 weeks)	Read	Reading/Writing Strategies
	The Crystal Drop (class set in basal program)	• Introduce theme and solving problems • Small-group discussion skills • Point of view • Descriptive language
Literature circles/book clubs, read three of four selections from basal (3 weeks)	"Kinship" "Leader of the Pack" "The Grandfather Tree" "Four Against the Sea"	• Reinforce theme and problem solving • Theme/main ideas • Draw conclusions, make inferences • Using descriptive language (sensory, setting, and so on)
Reader's workshop or independent reading (1 week)	Wide selection of books, magazines, newspapers, guides related to topic	• Apply strategies independently • Focus on sustained reading/writing • Conference once with each student

1993). The series authors have developed a lesson plan for literature study that links this text to the theme, as well as to other curriculum areas. The lesson plan includes a chart that provides chapter summaries, key vocabulary, strategic reading suggestions, and response options.

Response options are divided between personal response, reader response groups, and critical/creative responses. These divisions provide ideas for possible journal/log entries and small-group discussions as a follow-up to the whole-class reading. We can develop discussion guides from the response options to support small-group discussions, just as we did for *Hatchet* (Chapter 4) and for *A Taste of Blackberries* (Appendix A).

LITERATURE CIRCLES/BOOK CLUBS

After completing the whole-class study, several weeks of small-group study provide opportunity for more focused interaction with students. In this survival unit, 3 weeks out of 6 will be allotted for small-group work. Literature circles allow students to select the literature they prefer to read, or we may form book clubs, with everyone reading the same selections. (See Chapter 5 for more small-group possibilities.) The lesson plans developed by the series authors are full of ideas that we may use for small-group discussions, learning logs, and extension activities. Refer to the "Kinship" selection as an example.

READER'S WORKSHOP/INDEPENDENT READING

The culmination of the "Survival" unit is a week of reader's workshop or independent reading in books related to the theme, providing opportunity for students to select their own "survival" reading. During the other 5 weeks of the unit, students should have time for daily independent reading, but that reading need not be connected to a unit of study.

The More Books and Technology section of the theme plan includes suggestions for 17 additional books on a variety of levels. We will, however, need more than 17 books for reader's workshop. We might choose from the following additional titles:

Between a Rock and a Hard Place by Alden Carter (1999, Scholastic)

Brian's Winter by Gary Paulsen (1998, Laureleaf)

The Camp Survival Handbook by Katie Hall and Lisa Eisenberg (1995, HarperCollins)

The Cay by Theodore Taylor (1995, Avon)

Danger in the Desert by Terri Fields (1997, Rising Moon)

Floodland by Marcus Sedgewick (2001, Delacorte Press)

Frantic: Lightning Strike and Other Tales of Survival by Larry Straus (1996, Lowell House)

Island of the Blue Dolphins by Scott O'Dell (1990, Houghton Mifflin)

Kid's Survival Handbook by Claire Llewellyn (2002, Tangerine Press)

Nim's Island by Wendy Orr (2001, Knopf)

The River by Gary Paulsen (1993, Yearling Books)

The Shark Callers by Eric Campbell (1993, Harcourt)

Survival: Island by Gordon Korman (2001, Apple)

Survival on Cougar Mountain by Jerry Cunnyngham (1996, Soho Press)

Tested Man by John Christopher Fine (1994, Windswept House)

Thunder Cave by Roland Smith (1999, Econo-Clad Books)

Timothy of the Cay by Theodore Taylor (1995, Camelot)

Toughboy and Sister by Kirkpatrick Hill (2000, Aladdin Paperbacks)

Trial by Wilderness by David Mathieson (1990, Houghton Mifflin)

The Voyage of the Frog by Gary Paulsen (1990, Yearling)

When the Road Ends by Jean Thesman (1995, Camelot)

Wish Me Luck by James Henegan (1998, Laureleaf)

The week of independent reading can include the following:

- Whole-class meetings and minilessons to support continued development of independent reading strategies,
- Students self-selecting books and reading silently for a sustained period, and
- Opportunity for students to have personal conferences with you about their reading.

WRITER'S WORKSHOP

Students should continue to participate in writer's workshop throughout the 6-week unit. The series authors have provided suggestions for one extended piece of writing as well as for informal pieces that build background for that writing experience. These suggestions, along with grammar and spelling lessons and activities, are most useful to students if we integrate them into the writer's workshop. We also may include minilessons for grammar, mechanics, and word choice. Revising and editing groups can help students apply their knowledge from the minilessons.

WORD STUDY

If we want students to grow as both readers and writers, we must continue daily word study throughout the unit. Remember, we have a dual focus in word study of both reading and writing. For reading, we consider the vocabulary and word study activities that are already developed by the series authors. In addition, we may add words from the basal selections or other literature of interest to students.

With the range of readers and writers that are likely to be in our classrooms, we should continue to use a multilevel approach to spelling by developing our own lists for study each week. The list suggested by the basal authors may be appropriate for one or more of our word study groups. If so, we should certainly consider the suggested activities.

RESPECTING DIVERSITY IN BASAL INSTRUCTION

Like most facets of our society, basal series are showing greater sensitivity to the diverse needs and interests of middle grade learners. For example, the following activities to meet individual needs are suggesteed throughout the "Kinship" lesson plan:

- ESL language support for building fluency,
- Varied reading options depending on the type of text,
- Appreciating multilingualism,
- Challenging students,
- Providing additional support, and
- Appreciating cultural diversity.

The main characters in the literature selections across the unit represent a range of differences in gender, ethnicity, cultural groups, and time periods. Basal materials provide an opportunity to address issues of diversity and urge teachers to be the decision makers.

ASSESSMENT AND EVALUATION IN BASAL PROGRAMS

In previous chapters we have explored observation, conferences, and collecting samples of students' work as key sources of information we need to monitor their progress in reading and writing. In a basal language arts series, we add a fourth dimension, the series' own assessment materials.

In *Literature Works*, assessment is ongoing and includes both informal and formal assessment, as well as portfolio assessment. Informal assessment includes conferences and student self-assessment, both of which are familiar to us. Formal assessments, typically paper-and-pencil assessments, are available for reading, language arts, spelling, and writing. We are encouraged to maintain student portfolios.

When a school district adopts a basal series, teachers are often required to use all or part of the assessment program. Before teaching with a basal series, we would want to be aware of what skills/strategies will be assessed and be sure to include them in our plans for learning activities.

■ *TAKE A MOMENT TO REFLECT . . .*

■ *A basal language arts series is:*

- A set of sequential instructional materials; and
- Organized around a hierarchy of reading and language arts skills and strategies.

Since their inception, basal readers have dominated reading instruction in the United States.

■ *The content and organization of basal reading series are being influenced by the movement in literature-based reading:*

- More authentic literature is being included.
- Fewer adaptations of literature occur.
- Fewer controls on vocabulary exist.
- Suggestions to teachers are less prescriptive.
- Skill/strategy instruction is less isolated, more meaningful.
- The language arts are more integrated.

Basal series are comprehensive and include a range of materials to meet the varied needs and interests of students.

■ *Planning for basal themes or units should include:*

- Determining what students need to learn;
- Gathering resources for learning;
- Selecting activities that are appropriate for students; and
- Considering how to assess student learning.

■ *Basal themes/units frequently have most of the components of teacher-developed themes:*

- Introductory engagements;
- Extension activities;
- Varied reading and writing activities; and
- Open-ended activities.

The writing process, including attention to grammar and spelling, is encouraged as part of the basal lesson.

The teacher's edition does not make decisions! Teachers must make decisions about which activities best meet instructional goals, as well as student needs and interests.

■ *A basal lesson plan includes several components:*

- Reading and responding;
- Development of skills and strategies in literature, comprehension, work study, and study skills; and
- Cross-curricular connections.

■ *A basal theme or unit can include a variety of instructional formats:*

- Whole-class literature study (large group);
- Literature circles/book clubs (small group); and
- Readers' workshop (individual).

Basal programs show sensitivity to diversity through suggested activities for meeting individual needs.

■ *To assess and evaluate student progress, basal programs include suggestions for:*

- Informal assessment;
- Formal assessment; and
- Portfolio assessment.

■ REFERENCES

Apple, M. (1982). *Education and power.* Boston: Routledge & Kegan Paul.

Aukerman, R. (1981). *The basal reader approach to reading.* New York: Wiley.

Betts, E. A. (1946). *Foundations of reading instruction.* New York: American Book Company.

Bohning, G. (1986). *The McGuffey Eclectic Readers: 1836–1986. The Reading Teacher, 40,* 263–269.

DeLain, M. T., Englebretson, R., Florio-Ruane, S., Galda, L., Grant, C., Hiebert, E. H., Juel, C., Moll, L. C., Paratore, J., Pearson, P. D., Raphael, T. E., & Rueda, R. (1996). *Literature works: Grade 6, volume 2.* Needham, MA: Silver Burdett & Ginn.

Farr, R., Tulley, M. A., & Powell, D. (1987). The evaluation and selection of basal readers. *The Elementary School Journal, 87*(3), 276–279.

Gates, A. I. (1935). *The improvement of reading.* Upper Saddle River, NJ: Merrill/Prentice Hall.

Goodman, K. S., Shannon, P., Freeman, Y. S., & Murphy, S. (1988). *Report card on basal readers.* New York: Richard C. Owens.

McCallum, R. D. (1988). Don't throw the basals out with the bath water. *The Reading Teacher, 42,* 204–209.

McCarthey, S. J., & Hoffman, J. V. (1995). The new basals: How are they different? *The Reading Teacher, 49,* 72–75.

Ogle, D. (1986). K-W-L: A teaching model that develops active reading of expository text. *The Reading Teacher, 39,* 364–370.

Reutzel, D. R. (1991). Understanding and using basal readers effectively. In B. Hayes (Ed.), *Effective strategies for teaching reading* (pp. 254–280). Boston: Allyn and Bacon.

Reutzel, D. R., & Cooter, R. B. (1992). *Teaching children to read.* Upper Saddle River, NJ: Merrill/Prentice Hall.

Shannon, P. (1989). *Broken promises.* Granby, MA: Bergin & Garvey.

Shannon, P. (1990). *The struggle to continue.* Portsmouth, NH: Heinemann.

Texas Education Agency. (1990). Proclamation of the State Board of Education advertising for bids on textbooks: Proclamation 68. Austin, TX: Author.

■ CHILDREN'S LITERATURE

Hamilton, V. (1992). *Drylongso.* New York: Harcourt Brace.

Hughes, M. (1993). *The crystal drop.* New York: Simon & Schuster.

Paulsen, G. (1999). *Hatchet.* New York: Viking Penguin.

Paulsen, G. (1990). *Woodsong.* New York: Viking Penguin.

— (1996). *Brian's winter.* New York: Laureleaf Publishers.

chapter *13*

Integrating Learning Experiences: Linking Language Learning Opportunities

In this chapter . . .

We explore combining time and subject matter to create cohesive units of instruction that provide integrated learning experiences for middle grade students, including:

- Answering the question "What is integration?",
- Types and levels of integration,
- The role of language arts in integration, and
- Planning, organizing, and implementing an integrated unit.

Looking into Classrooms . . .

Following almost 4 weeks of study about the people and culture of ancient Egypt, the students in Jasmine's sixth-grade classroom are preparing a Living Museum to demonstrate aspects of their learning. They have invited students from other classrooms to take a field trip to their museum. In the museum Jasmine's students take on the roles of artisans and craftsman carving statues of the gods and goddesses and creating jewelry; scribes with scrolls made of papyrus, recording important events in hieroglyphs; farmers preparing to plant crops in the fertile silt left after the flooding of the Nile; Ra, the sun god, being worshipped by a priest; and, of course, pharaoh with his judges, tax collectors, and chief of treasury. The Living Museum is but one of the many integrative learning experiences that motivated these students to use reading, writing, listening, speaking, and viewing to expand their knowledge of themselves and their world.

Building a Theory Base . . .

In this chapter, we focus on linking opportunities for learning about oral and written language through integrated/interdisciplinary learning experiences. These types of learning experiences are identified in a variety of ways:

- "The term integrated curriculum is often interchangeable with integrated instruction, thematic instruction, theme immersion, project-based learning, and inquiry learning. These approaches usually organize learning in various content areas around a single theme" (Bromley, 2000).

- Content areas are blended through "overlapping skills, concepts and attitudes" (Fogarty, 1991, p. 64).

- The teacher "applies methodology and language from more than one discipline to examine a central theme, issue, problem, topic, or experience" (Jacobs, 1989, p. 8).

- "Interdisciplinary instruction is equally concerned with the learning processes, skills, and ways of knowing that are unique to the different disciplines, subjects, or domains" (Wood, 1997, p. 3).

- Regardless of the term we use, linking learning experiences for students makes learning more authentic, meaningful, and efficient (Gavelek, Raphael, Biondo, & Wang, 2000).

INTEGRATING LEARNING EXPERIENCES

As we explore the possibilities of connected learning experiences, we will focus on the necessary tools for such study, the language arts: listening, speaking, reading, writing, and viewing. Viewing has taken on new importance because of the pervasiveness of electronic media in students' lives. We must help them develop strategies for critical thinking as they navigate electronic text that is accompanied by pictures, animation, and sound (Leu, 1997; Leu & Leu, 1997). Through integration the language arts become "functional tools, rather than curricular entities to be studied or mastered in their own right" (Pearson, 1994, p. 19).

Two language principles will guide our planning for integrating learning experiences, the beliefs that:

- Learning results when demonstration and immersion are coupled with engagement (Cambourne, 1988), and
- Students learn a great deal about language as they work and talk together to accomplish goals (Wells & Chang-Wells, 1994).

INTEGRATION IS WHOLE LEARNING

Tarry Lindquist, a fifth-grade teacher and author of *Seeing the Whole Through Social Studies* (1995), states that integration is whole learning. She describes *whole learning* as "a way of balancing content and instructional strategies to nurture and nudge the whole child away from self-centeredness toward self-realization and self-actualization" (p. 5). Isn't this the place where we find our middle grade students—pulled back to childhood by self-centeredness, while desperately seeking the self-realization of adulthood? Perhaps more than any other age group, middle grade students should be engaged in whole learning that nurtures and nudges them as learners.

INTEGRATION IS THE FABRIC, NOT THE THREADS

Integration is the key to whole learning. Imagine that integration is represented by a loom:

Think of language arts skills and processes as the warp of learning, with each specific skill or understanding symbolized by a thread running vertically through the loom. Then picture another discipline, such as social studies, as the horizontal threads providing the pattern and individuality of the fabric eventually woven by the learner. (Lindquist, 1995, p. 5)

This is integration—the fabric of learning in which we see and appreciate the pattern in the fabric, rather than the individual threads. We weave our knowledge of language, communication, and thinking around and through other content.

INTEGRATION IS A PROCESS

Integration is the process of how we go about planning, developing, implementing, and evaluating learning experiences, rather than being only the product of the experience.

Integration is the process of making connections. "Integration calls upon the teacher, initially, and later the students to identify the connections or overlaps between content areas, between similar processes of applications of skills, and then build on those connections" (Lindquist, 1995, p. 7). In an integrated curriculum, units of study focus on "how concepts and ideas in one curriculum area are related to those in another area" (Morrison, 1993, p. 87).

TWO TYPES OF INTEGRATION

The most obvious type of integration is an *integrated curriculum*. Shoemaker (1991) identifies a number of ways in which teachers integrate the curriculum:

- Teachers select an organizing theme or topic, such as "Working Together" or "Ancient Egypt," and then select subject matter appropriate to the organizing topic.
- Teachers look for ways to infuse skills from one curriculum area into another, such as using critical thinking skills in social studies.
- Teachers organize the entire school year around a concept or theme, such as change or habitats.
- Teachers take advantage of natural links between subject areas, such as integrating the language arts together, using mathematical calculations to solve problems in science, or using writing to explore thinking in mathematics.

A second type of integration is *integrated learning*, which "occurs when we specifically consider and plan for the continued development of the cognitive, physical, affective, and moral dimensions of each child" (Shoemaker, 1991, p. 793). Integrated learning occurs when we use what we know about our students to consciously select learning experiences that enhance and extend their individual growth and ability to learn.

LEVELS OF INTEGRATION

Selecting a topic, usually from science or social studies, and using the language arts to support learning in that topic was my first conscious step into integrating the curriculum. From there I moved on to making links across several subject areas, committing larger and larger blocks of time to integration each day. As a teacher, I did not integrate all subjects or learning experiences in the same way.

We can provide integrated learning experiences at several levels for our students. Lindquist (1995) identifies four levels in her own development as a teacher:

- Level 1—few connections, carefully planned, rather formal;
- Level 2—blending skills and content, connecting subject areas;
- Level 3—highly integrative, natural connections, no longer focus on consciously connecting subjects because learning is not seen as subjects, but rather concepts, behaviors, ways of thinking; and
- Level 4—the whole student, not the subject or topic, is the focus of the planning.

The level of integration at which we function has a lot to do with our knowledge of (and comfort with) the curriculum at the particular grade level we teach, the depth of our understanding about human development and learning, and our knowledge of our students as individual people and learners. As we examine our school year (or any other increment of time), we can find ourselves working at various levels of integration. As elementary or middle school teachers, we know a little about a lot of topics, but those topics we know intimately enable us to function at a higher level of integration than those we merely "know about."

INTEGRATION AND THE LANGUAGE ARTS

Reading, writing, listening, speaking, and viewing are integral to all learning. In units of study, the language arts are integrated, drawing on listening, speaking, reading, writing, and viewing to explore and inquire. Without the language arts, the construction of meaning would be virtually impossible. The language arts are vehicles for exploring one's own thinking and inquiring into the thinking of others. Oral and written languages become tools for exploration and inquiry in integrated units.

Listening and speaking are the easiest links for us to make. These modes of communication enable us to receive the thinking of others and to share our own. We often do not think of using these modes as part of integration. However, the possibilities for integrated learning would be truly limited without verbal communication.

Reading is a link we make with other subject areas when firsthand experience is either not practical or possible. We read to inquire into new areas of knowledge, to expand our background knowledge, to solve problems, and the like. Abundant literature for children and young adults, both narrative and informational, now makes the reading link even stronger than in the past.

Writing is the link we use when we need to re-collect, re-create, and re-construct our thinking in subject areas. Getting our ideas outside of ourselves enables us to "see" what we know, to step back and reflect, to understand our own thinking, and to see our thinking in a new way (revision).

Viewing is an excellent way to acquire information in new forms. Developing skills in viewing require us to integrate information that is presented in a variety of media. We must understand the possibilities for organization of ideas in a particular type of media, such as video or the Internet. Integrating ideas presented in a visual form, supported by oral or written language, enhances students' ability to think critically.

THE ROLE OF LITERATURE

Literature, both narrative and informational, is a mainstay for most integrated units. Allen and Piersma (1995) suggest that the literature be used in units either as the central focus, as a supplement to content study, or infused into content area study:

- A *literature-centered model* focuses primarily on the literary value of narrative literature. While some students may explore content that is embedded (such as by exploring survival while reading *Hatchet* [Paulsen, 1999]), such content is not the main focus of the unit.

- A *literature-supplemented model* uses literature to supplement content area instruction. Literature is used to create interest and motivate students to engage in content study. The literary value of text, however, is not the focus of the unit.
- A *literature-infused model* places equal importance on narrative and information texts in the development of concepts in the unit. Information texts are integral to developing content background. Narrative texts play a vital role by helping students understand and appreciate content through interactions with characters and themes that relate to unit concepts.

In this chapter we will examine an example of a literature-infused unit, balancing our use of narrative and information texts. We have seen examples of a literature-centerd unit in Chapter 12, Survival.

Putting Theory into Practice . . .

Linking learning experiences is a process, not a product. Planning a unit of study is a complex process of selecting and organizing materials and activities that will have the greatest impact on student attitude and learning. As we explore the possibilities for integrating learning experiences in this chapter, we will follow Jasmine, a sixth-grade teacher, as she prepares for a unit of study about ancient Egypt.

PLANNING AN INTEGRATED UNIT

In her process of developing interdisciplinary theme studies, Jasmine will:

- Consider the required curriculum areas, topics, and academic standards.
- Brainstorm possibilities for units throughout a school year, including purposes for the use of the language arts in a unit.
- Identify available and appropriate resources, especially literature.
- Decide on an overarching concept and questions to guide planning.
- Match curriculum standards and resources.
- Select appropriate organizing ideas and activities that meet learning objectives.
- Decide on a time frame for the unit.
- Organize and implement unit activities.
- Assess students' progress during the unit.
- Evaluate the unit's overall effectiveness.

CONSIDER THE CURRICULUM

Topics of content area study are usually clearly identified by a school district's academic standards. Figures 13.1 and 13.2 show a sample of academic standards that Jasmine selected for focus during the unit. Even though she chooses to design instructional experiences for her students through integrated units, Jasmine must still support students' learning in all required areas.

■ **FIGURE 13.1**

Possible sixth-grade standards for "Ancient Egypt" unit

Social Studies – Geography
1. Describe how a natural hazard affects human activity and the earth's physical systems.
2. Identify how the characteristics of a region are related to its primary economic activity.

Social Studies – History
1. Evaluate sources of historical information based on bias, credibility, cultural context, reliability, or time period.
2. Read and use informational tools, including charts, diagrams, graphs, maps, political cartoons, photographs, or tables.
3. Locate ancient civilizations in time and place.
4. Identify significant characteristics of early agricultural societies.
5. Describe achievements made by ancient civilizations.

Social Studies – Civics
1. Explain the difference between the rule of law and the rule of man.

Science
1. Distinguish between fact and opinion when responding to information.
2. Investigate and describe how chemical reactions can be fast or slow.

As a starting point, think about what you would want your students to know and understand about ancient Egypt. Which of the skills and strategies identified in the standards would you select for a focus in this unit?

• • •

Many of the standards listed under social studies, science, and language arts could potentially appear in an ancient Egypt unit, although Jasmine emphasizes some more than others. She decides to focus more on the social studies standards that relate to cultural and historical understanding. The langauge arts standards should relate to the types of texts Jasmine selects to engage students and the type of thinking she wants to emphasize with them. As Jasmine gathers information and develops a clearer sense of the unit's focus, she returns to the standards and identifies those that will receive greater emphasis.

Notice the verbs in each standard. These verbs remind Jasmine of the thinking skills students should develop:

identify	describe	use	evaluate
read	locate	explain	analyze
investigate	determine	confirm	summarize
verify	organize	develop	produce
formulate	document	record	present

These verbs guide Jasmine to consider the processes she should select to help students address the content of the unit.

• • •

■ FIGURE 13.2

Possible sixth-grade
literacy standards for
"Ancient Egypt" unit

Reading

1. Determine how the function of a word changes when a suffix is added.
2. Develop a plan for reading that includes the determination of purpose, appropriate reading strategies, appropriate reading rate, and use of related graphic organizers.
3. Confirm and deny predictions while reading.
4. Identify and explain the relationships between main ideas and supporting details in text.
5. Summarize information from several sources by comparing and contrasting various texts to construct deeper meaning.
6. Find similarities and differences among texts in the treatment, scope, or organization of ideas.
7. Verify information from one source by consulting other sources.
8. Analyze the influence of setting on characters and how the problem or conflict is resolved.
9. Make logical predictions about characters' actions based on evidence from the text.

Writing

1. Organize ideas using graphic representations.
2. Write informative papers that develop a clear topic with appropriate facts, details, and examples from a variety of sources and have a distinct beginning, middle, and end.
3. Write paragraphs and compositions with clear transitions between ideas.
4. Produce writing with a voice that shows awareness of an intended audience and purpose.
5. Revise compositions to improve organization and consistency of ideas.
6. Edit for use of standard English.
7. Use verb tense correctly and consistently in writing.
8. Identify and correct fragments and run-on sentences in writing.
9. Use rules of capitalization, punctuation, and spelling correctly.

Listening/Speaking/Viewing

1. Use situationally appropriate language.
2. Participate in conversations and group discussions to develop active listening skills.

Research

1. Formulate a plan for research to answer a focused question.
2. Document research sources in order to prevent plagiarism.
3. Record information using note-taking and organizational formats.
4. Present research findings using written text or multimedia.

CONSIDER ADOPTED TEXTBOOKS

Jasmine's school district has an adopted textbook for both language arts and social studies. She knows that a textbook is not "the curriculum," but finds it to be a valuable resource as she is learning about integration. The adopted sixth-grade social studies textbook focuses on world history, with unit topics such as the rise and spread of civilizations, and the continents of Europe, Africa, Asia, Australia, Central and South America, and the Caribbean in the modern age. The adopted language arts text is divided into six units, one of which is focused on Egypt.

Jasmine views textbooks as a starting point for her planning. As an example, the authors of the social studies textbook adopted by Jasmine's district identify content objectives for the study of ancient Egypt:

Students should identify and describe:

- Special features of the Nile River,
- Differences between lifestyles of rulers and common citizens,
- Some key achievements of the Egyptians,
- Egyptian's religious beliefs, and
- Clues to culture provided by the contents of newly discovered tombs.

The authors of the language arts textbook have selected pieces of literature that Jasmine will consider as she identifies instructional materials. She knows that she automatically has a class set of several pieces of literature for the unit. She also realizes that the literature is too challenging for some of her students.

What do you think of the textbooks that Jasmine has to work with? Do you think your students would benefit by studying the objectives in the social studies text? How do you think the textbook objectives compare with the school district's social studies standards? Do you think that the literature selection in the language arts textbook might be helpful?

• • •

MY TURN...

The textbook provides some background about the geography and culture of Egypt. Half of the chapter, however, is devoted to the discoveries of the contents of pyramids and hidden tombs. The school district's standards go beyond what the textbook provides. Jasmine feels that she must supplement the information in the textbook to meet the school district's goals and standards for sixth grade. The standards also rely on her ability to develop thinking processes with students.

As learning experiences are planned, Jasmine will integrate content standards (social studies/science) with language and learning processes (language arts). While students explore characteristics of ancient Egyptian civilization (content), they will use language and thinking skills to determine what is significant (process). She will probably be able to integrate some of the ideas in the language arts textbook with the content of the social studies.

• • •

REVIEW AND SELECT LITERATURE RESOURCES

For most units, more literature will be available than we can possibly use. Some resources, but not all, will be useful for our students and/or the topic. It is important to carefully review the available narrative and information texts and select appropriate ones that meet the scope of the unit and the diverse reading levels and interests of the students.

Norton and Norton (1998) suggest the following guidelines to help us select quality information texts:

- All facts are accurate.
- Stereotypes have been eliminated.
- Illustrations enhance and clarify the text.
- Analytical thinking is encouraged.
- The organization of the text aids understanding.
- The style of writing stimulates interest.

For the unit that focuses on ancient Egypt, Jasmine thinks that it is particularly important to have texts with excellent photographs and drawings of the art and artifacts from that period to help her students develop a sense of the culture.

As Jasmine selects appropriate literature, she wants to ensure variety of use:

- Texts to read aloud to the whole class,
- Texts to be studied by a small group, and
- Texts to support individual/small-group study and research.

Such variety will enrich the way Jasmine uses literature to engage students in the unit topic and to meet reading/language arts and social studies standards at the same time.

Jasmine also considers the merits of the selections in the language arts textbook, which include three information texts and one narrative:

- "A Walking Tour of the Pyramids" (excerpt from *A Short Walk Around the Pyramids and Through the World of Art*) by Phillip Isaacson,
- "The Secret Chamber" (an excerpt from *Into the Mummy's Tomb*) by Nicholas Reeves with Nan Froman,
- "Revealing the Mysteries of Mummies" (excerpt from *Mummies and Their Mysteries*) by Charlotte Wilcox, and
- *The Winged Cat: A Tale of Ancient Egypt* by Deborah Lattimore.

The literature possibilities that Jasmine identified for ancient Egypt are listed in Figures 13.3 (information books) and 13.4 (narratives). In addition, examples of websites, useful for student research, are listed in Figure 13.5.

MAPPING UNIT CONCEPT

To focus on the most important outcomes for a unit, Jasmine decides on the overarching concept she will work toward with her students. She reviews the selected academic standards and decides that she wants her students to complete the unit of study with the understanding that civilizations such as ancient Egypt develop through the interactions of people and the region in which they live. She wants her students to appreciate the ingenuity, creativity, and problem-solving abilities that people have demonstrated throughout history. She identifies the overarching unit concept as "Life = People + Environment + Problem Solving." Jasmine will focus on the same overarching concept as she develops units about other civilizations. She develops a concept map to show the progression of thinking she will encourage in her students. She frames the concept map in questions that lead to the overarching goal (see Figure 13.6).

Read Aloud:

Week 1
Ancient Egyptian Places (Howarth, 1997)
*Daily Life of the Ancient Egyptians: Gods and
   Goddesses* (McCall, 2002)
The Egyptian Kingdoms (David, 1988)
Great Rivers of the World (National Geographic, 1984)
How We Know About the Egyptians (James, 1997)
The River Nile (Brander, 1993)

Week 2
Ancient Egyptian People (McNeill & Howarth, 1997)
Art and Civilization: Ancient Egypt (Moris, 2000)
Egyptian Town (Steedman, 1998)
Hieroglyphs: The Writing of Ancient Egypt (Katan,1981)
Slavery in Ancient Egypt and Mesopotamia
   (Green, 2000)

Additional Texts for Research:
Adventures in Ancient Egypt (Bailey, 2000)
Ancient Egypt (Cole, 2001)
Ancient Egypt (Crosher, 1993)
Ancient Egypt (Cultural Atlas for Young People)
   (Millard, 1990)
Ancient Egypt (Millard, 1995)
The Ancient Egyptians (Marston, 1996)
The Ancient World of the Egyptians (Odijk, 1989)
The Atlas of Ancient Egypt (Rosati & Morris, 2000)
Cat Mummies (Trumble, 1996)
Cleopatra (Stanley & Vennema, 1997)
Cleopatra: The Queen of Kings (McDonald, 2001)
Cleopatra VII: Daughter of the Nile (Gregory, 1999)
Clothes and Crafts in Ancient Egypt (Balkwill, 2000)
A Dictionary of Egyptian Gods and Goddesses
   (Hart, 1991)
Egyptian Art (Aldred, 1980)
The Egyptian News (Steedman, 2000)
The Egyptian World (Oliphant, 1989)
The Egyptians (Allard, 1997)
The Egyptians (Chapman, 1997)
Eyewitness Books: Ancient Egypt (Hart, 1990)
*The Great Pyramid: The Story of the Framers, the God-
   King, and the Most Astounding Structure Ever Built*
   (Mann, 1996)
The Great Wonder: Building of the Great Pyramid
   (Howard, 1998)
Hatshepsut and Ancient Egypt: Rulers and Their Times
   (Greenblatt, 2000)
Hieroglyphics for Fun (Scott & Scott, 1974)
I Wonder Why the Pyramids Were Built (Steele, 1995)
In the Footsteps of the Mummy (Roden, 1996)
*Into the Mummy's Tomb: The Real-Life Discovery of
   Tutankhamen's Treasures* (Reeves, 1992). (Excerpt,
   "The Secret Chamber," in language arts textbook)

Literature Circles:

Week 1
The Ancient Egyptians: Life in the Nile Valley
   (Koenig & Ageorges, 1992)
Egyptian Life (Guy, 1998)
Everyday Life in Ancient Egypt (Harris, 1990)
Growing Up in Ancient Egypt (David, 1993)
How Would You Survive as an Ancient Egyptian?
   (Morley, 1996)

Week 2
Ancient Egyptian Art (Hodge, 1997)
An Egyptian Craftsman (Caselli, 1986)
Fun with Hieroglyphics (Roehrig, 1990)
Gods and Goddesses of Ancient Egypt (Fisher, 1997)
Hatshepsut, His Majesty, Herself (Andronik, 2001)

The Land of the Pharaohs (Terzi, 1992)
Life of the Ancient Egyptians (Strouhal, 1992)
Made in Ancient Egypt (Price, 1990)
Mummies and Their Mysteries (Wilcox, 1993). (Excerpt,
   "Revealing the Mysteries of Mummies" in language
   arts textbook)
Mummies in the Morning (Osborne, 1993)
Mummies Made in Egypt (Brandenberg, 1985)
Mummies, Masks, and Mourners (Berrill, 1990)
Mummies, Tombs, and Treasures (Perl & Weihs, 1991)
Mysteries of the Pyramids (Millard, 1995)
Myths and Civilization of the Ancient Egyptians
   (Hart, 1991)
Nefertiti: The Mystery Queen (Holmes, 1977)
New Book of Pharaohs (Millard, 1998)
Pharaohs and Embalmers: All in a Day's Work
   (Ganeri, 2001)
Pyramid (MacAulay, 1982)
Pyramids (Jeunesse, Delafosse, & Biard, 1995)
Queen Cleopatra (Streissguth, 1999)
Read About Ancient Egyptians (Jay, 2000)
The Riddle of the Rosetta Stone (Giblin, 1990)
Science in Ancient Egypt (Woods, 1988)
Secrets of the Mummies (Tanaka, 2000)
*Sightseers Guide — Ancient Egypt: A Guide to Egypt in
   the Time of the Pharaohs* (Tagholm, 1999)
Tales of Ancient Egypt (Green, 1996)
Tales Mummies Tell (Lauber, 1983)
Tutankhamen's Gift (Sabuda, 1997)
The Valley of the Kings (Clayton, 1996)
A Walking Tour of the Pyramids (excerpt from "A Short
   Walk Around the Pyramids and Through the World
   of Art) (Isaacson, 1993)
Who Built the Pyramids? (Hooper, 2001)
The World of the Pharaoh (Millard, 1998)

■ **FIGURE 13.3**

Literature possibilities — information books

Read Aloud:

Week 1
  Bill and Pete Go Down the Nile (dePaola, 1987)
  Gift of the Nile (Mike, 1992)
  Zekmet, The Stone Carver (Stolz, 1988)

Week 2
  Ancient Egyptian Myths and Legends (Spence, 1991)
  The Egyptian Cinderella (Climo, 1989)
  I Am the Mummy Heb-Nefer (Bunting, 1997)
  The Winged Cat: A Tale of Ancient Egypt (Lattimore, 1992)
    (language arts textbook selection)

Weeks 3 and 4
  The Egypt Game (Snyder, 1976)

Literature Circles:

Weeks 3 and 4
Less Challenge:
  A Place in the Sun (Rubacalba, 1998)

Average Challenge:
  Mara, Daughter of the Nile (McGraw, 1988)
  Pharaoh's Daughter (Lester, 2002)
  A Place of Darkness: A Mystery About Ancient Egypt (Haney, 2001)

More Challenge:
  The Gilded Cat (Dexter, 1992)

Additional Texts for Independent Reading:

  The Curse of the Mummy's Tomb (Stine, 1993)
  The Golden Goblet (McGraw, 1986)
  The Reluctant God (Service, 1988)
  Tut Tut (Time Warp Series) (Scieszka, 1998)

For Teacher Planning and Preparation, with Links to Student Websites:

  http://www.focusmm.com.au/egypt/eg_giamn.htm
  http://www.oi.uchicago.ed/OI/DEPT/RA/ABZU/YOUTH_RESOURCES.HTM
  http://www.geocities.com/Athens/Academy/7357/builder.html
  http://www.pbs.org/wgbh/nova/pyramid
  http://interoz.com/egypt/construction/index.html
  http://carlos.emory.edu/ODYSSEY/
  http://www.ancientegypt.uk/geography/story/main.html
  http://neferchichi.com/
  http://www.cmi.k12.il.us/Urbana/projects/AncientCiv/
  http://tlc.ousd.k12.ca.us/cv/projects/egypt
  http://www.teachers.k12.sd.us/
  http://www.framingham.k12.ma.us/webquest/egypt.html
  http://teacherlink.ed.usu.edu/TLresources

■ **FIGURE 13.6**

Concept map for "Ancient Egypt" unit

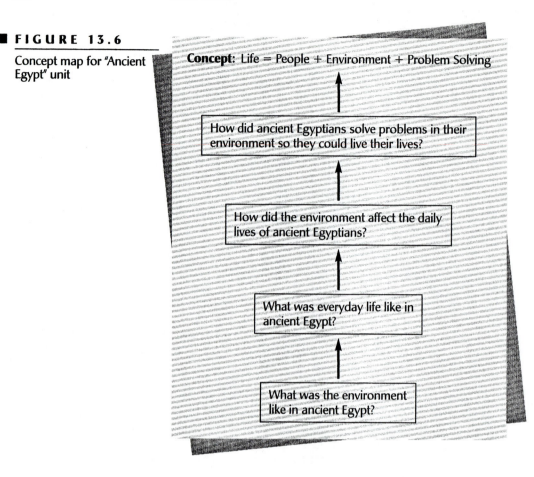

Concept: Life = People + Environment + Problem Solving

How did ancient Egyptians solve problems in their environment so they could live their lives?

How did the environment affect the daily lives of ancient Egyptians?

What was everyday life like in ancient Egypt?

What was the environment like in ancient Egypt?

INVOLVE STUDENTS IN PLANNING

A few weeks before Jasmine plans to implement the unit, she discusses the topic/concept with the students, exploring what they already know about Egypt. She wants the unit to reflect students' needs and interests, so she also solicits what they want to learn about Egypt. Sometimes she begins the K and W portions of a K-W-H-L (Bromley, 2000) or a K-W-L-Q (Schmidt, 1999) activity, recording students' responses (see Chapter 9). Her sixth-grade students raise questions about things they would like to learn:

- What was ancient Egypt like?
- How did the Egyptians make a mummy?
- Why did the Egyptians mummify people?
- Who got to be mummified?
- Who built the pyramids?
- How did the Egyptians make the pyramids without machines?
- Why did the Egyptians build the pyramids?
- Were all pharaohs buried in pyramids? Was King Tut?
- How did people figure out hieroglyphs? Why didn't Egyptians write with letters?

It is typical for students' interests in ancient Egypt to focus on pyramids and the mummification process. Jasmine's challenge is to find ways to weave their interests with her goals and the district's academic standards.

Look back at the school district's academic standards in Figures 13.1 and 13.2. What might you do to weave students' interest in mummies and pyramids into the standards listed?

• • •

Students' interests easily link to the academic standards:

- The discovery of Tutankhamen's tomb certainly provided a better understanding of this early civilization (History—4).
- The pyramids were an architectural and scientific feat (Science—1 & 3).
- The mummification process required chemical reactions (Science—4) and resulted from religious and cultural beliefs (History—5).
- Materials to build the pyramids and treasures in the tomb were related to natural resources and economics (Geography—3).
- Who was buried in pyramids and tombs related to the laws of the civilization (Civics—1).

• • •

DEVELOP ORGANIZING IDEAS AND ACTIVITIES

By now, Jasmine has some basic ideas around which she can begin to organize this unit. As she finds out more about students' knowledge and interests, she can add to or revise her plans. She does need, however, to make decisions about the following areas:

- The basic organization and scope of the unit,
- Initiating activities for the unit,
- Activities that will be important for all students, and
- Activities that could be choices for students.

Overall Organization. Considering the academic standards identified in an earlier section, what the adopted textbook offers, and the literature that is available, Jasmine could organize the unit around three central ideas:

Life Along the Nile River
Academic standards:
- Identify the impact of natural hazards (flooding of Nile) on people and the earth.
- Identify the characteristics of a region related to primary economic activity (farming).
- Locate ancient civilizations in time and place.
- Identify the significant characteristics of early agricultural societies.

The Social Pyramid in Ancient Egypt
Academic standards:
- Evaluate sources of historical information based on cultural context or time period.
- Explain difference between rule of law and rule of man.

Pyramids and the Valley of the Kings

Academic standards:

- Describe achievements made by ancient civilizations.
- Distinguish between fact and fiction when responding to information.
- Investigate how chemical reactions can be fast or slow.

Jasmine could develop the concept of civilization through the study of the Nile, including the influence of the geography on life and culture. Both the pyramids and the social pyramid could be related to students' interest in mummies and the mummification process, since only pharaohs were honored in this manner. Exploring the social pyramid will allow Jasmine to focus on Egyptian culture, including writing and religion.

Initiating Activities. Believing that the language arts undergird all learning, Jasmine chooses to begin with a whole-class literature selection to capture interest and set the tone for the unit. Figures 13.3 and 13.4 identify several whole-class books. While accurate information is very important, Jasmine knows that narrative selections will provide a good feel for life in another time. She knows that probing students' background knowledge is also important and there a number of ways she can do that: web/cluster, K-W-H-L (Bromley, 2000) or K-W-L-Q chart (Schmidt, 1999), or annotated drawings. Annotated drawings of the images that come to mind when students hear "ancient Egypt" can provide some insight into how their knowledge may be influenced by images in the media.

Activities for All Students. Jasmine believes that it is important for all students to participate in discussions that process the information being found during small groups and independent research. In addition, she wants all students to participate in some form of reading experience that provides opportunity for discussion and reflection through writing. New vocabulary will be abundant in this unit and her students who are learning English will need connected learning experiences that frequently recycle the important language of the unit. All of Jasmine's students need opportunities to collect and consider new words, especially words that are related to contemporary language.

Activities for Choice. Middle grade students need the sense of becoming independent and making successful decisions. Choice must be an integral part of any unit. With the wealth of information available on this topic, Jasmine will focus all students on learning outcomes to meet academic standards, but she will also provide opportunities for all students to pursue an area of personal interest as they apply reading, writing, and thinking strategies. Students can share what they learn in a variety of forums.

PLAN FOR ADEQUATE TIME

As Jasmine selects a theme/topic and begins to collect resources to plan for possible activities, she has a general sense of the time that she can devote to the theme study. She thinks about both the duration of the unit and the daily time devoted to unit activities. At the beginning of each school year, Jasmine reviews the curriculum and anticipates the units she might teach during the year. After reviewing the major concepts to be developed during the year, Jasmine decides to devote 3 to 4 weeks to this unit about ancient Egypt.

How we organize daily time for a unit depends, in part, on the organization of the school:

- If we have one class of students for the entire day (self-contained), we have the choice of integrating within time blocks or across time blocks in the daily schedule.

- If we have a class for a block of time, such as when departmentalizing by subject areas, we can plan jointly with other teachers to accomplish the unit goals.

In a self-contained classroom, we typically will have blocks of time for reading/language arts, mathematics, and science/social studies experiences. In an integrated unit, we must decide how much time to devote each day to unit activities. Will we use only science/social studies time or will we also think of language arts and/or mathematics instruction time as possibilities for inclusion? We will make these decisions as the unit takes shape.

ORGANIZING AND IMPLEMENTING THE UNIT

Starting with organizing ideas and activities, Jasmine plans the basic structure of the unit. She is aware of a variety of ways to organize instructional time. When integrated teaching was new for Jasmine, she considered keeping the daily schedule that was already established and use the time in one or more blocks to explore unit concepts. If she used existing time blocks for this unit, instructional time might be organized as follows:

- *Reading/language arts block.* Whole-group, small-group, and/or independent study of information and narrative texts about Egypt, write in response to reading, and make records of learning about Egyptians.
- *Science/social studies.* Whole-group background-building activities, time for independent/small-group exploration and research related to ancient Egypt.
- *Independent reading.* Self-selected reading in books related to the unit, continuation of reading for literature groups, or independent research.
- *Read-aloud.* Reading and rereading of texts that contribute to unit theme.

Now, after developing several units of study, Jasmine uses a workshop framework, similar to reader's and writer's workshop (see Chapters 6 and 10), to arrange content area work time:

- Whole-class activities set a focus,
- Followed by small-group and independent activities, then
- A return to the whole-class setting to process the activities and bring the work period to a close.

Depending on the daily schedule, Jasmine has one or more workshop periods during a day (language arts, unit study).

The more that Jasmine experiments with integration and the more familiar she becomes with the unit topic, the more she is able to think flexibly about daily instructional time and "blur" the lines that traditionally divide subject areas.

GROUPING FOR INSTRUCTION

In the ancient Egypt unit, Jasmine considers ways that she can arrange learning experiences as combinations of whole-group, small-group, and independent activities.

- *Whole group.* Introductory experiences are whole-class activities to help students become aware of concepts in the theme and possibilities for activities within the theme.

- *Small group.* Processing experiences are small-group activities to interact more closely with students, providing support to extend their thinking.
- *Independent.* Exploration and personal interest experiences are partner/ independent activities, giving individual students the time they need to learn.

We turn our attention now to the unit that Jasmine developed. Most blocks of time begin in some form of a whole-class experience to focus students' attention, then activities move to small group or independent work, and, finally, back to whole-class for processing and closure. In this 4-week unit she organizes learning experiences mainly around a social studies workshop, literature circles or reader's workshop, and writer's workshop:

- Week 1 engages students in a social studies workshop to activate and build their background knowledge for unit content. In addition, they join a literature circle to discuss a book of their choosing.
- In Week 2 students conduct research on Egyptians' roles in the social pyramid and communicate their learning through perspective-taking in writer's workshop. Building on week 1, students select a new book for literature circle.
- In weeks 3 and 4 of social studies workshop students join a focus group to research one of three main topics — pyramids, burial customs, or gods and goddesses. Independent/small-group reading and writing are woven throughout the 2 weeks of research. Students attend conferences with the teacher about their reading and writing.
- To culminate the unit, students prepare a Living Museum.

Figure 13.7 provides a visual overview of the unit. Note that daily instruction in mathematics and word study continues outside of the unit because the content of the unit does not provide enough developmentally appropriate opportunities for all students in these areas.

SAMPLE UNIT: ANCIENT EGYPT, SIXTH GRADE

Week 1

Monday

Annotated Drawing

- "What comes to mind when you think of ancient Egypt? What do you think life was like? Draw a picture of your thinking. Label your drawings to tell more about your thinking."
- Drawing will allow students who are acquiring English to share what they think. Set aside for now.
- Will be used to assess students' beginning conceptions and misconceptions.

Opening Read-Aloud

- Whole-class read-aloud of *Bill and Pete Go Down the Nile* (just for fun!).
- This text is engaging, has both humor and content.

Video—*What Was Ancient Egypt Like?* (Pyramid School Kit, PBS)

- Guided viewing of video, content ML-TA procedure (predict–view–explain–connect cycles) to focus attention and support on vocabulary and comprehension of verbal text.

■ **FIGURE 13.7**

Overview of unit, "Ancient Egypt", sixth grade

Week 1	Week 2	Weeks 3 & 4
Geography of Ancient Egypt	**Everyday Life/Social Roles**	**Digging into the Past**
Annotated drawing	**Read Aloud – ML-TA**	**Read Aloud and Videos**
Read Aloud	Background for life and social roles	Add to background
Information and narrative texts	**Group research**	**Research Projects**
Video –*What Was Ancient Egypt Like?*	All facets of a social role	Pyramids
Literature circles	Prepare display	Burial customs
Information texts	**Literature circles**	Gods and goddesses
Life in Nile River valley	Information texts	**Literature circles**
Learning Log	arts, crafts, hieroglyphics, pharaohs, gods and goddesses	Variety of novels
Response, words, facts, graphic organizers		**Writer's workshop**
Guided reading	**Literature log**	Research report
Social textbook	Response, words, facts, graphic organizers	**Living Museum**
Group research	**Writer's workshop**	Verbal presentation
Geography of Egypt	Perspective of a social role	Artifacts
Data Disk		Display of reports

- Move to small-group discussions, complete discussion guide (see Figure 13.8).
- Return to whole class, share discussion guides, record main ideas on large chart.
- Place discussion guide in learning log.

Learning Log
- Discuss purposes for each type of response that could be in the log for this unit:

    I Think . . . pages — Open response to reading.

    What's the Word? pages — Select three to five new words or interesting phrases for class discussions.

    That's a Fact! pages — Collect interesting facts about Egyptian life (may be accompanied by annotated drawings).

    I Wonder . . . pages — Raise questions for further discussion/exploration.

    Getting organized — various graphic organizers that help students relate information.
- Make daily entries during discussions and in preparation for literature circles.

Literature Circles
- Information book choices for Week 1:

    The Ancient Egyptians: Life in the Nile Valley by Viviane Koenig & Veronique Ageorges (1996, Millbrook)

■ **FIGURE 13.8**

Small-group discussion
guide following video

Video Dicussion Guide:

What Was Ancient Egypt Like?

1. Why is Egypt called "the gift of the Nile"?

2. What were Upper Egypt and Lower Egypt?

3. Why did ancient Egyptians live close to the Nile?

Ancient Egyptian People by Sarah McNeill and Sarah Howarth (1997 Millbrook)

Everyday Life in Ancient Egypt by Nathaniel Harris (1994, Watts Franklin)

Growing Up in Ancient Egypt by Rosalie David (1993, Troll Associates)

How Would You Survive as an Ancient Egyptian? by Jacqueline Morley (1996, Franklin Watts)

- Give book talks to provide overview of text.
- Provide time for students to examine each book, focusing on particular content that might be of interest to the student and reading level.
- Students select book, which determines group composition.
- Class discussion of developing a reading plan that includes purpose for reading, using appropriate reading strategies, appropriate reading rate, and making notes to support comprehension.
- Each book group meets, develops a plan to complete reading of text by Thursday.
- Discuss first impressions, make predictions, share background knowledge.

Daily Closure

- Read-aloud, ML-TA, *How We Know About the Ancient Egyptians* by Rosalie David (1988 Troll Associates).
- Discuss reading plans developed in literature circle.
- Preview and plan for Tuesday's events.

Tuesday

Whole-Class Opening

- Recall video highlights of the Nile and early Egypt.
- Begin a web of ideas to activate specific prior knowledge about the geography of ancient Egypt.

Content MR–TA
- Guided reading of sections of the social studies textbook, focusing on the geography of the Nile, farming, and irrigation (see Figure 13.9, repeated from Chapter 7).
- Add to/revise web throughout content MR–TA (see Figure 13.10).
- Cut web apart and reconstruct to emphasize how information is related (see Figure 13.11).

Independent Reading
- Read pages according to reading plan.
- Prepare for literature circle meeting.

Learning Log
- Record responses, vocabulary, facts, and so on, in learning log.

Literature Circles
- Groups meet for discussion, share learning log entries.
- Teacher observes interaction of groups, content of discussion, implementation of reading plans.

Whole-Class Closure
- ML–TA, *Gift of the Nile* by Jan M. Mike (1992, Troll Associates), a folktale of ancient Egypt.
- Review student learning for the day, paying particular attention to students' awareness of stratgeies used during independent reading and vocabulary being encountered.
- Shared writing, list of strategies used during independent reading.
- Begin chart to collect words and phrases that are new/challenging, identified in students' learning log "What's the Word" pages. Discuss strategies students used to figure out words (e.g., cataract, papyrus).
- Process positive aspects of group work.
- Make constructive suggestions for Wednesday groups.

Wednesday

Whole-Class Opening
- Content ML–TA, read selected portions of *Great Rivers of the World* by National Geographic (1984 National Geographic) and *The Nile* by Michael Pollard (2000, Benchmark Books) guide discussion.
- Introduce data disk for recording facts about a topic (see Figure 13.12). Brainstorm possible categories to create on a data disk (e.g., farming, transportation, Nile River, climate, the land).
- Discuss how to identify books that might have desired information.

Small-Group Research
- Research something of interest related to Egypt's geography. Make notes, sketches, charts, and so on, in learning log to retain information.
- Synthesize research onto a group data disk, creating relevant categories for information.
- Share data disks during closure.

Sample C–MR–TA for
*The Geography of
Ancient Egypt*

Before Reading:

Predict: Let's think about how we make predictions before we begin to read. The heading of this section of the text is "The Geography of Ancient Egypt." I'm thinking about this heading as I read the other subheadings on pages 65–69. I'm asking myself, "What do I think I might learn about Egypt?" The heading tells me that the focus is on geography, so I ask myself, "What do I know about geography?" I know it has something to do with the land and how the people are able to live in that environment. What predictions are you making as you preview this section? *(takes responses from students, queries students about what influenced that prediction)* How do these predictions compare to the Nile web that we started? *(Students make comparisons and contrasts.)*

During Reading:

Read: Let's look at the first subheading, "The Nile River Valley." Here we want to listen carefully to see if our ideas are on track with what the author thinks is important about the Nile. *(Jasmine reads the first three paragraphs out loud to set the tone for the reading. She refers students to the map on page 66 as suggested in the second paragraph. She reminds students that textual aids, like maps, can help make visual links with the author's ideas. Then she continues to read aloud.)* What do we know so far? *(She takes students' responses.)* I noticed how the author of this textbook reminds us how much the geography of a place influences people's lives. What ideas are important to remember about the influence of the geography? Please read the remainder of this subsection silently.

Explain: What did we find out about the Nile? *(takes students' responses, queries for students' awareness of text and head cues that lead to those ideas)*

Connect: *Should we add to or revise our web? Why do we think these ideas are important? What clues in the text and in our heads lead us to say that?* (Adds to the web *flows from south to north, and *Egypt divided into Upper and Lower).

Predict: Look at the map on page 66. What differences might there have been between Upper and Lower Egypt? What do we notice on the map that might give us some ideas? *(takes responses)* What does the next subheading make you think about? *(takes responses)*

Read: Let's read "The Overflow of the Nile" silently to check our ideas.

Explain: What did we find out about the overflow? *(takes responses)* Does the text explain why the overflow happened every summer? *(takes responses)* Perhaps we should reread the last few paragraphs to see if we can clarify our thinking. Did that help? Sometimes authors are inconsiderate and don't tell us everything or they think we know more about the topic than we do. Where else can we look for information to help us? *(Guides students to look at geographical areas of central Africa on the classroom map.)*

Connect: Do we need to add to or revise our cluster? *(takes responses)* The next section is titled "The Nile Delta." We should ask ourselves what we already know about that. *(Students refer back to the web and the map on page 66.)*

■ **FIGURE 13.9**

(Continued)

Predict:	What else might we find out about the Nile Delta in this section? What makes us think that? the text? our heads? *(takes responses)*
Read:	Please read this section on page 67 silently.
Explain:	What do we know about the delta? *(takes responses)* What did you find out about the comparison of the delta to the lotus flower? Does that seem important for us to remember? Why or why not? *(takes responses)*
Connect:	How do these ideas compare to the ideas on our web? *(takes responses)*
Predict:	We can tell from the subheadings and illustrations that the remaining sections have something to do with farming. Why do you think the textbook author put these sections next? *(takes responses)* As you read silently, it is important to make note of the details about farming and the Nile that you think are important to add to your understanding of life during this time in Egypt.
Read:	Students read pages 68 and 69 silently.
Explain:	What details did you notice as you read? *(takes responses)* Did anyone use the drawing on page 69 to better understand the way ancient Egyptians use irrigation? How did the drawing help? *(takes responses)* The drawing is another text aid that the authors give us to add to what we learn from the words in the text. The author expects us to use these aids to add to or revise our understanding.

After Reading:

Connect:	In the last paragraph on page 69, the textbook authors state that the Nile helped to unite Egypt. What do we know that could support that statement? Where did we get our ideas? *(takes responses)* Do we need to make any other revisions to our web for today? *(takes responses)* When we finish reading it is important to try to connect the most important ideas together to make it easier to remember. What are the most important ideas we want to remember from this reading? *(takes responses)* Let's highlight those important ideas on our cluster.

Independent Reading
- Prepare for literature circle meeting.
- Make notes in learning log as needed.

Literature Circles
- Groups meet, discuss section read.
- Share learning log entries.
- Discuss strategies that were helpful in reading text.

Whole-Class Closure
- ML–TA, *The Egyptian Kingdoms* by Rosalie A. David (1990, Peter Bedrick Books).
- Present results of research and group data disks.
- Create display, with scene of the Nile River and the data disks students made.
- Plan for Thursday.

FIGURE 13.10

Web created from video and textbook reading

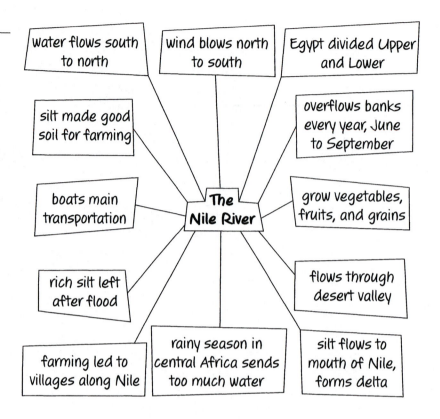

Thursday

Whole-Class Opening

- Minilesson, separating fact from fiction, verifying facts in more than one source.
- ML-TA, compare information presented in similar sections of *Ancient Egypt* (Cole, 2001) and *Ancient Egypt* (Crosher, 1993). Use overhead transparency for shared reading of texts. Students also have a copy. What leads us to believe that the authors are presenting accurate information? List facts from one book, then compare to second book.

Fact Search

- Groups identify three facts about Egypt presented in one source. Search for same facts in two other sources. Make a chart to compare findings.
- Share findings with class. What clues suggest that the information in a text is reliable? Why is it important to verify information in more than one source?

Independent Reading

- Complete the reading of text for literature circles.
- Make learning log entries.

Literature Circles

- Complete discussion of text.
- Share learning logs.

■ FIGURE 13.11

Ideas on web reconstructed
into chart for research

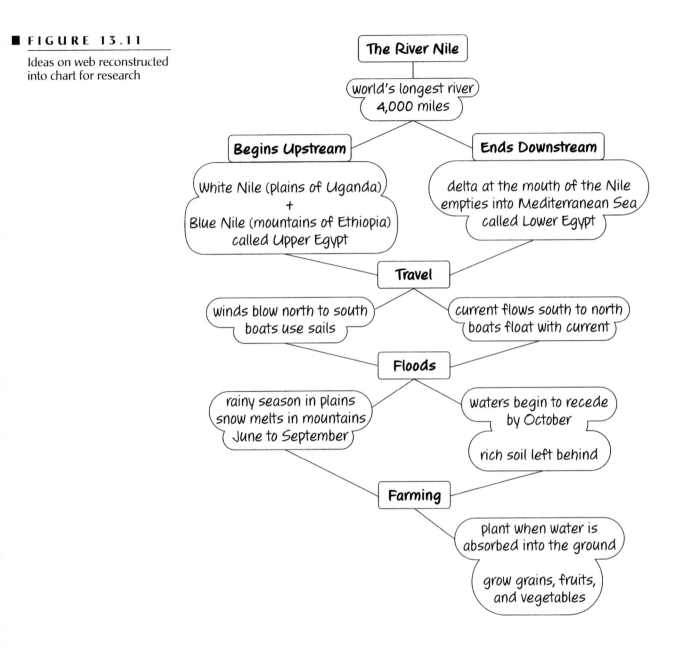

- Make a group list of five challenging words.
- Prepare to discuss clues for decoding and meaning, and questions raised by the reading on Friday.

Daily Closure
- Read-aloud, ML–TA, *Ancient Egyptian Places* (Howarth, 1997).
- Discuss new facts presented by the author.
- Review plans for Friday.

■ **FIGURE 13.12**

Data disk for the Nile River

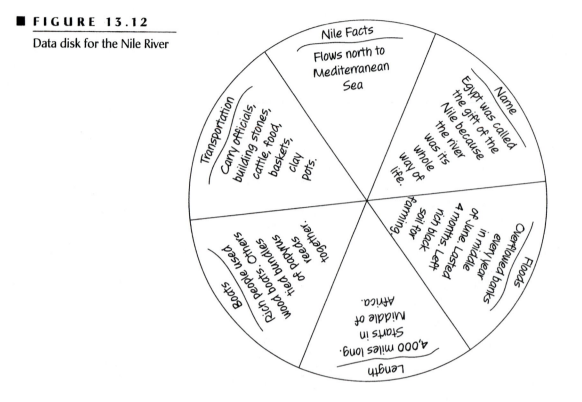

Friday

Whole-Class Opening

- Minilesson, finding information in narratives.
- ML–TA for *Zekmet, The Stone Carver* (Stolx, 1988).
- Role-play to retell story, extract information about social class in ancient Egypt:

  Khafre (pharaoh),

  Ho-tep (vizier),

  Zekmet (stone carver), and

  Senmut (Zekmet's son).
- Small-group discussions about impact of class distinctions, use discussion guide (see Figure 13.13).
- Return to whole class to share results of dicussions.
- Divide class by lottery into social groups (farmer, slave, pharaoh, scribe, artisan, priest, embalmer, and so on).
- Students prepare to research social roles in week 2 and take the perspective of that person.

Whole-Class Minilesson and Shared Reading — Writing a Summary

- How to reconstruct details into a summary.
- Shared reading of social studies textbook section, "Daily Life of Citizens" (five paragraphs), use copy on overhead projector, students have individual copies. Identify most important words and phrases through shared reading. Make a list of

■ **FIGURE 13.13**

Discussion guide, social class in ancient Egypt

Discussion Guide

Social Class in Ancient Egypt

1. What did you learn about social class in ancient Egypt?

2. What would you like to learn about the people of ancient Egypt?

those words and phrases. Expand words and phrases into sentences, arrange sentences into a logical order for summary paragraph.

Literature Circles

- Construct a group summary of the most important ideas in the text completed that week.

- Students teach each other how they figure out the five unfamiliar words selected on Thursday, both decoding and meaning. Share context in which the word was found in the text.

Daily Closure

- Give book talks for next week's literature circles; students select books by ballot.

- Groups share discussion of decoding challenging words.

- Add useful words to class list.

- Preview of week 2.

Week 2

Daily Opening and Closing

- Read-Aloud, ML–TA, at opening and closing of each day.

  Information texts

  Ancient Egyptian People (McNeill & Howarth, 1997)

  Art and Civilization: Ancient Egypt (Morris, 2000)

  Daily Life of Ancient Egyptians: Gods and Goddesses (McCall, 2002)

  Egyptian Town (Steedman, 1998)

  Hieroglyphics: The Writing of Ancient Egypt (Katan, 1981)

  Slavery in Ancient Egypt and Mesopotamia (Green, 2000)

  Narrative texts

  Ancient Egyptian Myths and Legends (Spence, 1991)

  The Egyptian Cinderella (Climo, 1989)

  I Am the Mummy Heb-Nefer (Bunting, 1997)

  The Winged Cat: A Tale of Ancient Egypt (Lattimore, 1992)

- Information texts to support and extend: knowledge of social roles in everyday life and impact of environment on everyday life and roles.
- Relate to students' research.

Group and Individual Research

- Use exploration of social roles to examine Egyptian culture and impact of environment on daily lives.
- Students find facts about specific role on the social pyramid.
- Verify in more than one source, make notes, note sources.
- Create an icon (about 6 inches tall) that represents their assumed social class.
- Summarize notes on an attribute card (3-inch by 5-inch card).
- Group members summarize different aspects of the assigned social role.
- On Friday of week 2, students create a social pyramid display by placing their icon and attribute card in the appropriate place on the social pyramid (see Figure 13.14).
- Class discussion of the impact of being assigned to a particular social class by birth.

Literature Circles

- Five groups, students select books, same format as week 1.
- Book choices: Information
  Ancient Egyptian Art (Hodge, 1997)
  An Egyptian Craftsman (Caselli, 1986)
  Fun with Hieroglyphics (Roehrig, 1990)
  Gods and Goddesses of Ancient Egypt (Fisher, 1997)
  Hatshepsut, His Majesty, Herself (Andronik, 2001)

Learning Log

- Continue to use same formats as week 1.
- Discuss entries during literature circles and whole-class meetings.

Writer's Workshop

- Writing from a perspective, taking a role in the social pyramid of Ancient Egypt.

■ **FIGURE 13.14**

Framework for display—social pyramid

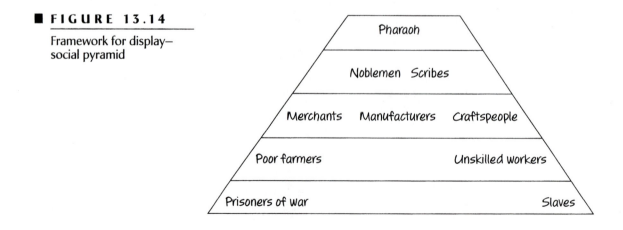

- Minilessons:
  Examples of writing in first person.
  Example of a poem as a possible format for writing (see Figure 13.15).
- Form is student's choice (diary, personal narrative, poem, letter, and so on).
- Move through writing process during week 2: rehearsal, draft, revise, edit, and share.

Weeks 3 and 4
Daily Opening and Closing
- Read-aloud, ML–TA, to build general background about the exploration of tombs in the Valley of the Kings.

■ **FIGURE 13.15**

A poem for two voices—
the social pyramid

Pharaoh's Voice	Both Voices	Slave's Voice
	1. What makes us different; we are so much the same	
2. I am pharaoh.		
		3. I am a slave.
4. Our worlds must be separate.		
	5. We both marvel at the beauty of the Nile.	
		6. Why can't we live together?
7. Because we are not equal.		
		8. But I am human just as you.
9. You are less.		
		10. I wish I was more.
11. I look forward to the life hereafter.		
		12. So do I.
	13. What makes us different; We are so much the same.	

Information Texts

The Great Pyramid: The Story of Farmers, the God-King, and the Most Astounding Structure Ever Built (Mann, 1996)

Into the Mummy's Tomb: The Real-Life Discovery of Tutankhamen's Treasures (Reeves, 1992)

Mummies, Masks, and Mourners (Berrill, 1990)

Science in Ancient Egypt (Woods, 1998)

The Valley of the Kings (Clayton, 1996)

Videos

- Guided viewing, ML–TA:

  Mysteries of Egypt (National Geographic, 1999)

  Egypt: Secrets of the Pharaohs (National Geographic, 1998)

- Add to mental images for research.

Interest Research Groups

- In-depth research, formalized through writing process in writer's workshop over weeks 3 and 4.

- Interest group discussions over weeks 3 and 4 to support student application of reading and informal writing strategies to research process.

- Opportunity to apply reading strategies over extended period of study.

  Pyramid Group

- Research questions:

  How were the pyramids built?

  Why are there different types of pyramids?

- View video on the making of the pyramids (Pyramid School Kit, PBS).

- Simulate building procedures, build a replica pyramid.

- Make records in "Architect's Manual" (learning log).

- Become an "expert" on a tool used for building.

  Burial Customs Group

- Research questions:

  Why were pyramids built?

  What was the significance of items placed in the tomb?

- View video on mummification (Pyramid School Kit, PBS).

- Research mummification process. Explore chemical change through mummification of an orange. Step-by-step process can be found at http://neferchichi.com/fruitystep1.html.

- Prepare a "How to" book for burial and mummification, a "Book of the Dead," or a stela or mural of important life events.

  Gods and Goddesses Group

- Research questions:

  What did Egyptians believe about life and afterlife? Why did the Egyptians have so many gods and goddesses?

- Read myths and legends about gods and goddesses.

- Compile information on data disks or make a "Guide to Gods and Goddesses."
- Write a myth that demonstrates the power of a particular god or goddess.

Literature Circles

- Narrative texts — Novels

  Less Challenge:

  > *A Place in the Sun* (Rubacalba, 1998)

  Average Challenge:

  > *Mara, Daughter of the Nile* (McGraw, 1988)
  >
  > *A Place of Darkness: A Mystery About Ancient Egypt* (Haney, 2001)
  >
  > *Pharaoh's Daughter* (Lester, 2002)

  More Challenge:

  > *The Gilded Cat* (Dexter, 1992)

- Whole-class minilessons focus on making logical predictions about characters' actions based on evidence from the text and on analyzing the influence of setting on characters' actions and how the problem or conflict is resolved.
- Groups meet according to reading plan, possibly alternating independent reading days and discussion days to allow the teacher to more closely observe and interact with groups.
- Predictions, responses, and vocabulary recorded in learning log to prepare for group meetings.
- Groups develop a character/setting interaction chart to show the impact of setting on character. Charts are discussed in whole-class meetings. Class chart constructed to allow for comparison of texts.

Writer's Workshop

- How Egyptians worked with their environment to solve problems in their lives, according to their beliefs.
- Minilessons:

  Effective spatial organization of information (in preparation for sharing with class).

  Selecting a form of writing that fits the author's intention.

- Topic and form is guided by work in interest group.
- Use informal writing in research group as rehearsal for research report.
- Group members divide topic into sections for individual or partner research reports.
- Group members provide revision and editing feedback to author.
- Individuals/groups have conferences with teacher at least once during 2 weeks.
- Final product to be shared through display and presentation during Living Museum.

Culminating Activity

- Create a Living Museum, vignettes of Egyptian life, including student-created art, models, poetry, and so on.
- Practice speaking skills by presenting to other classes.

Now that you have reviewed Jasmine's planning processes and the structure and content of the unit about ancient Egypt, what thoughts do you have about integrating learning experiences for students? Do you think linking learning experiences for her students increases opportunities for all of Jasmine's students to become engaged in the unit content and learn more about themselves as readers and writers? Explain your thinking to someone else.

• • •

RESPECTING DIVERSITY IN INTEGRATED UNITS

Integrated units may be the most genuine way for us to respect and support diversity in the classroom. The range of curricular experiences in a well-planned integrated unit makes it possible to meet the diversity of our students' interests and needs. Every student should find success in the range of unit activities and projects. Including students in developing and planning units enhances our opportunities for success.

Consider for a moment the chapter's sample integrated unit on ancient Egypt. This unit drew on nearly all of the instructional strategies and approaches that we have discussed in this text:

- Reading experiences combined whole-class, small-group, and independent opportunities, as well as reading aloud to students, in a variety of narrative and information texts.

- Writing experiences included both writing process and informal writing. The teacher mediated some experiences, while others were initiated and guided by students.

- Many activities were open ended to allow for diversity in student thinking.

What other types of activities could Jasmine have included to support and extend the knowledge and skills of the diverse learners in her classroom? In each chapter of this text we have considered issues of diversity. It may be helpful to reread the "Respecting Diversity" sections at the end of other chapters to recall the range of possibilities we have for meeting the needs and interests of diverse groups of middle grade students.

ASSESSMENT AND EVALUATION IN INTEGRATED UNITS

In past chapters we have organized assessment around observing students at work, holding conferences with them about their work, and collecting samples of their work over time. In integrated units, we will use those same procedures to consider students' growth in the language arts and content areas.

OBSERVING STUDENTS

During the 4 weeks of this unit, Jasmine would have opportunities to observe students in guided whole-group activities, in cooperative small-group activities, and in independent reading and writing activities. She can make anecdotal records of students during the unit to see patterns of learning behavior, while maintaining individual record forms. She also may make records of learning behavior that meet her instructional goals. Unit standards become a frame of reference for observing students' progress. A simple form that lists the various standards to be achieved, with space to record notes, can focus observations on the goals of the unit.

CONFERENCES WITH STUDENTS

During independent reading, writer's workshop, and personal research time, Jasmine has opportunities to hold conferences with students about their progress in learning, focusing on the students as learners, as well as on the concepts they are acquiring. In the ancient Egypt unit, conferences are most practical during weeks 3 and 4 when students are engaged primarily in independent work. Even though our standards address more than one subject area, one general conference record per student should suffice for this unit.

SAMPLES OF STUDENT WORK

As we think back over the unit, what samples of work could Jasmine save to reflect student learning?

Week 1: Learning Log
> Response to literature
> Information from research

Data Disk
> Accurately organized information

Week 2: Learning Log
> Response to literature
> Vocabulary
> Information

Writer's Workshop
> Writing from a perspective (evaluate for writing traits, especially voice)

Weeks 3 & 4:
Literature Log
> Notes on character and influence of setting

Writer's Workshop
> Evaluate for writing traits, especially ideas and content, organization, and conventions

Living Museum
> Verbal presentation/demonstration of learning

As work samples are selected for the portfolio, Jasmine might ask students to select one or two other samples of work that will show the following:

- Effort during the unit,
- Creative or critical thinking,
- Something that was hard to accomplish, and
- Something the student is most proud of.

Jasmine will also invite students to evaluate their work according to unit goals, as well as their personal goals.

Observing, conferring, and collecting samples of students' work during integrated units enable us to help students reflect on their own growth, as well as to share their progress with parents and administrators. While we may be able to "blur" the lines among subject matter in unit activities, we are still accountable for documenting growth on report cards and other evaluation systems used by the school district.

EVALUATING AN INTEGRATED UNIT

As Jasmine monitors students' progress in a unit, she also gathers information that enables her to evaluate the unit's effectiveness. Jasmine tries to develop a unit plan that is engaging and beneficial for learning, but how can she be sure that actually happens? To evaluate the effectiveness of the ancient Egypt unit, Jasmine asks herself the following questions at the completion of the unit:

- Were the unit goals/standards and activities appropriate for the needs and interests of the students?
- Did students have adequate learning time to meet the desired unit outcomes?
- Did I provide appropriate support to enable all students to be successful in gaining new knowledge and connecting their past experiences to that new knowledge?
- Did the instructional materials I selected meet the varying needs and interests of my students?

Evaluation should focus heavily on the decisions that we make while planning and implementing instructional activities. When instruction is not as successful as we hope, the cause may lie in not understanding enough about our students as individuals and as learners. That understanding should influence our goals for instruction, the materials we select to help meet those goals, and the instructional strategies we use to engage students in learning. Here we are evaluating our decision-making processes.

As Lindquist (1995) stated at the beginning of this chapter, the more knowledgeable we are about curriculum, teaching strategies and materials, and our students, the more natural teaching through integration will become, and the more we will grow to respect the wonderful diversity of our students.

■ TAKE A MOMENT TO REFLECT . . .

■ *Integration is:*

- Whole learning;
- The woven fabric, not the individual threads; and
- A process.

■ *Two types of integration are:*

- Integrated curriculum, including
  - Selecting appropriate subject matter for a topic;
  - Infusing skills from one area to another;

- Organizing the school year around a theme; and
- Natural links between subject areas.
- Integrated learning that focuses on the child.

■ *Levels of integration include:*

- Few connections, formal planning;
- Blending skills and content, connecting subject areas;
- Natural connections, focus is not on subjects; and
- Focus on whole student.

The language arts are naturally integrative and support all learning.

■ *Use of literature in units serves different purposes:*

- Focus on literature and literary value.
- Use literature to supplement content.
- Blend literature and content experiences.

■ *To develop units of instruction, we:*

- Consider the required curriculum areas, topics, and academic standards.
- Consider content of adopted textbooks.
- Brainstorm possibilities for units, including purposes for using language arts to support learning.
- Identify available and appropriate resources, including literature.
- Involve students in planning.
- Match curriculum standards and resources.
- Select appropriate activities that meet our goals or learning outcomes.
- Plan adequate time for the unit.
- Organize and implement unit activities.
- Monitor students' progress during the unit.
- Evaluate the effectiveness of the unit.

■ *Integrated units:*

- Maximize instructional time in an already crowded school day.
- Balance the use of narrative and informational texts to better meet students' needs and interests.
- Use reading and writing as tools for learning rather than focusing on the processes of learning to read and write.

■ *Assessment and evaluation of an integrated unit:*

- Make records of students' progress toward the learning outcomes or standards for the unit.
- Find time to conference individually with students to provide guidance and document progress.
- Collect varied samples of each student's work throughout the unit for both student and teacher evaluation.
- Take time to evaluate the overall effectiveness of the unit in light of students' needs, interests, and learning outcomes.

■ REFERENCES

Allen, D. D., & Piersma, M. L. (1995). *Developing thematic units*. Albany, NY: Delmar.

Bromley, K. (2000). Integrating language arts with the content areas. In K. Wood & T. S. Dickinson (Eds.), *Promoting literacy in grades 4–9: A handbook for teachers and administrators*. Boston: Allyn and Bacon.

Cambourne, B. (1988). *The whole-story: Natural learning and the acquisition of literacy in the classroom*. Auckland, New Zealand: Scholastic.

Fogarty, R. (1991). Ten ways to integrate curriculum. *Educational Leadership, 49*(2), 61–65.

Gavelek, J. R., Raphael, T. E., Biondo, S. M., & Wang, D. (2000). Integrated literacy instruction. In K. L. Kamil, P. B. Mosenthal, P. D. Pearson, & R. Barr (Eds.), *Handbook of reading research* (Vol. 3, pp. 587–607). Mahwah, NJ: Lawrence Erlbaum Associates.

Jacobs, H.(1989). *Interdisciplinary curriculum: Design and implementation*. Alexandria, VA: Association for Supervision and Curriculum Development.

Leu, D. J. (1997). Caity's questions: Literacy as deixis on the Internet. *The Reading Teacher, 51*(1), 62–67.

Leu, D. J., & Leu, D. D. (1997). *Teaching with the Internet: Lessons from the classroom*. Portsmouth, NH: Heinemann.

Lindquist, T. (1995). *Seeing the whole through social studies*. Portsmouth, NH: Heinemann.

Moore, D. W., Moore, S. A., Cunningham, P. M., & Cunningham, J. W. (1998). *Developing readers & writers in the content areas K–12*. New York: Longman.

Morrison, G. S. (1993). *Contemporary curriculum K–8*. Boston: Allyn and Bacon.

Norton, D. E., & Norton, S. E. (1998). *Through the eyes of a child: An introduction to children's literature* (5th ed.). Upper Saddle River, NJ: Merrill/Prentice Hall.

Pearson, P. D. (1994). Integrated language arts: Sources of controversy and seeds of consensus. In L. M. Morrow, J. K. Smith, & L. C. Wilkinson (Eds.), *Integrated language arts: Controversy to consensus* (pp. 11–31). Needham Heights, MA: Allyn and Bacon.

Schmidt, P. R. (1999). KWLQ: Inquiry and literacy learning in science. *The Reading Teacher, 52*(7), 789–792.

Shoemaker, B. J. E. (1991). Education 2000 integrated curriculum. *Phi Delta Kappan, 73*, 793–797.

Wells, G., & Chang-Wells, G. L. (1994). *Constructing knowledge together: Classrooms as centers of inquiry and literacy*. Portsmouth, NH: Heinemann.

Wood, K. E. (1997). *Interdisciplinary instruction: A practical guide for elementary and middle school teachers*. Upper Saddle River, NJ: Merrill/Prentice Hall.

■ CHILDREN'S LITERATURE

Paulsen, G. (1999). *Hatchet*. New York: Viking Penguin.

Whole-Class Literature Study: A Taste of Blackberries*

by Doris Buchanan Smith
(New York: Harper Collins Children's Books, 1988)

This study includes:

- Chapter lesson plans,
- Discussion guides, and
- Sample forms for literature log entries.

Recommended for students reading at fourth- or fifth-grade level.

CHAPTER 1 LESSON PLAN

SUMMARY

We meet Jamie and the unnamed narrator ("I") and learn of their friendship, woven around picking blackberries, stealing apples, and rock-hopping a creek. Narrator agrees to get children to pick Japanese beetles off of Mrs. Houser's grapevines.

---

* Developed by Ginny Beck, Vickie Cannon, Martha Combs, Janet DeLano, Stacy Drum, Liz Lean, Paula McLaughlin, Kae Moreno, Lisa Reger, and Judy Smith.

DISCUSSION POINTS AND KEY WORDS

BEFORE READING

- Read the title and information about the book available on the dust jacket. From the title and jacket copy, what do we know so far about this story? What do you think might happen?

DURING READING

- Read the first two paragraphs. Clarify the point of view. Who is "I"?
- Note how Jamie and "I" overhear other children talking about them while in the blackberry thicket.
- Pause at the beginning of the apple stealing incident (after Jamie "up-and-overed" the fence) for children to anticipate what is going to happen, and why "I" didn't join in.
- After the stealing incident, encourage brief responses. Note the statement, "My heart was beating *paradiddles*," to emphasize how "I" felt.
- Pause after Mrs. Houser calls to "I"; anticipate what might happen (we already know that "I" is afraid of her).

AFTER READING

- Engage in brief retelling of the key ideas before children go to small groups.
- Children respond to the chapter in small groups using the discussion guide.
- Return to whole class for in-depth discussion using discussion guides.
- Additional suggestions for discussion:
    1. What do we know so far about Jamie? About "I"?
    2. Hyphen-words from Chapter 1:

       every which-a-way   sat down cross-legged
       rock-hopped the creek   across-the-street neighbor
       up-and-overed the fence   far-away feeling
       playground merry-go-round
       sour-sweetness spilled into my mouth

- Anticipate what might happen in the next chapter. Say, "What do you think might happen in the next chapter? What makes you think that?" Think back to "I"'s conversation with Mrs. Houser.

DISCUSSION GUIDE

After reading this chapter, I wonder . . .

1. Do Jamie and "I" seem like good friends? What parts of Chapter 1 make you think that?
2. Would you have gone over the fence to get the apples? Why/why not?

3. When Doris Smith (author) writes, she likes to use hyphens(-) to make up words that fit her purpose, such as

We *rock-hopped* the creek and sat down on the other side where there was a fence to lean on. (p. 3)

The word *rock-hopped* lets you know exactly what the boys did and it is more interesting than just saying the boys hopped on rocks. Find other hyphen-words in Chapter 1 and talk about their meaning. Make up a hyphen-word and be ready to tell what it means to you.

4. Our group also talked about. . . (group members can add to teacher prompts).

LITERATURE LOG POSSIBILITIES

- Start a character chart to show what you are learning about Jamie and "I" as people and as friends (see sample log form, Figure A.1). What have you learned about them in Chapter 1? (*Suggestion:* Begin this as a whole class, then move to independent recording.)
- Start lists of words on separate pages (see sample log forms, Figures A.2 and A.3):

Interesting words and phrases

Words I want to know more about

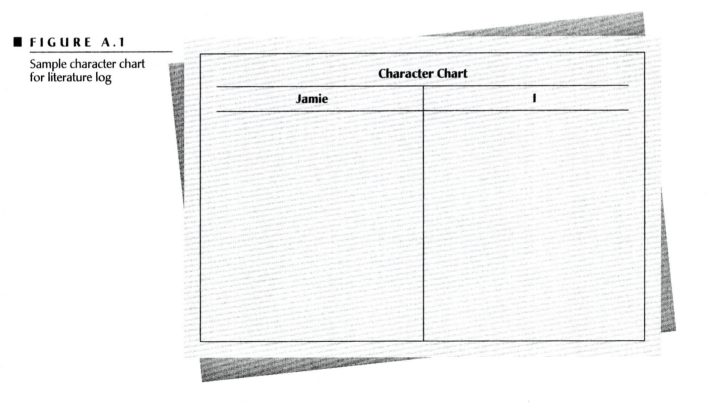

■ **FIGURE A.1**

Sample character chart
for literature log

| Character Chart | |
Jamie	I

Sample form for collecting
words and phrases

Interesting words and phrases

Page _____

Word/phrase _____

To me, it means _____

Page _____

Word/phrase _____

To me, it means _____

Page _____

Word/phrase _____

To me, it means _____

Sample form for collecting
words for personal
learning

Words I want to know more about

Page _____ Word/phrase _____

In the dictionary it means _____

Page _____ Word/phrase _____

In the dictionary it means _____

Page _____ Word/phrase _____

In the dictionary it means _____

Page _____ Word/phrase _____

In the dictionary it means _____

Page _____ Word/phrase _____

In the dictionary it means _____

CHAPTER 2 LESSON PLAN

SUMMARY

Jamie and "I" take Martha, Jamie's 4-year-old sister, for a walk as they get children to pick beetles off Mrs. Houser's grapevines. Heather, the boys' best friend, is the first one they ask. Trying to show Martha their school, the children get stuck in a storm and "hitch" a ride from a stranger who is actually the father of a schoolmate.

DISCUSSION POINTS AND KEY WORDS

BEFORE READING

- Read the first two sentences of the chapter, then recall the end of Chapter 1, where "I" volunteers to get other children to help remove the Japanese beetles from Mrs. Houser's grapevines.

DURING READING

- Pause before Jamie and "I" start toward their school with Martha, and discuss how the boys feel about helping Mrs. Houser. Note the description, "She guarded her property as if every inch was a diamond mine."
- Pause when the stranger stops and offers a ride. Anticipate what might happen.
- Note narrator's reaction to his mother standing at the door and his feeling that "She had the *uncanniest* ability to suspect things. . . ."

AFTER READING

- Brief retelling to confirm important events in chapter.
- Children meet in small groups with discussion guide.
- Return to large group for in-depth discussion.
- Additional suggestions for discussion:
    1. Did anything the author said make you anticipate that something bad might happen?
    2. How words can make images in our minds ("streaks of angel wings").
    3. More hyphen-words:

       four-year-old sister   Jamie *big-mouth*

       I was *tongue-tied*
- Anticipate what might happen in the next chapter.

DISCUSSION GUIDE

After reading this chapter, I wonder . . .

1. How does Jamie feel about his sister, Martha? What happens in Chapter 2 that helps you know that?

2. Would you have hitchhiked in the thunderstorm? Why/why not?

3. While the children are riding with the stranger, you read:

   "Here's the turn," Jamie said. His voice squeaked. I didn't breathe until the man slowed the car and began to turn. Then Jamie and I looked at each other and grinned. At the same time the sun burst through the clouds in streaks of angel wings. (p. 14)

   What kind of pictures do you get in your mind when the author talks about the sun? On the back of this paper, make a sketch of the picture you have in your mind. Be ready to share your sketch.

4. Our group also talked about. . . .

LITERATURE LOG POSSIBILITIES

- Begin a double-entry log, which allows readers to select specific quotes from the text or an event to which they wish to respond (see sample log form, Figure A.4).

  Example:

In the text	*My response (student)*
Mrs. Houser "guarded her property as if every inch was a diamond mine."	The lady on my corner was like that. Once my ball got in her yard. She wouldn't give it back to me. My dad went to see her. He got it back!

- Add to the character chart and word lists in the log.

■ **FIGURE A.4**

Sample double-entry form for literature log

Double-entry Log	
In the text	**My response**

CHAPTER 3 LESSON PLAN

SUMMARY

While the children are scraping Japanese beetles off of Mrs. Houser's grapevines, Jamie pokes a stick in a hole where bees live and is stung. He has an acute reaction. "I" thinks Jamie is acting, so he goes home and eats a popsicle. An ambulance comes and takes Jamie away. "I" returns to scraping beetles.

DISCUSSION POINTS AND KEY WORDS

BEFORE READING

- Recall how the chapter ended yesterday (collecting children to pick off the beetles).
- The chapter opens with a foreshadowing of Jamie's death. Read the first paragraph aloud, then pause and ask children what this paragraph might mean, and why the author might have started the chapter this way.

DURING READING

- Pause after, "It's just a bunch of Heather-bees" to anticipate what might happen. Why did the author use the word *Heather-bees*?
- Note the language used to describe the bees: "The bees came swarming up out of the hole in *a ball of fury*. . . . Those bees went after the kids in *arrow formation*; just like in the cartoons."
- Discuss narrator's reaction to Jamie's falling down. What does "I" know about Jamie that would make him think Jamie is acting?
- Pause after "I" finds out the ambulance is for Jamie and discuss his reaction.

AFTER READING

- Brief retelling to confirm important events in the chapter.
- Children meet in small groups with the discussion guide.
- Return to large group for in-depth discussion.
- Additional suggestions for discussion:
    1. Return to the foreshadowing and discuss how authors use this literary device.
    2. Why did the author spend time describing the popsicle scene? What purpose did it serve?
    3. More hyphen-words:
       Heather-bees   *whoop-whoop-whoop*
- Anticipate what might happen in the next chapter.

DISCUSSION GUIDE

After reading this chapter, I wonder . . .

1. How did "I" react to Jamie's falling down act and being taken away in the ambulance? Were you surprised by the way that "I" reacted? Why/why not?

2. Did the author help you make a picture in your head when she wrote the following?

    The whole neighborhood flowed down the hill like water behind a moving dam. (p. 23)

    How did you picture the neighborhood?

3. What did the author mean by the italicized phrase in this quote?

    In the distance I heard a siren wail and *cocked my ear* to decide if it was the police, a fire engine or an ambulance. (p. 21)

    What clues did you use to help you figure out this phrase? Were the clues in the book? Were some of the clues in you from things you already know?

4. Our group also talked about. . . .

LITERATURE LOG POSSIBILITIES

- Start collecting phrases and sentences that make pictures in your head (see sample log form, Figure A.5). You might begin with the description of the sun from Chapter 2:

    At the same time the sun burst through the clouds in streaks of angel wings.

■ **FIGURE A.5**

Sample form for collecting interesting phrases

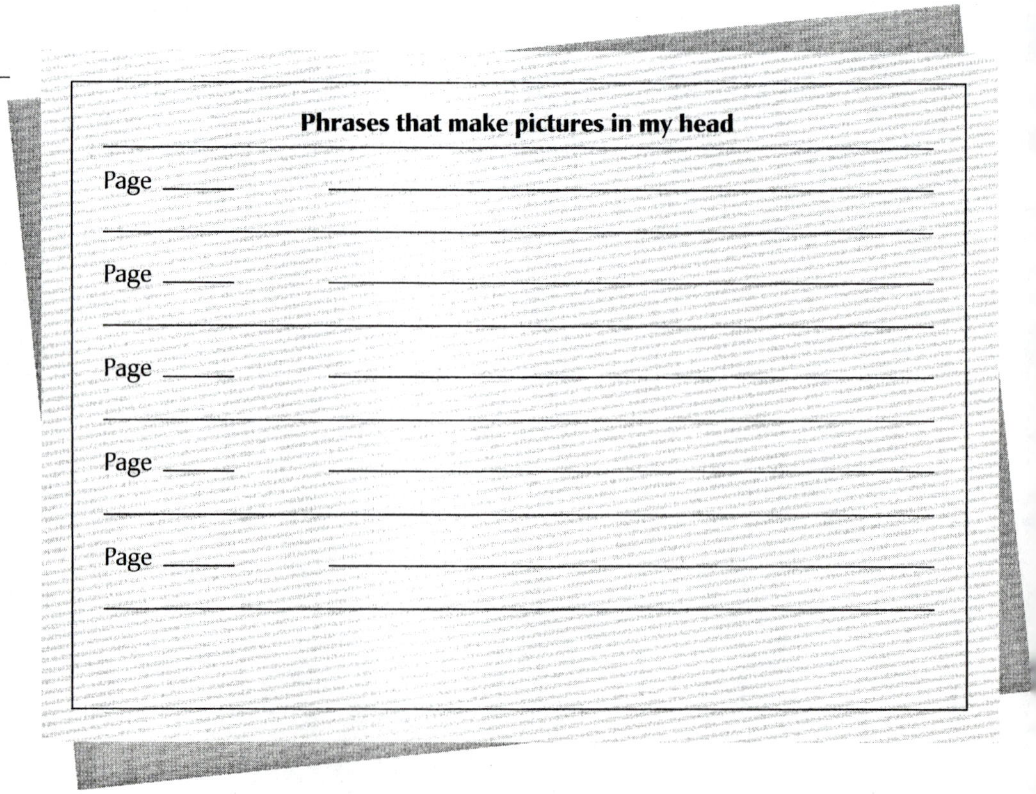

Phrases that make pictures in my head

Page _____

Page _____

Page _____

Page _____

Page _____

Possibilities from Chapter 3:

arrow formation

the neighborhood flowing down the hill like water behind a moving dam

- Add to character chart and word lists.
- Make a double-entry log entry.

CHAPTER 4 LESSON PLAN

SUMMARY

"I" finds out that Jamie is dead. He thinks back on the event and considers what being dead really means.

DISCUSSION POINTS AND KEY WORDS

BEFORE READING

- Read aloud the first paragraph, pause, and help children connect back to Chapter 3. Realize that it is still the same day. Recall predictions from yesterday.

DURING READING

- Pause just after narrator's mother tells him Jamie is dead and question whether "I" knew. What in the text makes you think that?
- Discuss the meaning of *allergic:* "It wasn't the number of stings, it was that Jamie was *allergic* to them."
- Discuss the meaning of *freak:* "It was a *freak* accident. It hardly ever happens." Contrast with previous use, "Jamie was a *freak*."
- Help children realize that narrator's thoughts about making a string telephone and learning Morse code to communicate across the street is really his thinking back to something that happened in the past (flashback).

AFTER READING

- Brief retelling to confirm important events in the chapter.
- Children meet in small groups with the discussion guide.
- Return to large group for in-depth discussion.
- Additional suggestions for discussion:
  1. Revisit portions of the chapter that describe narrator's actions and feelings.
  2. Why "I" would think back over the event and other past experiences with Jamie.
  3. More hyphen-words:

     show-off   *blue-sky* and *white-cloud* day   *floppy-eared* dogs
- Anticipate what might happen in the next chapter.

Discussion Guide

After reading this chapter, I wonder . . .

1. How did "I" act when he heard that Jamie was dead? Why do you think he acted that way?
2. Have you ever known someone who is *allergic* to something? What was he or she allergic to? How did the allergy affect him or her?
3. What do you think you might have done if you were the narrator?
4. Our group also talked about. . . .

Literature Log Possibilities

- Personal response to Jamie's death.
- Add to the character chart and word lists.
- Make a double-entry log entry.

Chapter 5 Lesson Plan

Summary

"I" begins to realize that Jamie is dead and starts to deal with his grief and with his view of death, which is based on his experience at his uncle's funeral.

Discussion Points and Key Words

Before Reading

- Reread the last paragraph of Chapter 4; ask for predictions about Chapter 5.

During Reading

- Why do you think "I" decided to go to the funeral parlor? Why would he have felt panicky? What does *panicky* mean?
- How did Jamie look in his casket to the narrator? Discuss the meaning of *casket*.
- Before the setting shifts from the funeral parlor to home, pause to make clear that this is a viewing and not the funeral.

After Reading

- Brief retelling to confirm important events in the chapter.
- Children meet in small groups with the discussion guide.
- Return to large group for in-depth discussion.
- Additional suggestions for discussion:
    1. Notice word pictures the author uses to help us "see" and "feel":

Soapy whiskers covered my chin.

Jamie slept all bunched up.

I imagined the crack of light slicing across the room.

The sight of her turned my tear faucets on so suddenly that I was surprised.

My face was tight where the tears had dried.

He sat me on his lap and cradled my head to his chest.

2. Did you think "I" would go to the funeral?

3. What does "I" discover about his dad's lap?

4. Why do you think "I" tears up the yellow flower?

- Anticipate what might happen in the next chapter.

DISCUSSION GUIDE

After reading this chapter, I wonder . . .

1. How did "I" see Jamie in a different way than other people?

2. Why do you think "I" doesn't want his parents to know that he is awake?

3. Explain what you think "I" meant when he said, "I wasn't glad the bees were dead" (p. 34).

4. Our group also talked about. . . .

LITERATURE LOG POSSIBILITIES

- When you feel sad, what do you do to make yourself feel better?
- If you sent a sympathy card to Jamie's family, what would you say?
- Add to the character chart and word lists.
- Make a double-entry log entry.

CHAPTER 6 LESSON PLAN

SUMMARY

"I" is having trouble with the fact that everything is remaining the same after Jamie's death. People and things are continuing as if Jamie had never died. "I" sneaks into Mrs. Mullins's garden to sit and think and ends up having a conversation with her about Jamie and death.

DISCUSSION POINTS AND KEY WORDS

BEFORE READING

- Share literature log entries from the previous day.
- When you feel sad, what do you do to make yourself feel better?
- Based on what we know about ourselves and "I", what do you think "I" might do to help himself feel better about Jamie's death?

DURING READING

- Pause after "I" talks about going into the garden (end of p. 39).
- What do we already know about Mrs. Mullins's garden? Reread the description of the garden from Chapter 3. Have children close their eyes to visualize. Ask, Do you think "I" will go into the garden?
- Note the words used to describe objects in the garden.
  [The granite] was *speckledy black and white.*
  I could almost *hear the colors in my ears.*
  And there was a hummingbird, *hovering like a helicopter.*

AFTER READING

- Brief retelling to confirm important events in the chapter.
- Children meet in small groups with the discussion guide.
- Return to large group for in-depth discussion beginning with the discussion guide.
- Additional suggestion for discussion: Are there times when you needed to talk with someone else, and doing it helped you feel better?
- Anticipate what might happen in the next chapter.

DISCUSSION GUIDE

After reading this chapter, I wonder . . .

1. In this chapter "I" talks about not wanting things to be the same since Jamie died. Why do you think he feels this way? Would you feel the same? Why/why not?
2. On page 40, what do you think the word *speckledy* means? "At first glance it looked gray, but if you looked closely it was *speckledy* black and white." Use the word in a sentence of your own.
3. Discuss what you think the author means when she writes the following:
   The air felt empty (p. 42).
   This time the air didn't need to be filled (p. 43).
4. Our group also talked about. . . .

LITERATURE LOG POSSIBILITIES

- The author uses a lot of words and phrases in this chapter that help to make pictures in your head. Look back through the chapter. Add to your list of words and phrases that help you make pictures in your head.
- In this chapter, and also in Chapter 3, the author vividly describes Mrs. Mullins's garden. It is bright compared to the narrator's dark mood. The book's illustrations are in black, white, and gray. Draw a picture of Mrs. Mullins's garden. Go back through the chapter and look for the descriptions of the flowers and creatures in the garden: colors, shapes, animals, and insects that are there.
- Add to the character chart and word lists.
- Make a double-entry log entry.

CHAPTER 7 LESSON PLAN

SUMMARY

"I" is coming to terms with Jamie's death by talking to Martha, attending Jamie's funeral, and going to the cemetery.

DISCUSSION POINTS AND KEY WORDS

BEFORE READING

- Ask students to share any experience they have had with someone dying, such as attending a viewing or a funeral, or going to a cemetery. Think back to Chapter 5 and the viewing.

DURING READING

- Pause after Martha says "Heaben." What is the word supposed to be? Why did the author spell it like that?
- In the scene during the funeral, after reading the paragraph that begins, "I be-gan . . ." (p. 49), pause to discuss the meaning of two phrases:
  brace myself against time
  reverse gravity
- Discuss other interesting words:
  procession—What is a procession?
  strictly taboo—What does that mean?
  foxholes—What is a foxhole? What might have they been playing if they dug foxholes?

AFTER READING

- Brief retelling to confirm important events in the chapter.
- Children meet in small groups with the discussion guide.
- Return to large group for in-depth discussion.
- Additional suggestions for discussion:
  1. While narrator's mind was wandering during the funeral and at the cemetery, what was really happening?
  2. "I" talked about wanting to be near his family during the funeral and in the car. Why do you think he wanted to be with his family instead of his friends?
- Anticipate what might happen in the next chapter.

DISCUSSION GUIDE

After reading this chapter, I wonder . . .

1. Reread the three paragraphs (pp. 46–47) that begin "Where is Martha?"
   Do you think Martha understood what had happened to Jamie? What makes you think that?

Do you think Martha should have gone to the funeral? Why or why not?

Does it help someone to go to the funeral of someone he or she cared for? Why do you think that?

2. Make a list of things that "I" was noticing and thinking about during the funeral and at the cemetery.

3. Our group also talked about. . . .

LITERATURE LOG POSSIBILITIES

- Follow up the small-group discussion of the things "I" noticed during the funeral. Ask students to sit quietly and write for 10 minutes (Graves, 1994) about things they notice and/or think about. Encourage them to think of a recent event that they have strong memories about.

- Write about a time when you were happy to be with your family. What were you doing? Why did you want to be with your family?

- Add to the character chart and word lists.

- Make a double-entry log entry.

CHAPTER 8 LESSON PLAN

SUMMARY

This is a turning point for the narrator's acceptance of Jamie's death. "I" gives into his hunger. He picks blackberries and takes them to Jamie's mother. After talking briefly to her, "I" runs off to play.

DISCUSSION POINTS AND KEY WORDS

BEFORE READING

- Briefly review what happened in Chapter 7.
- Encourage predictions. This is the last chapter of the book. Remember, "I" hasn't eaten, played, or talked to Jamie's mother. What things do you think "I" still needs to deal with? How do you think the author will tie everything together in this last chapter?

DURING READING

- Pause and discuss the meaning of the following:

Suddenly I thought about blackberries. They'd be ripe now. It seemed important to pick blackberries.

I wished I was invisible. I didn't want anyone to see me, even Heather. I wanted to go blackberry picking with Jamie.

And you be sure to come slam the door for me now and then.

- Discuss the following key words as they appear in the chapter:
  I *rummaged* under the sink and brought out two *peck* baskets.
  It seemed a long time since Jamie and I had *snickered* while the kids talked about us from the outside edge of the *thicket*.

AFTER READING

- Brief retelling to confirm important events in the chapter.
- Children meet in small groups with the discussion guide.
- Return to large group for in-depth discussion.
- Additional suggestions for discussion:

  1. What do you think about the way the story ended?
  2. Solicit open responses to the story as a whole, and to favorite parts.

DISCUSSION GUIDE

After reading this chapter, I wonder . . .

1. Look back at your character chart of Jamie and "I". Talk about how you think "I" has changed since the beginning. Find examples in the story to support your ideas.
2. Why was it important for "I" to pick blackberries in the last chapter?
3. How did it help "I" end the "main sadness" when Jamie's mother said, "And be sure to come slam the door for me now and then" (p. 56)?
4. Our group also talked about . . . .

LITERATURE LOG POSSIBILITIES

- Do you think "I" will still think of Jamie? What kind of things do you think he will remember and feel?
- Imagine you are the narrator. Write a letter to Jamie's mother explaining why it took you so long to go over to her house and talk to her.
- Make the following double-entry log entry:

In the text	My response
At supper I no longer felt it was disloyal to eat. If a miracle could have brought Jamie back, it would have been done already.	_____ _____ _____ _____

Suggested Literature by Category

RECENT FAVORITES/RECOMMENDED TITLES

Almost a Hero
(John Neufeld, 1995, Gr. 5–8)

The Arkadians
(Lloyd Alexander, 1995, Gr. 6–9)

The Barn
(Avi, 1994, Gr. 6–8)

The Booford Summer
(Susan Mathias Smith, 1995, Gr. 4–6)

Chicken Soup for the Kid's Soul
(Jack Canfield, Mark V. Hansen, Patty
Hansen, & Irene Dunlap, 1999, Gr. 5–8)

Clockwork
(Philip Pullan, 1999, Gr. 5–8)

Deep Dream of the Rain Forest
(Malcolm Bosse, 1994, Gr. 6–8)

Dragon's Gate
(Lawrence Yep, 1994, Gr. 6–8)

Fig Pudding
(Ralph Fletcher, 1995, Gr. 3–5)

Flip-Flop Girl
(Katherine Paterson, 1994, Gr. 5–8)

Frankenlouse
(Mary James, 1994, Gr. 6–8)

The Ghost of Popcorn Hill
(Betty Ren Wright, 1993, Gr. 3–5)

The Giver
(Lois Lowry, 1993, Gr. 5–8)

Goodbye, Vietnam
(Gloria Whelan, 1994, Gr. 3–5)

Harris and Me: A Summer Remembered
(Gary Paulsen, 1994, Gr. 6–8)

Heart of a Champion
(Carl Deuker, 1994, Gr. 6–8)

Here There Be Angels
(Jane Yolen, 1998, Gr. 7–9)

How I Survived Being a Girl
(Wendelin Van Draanen, 1998, Gr. 5–8)

In the Middle of the Night
(Robert Cormier, 1995, Gr. 6–8)

The King's Shadow
(Elizabeth Alder, 1995, Gr. 6–8)

A Knock at the Door
(Eric Sonderling, 1998, Gr. 3–5)

The Midwife's Apprentice
(Karen Cushman, 1995, Gr. 6–8)

My Brother, My Sister and I
(Yoko Kawashima Watkins, 1994,
Gr. 6–8)

Oops! The Manners Guide for Girls
(Nancy Holyoke, 1998, Gr. 5–8)

Out of the Storm
(Patricia Willis, 1995, Gr. 5–7)

Phoenix Rising
(Karen Hesse, 1994, Gr. 6–8)

Pop-O-Mania: How to Create Your Own Pop-Ups
(Barbara Valenta, 1998, Gr. 5–8)
Seedfolks
(Paul Fleischman, 1998, Gr. 5–8)
Somewhere Around the Corner
(Jackie French, 1994, Gr. 6+)
Songs in the Silence
(Catherine Murphy, 1994, Gr. 4–6)
Squids Will Be Squids
(Jon Scieszka, 1999, Gr. 3–5)
Super Slumber Parties
(Brooks Whitney, 1998, Gr. 5–8)
The Tent: A Parable in One Sitting
(Gary Paulsen, 1995, Gr. 6–8)
Tiger, Tiger, Burning Bright
(Ron Koertge, 1994, Gr. 6–8)

A Time for Andrew: A Ghost Story
(Mary Downing Hahn, 1995, Gr. 4–7)
Timothy of the Cay
(Theodore Taylor, 1994, Gr. 5–8)
Toning the Sweep
(Angela Johnson, 1994, Gr. 6–8)
Under the Blood-Red Sun
(Graham Salisbury, 1994, Gr. 6–8)
Venus Among the Fishes
(Elizabeth Hall & Scott O'Dell, 1994, Gr. 5+)
Walk Two Moons
(Sharon Creech, 1994, Gr. 6–8)
The Well
(Mildred Taylor, 1995, Gr. 6–8)
White Lilacs
(Carolyn Meyer, 1994, Gr. 6–8)

AFRICAN AMERICANS

African Migrations
(Hakim Adi, 1994, Gr. 5+)
Amistad: A Long Road to Freedom
(Walter Dan Myers, 1999, Gr. 5–8)
The Ballad of Belle Dorcas
(William Hooks, 1990, Gr. 4–6)
Barefoot: Escape on the Underground Railroad
(Pamela D. Edwards, 1998, Gr. 3–5)
Black Eagles: African Americans in Aviation
(Jim Haskins, 1994, Gr. 6–8)
Black Stars in Orbit: NASA's African American Astronauts
(Khephra Burns & William Miles, 1994, Gr. 4+)
Circle of Fire
(William Hooks, 1982, Gr. 5–8)
Come a Stranger
(Cynthia Voight, 1986, Gr. 5+)
Cousins
(Virginia Hamilton, 1990, Gr. 6–9)
The Day That Elvis Came to Town
(Jan Marino, 1991, Gr. 6–9)
Down in the Piney Woods
(Ethel Smothers, 1992, Gr. 6–8)
Finding Buck McHenry
(Alfred Slote, 1991, Gr. 4–6)
Fish & Bones
(Ray Prather, 1992, Gr. 6–9)
The Friendship
(Mildred Taylor, 1987, Gr. 4–6)
From AFAR to ZULU: A Dictionary of African American Cultures
(Jim Haskins & Joann Biondi, 1994, Gr. 5+)

From Slave Ship to Freedom Road
(Julius Lester, 1999, Gr. 5–8)
The Gift-Giver
(Joyce Hansen, 1980, Gr. 4–6)
A Girl Called Bob and a Horse Called Yoki
(Barbara Campbell, 1982, Gr. 4–6)
The Glory Field
(Walter Dean Myers, 1994, Gr. 5+)
The Green Lion of Zion Street
(Julia Fields, 1988, Gr. 3–5)
Have a Happy . . . A Novel
(Mildred Pitts Walter, 1989, Gr. 6–8)
Hold Fast to Dreams
(Andrea Pinkney, 1995, Gr. 5–7)
I Have a Dream
(Dr. Martin Luther King, Jr., 1998, Gr. 3–5)
I Have Heard of a Land
(Joyce Carol Thomas, 1999, Gr. 3–5)
I Thought My Soul Would Rise and Fly: The Diary of Patsy, a Freed Girl
(Joyce Hansen, 1998, Gr. 5–8)
Jackie Robinson: Baseball's Civil Rights Legend
(Karen Mueller Coombs, 1998, Gr. 5–8)
Julian, Dream Doctor
(Ann Cameron, 1990, Gr. 3–5)
Just an Overnight Guest
(Eleanora Tate, 1980, Gr. 4–6)
Just Like Martin
(Ossie Davis, 1992, Gr. 6–9)
Just My Luck
(Emily Moore, 1983, Gr. 4–6)
Justin and the Best Biscuits in the World
(Mildred Pitts Walter, 1986, Gr. 3–6)

*The Last Safe House: A Story of the
Underground Railroad*
(Barbara Greenwood, 1999, Gr. 3–5)
Leon's Story
(Leon W. Tillage, 1998, Gr. 3–5)
Lives of Our Own
(Lorri Hewett, 2000, Gr. 7–9)
Mariah Loves Rock
(Mildred Pitts Walter, 1988, Gr. 3–6)
Mississippi Bridge
(Mildred Taylor, 1990, Gr. 4–6)
The Mouse Rap
(Walter Dean Myers, 1990, Gr. 6–10)
Paris, Pee Wee, and Big Dog
(Rosa Guy, 1985, Gr. 3–5)
The Righteous Revenge of Artemis Bonner
(Walter Dean Myers, 1992, Gr. 7–10)
The Road to Memphis
(Mildred Taylor, 1990, Gr. 6–8)
Roll of Thunder, Hear My Cry
(Mildred Taylor, 1976, Gr. 5–8)
Scorpions
(Walter Dean Myers, 1988, Gr. 6–8)
The Secret of Gumbo Grove
(Eleanora Tate, 1987, Gr. 5–8)
The Shimmershine Queens
(Camille Yarborough, 1990, Gr. 6–8)

Skeeter
(K. Smith, 1989, Gr. 7–10)
Somewhere in the Darkness
(Walter Dean Myers, 1992, Gr. 6–8)
Sort of Sisters
(Stacie Johnson, 1992, Gr. 6–8)
Sweet Whispers, Brother Rush
(Virginia Hamilton, 1982, Gr. 5–8)
Talking Turkey
(Lila Hopkins, 1989, Gr. 6–8)
Thank you, Dr. Martin Luther King, Jr.
(Eleanora Tate, 1990, Gr. 3–5)
Tough Tiffany
(Belinda Hurmence, 1980, Gr. 5–7)
*True North: A Novel of the Underground
Railroad*
(Kathryn Lasky, 1998, Gr. 7–9)
The Underground Railroad
(Raymond Bill, 1994, Gr. 3–6)
The Ups and Downs of Carl Davis III
(Rosa Guy, 1989, Gr. 6–9)
Washington City Is Burning
(Harriette Gilllem Robinet, 1998, Gr. 7–9)
When the Nightingale Sings
(Joyce Thomas, 1992, Gr. 6–8)
Willy's Summer Dream
(Kay Brown, 1990, Gr. 6–8)

ASIAN AMERICANS

April and the Dragon Lady
(Lensey Namioka, 1994, Gr. 6+)
Baseball Saved Us
(Mochizuki, 1993, Gr. 6+)
The Best Bad Thing
(Yoshiko Uchida, 1983, Gr. 4–6)
The Chi-Lin Purse
(Linda Fang, 1994, Gr. 4–7)
Children of the River
(Linda Crew, 1989, Gr. 5+)
Cranes at Dusk
(Hisako Matsubara, 1985, Gr. 6+)
Dara's Cambodian New Year
(Sothea Chiemroum, 1992, Gr. 3–5)
Dragonwings
(Lawrence Yep, 1975, Gr. 6+)
El Chino
(Allen Say, 1990, Gr. 3–5)
Hello, My Name Is Scrambled Eggs
(Jamie Gilson, 1985, Gr. 6–8)
Her Own Song
(Ellen Howard, 1988, Gr. 3–6)

*I Am an American: A True Story of Japanese
Internment*
(Jerry Stanley, 1994, Gr. 4+)
In the Eye of the War
(Margaret Chang, 1990, Gr. 4–6)
In the Year of the Boar and Jackie Robinson
(Bette Bao Lord, 1984, Gr. 4–6)
The Invisible Thread
(Yoshiko Uchida, 1991, Gr. 4–6)
A Jar of Dreams
(Yoshiko Uchida, 1981, Gr. 4–6)
Journey to Topaz
(Yoshiko Uchida, 1971, Gr. 4–6)
Kim/Kimi
(Hadley Irwin, 1987, Gr. 6+)
Michelle Kwan: Heart of a Champion
(As told to Laura James, 1999, Gr. 7–9)
Molly by Any Other Name
(Jean Davies Okimoto, 1990, Gr. 7–10)
My Name Is San Ho
(Jayne Pettit, 1992, Gr. 6–8)

Passage to Freedom: The Sugihara Story
  (Ken Mochizuki, 1998, Gr. 3–5)
The Rainbow People
  (Lawrence Yep, 1989, Gr. 6–8)
Sadako and the Thousand Paper Cranes
  (Eleanor Coerr, 1977, Gr. 3–5)
Shortstop from Tokyo
  (Matt Christopher, 1988, Gr. 6–8)
So Far from the Bamboo Grove
  (Yoko Kawashima Watkins, 1986, Gr. 4–6)
The Star Fisher
  (Lawrence Yep, 1991, Gr. 6–8)

*Tales from Gold Mountain: Stories of the
  Chinese in the New World*
  (Paul Yee, 1990, Gr. 6–8)
A Time Too Swift
  (Margaret Poynter, 1990, Gr. 7–10)
When Justice Failed: The Fred Korematsu Story
  (Steven Chin, 1993, Gr. 6–8)
Yang the Youngest and His Terrible Ear
  (Lensey Namioka, 1992, Gr. 6–8)
Year of Impossible Goodbyes
  (Sook Nyui Choi, 1991, Gr. 6–10)
Youn Hee & Me
  (C. S Adler, 1995, Gr. 3–6)

COMING OF AGE

Across the Grain
  (Jean Ferris, 1990, Gr. 8+)
Against the Storm
  (Gaye Hicyilmaz, 1990, Gr. 7–9)
Are You Alone on Purpose?
  (Nancy Werlin, 1994, Gr. 5+)
Athletic Shorts: Six Short Stories
  (Chris Crutcher, 1991, Gr. 8–12)
Becoming Gershona
  (Nava Semel, 1990, Gr. 6–8)
Bloomability
  (Sharon Creech, 1999, Gr. 5–8)
Blue Skin of the Sea
  (Graham Salisbury, 1992, Gr. 8+)
Canyons
  (Gary Paulsen, 1990, Gr. 7–10)
Celine
  (Brock Cole, 1989, Gr. 8+)
Chasing Redbird
  (Sharon Creech, 1998, Gr. 5–8)
The Crystal Garden
  (Vicki Grove, 1994, Gr. 5–8)
Dawn River
  (Jan Hudson, 1990, Gr. 5–8)
The Dying Sun
  (Gary Blackwood, 1989, Gr. 7–10)
Fools' Hill
  (Barbara Hall, 1992, Gr. 7–10)
Funnybone
  (William Coles & Stephen Schwandt, 1992,
  Gr. 7–10)
A Hand Full of Stars
  (Rafik Schami, 1990, Gr. 7–10)

Haunted Journey
  (Ruth Riddell, 1988, Gr. 7–12)
In Your Dreams
  (Colin Neeman, 1994, Gr. 6+)
Julie's Wolf Pack
  (Jean Craighead George, 1999, Gr. 7–9)
Looking at the Moon
  (Kit Pearson, 1992, Gr. 7–10)
Me and the End of the World
  (William Corbin, 1991, Gr. 6–8)
Newfound
  (Jim Miller, 1989, Gr. 8+)
*The Last Safe House: A Story of the
  Underground Railroad*
  (Barbara Greenwood, 1999, Gr. 3–5)
The Original Freddie Ackerman
  (Hadley Irwin, 1992, Gr. 6–8)
*Rattlesnake Dance: True Tales, Mysteries, and
  Rattlesnake Ceremonies*
  (Jennifer Owings Dewey, 1998, Gr. 3–5)
Shabanu: Daughter of the Wind
  (Suzanne Staples, 1989, Gr. 7–10)
The Shadow Brothers
  (A. E Cannon, 1990, Gr. 7–10)
Twisted Summer
  (Willo Davis Roberts, 1998, Gr. 7–9)
*When I Was Your Age: Original Stories About
  Growing Up*
  (Amy Ehrlich (ed.), 1998, Gr. 7–9)
Willie and the Rattlesnake King
  (Clara Gillow Clark, 1999, Gr. 7–9)

CONTENT AREA STUDIES

Science

Alex and Friends: Animal Talk, Animal Thinking
 (Dorothy Hinshaw, 1999, Gr. 5–8)
Astronauts: Training for Space
 (Michael D. Cole, 2000, Gr. 5–8)
Bald Eagles
 (Karen Dudley, 1999, Gr. 5–8)
Deep Space Astronomy
 (Gregory Vogt, 2000, Gr. 5–8)
Disappearing Lake: Nature's Magic in Denali National Park
 (Debbie S. Miller, 1998, Gr. 3–5)
Discovering the Iceman
 (Shelly Tanaka, 1998, Gr. 5–8)
Dive! My Adventures in the Deep Frontier
 (Sylvia A. Earle, 2000, Gr. 3–5)
A Drop of Water
 (Walter Wick, 1998, Gr. 3–5)
About the Titanic
 (Hugh Brewster & Laurie Coulter, 2000, Gr. 3–5)
882½ Amazing Answers to Your Questions Exploring the Deep, Dark Sea
 (Gail Gibbons, 2000, Gr. 3–5)
An Extraordinary Life: The Story of the Monarch Butterfly
 (Laurence Pringle, 1998, Gr. 3–5)
Graveyards of the Dinosaurs
 (Shelly Tanaka, 1999, Gr. 5–8)
The Kid Who Invented the Popsicle
 (Don L. Wulffson, 1998, Gr. 5–8)
Light Shining Through the Mist: A Photobiography of Dian Fossey
 (Tom L. Matthews, 1999, Gr. 5–8)
Lightning
 (Seymour Simon, 1998, Gr. 3–5)
National Audubon Society First Field Guide: Reptiles
 (John L. Behler, 2000, Gr. 3–5)
National Audubon Society First Field Guide: Trees
 (Brian Cassie, 2000, Gr. 3–5)
Questions Your Brain Has Asked Itself But Couldn't Answer. . .Until Now
 (Faith Hickeman Brynie, 1999, Gr. 5–8)
The Scholastic Encyclopedia of Space
 (Jacqueline Mitton & Simon Mitton, 2000, Gr. 3–5)
Seeing Stars
 (James Muirden, 1999, Gr. 3–5)
What's Bugging You?
 (James Preller, 1998, Gr. 3–5)

Social Studies

The Adventures of Sojourner
 (Susi Trautmann Wunsch, 1999, Gr. 5–8)
Amistad: A Long Road to Freedom
 (Walter Dan Myers, 1999, Gr. 5–8)
Ancient Greece
 (Judith Crosher, 1999, Gr. 5–8)
Angels in the Dust
 (Margot T. Raven, 1998, Gr. 3–5)
Art of the Far North: Inuit Sculpture, Drawing, and Printmaking
 (Carol Finley, 1999, Gr. 5–8)
Barefoot: Escape on the Underground Railroad
 (Pamela D. Edwards, 1998, Gr. 3–5)
From Slave Ship to Freedom Road
 (Julius Lester, 1999, Gr. 5–8)
Joan of Arc
 (Diane Stanley, 1999, Gr. 3–5)
Journey to Ellis Island: How My Father Came to America
 (Carol Bierman, 1999, Gr. 3–5)
Lives of the Presidents: Fame, Shame (and What the Neighbors Thought)
 (Kathleen Krull, 1999, Gr. 3–5)
Mapping Our World
 (Martyn Bramwell, 1999, Gr. 5–8)
Safari
 (Robert Bateman & Rick Archbold, 1999, Gr. 3–5)
The Scrambled States of America
 (Laurie Keller, 1999, Gr. 3–5)
Ten Queens: Portraits of Women of Power
 (Milton Meltzer, 1999, Gr. 5–8)
Witness to War: Eight True-Life Stories of Nazi Persecution
 (Michael Leapman, 1999, Gr. 5–8)

Mathematics

The *Amazing Pop-up Multiplication Book*
 (Kate Petty & Jennie Maizels, 1999, Gr. 3–5)
A Visit from Grandfather Abacus
 (Keely Hoffman, 2000, Gr. 5–8)

Technology

Creating and Publishing Web Pages on the Internet
 (Art Wolinsky, 2000, Gr. 5–8)
How the Future Began: Communications
 (Anthony Wilson, 2000, Gr. 5–8)
The New Way Things Work
 (David Macaulay, 1999, Gr. 5–8)

Family Relationships/Problems

The Absolutely True Story
   (Willo Roberts, 1994, Gr. 3–6)
Alida's Song
   (Gary Paulsen, 2000, Gr. 5–8)
Amazing Gracie
   (A. E. Cannon, 1991, Gr. 6–9)
Ask Me Something Easy
   (Natalie Honeycutt, 1991, Gr. 7–10)
The Baby Grand, the Moon in July, & Me
   (Joyce Barnes, 1994, Gr. 4–6)
Babyface
   (Norma Fox Mazer, 1990, Gr. 7–10)
The Best School Year Ever
   (Barbara Robinson, 1994, Gr. 3–6)
Beyond the Mango Tree
   (Amy Zemser, 1999, Gr. 5–8)
Bloomability
   (Sharon Creech, 2000, Gr. 7–9)
Blue Heron
   (Avi, 1992, Gr. 6–9)
The Brightest Light
   (Colleen O'Shaughnessy McKenna, 1992,
   Gr. 7–10)
C, My Name is Cal
   (Norma Fox Mazer, 1990, Gr. 7–9)
Cages
   (Peg Kehret, 1991, Gr. 6–9)
Chasing Redbird
   (Sharon Creech, 1998, Gr. 5–8)
Come the Morning
   (Mark Harris, 1989, Gr. 5–8)
Cruise Control
   (Lisa Fosburgh, 1988, Gr. 7–10)
Danger Zone
   (David Klass, 1998, Gr. 7–9)
Danny Ain't
   (Joe Cottonwood, 1992, Gr. 7–10)
Del-Del
   (Victor Kelleher, 1992, Gr. 7–10)
Dixie Storms
   (Barbara Hall, 1990, Gr. 7–10)
Don't You Dare Read This, Mrs. Dunphrey
   (Margaret Peterson Haddix, 1998, Gr. 7–9)
Earthshine
   (Theresa Nelson, 1994, Gr. 5–8)
Eclipse
   (Kristine Franklin, 1994, Gr. 6–9)
Elizabeth, Who Is Not a Saint
   (Kathleen C. Szaj, 1998, Gr. 3–5)
Fallout
   (Jim Lester, 1998, Gr. 7–9)
Fig Pudding
   (Ralph Fletcher, 1994, Gr. 3–6)

Free Fall
   (Elizabeth Barrett, 1994, Gr. 6+)
From the Notebooks of Melanin Sun
   (Jacqueline Woodson, 1995, Gr. 6+)
The Glass House People
   (Kathryn Reiss, 1992, Gr. 7–10)
Going the Distance
   (Mary Jane Miller, 1994, Gr. 4–6)
Gruel and Unusual Punishment
   (Jim Arter, 1991, Gr. 7–9)
Homecoming
   (Cynthia Voigt, 1981, Gr. 5–8)
How Could You Do It, Diane?
   (Stella Pevsner, 1989, Gr. 7–10)
I Am the Universe
   (Barbara Corcoran, 1986, Gr. 5–8)
I Can't Believe I Have To Do This
   (Jan Alford, 1999, Gr. 7–9)
If I Forget, You Remember
   (Carol Lynch Williams, 1999, Gr. 3–5)
If You Need Me
   (C. S Adler, 1988, Gr. 6–8)
Jaguar
   (Rolland Smith, 1999, Gr. 7–9)
Jason and the Losers
   (Gina Willner-Pardo, 1995, Gr. 4–6)
Journey to Nowhere
   (Mary Jane Auch, 1999, Gr. 7–9)
Junglerama
   (Vicki Grove, 1989, Gr. 6–9)
Just an Overnight Guest
   (Eleanora Tate, 1980, Gr. 4–6)
Just as Long as We're Together
   (Judy Blume, 1987, Gr. 6+)
The Kite Song
   (Margery Evernden, 1984, Gr. 6–7)
The Koufax Dilemma
   (Steven Schnur, 1999, Gr. 7–9)
The Last Safe Place on Earth
   (Richard Peck, 1995, Gr. 6+)
The Latchkey Kids
   (Susan Terris, 1986, Gr. 4–7)
The Leaves in October
   (Karen Ackerman, 1991, Gr. 5+)
Like Seabirds Flying Home
   (Marguerite Murray, 1988, Gr. 7–10)
Linc
   (Mary Christian, 1991, Gr. 7–10)
Love, David
   (Dianne Case, 1991, Gr. 6–8)
Maizie
   (Linda High, 1994, Gr. 4–6)
Mama's Going to Buy You a Mockingbird
   (Jean Little, 1984, Gr. 5–8)

The Maze
(Will Hobbs, 1999, Gr. 5–8)
Missing Pieces
(Norma Fox Mazer, 1995, Gr. 6+)
The Mona Lisa of Salem Street
(Jan Marino, 1994, Gr. 5+)
More Than a Name
(Candice Ransom, 1995, Gr. 3–6)
Out of the Dust
(Karen Hesse, 1998, Gr. 5–8)
Past Forgiving
(Gloria Miklowitz, 1995, Gr. 6+)
River Thunder
(Will Hobbs, 1999, Gr. 7–9)
Several Kinds of Silence
(Marilyn Singer, 1988, Gr. 7–10)
Shadows
(Dennis Haseley, 1991, Gr. 3–5)
The Solitary
(Lynn Hall, 1986, Gr. 6+)
Something Terrible Happened
(Barbara Porte, 1994, Gr. 6+)
Sunny, Diary 3 (California Diaries # 12)
(Ann M. Martin, 2000, Gr. 5–8)
Tallahassee Higgins
(Mary Downing Hahn, 1987, Gr. 5–7)
Tangerine
(Edward Bloor, 1999, Gr. 7–9)
Thomás and the Library Lady
(Pat Hora, 1998, Gr. 3–5)
Tree by Leaf
(Cynthia Voight, 1988, Gr. 7–9)
Under Seige
(Elisabeth Mace, 1988, Gr. 7–10)
Vikki Vanishes
(Peni Griffin, 1994, Gr. 5–8)
The Voice on the Radio
(Caroline B. Cooney, 1998, Gr. 7–9)
With a Wave of the Wand
(Mark Harris, 1980, Gr. 4–6)
You'll Miss Me When I'm Gone
(Stephen Roos, 1988, Gr. 7–10)
You're Dead David Borelli
(Susan Brown, 1994, Gr. 4–7)

Fantasy/Science Fiction
An Acceptable Time
(Madeleine L'Engle, 1989, Gr. 8+)
Ambrosia and the Coral Sun
(Sherri Board, 1994, Gr. 6+)
The Ancient One
(Thomas Barron, 1992, Gr. 7–10)
The Andalite's Gift: Megamorphs # 1
(K. A. Applegate, 1998, Gr. 5–8)

Antar and the Eagles
(William Mayne, 1990, Gr. 6–9)
Bailey's Window
(Ann Lindbergh, 1984, Gr. 3–6)
Below the Root
(Zilpha Keatley Snyder, 1975, Gr. 5–7)
Castle in the Air
(Diana Jones, 1991, Gr. 7–12)
The Castle in the Attic
(Elizabeth Winthrop, 1985, Gr. 4–6)
The Chronicles of Narnia (7 vols.)
(C. S Lewis, 1950–1956, Gr. 3–6)
The Crystal Stair
(Grace Chetwin, 1988, Gr. 6–8)
Curses, Inc. and Other Stories
(Vivian Vande Velde, 1999, Gr. 7–9)
Dark Heart
(Betsy James, 1992, Gr. 7–10)
The Dark Is Rising
(Susan Cooper, 1973, Gr. 5–7)
Diggers
(Terry Pratchett, 1991, Gr. 6–9)
Dr. Gravity
(Dennis Haseley, 1992, Gr. 7–10)
The Dragon and the Thief
(Gillian Bradshaw, 1991, Gr. 7–10)
Ella Enchanted
(Gail Carson Levine, 1999, Gr. 7–9)
Everworld: Search for Senna
(K. A. Applegate, 2000, Gr. 5–8)
Follow a Shadow
(Robert Swindells, 1990, Gr. 7–10)
Gallows Hill
(Lois Duncan, 1999, Gr. 7–9)
Gameplayers
(Stephen Bowkett, 1986, Gr. 7–10)
Gemini Game
(Michael Scott, 1994, Gr. 6+)
The Gold Dust Letters
(Janet Lisle, 1994, Gr. 4–6)
Harry Potter and the Chamber of Secrets
(J. K. Rowling, 2000, Gr. 5–9)
Harry Potter and the Prisoner of Azkaban
(J. K. Rowling, 2001, Gr. 5–9)
Harry Potter and the Sorcerer's Stone
(J. K. Rowling, 1999, Gr. 5–9)
Hero's Song
(Edith Pattou, 1991, Gr. 7–10)
Hexwood
(Diana Jones, 1994, Gr. 6+)
Hob and the Goblins
(William Mayne, 1994, Gr. 5+)
Insomniacs #1: Road Kill
(S. R. Martin, 2000, Gr. 5–8)

Into the Land of the Unicorns
  (Bruce Corville, 1994, Gr. 3–6)
Into the Under World
  (Gillian Clements, 2000, Gr. 3–5)
Lizard Music
  (Daniel Pinkwater, 1976, Gr. 4–8)
Long Night Dance
  (Betsy James, 1989, Gr. 8–12)
The Long Patrol: A Tale From Redwall
  (Brian Jacques, 2000, Gr. 7–9)
Mazemaker
  (Catherine Dexter, 1989, Gr. 6–8)
Minnie
  (Annie Schmidt, 1994, Gr. 3+)
My Name Is Amelia
  (Donald Sobol, 1994, Gr. 4–7)
One Good Turn Deserves Another
  (Eric Kimmel, 1994, Gr. 5–7)
The Phantom Tollbooth
  (Norton Juster, 1961, Gr. 4–8)
The Promise
  (Monica Hughes, 1992, Gr. 6–8)
The Same But Different
  (Perry Nodelman, 1994, Gr. 3–6)
Sandwriter
  (Monica Hughes, 1988, Gr. 7–10)
The Seven Songs of Merlin
  (T. A. Barron, 1999, Gr. 7–9)
Sirena
  (Donna Jo Napoli, 1999, Gr. 5–8)
The Sleep of Stone
  (Louise Cooper, 1991, Gr. 7–12)
The Stone in the Sword: The Quest for a Stolen Emerald
  (Deri & Jim Robbins, 1999, Gr. 3–5)
Touch the Moon
  (Marion Dane Bauer, 1987, Gr. 3–5)
Tuck Everlasting
  (Natalie Babbit, 1975, Gr. 5–7)
2099: Doomsday
  (John Peel, 2000, Gr. 5–8)
The Van Gogh Cafe
  (Cynthia Rylant, 1994, Gr. 3–6)
Wings
  (Bill Brittain, 1991, Gr. 5–7)
A Wizard of Earthsea
  (Ursula Le Guin, 1968, Gr. 5+)

Friendship
Across the Creek
  (Myra Smith, 1987, Gr. 5–7)
Afternoon of the Elves
  (Janet Lisle, 1989, Gr. 5–8)

Alice in Lace
  (Phyllis Reynolds Naylor, 1998, Gr. 7–9)
All But Alice
  (Phyllis Naylor, 1992, Gr. 6–8)
Always and Forever Friends
  (Carol Adler, 1988, Gr. 5–8)
And One for All
  (Theresa Nelson, 1989, Gr. 6–10)
Angela and Diabola
  (Lynne Reid Banks, 1998, Gr. 5–8)
Anne of Green Gables
  (L. M. Montgomery, 1908, Gr. 5–9)
Backfield Package
  (Thomas Dygard, 1992, Gr. 7–10)
The Beasties
  (William Sleator, 1999, Gr. 7–9)
The Berkley Street Six Pack
  (Mary Francis Shura, 1979, Gr. 3–5)
Best Friend Insurance
  (Beatrice Gormley, 1983, Gr. 5–7)
Best Friends Tell the Best Lies
  (Carol Dines, 1989, Gr. 7–10)
The Best of Friends
  (Margaret Rostkowski, 1989, Gr. 6–12)
Better Than a Brother
  (Edith McCall, 1988, Gr. 6–9)
Between the Cracks
  (Joyce Wolf, 1992, Gr. 6–8)
Bones on Black Spruce Mountain
  (David Budbill, 1978, Gr. 5+)
Bridge to Terabithia
  (Katherine Paterson, 1977, Gr. 5–7)
The Broken Boy
  (Karen Ackerman, 1991, Gr. 6–8)
Buddies
  (Barbara Park, 1985, Gr. 5–8)
Came Back to Show You I Could Fly
  (Robin Klein, 1990, Gr. 6–10)
Changeling
  (Zilpha Keatley Snyder, 1970, Gr. 5–8)
Charlotte's Web
  (E. B White, 1952, Gr. 3–6)
The China Year
  (Emily Neville, 1991, Gr. 7–9)
Class Pictures
  (Marilyn Sachs, 1980, Gr. 5–6)
The Cold and Hot Winter
  (Joanna Hurwitz, 1988, Gr. 4–6)
Commander Coatrack Returns
  (Joseph McNair, 1989, Gr. 6–9)
Cricket and the Crackerbox
  (Alane Ferguson, 1990, Gr. 5–6)

Crutches
(Peter Hartling, 1988, Gr. 6+)
Cute Is a Four Letter Word
(Stella Pevsner, 1980, Gr. 5–6)
The Cybil War
(Betsy Byars, 1981, Gr. 4–6)
Daphne's Book
(Mary Downing Hahn, 1983, Gr. 5+)
Diving for the Moon
(Lee Bantle, 1994, Gr. 5+)
The Divorce Express
(Paula Danziger, 1982, Gr. 5–6)
Dog Days
(Colby Rodowsky, 1990, Gr. 4–6)
The Double Life of Angela Jones
(Hila Colman, 1988, Gr. 7–10)
Dump Days
(Jerry Spinelli, 1988, Gr. 4–7)
Dynamite Dinah
(Claudia Mills, 1990, Gr. 5–6)
Eben Tyne: Powdermonkey
(Patricia Beatty, 1990, Gr. 5+)
The Empty Window
(Anne Evelyn Bunting, 1980, Gr. 3–5)
An End to Perfect
(Suzanne Newton, 1984, Gr. 6–8)
Enemies
(Robin Klein, 1989, Gr. 3–5)
Eunice (the Egg Salad) Gottlieb
(Tricia Springstubb, 1988, Gr. 4–6)
A Fine White Dust
(Cynthia Rylant, 1986, Gr. 5–7)
The Flying Fingers Club
(Jean Andrews, 1988, Gr. 3–5)
Fourteen
(Marilyn Sachs, 1983, Gr. 5–8)
Fourth Grade Celebrity
(Patricia Reilly Giff, 1979, Gr. 4–5)
Friends First
(Christine McDonnel, 1990, Gr. 6–8)
Golden Girl
(Nancy Tilly, 1985, Gr. 5–8)
Good-bye, Billy Radish
(Gloria Skurzynski, 1992, Gr. 6–8)
The Great Gilly Hopkins
(Katherine Paterson, 1978, Gr. 5–6)
Hear the Wind Blow
(Patricia Pendergraft, 1988, Gr. 5–7)
The Hermit of Fog Hollow Station
(David Roth, 1980, Gr. 4–6)
Honus & Me
(Dan Gutman, 1998, Gr. 5–8)
Hunt for the Last Cat
(Justin Denzel, 1991, Gr. 6–8)

I Hate Being Gifted
(Patricia Hermes, 1990, Gr. 4–6)
The Iceberg and Its Shadow
(Jan Greenberg, 1980, Gr. 5–6)
Instant Soup
(Brenda Guiberson, 1991, Gr. 5–7)
Jennifer, Hecate, Macbeth, William McKinley and Me, Elizabeth
(E. L. Konigsburg, 1967, Gr. 3–5)
The Josey Gambit
(Mary Francis Shura, 1986, Gr. 5–7)
Just as Long as We're Together
(Judy Blume, 1978, Gr. 6+)
Just Between Us
(Susan Pfeffer, 1980, Gr. 5–6)
Just Good Friends
(Dean Marney, 1982, Gr. 5–8)
Just Like a Friend
(Marilyn Sachs, 1989, Gr. 7–9)
Just Like Always
(Elizabeth-Ann Sachs, 1981, Gr. 5+)
The Kid in the Red Jacket
(Barbara Park, 1987, Gr. 4–6)
Kiss Me, Janie Tannenbaum
(Elizabeth-Ann Sachs, 1992, Gr. 6–8)
Libby on Wednesday
(Zilpha Keatley Snyder, 1990, Gr. 5–6)
Like Everyone Else
(Barbara Girion, 1980, Gr. 5–6)
Lily's Crossing
(Patricia Reilly Giff, 1998, Gr. 5–8)
Losing Joe's Place
(Gordon Korman, 1990, Gr. 6–9)
Ludie's Song
(Shirlie Herlihy, 1988, Gr. 6–8)
Mariposa Blues
(Ron Koertge, 1991, Gr. 7–9)
Maybe I'll Move to the Lost and Found
(Susan Haven, 1988, Gr. 7–9)
My Life in the Seventh Grade
(Mark Geller, 1986, Gr. 5–7)
My Summer Brother
(Ilse-Margaret Vogel, 1981, Gr. 3–5)
Next Thing to Strangers
(Sheri Sinykin, 1991, Gr. 6–9)
Nothing's Fair in Fifth Grade
(Barthe DeClements, 1981, Gr. 4–6)
One of Us
(Nikki Amdur, 1981, Gr. 4–6)
The Other Side of the Fence
(Jean Ure, 1988, Gr. 8–10)
Part-Time Boy
(Elizabeth Billington, 1981, Gr. 3–4)

Philip Hall Likes Me, I Reckon Maybe
(Bette Greene, 1974, Gr. 5–6)
The Pinballs
(Betsy Byars, 1977, Gr. 5–6)
Pink Slippers, Bat Mitzvah Blues
(Ferida Wolff, 1989, Gr. 6–8)
The Planet of Junior Brown
(Virginia Hamilton, 1971, Gr. 5+)
Rabble Starkey
(Lois Lowry, 1987, Gr. 5–6)
Ramona's World
(Beverly Cleary, 2000, Gr. 3–5)
Remember Me to Harold Square
(Paula Danziger, 1987, Gr. 4–6)
Rhonda, Straight and True
(Roni Schotter, 1986, Gr. 5–7)
Rish 'n Roses
(Jan Slepian, 1990, Gr. 5–7)
Sam and the Moon Queen
(Alizon Herzig & Jane Mali, 1990,
Gr. 6–8)
Sarah and Me and the Lady from the Sea
(Patricia Beatty, 1989, Gr. 6–8)
Shoeshine Girl
(Clyde Bulla, 1975, Gr. 3–5)
The Silent Treatment
(David Carkeet, 1988, Gr. 7–10)
Soup
(Robert Newton Peck, 1974, Gr. 3–6)
The Strange Case of the Reluctant Partners
(Mark Geller, 1990, Gr. 6–8)
Stuart Little
(E. B White, 1945, Gr. 3–6)
Such Nice Kids
(Eve Bunting, 1990, Gr. 7–10)
Thatcher Pain-in-the-Neck
(Betty Bates, 1985, Gr. 4–6)
The Trouble with Lemons
(Daniel Hayes, 1991, Gr. 7–9)
What If They Knew?
(Patricia Hermes, 1980, Gr. 4–5)
The Young Landlords
(Walter Dean Myers, 1979, Gr. 5–7)
Zucchini
(Barbara Dana, 1982, Gr. 3–5)

Hispanic Americans
All For the Better: A Story of El Barrio
(Nicholasa Mohr, 1993, Gr. 3–5)
Baseball in April and Other Stories
(Gary Soto, 1990, Gr. 6–10)
Best Friends Tell the Best Lies
(Carol Dines, 1989, Gr. 7–10)

Centerfield Ballhawk
(Matt Christopher, 1992, Gr. 6–8)
*Champions of Change: Biographies of Famous
Hispanic Americans*
(Thomas Powers & José Galvan, 1989,
Gr. 3–5)
Class President
(Joanna Hurwitz, 1990, Gr. 3–5)
*Crews: Gang Members Talk to Maria
Hinojosa*
(Maria Hinojosa, 1994, Gr. 6+)
Don't Look at Me That Way
(Caroline Crane, 1970, Gr. 6–8)
El Bronx Remembered: A Novela and Stories
(Nicholosa Mohr, 1975, Gr. 6–8)
Everett Alvarez, Jr: A Hero of Our Time
(Susan Clinton, 1990, Gr. 3–5)
Extraordinary Hispanic Americans
(Susan Sinnott, 1991, Gr. 6–8)
Felita
(Nicholosa Mohr, 1989, Gr. 4–6)
A Fire in My Hands: A Book of Poems
(Gary Soto, 1990, Gr. 6–8)
Gaucho
(Gloria Gonzalez, 1977, Gr. 4–6)
Going Home
(Nicholasa Mohr, 1986, Gr. 6–8)
Gonzalo: Coronado's Shepherd Boy
(Mary Clendenen, 1990, Gr. 6–8)
Hispanic, Female and Young
(Phyllis Tashlik, 1994, Gr. 7+)
I Speak English for My Mom
(Muriel Stanek, 1989, Gr. 3–5)
Jesse
(Gary Soto, 1994, Gr. 6+)
Juanita Fights the School Board
(Gloria Velasquez, 1994, Gr. 6+)
Leona
(Elizabeth de Trevino, 1994, Gr. 5+)
Local News
(Gary Soto, 1994, Gr. 6–8)
Lupita Manana
(Patricia Beatty, 1981, Gr. 6–8)
The Maldonado Miracle
(Theodore Taylor, 1973, Gr. 5–8)
Maria Luisa
(Winifred Madison, 1971, Gr. 5–6)
The Me Inside of Me: A Novel
(T. Ernesto Bethancourt, 1985, Gr. 6–8)
Momentos Magicos/Magic Moments
(Olga Loya, 1999, Gr. 7–9)
New York City, Too Far from Tampa Blues
(T. Ernesto Bethancourt, 1975, Gr. 5–8)

The One Who Came Back
  (Joann Mazzio, 1992, Gr. 7–10)
Our Tejano Heroes: Outstanding Mexican-Americans in Texas
  (Sammye Munson, 1989, Gr. 6–8)
Pacific Crossing
  (Gary Soto, 1992, Gr. 6–9)
Stories from El Barrio
  (Piri Thomas, 1978, Gr. 6–8)
Taking Sides
  (Gary Soto, 1991, Gr. 6–8)
Thomás and the Library Lady
  (Pat Hora, 1998, Gr. 3–5)
Vilma Martinez
  (Corinne Cody, 1991, Gr. 3–5)
Where Angels Glide at Dawn: New Stories from Latin America
  (Lori Carlson & Cynthia Ventura, 1990, Gr. 6–8)
Who Needs Espei Sanchez
  (Terry Dunnahoo, 1977, Gr. 6–8))

Historical Fiction
Across the Wide and Lonesome Prairie: The Oregon Trail Diary of Hattie Campbell, 1847
  (Kristiana Gregory, 1999, Gr. 7–9)
Beyond the Western Sea: Book One, The Escape from Home
  (Avi, 1998, Gr. 7–9)
Dreams of Mairhe Mehan
  (Jennifer Armstrong, 1998, Gr. 7–9)
Echohawk
  (Lynda Durrant, 1998, Gr. 7–9)
Four Perfect Pebbles, A Holocaust Story
  (Lila Perl & Marion Blumenthal Lazan, 1998, Gr. 7–9)
Freed Girl
  (Joyce Hansen, 1998, Gr. 5–8)
I Have Heard of a Land
  (Joyce Carol Thomas, 1999, Gr. 3–5)
Journey to Nowhere
  (Mary Jane Auch, 1999, Gr. 7–9)
Lily's Crossing
  (Patricia Reilly Giff, 1998, Gr. 5–8)
Nightjohn
  (Gary Paulsen, 1993, Gr. 5–8)
No Turning Back: A Novel of South Africa
  (Beverlley Naidoo, 1998, Gr. 5–8)
Number the Stars
  (Lois Lowry, 1989, Gr. 4–6)
Passage to Freedom: The Sugihara Story
  (Ken Mochizuki, 1998, Gr. 3–5)
Return to Hawk's Hill
  (Allan W. Eckert, 1999, Gr. 5–8)

Run Away Home
  (Patricia C. McKissack, 1998, Gr. 5–8)
Sarny, A Life Remembered
  (Gary Paulsen, 1999, Gr. 7–9)
So Far from Home: The Diary of Mary Driscoll, An Irish Mill Girl
  (Marry Denenburg, 1999, Gr. 7–9)
Soldier Boy
  (Brian Burks, 1999, Gr. 7–9)
Soldier's Heart
  (Gary Paulsen, 1999, Gr. 5–8)
SOS Titanic
  (Eve Bunting, 1998, Gr. 7–9)
Standing in the Light: The Captive Diary of Cathering Carey Logan
  (Mary Pope Osborne, 1999, Gr. 3–5)
To See with the Heart: The Life of Sitting Bull
  (Judith St. George, 1998, Gr. 7–9)
True North: A Novel of the Underground Railroad
  (Kathryn Lasky, 1998, Gr. 7–9)
The Voices of Silence
  (Bel Mooney, 1998, Gr. 5–8)
Washington City Is Burning
  (Harriette Gilllem Robinet, 1998, Gr. 7–9)

Humor
Agnes the Sheep
  (William Taylor, 1991, Gr. 6–8)
Alan Mendelsohn, The Boy from Mars
  (Daniel Pinkwater, 1979, Gr. 5–8)
Alias Madame Doubtfire
  (Anne Fine, 1988, Gr. 6–9)
Almost Starring Skinnybones
  (Barbara Park, 1988, Gr. 4–6)
The Amazing and Death-Defying Diary of Eugene Dingman
  (Paul Zindel, 1987, Gr. 7–10)
Andie and the Boys
  (Janice Harrell, 1990, Gr. 7–10)
Be a Perfect Person in Just Three Days
  (Stephen Manes, 1982, Gr. 3–5)
Billy the Ghost and Me
  (Gery Greer & Bob Ruddick, 1998, Gr. 3–5)
Bingo Brown and the Language of Love
  (Betsy Byars, 1989, Gr. 6–8)
Borgel
  (Daniel Pinkwater, 1990, Gr. 6–8)
The Boy Who Owned the School
  (Gary Paulsen, 1990, Gr. 7–10)
Buffalo Brenda
  (Jill Pinkwater, 1989, Gr. 7–9)
Cinderella Bigfoot
  (Mike Thaler, 1998, Gr. 3–5)

Dear Mom, You're Ruining My Life
  (Jean Van Leeuwen, 1989, Gr. 4–7)
Dracula's Tomb
  (Colin McNaughton, 1999, Gr. 3–5)
Family Reunion
  (Caroline Cooney, 1989, Gr. 7–10)
Fat Men from Space
  (Daniel Pinkwater, 1977, Gr. 3–6)
Fudge-a-Mania
  (Judy Blume, 1990, Gr. 3–6)
Funny You Should Ask
  (David Gale, 1992, Gr. 5–8)
The Ghost Belongs to Me
  (Richard Peck, 1975, Gr. 5–9)
The Hoboken Chicken Emergency
  (Daniel Pinkwater, 1977, Gr. 3–5)
How to Eat Fried Worms
  (Thomas Rockwell, 1973, Gr. 3–5)
If Pigs Could Fly
  (John Lawson, 1989, Gr. 6–8)
Just the Two of Us
  (Jan Greenberg, 1988, Gr. 6–8)
Like Some Kind of Hero
  (Jan Marino, 1992, Gr. 7–10)
Lizard Music
  (Daniel Pinkwater, 1976, Gr. 4–6)
Mariah Delaney's Author-of-the-Month Club
  (Sheila Greenwald, 1990, Gr. 4–6)
Matilda
  (Roald Dahl, 1988, Gr. 4–7)
McBroom Tells the Truth
  (Sid Fleischman, 1999, Gr. 3–5)
Mom Is Dating Weird Wayne
  (Mary Jane Auch, 1988, Gr. 6–8)
The Richest Kid in the World
  (Robert Hawks, 1992, Gr. 6–8)
*Seuss-isms (Wise and Witty Prescriptions for
  Living from the Good Doctor)*
  (Dr. Seuss, 1998, Gr. 5–8)
Sideways Stories from Wayside School
  (Louis Sachar, 1989, Gr. 3–6)
Sixth Grade Secrets
  (Louis Sachar, 1987, Gr. 4–6)
The Snarkout Boys and the Avocado of Death
  (Daniel Pinkwater, 1982, Gr. 5–9)
*The Snarkout Boys and the Baconburg
  Horror*
  (Daniel Pinkwater, 1984, Gr. 5–9)
Something's Rotten in the State of Maryland
  (Laura Sonnenmark, 1990, Gr. 7–10)
Summer of the Monkeys
  (Wilson Rawls, 1976, Gr. 4–6)
There's a Girl in My Hammerlock
  (Jerry Spinelli, 1991, Gr. 6–9)

Wanted: Mud Blossom
  (Betsy Byars, 1991, Gr. 6–8)
*Who Ordered the Jumbo Shrimp? And
  Other Oxymorons*
  (John Agee, 1999, Gr. 3–5)
You'll Never Guess the End
  (Barbara Wersba, 1992, Gr. 7–10)
Young Adults
  (Daniel Pinkwater, 1985, Gr. 6–8)
The Zucchini Warriors
  (Gordon Korman, 1988, Gr. 6–8)

Mystery/Suspense
A to Z Mysteries: The Haunted Hotel
  (Ron Roy, 2000, Gr. 3–5)
The Accident
  (Todd Strasser, 1988, Gr. 7–10)
Adventure in Granada
  (Walter Dean Myers, 1985, Gr. 5–8)
Altered Voices: Nine Science Fiction Stories
  (Compiled by Lucy Sussex, 2000,
  Gr. 5–8)
Beyond the Magic Sphere
  (Gail Jarrow, 1994, Gr. 3–6)
The Blue Empress
  (Kathy Pelta, 1988, Gr. 4–6)
The Bones in the Cliff
  (James Stevenson, 1995, Gr. 5+)
The Boxes
  (William Sleator, 1999, Gr. 5–8)
Breaking the Ring
  (Donna Inglehart, 1991, Gr. 7–10)
Callender Papers
  (Cynthia Voigt, 1983, Gr. 5–8)
Cameo Rose
  (Robbie Branscum, 1989, Gr. 6–8)
A Candidate for Murder
  (Joan Lowery Nixon, 1991, Gr. 7–12)
The Case of the Crooked Candles
  (Johnathan V. Cann, 1998, Gr. 3–5)
Cold as Ice
  (Elizabeth Levy, 1988, Gr. 7–9)
Companions of the Night
  (Vivian Velde, 1995, Gr. 6+)
Deadly Games
  (Peter Nelson, 1992, Gr. 8–12)
Finders
  (Jan Dean, 1994, Gr. 6+)
Fire in the Heart
  (Liza Murrow, 1989, Gr. 7–10)
Following the Mystery Man
  (Mary Downing Hahn, 1988, Gr. 5–7)
The Ghost Children
  (Eve Bunting, 1989, Gr. 5–7)

Graven Images
(Paul Fleischman, 1983, Gr. 5–8)
The Haunting of Holroyd Hill
(Brenda Seabrooke, 1995, Gr. 4–6)
High Trail to Danger
(Joan Lowery Nixon, 1991, Gr. 4–6)
Interstellar Pig
(William Sleator, 1984, Gr. 6–9)
Into the Candlelit Room and Other Strange Tales
(Thomas McKean, 2000, Gr. 5–8)
Is Anybody There?
(Eve Bunting, 1988, Gr. 6–8)
Jaguar
(Roland Smith, 1998, Gr. 5–8)
Keeper of the Light
(Jan Klaveness, 1990, Gr. 7–10)
Lake Fear
(Ian McMahon, 1985, Gr. 5–7)
Legends of Dracula (A&E Bibliography Series)
(Tom Streissguth, 2000, Gr. 5–8)
Marty Frye, Private Eye
(Janet Tashjian, 1999, Gr. 3–5)
The Mystery of the Treasure Map
(Andrew Richardson, 1998, Gr. 3–5)
Mystery on Ice
(Barbara Corcoran, 1985, Gr. 5–8)
Nightmare Hour
(R.L. Stine, 2000, Gr. 5–9)
On the Edge
(Gillian Cross, 1984, Gr. 5–6)
Reef of Death
(Paul Zindel, 1999, Gr. 5–8)
Sammy, Dog Detective
(Colleen Stanley Bare, 1999, Gr. 3–5)
The Sandman's Eyes
(Patricia Windsor, 1985, Gr. 6–10)
The Search for Jim McGwynn
(Marcia Wood, 1989, Gr. 5–8)
Show Me the Evidence
(Alane Ferguson, 1989, Gr. 7–10)
Something Suspicious
(Kathryn Galbraith, 1985, Gr. 4–6)
The Spirit House
(William Sleator, 1991, Gr. 7–10)
Steal Away Home
(Lois Ruby, 1995, Gr. 3–6)
Terror Train
(Gilbert Cross, 1987, Gr. 4–6)
Tom Tiddler's Ground
(John Townsend, 1986, Gr. 4–7)
Trapped in Death Cave
(Bill Wallace, 1984, Gr. 5–8)
The Turquoise Toad Mystery
(Georgess McHargue, 1982, Gr. 4–6)

Up from Jerico Tel
(E. L. Konigsburg, 1986, Gr. 4–6)
Vampire and Werewolf Stories
(Alan Durant, 1999, Gr. 5–8)
The Vandemark Mummy
(Cynthia Voigt, 1991, Gr. 6–9)
The Watcher in the Garden
(Joan Phipson, 1982, Gr. 5+)
The Way to Sattin Shore
(Philippa Pearce, 1984, Gr. 5–8)
The Westing Game
(Ellen Raskin, 1978, Gr. 5–6)
The Window
(Jeanette Ingold, 1998, Gr. 7–9)
The Woman in the Wall
(Patrice Kindl, 1999, Gr. 7–9)

Native Americans
Ashana
(E. P. Roesch, 1990, Gr. 7+)
Bearstone
(Will Hobbs, 1989, Gr. 6–9)
The Bone Wars
(Kathryn Lasky, 1988, Gr. 8+)
The Brave
(Robert Lipsyte, 1991, Gr. 8+)
Brother Moose
(Betty Levin, 1990, Gr. 6–9)
A Brown Bird Singing
(Frances Wosmek, 1986, Gr. 4–6)
Canyons
(Gary Paulsen, 1990, Gr. 7–10)
Cherokee Summer
(Diane Hoyt-Goldsmith, 1993, Gr. 3–5)
A Circle Unbroken
(Sollace Hotze, 1988, Gr. 7–10)
Crossing the Starlight Bridge
(Alice Meade, 1994, Gr. 4–6)
The Crying for a Vision
(Walter Wangerin, Jr., 1994, Gr. 6–9)
Dawn Rider
(Jan Hudson, 1990, Gr. 5+)
Echohawk
(Lynda Durrant, 1998, Gr. 7–9)
Eyes of Darkness
(Jamake Highwater, 1985, Gr. 6–8)
False Face
(Welwyn Katz, 1988, Gr. 7–10)
The Fledglings
(Sandra Markle, 1992, Gr. 7–9)
The Ghost of Eagle Mountain
(L. E. Blair, 1990, Gr. 5+)
Gone the Dreams and Dancing
(Douglas C. Jones, 1985, Gr. 8+)

Guests
   (Michael Dorris, 1994, Gr. 3–6)
I Am Regina
   (Sally Keehn, 1991, Gr. 7–10)
Jenny of the Tetons
   (Kristiana Gregory, 1989, Gr. 6–9)
Kunu: Escape on the Missouri
   (Kenneth Thomasma, 1989, Gr. 6+)
Legend Days
   (Jamake Highwater, 1993, Gr. 6–8)
The Legend of Jimmy Spoon
   (Kristiana Gregory, 1990, Gr. 6–8)
Maggie Among the Seneca
   (Robin Moore, 1990, Gr. 5+)
Mother's Blessings
   (Penina Keen Spinka, 1992, Gr. 6–9)
Music from a Place Called Half Moon
   (Jerrie Opughton, 1994, Gr. 5–8)
Navajo Code Talkers
   (Nathan Aaseng, 1992, Gr. 5+)
Only Brave Tomorrows
   (Winifred Luhrman, 1989, Gr. 6–9)
The People Shall Continue
   (Simon Ortiz, 1988, Gr. 3–5)
The Primrose Way
   (Jackie French Koller, 1992, Gr. 7–10)
Quiver River
   (David Carkeet, 1991, Gr. 7–10)
Racing the Sun
   (Paul Pitts, 1988, Gr. 5–7)
The Rattle and the Drum
   (Kisa Sita, 1994, Gr. 4–6)
Run Away Home
   (Patricia C. McKissack, 1998, Gr. 5–8)
Sarah Winnemucca
   (Mary Morrow, 1992, Gr. 3–5)
Saturnalia
   (Paul Fleischman, 1990, Gr. 7–10)
The Secret of the Eagle Feathers
   (Maura Elizabeth Keleher McKinley, 1998,
   Gr. 3–5)
The Secret of the Seal
   (Deborah Davis, 1989, Gr. 6–8)
The Shadow Brothers
   (A. E. Cannon, 1990, Gr. 5+)
Sing Down the Moon
   (Scott O'Dell, 1970, Gr. 5–7)
Sing for a Gentle Rain
   (J. Alison James, 1990, Gr. 8+)
Smoke on the Water
   (John Ruemmler, 1992, Gr. 8+)
So Sings the Blue Deer
   (Charmayne McGee, 1994, Gr. 3–6)

Speak to the Rain
   (Helen Passey, 1989, Gr. 7–10)
Sweetgrass
   (Jan Hudson, 1989, Gr. 6–10)
The Talking Earth
   (Jean Craighead George, 1987, Gr. 6–8)
Thunder Rolling in the Mountains
   (Scott O'Dell & Elizabeth Hall, 1992,
   Gr. 6–9)
*To See with the Heart: The Life of
   Sitting Bull*
   (Judith St. George, 1998, Gr. 7–9)
*Turtle Dream: Collected Stories from the Hopi,
   Navajo, Pueblo, and Havasupai People*
   (Gerald Hausman, 1989, Gr. 6–8)
*Uncle Smoke Stories: Nehaawka Tales of
   Coyote the Trickster*
   (Roger Welsch, 1994, Gr. 3–6)
Vision Quest
   (Pamela Service, 1989, Gr. 6–9)
A Woman of Her Tribe
   (Margaret Robinson, 1990, Gr. 7–10)

Poetry/Language Play
*The Beauty of the Beast: Poems from the
   Animal Kingdom*
   (Jack Prelutsky, 1998, Gr. 3–5)
Classic Poetry: An Illustrated Collection
   (Michael Rosen, 1999, Gr. 5–8)
I Have Heard of a Land
   (Joyce Carol Thomas, 1999, Gr. 3–5)
The King's Beard
   (Tish Rabe, 1998, Gr. 3–5)
Laugh-eteria
   (Douglas Florian, 2000, Gr. 3–5)
Look-Alikes
   (Joan Steiner, 1999, Gr. 3–5)
Marty Frye, Private Eye
   (Janet Tashjian, 1999, Gr. 3–5)
Popcorn
   (James Stevenson, 1999, Gr. 3–5)
Sit on a Potato Pan, Otis! More Palindromes
   (Jon Agee, 2000, Gr. 3–5)
Z Is for Zombie
   (Merrily Kutner, 2000, Gr. 3–5)

Sports
The Atlanta Braves Baseball Team
   (Thomas S. Owens, 1999, Gr. 5–8)
Bradley and the Billboard
   (Mame Farrell, 1999, Gr. 5–8)
The Chicago Bulls Basketball Team
   (Thomas S. Owens, 1998, Gr. 5–8)

The Dallas Cowboys Football Team
    (William W. Lace, 1998, Gr. 5–8)
Derek Jeter: Surefire Shortstop
    (Bob Schnakenberg, 2000, Gr. 3–5)
Dribble, Shoot, Score! Introduction to
    NBA Basketball
    (Joe Layden, 1998, Gr. 3–5)
Home Run Heroes: Mark McGwire &
    Sammy Sosa
    (Mark Stewart & Mike Kennedy, 2000,
    Gr. 5–8)
Home Run: The Story of Babe Ruth
    (Robert Burleigh, 1999, Gr. 3–5)
Honus & Me
    (Dan Gutman, 1998, Gr. 5–8)
Hoops
    (Robert Burleigh, 1998, Gr. 3–5)
Jackie & Me
    (Dan Gutman, 2001, Gr. 7–9)
Jackie Robinson: Baseball's Civil Rights Legend
    (Karen Mueller Coombs, 1998, Gr. 5–8)
The Koufax Dilemma
    (Steven Schnur, 1999, Gr. 7–9)

Mark McGwire: Home Run King
    (Jeff Savage, 2000, Gr. 5–8)
Michael Jordan: Basketball Skywalker,
    Revised, 3rd Edition
    (Thomas R. Raber, 2000, Gr. 5–8)
Michelle Kwan: Heart of a Champion
    (As told to Laura James, 1999, Gr. 7–9)
NBA Action from A to Z
    (James Preller, 1998, Gr. 3–5)
Roughnecks
    (Thomas Cochran, 1999, Gr. 5–8)
Snowboarding
    (Larry Dane Brimner, 1998, Gr. 5–8)
Snowboarding: A Complete Guide for
    Beginners
    (George Sullivan, 1998, Gr. 5–8)
Sports Great Muggsy Bogues
    (George Rekela, 1998, Gr. 5–8)
Tangerine
    (Edward Bloor, 1999, Gr. 7–9)
Top 10 Baseball Home Run Hitters
    (Bill Deane, 1998, Gr. 5–8)

Morphemic Patterns for Study in the Middle Grades

SAMPLE LISTS FOR WORD STUDY

The sample word lists in Appendix C will help you construct your own lists of words appropriate for your students. The number and type of words you select will depend on your assessment of how students are progressing in weekly word study activities.

When sorting words, always provide students with the option of a "discard pile" for words they believe do not fit the pattern(s) being studied. To encourage such comparisons, it is appropriate to provide words from patterns students have already studied.

MULTISYLLABLE PATTERNS STAGE

1. Compound Words

Literal Meaning

bedroom	playground	goldfish
daydream	houseboat	baseball
doghouse	snowman	daytime
armchair	textbook	twenty-four
wheelchair	round-trip	evergreen

Implied Meaning

starfish	hardship	butterfly
uproar	homesick	however
software	fallout	overdrawn
everywhere	drumstick (chicken)	breakfast

Base + Base		Base + Affix(es)	
Compound Words	**Contractions**	**Prefixes**	**Suffixes**

Compound Words	Contractions	Prefixes	Suffixes

literal meaning concrete object
dog+house
bed+room
gold+fish
police+man
play+ground
	not family
	are+not = aren't
	can+not = can't
	have+not = haven't
	do+not = don't
	will+not = won't
	would+not = wouldn't
	could+not = couldn't
	should+not = shouldn't
		**independent—
		not bound to base**
		dis disobey
		en enjoy
		for forgive
		fore foretold
		im impure
		in inactive
		inter interview
		mis mislead
		non nonstop
		pre* preview
		re repay
		un undo
			inflectional nouns
			s dog+s
			es dish+es
			   horse+es
			's one boy's
			   two boys'

literal meaning, not concrete
bed+time
after+noon
play+time
eye+sight
wild+life
	are family
	you+are = you're
	they+are = they're
	we+are = we're
	
	will family
	I+will = I'll
	you+will = you'll
	we+will = we'll
	they+will = they'll
			verbs
			s jump+s
			ed jump+ed
			   bat+t+ed
			   bake+ed
			ing jump+ing
			   hit+t+ing
			   bake+ing

known words, implied/accepted meaning
every+one
out+side
run+away
over+drawn
fall+out
soft+ware
butter+fly
	is family
	he+is = he's
	she+is = she's
	it+is = it's
	I+am = I'm
	
	have family
	I+have = I've
	you+have = you've
	we+have = we've
	they+have = they've
		**dependent—
		bound to base/root**
		com combine
		con concern
		de decide
		ex excuse
		pre* prefer
		pro process
		
		*can be both independent and dependent
			adjective
			er tall+er
			   big+g+er
			   pretty+er
			   nice+er
			est tall+est
			   big+g+est
			   pretty+est
			   nice+est

			derivational able comfortable ance allowance ess princess ful careful ify classify ion addition division ish foolish ism criticism ist finalist ity ability ive productive ize organize less painless ly friendly ment payment ness kindness ogy biology ous joyous

Overview of morphemic patterns in the middle grades

2. Contractions by Families

not	is/am	are	will	have
aren't	he's	you're	I'll	I've
can't	she's	we're	you'll	you've
don't	I'm	they're	we'll	we've
doesn't				they've
haven't				
shouldn't				
couldn't				

3. Base + Inflected Suffix Words (no change to base)

s/es	ed	ing	er	est
sheriffs	attached	barking	taller	tallest
alleys	spoiled	matching	shorter	shortest
patios	started	whispering	smarter	smartest
heroes	collected	answering	nicer	nicest

4. Base + Inflected Suffixes (base changes)

e drop

raked	horses	received	places
created	making	hoping	freezing
using	smiling	created	guiding
dangling	preparing	balancing	arranging

consonant double

hitting	rubbed	runner	chopped
hottest	hopping	stopping	bigger
gripping	trimmed	batted	popping

y to i

babies	tried	candies	flies
cried	puppies	prettiest	supplies
tiniest	copied	chillier	diaries
horrified	buried	carried	victories

5. Independent Prefix + Base

un	re	pre	dis
untie	reuse	preview	discuss
unkind	review	prepay	dismiss
unload	repay	preschool	discover
undo	recall	presume	discovery
unhappy	repeat	prehistoric	dissolve
unknown	relief	prearrange	disrupt
unwrap	rejoice	precinct	disapprove
unsure	remark	precaution	disappear
unhealthy	refresh	prerecorded	discard
unexpected	reappear	precede	disagree
unreliable	rearrange	preparing	disappoint
unfortunate	retrieve	precipitation	discriminate

in	inter	en
invite	interview	enlist
include	interfere	enroll
inspire	interrupt	enable
incomplete	interaction	endanger
incorrect	intercept	enlarge
inevitable	intersection	engrave
inferior	intervene	enrich
inquiry	intermittent	enclose

6. Base Words + Derivational Suffixes

-ful	-ly	-less	-ness
useful	really	spotless	brightness
beautiful	lightly	hopeless	kindness
sorrowful	finally	timeless	darkness
handful	angrily	helpless	emptiness
hopeful	hopefully	restless	quickness
harmful	apparently	penniless	stubbornness
doubtful	silently	relentless	happiness
skillful	hesitantly	careless	selfishness

-ent	-ant	-able	-ible
parent	servant	favorable	flexible
decent	merchant	reasonable	sensible
present	radiant	comfortable	edible
absent	observant	remarkable	legible
talent	distant	capable	horrible
efficient	pleasant	changeable	convertible
obedient	occupant	valuable	irresistible
ingredient	assistant	admirable	
continent		lovable	
permanent			

-ion	-tion		-sion
collection	elevation	determination	tension
confession	protection	mention	possession
association	connection	position	extension
reaction	action	condition	decision
infection	operation	addition	persuasion
discussion	creation		mission
pollution			permission

7. Syllabication Generalizations

base + base	prefix + base	base + suffix
starfish	untie	swimming
didn't	prepay	horses
I'll	recall	washed
daydream	forgive	careful
you're	unkind	slowly
houseboat	kindness	
weekend		

VC/CV (same letters)

kitten	pretty
summer	yellow
rabbit	lesson
pillow	hammer
little	dollar
platter	balloon
issue	villain
carrot	barrel
dinner	arrive
attempt	

VC/CV (different letters)

picnic	winter
pencil	monkey
garden	person
circus	signal
doctor	after
basket	captain
chimney	harvest
hungry	active
capture	distant

V/CV

cider	defeat
notice	patience
ocean	meter
music	female
polar	vacate
pilot	notice
open	library
secret	hotel
student	puny
cement	cubic
receive	weapon
afraid	cement
diner	equal

VC/V

balance	gravel
second	minute
clever	relish
sugar	comic
ticket	finish
travel	feather
rocket	novel
linen	nephew
lizard	popular
pocket	meadow
radish	melon
cousin	figure
never	promise

V/CV schwa

about	stomach
afraid	banana
apart	lagoon
against	brother
asleep	ability

C + le

fiddle	purple	eagle	fable
pebble	turtle	candle	cycle
needle	whistle	trouble	terrible

Morphemic Patterns Stage

1. Dependent Prefix + Root

com	con	de
compress	continue	design
compute	conference	deprived
common	contestant	depress
comma	control	desirable
comrade	confine	descent
comic	convince	departure
compound	contract	devotion
commendable	condense	devour

ex	pro
example	program
examination	procedure
exercise	protection
exploration	prolong
expression	proportion
exhaust	propeller
expensive	profound
excellent	pronounce

2. Pronunciation Change

change in stressed syllable, changes sound

combine	combination	disable	disability
inspire	inspiration	stable	stability
prepare	preparation	repeat	repetition
confide	confident	reform	reformation
product	production	local	locality

syllable division changes sound

crumb	crumble	mortal	mortality
magic	magical	family	familiar
crime	criminal	electric	electricity
compete	competent	divide	division
magic	magician	music	musician

3. Greek Combining Forms

uni (one)	bi (two)	tri (three)
unicorn	biannual	tricycle
unified	bicycle	triangle
uniform	biceps	triceps
unity	bicentennial	tripod
unilateral	biennium	trio
unicycle		triple

auto (self/same)	astro (star)	bio (life)
autobiography	astronomy	biography
autocratic	astronomer	biology
autograph	astronomical	biopsy
automatic	astrological	biosphere
autopsy	astrophysics	biosynthesis
automobile	astronaut	

tele (far)	thermo (heat)	photo (light)
telecast	thermal	photo finish
telegraph	thermometer	photograph
telephone	thermostat	photographer
telephoto		photogenic
telescope		photosynthesis
telescopic		

-phon- (speech/sound)
homophone
microphone
megaphone
saxophone
symphony
telephone
phonograph

-graph (write/record)
autograph
telegraph
paragraph
geography
photograph
biography

hydro (water)
hydrant
hydrogen
hydroelectric

4. Latin Roots and Related Words

aud (hear)
audible
audio
audition
auditorium
audience

aqu (water)
aquarium
aquatic
aquamarine

cis (cut/kill)
scissors
precise
incisor
incision
exercise

jec (throw/lay/lie/extend)
reject
eject
projector
object
injection

mit/mis/miss (send/do)
dismiss
mission
admit
submit
missionary
transmit

ped/pod/pus (foot)
centipede
pedal
pedestrian
pedestal
podiatrist

port (carry)
important
reporter
support
portfolio
import

spect (to look)
spectator
inspection
spectacles
suspect
expectation

scrib (write)
prescribe
manuscript
subscribe
scribble
describe

appendix *D*

Phonics Patterns: Background Knowledge to Support Instruction

This appendix provides additional background in phonics and is intended for individual use. While most middle grade students will be quite proficient in using letter–sound relationships to decode unfamiliar words, some students will need explicit instruction in the background knowledge provided here.

OVERVIEW OF PHONICS PATTERNS

Phonics patterns are divided between consonants and vowels. Figure D.1 shows an overview of the possible combinations of each.

CONSONANT PATTERNS

Consonants, of which there are 21 in the alphabet, are fairly stable in the sounds they represent. Consonants fall into two basic categories, single and double. What do we know about these categories?

Single-consonant patterns include the following:

- Consonants that are consistent in the sounds they represent.
- Those that vary depending on the placement of the consonant(s) within a syllable and/or the letters that follow the consonant(s).

Consonants		Vowels	
Single	**Double**	**Single**	**Double**
Consistent Letter names sound Letter does not name sound	2 Consonants–2 Sounds Blends/Clusters initial & final	Long CV CVCe	Long—Consistent Vowel Digraphs
Vary Vary by position Vary by vowel that follows	2 Consonants—1 Sound Double Consonants Consonant Digraph H digraphs Silent letter digraphs	Short CVC	Long–Short Vary Vowel Digraphs
		Neither Long nor short R-controlled	Neither Long nor short Diphthongs R-controlled

■ FIGURE D.1

Phonics patterns

Double-consonant patterns include the following:

- Blends or clusters, combinations of two- or three-consonant letters in which each letter represents a sound, as in *bread, clap,* and *street.* Within the syllable, blends/clusters work as a unit.
- Double consonants, two of the same consonant letters together, such as *egg* or *dress,* that represent one sound. One consonant is sounded and one is silent.
- Consonant digraphs, units of two consonants that represent one sound, either a new sound not represented by either of the letters in the unit, such as *sh* in *ship,* or the sound of one of the letters in the unit, with the other letter being silent, such as *wr* in *write.*

SINGLE CONSONANTS

Single consonants often represent the sound we hear when we say the name of the letter. For example, when we say the name of the letter *b,* we make a "buh" sound that represents the sound of the consonant within a syllable. The letter *b* not only names its sound but also is fairly consistent in the sound it represents at both the beginning and end of a syllable.

Single consonants that name their sound will usually be the easiest letter–sound correspondences for children to distinguish. Figure D.2 identifies the consonants that name their sound. When children first begin to notice letter sounds, they are also learning about the names of the letters of the alphabet. Children give so much attention to naming letters that it makes sense to them that the sounds of the letters should relate to their names. Working to make sense out of the abstract nature of written language, children tend to generalize from naming letters to naming consonant sounds. Early spelling attempts also focus on letter-naming strategies. Effective early consonant instruction thus will focus on the letters whose name and sound are similar.

Some single consonants also represent sounds that vary depending on their placement in the syllable. The letter *s* can represent the sounds of /s/, /z/, or /sh/ depending on position.

Pronunciation of some consonants is influenced by the letters that immediately follow. The letters *c* and *g* can each represent two different sounds depending on the vowel that follows. The sound represented is described as a *hard* sound when followed by the letters *a* (*cane/gate*), *o* (*cone/gone*), or *u* (*cute/gun*), and as a *soft* sound when followed by *e* (*cent/gem*), *i* (*city/giant*), or *y* (*cycle/gym*). The terms *hard* and *soft* refer to the formation of the sound in the mouth.

DOUBLE CONSONANTS

After students know single consonants fairly well, we may introduce *blends* or *clusters*. Blends and clusters do not require new consonant knowledge, but do require that students understand that letters can work as a unit. Teaching blends in the *r*, *l*, *s*, and *w* families facilitates generalizations about the sounds represented. Knowing how to think of the blend *br* as a unit facilitates knowing *cr*, *dr*, *fr*, *gr*, *pr*, and *tr* as sound units.

Double consonants, which usually appear at the end of a syllable (*ball*) or are divided between two syllables (*supper*), may be children's first introduction to the concept of silent letters. The concept of a silent letter is very abstract and children may initially find it confusing.

In a *consonant digraph*, two consonant letters typically represent one sound. The digraph may represent either a new or a familiar consonant sound. For example, digraphs made with the letter *h*, such as *sh*, do not represent the common sounds of *s* or *h*, but instead represent a new phoneme. In contrast, silent letter digraphs, such as *kn* or *ck* (*knock*), include a familiar consonant sound and a silent letter (in *kn*, the *k* is silent and the *n* is sounded).

ONSETS

Syllables divide into two parts: *onsets* and *rimes*. The consonant(s) found at the beginning of a syllable, preceding the vowel, is called the *onset*. In the word *bake*, the letter *b* is the onset of the syllable and occurs before *ake*, which is the *rime*, the rhyming portion of the syllable. Working with onsets and rimes can be a productive way to help children learn phonics at the syllable level and see letter patterns as units of sound.

Onsets can be single or double consonants, but they always occur before the vowel in the syllable. What letters represent the onsets in the following words?

mail   *street*   *bump*   *when*

Single Consonants		Double Consonants	
Consistent Sound	**Variant Sound**	**2 Consonants—2 Sounds**	**2 Consonants—1 Sound**
letter names sound	**vary by position and vowel that follows**	**initial blends**	**double consonants (1 silent letter)**
b bat, cab	c (hard c=/k/)	**r family**	bb rabbit
d dot, mad	cage	br break	dd add
f fan, leaf	cone	cr crown	ff cuff
g bag	cut	dr drop	gg egg
j jam		fr frog	ll ball
k kid, peek	c (soft c=/s/)	gr grapes	nn inn
l lid, pail	cent, face	pr prize	ss dress
m man, ham	city	tr tree	zz fuzz
n nut, bun	cycle	**l family**	
p pin, map		bl blue	**H digraphs (new sound)**
r rug, car	g (hard g = /g/)	cl clown	ch chip, each
t tag, cat	gate, bag	fl flag	chef —
v van, love	girl	gl glass	school —
z zoo, quiz	gone	pl play	gh —, laugh
	gum	**s family**	ph phone, graph
letter doesn't name sound		sc scarf	sh ship, dish
h hat	g (soft g = /j/)	scr scrap	th this, breathe
w win	gem, cage	sk skip	thin, breath
y yes	giant	sl slide	
	gym	sm smile	**digraph with silent letters**
		sp spoon	ck — duck
	s sand, bus	spr spray	dge — fudge
	sure -	st stop	gh ghost —
	- his	str street	gn gnat sign
		w family	kn knock —
	x x-ray, fox	dw dwell	ng — ring
	xylophone	sw swim	tch — match
		tw twin	wr write —
			wh what —
		qu quick (/kw/)	who —
		squ squirrel	
		final blends	
		lb bulb	
		ld hold	
		lk milk	
		lt belt	
		nd hand	
		nk pink	
		nt went	

■ **F I G U R E   D . 2**

Overview of consonant patterns

The onsets are *m*-ail, *str*-eet, *b*-ump, and *wh*-en. The onsets are the same single and double initial consonant patterns we have been discussing. We will return to onsets as we discuss the development of students' knowledge about vowels and vowel patterns.

VOWEL PATTERNS

Students must know the following to understand vowel patterns in words:

- Vowels are letters that vary and represent phonemes that are long (sound names the vowel letter), short (as in *bag, beg, big, bog, bug*), or neither.
- The position of letters in words influences the vowel's sound. For example, in the word *cane* we cannot know the sound of the letter *a* until we look past it and see the letter *e* at the end that indicates the possibility of a long vowel pattern.
- Some vowel patterns represent a consistent sound (*ai* is usually always long *a*), while other patterns (*ea* in *meat, head, steak*) may represent one of several sounds.
- In multisyllable words the sounds that vowels represent in unstressed syllables are often not the expected sounds. For example, the *e* in *pen'*-cil has the expected sound of short *e*, but the *i* in the unstressed syllable is sounded like short *u* instead of short *i*.

Like consonants, vowels can be divided into two basic categories, single and double, as shown in Figure D.3. Within each category there are short vowel patterns, long vowel patterns, and patterns that are neither short nor long.

SINGLE VOWELS

Single vowels can represent a variety of phonemes:

- *Short vowel* patterns are often found in closed syllables that end with a consonant, such as *up, big,* and *stamp*.
- *Long vowel* patterns are often found in open syllables that end with a vowel, such as *me* or *game*.
- *R-controlled single vowel* patterns are found in syllables in which the letter *r* follows a single long or short vowel and modifies its sound, such as *car, care, bird, store,* and *fur*.

DOUBLE VOWELS

Double vowels can represent a variety of phonemes:

- *Vowel digraphs* are two vowels or a vowel plus a semi-vowel (a consonant that takes on the characteristics of a vowel, usually *w* or *y*) that represent one phoneme that is usually either a long or short vowel sound, such as *rain, they, pie, boat,* or *soul*.
- *Diphthongs* are two vowels or one vowel with a semi-vowel in which one vowel sound slides into another, producing a phoneme that is often neither long nor short, as in *saw* and *tool*.
- *R-controlled double vowel* patterns are vowel digraphs and diphthongs followed by the letter *r* that modify the vowel sound, such as *fair, steer,* or *oar*.

Single Vowels			Double Vowels		
Short	**Long**	**Neither Long nor Short**	**Long–Consistent**	**Long–Short Vary**	**Neither Long nor Short**

vc   cvc
a at, bag
e egg, bed
i in, hit
o on, log
u up, sun
	cv, vce
	a cake
	e me
	i hide
	o go, rope
	u cute
	    rude
	
	y fly (i)
	    baby (e)
		r-control
		ar car
		er her
		ir bird
		or for
		ur fur
		
		are care
		ere here
		     there
		ire fire
		ore horse
		ure sure
			vowel digraph
			ai rain
			ay may
			ee feet
			igh night
			oa boat
				vowel digraph
				ea meat
				     bread
				     great
				
				ei vein
				    ceiling
				
				ey key
				    they
				
				ie pie
				    chief
				
				oe toe
				    shoe
				
				ou soul
				    young
					diphthong
					au haul
					aw saw
					
					oi oil
					oy boy
					oo boot
					    foot
					ou through
					    round
					ow grow
					    cow
					ui fruit
					ue blue
					ew flew
					
					r-control
					air fair
					ear hear
					     bear
					     learn
					eer peer
					oar roar

■ FIGURE D.3

Overview of vowel patterns

RIMES

The rime portion of a syllable, such as *ake* in *bake*, provides more stable and predictable vowel patterns. Adams (1990) suggests that vowel sounds are more stable and predictable when they are a part of rimes than when they are viewed in isolation, and that of the 286 phonograms that appear in primary grade texts, 95% were pronounced the same in every word in which they appeared.

To support word learning for less experienced readers, nearly 500 words can be made from 37 rimes (Stahl, 1992; Wylie & Durrell, 1970):

A: *-ack, -ail, -ain, -ake, -ale, -ame, -an, -ank, -ap, -ash, -at, -ate, -aw*

E: *-eat, -ell, est*

I: *-ice, -ick, -ide, -ight, -ill, -ine, -ing, -ink, -ip, -ir*

O: -ock, -oke, -op, -or, -ore

U: -uck, -ug, -ump, -unk

In contrast to the great variability that Clymer (1963) found in vowel generalizations used in vocabulary in basal reading materials, rimes offer promise for helping students see vowel patterns as more predictable and useful in unfamiliar words. Using rimes, students learn to work from syllables to phonemes and to see the importance of the position of letters within a syllable. Rimes also offer a means of teaching spelling patterns that correspond to frequent, coherent, syllabic units needed in writing.

Sequence for Study

Single Long Vowels—CVCe.
Suggested sequence for word sorts:

- Long *a*____*e*, short *a*, discard pile.
- Long *i*____*e*, short *i*, discard pile.
- Long *a*____*e*, long *i*____*e*, discard pile.
- Long *o*____*e*, short *o*, discard pile.
- Long *o*____*e*, long *a*____*e*, long *i*____*e*, discard pile.
- Long *u*____*e*, short *u*, discard pile.
- Long *e*, short *e*, discard pile.
- Long *u*____*e*, long *e*, discard pile.

Notes:

- Sorts begin with single long vowels—CVCe and CCVCe. Begin with long *a* (*gate*) versus not long *a* (discard pile). The basic sorting sequence for one vowel:
  long, not long (*gate*, not *gate*)
  long, short, neither (*gate*, *hat*, neither)
- Single long vowel *u* can represent two sounds, /*u*/ (*cute*) and /*oo*/ (*rude*). Encourage students to try an "either–or" strategy (try /*u*/, then try /*oo*/) and select the appropriate sound, checked by context.

Double Vowels—Common Vowel Digraphs.
Suggested sequence:

- *ai*/*ay*, *a*____*e*, short *a*, discard pile.
- *ee*, short *e*, discard pile.
- *oa*, *o*____*e*, short *o*, discard pile.
- *igh*/*ight*, *i*____*e*, short *i*, discard pile.
- *ea* (long *e*), *ea* (short *e*), *ea* (long *a*), short *e*, discard pile.

Notes:

- After single long vowel patterns are under students' control, begin the study of the most consistent vowel digraphs. Don't spend time studying a pattern unless students are reading or writing it.
- Whenever possible, emphasize frequently used rimes (*aid*, *ail*, *ain*). Identify a specific phoneme, then sort against other known patterns that have similar vowel letters.

- Note that the common "rule," "When two vowels go walking, the first one does the talking (long sound)," is largely untrue. The first letter of a vowel digraph has a long vowel sound only about 45% of the time, more frequently with certain patterns than with others.

Double and Variant Consonants.

Suggested sequence:

- Final double consonant, discard pile.
- Single and double consonants (same sound), discard pile.
- Hard *c*, soft *c*, discard pile.
- Hard *g*, soft *g*, discard pile.
- Final *s* /z/, *s* /s/, discard pile.
- Final consonant blends (*d, l, n, t*), discard pile.

Notes:

- Sort single and double consonants that represent the same phoneme in one-syllable words (*doll, dress*). Do not introduce double consonants in two-syllable words, such as *rabbit*. This pattern introduces the concept of silent letters and more than one syllable. Sorting activities should confirm that only one consonant is sounded.
- Knowledge of single short and long vowels is needed to study single variant consonants (*c, g*). When *c* or *g* is followed by *a, o,* or *u*, the vowel sound is usually "hard," as in *can* or *gate*; when followed by an *e, i,* or *y*, the vowel is usually "soft," as in *cent* and *gem*.
- The variation in sound for *s* and *x* is determined by placement in a syllable:

    initial /s/ (*sun*), or /sh/ (*sugar*)

    final /s/ (*bus*) or /z/ (*his*)

    initial /ks/ (*x-ray*) and /z/ (*xylophone*)

    final /ks/ (*fox*)

- When the letters that are difficult to hear in final blends are beginning to show up in students' writing, study of final blends is appropriate (*ld, lt, lk, mp, nd, nk, nt*). Sorting activities should help students contrast the blend to the dominant single consonant, such as for the blend *ld*:

    ld, not *ld* (crazy pile)

    ld, *-d*, neither (discriminate *l*)

    ld, lt, lk, none (discriminate family)

Single R-Controlled Vowels (from Short Vowel Patterns).

Suggested sequence:

- *ar*, short *a*, crazy pile.
- *or/ore*, short *o*, crazy pile.
- *er/ir/ur*, short *e*, short *i*, short *u*, crazy pile.

Notes:

1. When single short and long vowels are well understood, students are usually able to begin work with the single-vowel *r*-controlled patterns (*ar, or, ie, er, ur*).

2. Begin with *ar*. Sort /ar/, not /ar/ to distinguish its unique sound, then compare to the other known patterns with the letter *a*, such as long and short *a*. Follow a similar pattern with *or*.

3. The sounds of *er*, *ir*, and *ur* are the same and should be studied together. Compare to short *e*, *i*, and *o* to help students distinguish the influence of the letter *r*.

Variant Double Vowels—Long and Short.
Suggested sequence:

- *a____e, ai, ay, ea, ei, ey* (long *a*), short *a*, crazy pile.
- *e, ee, ea, ie, ey* (long *e*), short *e*, crazy pile.
- *i____e, y, ie, igh* (long *i*), short *i*, crazy pile.

Notes:

1. Study other less consistent vowel digraphs (*ea, ie, ei, ey*). Work with vowel digraphs that are related by either sound or visual pattern.

2. Study the visual pattern (look the same—sound different). The visual pattern of these words will not help children with decoding. Use the "either–or" strategy with the possible sounds, checked by context.

  ea = long *e* (*meat*), short *e* (*bread*), long *a* (*great*)
  ei = long *e* (*receive*), long *a* (*vein*)
  ey = long *e* (*key*), long *a* (*prey*)
  ie = long *e* (*believe*), long *i* (*tie*)
  ou = long *o* (*soul*), short *u* (*rough*), *ow* (*out*), *oo* (*soup*)

3. Study the sound pattern (look different—sound the same). With this type of pattern, it is important for children to know that a single sound can be spelled in different ways. Sort for one sound (long *a* sound vs. not long *a*), then examine the words in the long *a* column to identify visual patterns. Re-sort by visual patterns.

Consonant Digraphs with Silent Letters.

1. Once students are familiar with silent letters, introduce consonant digraphs in which one letter is silent (*wr, kn, ck*). Sort one-syllable words with silent consonant digraphs in the initial, then final, positions in words.

2. If students have difficulty with the silent letter, sort words that begin with the single consonants. For example, for *wr* sort *wr* and *w* words to help them segment the /r/ sound.

3. Continue to examine other silent digraph patterns (*-ck, kn-, -gn, pn-, -ng, -dge, -tch*) as appropriate words are identified.

Variant Double Vowels—Neither Long nor Short.
Suggested sequence:

- *oo* (long), *oo* (short), long *o*, short *o*, crazy pile.
- *ow* (ow), *ow* (long *o*), short *o*, crazy pile.
- *au/aw*, long *a*, short *a*, crazy pile.

- *oi/oy*, long *o*, short *o*, crazy pile.
- *ou* (*ow*), (long *oo*), (short *oo*), (long *o*), (short *u*), crazy pile.
- *ui/ue/ew/u____e*, short *u*, crazy pile.

Notes:

1. While working with the vowel digraphs, you will have opportunities to study diphthongs that are appearing in students' reading and writing.
2. Look for visual patterns (look the same—sound different). With two sounds possible, encourage students to use the "either–or" strategy, checking for meaning.
3. Sorting activities should compare the different sounds for one letter pattern, then compare other vowel patterns with similar letters:

   boot, foot, crazy pile

   boot, foot, long *o*, short *o*, crazy pile
4. Listen for sound patterns (look different—sound the same):

   au (*haul*), *aw* (*saw*)

   oi (*oil*), *oy* (*boy*)

   ui (*fruit*), *ue* (*blue*), *ew* (*flew*)

   Sorting activities should compare letter patterns to show they produce the same sound, then compare the diphthong to other patterns to show the differences:

   au/aw, not *au/aw* (crazy pile)

   au/aw, long *a*, short *a*, crazy pile

R-Controlled Vowels—From Long and Double Vowels.
Suggested sequence:

- *are/air, ar,* crazy pile.
- *ear/eer/ere* (*eer*), *ear* (*er*), *ear* (*air*), *ear* (*ar*), crazy pile.
- *ire, ir,* crazy pile.
- *ure, ur,* crazy pile.

Notes:

1. When students are working confidently with double vowels, study those same patterns when they are influenced by the letter *r*. Sort the long *r*-controlled pattern (*are, air*) versus not long, to segment the sound.
2. Then compare the long *r*-controlled pattern to the short *ar* pattern, as well as other long and short vowel patterns.

■ REFERENCES

Adams, M. J (1990). *Beginning to read: Thinking and learning about print.* Cambridge, MA: MIT Press.

Clymer, T. (1963). The ability to use phonics generalizations in the primary grades. *The Reading Teacher, 16,* 252–258.

Graves, D. (1994). *A fresh look at writing.* Portsmouth, NH: Heinemann.

Stahl, S. A. (1992). Saying the "p" word: Nine guidelines for exemplary phonics instruction. *The Reading Teacher, 45,* 618–625.

Wylie, R. R., & Durrell, D. D. (1970). Word recognition and beginning reading. *Elementary English, 47,* 787–791.

Author Index

Subject Index